Revolution
in
Central
America

Also of Interest from Westview Press

† Available in hardcover and paperback.

About the Book and Editors

Revolution in Central America

edited by Stanford Central America Action Network

Central America, though affected for decades by profound socioeconomic transformations, has been more or less quiescent politically. The sudden eruption of revolutionary turmoil in the region, as seen in recent events in Nicaragua, El Salvador, and Guatemala, has shattered the political status quo and cast Central America into the U.S. foreign policy spotlight—a spotlight intensified by the Reagan administration's determination to make the isthmus a flashpoint in the precarious U.S.-Soviet relationship.

Revolution in Central America is the first book to explore these recent developments from a genuinely regional perspective. Topically comprehensive, it covers Central America's economic evolution, social conditions, and political changes, as well as the status of human rights and U.S. policy vis-à-vis the area. Special attention is given to the role of women and the Church and to the reconstruction problems of post-Somoza Nicaragua. The contributions in this critical anthology have been selected from a wide variety of sources to present an overview of the origins and nature of Central America's regional crisis that will be useful in the undergraduate classroom.

The Stanford Central America Action Network is a research and political education resource center based at Stanford University.

Revolution
in
Central
America

Edited by
Stanford Central America Action Network

Editorial Staff

John Althoff
Stephen Babb
Philippe Bourgois
Fatma N. Çağatay
David Dye
Hans Ulrich Hornig

María Angela Leal
David Lowe
Craig Richards
Diann Richards
Jo-Anne Scott

Westview Press / Boulder, Colorado

Copyright © 1983 by Westview Press, Inc.

Published in 1983 in the United States of America by
  Westview Press, Inc.
  5500 Central Avenue
  Boulder, Colorado 80301
  Frederick A. Praeger, President and Publisher

Library of Congress Catalog Card Number 82-61799
ISBN 0-86531-540-X
ISBN 0-86531-541-8 (pb)

Composition for this book was provided by the Stanford Central America Action Network
Printed and bound in the United States of America

10   9   8   7   6   5   4   3   2

Contents

Foreword

In the second half of the 20th century, crises are frequent but revolutions are rare. Central America is today a region in both crisis and revolution. Thus, what need to be explained are not only the multiple crises gripping the five republics, but also the roots and consequences of the revolutionary struggles now sweeping Nicaragua, El Salvador and Guatemala. As this is written, Honduras is also teetering on the brink of a revolutionary upheaval, and even Costa Rica is more severely stressed, politically and economically, than anytime in the past 35 years.

Although there can be no all-encompassing or final explanation for the crisis/revolution relationship, the recent history of Central America strongly supports the following assertion: Repeated and brutal denials of the most elementary social, economic, and political rights create the conditions under which mass revolutionary movements can (but not always do) flourish. Revolutionary movements are, in this sense, dramas of last resort. Their histories are crucial, for only when seen in the light of the past does their desperate yet hopeful character become understandable. In Nicaragua it took 45 years of Somocista dictatorship, murder, and pillage (as well as many years of organizational work by the Sandinists) to create the conditions that made possible the victorious popular insurgency of 1978-79. In El Salvador it took almost 50 years of military government, thousands of assassinations, fraudulent elections, and failed reformism to create the conditions for a broadly based mass struggle. In Guatemala it took U.S. intervention and a coup against a progressive government, widespread killing of moderate politicians, and the wholesale extermination of peasants and Indians to exhaust the possibilities for a peaceful transformation of the social and economic system.

To emphasize the political-historical aspect of the revolutionary process is not to underplay the depth of poverty, inequality, and social injustice in the region. On the contrary, the political and social factors are intimately related. For elites, both military and civilian, who have no desire to see social and economic conditions change in basic ways, a politics of exclusion, repression, and ultimately mass murder is a "logical" response. But the interplay of injustice and repression is explosive over the long run. Vast numbers of Central Americans have come to feel that revolutionary violence is the only possible response to the institutionalized, official violence to which they are subjected on a daily basis.

Despite the amount of violence in North American life, there is little in our recent national experience which prepares us to understand what institutionalized repression and state terror in Central America really mean. The Nicaraguan revolution left almost two percent of the population dead, another four percent wounded, most of them victims of Somoza's air and land attacks on urban areas. Proportional figures in the United States would be approximately four million dead and another nine million wounded. But these are just the aggregate statistics, in essence the statistics of war. To grasp the flesh-and-blood meaning of state terrorism, the Amnesty International report, "Guatemala: A Government Program of Political Murder," included in Chapter Five of this book, should be required reading. On any given day the security forces of El Salvador and Guatemala kill or torture dozens of persons in the ways described in the Amnesty report. For them, murder is "politics as usual."

Of particular importance to North American readers is the deep level of complicity of United States administrations, past and present, in this state of affairs. As the readings make clear, this complicity is neither complete nor always immediately evident. But the historical record overwhelmingly suggests that the massive economic, political, and military power of the United States has almost always been used on the side of the conservative status quo in Central America. Of course this status quo varies from time to time and place to place. Today's murderous Guatemalan military establishment is not the same as the fragile civilian administration currently holding nominal power in Honduras. Nor is U.S. power always used in the same way. The Carter administration's policy of seeking a modus vivendi, however conflictual, with the Nicaraguan Revolution is not the same as the Reagan administration's policy of seeking to destabilize and (it hopes) overthrow the Sandinists. But in the sweep of historical time, the continuities of imperialist practice are much more in evidence than are meaningful policy shifts. When viewed from Washington, Central America has been and continues to be a region where U.S. interests come first and the lives and futures of the local majority come second—if at all.

In this context of violence, revolutionary upheaval, and imperialist practice, one has to take sides. Certainly the Reagan administration has taken sides, vigorously promulgating its version of reality, vigorously supporting militarized regimes and solutions in El Salvador and Guatemala—to the extent that public opinion and congressional opposition permit. It is to the credit of the editors of this volume that they too have made choices and make no attempt to hide their sympathies. They are *for* the Nicaraguan Revolution, *for* the popular movements in the rest of Central America, and *against* U.S. imperialism. This does not mean, nor should it, that they always agree with each other, with the tactics adopted by various revolutionary movements, or with every criticism of U.S. policy. But it does mean that their choice of materials has been guided by quite explicit ethical and political criteria.

Some—perhaps many—will say that this is not a "balanced" selection. If by that they mean that the propagandists of the Reagan administration have not been given equal time, or the apologists for the Guatemalan military have not been invited to refute the Amnesty charges, they are obviously correct. But it is important to remember that the classic liberal definition of "balance" never included the notion of pleading your opponent's case. And certainly in this instance, given the financial and newsmaking resources at the disposal of the administration's propagandists, no one can claim that official U.S. explanations of the Central American crisis have not been widely disseminated. If such explanations fail to sway large segments of the American public it is because they are unconvincing and at times downright false.

So, in John Milton's famous phrase, "let truth and falsehood grapple." If readers of this book emerge with a clearer understanding of the nature of the Central American crisis and the reasons why revolutionary struggles are sweeping the region, then truth will have been served. And if, additionally, they emerge with a clearer understanding of why the United States government falsifies much of what is happening, blaming revolutionary upheavals on the Cubans and the Soviets, this too serves the cause of truth. Above all, if readers leave this volume convinced that they too must do their part to lift the burdens of state terror and imperialism from the backs of millions of their fellow Americans, then justice will have been served as well. In Central America today, the truth cries out for action.

Richard R. Fagen
Palo Alto, California

Acknowledgements

This book was collectively compiled and edited by the Stanford Central America Action Network (SCAAN) over a period of about one year and benefited from the knowledge, skill and energy of a large number of people. We would like to give special thanks to Craig Richards for initiating this project, encouraging us with his boundless energy, securing funds and writing the introduction to this book. Each chapter was assembled by one or more editors, who selected the articles, wrote the chapter introductions, and carried out the many other tasks involved in the production of this reader. Listed by chapter, the editors were: Chapter 1: "The Rise of Revolution," María Angela Leal; Chapter 2: "U.S. Policy: The Politics of Intervention," David Dye; Chapter 3: "Dependent Development and Economic Imperialism," Craig Richards; Chapter 4: "Heritage of Hunger: Population, Land and Survival," María Angela Leal and David Lowe; Chapter 5: "Violations of Human Rights: The Price of Stability," Diann Richards and Stephen Babb; Chapter 6: "The Church and Liberation," John Althoff; Chapter 7: "Women and Revolution," Jo-Anne Scott and Fatma N. Çağatay; Chapter 8: "Nicaragua: The Revolutionary Option," Philippe Bourgois, Hans Ulrich Hornig and David Dye. In addition, we appreciate the essential contributions made by David Lowe in producing many versions of the manuscript, David Dye in preparing the index, Mikell Seely in producing the maps, Julie Pearl in translating articles, and the many other people who helped in various ways.

Funding for this book was obtained from several sources. Stanford Workshops on Political and Social Issues (SWOPSI) supported our work as part of an on-going effort to stimulate informed analysis of and action on political and social problems. SWOPSI is a student-initiated program, begun in 1969, that also sponsors collaborative workshops and diverse public events on contemporary political and social issues. In addition to providing us with funding, SWOPSI provided us with a course setting in which to teach a course on Revolution in Central America based on the readings appearing in this book.

In addition, we are indebted to Dr. Richard Fagen, Gildred Professor of Latin American Studies at Stanford University; Dr. Arturo Pacheco, Associate Dean of the Stanford School of Education; and the Stanford Graduate Students Association for their support.

We want to tender special thanks to the North American Congress on Latin America (NACLA) for allowing us to make extensive use of their material. NACLA has consistently provided us with the single best source of information on Central America.

We also want to thank our friends and colleagues who gave so readily of their time, experience and knowledge, and without whom this book would not have existed: Bradford Barham, Jennifer Read, Isabel Alegría, Jean Kimmel, Rob Stevens, N.K. Erkip, Mary Smathers, and Rev. Manfred K. Bahmann.

Finally, to all the authors who generously gave us free access to their articles, we extend our gratitude: Harald Jung, Roger Burbach, Patricia Flynn, Robert Henriques Girling, Philip Wheaton, Frank Viviano, Joseph Collins, and especially to Norma Stoltz Chinchilla for her kind assistance.

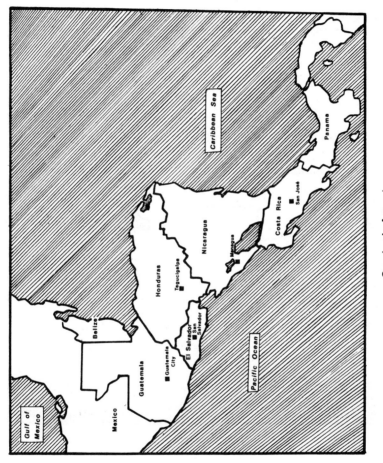

Central America

Guatemala

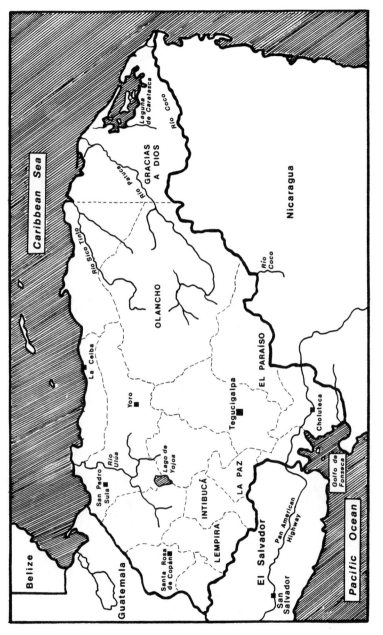

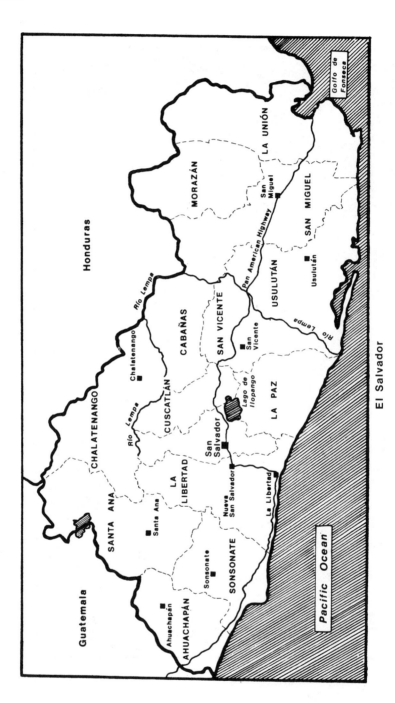

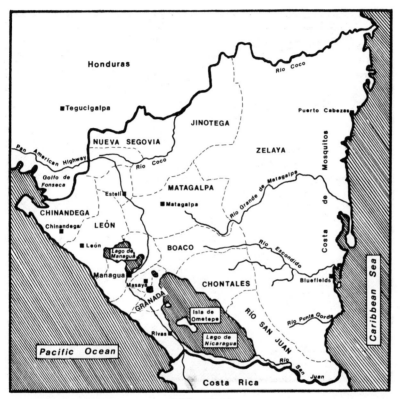

Nicaragua

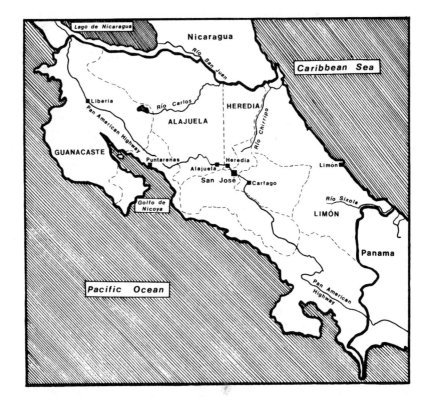

Costa Rica

Introduction

At the time of this writing, the political and military conflicts surrounding the small nation of El Salvador are center stage in the American public mind. Yet even a superficial observer of Central American affairs would agree that not only El Salvador, but the entire Middle American isthmus, is embroiled in a crisis of staggering proportions. The roots of this crisis reach deeply into the heart of the political, economic, and social institutions of the five nations—Guatemala, Honduras, El Salvador, Nicaragua and Costa Rica—which are the subject of this reader.[1]

Although important elements of this crisis are unique to each of these troubled nations, Central Americans share a common experience of neo-colonial relations with the United States that has remained essentially unaltered since President Monroe's imperial "doctrine"—with the notable exception of the recent Sandinista victory in Nicaragua. Similarly, they share a common pattern of dependent capitalist development that is a direct consequence of U.S. domination of the region. However, the same forces which thrust these Central American nations together in a desperate quest for external economic resources have served to tear them asunder politically. Those contradictory forces can be seen most clearly in the repeated historical failure to form a United States of Central America as a vehicle for political and economic unification.

Such unification is even less likely today given the diversity of political regimes currently coexisting in the region. On the extreme right end of the political spectrum are Guatemala and El Salvador, dominated by regimes which sustain their power through a system of overt military repression in alliance with traditional landowning oligarchies. By contrast, Honduras has recently taken tenuous steps in the direction of electoral politics with what appears to be relatively honest balloting. Costa Rica has been unique in the Central American political arena because of its strong social democratic tradition and a relatively stable political system. Even Costa Rica, however, is experiencing an unprecedented degree of political unease and economic disintegration as an explosive combination of world economic recession and regional political crisis deepens.

---

[1] The editors regret that both page constraints and political focus compelled us to exclude Panama and Belize from this reader. (See recommended readings at the back of this volume.) The crisis in Costa Rica is an extremely recent development, hence the paucity of literature on the subject. In this volume, most of the references to Costa Rica are embedded in articles whose scope includes Central America as a whole.

1

Meanwhile, Nicaragua stares across a chasm of successful popular revolution at the rightist regimes of Guatemala and El Salvador. For Nicaraguans, this gulf is widened by their absolute conviction that neither the United States nor its repressive neighbors to the north (with the exception of Mexico) will allow Nicaragua's progressive social experiment to proceed. It is, of course, the Sandinistas' good faith efforts to redistribute wealth and political power, far more than the lack of a functioning American-style political democracy, which threaten the status quo. After all, democratic political practices in Central America have historically been neither the norm nor a serious agenda item between the U.S. and the region's ruling oligarchies. Unfortunately, normalization in Nicaragua must at this juncture be viewed from the narrow frame of the 'state of emergency' declared in the spring of 1982 following public disclosure of a multi-million dollar United States destabilization effort. According to U.S. press reports, former *Somocista* national guardsmen, in collaboration with Argentine and U.S. commando teams, are launching attacks against Nicaragua from Honduran sanctuaries.

Much of Central America's current political upheaval can be traced to the development of agricultural export commodities, the land-based oligarchies that produce them, and the accompanying military regimes required to enforce the land seizures and exploitation of cheap labor necessary to sustain profits. Accordingly, a major part of the story to be told in the following pages will focus on the history of dependent development in the region. It is this structure of dependency which explains why, despite deep political differences, Nicaragua and Costa Rica joined their repressive neighbors on the isthmus in the fall of 1981 and presented a united front to the co-sponsors of the Caribbean Basin Plan, asking for $5 billion in emergency aid and $15 billion in long-term developmental aid. This program suffered a setback when the Reagan administration refused to consider Cuba and Nicaragua as equal partners in the recovery program and key donor nations like Mexico consequently refused to participate; it is nevertheless being advanced as a unilateral U.S. initiative.

Complicating this general pattern of dependency, the agrarian-based export economies of Central America, almost without exception, have been ravaged over the last three years by high oil prices, depressed commodity prices, high interest rates and an acute shortage of foreign credit. Vulnerability to world market prices for coffee, cotton, bananas and meat exports—the four major cash crops in Central America—leaves these troubled nations with little internal control over their economies. Even the limited cooperation stimulated by dire necessity has been threatened by collapse as a series of events in the spring of 1982 have served to heighten rather than diminish the brewing regionalization of war.

First, and most troublesome, border disputes between Honduras and Nicaragua have escalated to the point that Nicaragua has been forced to relocate Miskitu Indian villages to the interior and to recall the Nicaraguan ambassador to Honduras. The border clashes have been attributed to former Somocista national guardsmen using Honduras as a military sanctuary. Second, a coup in Guatemala following the fraudulent 1982 spring elections adds to the unpredictability of intra-regional relations and threatens an increased U.S. presence to protect military domination of the country. Finally, U.S.-orchestrated elections in El Salvador have backfired by consolidating the power of the ultra-rightist parties under the leadership of Roberto d'Aubuisson. The elections have destroyed what remained of Napoleón Duarte's and the Christian Democratic Party's tenuous hold over El Salvador's atrophied political institutions. The results also complicate U.S. strategy in the region because past U.S. military and economic assistance relied upon a Christian Democratic figleaf of moderation to obscure the naked brutality of El Salvador's military junta. It remains to be seen whether the American public will tolerate open military support for the ultra-right in El Salvador.

International Implications of the Crisis

The crisis in Central America is not merely regional; it has political and economic implications for the rest of the Americas. Predictably, American nations with a geopolitical interest in Central American regional stability are being drawn into the picture. Most immediately this includes the United States, Venezuela, Argentina, Mexico and Cuba. Interest in Central American affairs is not, however, restricted to the geo-political terrain of the Americas. For example, throughout the past decade, while the U.S. has been forced to limit its weapons sales because of public outcry over human rights abuses, Israel has taken up the slack, selling military hardware even to the worst human rights violators in the region—Guatemala and Somoza's Nicaragua. On the other hand, the new Socialist government in France supplies weapons and diplomatic support to the Sandinista government, arguing that this will aid the U.S. (which furiously protested the arms sales) by sparing Nicaragua excessive dependence on the Soviet Union. Mexico has also been a strong supporter of the Sandinistas and of El Salvador's Revolutionary Democratic Front (FDR), while Venezuela and Costa Rica supported the rule of El Salvador's Christian Democratic junta president Duarte and are decidedly hostile to the Sandinistas. Clearly, the resolution of the Central American crisis has transcended the narrow limits defined by U.S. hegemonic interests.

While the United States has historically been the key actor in the Central American theater, in the past decade it has been increasingly unsuccessful in directing events there. Indeed, if this collection of essays reaches a common conclusion, it is that the U.S., in collaboration with the region's dictators and oligarchies, has only succeeded in forestalling a resolution to the volcanic political pressures which have been building in Central America for the past half century. Perhaps the most significant and tragic intervention in the region by the United States occurred in 1954 when the Central Intelligence Agency, at President Eisenhower's direction, organized the overthrow of Guatemala's reform-minded President Jacobo Arbenz. Arbenz had been the only legitimately elected President in Guatemala's troubled political history, and the modest social reforms he encouraged stimulated parallel reformist pressures in other Central American nations. Had Arbenz been allowed to remain in power, Guatemala may well have become a stable social democracy. This repression of the impulse for social reform by the U.S. has left a legacy of corruption, human rights abuse, poverty and exploitation, both in Guatemala and in the rest of the region. Not surprisingly, such unrelenting oppression has intensified anti-North American sentiments and intensified the resistance and determination of opposition forces.

In addition to the growing hostility of Central Americans to U.S. military intervention in their region, the U.S. government has been stymied by a growing reluctance on the part of the American people to repeat the ignominy of the Vietnam War. Despite the arguments of State Department officials and some members of the academic community that the Vietnam analogy is inappropriate, similarities in the patterns of escalation increasingly haunt the American public. Public distrust is not without justification: witness U.S. arms sales to Honduras and El Salvador in 1982 of over $90 million—more than the combined sales to these two nations over the past 27 years—or the modeling of El Salvador's agrarian reform on the "Land to the Tiller" program which Roy Prosterman first designed to neutralize peasant leaders in Vietnam. (See Philip Wheaton's article in Chapter 4.) Even the widely publicized fictional invasion of El Salvador by Nicaraguan guerrillas via the Gulf of Fonseca reminds one of a similar fabrication in Indochina's Gulf of Tonkin—a fabrication which resulted in an escalation of the Vietnam War and led Congress to surrender its war powers to former President Lyndon Johnson.

One cannot deny that the crisis in Central America has rent the social fabric of the region's people and threatens the cohesion of family, church, and peasant culture. The depth of the suffering defies imagination. Nevertheless, the men, women and youth who comprise the popular resistance, along with the progressive elements of the church, are now knitting together a new social fabric in the very midst of civil war. While liberation theology has split the church hierarchy from its roots among the people, it has also deepened and revitalized those roots. And women, confronted with the harsh realities of war and repression, have forsaken traditional roles to inspire their people with bravery and leadership as revolutionary soldiers. In Nicaragua today, the people participate at all levels of economic, political and social life as the reconstruction of their war-torn nation proceeds. If El Salvador embodies the pain of the region, it is Nicaragua which symbolizes the promise.

It is the editors' hope that a careful study of this book will reward its readers with insight into the political and economic origins of the Central American crisis as well as an appreciation of the struggles of the Central American peoples and their hopes for a better future.

—*Craig Richards*

1

The Rise of Revolution

The resurgence of revolutionary movements in Central America comes as no surprise to those familiar with the history of the region. But because textbook histories and press accounts have traditionally ignored the voice of the majority of Central Americans—not big landowners and business sectors, but indigenous peoples, peasants, workers and students—many North Americans are puzzled and confused by the explosion of popular rebellion, seemingly sudden and out of nowhere. The *fait accompli* of the Sandinista triumph in Nicaragua, and decisive advances by the popular movements in El Salvador and Guatemala, have exposed as woefully inaccurate the patronizing (and for many, comforting) made-in-USA image of the "banana republic." Even Honduras, the original inspiration for this image, has long harbored the potential for transcending it—a fact which has acquired heightened importance in the context of growing regionalization of the conflicts in Guatemala and El Salvador.

Today, in defiance of ever-louder efforts by the U.S. foreign policy establishment to downplay and even deny the indigenous roots of their struggle, the popular majorities of Central America have begun to break the silence imposed on their history. They are determined to overturn centuries of exploitation and to resist newly intensified government repression, and they have formed mass revolutionary movements whose sheer size and level of organization have made it impossible for the international community to ignore their existence. But perhaps more important than the international recognition these groups have gained is the fact that they have achieved unprecedented levels of coordination and unity within their own ranks and have extended the base of their political support across a broad social spectrum.

The articles in this section provide documentation which helps to explain why the impulse to revolution has grown so strong at this particular time. In her overview, Chinchilla maps out the crucial convergence of three historical developments: (1) the contradictions inherent in Central America's capitalist development strategy; (2) the decline in the United States' capacity for direct military intervention in the domestic crises of other countries; and (3) the ability of revolutionaries, operating as ever within an extremely narrow margin of error, to adapt both philosophy and tactics to a changing social, political and economic environment. The remaining articles elaborate these points with respect to each of the main

5

actors in the current regional conflict—El Salvador, Guatemala, Honduras and Nicaragua—and point to two additional factors: (4) the adoption of a progressive stance by important sectors of the Church; and (5) intensified repression (official and "unofficial") directed not only against individuals actively seeking social change, but on an even greater scale against the civilian population at large. Paradoxically, thanks to the confluence of factors (1) through (4), repression has served to fuel rather than smother the impulse to revolution in Central America.

In its unique as well as its more universal aspects, the Nicaraguan experience has served as an inspiration and a lesson to revolutionary movements in other Central American countries. Under Somoza, leading sectors of the business community grew alienated by the dictatorship's virtual monopoly over much of the economy and eventually opted for the only remaining viable path of resistance—alliance with the popular struggle. This unification of the opposition clearly helped to hasten the victory against Somoza at home. It also had the equally important effect of catalyzing Somoza's defeat abroad, as few countries, with the notable exception of a confused United States, could any longer stomach a dictatorship so widely and so demonstrably hated.

As in pre-revolutionary Nicaragua, the popular majorities of El Salvador and Guatemala have long been subject to the exploitative rule of a small minority buttressed as needed by the overt and covert intervention of the United States. But unlike in Nicaragua, the dominant economic sectors in El Salvador and Guatemala have historically maintained a symbiotic relationship with the military, experiencing occasional but far less significant internal divisions. For that reason, the popular struggles being waged there are more starkly defined along class lines than was the case in Nicaragua. In the absence of a single dictatorial dynasty, such struggles more clearly take the form of a class war between an oligarchic minority of privileged agrarian and industrial elites and a vast majority of dispossessed peasants and workers.

The first lesson to be learned from all this has quickly impressed itself on revolutionaries in El Salvador and Guatemala: international support for the progressive side in a more clearly defined class conflict will be harder to come by than it was for the Sandinistas. Moreover, the defeat of Somoza has only sharpened the U.S.'s determination to prevent further popular victories in Central America. For these reasons, it is crucial for revolutionary movements to continue broadening and deepening their social base. In both El Salvador and Guatemala, this has effectively occurred. Historic alliances have been formed between the popular movements and major sectors of the professional classes and petite bourgeoisie, as the latter have found themselves shut out by the ruling oligarchic sectors, and all other avenues to political and economic change have been closed.

In El Salvador, this process culminated in April 1980 with the formation of the Democratic Revolutionary Front (FDR), a broad coalition of peasant, labor, professional, student, small business and church groups and left-of-center political parties fighting for an end to 50 years of military dictatorship and for the establishment of a mass-based democratic regime. In Guatemala, meanwhile, centuries of mutual isolation between indigenous and *ladino* groups have given way to an alliance embracing peasants, workers, teachers, professionals, and church and political leaders. Formed in February 1982, the Guatemalan Committee for Patriotic Unity (CGUP) aims to overthrow the governmental reign of terror that has taken an estimated 80,000 lives since 1954, when a U.S.-sponsored military coup ousted the democratically elected government of Jacobo Arbenz.

But if the difficulty of forging alliances with leading bourgeois sectors in Guatemala and El Salvador seems to pose unique impediments to popular victory, it has also impelled the revolutionaries towards a strategy of struggle that emphasizes consolidation of a mass political base as a precondition for establishing and maintaining military control. Thus, at the same time that progress is made toward a popular victory, the basis for the revolutionary transformation of these societies is being laid. This strategy, made famous in the Chinese and Vietnamese revolutions of this century, is known as "prolonged people's war" (or GPP in its Spanish acronym). The experience of Nicaragua, where revolutionary victory was achieved ultimately through other means, suggests some potential advantages of GPP. In Nicaragua, a hastily organized insurrection, made possible by transitory alliances with non-revolutionary sectors, was an effective means of deposing a dictatorship, but this was accomplished while large segments of the population remained unincorporated into the revolutionary struggle. Revolutionaries who achieve victory under such circumstances may have greater difficulties politically in resolving questions of resource allocation, in meeting massive expectations awakened in the popular classes, and in maintaining national unity in the face of foreign attempts at subversion, than would a similar movement which succeeds in building a more extensive social base before taking power. This speculation has led many to consider prolonged people's war as the only sure means of mitigating some of the sharp contradictions which inevitably succeed any revolutionary victory.

Elsewhere in Central America, the challenge to the established order has not attained such dramatic proportions. Yet it is nevertheless being fueled by deteriorating economic conditions and a concomitant increase in popular discontent. In Honduras, where the presence of thousands of refugees fleeing the war in El Salvador has strained local resources and threatens to erode public confidence in government promises of reform, popular movements are consolidating their strength. And in Costa Rica, an unprecedented economic crisis threatens to undermine the political stability that once seemed guaranteed by virtue of that country's less unequal distribution of income and wealth and its formally democratic system of government. As long as the dominant power in the hemisphere insists on imperialist military solutions to indigenous social crises abroad, the resolution of these dilemmas may remain dangerously beyond the reach of those most affected by them.

—María Angela Leal

Class Struggle in Central America:
Background and Overview*

By Norma Stoltz Chinchilla

Norma Stoltz Chinchilla is Professor of Social Relations at the University of California, Irvine.

Introduction

Ten years ago, the locus of intense anti-imperialist and anticapitalist conflict in the Western Hemisphere was in the southern cone of South America—Chile, Argentina, Brazil, Uruguay. Now, a decade later, the weakest links in the chain of U.S. imperialism are Central America and the Caribbean. In the relatively small but, from the U.S. point of view, geopolitically important countries of Central America and the islands of the Caribbean, U.S. hegemony is being fiercely challenged with a strength that many people find surprising. For those who have followed the history of the region, however, there was never any doubt that, sooner or later, several centuries of unfinished revolutions would eventually come together in explosive revolutionary upheavals. Nor should there be amazement that revolutionary forces in Central America seem to be so successful at taking advantage of this conjuncture. They have, after all, paid an enormous price for past mistakes. Their margin for error has always been small; rarely have they enjoyed even the limited space of bourgeois democracy. Faced with a notoriously ruthless and seemingly invincible enemy, they have had only the potential of superior numbers and the ingenuity and resourcefulness of the revolutionary movement on which to rely. If they are successfully intervening in determining the course of their own history at this moment, it is only the result of years of groundwork, sacrifice, and patient assimilation of lessons from their own and other revolutionary movements.

But even granting years of rumblings, tremors, and even premature eruptions, the question remains: why has the volcano exploded so forcefully at this particular time? In part, it is a reflection of the overall decline in U.S. imperialism and the obstacles to its being able to intervene militarily at a particular moment. In large part, it is due to the internal contradictions that capitalist expansion in the region itself has created: the particular model of industrial expansion (heavy doses of foreign investment with little or no redistribution of the wealth), capitalist agricultural development for export (dependent on a large seasonal workforce paid below the cost of its reproduction), heavy repression to insure the model of growth, and the growth of a more concentrated and modern urban and rural working class that responds to contradictions with greater organization and militancy than ever before.

---

*Excerpted from *Latin American Perspectives*, Issues 25 and 26, Spring-Summer 1980, Vol. 7, Nos. 2 and 3.

Finally, and most importantly, the popular and revolutionary movements have prospered as a result of qualitative changes in the character of the working class and in the turn to an emphasis on mass organization after the defeat of the guerrilla *focos* in the late 1960s. The most advanced detachments of the popular movement are no longer only artisans, peasants, and white-collar workers but urban wage workers, miners, and permanent and seasonal rural wage laborers. The political line guiding the revolutionary movements and their relationship to the popular movement has changed considerably. There is, by and large, a deeper appreciation of the relationship to each other of different forms of struggle ("people's war") than there was in the "foquista" celebration of the military aspect over all else (although there are still different degrees of emphasis on the relationship of armed guerrilla actions relative to other forces within different political tendencies). There is a much more sophisticated approach to the question of alliances, the growth of a perspective that neither falls into purist rejection of cross-class alliances nor naive conciliations to bourgeois forces that restrict the independent organization of the working class. There is also a growing understanding of the complex relationship of particular forms of oppression (racism and sexism) to class oppression and an openness to ideas from other philosophical traditions (such as liberation theology) incorporated into the basic framework of a Marxist-Leninist approach. All of these changes have made it possible for revolutionaries to stimulate, learn from, and guide the mass movements to an unprecedented degree. The emphasis on "subjective factors" (political line, organization, and ideological struggle) in the context of an unwillingness or inability of the bourgeoisie to make even the most minimal reforms, have swelled the ranks of the mass movement within an exceedingly short period of time.

Crisis in the Modes of Accumulation: Common Market Industrialization and Capitalist Export Agriculture

For long periods of their history, the Central American countries have remained relatively isolated, trading and communicating more directly with Mexico, Europe, and the United States than with each other (even to the extreme of having to telephone each other until recently via Miami as the result of a communications system set up by the United Fruit Company). With the creation of the Common Market in the 1960s, however, Central America became more economically integrated than it was ever before in its history.

The Common Market strategy for industrial growth was based on a conscious plan to enlarge existing markets by linking them to each other as an alternative to broadening each internal market through higher wages, more government services, and agrarian reform. Underlying the strategy was an agreement to maintain the power of existing economic groups and avoid, or at least stave off, pressures for potentially unsettling redistributions of wealth. Although the plan originally had a nationalist context in which imported products would be gradually substituted by regionally produced ones under conditions of careful planning and a certain degree of control over foreign investment, the eventual active participation of U.S. advisors in the final formulation of the plan changed its philosophy from planning and state control to laissez-faire capitalism with open doors and generous incentives for foreign (primarily monopoly) capital.[1]

Parallel to the process of growing inequality and uneven development internal to each country was a process of conflict between the bourgeoisies of different countries and within the bourgeoisie of a single country. Where local bourgeoisies participated in the new forms of production and commerce, there was rivalry over who would control which markets and whose surplus population would be allowed to migrate where. (There were also corresponding problems in breaking down national rivalries among military officers participating in the Central American Defense Council.) The most dramatic example of this type of conflict was the 1969 war between Honduras and El Salvador which was trivialized by the U.S. press as a "soccer war" but in fact was the surface manifestation of some deep intraregional contradictions.

While the intention of the Common Market strategy was to link existing markets, it also had the effect of increasing overall dependence on the market by destroying artisan industries and restricting access to land. More important, the period of industrial and agricultural growth of the 1960s transformed a greater proportion of urban workers into pure wage laborers in concentrated modern industries and forced a greater proportion of rural workers into full or partial dependence on wages for their subsistence. The particularities of this type of dependent capitalism ("disarticulated" to a certain degree from demand and supply in the local market) dictated that they frequently be paid below the costs of their subsistence. But the very conditions that made their labor so exploitable in the first place (the use of the power of the state to repress organization and keep wages low) created its own contradiction—a popular and revolutionary movement.

Although the Common Market became a boon to foreign capital and many of its original nationalist objectives were compromised early on, the importance of the accompanying accelerated capitalist development in many parts of the region should not be downplayed. Substantial industrialization and a large measure of economic integration altered the class configuration of Central America. The major consequence was the increase in proletarianization in countries which had heretofore been among Latin America's weakest and most backward. Not only did the strengthened urban working class assume a more central political role, but the class outlook of many peasants changed as they were pulled into an expanding rural proletariat and semi-proletariat.

Secondly, economic development spawned the growth of new sectors within the Central American bourgeoisies and created new intra-bourgeois contradictions which the traditional political order was ill equipped to

---

[1] For a detailed analysis of the origin and development of the Central American Common Market see "Masterminding the Mini-Market: U.S. Aid to the Central American Common Market" in Chapter 3 of this book. —Ed.

resolve. Tyrants lording over banana republics on behalf of United Fruit was a stereotype which never accurately portrayed class rule in Central America, but the scarcity or absence of bourgeois democracy certainly favored continued political dominance by the older agro-exporting oligarchies to the detriment of newer local and foreign interests expanding through the Common Market. By the time the U.S. government realized that political reforms were urgently required to stem the revolutionary tide, it was too late in Nicaragua, El Salvador, and probably also Guatemala.

Finally, while the Common Market strategy only accentuated pre-existing differences and heightened unequal development, it did link the destinies of the different Central American nations more tightly than ever before in their history. Just as it created open markets and free trade, it also created a certain commonality of ties to the capitalist organization with all its crises as well as its changes in the relations of production. While each revolutionary movement in the different countries of the region arises out of particular conditions and addresses particular issues, it shares with the others a common origin in a common market period and with the particular type of capitalist development. Just as bourgeois interests have become more interdependent, so have those of the revolutionary movements. If there is, in fact, a domino effect in Central America, the blame or thanks are due to this stage of capitalism itself.

Crisis in the Mode of Domination

The model of industrial expansion without redistribution (in the context of massive foreign investments, use of the state apparatus to keep wages low, and reinforcement of the political and economic power of the agro-export bourgeoisie) required a corresponding political, ideological, and military apparatus to make it work. Politically, this meant use of state power to curtail union organization, break up strikes, and isolate or eliminate left political organizations while co-opting or corrupting trade unions and nonrevolutionary opposition parties. Ideologically, it meant the infusion of massive doses of anticommunist ideology, through school textbooks, teacher training programs, Protestant evangelical missionaries, and U.S.-financed institutes for training potentially friendly trade-union activists. Militarily, it meant systematic training and equipping of local security forces, the creation of special units (such as the Guatemalan Kaibiles) designed to carry out counterinsurgency operations with the assistance of U.S. advisors, and coordination of military high commands at the regional level through the Central American Defense Council.

Just as the modes of accumulation and the composition of the class benefiting from the accumulation process differ to some extent from country to country, the particular mix of military vs. civilian control, repression vs. limited formal democracy, legal vs. extra-legal force, elections vs. open dictatorship, and "law and order" vs. reformist rhetoric has varied within the Central American region in the post-war period. In El Salvador, for example, vacillations between hard-line conservative and liberal reform strategies have occurred within the relatively unchallenged context of 50 years of military rule (the bourgeoisie's answer to the ill-fated peasant uprising of 1932). Geographic, demographic, and political conditions never favored the development of armed guerrilla forces in the 1960s, but open mass political organizations were allowed to function, and the left was able to take advantage of the situation to help them grow. In Guatemala, by contrast, formal democracy exists (there are elections in which a limited number of political parties are allowed to participate but candidates are usually military men), but any opposition party and all left and working class organizations are seen as potential threats and subject to fierce repression. In Nicaragua under Somoza, on the other hand, little pretense of bourgeois democracy was ever made and Somoza's group made open legal organization, even by other sectors of the bourgeoisie, practically impossible. Only in Costa Rica has there been fertile ground for the growth of a social democratic political alternative, a result, among other factors, of a smallholding family-farm economy for long periods of its history,[2] of the reform initiatives taken early on by the Costa Rican bourgeoisie after independence from Spain, and of a continued flexibility that has allowed it to undercut potential demands from any left movement.

While repression by the state and by official military groups operating under the guise of civilians has been a characteristic of attempts to control labor, reform, and revolutionary movements in most of the Central American countries since the 1950s, the most consistent and intense application of terror and violence as a method of counterinsurgency has occurred in Guatemala since the 1960s. There are several reasons why this has been the extreme case. In the first place the agro-export bourgeoisie and its U.S. allies saw outright repression as the most efficient and, to a large extent, only effective means of dismantling the militant mass and political organizations that were built during the democratic reform movement of 1944-1954. Likewise, the armed guerrilla groups that emerged to take their place in the decade of the 1960s had to be isolated from potential links to the popular movement if the demobilization was to be maintained. During the same period, the agro-export bourgeoisie found it necessary to resort to physical force and intimidation to usurp lands occupied by small peasants and coerce a small peasant labor force to supply both the permanent and seasonal labor needed to expand their labor intensive agriculture production (the violent process of "primitive accumulation" described by Marx). The terror and violence used to break up strikes and pick off union leaders and sympathizers became part of the same system of institutionalized violence used directly for counterinsurgency.

Since the first guerrilla organizations were largely demolished in the late 1960s, terror and violence on the part of the Guatemalan government, military and large landowners continue to be the dominant mode of control both against the open mass movement and against the clandestine guerrilla

---

[2] See Anthony Winson, "Class Structure and Agrarian Transition in Central America," *Latin American Perspectives*, Vol. 5, Fall 1978, pp. 27-48.

groups. During the early guerrilla period and now during the revival of above-ground popular organizations and mobilizations, it has robbed the movement of layer upon layer of the most militant and experienced activists, making it much more difficult to sustain open popular organizations than in countries where there is still a margin of formal democracy. But in spite of the fierce repression, the last five years have seen a tremendous growth in open protests, mass mobilizations, strikes, and popular organizations as well as the appearance of guerrilla organizations (the *Ejército Guerrillero de los Pobres* [EGP], *Organización Revolucionaria del Pueblo en Armas* [ORPA], and a reconstituted *Fuerzas Armadas Rebeldes* [FAR]) that are as sophisticated politically as they are militarily. The ability of the Guatemalan mass movement to survive and grow and for new guerrilla organizations to arise from the ashes of the old is due not only to the polarization and eventual loss of fear created by the decade of official violence but, more importantly, to a new perspective on how to wage revolutionary struggle under these type of conditions, that of "people's war" or "prolonged people's war."

"People's war" is a philosophy and methodology of revolutionary struggle that emerges out of the experiences of the Vietnamese in their battles first against the French and then the United States. Its increasing influence on the thinking of Latin American revolutionaries came only after a painful and sobering examination of the "foquista" guerrilla experiences of Che Guevara in the 1960s. The guerrilla *foco*—a small group of militarily trained armed professional revolutionaries—was seen as capable of creating the subjective conditions for convincing the masses of people to revolt, of setting off the spark that would light the revolutionary fire. In contrast to the traditional communist parties, which refused to accept the necessity of armed struggle by refusing to prepare for it either in theory or in practice, the guerrilla army was seen as a proto-party organization, a fighting unit that could unite in a single command the political and military leadership for an embryonic vanguard party.

But the foco conception, encouraged by Regis Debray's writings on the Cuban revolution, suffered from what turned out to be fatal distortions: it emphasized military-tactical training and perspectives over political-ideological ones. Foco groups failed to analyze carefully the objective economic and political factors or to build patiently on the existing levels of organization and consciousness of the mass movement and generally left an active, conscious working class out of the formula. The resulting ease with which the military isolated foco guerrillas from their urban or rural bases of support—even using peasants to track them down—was more a result of their own weaknesses in understanding the complex relationship between armed guerrilla actions and other forms of struggle—political, economic, and diplomatic, internal and external, rural and urban, reform and revolutionary, peasant and worker—than it was the overwhelming strength and efficiency of the armed forces and their U.S. advisors. The latter were and are certainly formidable—with their crack counterinsurgency units and high-powered technology—but they can only succeed where military aspects predominate over political ones and when the roots of the guerrillas in the mass movements are weak.

The philosophy of "people's war," in contrast, is one which lays out the necessity of developing and coordinating different parts of a multi-sided struggle: different sectors such as men and women, young and old, peasants and workers, salaried workers and small merchants, rural and city dwellers, patriots and communists; different forms of struggle such as armed and legal, political and military, labor union and cultural, commando and masses, violent and nonviolent; and tactical flexibility (through strategic intransigence or emphasis on diplomatic vs. military, rearguard vs. vanguard, etc.) at any one point in time.

The Central American Labor Movement

Although capitalism is relatively recent in Central America and wage laborers are still less than half of the overall workforce, the origins of the labor movement and a militant tradition of struggle go back to the beginning decades of this century. Lacking the impetus provided in other Latin American countries by European immigrants with a strong labor tradition, the Central American labor movement has had from its inception a strong identification with socialist ideas and links to socialist organizations. The first labor organizations gave rise to the first communist parties.

Nevertheless, in spite of early successes, the Central American labor movement faced formidable obstacles to creating strong workers' organizations prior to the Second World War. In addition to the small size of the working class, its largely artisan and unconcentrated character, and the predominance of relations of paternalism, there were serious problems of repression from personalistic dictatorial regimes who ruled unrestrained by any provisions for legal rights. Landowners and the government in Guatemala cooperated in enforcing de facto forced labor throughout the 1920s and 1930s, the former using indigenous labor on farms and the latter on public works projects. Forced labor in both cases was assured by means of arbitrary military control.

In El Salvador, conditions favored the emergence of "free" wage labor on the one hand (over half of the rural population was landless by 1881), and a strong and relatively consolidated bourgeoisie, one relatively undifferentiated into separate agrarian, commercial, or industrial interests, on the other. In the early days of the Central American labor movement, the Salvadorean section of the Regional Workers Confederation made the rapid gains referred to above. But the ill-fated attempt to set up rural "soviets" in 1932, encouraged by the desperate conditions of the depression and the Communist Party's premature anticipation of a socialist revolution, proved to be a disastrous setback that strengthened the resolve of the Salvadorean bourgeoisie to avoid social reforms wherever possible and rule through military force—a resolve that exists, with occasional fluctuations between conservative and moderate, to the present day. The massacre of peasants that resulted in 1932 may have been the worst in Latin American history (as many as 40,000 people—or 4 percent of the population—were killed). As a consequence, repression came down on other Central American labor movements; union activity virtually stopped for twelve years within El Salvador,[3] and Salvadorean peasants remained understandably suspicious of political and labor involvement for a long time. In many ways the Salvadorean labor movement only began to recover its militant strength in the mid-1960s. But even at its low points, it has been one of the strongest and most consistently militant and class-conscious movements in the region, undoubtedly in part because of the relative intransigence of the bourgeoisie.

Early gains were also characteristic of the Costa Rican labor movement. Influenced by anarchist ideas introduced by European immigrant labor, it pulled off its first general strike as early as 1921 and, as a result, won the right to an eight-hour day and a country-wide wage increase of 40 percent.[4] On the other end of the spectrum in terms of gaining the legal right to organize is the Honduran labor movement. In spite of strong workers' organizations in the banana industry and among railroad workers, United Fruit strongly resisted efforts of workers to organize. The right to legal recognition of workers' organizations was won only as a result of a strike in 1954 in which the Latin American labor organization sympathetic to and assisted by the United States, the *Organización Regional Interamericana de Trabajadores* (ORIT), intervened with the government on behalf of the workers. As a result of this successful intervention, ORIT was granted an official monopoly on the right to organize all workers in the country, which it did with large amounts of aid from the United States government and labor federations. The Honduran labor movement became a testing ground for tactics and laws that would remove leaders who believed in class-struggle unionism or who were suspected of being sympathetic to the Communist Party. This stranglehold over the once militant union movement was eventually broken during the 1970s, leading to the emergence of a number of independent unions and confederations.[5]

Labor movements in Nicaragua and Panama have been shaped by certain internal and external factors that have no parallel in the other Central American countries. In Nicaragua, the weakness of liberal forces and the resulting limited character of liberal reforms resulted in a labor movement with relatively weak roots in the pre-Second-World-War period. After 1943, it was Somoza himself, anxious to impress the United States and cover his profascist tracks, who initiated a new labor code and provided the opening for union organization. When it became clear that the U.S. was going to be more worried about communism than fascism, Somoza availed himself of the opportunity to practically annihilate the union movement. The weakness of the union movement throughout the 1960s and the conciliatory posture of its Communist Party leadership prevented it from playing an active role and encouraged the establishment of an equally weak Social Christian

---

[3] Mario Monteforte Toledo, *Centroamérica: subdesarrollo y dependencia,* Vol. 2 (Mexico City: UNAM, 1972), p. 124.

[4] *Ibid.,* p. 123.

[5] Mario Posas, "Tres ideologías actuales en el movimiento obrero hondureño: notas preliminares de una investigación," unpublished manuscript.

influence in the labor movement. Only in the 1970s did the Nicaraguan labor movement really come into its own as an independent force, and even then it was primarily the actions of rural and urban workers organized into other forms and on their own that gave the greatest impetus to the Nicaraguan revolution.

After the Second World War the labor movement in Central America experienced substantial gains, particularly in Costa Rica and Guatemala. The Communist Party emerged as the dominant influence in the Costa Rican labor movement and apparently remains so today. At various times different ideological tendencies have attempted to challenge this influence. The ability of the Costa Rican bourgeoisie to initiate or respond to pressures for social reforms at crucial times in its post-independence history has provided favorable conditions for the existence of social and Christian democracy and has blunted the potential for militant class conflict to the present day.

The post-war pressure for democratic and nationalist reforms in Guatemala, on the other hand, provided the opening for the long-delayed development of strong rural and urban unions and, under the Presidency of Jacobo Arbenz after 1950, the conditions for an increasingly active and militant role for urban and rural workers. The overall strategy within which this radicalization occurred, however, was limited by its adherence to a Third International perspective on popular fronts (in which progressive sectors of the bourgeoisie were seen as allies and efforts were made not to alienate them). Workers were neither in control of the government nor sufficiently in opposition to it to pull it in their direction. When the landed oligarchy attempted to overthrow the government with CIA assistance, workers and peasants were never supplied the arms they were promised.

Nevertheless, in spite of the limitations of the 1944-1954 reforms in Guatemala, the legal and political advances made were substantial; so substantial, in fact, that a massive campaign of anticommunism, terror, and destruction of labor organizations had to be waged to weaken them. The first period (1954-1962) consisted primarily of demobilizing mass organizations and crippling the unions, replacing them in a few cases with company- (and U.S.-) oriented unions but in most cases with no organization at all. Many of the highly progressive provisions of the Labor Code were chipped away one by one, and others were simply removed de facto by lack of institutional support or by intimidation. The AFL-CIO and advisors from the Cuban Federation of Labor under Batista were invited to create an anticommunist labor movement. Although the tactic of terror took its toll in the early period, particularly by eliminating the best activists and leaders, ORIT-affiliated unions never achieved much importance. The Christian Democratic tendency emerged as a more important force. Increasingly, as the mass movement began to recover in 1962 and after the defeat of the foco guerrilla strategy in the late 1960s, the labor movement began to recover with the establishment of a number of unions and confederations free of bourgeois control.[6]

By the mid-1970s all over Central America there was a revival of labor struggles with much tighter links to other forms of mass struggle than ever before.

The recent period of the Central American labor movement, particularly in Guatemala and El Salvador, has been an extremely dynamic one of growth and experimentation, even though this has taken place under conditions of severe repression. Alliances between urban and rural unions are closer than ever before, and in the case of Guatemala, the historic division between Indian and mestizo workers seems to be narrowing.

Popular Organizations

Complementing the work of labor unions in Central American countries are a variety of mass organizations including peasant committees, neighborhood and slum-dweller organizations, housewife and consumer committees, student and professional organizations (teachers, doctors, lawyers, etc.), committees of relatives of the disappeared, groups of indigenous people, etc. These organizations take on a particular importance in the region where the organized labor movement is small and the proportion of the population outside of wage or salaried work is high (because of the high number of artisans, "self-employed," and outright unemployed).

Peasant organizations are made up of small peasant producers, semi-wage or full-wage workers in agriculture, in proportions that vary from country to country. (In El Salvador, for example, the number of permanent wage workers in agriculture is high, whereas in Guatemala, the majority combine seasonal wage labor with artisan or small producer activities). In the case of Guatemala, where the representation of different ethnic groups in the rural population is high, peasant organizations also serve to link the special concerns of indigenous peoples to overall rural concerns. They also serve to link the villages of the highlands to the plantations of the coast so that as workers migrate, an infrastructure of organization is carried with them.

Another group of people who play an important role in the movement for fundamental social change in Central America are the progressive and revolutionary Christians. In the case of El Salvador, for example, the most important peasant organization was started by Christians. Liberation theology—a doctrine that tries to analyze Christian principles from the point of view of the oppressed and exploited—has helped blunt the traditional anticommunist arguments that ruling classes have used to oppose social change and has facilitated the participation of Christians in the popular movement.

Women are unusually active in the popular and revolutionary movements of Central America. They participate as militants, members of

[6] CIDAMO (Centro de Información, Documentación y Análisis sobre el Movimiento Obrero Latinoamericano), "The Workers' Movement in Guatemala" in *NACLA Report on the Americas*, Vol. 14, No. 1, January-February 1980.

peasant and indigenous communities (the leader of the protesting peasants who were massacred at Panzós, Guatemala, was an Indian woman, and five out of the thirty-two who died when the Guatemalan police stormed the Spanish embassy were women), organizers of neighborhood committees (especially in Nicaragua), and as relatives of the dead and disappeared who pressure the governments and appeal to international public opinion.[7]

The Significance of the Nicaraguan Revolution

Almost exactly twenty years after the victory of the Cuban revolution, the Nicaraguan revolution led by the Frente Sandinista de Liberación Nacional (FSLN) came to power. The extent of the victory was surprising. Everyone believed Somoza's days were numbered, but few imagined that the end was quite so near or that the schemes of pro-Somoza and U.S. imperialist forces to leave intact the National Guard and elements of the pro-Somoza bourgeoisie would disintegrate so quickly. It was a remarkable achievement for the FSLN, an organization established two decades ago, that had suffered in the past from some of the same defeats, dead-end paths, and problems of isolation from the masses that had plagued other Central American and Latin American revolutionary organizations.[8]

Revolutionary Strategy

The main strategic perspective of the Frente after 1970—that of the *Guerra Popular Prolongada* (GPP) or "prolonged people's war"—allowed the nucleus of the Frente to develop in the protective geography of the rural areas and develop strong roots among the rural population in addition to some organization in urban neighborhoods. It saw the guerrilla as the vanguard and emphasized the need for sophisticated military organization to confront the National Guard. It enjoyed a great deal of popularity and prestige among the masses for its military skill and its well-known leaders, Tomás Borje, Henry Ruiz, Bayardo Arce, etc.[9]

On the other hand, it is possible to look backwards and see how the GPP strategy underestimated both the potential for urban working-class organization through labor unions (advocated by the *Tendencia Proletaria* or Proletarian Tendency) and the spontaneous insurrectional currents in the masses (advocated by the insurrectional or *Tercerista* tendency). The proletarian perspective focused on the change that had occurred in the Nicaraguan social formation in the last twenty years as a result of the introduction of cotton production and the Central American Common Market, arguing that the emergent process of proletarianization among urban and

[7] See Chapter 7 of this book for a specific treatment of women's participation in revolutionary movements. –Ed.

[8] See FSLN (Frente Sandinista de Liberación Nacional), "On the General Political-Military Platform of Struggle of the Sandinista Front for National Liberation for the Triumph of the Sandinista Popular Revolution," Resistance Publications (P.O. Box 116, Oakland, California 94604), 1979.

[9] Nelson Minello, "Antecedentes y características del proceso revolucionario," *Cuadernos de Marcha*, Segunda Epoca, 1, January-February 1980, pp. 55-62.

rural workers made the construction of something more than a "frente" (i.e., a Leninist party) a desirable possibility. The insurrectionists, or Terceristas, while emphasizing military firepower almost to the exclusion of ideological development and political work among the masses, correctly perceived the vulnerability of the Somoza regime in that particular conjuncture, the insurrectional possibilities of the masses, and the usefulness of broad international support such as that actually given by the countries and parties of the Socialist International.

Unity Among Revolutionaries

A second key contribution of the Nicaraguan experience—one which has already had a positive effect on the struggles in El Salvador and Guatemala—was the successful process of reuniting three tendencies that had developed their own leadership, organizational structures, military units, and international support systems. The conditions under which this extraordinary and critical process of unity was forged have yet to be fully studied or revealed. But several contributing factors can be singled out.

In the first place, there was relatively little sectarianism or dogmatism characterizing the different tendencies when they were operating separately. In part, experience itself convinced the different tendencies of a more multidimensional view of revolutionary strategy. None of the tendencies apparently interfered with each others' work, even during the period of separation, and the degree to which they all were firmly oriented to Nicaraguan reality, rather than some invariant formula, made it possible to assimilate the results of new experiences when those experiences began changing. Most important of all, however, was the growing momentum of the mass movement which increasingly resolved the question of whether the masses were ready to fight. Popular organizations in the *Movimiento Pueblo Unido* demanded the unity of revolutionaries.

The Relationship of the Vanguard to the Masses

Unity among revolutionaries was encouraged by the spontaneous movements of the masses, and this unity, in turn, gave cohesion and direction to the spontaneous rebellions of the people.

Ortega comments on the way the relationship developed. In October 1977, for example, when the FSLN ended a period of relative stagnation by capturing the National Guard garrison at San Carlos near the Costa Rican border and continued with attacks on the main garrison in Masaya, the action was not only an action by a vanguard but one which

> *frustrated the schemes of reaction and enabled the vanguard to gather renewed strength, e.g., begin to strengthen a series of activities that the masses had been carrying out, in spite of the repression, and which consisted of struggles for social gains, trade-union and political struggles. Therefore, these actions strengthened the mass movement, which later*

became openly insurrectional.[10]

In the end, actions on the part of the masses were determinant in the outcome of the struggle. Ortega comments:

I myself feel that it is very difficult to take power without a crea-tive combination of all forms of struggle wherever they can take place: countryside, city, town, neighborhood, mountain, etc., but always based on the idea that the mass movement is the focal point of the struggle and not the vanguard with the masses limited to merely supporting it.[11]

These views of the relationship between mass and vanguard represent a qualitative change from the days of the conception of the guerrilla foco where the vanguard was seen as acting almost alone (an error referred to as "vanguardism"). At the same time, it represents a variation on the classical Leninist conception of the vanguard as a party of the working class and peasantry formed as a precondition for taking power. Just why this is the case and what its implications are remains to be fully explained. But it is a fact that party formation in Nicaragua, and probably in a number of future revolutions in Latin American countries, will be seen as a task corresponding to the period of consolidation of revolutionary power rather than as an indispensable precondition for achieving it.

National Unity: The Question of Alliances

The Sandinistas have revealed themselves to be artists in "uniting all who can be united" around a particular platform or program. Their ability to ally with sectors of the bourgeoisie, not only to overthrow Somoza but to contribute to a mixed economy during a crucial period of reconstruction and to do so under conditions essentially controlled by the Frente, opens a whole new chapter in the art of making revolution in Latin America. Their in-timate relationship with progressive and revolutionary sectors of the Chris-tian church—a relationship that Tomás Borje has assured is neither tactical nor short-term—has undercut and helped to neutralize the hysterical anti-communist propaganda that has bombarded Central American societies since the beginning of the Cold War. Internationally, the FSLN has pursued the same policy of uniting all who can be united in support of the revolu-tion. The result was the greatest outpouring of international solidarity since the Spanish Civil War. The very effectiveness of those alliances during the period of insurrection is the reason for the increasing pressure on them by U.S. imperialism in the period of reconstruction, leading to some defections or vacillations by members of the Socialist International camp (Costa Rica and Venezuela, for example).

Conclusion

Because of the high degree of international solidarity and because of

---

[10] Marta Harnecker, "Nicaragua: The Strategy of Victory" (interview with FSLN Com-mander Humberto Ortega), *Intercontinental Press*, 18, February 18, 1980, p. 151.
[11] *Ibid.*, p. 155.

the instantaneous transmissions of international news agencies (distorted though their accounts may often be), we are probably closer to the unfolding of the Nicaraguan revolutionary process and to current events in El Salvador and Guatemala than we have been to any comparable development in Latin America during this century. This intimacy affords a unique opportunity for learning about social and political processes and the ability of people to shape them. If there is one lesson that has been learned at great cost as a result of mechanical attempts to repeat the Cuban revolution, it is that successful interventions into the course of history depend on a careful mastering not only of universal principles but of concrete conditions. The significance of the Nicaraguan revolutionary process so far is precisely its ability to absorb the lessons of Sandino, a revolutionary fighter who knew the social and geographical terrain of his country like the palm of his hand, and the insights of other revolutionary movements. The Sandinistas have affirmed the principle that theory is not a dogma but a guide to action and that tactics must be flexible and creative even while the overall strategic perspective is constant and firm. It is safe to say that the same degree of grounding in knowledge of concrete conditions will be true of any successes of the revolutionary movements in El Salvador and Guatemala.

Behind the Nicaraguan Revolution*

By Harald Jung

Harald Jung is a Researcher for Fundación IESA (Investigaciones Económicas y Sociales Aplicadas) *in Madrid, Spain.*

The first decades of the 20th century saw the transformation of Nicaragua into one of the so-called banana republics of Central America, though it was not so much banana companies who took charge of the country's political and economic destiny as United States wood and mining interests. As the mining labor force expanded, these companies found themselves faced with a proletariat that was extremely rebellious by Central American standards, launching no less than ten armed insurrections against the U.S. companies and their puppet governments between 1914 and 1925, in union with sections of the peasantry and national bourgeoisie, as well as a large number of major strikes.

The response of the Nicaraguan government was to call in the U.S. Marines, in 1912, and for the next sixteen years the presidential office was generally occupied by an accountant for one of the U.S. mining companies, or else by one of his subordinates. When in 1927 this government was no longer able, despite repeated U.S. military support, to resist a rebel army composed of sections of the liberal national bourgeoisie together with workers and peasants, the United States managed to purchase an armistice and peace agreement with the bourgeois commanders of the rebel army. In

---

*Excerpted and abridged from *New Left Review*, No. 117, September-October 1979, pp. 69-89.

the most literal sense of the term, the Nicaraguan bourgeoisie sold out and ended their war.

The workers' and peasants' section of the rebel force, however, did not go along with this deal. Under the leadership of Augusto César Sandino, a former plantation worker, oil-field worker and petrol salesman, they retreated into the mountains and there began an almost six-year *guerrilla*. This broadened out into a people's war, aiming to bring about the withdrawal of the U.S. Marines and establish true national sovereignty. After heavy losses by the Marines, and growing opposition in the U.S.A. itself against this military presence, the Marines built up a local professional army, the *Guardia Nacional*, and withdrew from the country in 1932. In the elections held in November of that year, the Liberal politician Sacasa was elected president.

Sandino, whose army was by now the preponderant military force in Nicaragua, and could not have been successfully resisted, saw his goal as attained. He recognized the Sacasa government and signed a peace treaty in February 1933, disarming his soldiers and dissolving his force.

In the course of the war Sandino's national revolutionaries had developed into social revolutionaries, in a spontaneous fashion conditioned by their class origin and without much theoretical consciousness of their own development. In the districts which they controlled, they began to reorganize agriculture along collective lines. After the war was over, they continued working to build a comprehensive cooperative movement. Their ideas on agricultural collectivization undermined the private economy and they came to be regarded as heroes by the workers and peasants.

In February 1934, accordingly, the National Guard (now the only armed force in the country) seized Sandino and his former commanders and shot them on the spot, beginning a merciless hunt for the disarmed and scattered Sandino supporters. They broke up the cooperatives, killing hundreds of families in the process, and finally, in 1936-1937, their American-appointed commander-in-chief overthrew the government and took over the presidency. His name: Anastasio "Tacho" Somoza.

The Somoza Clan and the National Guard

Once in power, Somoza, and after his assassination in 1956 his two sons Luis and Anastasio "Tachito" Somoza (the recent president), used their positions as head of state (Luis) and commander-in-chief of the National Guard (Anastasio) to fill all important posts either with members of their own family or business friends, or else with officers of the National Guard.

Control of these positions enabled the clan to directly appropriate other people's property through politically sanctioned robbery and theft, to monopolize especially profitable branches of the economy for themselves, and to obtain limitless competitive advantages. They forced unequal business deals on the bourgeoisie, and enriched themselves by corruption, embezzlement, blackmail, murder, and every conceivable form of economic and ordinary crime.

Since such methods provoked an always latent and often violent resistance from the non-Somoza bourgeoisie, the Somozas needed an armed force that would stand faithfully by their clan. This force was the National Guard. The Somozas made sure of its fidelity by involving the majority of officers and a large section of the rank and file in their machinations, besides providing the National Guard with its own independent means of enrichment, from corruption through to robbery and murder.[1]

Through such Mafioso methods, the clan succeeded by the mid 1970s in bringing some 60 per cent of the national economy into its own hands or under its majority control, and becoming the dominant force in all spheres of the Nicaraguan economy.

The Non-Somoza Bourgeoisie and Middle Strata

Alongside the Somozas there were two other great bourgeois families who were exempt from the clan's criminal methods, and who continued to profit from Somoza's policies until the mid-1970s, being tied to the clan by common business interests. One of these is the group around the Banco de América (led by the Pellas Chamorro family), the other that around the Banco Nicaragüense (led by the Montealegre Callejos family).

The third pillar of capital in Nicaragua is foreign capital, its investments shifting during the 1960s from the traditional agricultural and service sectors into the foodstuffs, chemical, textile and electrical industries. In 1976 this foreign capital amounted to some $125 million (70 per cent being United States). If this foreign capital had to give the clan bribes and a share in its profits, it was rewarded by wide-ranging freedom from taxation, it received privileges and guarantees that were secured by the state, it could obtain public contracts through corruption, and it had no restrictions placed on the transfer of capital or profits.

Finally, there is a further fraction of the bourgeoisie that can best be described as marginal, playing only a subordinate economic role in comparison to the Somozas, the military bourgeoisie, the two other major financial families and foreign capital. This stratum is also underrepresented in precisely the more dynamic and expanding sectors. And it was this fraction of the bourgeoisie whose economic opportunities came to be ever more restricted by the criminal methods of the Somoza clan.

Nicaragua's entry into the Central American Common Market in 1963 set under way a process of industrialization and economic boom, giving rise to a large urban middle stratum made up of the smallest entrepreneurs, handicraft and petty service undertakings, employees in the banks and insurance companies, teachers, middle-rank officials in the administration and other intellectual professions. This stratum, which shades easily into the marginal bourgeoisie on the one hand and the urban working class on

---

[1] To give one example, between June and November alone, 312 peasants vanished without trace in the department of Zelaya. Their homes subsequently became the property of National Guards. (*Los Derechos Humanos en Nicaragua*, published by the Informe Oficial CPDH de Nicaragua, April 1977-February 1978.)

the other, comprised in 1973 somewhat less than a fifth of Nicaragua's 544,000 economically active population (out of a total population of 2.02 million), so that it is a significant political factor by size alone. It was exposed to the arbitrary machinations of the middle and lower ranks of the Somoza clan's retinue and the National Guard, and was blocked by the regime in its economic, cultural and political development. Since it enjoys a higher educational standard than the rest of the oppressed population, it is principally from its ranks that the leading members of the opposition and the resistance movement have been recruited.

The Development of the Opposition

During the liberation war under Sandino, all the subaltern sectors of Nicaraguan society, which had previously acted in isolation from one another, or under the leadership of a fraction of the bourgeoisie, emerged as a single, autonomous historical subject, acting independently of the bourgeoisie for the first time in the country's history. After all but a few remnants of the Sandinistas had been destroyed, the popular resistance came in the 1940s to follow in the wake of the Conservative bourgeois opposition, and was channelled and used by these forces.[2] Both the Communist party and the trade-union movement were crushed by Somoza immediately after the Second World War.

The first steps towards the beginning of a new autonomous labor movement were taken by the transport workers in 1950, with the foundation of a national union.

The emancipation of the agricultural population from the tutelage of the Conservative opposition began with the cotton boom of the first half of the 1950s. This led to a pact between the Conservative cotton bourgeoisie and Somoza, and, with the extension of cotton-growing, to the proletarianization of former small peasants and evictions from the land. The victims of this process could not but take an opposition stance against its initiators. When falling cotton and coffee prices led to an economic crisis in the second half of the 1950s, and the assassination of Tacho Somoza also brought the regime into political crisis, this emancipation led to a large number of strikes, mass struggles and the refounding of trade-unions and workers' and peasants' associations. The Conservatives were now unable to control and channel this movement.

From this peasants', workers' and students' movement of the late 1950s grew the first—chiefly student—guerrilla groups, coming together in 1961-62 to form the *Frente Sandinista de Liberación Nacional* (FSLN). The same movement led to the reconstruction of the Communist party, the *Partido Socialista Nicaragüense* (PSN). From the movement, too, there arose the forerunners of the three major Nicaraguan trade-union associations of

---

[2] Somoza converted the Liberal party into his private party. The bourgeois opposition thus gathered around the Conservatives. The political content of these two major traditional political tendencies, however, had long since shifted. The Conservatives no more pursue a consistently conservative policy than the Somozists a liberal one.

today: the *Confederación General de Trabajadores* (CGT), the *Central de Trabajadores de Nicaragua* (CTN), and the *Confederación Unificación Sindical* (CUS).[3]

In the countryside, it was chiefly the Sandinistas and philanthropic Christians who organized workers into unions and gave them their political education. Monastic orders organized peasant cooperatives and in this way took over the vision of a society based on cooperation which Sandino's original peasant and worker soldiers had already dreamed of.

In the cities, the same period saw the implantation of the Communist party and the small left-wing Catholic *Partido Social Cristiano* (PSC), the Communist party later splitting into an orthodox and a "nationally independent" wing. The PSC led the CTN trade-union federation, and the Communists the CGT. From 1972 on, these trade unions were increasingly able to stage large-scale and comprehensive strikes and mass demonstrations, making social, economic and specific political demands on the regime.

Until 1974, the political groupings of the bourgeoisie followed a very disunited, vacillating and contradictory policy vis-á-vis the Somoza clan and its Mafia regime. The clan was well aware of this, and alternately involved different fractions of the bourgeoisie in its criminal deals, seeking always to break up the bourgeois opposition.

The most important points in this policy of vacillation—in actual fact a struggle for the trough—were as follows. In 1948 the Conservative opposition led a broad popular movement against Somoza. By 1950, however, with the cotton boom impending, it had already made a deal with Somoza, as his National Guard was needed to drive the peasants off the land. Scarcely was the boom over, when the Conservatives got involved in an assassination plot against Somoza. In 1959-1960 they led armed invasions and insurrections, only to cease virtually all opposition in the second half of the 1960s. This was again a time of economic boom. In 1967 the Conservatives organized mass demonstrations for the holding of genuine free elections. The National Guard fired on the crowd, killing or wounding more than 300 people, but this did not prevent the Conservatives, later the same year, from entering into an armistice with Somoza in return for a few seats in congress (blatant sinecures). In 1971 a new deal was made for the elections due to be held in the following year. This time the Conservatives were promised in advance some 40 per cent of the seats.

Opposition Strategies from the Mid-1970s

From 1973 on, the political crisis came increasingly to a head. Four factors were responsible for this.

(1) After the devastating Managua earthquake of December 1972, the Somoza clan used the resultant international aid chiefly for its own enrichment. The Somozas misappropriated to their own advantage a good half

---

[3] The CGT, the largest trade-union association, belongs to the World Federation of Trade Unions, the CTN to the World Confederation of Labor, and the CUS to the International Confederation of Free Trade Unions.

of all aid received. The National Guard also looted. While victims of the earthquake were bleeding in Managua, the clan were selling the blood plasma received from international aid organizations at a good price in the U.S.A. This made it clear to all that the Nicaraguan government was in actual fact nothing but a criminal syndicate. (Here is the reason, incidentally, why subsequently even reactionary Latin American regimes began to distance themselves from Somoza.)

(2) With the build-up of the military bourgeoisie after 1972, government corruption and economic crime increased to such an extent that properly conducted business transactions became virtually impossible. Even the Somoza clan was no longer in a position to control the access of certain fractions of the bourgeoisie to crooked deals. The mechanism that had previously blocked the emergence of a united bourgeois opposition now began increasingly to fail.

(3) To support this military bourgeoisie and make repayments on government-backed foreign debts,[4] the regime steadily increased taxes on production and consumption. This ever-rising tax burden, together with a rate of inflation that had reached almost 35 per cent by 1977, and the spread of criminal "competition" by the military bourgeoisie, brought the marginal and petty bourgeoisie, in particular, to the verge of economic collapse.[5]

(4) A liberal policy on prices, combined with restriction on wages, led from the mid-1970s to an increasing decline in real purchasing power for wage-earners, nominal wage increases failing to keep pace with inflation.

Against this background, all the opposition tendencies succeeded from the mid-1970s onwards in gaining support among those sections of the population they represented, on a scale they had not enjoyed for decades. The opposition was essentially divided into two sections, represented on the one hand by the bourgeois-dominated *Unión Democrática de Liberación* (UDEL), and on the other by the *Frente Sandinista de Liberación Nacional* (FSLN).

In the early 1970s, those parts of the bourgeois opposition who were no longer prepared to continue the unprincipled struggle for the trough of the previous decades came together in an opposition coalition, and at the end of 1974 formed UDEL. This embraced a total of seven parties and trade unions. The Communist party and its trade-union confederation also joined UDEL. The party had stood since its reconstruction for the thesis that,

---

[4] The industrialization of the 1960s was largely financed by government loans from abroad, on account of the low level of local savings. After 1975, the government attempted to stabilize economic development in a similar way. In 1977 the publicly guaranteed foreign debt stood at 836 million dollars, as against a total GNP of only 2 billion. Debt servicing cost 104 million dollars in 1977, i.e., 15.8 per cent of total receipts from exports.

[5] In Managua, for example, officers sold vast quantities of electrical goods that had been smuggled into the country free of duty and at far below their usual market price. Taxi and bus firms were monopolized by National Guard officers, and several large estates were also distributed to officers.

without abandoning its "historic revolutionary and socialist perspective," it had initially to unite with the bourgeois-democratic forces and wage with them a preparatory struggle against the dictatorship and for a democratic renewal.[6]

The UDEL expressly saw itself as a collaboration of labor and capital for the overthrow of the Somoza government, and had no program of social transformation. It set its sights on the establishment of a capitalism functioning according to market mechanisms, with a democratic form of bourgeois rule, in which exchange relationships between economic subjects would obey the the principles of freedom and equality, and not be overshadowed and made impossible by corruption, blackmail and dictatorial caprice. UDEL's strategy was designed to strengthen the opponents of Somoza in the U.S.A. by exposing the atrocities of his regime, and subsequently to force the dictator's resignation by a general strike with United States backing.[7]

The FSLN had originally operated on the lines of Che Guevara's theory of the *foco*, but by 1964 had been almost destroyed, so that it then began intensive political work among students and peasants. In 1966-67 it launched a new guerrilla war, was again defeated, and subsequently came to place the major weight of its activity on political work among peasants and agricultural workers, whom it intended to organize and educate for a protracted people's war (*guerra popular prolongada*).

The tremendous growth of the marginalized masses in the urban slums, and the economic and political development since 1973 already sketched, gave rise to a massive resistance potential in the cities also. In 1975, this development led to a new discussion on strategy in the FSLN, ending with the emergence of three distinct fractions. The majority fraction, the "*Tendencia Insurreccional*" (TI), maintained that the guerrilla struggle had to be brought into the cities, mass work intensified in the countryside, and mass organizations built up in factories, educational institutions, offices and residential districts, with a view to preparing the population for a new insurrection. The "*Guerra Popular Prolongada*" fraction continued to stand for the strategy of a protracted people's war in the countryside, while the "*Tendencia Proletaria*" fraction held that guerrilla warfare should be abandoned and devoted itself to the construction of a revolutionary proletarian party.

After 1975, the national leadership of the majority fraction opened up the FSLN to non-Marxist, politically committed Christians, who worked for liberation from the Somoza regime and for a socialism based on cooperatives. In this way it managed to win the support of important sections of the church, which since the late 1960s had turned more strongly against the regime on humanitarian grounds. At the same time, the majority fraction began to construct a political as well as a military organization in

---

[6]L. Sanchez, "El programa de UDEL como alternativa para la democratización y la liberación de Nicaragua," in *Alianzas políticas en Centroamérica*, Guatemala City, 1975.

[7]UDEL, *El programa de UDEL*, Managua, 1974; and *Pronunciamiento*, Managua, 24 August 1977.

the cities, to initiate and press forward the mass organization needed for popular insurrection.[8]

The FSLN undoubtedly pursued the goal of a socialist revolution in Nicaragua. But it saw as a necessary intermediate stage the destruction of the Somoza regime together with its economic and military power base. Its minimal program for the post-Somoza government accordingly involved the nationalization of the Somoza clan's property and the dissolution of the National Guard.[9]

For the overthrow of the Somoza dictatorship—so ran the strategy of the majority fraction—the "popular political forces" (i.e., the FSLN itself, the trade unions, the various mass organizations, and the Communists) should enter a tactical alliance with the "bourgeois opposition forces," and form together with them the post-Somoza transitional government. So that the popular forces should win the upper hand in this "democratic popular government," and be able to transform an originally mixed economic system into a socialist economic order on the basis of the nationalized Somoza property, they should be organized already before the uprising in as united and comprehensive a fashion as possible.[10]

The result of this strategy was the formation of numerous new mass organizations, and finally, in late summer of 1978, the constitution of the *Movimiento Pueblo Unido* (MPU) with the adherence of more than 22 organizations. The MPU stood still more clearly than the FSLN for a socialist perspective on the basis of the nationalization of all basic branches of the economy.[11] The Communists and their trade-union confederation also joined the MPU.

U.S. Opposition to Somoza

The Somozas sought to make themselves as independent as possible from the U.S.A., and the U.S.A. as dependent as possible on them. The clan reduced as much as it could its one-time total dependence on the U.S.A. in the field of foreign trade. On the other hand, it most willingly developed the role of a counter-revolutionary force of order, using the National Guard for this purpose in a region that is of extreme strategic importance for the U.S.A., so that the latter became to a significant extent dependent on it. The National Guard was built up by the United States into the most powerful army in Central America, and became the backbone of the Central American military alliance CONDECA, whose primary purpose was the collaboration of the small Central American armies in combating guerrilla activity. From 1964 on, more than ten anti-guerrilla actions were jointly

---

[8] C. Fonseca Amador, "Zero Hour in Nicaragua," *Tricontinental*, Havana, September-October 1969; D. Waksman Schinca, "Entrevista con Plutarco Hernández," *El Gallo Ilustrado*, Mexico City, 6 August 1978.

[9] FSLN, "Por que lucha el FSLN junto al pueblo," *Lucha Sandinista*, somewhere in Nicaragua, June 1978.

[10] "El Frente Amplio, el pueblo a la cabeza," *Lucha Sandinista, loc. cit.*, May 1978.

[11] MPU, "Programa de MPU," Managua, July 1978.

conducted by the armed forces of Guatemala, El Salvador, Honduras and Nicaragua.[12]

It goes without saying, moreover, that a United States government could only be seriously interested in Somoza's resignation if a bourgeois alternative to Somoza were available, and Sandinista or other forces with a socialist or communist orientation were not automatically catapulted to power as a result.

Only against this background is it possible to understand why the history of relations between the Somoza clan and the U.S.A. shows a steady alternation of phases in which the clan enjoyed the unconditional support of the U.S. government, with phases in which the United States withdrew this support and even sought to expel Somoza from power. This policy continued under the Carter Administration.

From Bourgeois Opposition to Sandinista Insurrection

As far back as 1976 UDEL was already organizing a human rights campaign against Somoza among North American public opinion, and even before Congressional committees. After heated discussions and intrigues in the U.S. State Department, in Congressional committees and on the floor of Congress itself, Congress still voted in June 1977 to continue military support to Somoza. The UDEL's hope of forcing Somoza to resign by way of United States pressure thus came to a temporary dead-end.

The Sandinistas now took the initiative. Starting in October 1977, their military organization incessantly attacked the National Guard, imposing heavy losses; it temporarily occupied several towns, expropriating weapons from the National Guard there, opening prisons, holding political meetings and recruiting new soldiers before vanishing once again. Its political organization held meetings of peasants and agricultural workers, organized land occupations, strikes in the factories and mass demonstrations, which rapidly overspilled their immediate pretexts and set themselves directly against the regime.

The church and the trade unions were particularly active in supporting such actions and contributing to the formation of new popular organizations. At the same time, a group of prominent individuals from Nicaragua's economic and cultural life, the "Group of Twelve," declared that no solution was possible for the country without the participation of the FSLN, and that the entire opposition, including the Sandinistas, should combine in a common opposition front for the overthrow of the regime. The group subsequently went into exile. High bourgeois dignitaries, members of the UDEL and sections of the church leadership sought to stir the dictator to a "national dialogue" and to reforms.

On 10 January 1978 the UDEL chairman, Pedro Joaquín Chamorro, was shot. The bourgeois opposition blamed Somoza, withdrew its proposal for a national dialogue with the dictator, and called a general strike on 22 January, to last until Somoza resigned. The trade unions and several

---

[12] G. Aguilera, *La integración militar en Centroamérica*, Guatemala City, 1975.

mass organizations added their voices to this call. When the strike became ever more militant, around the end of the month, and began to assume the forms of a violent popular insurrection, the U.S. embassy in Managua prevailed on the opposition to end the strike. On 5 and 6 February the embassy declared that the U.S.A. would cease military aid to Somoza for the rest of the year and support a reform of the regime, but was not willing to see a revolution. On 7 February the bourgeois-dominated "National Strike Committee" called off the strike. A conflict now broke out in the UDEL between the "bourgeois" and the "popular" sectors. The former called for an end to the strike, the latter for its continuation. The church, too, took up a clear position, the Archbishop of Managua declaring the right of a people to collective armed resistance. And while control of the continuing strike slipped away from the bourgeoisie, the people began to make use of this right. The period between 12 and 20 February saw mass demonstrations right across the country, together with violent clashes between demonstrators and National Guard, and acts of sabotage against Somoza property.

The first insurrection then broke out. In Masaya the National Guard fired on a demonstration with machine-guns. The citizens built barricades and defended themselves with stones, cudgels and old rifles. The Indian quarter of Monimbó was sealed off by its inhabitants and became the heart of the town's resistance, being bombed by Somoza's air force and shelled by the artillery. March 3 saw the end of seven days of constant battle. The National Guard reconquered Monimbó, where there were some four to five hundred victims.

The Carter Administration stood fast on its line of "reform yes, revolution no." On 16 February, after the bourgeoisie had lost control of the strike, the U.S.A. announced that it would not after all suspend military aid to Somoza for 1978, but only for 1979. After the Monimbó insurrection, and the National Guard's mass murder, high U.S. functionaries spoke publicly on various occasions of an improvement in the human rights situation in Nicaragua. Somoza also continued to receive economic aid from the U.S.A. to make good the earthquake damage of 1972-3, though everyone now knew how conscientiously Somoza misappropriated such donations.[13]

From Monimbó to September 1978

By July, further clashes of a civil war character had taken place in Managua, León, Rivas, Granada, Jinotepe and Estelí. The FSLN extended its guerrilla war, with ever greater support from the population, who built roadblocks and acted as scouts. The peasant movement advanced to large-scale land occupations.[14] The "Group of Twelve" returned from exile in

---

[13] Comisión del FSLN, *Boletín Informativo* No. 3, "Somewhere in Nicaragua," February 1978; "La situación en Nicaragua a partir de octubre 1977," *Gaceta Sandinista*, Mexico City, October 1977-March 1978; M.G. Del Cueto, "Nicaragua, El crimen fue en Masaya," *Bohemia*, Havana, 10 March 1978; Infopress Centroamericana No. 309, Guatemala C.A., September 14, 1978, p. 4.

[14] M.G. Del Cueto, "Nicaragua, rebeliones campesinas," *Bohemia*, 23 June, 1978.

July, despite threats of imprisonment from Somoza, and were welcomed by 60,000 enthusiastic Nicaraguans. In the same month, the broad front of all opposition groups which the Group of Twelve had called for was finally formed, the *Frente Amplio de Oposición* (FAO), on a bourgeois-democratic platform of national renewal.[15] The FSLN participated in the FAO, represented by the Group of Twelve.

In the middle of the year it became clear to the entire opposition that the U.S.A. was once more placing itself behind Somoza, as a result of the radicalization of the popular movement. In May, the Nicaraguan government received a 12 million dollar credit from the United States. In August, after Somoza had been in Washington, three loans of 40, 50 and 60 million dollars were announced, obtained in the U.S.A. by private Nicaraguan banks. Carter himself wrote a personal letter to Somoza, congratulating him for the improvement in the human rights situation in his country.[16]

The opposition now abandoned all hopes for a peaceful solution, the FSLN counting solely on the violent overthrow of the Somoza regime. On 22 August a twenty-five strong FSLN force occupied the National Palace, taking some 2000 politicians and their staff hostage. They obtained a ransom in money and the release of sixty political prisoners before setting off for Panama and Venezuela by plane amid the rejoicing of tens of thousands of Nicaraguans, who jammed the streets in massed ranks.[17]

On 25 August, after a call from the FAO, a general strike of labor and capital was launched. Somoza had several bourgeois oppositionists imprisoned, including the Nicaraguan head of Coca-Cola. In the meantime, district committees had been formed in almost all towns in the country, coordinated by the MPU, in which all opposition organizations worked together, taking concrete steps to prepare for insurrection: medical and surgical posts were set up, and the population instructed in first aid. "Popular brigades" expelled Somoza supporters and seized their houses and offices.[18] A general insurrection then broke out. On 28 August the population of Matagalpa rose up spontaneously and were indiscriminately bombed by Somoza's air force, just as in Masaya-Monimbó. The FSLN found itself under pressure to move, and called for a general popular insurrection on 9 September. By 15 September the inhabitants of 15 towns had revolted. In most cases, the FSLN forces succeeded at first in occupying the National Guard garrisons. Then Somoza's aerial bombing started. The population sealed off the towns. The MPU and FSLN began to evacuate those people in greatest danger, and subsequently to withdraw. But the bombing continued even after the FSLN had withdrawn. After the towns had been recaptured, the National Guard systematically massacred all young people

---

[15] FAO, "16 Puntos para el gobierno nacional," Managua, 17 August 1978.

[16] G. García Márquez, "El ataque sandinista en Managua" (4 parts), *El Gráfico*, Guatemala City, 5-8 September 1978; NLR translation, No. 111 (Sept.-Oct. 1978).

[17] *Ibid.*

[18] A. M. Mergier, "Cada casa, un cuartel sandinista," *Alternativa*, Bogotá, 25 September 1978.

who had not fled with the FSLN into the mountains, in so-called "mop up" operations.[19] The number of dead is estimated at 6,000 insurrectionists and civilians. The FSLN claims to have lost only 33 *guerrilleros*, as against 1,200 National Guard killed and 700 deserted, some of these going over to the FSLN complete with their weapons.[20] Meanwhile 60,000 Nicaraguans fled into adjacent countries.

From September 1978 to June 1979

After the defeat of the September insurrection, the U.S.A. sought to mediate between Somoza and the FAO, with the aid of the Dominican Republic and Guatemala. These mediators sought the resignation of Somoza while maintaining the National Guard as a last bastion against a Sandinista seizure of power, and the installation of a non-Sandinista government acceptable to the United States. The Group of Twelve withdrew from the negotiations in October. It was essentially only those groups within the FAO who stood close to the two non-Somoza financial families that continued to negotiate on the basis of this plan. The Group of Twelve subsequently broke with the FAO, which it charged with betraying the interests of the Nicaraguan people. It was followed by the trade unions, the Communists, and almost all the bourgeois parties, with the exception of those groups closest to finance capital.[21] In January 1979, Somoza brought negotiations with the rump of the FAO to a halt. This meant an end to the solution sought by the Nicaraguan financial bourgeoisie and the U.S.A.

While the FAO broke up in disarray, a new opposition front was formed on 1 February 1979, the *Frente Patriótico Nacional* (FPN). The FPN explicitly shared the Sandinista perspective, and accepted the three fundamental points of the Sandinista program: disbandment of the National Guard, nationalization of all property belonging to the Somoza clan, and the establishment of a democratic popular government with the participation of all major social and political sectors. With the exception of Nicaraguan finance capital, almost all organizations and parties of the bourgeoisie, the working class, the peasants, the marginalized population and the intellectuals adhered to the FPN.[22]

In the meantime, the FSLN was preparing for its final offensive: thousands of young men and women who had fled from the towns after the September insurrection poured into the ranks of the FSLN, which began to build up a Sandinista army alongside its guerrilla force. In the working-class and poor districts of the towns it organized Sandinista people's militias, established supplies of weapons, medicines, and provisions, and prepared the population for the uprising.

---

[19] (Por la) Dirección Nacional del FSLN, *Parte de Guerra* nos. 1-9, somewhere in Nicaragua, 10-17 September 1978.

[20] *Ibid.*

[21] These groupings were led by the *Movimiento Democrático Nicaragüense* (MDN), a center-right party of dignitaries founded in February 1978.

[22] FPN, *Constitution of the National Patriotic Front*, Managua, January 1979.

From December 1978 on, it gradually intensified the guerrilla war step by step, so as to weaken and demoralize the National Guard and obtain weapons. The Central American neighbor states became ever more drawn into the war. The right-wing dictatorships of El Salvador and Guatemala sent troops to Nicaragua to support Somoza, as provided for by the CON-DECA agreement. The Sandinistas for their part received political support from Costa Rica, Panama and Venezuela.[23]

The defeat of the September insurrection and the continuation of the guerrilla war brought the Nicaraguan economy to the point of collapse. Six hundred sixteen businesses were physically destroyed, and 30 factories and large parts of the transport system and other infrastructural installations had to cease operation. The unemployment figure rose to 50 or even 60 per cent by the end of November.[24] During 1978, some 233 million dollars were taken out of the country in a flight of capital. At the same time Somoza began to double the National Guard to a total of 15,000 men, hiring foreign mercenaries and purchasing new weapons from Israel.

These military expenditures, and an economic growth rate of *minus* 5 per cent in 1978, exhausted state funds despite new increases in taxation. Reserves fell to a twentieth of the governmental foreign debt. After November, the Nicaraguan central bank was no longer able to meet the debt payments.

The Liberation War of Summer 1979

Whereas until late 1977 the marginal and petty bourgeoisie, the urban middle strata and the industrial proletariat originally followed the opposition perspective of the big bourgeoisie, during the course of 1978 they shifted overwhelmingly over to the Sandinista camp. There were several reasons for this. Firstly, the bourgeois perspective came to an untimely end due to the position taken by the U.S.A., and later due to Somoza's own obstinacy, which enabled the Sandinistas to take the initiative politically as well as militarily. Then the economic decline, the defeat of the insurrections, and the continuing guerrilla war not only led to an impoverishment of the urban middle strata, but deprived numerous middle and petty-bourgeois elements of the very economic basis of their class existence and interests.[25] And last but not least, it was the sons and daughters of the bourgeoisie who had left the universities to join the guerrillas, and in the heat of the

---

[23] The Sandinistas claim to have received no military aid from these countries. The opponents of the new Panama Canal treaty in the U.S.A. maintain that Panama armed the Sandinistas, and that Cuban military aid was sent to the FSLN via Panama and Costa Rica. There is however no evidence for this. What is established is that (1) a detachment of Panamanian volunteers was fighting with the FSLN, (2) early in 1979 several Panamanians were arrested in Florida on suspicion of having bought weapons for the FSLN on the black market in the U.S., and (3) the FSLN maintained bases in Costa Rica.

[24] W. Chislett, "Somoza Clings to Power," *Financial Times*, 28 November 1978.

[25] In September Somoza deliberately shelled businesses belonging to bourgeois oppositionists, with a view to destroying their social position.

struggle the family solidarity of their fathers and mothers often triumphed over rational economic interests.

The stronger the Sandinistas became, the more the big bourgeoisie and financial bourgeoisie were driven to rely on Somoza's National Guard. This is the only way to explain the plan of August 1978, and to understand the attempts at mediation after the September insurrection. The goal of this section of the bourgeoisie had long since ceased to be simply Somoza's resignation. Their immediate goal was the weakening or destruction of the FSLN and the preservation of the National Guard, and only subsequently Somoza's resignation and replacement by a "moderate" regime. This was also the line of the U.S.A. and the non-Somozist big bourgeoisie, represented politically by the (rump) FAO, and continued even during the popular insurrection and liberation war of June-July 1979.

From the beginning of April 1979, it was common knowledge that the Sandinistas and the FPN were planning a new insurrection for May. It was impossible to overlook the FSLN's preparations and proclamations, while the FPN had formed more than 130 "workers' commissions" in the country's factories, with the aim of organizing the intended general strike.

Even though the prospects of economic recovery were still worse now than in November 1978, when the IMF had refused Somoza further credit, Somoza received from the IMF in April 1979 a loan of 40 million dollars, followed in May by further loans to a total of 25 million dollars. At the beginning of April Somoza left for a "vacation" in the U.S.A. In April, too, Israeli military experts arrived in Nicaragua to install for Somoza a mobile "air defense system."

The proposal for unity of action which the FPN sent to the (rump) FAO in May was rejected. On 2 June the FAO made its own proposal for solving the crisis. The post-Somoza government would have seven heads, provided one each by Somoza's Liberal party, the National Guard, the FAO, the "entrepreneurs," the "free professions," and the trade unions. The FPN and FSLN, for their part, would also be represented by one joint representative.

At the end of May the FSLN announced the start of its offensive, and called a general strike for 4 June, which the FAO joined so as to avoid losing all its support. At the end of May, too, Somoza's son, who commanded an elite unit of 3,000 men, flew to the U.S.A. to seek new weapons. Managua airport was also closed, though it was not under attack. From early on 30 May military equipment from El Salvador began to be landed, destined for the National Guard.[26] In the far east of the country, in the vicinity of Bluefields, a U.S. military aircraft arrived from the Panama Canal Zone bringing weapons for the National Guard.[27] On 6 June Guatemalan soldiers gathered in Corinto to support Somoza.[28]

By the middle of June, the insurrectionary forces under the leadership

---

[26] FSLN telex to Europe, somewhere in Costa Rica, 30 May 1979.
[27] *Ibid.*, 7 June 1979.
[28] Radio Sandino, somewhere in Nicaragua, 6 June 1979.

of the FSLN controlled not only the agricultural districts and several small communities, but also the working-class and poor quarters of the big towns. By the beginning of July, León, Masaya, Matagalpa and Diriamba were all in the hands of the insurrectionists, as well as a further 20 smaller towns. Yet the FSLN's insurrection plan was not completely successful.

The FSLN had assumed that it could defeat the National Guard militarily within a short period of time. On 10 June it still believed that the fall of the regime could only be a matter of days away.[29] On 16 June it formed a five-person Government Council of National Reconstruction, made up of the widow of the former murdered chairman of the UDEL, a Conservative entrepreneur of the (rump) FAO, a representative of the FPN, one of the "Group of Twelve" and one for the FSLN itself.

When a military victory of the Sandinistas appeared possible in mid-June, and the Somoza regime found itself ever more isolated internationally (the Council of Government and the FSLN having rejected any "mediation offer" on the part of the U.S.A.),[30] the United States tried to gain OAS support for a military intervention. On 21 June, however, the OAS rejected such an intervention by majority vote. But even without this intervention, the Sandinistas were in no position to win rapid military victory. They were forced to withdraw from Managua.

The failure of this victory to materialize gave the U.S.A. and the Nicaraguan big bourgeoisie the chance to reanimate their own perspective. Somoza was to resign, but his Liberal party and National Guard to remain intact. On 6 July Somoza gave in and declared his readiness to resign. He left the timing of his resignation to the United States. After 6 July the National Guard was no longer fighting for Somoza, but for the interests of the U.S.A. and the Nicaraguan financial bourgeoisie.

On the same day, the Panamanian newspaper *La Estrella de Panamá* published a list obtained from the Panamanian secret service, which detailed the continuing flights made by the U.S. Air Force to supply the Nicaraguan National Guard.[31] Other United States weapons reached the National Guard via Guatemala and El Salvador, while Spanish military equipment arrived for Somoza via Portugal and Guatemala.[32] This military aid was designed to halt the further advance of the Sandinistas, to force them to coopt two more pro-United States representatives onto the Council of Government (one each for the Liberal party and the National Guard) and accept the National Guard's continued existence. Venezuela was also seeking to move the FSLN to make these concessions, from its position as a Sandinista sympathizer.[33]

On 10 July, however, the FSLN appeared to be marching successfully back to Managua. A military putsch by sections of the National Guard,

---

[29] *Ibid.*, 10 June 1979.
[30] Communiqué No. 3 of the Government of National Reconstruction, 20 June 1979.
[31] *La Estrella de Panamá*, Panama City, 6 July 1979.
[32] "Portugal y Guatemala exportaron armas españolas a Nicaragua," *El País*, Madrid, 6 July 1979.
[33] FSLN telex to Europe, somewhere in Costa Rica, 26 June 1979.

as planned since the middle of June, appeared likely. Also in June Senator Edward Kennedy (no cold warrior by U.S. standards, and a sworn enemy of Somoza) called for "any means, including military" to be used to prevent "the establishment of a Marxist regime" in Nicaragua.

The putsch did not in fact take place, and the United States did not intervene militarily. However, the threat was sufficient to force the Government Council of National Reconstruction into readiness for compromise and negotiation with the U.S.A. On 14 and 15 July the junta appointed a provisional Cabinet of 18 ministers, in which the Sandinistas joined up with conservative and social-democratic elements and in no way played a leading role. The agricultural, cultural, interior and foreign ministries were taken by Sandinistas or their sympathizers, but the economic and finance ministries were occupied by representatives of the bourgeoisie.

Moreover, it is only thanks to the megalomania and stupidity of one Somoza supporter that the Sandinistas have not been compelled to accept the continued existence of a lightly-purged National Guard. The U.S. and Somoza had agreed that the latter should resign and hand over power to an interim President. The older *Guardia* officers were to leave alongside the dictator, and transfer leadership to younger men "trained in the U.S.A." (the phrase was supposed to suggest true gentlemen, as distinct from corrupt and criminal elements!).

But when Somoza did go, on 16 July, his "interim" successor Francisco Urcuyo announced that he planned to stay on until 1981, and had no intention whatever of transferring power to any junta. This proved too much. His support dissolved, and at the same time the *Guardia*, deprived of its top command structure, showed it was no longer capable of serious resistance to the FSLN. It melted away; some Guardsmen surrendered to the Sandinistas, and the majority simply took to their heels. Urcuyo followed Somoza into exile, and by July 19th Managua was completely under FSLN control.

Thus, the two political tendencies which have both opposed Somoza and quarrelled with one another over the last few years are now involved in a common government. They have to continue their struggle for the future social order of the country against the background of an almost totally destroyed economy. At the beginning of this new battle, the Sandinistas have scored at least one very important gain: the first decree of the ruling junta provides for the dissolution of the National Guard, and the state take-over of all the property of the Somoza clan. In addition, the Sandinistas enjoy great assets not to be underestimated: leadership of an authentically pluralist revolutionary movement which mobilized the overwhelming majority of the population behind it; the prestige of having reversed—albeit in the specific circumstances of one small country—the general reactionary deadlock of the Latin American political world; and widespread international support. In spite of its problems, the Nicaraguan Revolution may not be fated merely to repeat the errors of its revolutionary ancestors. Within its peculiar evolution, the seeds of a more advanced socialist democracy may have been sown.

Guatemala: Crisis and Political Violence*

By Edelberto Torres-Rivas

Edelberto Torres-Rivas teaches sociology at the Consejo Superior Universitario Centroamericano (CSUCA) in San José, Costa Rica. He has published numerous essays and books on dependent development in Central America. This article, edited by NACLA, is a shortened version of a paper presented at the Latin American Sociology Conference held in November 1979, in Panama.

Guatemala is legally organized as a democratic republic. According to the newspapers, Guatemala has been ruled in the 1970s by a series of democratically elected governments. The fact that its presidents wear uniforms and that military titles precede their names is coincidental.

The realities of Guatemalan political life are quite different. One reality is that democracy consists of rigged elections and the assassination of opponents, be they prominent politicians or rebellious peasants. Another is that one-quarter of the population earns 66.5% of the national income, while another quarter earns only 6.7%.[1] The lists of "disappeared persons" are a reality, too, as is the fact that 50% of the adult members of this "democracy" can't read or write. In short, Guatemala's political reality has been dominated for a century by a defiance of democratic norms, in social, political and economic terms.

A progressive interlude in Guatemalan history came in the 1940s and early 1950s. Under the banner of revolutionary nationalism, the democratically elected governments of Arévalo (1945-51) and Arbenz (1951-54) enacted significant political and economic reforms. But the interlude came to a bloody end in 1954, when direct U.S. intervention installed a CIA protégé in the presidential palace.[2]

Colonel Carlos Castillo Armas was flown in from Honduras, on a U.S. embassy plane, to head the first in a succession of rabidly anti-communist regimes. They would all fail miserably in their attempts to stabilize the country, while exacerbating the very causes of social unrest. The growth of a strong guerrilla movement in the early 1960s was used as an excuse for failure, and as an argument for the need to intensify repression. Behind a constitutional-democratic facade, the counterrevolution sought to consolidate a new pact of class domination. But official violence and terror failed to eliminate the source of instability within the dominant class itself.

---

*This article consists of brief excerpts from "Latin America 1980," *NACLA Report on the Americas*, Vol. XIV, No. 1 (January-February), 1980 (52 pages, illustrated). NACLA publications may be ordered directly from NACLA, 151 W. 19th St., N.Y., N.Y. 10011.

[1] The World Bank, *Guatemala: Economic and Social Position and Prospects* (Washington, D.C.: 1978), p. 12.

[2] For an extensive analysis of the reformist period and the U.S. role in overthrowing the Arbenz regime, see NACLA's 265-page book entitled *Guatemala*, edited by Susanne Jonas and David Tobis (1974).

The Castillo Armas government (1954-57) tried to legitimize its rule by holding a plebiscite in 1954. It was a yes/no proposition, with no alternative candidates, and with "votes" cast orally and in public. Three years later, the president was assassinated by a member of his own party, over a petty conflict of interests. Elections to fill the vacancy were blatantly rigged. The Movement of National Liberation (MLN), the extreme-right "party of organized violence," was defeated after two months of popular unrest that ended with the election of General Ydígoras Fuentes, a conservative opponent of Castillo Armas' party.

Ydígoras, in turn, was overthrown by a coup d'etat engineered by his own Minister of Defense in 1963. For the first time, the Army broke with its tradition of *caudillismo* and acted with institutional unity. Colonel Peralta Azurdia governed for a thousand days, with no constitution or parliament, while Guatemalans lived under a "state of siege."

An internal crisis, provoked by the guerrilla movement, eventually forced the regime to hold elections. Again, the results were unfavorable to the MLN and groups of the extreme right. Méndez Montenegro, a civilian, defeated two military candidates in 1966. But this victory for civilian rule was illusory. As a pre-condition for taking office, Méndez was forced to accept certain conditions imposed by the military and to relinquish important decision-making powers. In addition, the military was given a free hand to expand the repressive apparatus of the state. Since power tends to become concentrated, the end of the Méndez administration in 1969 coincided with the demise of civilian rule in Guatemala. It was replaced by raw, military power.

Military Campaigns

The 1970s saw a series of military regimes come to power in Latin America. But in Guatemala, it was military rule with a difference. The periodic changing of the guard was achieved by *electoral* means, as the dictatorship sought to hide its face behind a democratic facade.

The crystallization of military power in this decade cannot be understood without examining the nature of the relationship between the Army and political parties. In Guatemala this relationship is built upon electoral deals and alliances of convenience. The Guatemalan military doesn't have its own party; it does, however, have its own presidential candidates, and their election can easily be secured by a transitory alliance with one of several right-wing groups. In 1970, General Arana Osorio relied on the MLN, an avowedly extremist party of the right. In 1974, a coalition of the MLN and the Institutional Democratic party (PID) elected General Kjell Laugerud. And in 1978, an alliance of the PID and the Revolutionary Party (PR) nominated General Lucas García. In 1970, the PR was in the opposition; today the MLN plays that role. Either one will do, depending on the circumstances, since opportunism is their *raison d'etre*.

In nominating its candidate, the Army effectively chooses the titular head of state; then, the party (any one of the three main right-wing parties) provides electoral backing and legal sanction.

A military man as head of state is a perverse tradition of Guatemalan political life. However, the electoral victory of General Arana Osorio in 1970 marked the first time in 40 years that a reactionary candidate gained office by electoral means.[3] Until that date, the military had been able to secure power only by means of coups d'etat, phony plebiscites or rigged elections, that is, by abandoning constitutional legality altogether.

Obviously, Arana's election did not restore democratic rule. He won because the Méndez government had been totally discredited as repressive and incompetent. Moreover, a climate of terror had enveloped the country, with Arana himself a leading figure in its creation. Between 1966 and 1970, Arana was commander of the Zacapa region of Guatemala, a major stronghold of the guerrilla forces. He directed an anti-guerrilla campaign, with material and logistical support from the United States, that took the lives of 15,000 in three years. U.S. advisors and the CIA dubbed it "Operation Guatemala," modeled after the early U.S. activity in Vietnam.[4]

Arana, as well as his successors, Kjell Laugerud and Lucas García, were all Army candidates, backed by precarious minorities, operating within a narrow, anti-communist framework. No party of the left has been allowed to register for elections. In March 1979, the United Revolutionary Front (FUR), a moderate, centrist group, was finally allowed to register after 14 years of struggle and negotiation. Its leader, Manuel Colom Argueta, was promptly assassinated. The Christian Democratic Party, which has been registered for some time, has achieved neither a stable, programmatic presence nor a popular base of support.

In summary, liberal democracy—a mechanism that organizes relations of domination among social classes—has not developed, and force has filled the void. Both the state and the economy in Guatemala function entirely at the service of a bourgeoisie that is nourished ideologically and financially from abroad, and that basks in the climate created by counterrevolution and maintained by counterinsurgency.

In recent years, the different fractions of the Guatemalan bourgeoisie have become strengthened. They have created their own organizations to fiercely defend bourgeois interests against all threats, imagined or real, and to develop a *defensive* consciousness of their status. The bourgeoisie has declared a veritable war against the trade union movement, the peasantry, student protestors—in short, against the political representatives of the dominated classes.

In the first 52 days of 1979, for example, a *daily* average was reported of 10.5 political deaths in the Guatemalan countryside. Press reports, which are not necessarily complete or reliable, indicate that 546 people were assassinated for strictly political reasons within this same two-month

---

[3] General Jorge Ubico was the only candidate and winner of the 1931 elections. In 1958, General Ydígoras Fuentes won the election as an opposition candidate, on a bourgeois-nationalist platform.

[4] See NACLA, "The Vietnamization of Guatemala: U.S. Counterinsurgency Programs," in *Guatemala*, pp. 193-203.

period. It is this situation which is now being pushed to its logical limits.

The Nature of the Crisis

The crisis that consumes Guatemalan society, and that has an immediate political expression, cannot be explained solely by reference to the configuration of state power, or to the agrarian character of the economy. Rather, throughout its history, different fractions of the bourgeoisie have had great difficulty in constituting a stable power based on consensus. Hence, what's at stake is a crisis internal to the dominant power bloc, which results in a lack of cohesion at critical junctures. The political crisis, then, can be explained by the persistent problem of establishing a legitimate form of domination. Underlying this difficulty, and inherent in the very existence of diverse bourgeois fractions, is a "style" of development that, in the long run, is totally insufficient in its dynamics and negative in its results.

Since 1960, the economy has grown at an average rate of 5.7% a year, approximating the average rate for Latin America as a whole.[5] But the case of Guatemala presents daily, incontrovertible proof that economic growth alone cannot resolve social problems. On the contrary, it tends to aggravate them. If the economy turns on the export of agricultural production, based on concentrated ownership of land, capital, marketing networks, etc; if industrial development, under the control of foreign capital, is monopolized at birth; and if to this we add a state that is decidedly on the side of private enterprise, the result can only be growing inequalities and social tensions. The state's commitment to so-called "private initiative" is such that capital's assault on the working class is actually led by the state.

Social and regional inequalities in Guatemala are growing. Over the last 15 years, poverty has deepened and spread at an amazing pace. It is even more glaring in contrast to the growth of ostentatious, imprudent and provocative wealth. In the mid-1970s, 5% of the population absorbed 34% of the national income. Moreover, the top 1.5% alone accounted for 23% of this wealth. Meanwhile, 70% of a population totaling 6.5 million were obliged to live on an average annual income of U.S.$74 per capita.

These disparities are sharper still in the countryside. Capitalist modernization of agriculture has given rise to a new social structure, a qualitative redistribution of rural misery. The peasant producer has been replaced by a hybrid type—the rural semi-proletariat. Unable to eke out an existence on their own tiny parcels of land, peasants have become seasonal laborers on larger holdings. In the early 1970s, 48.8% of the rural work force were semi-proletarians, while 41.3% were rural proletarians in the strict sense, owning no land of their own. According to official statistics, to be approached with caution, both groups earn an average per capita income of $35 a year, while the agrarian bourgeoisie receives an average of $2,591—or 64 times more than the population they exploit. Other figures can be used to describe the same situation: 83.3% of the economically ac-

---

[5] The World Bank, *Guatemala*, p. 25.

tive population in the countryside earn 34.8% of the total rural income; 1.8% of that population receive 40.7%.

The conditions of the poor in Guatemala include massive and permanent unemployment, incomes eaten up by inflation, acute housing shortages and hunger as a mass phenomenon. The consequences of such conditions are only beginning to be felt, adding a potentially explosive dimension to the intra-bourgeois crisis that has been a permanent feature of political life since 1954.

Escape Valves

The misery and the desperation of millions of Guatemalans are expressed in a variety of ways. A conservative adaptation to dire conditions has taken a religious, millenary form. The proliferation of new sects among the poorest sectors is alarming, as individual desperation is channeled into collective faith.

Yet recently, some religious groups have adopted a sympathetic stance toward the problems of the poor, and are attempting to organize an expression of popular unrest. The Catholic Church is no longer the willing accomplice of the powerful; its traditional contribution to "established order" is rapidly fading. Priests and nuns have been persecuted, and even executed, for their activities in support of the poor.

A second escape route leads to personal disintegration and indicates pervasive social disintegration. Severe alcoholism, drugs, prostitution and various forms of delinquency are rampant among the poorest sectors of society. Statistics confirm the extent of the problem. Between 1960 and 1976, the index of criminality rose by 760%. The official response to this increase was direct, physical repression. Laws, courts, and police were overshadowed by the appearance of Mano Blanca (literally, White Hand) and other para-military organizations that modeled themselves on Brazil's notorious Death Squad.

Finally, there has been a third response to misery and repression that is not an individual form of escape, but a collective form of struggle: the trade union and political struggle. In a different context, trade union organization can serve to stabilize the system. The institutionalized and legal defense of group interests are tried-and-true ways for the bourgeoisie to legitimize its political domination. And political participation is always susceptible to being manipulated, formalized and reduced to mere ritual; it can minimize tensions by giving people a mere "sense" of participation.

The bourgeoisies of Central America, however, are not ready for democratic pluralism under their control. Coercion takes primacy over ideology, and power no longer attempts to disguise the use of force for the sake of consensus. Repression of the union and peasant movements has become the key to political violence in Guatemala over the last few years.

The Guatemalan crisis originated in the bourgeoisie's inability to resolve internal class contradictions, contradictions hidden by its unrestrained use of violence against other classes. The crisis revealed itself in the bourgeoisie's failure to legitimize its rule and has only been accentuated with the passage of time. Social contradictions have sharpened as a result of capitalist economic growth in its most untamed form, in which the raw logic of dependent capital accumulation presides over all else. Moreover, the internal crisis has been reinforced by a crisis imported from abroad that now engulfs the capitalist world as a whole. This, combined with the effects of the Nicaraguan revolution, increasingly define the character of crisis in Guatemala.

"Operation Guatemala"

When "Operation Guatemala" was imported and instituted in the 1960s, the pretext was defense of the democratic order, threatened by the rise of the guerrilla movement. From 1965 to 1967, the Rebel Armed Forces (FAR) and the November 13th Movement (MR-13) controlled the mountains of Las Minas, disputed the Army's control of the Atlantic Highway, and camped at night with impunity in the towns of Zacapa, Chiquimula and Izabal. Nonetheless, the insurrectional armed struggle, in and of itself, never posed a real military threat to the Army, nor did it offer a political alternative to the system. It did, however, have the potential to become an important, destabilizing force—above all, in the context of repeated attempts by diverse bourgeois sectors to forge alliances and build a stable form of control and political domination.

The guerrilla threat unleashed a wave of political persecution and killings, in which the enemy was defined in the broadest possible terms. These counterinsurgency operations were inspired by the infamous "Operation Phoenix" that took the lives of 80,000 Vietnamese. They were carried out by the Guatemalan Army under the military leadership and with the logistical support of the United States Government.

The attitude of the civilian government of Méndez Montenegro (1966-1970) was more than one of guilt by complicity. It acceded to the tremendous growth of the repressive apparatus, far beyond the control of civilian authority, which proceeded to assassinate guerrillas, friends and family of guerrillas and, ultimately, threatened anyone suspected of democratic sympathies.

The extensive scope of counterinsurgency left an indelible mark on Guatemalan society. When death is a daily occurrence, it becomes an accepted dimension of personal life. Horror desensitizes and permeates all social relations (family, work, interpersonal, social, etc.) with what is called the "concentration camp mentality."

But it was not the psychological effects alone that enabled counterinsurgency to make death a symbol of victory. By institutionalizing repression to a degree unparalleled in the authoritarian tradition of the country, counterinsurgency engendered a dual simulation on the part of the state. First, public functions were seemingly transferred to private hands: the "paramilitary" bands began to function, clandestine cemeteries were created, and protection went on sale as a lucrative, new business. Second, the state pretended to take a neutral stance toward a conflict that, at worst, it seemed unable to control.

Contrary to appearances, however, the power of the state was not privatized. The Mano Blanca, for example, was a para-military organization from its very inception, disguised and out of uniform for the dirty work of torture and assassination. Ten years later, even the disguise was dropped and the names reverted back to the Army and police. Counterinsurgency did not succeed in stabilizing bourgeois rule. Instead, it destabilized the society as a whole.

The escalation of violence in Guatemala has passed through several stages. It began in July 1954, with the anti-communist revenge against the national-revolutionary program attempted by Arbenz. Aided by U.S. intervention in toppling that regime, power was assumed by the most reactionary sectors of the bourgeoisie, and counterrevolution focused its wrath on the agrarian sector. Large landowners took their revenge on those who had benefited from agrarian reform under Arbenz, expelling them from the land. It is estimated that 8,000 peasants were assassinated in the first two months of the Castillo Armas regime. There were urban victims as well, and victims from other social classes, but the repression of 1954-57 was primarily a "vendetta": a frightened and embittered bourgeoisie punishing the rebellion of their peons in the countryside.

The next stage was "Operation Guatemala," when class hatred was institutionalized as a public function of the state and implemented by the Army. In order to combat several hundred guerrillas, more than 18,000 Guatemalans were annihilated in the space of two years. To be sure, the guerrillas had killed off some military officers, a few landowners tightly linked to the repression, and many military *comisionados*.[6] But as the repression continued, year after year, what began as a specific campaign against the guerrillas became a political assault on the broad, democratic opposition. It became a weapon in the hands of right-wing forces against all political rivals.

The third stage began in the 1970s and continues to this day. Official violence—class violence—has always been aimed at the poor. But the repression of the 1970s, which regained homicidal furor in May 1978 (under the government of General Lucas García), has its own distinct character. This time, its main target is an *organized* popular movement: the trade unions, peasant organizations and popular sectors.

New Targets

For the first time in Guatemala's history, a broad mass movement, combining spontaneity and organization, has emerged. And it is all the more remarkable because consciousness and combativity have been forged in a thick atmosphere of terror. It is important to recall that the workers' movement that emerged in Guatemala between 1948 and 1954 had a very different character. It was born and bred in a complacent climate of bourgeois democracy, and learned to walk with official support. To be sure,

---

[6] These *comisionados militares*, or military agents, were local informers employed by the Army in the countryside to identify and eliminate guerrilla sympathizers.

it rapidly gained independence and formulated its own program. But it was a trade union movement of artisans on the one hand and "white collar workers" on the other, which remained trapped by its own petty-bourgeois base.

Today, the trade union, peasant and popular movement does not describe itself as anti-status quo. Yet this character has been imposed on the movement by the peculiar circumstances of political life in Guatemala. The trade union movement is illegal because the state refuses to legalize its existence, even within the narrow limits set by the state itself. In so doing, the state de-legitimizes its own role. In the myopic view of the ruling class, any sign of popular movement is considered subversive and demands swift repression.

Social problems that a bourgeois democracy would resolve and absorb as a matter of course appear on the Guatemalan political horizon as threats to the existing order. Neither a "social-democratic" style nor a reformist response to demands from below has ever emerged. The extreme sensitivity of the Guatemalan bourgeoisie, with its praetorian guard, maintains it permanently on the defensive and immune to any suggestion of compromise. There can be no "margin of tolerance" toward communism. The fear of what is subjectively accepted as an external threat prohibits the establishment of mechanisms and institutions that could mediate between classes, and between the state and society as a whole.

A second clarification refers to the increasingly working-class character of the popular movement. Industrial growth, the discovery of important mineral deposits in the last decade, and the relative modernization of export agriculture have altered, definitively, the class structure of the country in at least two ways. (1) A proletarian nucleus, in the strict sense, has been formed in the "integrated industries" producing for the regional market, in the nickel, copper and petroleum sectors, and on the banana, cotton and sugar plantations. (2) An "informal sector" has appeared in the cities—a mass of underemployed proletarians whose physical presence in the urban growth of Guatemala City could no longer remain hidden after the violent earthquakes of 1976.

All the immediate causes of social conflict cannot be discussed here. The ultimate source, however, can be traced to the nature of capitalism. In Central America today, it is the brutality of capitalism in its early epoch of industrial expansion that is being reproduced. The emergence of popular organizations, the growth of trade unionism and the awakening of the peasantry constitute a defensive reaction to the repression required to keep the system functioning.

On the whole, trade union and peasant conflicts have been motivated by the need to defend an already abysmal and still declining standard of living. These conflicts represent the difficult and partial defense of interests of the class as a corporative class, and not as a class engaged in establishing its hegemony, or that contemplates political power and the struggle to seize it.

The popular sectors have organized themselves in the defense of narrow economic interests. Many have died in a struggle still heavily weighted against them. The examples are too numerous to exhaust: protesting a rise in the cost of public transport, 47 people were killed within a two-month period in 1978. On May 28, 1978, defending their lands against the advance of agrarian capitalism, 102 peasant men and women were machine-gunned to death at Panzós. Fighting for the independence of their unions, two Secretaries General of the Guatemalan Bottle Workers Union (Coca-Cola) were assassinated and three members of the union's Executive Committee were sentenced to death.

Class Dictatorship

Since 1954, the Guatemalan regime has tried in vain to restore the old order. A democratic process—one that aimed at a model of economic development that would have altered the interests of the dominant classes— was violently interrupted. Historically, such interruptions have given rise to the *reactionary dictatorship of a class.*

The 1954 challenge was repeated in 1964-69, with the guerrilla insurgency. The reactionary class dictatorship took the form of a military government, in which the state assumed the task of defending the interests of the threatened classes, and ultimately became totally identified with them. State power was used to recreate the conditions for a new model of economic growth, offering political protection to the process of capital accumulation and the establishment of a capitalist economy. In an immediate sense, this took the form of a marriage between the military and the business sector, mediated by control of the state apparatus.

The Militarized State

Within this reactionary class dictatorship, military personnel have come to exercise more and more civilian functions in the administrative apparatus of the state. They now serve as provincial governors, directors of public enterprises, diplomats and deputy ministers. Only the judicial branch has, for the time being, escaped such penetration.

The term "militarized state" should be used with caution, and perhaps only to underline a growing *tendency* toward military assault on the administrative machinery of the state. The Army chief of staff, according to a 1979 decree, controls, registers and decides upon all appointments to the public bureaucracy; he has the power to summon the ministers of state and functions as a sort of super-minister. The current president of the Bank of Guatemala, the most modern and favored institution of the bourgeoisie, is a military man; the number of graduates of the Military Academy has tripled over the last ten years; and the duration of military service has doubled.

Secondly, it is important to mention the role being carved out for petty bourgeois intellectuals. Combining opportunism and technical training, a *service class* has emerged from the new ranks of the middle classes, providing low-level technocrats to fill the administrative posts of domination. In the eyes of these technocrats, the government is promoting a mesocracy (the rule of the middle classes). But nothing could be further from the truth. The bureaucracy, even at its highest levels, never defines the ultimate direction of the state. This historical function is determined by the dominant bourgeois interests, and does not presuppose their physical, direct participation in the public management of the state.

Nevertheless, the role of petty-bourgeois intellectuals and political cadres has become increasingly important since the 1940s. In Guatemala, the bourgeoisie no longer produces leaders. Ideological manipulation (not creation), political action, cultural life, are all the province of personalities that have emerged from the middle classes. Even military cadres are recruited from this source. The sons of the most powerful coffee growers never attend the Military Academy. Only those that need to climb the social ladder choose that path.

Thirdly, it is essential to determine what class the state serves as a reactionary class dictatorship. At the critical moment of the counterrevolution (1954-55), the diverse bourgeois fractions achieved a tenuous unity. But what fear served to unify, the inexorable logic of the market divided soon after. Internal struggles dating from that time explain the instability referred to in the first part of this exposition.

Contrary to some explanations, the agro-export fraction of the Guatemalan bourgeoisie has not been significantly weakened. Rather, a process of internal differentiation has taken place, both within the coffee-producing group itself and with the advent of new agricultural products for export. Furthermore, new avenues for investment, and hence for accumulation, have opened in the industrial and service sectors. The Central American Common Market stimulated the emergence of an industrial and commercial fraction of the bourgeoisie that has become increasingly powerful. Financial capital has grown as well, with banks and private finance companies controlling a wide range of economic activities. But financial capital is of agrarian/commercial origin, and is therefore connected to some of the most important economic groups in the country. It is among these groups that the struggles and conflict have taken place.

Today, there is also a sector of *nouveau riche* entrepreneurs who amassed their fortunes by influence-peddling and the like. Vulgar "perks," subtle bribes, bank loans without collateral, speculation based on inside sources, and a thousand other forms of corruption have become a means of vast personal enrichment, created by access to power. A sizeable group of these newcomers have invested their fortunes and used the strings of government to better compete in the market.

Another source of intra-bourgeois conflict is unequal access to international capital, which offers considerable advantages to certain industrial investments in the race to control the regional Common Market. The "old bourgeoisie," which preceded the growth of industrial investment in the region under a new international division of labor, often comes into conflict with the "new bourgeoisie," born into the Common Market structure. The latter group includes the mafia-type elements mentioned above, the politicians and military officers that have amassed illicit fortunes. Disagreements emerge continuously over specific policies of the state, which is incapable of attending to contradictory priorities at one and the same time.

In summary, the reactionary class dictatorship is at the direct and exclusive service of these sectors, and is incapable of resolving the secondary contradictions that exist among them. Power constituted in this way seeks to control society by any available means. Control is sought not through support, but through repression.

In this way, the state protects a process of pseudo-modernization from above, to the benefit of a bourgeois alliance in which foreign capital plays a decisive role. Over the last 18 months in particular, the inherent weakness of this form of domination has led to the intensification of repression. Trade union, student, and peasant organizations have increasingly begun to challenge the bourgeois pact of domination and death that has prevailed in Guatemala for decades.

The constitution of a Democratic Front against Repression, in March 1979, signals an important step forward in this confrontation. Under the leadership and initiative of the National Committee for Trade Union Unity (CNUS), the Democratic Front was formed by 167 organizations, including political parties, religious groups, worker and peasant organizations, and student associations. Attempts on the lives of its members have already been made, as the Guatemalan government moves against a new, more united opponent.

El Salvador: Why Revolution?*

By Robert Armstrong

Robert Armstrong, a lawyer active in the human rights and solidarity movement, lived in El Salvador as a Peace Corps member. He writes regularly on the region for NACLA Report on the Americas and for The Guardian.

In the Beginning There Was the Coffee Oligarchy

In the mid-19th century, coffee created its own labor force: communal lands (*ejidos*) were abolished by decree, to make way for large *fincas* in the cool highlands of western El Salvador. The scarcity of land, and dense population even in the 1800s, led to the rapid destruction of pre-capitalist forms of production. Commercial agriculture grew at the expense of—and not parallel to—the subsistence economy. As a result, wage labor and capitalist relations of production developed more rapidly and more extensively than elsewhere in Central America.[1]

---

*This article consists of brief excerpts from "El Salvador: Why Revolution?," *NACLA Report on the Americas*, Vol. XIV, No. 2 (March-April), 1980 (52 pages, illustrated).

[1] Hector Dada Hirezi, *La economía de El Salvador y la integración centroamericana 1945-1960* (San Salvador: UCA Editores), 1978.

Until 1932, politics was a game played by the oligarchy, involving inter-family struggles for control of the state. But capitalist agriculture had not been implanted without resistance. Rural uprisings had occurred at close intervals throughout the late 1800s. By 1912 a National Guard was created to maintain order in the countryside.

The "Golden Age," as the oligarchy came to view it, ended in 1932. The bottom fell out of the coffee market with the worldwide depression in 1929.

For the growing number of unemployed, the crisis was worse in El Salvador than in neighboring countries. There were no idle lands to provide subsistence, and thousands of Salvadoreans were forced to migrate. The crisis mobilized the small but growing working-class movement which had developed within the Regional Federation of Salvadorean Workers (FRTS). Initiated in the early 1920s, the FRTS defied a government ban on unions and organized textile and railroad workers, artisans, peasants and farmworkers. Its leadership was greatly influenced by several organizations loosely associated with the Communist International. In 1930, leaders of many of the local unions within the FRTS met to form the Salvadorean Communist Party (PCS). Among those present was Agustín Farabundo Martí.

Martí had been exiled in 1920 while still a university student. He traveled throughout Mexico and Central America in an effort to promote a regional perspective to the revolutionary upsurge in every country. To this end he was one of the founders in 1925 of the Central American Socialist Party. In 1928, he joined Sandino in Nicaragua, serving for two years as his personal secretary and lieutenant. Finally in 1930, Martí returned to ripening conditions in his native land.

The Uprising

The oligarchy, weakened by the economic crisis, sought the assistance of the Army. President Arturo Araujo, chosen in 1931 in what have been called the only free elections in El Salvador's history, was deposed. His Vice President, General Maximiliano Hernández Martínez, assumed power.

Revolutionary sentiment had risen palpably in early January 1932 when the government refused to recognize PCS victories in municipal and legislative elections. The Party set January 22 as the day of insurrection. The PCS had planned simultaneous uprisings in the cities, the rural areas and in military garrisons. Three days before the uprising was scheduled to take place, Martí and other leaders were arrested. The barracks revolt was betrayed by spies and crushed before it began. The PCS tried to call off the uprising in the rural areas, but communication had broken down. On the agreed-upon date, thousands of peasants and farmworkers, primarily Indians, left their homes to march into nearby cities. The pathetically-armed rebels stoned government offices, occupied city halls and police posts. They broke into shops and torched the houses of the rich.

Martínez brought the Army's full force against the rebels. Four thousand died and the uprising was crushed. Then the *matanza*—the massacre—began. Within weeks, the Army and the paramilitary forces organized by large landowners killed 30,000. Peasant leaders were hung in the town squares, the bodies left dangling for days to make the point. Persons with Indian features were lined up in groups of fifty and shot down by firing squads. The Communist Party was liquidated, its cadre killed or exiled. The FRTS was annihilated. Indians ceased to wear traditional dress, abandoned traditional customs and ceased to use their native language.

Martínez ruled for thirteen years. Laws were passed to impede mechanization, and only investments in industries that would not compete with artisan production were encouraged. Industrialization, it was feared, would only destroy the crafts sector and reactivate the worker-peasant alliance that had led to the uprising. The textile industry was the only sector that thrived. In the late 1930s and 40s, war-related shortages caused an increased demand for cotton, sparsely planted since the turn of the century. Again the peasantry was displaced, as cotton plantations took over the coastal lowlands. Again land was concentrated in the hands of a few. Again the country's dependence on foreign markets was heightened. Again, there was unrest.

In 1944 a small, democratic sector within the military launched a coup d'etat. Martínez was forced from office—but the military, not the masses, inherited his rule.

Thus Came the Modernizers

Emerging victorious from the power struggles of the late 1940s, a coalition of military men, technocrats, and a tiny industrial bourgeoisie made an alliance with a sector of the coffee oligarchy—principally those involved in export. Their project was to modernize Salvadorean capitalism through agricultural diversification, industrialization and political reform. What brought these disparate forces together and made the plan possible was the post-war boom in coffee prices from 1945 to 1950.

In the same period, U.S. investors were eager to invest abroad. U.S. capital, in El Salvador as elsewhere, would develop a strong stake in the economy and play a major role in making sure that politics protected that stake.

In 1950, Colonel Oscar Osorio became president in elections that were widely attacked as fraudulent. As the first order of business, the anti-industrial laws of Martínez had to be buried and replaced by strong incentives. A government office was created to coordinate the development of commerce, industry and mining. The power of the state was dramatically increased. New taxes were imposed on coffee exports to transfer resources to new areas of investment. A modern infrastructure was built, starting with the 5th of November Dam to generate electrical energy.

Politically, the official party was born—the Revolutionary Party of Democratic Unification (PRUD). Sponsored by the military and the modernizing bourgeoisie, it was designed to involve new sectors of society in the "Revolution:" professionals, a growing service sector linked to the phenomenal growth of the state, and the proletariat created by industrialization. To attract the latter, industrial unions were legalized but carefully controlled, and social security benefits were established.

Industrialization, the chief priority of the modernizers, took the form of import substitution, i.e., creating industries to produce manufactured goods that were previously imported.

Economic integration—a free trade zone that would permit the unrestricted flow of goods, capital and people among the five republics [of Central America]—became the chosen path toward industrialization. It would obviate the need for structural reform, or so it was thought by the bourgeoisie. Initially hostile to economic integration, U.S. policymakers soon realized that such a scheme could make political and economic sense under certain conditions. U.S. approval of the scheme meant that restrictions on foreign investment had to be scratched, alongside notions of mutual cooperation and balanced development. The Salvadorean bourgeoisie, enjoying a clear advantage over its neighbors, was also eager to give the free market its rein. In 1961, the Central American Common Market (CACM) was born.

Over half of all foreign investments in El Salvador during the 20th century were made in the 1960s. A large portion of foreign investment went into "last-touch" and highly import-intensive industries. That is, they conveniently required large amounts of industrial inputs not locally available—but easily supplied by U.S. sources. As a result, El Salvador and other countries began to experience severe strains in their balance of payments.[2]

The Five-Day War

The Honduran market was swamped with Salvadorean goods, while its raw materials went to feed Salvadorean industry. Domestically, the Honduran government was under pressure to carry out reforms and redistribute land.

In 1969, Honduras began a campaign against Salvadorean products, refused to renew a migration treaty and froze Salvadorean capital. The agrarian reform program was kicked off by expropriating the lands of Salvadorean immigrants. Three hundred thousand had settled in Honduras; many were descendants of those who fled the peasant massacres of 1932. The Honduran government began to drive out the Salvadorean settlers, who brought back terrible tales of atrocities that were exploited by the Salvadorean press. A soccer match added fuel to the fires. On July 14, 1969, the army of El Salvador invaded Honduras. Five thousand died.

El Salvador claimed victory, after the OAS declared a cease-fire and forced it to withdraw its troops. The entire country, save a tiny, unpopular few, had rallied to defend the *patria*.

---

[2] Marc Herold, unpublished manuscript on direct U.S. investment in El Salvador (March 1980), p. 21.

With Honduras, El Salvador lost its largest market for industrial goods. Honduras closed the road to Nicaragua and still more trade was affected. The forced return of farmworkers had a profound impact on the political crisis about to unfold. The Salvadorean government reneged on promises to give them land. Instead, they were herded into camps—and eventually dispersed to ancestral regions they had long forgotten.[3]

The memory of 1932 became more vivid as a series of protests began. They came close upon the heels of a strike wave in the cities, where teachers, bus drivers and industrial workers defied the labor laws and battled the National Police. The urban work force was still very small (less than 500,000 in 1971), with only 9% organized in unions.[4] Organization was hampered by restrictive labor laws, repression and the preponderance of small shops in the industrial sector. The labor movement was also divided into two competing factions. The General Confederation of Unions (CGS) was pro-government and heavily influenced by the AFL-CIO. The United Federation of Salvadorean Unions (FUSS) was influenced by the outlawed Communist Party. By the strikes of the late 60s, however, economic conditions had led to a radicalization of the movement as a whole.

In the countryside, the number of landless increased more than two-fold in the 1960s.[5] Migrants swelled the cities, living in *tugurios*, or slums, with no basic services and little hope of employment. New sectors had emerged in the 50s and 60s: the middle class, employed in the public sector, professionals, small merchants in the cities and towns.

The Electoral Opposition

In the late 50s, a fall in world coffee prices provoked renewed unrest. The regime of Osorio's successor, Colonel José María Lemus, was unacceptably corrupt. A coup was launched in 1961 by an alliance of petty-bourgeois reformers and democratic sectors of the military. The conspirators did not seek popular support and after three months, the modernizers reconstituted their coalition and installed a new government.

In 1962, the discredited PRUD was resurrected as the Party of National Conciliation (PCN)—the official party representing the interests of the bourgeoisie and running military candidates. The 1962 elections were uncontested, bringing Colonel Julio Rivera to power. In keeping with the semblance of political pluralism advocated by the United States, the Rivera government opened the way for the emergence of the first opposition parties and the first truly contested elections since 1931. Buoyed by the success of its industrialization scheme and the CACM, the PCN felt confident that

---

[3] Rafael Menjívar, "El Salvador: el eslabón más pequeño," *Le Monde Diplomatique en Español* (Mexico City), September 1979.

[4] Francisco Chavarría Kleinhenm, *Fundamentos políticos, económicos y sociales de la evolución y desarrollo del movimiento sindical en El Salvador* (unpublished thesis, University of Costa Rica), 1977, p. 451.

[5] Melvin Burke, "El sistema de plantación y la proletarización del trabajo agrícola en El Salvador," *Estudios Centroamericanos ECA*, No. 335/336 (September-October 1976), p. 483.

its program could withstand the electoral test.

In 1962, a group of professionals, many of them educated abroad, formed the Christian Democratic Party of El Salvador. Supported by Christian Democracy in Europe, its success was phenomenal. José Napoleón Duarte, mayor of San Salvador, became the most charismatic leader of the PDC. Politically, the PDC stood for a program of "national development" and reform within a capitalist framework. Its modernization program differed from that of the PCN by promising to share the benefits more broadly.

A second reformist party emerged in 1968, the National Revolutionary Movement (MNR). It remained small in numbers, comprising professionals and intellectuals, but it would play a significant role in formulating the strategy of the petty-bourgeois opposition.

Radical opposition to the PCN was focused first in the Party of Renovation (PAR) and later in the National Democratic Union (UDN). Both reflected the politics of the Salvadorean Communist Party, outlawed since 1932, and its emphasis on electoral struggle. PAR attracted radical professionals and sectors of the urban working class. Its presidential candidate, Dr. Fabio Castillo, placed a respectable third in the 1967 elections, despite intense harassment. Immediately after the elections, the party was officially banned and ceased to exist. In the late 60s, the Communist Party and remnants of PAR were influential in the formation of a new party, the National Democratic Union. UDN emphasized modernization, independent development and the electoral path.

Formation of the UNO

The 1968 elections marked the high point of the electoral opposition. But the war with Honduras changed the political climate abruptly. A nationalist euphoria pervaded all political discussion. The PCN ran heroes of the Honduran war as candidates. It won 60% of the vote and regained control of city halls and assembly seats. In defeat, the opposition found an impetus toward unity. The Christian Democrats, the MNR and the UDN formed a coalition—the National Opposition Union (UNO)—to prepare for the approaching presidential campaign.

Political-Military Organizations

The Communist Party (PCS) continued to insist on the peaceful road to change and to seek alliances with petty bourgeois sectors as the only way of defeating the oligarchy. The Popular Liberation Forces (FPL) developed from a split within the PCS, precipitated by the party's support for the government's war with Honduras. A second group had its roots in the left wing of the Christian Democratic Party. Other leftists joined them to form a federation of guerrilla groups called the People's Revolutionary Army (ERP).

One distinction between the two was the FPL's emphasis on mass organizing as well as military action. Within the ERP, disputes over the importance of mass work reportedly led to the execution in 1975 of ERP member and poet, Roque Dalton García, who saw it as a key element. His death caused a split within the ERP, with Dalton's supporters forming the National Resistance (RN), with its own armed wing, the Armed Forces of National Resistance (FARN). The early activities of these political-military organizations were small-scale, and without broad impact on the popular struggle.

Breaking Point

The 1972 elections—an enormous fraud favoring the PCN over the UNO—marked a definitive breaking point in El Salvador's saga of class struggle. The UNO's candidate in 1972 was José Napoleón Duarte, the Christian Democratic mayor of San Salvador. The PCN ran Colonel Arturo Molina, a semi-literate career soldier, representing the modernizing tendency. Wealthy landowners, portending a split with the modernizers, ran General José Alberto Medrano, war hero and former head of the National Guard.

The blatancy and extent of the fraud shocked even the most cynical. Once the doctored results were announced, militants of the UNO called on Duarte to declare a general strike. Duarte did nothing. One month later, a sector of the Army joined with civilian elements to attempt a counter-coup. The initiative failed, among other reasons, because Nicaragua (under Somoza) and Guatemala (under military rule) sent troops and planes. They did so under the aegis of the Central American Defense Council (CONDECA), founded and promoted by the United States to control subversion and police the region. U.S. military advisers reportedly coordinated these activities from their communications center at the U.S. embassy in San Salvador.[6]

A wave of repression was unleashed against the entire spectrum of opposition. Duarte and others were exiled; the National University was closed for two years; trade unions were taken over, their leaders imprisoned or exiled. Persecution of the Church and rural workers led to bloody massacres.

A Revolution Brews

Within the short space of several years, mass organizations have emerged in El Salvador. The first organizations to emerge in the mid-70s were the People's Revolutionary Bloc (BPR) and the Front for United People's Action (FAPU). The People's Leagues (LP-28) was formed in 1977. In contrast to the UNO concept of an electoral coalition, these mass organizations saw elections as a futile exercise, designed to divert the energies of the opposition. Moreover, they disagreed with the Communist Party's strategy of allying with mildly reformist parties, such as the PDC, instead of mobilizing the collective strength of the masses. They viewed armed struggle as the necessary answer to the intransigence of the bourgeoisie.

---

[6] Anderson, NACLA, *Guatemala* (Berkeley: NACLA, 1974), p. 157, citing Mauricio de la Selva, "El Salvador: tres décadas de lucha," *Cuadernos Americanos*, No. 21 (January-February 1962), p. 196-200.

In the mid-1970s, conditions in the cities and countryside had only continued to deteriorate. The strategy of the BPR was to focus on these conditions, and on immediate economic demands, as a means to create class consciousness and incorporate the masses into the revolutionary struggle. It organized land invasions; it led demonstrations demanding a minimum wage in the coffee fields, and lower prices for seed and fertilizer for the impoverished peasant. In the cities, the strategy was used effectively to organize industrial workers around wage demands, speed-up, bus fares and managerial abuse. Slum dwellers marched for housing and running water; market women staged sit-ins to demand lower rents for market stalls. The goal was a mass front, based on a worker-peasant alliance.

From 1975 on, the political-military organizations began operating in closer coordination with the mass movement. The People's Liberation Forces (FPL), operating as both a political formation and a guerrilla army, promoted and supported the work of the BPR. The political party, National Resistance (RN), and its military arm, the FARN, served a similar function for FAPU. After 1977, the People's Revolutionary Army (ERP) would begin to work with the People's Leagues (LP-28).

Militarily, FPL, FARN and ERP have used similar tactics. In retaliation for government repression and the uncontrolled activities of paramilitary bands, they have eliminated key figures in the repressive apparatus. They have attacked security forces through direct, armed confrontations and the bombing of strategic facilities. And they have used the ransoms collected from kidnapping to support the popular struggle.

The Molina Period

In response to growing unrest and economic crisis, a new formula for development was devised under the Molina government (1972-77). The government did its utmost to cater to foreign capital. Roads, ports and airports were modernized at state expense. Tax and exchange laws allowed foreign companies to increase and repatriate profits. New policies allowed the free entry of machinery, equipment and raw materials. State institutions were used to underwrite foreign investments. They gave long-term credits at low interest, with 100% guarantees by the Salvadorean state.[7] Conditions were even better in the San Bartolo free trade zone. There, strikes were outlawed, and companies could operate tax-free. San Bartolo became a haven for runaway garment shops and electronics plants. Maidenform, Texas Instruments and others made it their home.

Import substitution was no longer the operative model. Local and even regional consumption was incidental to the new scheme. El Salvador was now competing on the world market—on the basis of cheap and abundant labor. Workers received an average wage of $4 *daily*.[8]

---

[7] Burke, *op. cit.*, p. 481.

[8] *Women's Wear Daily*, March 3, 1980, p. 1.

The Death Squad

Selective repression had been an essential element of governing since the massacre of 1932. But as popular struggle continued to expand in the 1970s, the military answered with massive retaliation. To complement the brutality of the armed forces, the Molina government revitalized ORDEN, nominally a civic organization but in fact a para-military network of spies, informers and enforcers, founded by General Medrano in the mid-60s, to combat "subversion." By 1979, ORDEN would claim 100,000 members, recruited from the ranks of retired soldiers, small landowners, thugs and a frightened middle class.

Other death squads began to operate as well: White Warriors Union (UGB), Anti-Communist Armed Forces of Liberation-War of Elimination (FALANGE), and Organization for the Liberation from Communism (OLC). Sectors of the agro-bourgeoisie are suspected of financing the operations of these right-wing gangs.

Agrarian Reform

On June 29, 1976, Molina announced a meek project for agrarian reform, called the *Transformación Agraria*.[9] Only 4% of the country's land would be affected. Property owners would be amply compensated by the state, while a new caste of 12,000 small landowners would be created. El Salvador's internal market would expand and new investments would flow into industry from payments for "expropriated" lands. The project was supported only by a handful of the more visionary members of the bourgeoisie, with interests in industry; by technocrats in the state apparatus; and by the U.S. embassy. But the most reactionary sectors of the bourgeoisie—those dependent on growing coffee, cotton and cane— seized the initiative against the more diversified sectors of the ruling class. Molina himself was excoriated in the press as a communist. A successor had already been named—or rather a PCN candidate for the 1977 elections [General Carlos Humberto Romero]—who quickly made clear his opposition to agrarian reform. A coup would have been superfluous. The defeat of the *Transformación Agraria* signified the eclipse of the modernizing tendency within the bourgeoisie. Large landowners took firm control of the state apparatus—as always, through military intermediaries.

Growing unrest in the countryside was of paramount concern to the new regime. The Catholic Church was targeted as a major source of that unrest. Since the 1960s, priests and nuns had organized *comunidades de base*, a combination of study and social action groups composed of poor peasants and farmworkers. In April 1977, a Jesuit priest, Father Rutilio Grande, was machine-gunned to death on his way to Mass by unknown assailants. His work had radicalized a significant sector of the

---

[9] *Estudios Centroamericanos*, No. 335/336 (September-October 1976). The entire issue, devoted to the agrarian transformation, was written in the midst of the debate. It gives a cross-section of views and excellent articles on land tenure.

rural community. Land occupations and strikes for higher wages had begun to disturb the tranquility of Aguilares, located about 20 miles north of San Salvador. The BPR had become very active. The Jesuit's murder was followed by a military attack on the town. House-to-house searches allowed soldiers to steal what little the people had. Men were lined up in the streets and beaten; women were abused; hundreds were arrested. The Army called it Operation Rutilio. Simultaneously, the National Guard attacked numerous land occupations in the area, using modern weapons and helicopters to drive workers off the land.

Upper echelons of the Salvadorean Church were profoundly affected by these events. Aguilares marked a turning point for Archbishop Oscar A. Romero (no relation to the general), a conservative when he assumed the position in 1977. He [went on to] become one of the most outspoken critics of military rule and economic injustice.[10] The Archbishop used his weekly sermons, broadcast on radio, to attack the system of "institutionalized violence," the system of exploitation and repression which has kept the mass of Salvadoreans hungry and poor.

International Isolation

The excesses of the Romero regime brought it the condemnation of Amnesty International, the International Commission of Jurists, the Human Rights Commission of the OAS—and even the U.S. State Department.

The beginning of the end of the Romero period can be dated from May 1979. Plainclothesmen from the political police arrested the Secretary General and four principal leaders of the People's Revolutionary Bloc. The Metropolitan Cathedral was occupied in protest. Without warning and in full view of the TV cameras, National Police and Guardsmen opened fire on a crowd gathered on the steps. Twenty-four died.

The left retaliated by occupying embassies and assassinating key government figures. And the bloodiest period of repression under Romero began. In the first six months of 1979, the government killed 406 people.[11] The political-military organizations of the left became increasingly active as the only armed deterrent to government repression.

---

[10] Ivan D. Paredes, "La situación de la iglesia católica en El Salvador y su influjo social," *Estudios Centroamericanos*, No. 369-370 (July-August 1979).

[11] Italo López Vallecillos, "Fuerzas sociales y cambio social en El Salvador," *Estudios Centroamericanos* (July-August 1979).

El Salvador: A Revolution Brews*

By Robert Armstrong
and Janet Shenk

Robert Armstrong and Janet Shenk are Researchers for NACLA.

The Rise and Fall of the Center

In September 1979, William Bowdler flew to El Salvador to urge President Romero to resign for the good of his country. Bowdler—then special envoy, now Assistant Secretary of State for Inter-American Affairs—had been sent a few months earlier to save Nicaragua from the Sandinistas. He hoped for better luck in El Salvador.

On October 15, 1979, Romero was overthrown in a coup d'etat that surprised no one. With lightning and almost embarrassing speed, the U.S. government announced its support for the new junta: Colonels Adolfo Majano and Jaime Abdul Gutiérrez. Three separate coups had been in the works within the Army. One was led by the young officers, committed to structural reform; another by forces close to the U.S. Pentagon; and a third by the fascists. But to secure support, meaning U.S. approval, they enlisted the pro-Pentagon faction in their conspiracy. Gutiérrez would hold the key to the junta's future course.

Each faction of the military had its own allies and patrons, and the power struggle among them consumed the energies of the first junta. The young officers flirted with the opposition parties, dominated by the tiny middle class. The pro-Pentagon faction was content to link the country's development to the United States. They were modernizers; anti-communists but not fanatics. And they were supported by the "enlightened" bourgeoisie and, of course, the United States.

The fascists, temporarily on the sidelines, enjoyed the powerful backing of the agrarian bourgeoisie. They admired Hitler and Mussolini, read *Mein Kampf* and specialized in repression. On off-duty hours, they staffed the paramilitary gangs and composed death lists and slogans: "El Salvador is the tomb of the Communists. Prepare to end that race."

A Civilian Presence

Except for two brief periods, in 1960 and 1961, no civilian had occupied the highest office since 1931. But now it was obvious that the military could not rule alone. They were simply too despised. The new junta looked for respectable civilians to share the seat of power.

The three civilians chosen to fill out the five-man junta were Guillermo Ungo, leader of the small social democratic party (MNR); Román Mayorga, rector of the Central American University; and Mario Andino, manager of the local subsidiary of the Phelps-Dodge Corporation. The cabinet

---

*This article consists of brief excerpts from "El Salvador: A Revolution Brews," *NACLA Report on the Americas*, Vol. XIV, No. 4 (July-August), 1980 (52 pages, illustrated).

included representatives of the opposition parties, independents and the "enlightened" bourgeoisie.

The absence of Christian Democrats on the junta was striking. The party was caught off guard by the coup. Its leadership was in a period of transition. The old guard—Napoleón Duarte, Morales Erlich and others— were still in exile or were out of touch with active party life. A new generation of leaders was trying to make the party more responsive to the political climate created by the mass organizations. Many of them, generally associated with the party's left wing, accepted posts in the new cabinet.

The new government was impressive. Its civilian members were well educated, honest and committed to reforms. But they also harbored serious doubts as to the viability of the government they had agreed to join. They wanted to believe in the young officers, yet doubted their ability to withstand the pressures of pro-Pentagon and fascist sectors. And most of all, they were unconvinced that the oligarchy would stand by and allow their interests to be untouched.

The Popular Response

When the junta announced a platform of reforms—originally proposed by the Popular Forum[1] in the final days of Romero's regime—sectors of the left adopted different attitudes toward the new government. The UDN, legal arm of the Communist Party, accepted several cabinet positions. The LP-28, which had called for an insurrection immediately after the coup, now said that it would give the junta time. FAPU and the BPR maintained a position of staunch opposition to what they viewed as a U.S. maneuver to put the "enlightened" bourgeoisie in power and eliminate the popular organizations. The BPR strategy was to press the new government to keep its promises—knowing that it was powerless to do so.

Events in El Salvador quickly pushed the left toward a unified position. The death toll in the first two weeks of the junta exceeded the rate of deaths for the first 9-1/2 months of the year under Romero.[2] Daily, the mass organizations filled the streets with demonstrators, demanding a full accounting of the whereabouts of the "disappeared" and political prisoners of the Romero regime, demanding that the torturers be punished. The military quivered: pointing a finger at one of them would tangle hundreds in a web of murder and corruption.

The mass organizations used civil disobedience—occupying churches, ministries and markets—to press their demands for higher wages, lower rents, agrarian reform and an end to repression. They held public meetings

---

[1] The Popular Forum was a broad-based coalition formed in September 1979 to formulate and press for a program of reforms. It included members of the Christian Democratic Party, the MNR, the Communist Party, the LP-28 and a FAPU-related labor federation. Of the mass organizations, only the BPR did not join.

[2] Tommie Sue Montgomery, "Política estadounidense y el proceso revolucionario: el caso de El Salvador," *Estudios Centroamericanos*, Nos. 377-378, March-April 1980, pp. 241-252.

in movie theaters. Ten years of slow but steady organizing, under the most difficult and brutal conditions, were bearing fruit: the junta had opened a small democratic space for the first time in 50 years; the mass organizations were filling that space and moving beyond its bounds.

Power struggles within the military—reflecting larger struggles within the bourgeoisie—paralyzed all reforms. The bourgeoisie was outraged at the junta's "permissiveness" toward agitation in the streets. And the fine line between the "enlightened" sector and the old agrarian interests began to fade. All could agree that repression was the only effective response to the growing strength of the left. Day by day, the civilians on the junta could feel their influence waning. The pro-Pentagon faction of the military was in clear control of the junta, the fascist sectors were operating with impunity through the paramilitary bands, and the bourgeoisie was financing the death squads and controlling the economic program of the junta. Guillermo Ungo and Román Mayorga, two civilians on the junta, realized they were being used as window-dressing for international consumption—and nothing more.[3]

The U.S. Formula

The U.S. government embraced the new junta as the answer to its prayers for a centrist solution. U.S. Ambassador Frank Devine met privately with the business sector, urging them to cooperate, to sacrifice a part in order to preserve the whole. The United States was confident that a small dose of reform could woo the masses away from the left. But it grossly underestimated the loyalty of the masses to their own organizations and goals, and therefore the desperate belligerency of the right. As the terror intensified, U.S. officials continued to insist that the left was to blame.

As for the so-called center, the United States distrusted the civilian members of the junta—except for Andino. They couldn't be sold to the bourgeoisie, since the reforms they envisioned were more than cosmetic. So behind the smokescreen of even-handedness, the United States threw its weight to the colonels. In November, when Carter sent a Defense Survey Team to El Salvador to assess the situation, neither the U.S. embassy nor the colonels thought to inform Ungo or Mayorga of the delegation's visit.[4]

In case the reforms didn't work against the left, the United States resumed military aid to El Salvador to carry out what officials privately referred to as "clean counterinsurgency." While the left had to be cowed into submission, it had to be done with finesse. The Salvadorean Army, with 30 years of U.S. training behind it, was said to be more "professional" than the security forces—meaning less prone to "excess" in controlling opposition. New equipment would be channelled to the Army, while the National Guard and Police would be trained to use less barbaric methods. "The idea is that if a guy is standing with a protest sign, you don't have

---

[3] *NACLA* interview with Guillermo Manuel Ungo, New York City, July 28, 1980.

[4] Cynthia Arnson and Delia Miller, "Background Information on El Salvador and U.S. Military Assistance to Central America," Institute for Policy Studies, resource paper, June 1980, p. 7. Also, *NACLA* interview with Guillermo Manuel Ungo, July 30, 1980.

to cut him down with a machine gun," a U.S. official explained. "You just gas 'em."

The Center Collapses

By December, the autumn lull in the repression had ended. Demonstrators were fired upon by the National Guard. ORDEN, reconstituted as the Broad National Front (FAN), began to terrorize the countryside and eliminate key leaders of the popular organizations. And still there were no reforms. Then, to everyone's astonishment, during the first three days of January, virtually the entire cabinet resigned in protest. Ungo and Mayorga resigned from the junta. The civilian presence was gone. The center had collapsed.

As the junta disintegrated, the left began to coalesce. Long-standing debates over strategy and tactics were being decided by the test of practice, and certain common conclusions were being reached. The question of armed versus electoral struggle—which had divided the Communist Party from all the mass organizations—was settled by the fall of the first junta. The last chance for peaceful change had been lost; the CP admitted its errors and began military preparations. A people's army was taking shape.

The question of alliances with reformist sectors was settled by the preponderant strength of the popular organizations. The FPL had argued consistently—against the CP, FAPU and others—that alliances with the petty bourgeoisie had to be contingent upon the ability of the working class, allied with the peasantry, to lead a broader front. By January 1980, proletarian hegemony was a fact.

The question of divisions within the bourgeoisie—and the possibility of alliances with the "enlightened" sector—was settled by the bourgeoisie itself, as it closed ranks against reform and financed the growing terror. On January 10, the FPL, the RN and the Communist Party announced the formation of a coordinating council of the political-military organizations.[5] One day later, the BPR, FAPU, LP-28 and the UDN established the Coordinating Council of the Masses (CRM).

Repression (with a Dose of Reform)

The fall of the first junta gave the PDC [Christian Democratic Party] the chance it was waiting for and saved the U.S. government from having to abandon its centrist pretensions. The PDC had all the necessary qualities: a moderate image and the memory of popular support in the 1960s; an international network to complement its own structures; cordial relations with the business community; and, above all, a thirst for power.

The PDC filled two slots on the junta and packed the cabinet. Their rationale for entering as others resigned was simple: only they could prevent a civil war between left and right. Where the first junta had failed, they could succeed in pushing through reforms. U.S. officials admitted that the

---

[5] The People's Revolutionary Army (ERP) did not participate in the Political-Military Coordinating Council because of unresolved differences, especially with the RN.

"center" had shifted to the right—but "only slightly," they said.[6] A new ambassador, Robert White, with his human rights credentials earned in Paraguay, was brought in to win votes for U.S. policy among liberals in Congress.

The War Begins

Throughout the countryside, the fledgling people's army was testing its strength. The brutality of the Salvadorean military and its greater weaponry outgunned the guerrilla armies. Their targets were different. The guerrillas attacked the armed forces and members of the paramilitary squads. The military went after the unarmed members of the popular organizations.

The right was becoming more brazen as the left grew stronger. It found a champion in Roberto d'Aubuisson, a former intelligence officer in the National Guard, dismissed by the first junta as one of Romero's chief torturers. D'Aubuisson was handsome, charismatic and totally committed to the destruction of the left. He headed the Broad National Front (the reincarnation of ORDEN) and many said he led the death squads, the White Warrior Union and the Secret Anti-Communist Army.

D'Aubuisson had close ties to the American right. His first trip to the United States was sponsored by the American Security Council, a right-wing lobby group in Washington. He lunched with the American Legion, lobbied for more arms and accused the U.S. Ambassador of "leftist sympathies." D'Aubuisson's message was clear: get rid of the Christian Democrats and make way for a Chilean solution to the crisis.[7] In mid-February, he appeared on Salvadorean TV to denounce a list of persons who, he said, were linked to the political-military organizations of the left. Among them was Mario Zamora Rivas, then Solicitor General of the second junta. Zamora was a bridge between the left and right wings of the Christian Democratic Party. Destroying that bridge might force the party out of the junta. Several nights later, armed men entered Zamora's house through the roof and killed him with a tommy gun. The Christian Democrats were stunned and outraged. They pointed the finger at d'Aubuisson and threatened to resign if Zamora's killers were not brought to justice. But no one was arrested and the Christian Democrats stayed on. The party, however, could no longer stand the strain.

The Party Splinters

By May, the entire left wing of the party had resigned, as well as those associated with the Central American University. But there were others, less scrupulous than they, to fill the vacancies. Napoleón Duarte— the charismatic mayor of San Salvador in the 1960s, presidential candidate

---

[6] Memorandum of meeting with Robert White on June 4, 1980 with representatives of six Congresspeople, Washington, D.C.

[7] *Washington Post*, July 2, 1980.

in 1972—would now save the junta from total abandonment. He was joined by Antonio Morales Erlich, another stalwart of the party's right wing.

Again, the U.S. government breathed a sigh of relief. Duarte was well known internationally; the myth of a moderate center might still be swallowed. But time was running out. In mid-February, the U.S. ambassador had to summon the military high command, along with members of the oligarchy, to convey that the U.S. government would not tolerate a coup. It was high time for some dramatic strokes. So on March 9, the second junta announced a set of "sweeping reforms": land would be redistributed, banks and foreign trade would be nationalized, the power of the oligarchy would be broken, they said. And the people would desert the popular organizations, they believed.

The Carrot and the Stick

On paper, the agrarian reform seemed impressive, even drastic. First, all properties in excess of 1,250 acres would be expropriated to form peasant cooperatives. Owners would be generously compensated in cash and government bonds, and encouraged to invest in industry. At a second stage, properties of 250 to 500 acres would be affected; and later, the small plots would become the property of tenant farmers and sharecroppers. Mobilizing its forces like a military campaign, the junta rushed its reform into place. A state of siege was declared throughout the country and troops rolled into the largest haciendas, ostensibly to stop the landowners from fighting back. But there was no resistance. Most landowners took their compensation in cash, packed their bags and went to Miami. From there they would finance a more subtle resistance.

The real objectives of the military occupations became all too clear. Each hacienda was to be a military outpost in the junta's campaign to destroy the left. Each occupying force received a list, prepared by ORDEN, of suspected members of the popular organizations. Reform was a cover for repression.

The greatest sham of the agrarian reform was that the coffee oligarchs, the heart of bourgeois power, were not even touched. In 1971, 91% of all coffee holdings were less than 1,250 acres—the limit of the agrarian reform's reach. Since 1971, coffee magnates had further subdivided their estates among family members in anticipation of reform.

Vietnam Revisited

When the first phase of the agrarian reform failed to attract any popular support, the junta jumped to stage three: giving land to sharecroppers and tenant farmers. They called it "Land to the Tiller" and a U.S. official commented on the reform's intent: "There is no one more conservative than a small farmer. We're going to breed capitalists like rabbits."[8]

The original "Land to the Tiller" program was implemented in Vietnam. Its purpose was to politically isolate the Viet Cong by giving land

---

[8] *New York Times*, March 13, 1980.

to peasants in targeted areas. But it was one component of a larger "rural development" project that included the infamous Operation Phoenix, run by former CIA director William Colby. Approximately 30,000 people were murdered through Colby's efforts to eliminate Viet Cong supporters.

Counterinsurgency is also part of the package in El Salvador. On April 1, 1980, the U.S. government re-programmed another $5.7 million to El Salvador, for transport, communications and intelligence equipment.

Archbishop Romero had implored President Carter to halt the flow of arms. He had exposed the lies of U.S. policy, declaring that so-called reforms "had to be judged within a context of death and annihilation."[9] He decried the torture and killings from his pulpit and said defiantly, "When all peaceful means have been exhausted the Church recognizes the right to insurrection."[10] And finally, on March 23, he called on the National Guard to disobey the orders of their superiors and end the killings.

On March 24, Archbishop Romero was killed by an assassin's bullet as he offered Mass for the mother of a friend. His voice had expressed the hopes and determination of the Salvadorean people. But in Washington, it was ignored.

There's a War Going On

There is no one Somoza in El Salvador; there are many. The bourgeoisie is not divided as it was in Nicaragua. It is one and united against a vast popular movement, led by peasants and workers, and joined by large sectors of the middle class. Not able to paint a portrait of a heterogeneous struggle against a single dictator, the U.S. media—so sympathetic at one stage to the Sandinistas—refuses to accept the notion of a class war in El Salvador. It prefers the mythology of two tiny extremes, squeezing the honorable center.

Today, the myth of the "viable center" has been all but abandoned. A new rationale for supporting the junta has replaced the old. The *Washington Post* said it succinctly in a recent editorial: "... the United States has found it politically more feasible and ideologically less objectionable to support reform, even reform soiled by some repression, than to condone revolution, especially revolution stained by nihilism."[11] The left in El Salvador is being painted as irrational and crazy. "Even Fidel Castro can't control it," says a State Department leak. "We're not talking about pragmatic Sandinistas," they say. "This is a Pol Pot left."[12]

Even this rationale is getting harder to push on the American public. Recent events in El Salvador have made it eminently clear that the Salvadorean left is neither tiny nor crazy. A new coalition has been formed that incorporates broad sectors of society, exposing the total isolation of the

---

[9] *Miami Herald*, March 11, 1980.

[10] *This Week Central America and Panama*, February 4, 1980.

[11] *Washington Post*, July 23, 1980.

[12] *El Salvador News-Gazette*, English-language newspaper in San Salvador, April 27-May 5, 1980; *Washington Post*, July 2, 1980.

junta from all forces save the right. The program of the popular movement is public knowledge; it is anything but nihilism.

The Center Meets the Left

The difficult task of unifying the revolutionary and reformist forces in El Salvador has been accomplished, after nine months of intense debate. The result is the Democratic Revolutionary Front (FDR), which includes all the popular organizations and all the forces involved in the first junta; and the United Revolutionary Directorate (DRU), which includes all the political-military organizations of the left. The FDR is the future expression of a popular, anti-oligarchic, anti-imperialist government which the revolution has pledged itself to establish. The DRU is recognized as the political and military vanguard of the revolutionary process.[13]

The FDR

The Democratic Revolutionary Front was formed on April 18, 1980, when the Revolutionary Coordinating Council of the Masses (CRM), representing all the popular organizations, united with the Democratic Front (FD). The FD was a newly formed organization composed of trade unions, professional organizations, small business groups, student associations, the two major universities and, most significantly, the social democratic MNR and the Popular Social Christian Movement (a new group composed of the Christian Democrats who left the junta in March).

With the formation of the FDR, all of the important opposition forces in El Salvador for the last 20 years—save the handful of Christian Democrats still in the government—came together in a single body. Neither the military nor their bourgeois patrons could be found among them. The initiative to form the FDR came from the popular organizations, whose unity proclamation declared: "We call on all the sons, small and medium-sized business people, professionals, students, market women, etc., to close ranks against the enemies of the people so that we can form the broadest and most powerful unity of the revolutionary and democratic forces—a unity that will make possible the conquest of a truly revolutionary government and ... will make democracy and social justice a reality."[14]

The Front's first tasks have been to win recognition and support internationally, and to try by diplomatic means to reduce the bloodshed that must result from the stubborn U.S. support for the Christian Democratic-military junta. In June, the FDR won the endorsement of the Socialist International, whose resolution of support urges the United States to alter its policy toward the junta.

---

[13] The DRU was initially founded as a coordinating structure for building a united military and political front. This aim was realized in October 1980 with the formation of the Farabundo Martí National Liberation Front (FMLN), incorporating under a common strategy the membership of all the political-military organizations represented in the DRU. The DRU remains as the unified command structure of the FMLN. —Ed.

[14] Manifesto of the Revolutionary Coordinating Council of the Masses, San Salvador, January 11, 1980.

Washington has tried to discredit the FDR by saying that reformers joined out of weakness, capitulating to an extremist left. Rubén Zamora, leader of the dissident Christian Democrats, responded to that charge in a recent NACLA interview: "The State Department contradicts its own words. On one hand they tell us that we are so weak that some alleged madmen on the left will eat us alive. On the other hand, they urge us to go in with the junta so that it can rely on our strength to break the oligarchy."[15]

Is the alliance between reformers and revolutionaries as solid as it seems? Guillermo Ungo observed:

> This is not a tactical, but a strategic alliance. It is an absolute historic necessity, and it will be very resilient. In Nicaragua, for example, the alliances of classes in opposition to Somoza included the weakened national bourgeoisie. Right after the Sandinista victory, the bourgeoisie moved to recover its influence and had to be edged out, slowly and painfully. In El Salvador, the class alliance has been distilled. It has excluded the national bourgeoisie before the revolution. There can be few surprises we won't be prepared for now.[16]

The DRU

What the U.S. government fears most is represented by the DRU, comprising the three major political-military organizations and the Salvadorean Communist Party. The DRU is the unified political and military command of the revolution. All four member organizations describe themselves as Marxist-Leninist and have been responsible for guiding the revolutionary struggle over the last ten years. Four men form the central command: Salvador Cayetano Carpio of the FPL, Jorge Shafik Handal of the PCS, Ernesto Jovel of the RN, and Joaquín Villalobos of the ERP.

People's War

On the military front, militants of the popular organizations have taken up arms in the Liberation Army, under the joint command of the DRU, while others have stayed in their communities to form people's militias. The only outstanding question for the revolutionary forces is how the war will be conducted. Since October, there has been a continuing debate between the FPL and the RN over whether insurrection or prolonged people's war is the correct strategy. Insurrection would mean building to a major confrontation in the short term, while the latter would mean the continuing development of the mass organizations and the revolutionary armies, and a more gradual war of attrition and isolation of the enemy.

While the military struggle goes on, the diplomatic efforts of the FDR are aimed at peeling away the mask of respectability that the second junta has been allowed to maintain. They believe that international solidarity

---

[15] *NACLA* interview with Rubén Zamora, New York City, July 28, 1980.
[16] *NACLA* interview, Ungo.

is the only way to reduce the bloodshed. The task is ever more urgent as the U.S. government begins to arm El Salvador's neighbors for a Central American war.

What Is at Stake?

Why has the struggle of a country the size of Massachusetts caused so much panic in Washington? What is at stake that is so important that the United States is willing to provoke a regional war? U.S. economic investment in El Salvador is minimal compared to the rest of Latin America. Including foreign subsidiaries, it does not exceed $60 million. The State Department argues rather that "strategic interests" are at stake: a revolutionary victory in El Salvador would endanger the recently discovered oil fields in Guatemala and Mexico, as well as the Panama Canal.

Protecting oil fields has become a convenient rationale for imperialist intervention in many parts of the globe. But such arguments are specifically designed to appeal to the anxiety and chauvinism of the more reactionary segments of U.S. public opinion. They are rounded out by the old standby: Cuban expansionism.[17] In testimony before a Congressional subcommittee deciding on a military aid package to the Salvadorean junta, U.S. State and Defense Department officials accused Cuba of sending arms to insurgents through Honduran territory. In fact, the Salvadorean rebels are self-financed and quite able to purchase weapons on the open and black markets.

The Nicaraguan revolution was the first break in 20 years in the chain of control that the United States maintains in Latin America. It came in the same year that the U.S. empire suffered another defeat in Iran. It followed a decade of setbacks beginning in Vietnam. An empire is sustained, in part, by the image of its invincibility. If it suffers defeat in its own backyard, questions are raised about its strength throughout the world, both among its enemies and its allies. Herein lies the real U.S. stake in El Salvador.

Honduras: On the Border of War*
By Steven Volk

Steven Volk is Research Director of NACLA.

In most of the Central American nations, a native oligarchy arose in the late 1800s or, at latest, by the first third of the 1900s. In coordination with foreign firms which by that time were beginning to invest in the region, these oligarchies ruled for the mutual benefit of both. Honduras, on the other hand, has been characterized by the lack of a local economic oligarchy

---

[17] *New York Times*, March 26, 1980.

*This article consists of brief excerpts from "Honduras: On the Border of War," *NACLA Report on the Americas*, Vol. XV, No. 6 (November-December), 1981 (52 pages, illustrated).

until the late 1950s, by the predominance of the foreign agro-exporting firms, and by the continuation of precapitalist forms of land tenure. What accounts for this difference? The fundamental explanation resides in the agrarian structure of Honduras. Throughout the nineteenth century, Honduras was one of the most sparsely populated countries in Central America. In 1895, it was estimated to have a population slightly less than 400,000 compared to 700,000 in El Salvador, a country five and one-half times smaller. With little pressure on the land, there was less motivation to destroy older communal forms of landholding (the *ejido*) during the so-called liberal reform period in the nineteenth century.

One consequence was that a coffee oligarchy did not arise in Honduras as it did in most other Central American countries. While this was due in part to the fact that the coffee-producing areas were hard to get to, more importantly there was neither a pressure to use land more productively nor was there a large landless workforce which could be harnessed to capitalist agricultural production.

If the landed elite were not inclined to convert their landholdings into capitalist enterprises, the foreign fruit companies most certainly were. For one thing, they did not have to rely on local laborers. Instead, they imported large numbers of black workers from the Caribbean to work on their plantations. By 1910, 80% of all banana lands were under the control of U.S. firms. Four years later, the five principal concessionaires held more than one million acres of coastal land, much of it the most fertile land in the country.

As late as 1950, only 48% of the country's land was in private hands. The rest belonged to the state (31%), *ejidos* (17%), or other forms of communal holdings. But in that 48%, property ownership was very unevenly divided. According to the 1952 Agricultural Census, the top 4% of the farms spread over 57% of the territory while the smallest 65% of the farms occupied only 15% of the land.[1]

Dictatorships and Reformers

United and Standard Fruit ruled Honduras in the 1930s and 1940s, but it was Tiburcio Carías Andino whom they chose as their top banana. Elected to office in 1932 for a four-year term, Carías persuaded congress to extend his term, first to 1938, then to 1943, and then until 1949. Congress and the courts became tools of the presidency, and the country suffered through nearly 16 years of martial law.

In 1949, Carías' choice as successor, Juan Manuel Gálvez of the National Party, was elected president. The choice coincided with a desire on the part of the banana companies to diversify and reorganize their productive activities, a move which required a much more active presence of the government. The Gálvez government fostered the general conditions for the capitalist development of the countryside not only through the construction

---

[1] Mario Posas, "Política estatal y estructura agraria en Honduras (1950-1978)," *Estudios Sociales Centroamericanos* (Costa Rica), No. 24 (September-December 1979), p. 38.

of a necessary transport infrastructure, but also by providing easy financing and technical assistance.

The Strike of 1954

Although Honduran workers had been organizing and striking since the 1920s, only after a strike in 1954 did the government and private enterprise legally recognize trade union organizations, making Honduras virtually the last country in the hemisphere to accept unionization.[2] Workers at the Tela Railroad company's[3] north coast installations marched out on May 1 demanding a 50% wage hike, better conditions and, most importantly, legal recognition. Encouraged by a militant Central Strike Committee, the strike took hold among some 25,000 workers, including dockworkers at the northern ports.

Gálvez sent troops to the northern plantations, but leaders of the American Federation of Labor and its Latin American spinoff, the Inter-American Regional Organization of Labor (ORIT), sent advisers to Honduras to mediate the crisis. After a month on strike, the negotiators managed to remove the most militant leaders on the Central Strike Committee and replace them with known anti-communists. On July 9, the AFL and the CIO pressured United Fruit to settle the strike and the company agreed.

By forcing the fruit companies to recognize trade union organizations in 1954, the Honduran workers won an important victory. But it was clearly conditional. From the United Fruit strike of 1954 until the present day, conservative forces in the U.S. labor movement have continued to play a very active role in the Honduran workers' movement, both among industrial workers and the peasantry.

A First Attempt at Reform

One of the most important consequences of the 1954 strike was least expected by the workers. A reformer, Ramón Villeda Morales of the Liberal Party, slipped through a split in the National Party to be elected president in 1954. Villeda set about designing a public works program which would both provide the nation with some basic infrastructure and employ some of the thousands of dismissed banana workers. He also ordered a number of land colonization plans. Between 1958 and 1960 the government distributed nearly 75,000 acres of land. Further, in September 1962, Villeda shepherded through the country's first agrarian reform law.

Similar to other reform programs of the period, the 1962 law hoped to reach a number of goals. First, it tried to promote productive exploitation of the country's farmlands. Second, the law attempted to create a legal basis for the recuperation of national and *ejido* land which had been illegally occupied over the years. Finally, the agrarian reform law hoped to put a

---

[2] Mario Posas, "Tendencias ideológicas actuales en el movimiento obrero hondureño," *Anuario de Estudios Centroamericanos* [Costa Rica], No. 6 (1980), p. 25.

[3] The Tela Railroad Company was the name of the Honduran subsidiary of United Fruit. –Ed.

lid on an increasingly militant rural population. The anger of the landless and the peasant minifundistas had soared in the post-World War II period as population growth put a real pressure on the land. In 1952, 75% of Honduran farms were under 10 hectares and most averaged less than 4 hectares.

The 1962 agrarian reform met few of its goals. As was to be expected, the law immediately drew howls of protest from the large fruit companies and local ranchers who maintained extensive holdings. The National Agrarian Institute (INA), created in 1961 to oversee the new colonization projects and given authority over the reform process, was hamstrung by a lack of funds and the relative sympathy of many of its directors for the large landowners. Then on October 3, 1963, when Air Force Col. Oswaldo López Arellano seized power and deposed the Villeda government, the agrarian reform process begun in 1962 was abruptly halted.

New Crops and New Buyers

The forces which inspired the 1963 coup sought to destroy the impetus for change from below. But they nevertheless favored the modernization of the Honduran productive system. And this implied important changes in both the city and the countryside.

Some important changes had already been occurring in the rural sector since the end of the Second World War. Bananas, which represented 88% of the value of Honduran exports in the 1925-1939 period, declined to 70% of the total value of exports by 1950 and to 45% by 1960.[4] Pushed by international demand and supported by the state's credit mechanisms and technical aid, coffee, cattle, cotton and timber grew impressively after the war. Coffee more than doubled between 1945 and 1960. Land sown with cotton shot up almost 26 times between 1950 and 1965, creating a demand for nearly 30,000 seasonal laborers. In the 1960s, Honduras began to export beef, mainly to the United States, thanks to the installation of the country's first meat packing plants.

This was also a period of significant industrial growth in Honduras. Typical of industrialization programs throughout Latin America in the late 1950s and 1960s, the process was designed to allow local producers to manufacture some of the commodities which previously had been imported. And, similar to other such programs, the Honduran industrialization plan resulted not in a lessening of imports, but rather in an increasing penetration of foreign, particularly U.S., capital and capital goods imports into the manufacturing sector. Over 70% of Honduras' largest firms were founded between 1950 and 1968, and U.S. capital played a dominant role in the vast majority of them. By 1969, U.S. investments in Honduras totaled more than $200 million, in a country whose entire GNP was only slightly more than $500 million.[5]

---

[4] Daniel Slutzky and Esther Alonso, *Les transformations récentes de l'enclave bananière au Honduras* (Paris: CETRAL, 1979), Table 4.

[5] Víctor Meza, "Crisis del reformismo militar y coyuntura política en Honduras," ALAI [Montreal], Vol. 5, No. 3 (October 9, 1981), p. 41.

Land Hunger and Peasant Militancy

Smallholders and renters in El Salvador, Guatemala and Honduras maintain an equally precarious grip on their lands. But only in Honduras has the commercialization of agriculture disrupted communal forms of property-owning so late in the twentieth century. Many analysts see in this the reason why, in the 1960s, Honduras gave birth to the most militant and, before long, best organized peasant movement in Central America.[6]

The peasant movement was split into two main organizations. The National Association of Honduran Peasants (ANACH) was the larger but less militant of the two, tied as it was to the U.S.-dominated ORIT. Nevertheless, by the mid and late 1960s, it had been pressured by its members to play a more active role in the land invasions which were sweeping the countryside.

The National Peasant Union (UNC), on the other hand, played a leading part in the organization of the land seizures. It was founded in 1963, based on the peasant leagues begun by church activists in the departments of Valle and Choluteca. Internationally, the UNC was linked to the Latin American Confederation of Workers (CLAT), a Christian Democratic organization.

The wave of land seizures placed the government in an unusual position. Its neglect of the 1962 agrarian reform law had contributed to the radicalization of the peasant movement. At the same time, López Arellano, who halted the reform in 1963, now sought its reinitiation as part of his own search for a new political base. The government picked the inert National Agrarian Institute (INA) to implement its policy. For the next five years, INA would be a useful, if limited, ally of the peasants. It would not initiate actions on their behalf, but its support of land seizures would spell the difference between success and failure.

The Ranchers React

The most vehement opposition to the land seizures and INA policy in general came from the National Federation of Farmers and Ranchers (FENAGH), an association of large landowners founded in 1966. It continually took the government to task for supporting land seizures even though the government's record on this was spotty. In the late 1960s, FENAGH also began to blame the invasions on Salvadorean migrants. There was now pressure on the Honduran government to expel the Salvadoreans as "troublemakers" and "land usurpers." Further, the deportation of large numbers of rural dwellers would serve to relieve pressure on the land in the southern and western areas of the country.

Adding to the misfortunes of the Salvadorean settlers, Honduran authorities charged that El Salvador's development in the 1960s had taken place at the expense of Honduras, a well-founded accusation. Between 1960 and 1968, El Salvador quintupled its exports to Honduras, using its neighbor as

[6] Rafael del Cid, "Las clases sociales y su dinámica en el agro hondureño," *Estudios Sociales Centroamericanos*, No. 18 (September-December 1977), p. 154.

a captive market to vitalize its own industrialization. And, while Honduran exports also grew during the period, by 1969 the country was running a $20.6 million deficit in intra-CACM trade.

War and Its Consequences

On April 30, 1969, Honduran authorities gave the Salvadorean settlers in Honduras 30 days to get off the land. By late May, more than 11,000 refugees had re-entered El Salvador, propelled by the Honduran government's edicts and the vigilante tactics of the goon squad, *Mancha Brava,* which was organized by the National Party. Then, in early July, Salvadorean troops crossed into Honduras "to defend the human rights of their countrymen." Only after the OAS threatened to slap an economic boycott on El Salvador did that country agree to pull its troops back. Honduras closed its borders to Salvadorean traffic and, within time, a demilitarized zone was established between the two countries pending a final truce.

For Honduras, the war was nothing short of monumental. The defeat suffered by the Honduran troops during the short conflict revealed a command structure which was inefficient, backward and corrupt. Following the war, the Honduran officer corps would come increasingly under the influence of a group of younger officers who drew their inspiration (and, in some cases, training) from the military reformers in Peru and Panama. Many of the older, corruption-tainted officers were purged.

Changes at the Top

The war also furthered a process of realignment in the nation's bourgeoisie. Broadly speaking, we can identify two wings of the upper class. One was composed of the traditional oligarchs whose wealth was tied up in the land: cattle ranchers, large farmers and those linked to the banana companies. The other wing was smaller and less well articulated. It represented the interests of new industrialists centered in San Pedro Sula and Tegucigalpa and producing for the domestic market. Ironically, this sector was strengthened when Honduras pulled out of the Common Market[7] because Honduran manufacturers no longer had to compete with a huge influx of consumer goods from El Salvador and Guatemala. While momentary circumstances and a policy of alliances with the workers and peasants would propel this new bourgeoisie into a position of state control, it remained fundamentally weak given the underdevelopment of Honduran industry.

The Plan for National Unity

Political forces shifted rapidly in Honduras after the war with El Salvador. A reform movement coalesced, based on a common opposition to continued rule by the traditional conservative political parties. This movement took shape at the end of 1970 with the formal alliance of the Private Enterprise Council of Honduras (COHEP), a business association

---

[7] For a discussion of the contradictions in the Central American Common Market which led to this move, see Jonas, Chapter 3 of this volume. –Ed.

which often reflected the interests of the new industrialists; the Workers Confederation of Honduras (CTH), a 45,000-member labor organization founded in 1964 by the main urban labor and peasant federations linked to ORIT; and the armed forces, represented by General López Arellano, their commander-in-chief.

López joined with COHEP and the CTH in drafting a Colombian-style solution to the nation's problems known as the "Political Plan for National Unity." Under it, a single, non-partisan candidate would run for president in the June 1971 elections, and a program of reforms, albeit minimal, would be instituted.

Fearful of losing their place in the political game, [Honduras' two traditional parties, the National and Liberal,] expressed agreement with the national unity proposal, but rejected the notion of a single candidate. They wanted partisan elections for president. Given that the two parties could still muster a considerable amount of influence, the reformers accepted the compromise, and Ramón Ernesto Cruz, an old lawyer from the National Party, was elected president in 1971.

It did not take long for the reformers to realize that they had been taken. Even before the elections, the two parties divvied up all the important posts in the public administration, a move which would raise corruption by government officials to new heights. With Cruz in office, the agrarian reform, which had again picked up steam in the late 1960s, wheezed to a halt. The government stopped expropriating national and *ejido* lands illegally held by corporations and private ranchers, and began to jail peasants who took part in land seizures.

The Political Plan Disintegrates

On February 18, 1972, police killed six peasants who had settled on unused land on a large estate in the department of Olancho. The escalation of repression in the countryside sapped what little legitimacy remained of the Cruz government. The workers, in particular, felt cheated by the political parties, which had made a mockery of their own agreements.

Three factors lay behind this. First, neither the Liberal nor the National Party seemed to value the "labor vote." Second, since the end of the 1960s, workers had begun to present their political demands through union organizations rather than the classical party channels. Finally, the ORIT-linked union movement, as opposed to some smaller, militant unions, thought that the best interests of its members would be served by supporting the new industrial bourgeoisie.

López Arellano: Once More with Feeling

On December 4, 1972, as a "hunger march" of thousands of peasants demanding the application of the agrarian reform law neared Tegucigalpa, López Arellano dispatched the Defense Minister to inform [Ramón] Cruz that his services as president were no longer required. Shortly after taking over the presidency, López Arellano issued Decree Law 8, an emergency measure which gave the peasants immediate, if temporary, use of arable national and *ejido* lands held by INA until their rightful owners could be determined.

Decree 8 regulations expired in late 1974 and were replaced in early 1975 by a new agrarian reform law. As opposed to the 1962 reform law, this one placed limits on the size of most land holdings (500 hectares, except those dedicated to export crops). It promised to distribute within a five-year period almost 1.5 million acres (600,000 hectares) to 120,000 peasant families.

As mild as it was, the 1975 agrarian reform law was condemned by the Private Enterprise Council (COHEP), one of the original supporters of López Arellano's reform alliance in 1970. Further, as with the 1962 law, its application was dependent on the willingness of INA and the government to honor it.

Bananagate

On February 3, 1975, Eli Black, United Brands' chairman, tossed his briefcase through his sealed skyscraper window and followed it down 44 floors to the street below. His suicide piqued the curiosity of the Securities and Exchange Commission, which opened an investigation into the company's affairs. On April 9, they reported that United Brands had paid a $1.25 million bribe to an official of the Honduran government in exchange for relief from an export tax on bananas.[8] The new 50 cent-a-box tax had been levied by Honduras a year earlier as part of a plan by the seven Central and South American banana-producing countries (the Union of Banana Exporting Countries) to recoup some of their losses due to escalating fuel costs.

It was López Arellano who paid the price for the Bananagate affair. On April 22, he was removed in a bloodless coup by Col. Juan Alberto Melgar Castro, a conservative who had replaced López as military chief. Under Melgar Castro, the country swung sharply to the right.

The Horcones Massacre

With the ouster of López Arellano, the reform program again ground to a halt. Thus on May 18, 1975, the 38,000 member National Peasant Union (UNC) seized land throughout the country, withdrawing only when the government threatened to remove them by force. On June 25, they led a nationwide "hunger march" which was to converge on the nation's capital from five directions. One column had just reached Juticalpa, in Olancho, when the Army moved in to stop it. Five peasants were shot to death and nine others disappeared.

The Horcones massacre caused the Church to pull back some of its priests from Olancho and discouraged some others from social activism. But it had the opposite effect on the peasant movement. Within months various forces had united to confront the government from a position of greater strength.

---

[8] *Wall Street Journal,* April 9, 1975.

The leading force in this coalescence was the UNC, which had led the upsurge of peasant activities in the 1970s. The 80,000 member ANACH joined in as well. The Horcones killings put pressure on both ANACH and the Honduran Federation of Agrarian Cooperatives (FECORAH) to act lest they be abandoned by their members.

On October 9, 1975, the three organizations joined in a National Front of Peasant Unity and gave the government two weeks in which to distribute over 300,000 acres of land to 30,000 landless peasants. Melgar Castro ignored the deadline, and tensions in the countryside continued to build. In October 1975, the President sent Col. Maldonado, the progressive head of INA, to diplomatic exile in Washington, thus depriving the agrarian reform agency of its key leadership. He also created an Agrarian Policy Commission with the power to override any decision by INA's director, and stocked it with the country's most powerful landowners.

"Democratic Fronts"

The ranchers' and landowners' ability to halt the agrarian reform soon encouraged reactionary moves in other areas. In January 1977, conservative forces had managed to remove the last group of young officers who, from a position of strength in the Supreme Council of the Armed Forces, had directed the reformists' initiatives between 1972 and 1975. The hardliners soon turned their attention to the workers' movement. Melgar Castro set out to break the powerful unions on the banana plantations, which had become increasingly militant in the 1960s. With the approval of the Ministry of Labor, and funds and support from AIFLD, so-called "democratic fronts" arose in both unions. Through violence and intimidation, they managed to gain control of both.

Elections on the Agenda

As the government of Melgar Castro struck out against the peasant and workers' movement, it announced that general elections would be held in 1979. On the one hand, by moving toward civilian control, the military implicitly acknowledged that it was becoming increasingly unpopular. Besides growing public rejection of their sharp swing to the right, military officers were beset by charges of large-scale corruption.

Contrarily, those sectors of the traditional parties most fiercely opposed to the first phase of military reformism (1972-1975) were loudest in demanding a return to constitutionality as this was the only way in which they could gain control over the state apparatus. Thus, elections were one way to give a democratic facade to a conservative regime, a move seen as highly desirable by the U.S. government.

On August 7, 1978, weakened by continual charges of corruption as well as by an ongoing struggle for power in the military, General Melgar Castro was overthrown in a bloodless coup. He was replaced by a junta led by General Policarpo Paz García, the chief of the armed forces. The conservative junta immediately promised that elections would be held in

1980, a move which, according to many observers, was dictated by the Carter Administration in return for aid.[9]

Elections and Beyond

[A presidential election eventually took place in Honduras] on November 29, 1981. Prior to the elections, [Liberal Party leader Roberto] Suazo Córdoba and [National Party candidate Ricardo] Zúñiga were called in for meetings with military authorities at which they were told that an ongoing investigation of corruption by a civil commission only "played into the hands of the enemies of the country." If the elections were to proceed, the two majority party candidates would be obliged to sanction the reconstitution of the commission. The other condition imposed by the military was that the armed forces would have access to certain cabinet posts and veto power over others.

By all accounts the voting itself was honest. By the time it was over, the Liberal Party had won a stunning victory, polling more than 640,000 votes to the Nationals' 490,000. This gave them not only the presidency, but also an expected 44-46 seats in the 85-seat Chamber of Deputies.

President Suazo's campaign rhetoric had not been particularly impressive, proposing to combat endemic corruption by "making sure every public servant puts in an eight-hour day," to relieve the economic crisis "by increasing production and productivity," and responding to the U.S. presence in El Salvador with the bald statement that, "We believe that the United States is the defender of democracy and liberty in the world." [10]

Moreover, Suazo and his military backers immediately faced a major financial crisis. Low-interest, long-term loans from international lending institutions had dried up, as they had for the rest of Central America. Capital flight and a huge trade deficit had cut Honduras' foreign reserves from $150 million in 1980 to under $40 million at the end of 1981, less than necessary to cover two weeks' imports.

Under such doleful circumstances, a few eyebrows were raised when Finance Minister Práxedes Martínez returned triumphantly from New York a few days before the November 1981 elections to announce a new $100 million loan package from the United States—including a $50 million advance on the national coffee crop after a year of the lowest coffee prices in recent history.[11] Informed U.S. government sources predicted that Honduras' allocated economic aid for FY 1982, some $39 million, would actually be closer to $60 million when all was said and done.

The stakes, of course, were regional. There is a strong sector within the Honduran military that is eager to play a role in the regional Central American drama, in full collaboration with the military regimes of Guatemala and El Salvador, acutely aware of the short-term and long-term personal

---

[9] For details on U.S. pressure for elections, see Volk, "Into the Central American Maelstrom," Chapter 2 of this volume. –Ed.

[10] Roberto Suazo Córdoba, press conference, La Paz, Honduras, November 28, 1981.

[11] *Tiempo*, November 24, 1981.

benefits they could reap. An active commitment by the Hondurans would generate increased sums of U.S. aid—and the opportunities that would open for graft—as well as a likelihood that the military would again assume direct political power.

However, there is another sector of the Honduran military, composed of junior officers from captain-major up, that came of age in the aftermath of the 1969 war with El Salvador, passionate in its loathing of the Salvadorean Army and repulsed at the gory excesses of the Guatemalans. While these officers may be incapable of preventing an "Iron Triangle" military alliance with El Salvador and Guatemala, they will most certainly be capable of delaying it, especially since many of them will rise to more influential posts in a routine round of promotions soon after the inauguration.

Should U.S. policy-makers and the reactionary forces of Guatemala and El Salvador pull Honduras into the Central American wars, they may find that they have momentarily strengthened their forces in the region. But, ultimately, they will only prolong the conflicts and produce yet another crisis for the region, this time in Honduras itself.

2

U.S. Policy: The Politics
of Intervention

The articles included in the opening section of this book have amply documented, at the domestic political level, the genesis and development of
Central America's current revolutionary crisis. The present section addresses the crucial question of the United States response to the deepening
of that crisis—and its outbreak into revolutionary war—in the late 1970s
and early 1980s.

Although there is insufficient space in this reader to detail the commanding historical role which the U.S. has played in the Central American
region, it is necessary, in order to frame the analysis of recent U.S. behavior
toward the countries of the area which is contained in the articles below, to
establish a number of fundamental points of departure. These concern developments in U.S. policy toward Central America, developments in policy
toward Latin America more generally, and some of the global changes occurring in American foreign policy during the turbulent 1970s.

We will argue that once the crisis in Central America began to unfold,
U.S. policymakers (even those in the "progressive" Carter administration)
were unable to abandon an imperial preoccupation with the stability of
existing structures of power in the area. With that failure, the limits
to possible change in U.S. foreign policy were starkly illuminated. Our
contention will be that the source of those limits lies in the strength of
certain social and political forces in the United States, forces which have
been favored by the exercise of U.S. hegemony within the capitalist world
since the second World War and which oppose any move to weaken it.

To begin with, the U.S. foreign affairs establishment failed to come
to grips with the profound alterations occurring in the socio-economic
framework of Central American life after 1960, or with the implications of
those changes for the stability of the region's political structures. Despite
the fact that such alterations took the form of a socially and regionally unbalanced "modernization," one which inevitably produced pressures tending to burst the rigid boundaries of the majority of Central America'a
traditional regimes, American policy-makers acted as though they did not
realize that a basic problem of political control was in gestation, or that
they would ultimately have to respond to it with some sort of accommodation. Hence in 1972, a year of upheavals (in more than one sense), the
Nixon administration moved forcefully to shore up the U.S.'s traditional
regional allies. In El Salvador, which had just witnessed the nullification

of José Napoleón Duarte's election victory by the conservative military, the U.S. embassy actively assisted in putting down a progressive civilian-military revolt, thus upholding the rule of the Salvadorean oligarchy. In nearby Nicaragua, meanwhile, swift actions taken by Ambassador Turner Shelton, an ardently pro-Somoza sidekick of American billionaire Howard Hughes, prevented the Somoza tyranny from collapsing in the aftermath of the December Managua earthquake. Finally, having waged a successful counterinsurgency war in Guatemala in the late 1960s, the U.S. government, through AID, was busily engaged in helping the corrupt right-wing regime of General Carlos Arana to plan that country's development to the benefit of new groups of American investors, in utter disregard of the needs and protests of the Guatemalan people.

In setting its face against the slowly growing current of demands for progressive economic and political change in the nations of Central America, the Nixon administration helped to guarantee that the crisis in the region would deepen and mature. Nixon's policy, of course, was not unexpected. On the contrary, it reflected a traditional imperial disdain for and underestimation of the strength of Latin American popular movements. What emerges clearly in the readings included in this chapter is that such attitudes were not limited to the policy analysts of the Nixon administration, but in one or another guise characterized all of the administrations which have succeeded it.

If the Nixon administration's unwillingness to alter the traditional course of U.S. policy contributed to intensifying the conflict in Central America, its failures and misdeeds in other parts of the world ensured that once the crisis in the area erupted, it would do so within a partially transformed hemispheric and international setting. In this regard, the most significant development was the impending defeat of U.S.-backed forces in Southeast Asia; such defeat solidified a growing conviction among the American public that future overt interventions had to be rigorously avoided. Strengthening the impact of this decline in mass backing for an interventionist foreign policy were the revelations of governmental wrongdoing which occurred in the course of Congress' investigations into the Watergate affair, the overthrow of Salvador Allende in Chile, the CIA's plots to assassinate foreign leaders, and the whole array of official attempts to repress dissent domestically. As witnessed by the passage of the Clark Amendment, which prohibited the Ford administration from engaging in covert operations in Angola, the combined effect of these events was to place insurmountable short-term obstacles in the way of direct American military intervention virtually anywhere in the world, including the Western hemisphere.

The developments just mentioned also gave birth to a new dimension in U.S. foreign policy, the theme of "human rights." It was a dimension whose internal face—restoration of the tarnished legitimacy of the U.S. government in the eyes of its own people—did not escape the notice of skeptical commentators. Nevertheless, the coupling of these two concerns, the "Vietnam syndrome" and the politics of human rights, prepared the way for what was initially a less destructive than usual response by the U.S. to potentially destabilizing political changes in Central America. It is interesting to recall, in this connection, that the Somoza regime in Nicaragua was one of the earliest subjects of human rights concern, both because of the dictator's brazen manipulation of aid funds sent to help the Nicaraguan people after the 1972 earthquake and the violence inflicted by the National Guard against suspected FSLN sympathizers. As a result of these developments, not only did satrap Somoza come in for some intense criticism in the U.S. Congress, but the State Department, alarmed over the absence of advance intelligence on the strength of the Sandinistas, decided to replace its complacent ambassador with someone who could be counted upon to provide reliable reporting on Nicaraguan politics. By the end of the Ford administration, however, Somoza's position in Nicaragua, and with it the U.S. position in Central America, appeared to have stabilized, and official concern with events in the area ebbed.

In the context of the above-noted pressures to avoid new interventions and to refurbish the U.S. government's domestic image—and in the absence of any well-defined threat anywhere in the hemisphere—the stage was set in 1976 for a temporary and partial restructuring of U.S. policy toward Latin America. Taking its cues primarily from the recommendations of the two Linowitz reports, the incoming Carter administration embarked upon what promised to be a more humane and progressive course of policy toward the nations of the region. Not only were a rapprochement with Cuba and the successful completion of the Panama Canal treaties high on the hemispheric agenda, but the new administration also declared its willingness to tolerate a measure of ideological pluralism in countries close to U.S. borders (e.g., Jamaica). Most significantly, some of Carter's new Latin American specialists—the human rights proponents—appeared prone to move vigorously to apply sanctions against grossly repressive Latin American regimes which tortured and murdered their political opponents, and in general to promote "democratic change" wherever possible. Taken at face value, such postures appeared to herald a new era in hemispheric relations, one in which the dominant position of the U.S. would be secured by a politically pre-emptive, "social-democratic" strategy.

The general thrust of this new current of thinking might have been expected to prompt a relatively bold departure in the U.S. treatment of Central America's traditional right-wing dictatorships. In point of fact, a prominent Latin American analyst (Maira, 1980) relates that second-echelon State Department people appear to have drawn up an elaborate scenario for the "guided democratization" of the isthmus, complete with a four-country electoral timetable and an analysis of the political forces in each country which could be relied upon to carry it out. Had such a strategy actually been implemented, it would have constituted a major break with past patterns of policy. By the time the crisis in Nicaragua broke, however, it was clear that no such timetable and analyses (if they existed) were operative elements in American policy. Instead, once a vacillating "carrot-and-stick" application of human rights pressures had failed to achieve its intended purposes, U.S. policymakers found themselves in a familiar position—that of having to scramble in search of a strategy to head off the complete collapse of an embattled ally. Unwilling or unable to anticipate events, American foreign policy was forced once again to react to them.

Why Did Things Turn out This Way?

The key to understanding the inability of the Carter administration to implement a reformist course in its Latin American policy is ultimately to be found in the continuing position of the U.S. as the hegemonic power in the capitalist world, as well as in the actions taken, in the domestic and international conjuncture of the late 1970s, by internal political forces to which that position has historically given rise. In brief, the United States, though declining in economic weight, remains militarily pre-eminent within the Western capitalist alliance and must remain so if that alliance is to survive. This basic structural reality creates enduring pressures which work to block fundamental change in American foreign policy. Even before the Carter administration came into office, it was evident that the policy of detente, as conceived by Nixon and Kissinger, was encountering increasing opposition on the grounds that it weakened the U.S. role in the world. In particular, developments such as the changing nuclear balance between the superpowers and Cuban activities in Africa gradually tended to provoke the remobilization in the U.S. of "Cold War Liberalism" (Wolfe and Sanders, 1979). This term denotes a policy perspective uniting members of the post-war foreign policy elite who had been marginalized after Vietnam with certain sectors of labor and capital that had been nurtured in the prior period of undisputed U.S. hegemony and were unable to reconcile themselves to its loss. Subsequent setbacks to the U.S. global position—the Islamic Revolution in Iran and the ensuing hostage crisis, plus the Soviet intervention in Afghanistan—only strengthened the outcry in favor of a new defense buildup, including a revamping of America's intervention capabilities, and a reaffirmation of support for countries all over the world which had traditionally been U.S. allies. As the 1980 national elections approached, therefore, the Carter administration confronted the bleak prospect of having to defend itself against semi-McCarthyite charges of having "lost" one or more countries to forces inimical to U.S. strategic interests.

As the articles which follow illustrate, the Carter policy toward Central and Latin America was played out against the backdrop and under the influence of mounting pressures to rekindle the Cold War which emanated from the above mentioned sources. Opposition to Carter's Latin American initiatives was already very strong by 1977-78, when the administration barely managed to secure passage of the Panama Canal treaties and was forced to abandon its overtures to Cuba. Although the Carter Latin America policymakers could subsequently boast of several modest successes, including the salvaging of democratic elections in the Dominican Republic in the face of a coup threat, a political environment had been created in which proponents of a more forward-looking strategy were obliged periodically to give ground. We will see (LeoGrande, 1979, this volume) that by the time the Nicaragua crisis had to be dealt with, the Carter administration, fearing "another Cuba," was unable to break with past practice and force a now-spent ally out of power if doing so entailed the risk of seeing established political and military structures in Nicaragua collapse. Although "progressive" positions were able to reassert themselves briefly with regard to Nicaragua policymaking after the Sandinista triumph, leading to aid being granted to the revolutionary government (Jonas, 1981, this volume), those positions were ultimately checkmated and defeated after Reagan's election. When a revolutionary crisis emerged in El Salvador, a pattern of policy betraying a similarly conservative bias appeared once again; rather than take a chance on backing genuine reform, thus leaving itself open to domestic political risk, the Carter administration opted during 1979-80 for pseudo-reform and strengthening of the existing bulwarks of political and military power (LeoGrande, 1981, this volume). In Honduras, meanwhile, as is recounted below by Volk (1981), the Carter strategists engineered a "democratization" of the political realm which has left the conservative Honduran military free to support U.S. policy objectives in the other countries of the region.

Carter's right-wing critics, of course, were quick to charge that his responses to the crisis in Central America represented a repudiation of the whole prior foundation of U.S. policy in the Caribbean region (see Fontaine et al., 1980). In reality this was far from being the case. On the contrary, the analyses excerpted here indicate that the Carter administration was never able to place itself squarely and decisively behind those political forces which alone might have been able to effect a measure of social reform within the framework of Central America's dependent capitalism and thus temporarily stabilize the area for U.S. interests. The failure of the administration to strike out in this bold direction, one which would have gone beyond superficial and episodic concern with a narrowly-defined set of "rights," helped open the door to the victory of a new policy current, that unholy alliance of old Cold Warriors and the New American Right which today determines the foreign policy of Ronald Reagan. At present that alliance is not only trying to destabilize the Sandinista government in Nicaragua, but as the analyses by LeoGrande and Simons (see below) indicate, has hardened the Carter policy of reform with repression in El Salvador and gives every sign of trying to extend the same approach to Guatemala—all in the context of a classic Cold War analysis of the significance of Central America's revolutionary struggles. It is a strategy which threatens to plunge all of Central America into a devastating conflict. Whether or not such a conflict takes place will depend very centrally on the steps which we as Americans take to oppose the present Reagan administration policy.

—*David Dye*

The Revolution in Nicaragua: Another Cuba?*

By William M. LeoGrande

In this selection, William LeoGrande briefly reviews the record of American policy toward Nicaragua from the emergence of the revolutionary crisis up until the fall of Somoza. The evident unreality of much of the official analysis of what was happening in Nicaragua is explained by LeoGrande on the basis of selective and distorted perceptions among policymakers, grounded in the fear of "another Cuba." While LeoGrande only hints at the structural sources of such perceptions, other more detailed analyses of this period (see especially Lawton Casals, 1979) stress both the strong sensitivity of the policymaking process to political trends within the United States and the concomitant and widely-shared assumption among decision-makers that American hegemony must not be put at risk by adventurous policies which undermine the existing structures of power protecting U.S. interests.

Professor William LeoGrande is Director of Political Science in The School of Government and Public Administration, The American University. He is the author of Cuba's Policy in Africa, 1959-1980, as well as numerous articles on Latin American politics and U.S. foreign policy.

For two decades, the hemispheric policy of the United States has been haunted by the specter of "another Cuba." The fear that Cuba's revolutionary upheaval might be repeated elsewhere energized the Alliance for Progress and, when progress gave way to order, that same fear justified providing counterinsurgency assistance to a continent increasingly dominated by military dictatorships. Lyndon Johnson sent a force of 20,000 men to the Dominican Republic in 1965 to prevent "another Cuba," and Henry Kissinger unleashed the CIA on Chile for the same reason.

The collapse of the Somoza dynasty in Nicaragua has made this fear more palpable than ever. The United States labored mightily over the past year to prevent the accession of a Sandinista government in Nicaragua, but in the end was reduced to reluctantly arranging the terms of transition from Somoza to a provisional government appointed by the guerrillas. Preoccupied with isolating the Sandinistas, Washington policymakers consistently underestimated their strength and exaggerated that of Somoza. Now that he is gone, the Cuba specter still hovers, threatening to obscure U.S. understanding of the dynamics of post-Somoza politics just as it obscured the dynamics of his collapse.

Nicaragua's future course will be determined fundamentally by internal forces—how the revolutionary coalition breaks down into contending political camps, the relative strengths of those camps, and the issues around

*Excerpted and abridged from Foreign Affairs, 58:1 (Fall 1979). Reprinted by permission of Foreign Affairs. Copyright 1979 by the Council on Foreign Relations, Inc.

which the political battles of the future are fought. No external actor will be able to control this process, but the United States can have an impact on it by affecting the alignments of the political contenders and the issues which divide them. Whether Nicaragua becomes "another Cuba" will depend in no small measure on whether the United States reenacts the mistakes it made 20 years ago in its relations with the *first* Cuba.

Nicaragua, like Cuba, was victimized early in the century by the new "Manifest Destiny" which guided U.S. hemispheric policy during those years.[1] It became a virtual protectorate of the United States in 1912 when the Marines were dispatched, ostensibly to protect American property and citizens during a period of civil strife. In fact, U.S. interest in Nicaragua was primarily strategic. Considered for a time as a possible site for the canal across the isthmus, Nicaragua's location remained strategically important for defense of the canal in Panama. U.S. control over the customs houses of Nicaragua was established less to insure the loans of U.S. bankers than those of Europeans, whose potential for intervention the United States perceived as a strategic threat.

Except for a brief interlude in 1925-26, U.S. troops remained in Nicaragua until 1933. The second occupation never quite succeeded in pacifying Nicaragua. Augusto César Sandino, a general of the Liberal Party, refused to accept the imposition of a Conservative president, and for nearly six years he fought a guerrilla war against the Marines, achieving international stature as a nationalist and anti-imperialist. When the United States withdrew under the banner of FDR's Good Neighborism, it left the task of ensuring stability to the American-trained National Guard under the command of Anastasio Somoza García. One of Somoza's first achievements was to lure the legendary Sandino to Managua on the pretext of arranging peace, only to have him assassinated. In 1936, Somoza forced the civilian president from office, arranged his own election, and thus began a family dynasty which ruled Nicaragua for 43 years.

The Somoza dynasty rested upon two pillars of support: the National Guard, transformed by patronage into a personalistic instrument of political repression, and the backing of the United States, ensured by the Somozas' anti-communism and their ability to maintain order. Though their reign did little to alleviate the tremendous poverty of one of the hemisphere's poorest countries, the Somozas proved adept at personal enrichment. At the end, Anastasio Somoza Debayle, son of the Guard's first commander, controlled an economic empire estimated to be worth nearly a billion dollars, including one-third of the nation's arable land and many of the major industries. So complete was his economic control that foreign investors avoided Nicaragua for want of any reasonable investment opportunities.

During the first three decades of the postwar period, opposition to the dynasty was weak and divided. The moderates in the traditional opposition

---

[1] For an excellent history of early U.S.-Nicaraguan relations, see Richard Millett, *Guardians of the Dynasty*, Maryknoll, N.Y.: Orbis Books, 1977.

parties were paralyzed by the Somozas' close ties with the United States, and by their own fear of the more radical opposition—a fear which lured them, time after time, into unequal "alliances" with the government. The radical opposition, on the other hand, was contained by ferocious repression. Thus the future of the dynasty seemed secure when, on December 23, 1972, the earth began to move, changing not only the physical geography of Nicaragua, but its political geography as well.

The political aftershocks of the earthquake that destroyed Managua fatally weakened the structure of Somoza's rule. Turning adversity to advantage, Somoza and his associates enriched themselves shamelessly with the international aid intended for earthquake victims. The extent of corruption, together with the expansion of Somoza's economic empire into areas of economic activity previously reserved for other members of Nicaragua's bourgeoisie, alienated large sectors of both the middle and upper classes. Among Nicaragua's lower classes, the economic adversity caused by the earthquake stimulated more radical opposition, manifested in the wave of strikes, demonstrations and land seizures that swept the country in 1972-73.

The moderate opposition coalesced around the leadership of Pedro Joaquín Chamorro, editor of the anti-Somoza daily La Prensa, and a social democrat who in 1974 organized seven opposition political parties and two labor confederations into the Unión Democrática de Liberación. In the same month that Chamorro founded the UDEL, the nation's attention was fixed momentarily on a group which would eventually become the focal point of the more radical opposition—the Frente Sandinista de Liberación Nacional. On December 27, 1974, 25 FSLN guerrillas invaded a Managua Christmas party, capturing 12 of Nicaragua's most prominent business and political leaders. The guerrillas exchanged their hostages for 14 political prisoners, one million dollars in ransom, and safe passage to Cuba. The boldness of the Christmas operation brought the FSLN national recognition.

Somoza's embarrassment over the Christmas raid led him to embark upon a war of extermination against the FSLN. He declared a state of siege, created an elite counterinsurgency force within the National Guard, and obtained an 80 percent increase in U.S. military aid. The National Guard then proceeded to conduct a reign of terror in the northern departments of Zelaya, Matagalpa and Segovia, where the FSLN had been most active. For two years, peasants in those areas were subjected to a systematic campaign of torture and mass execution. To deprive the FSLN of support, 80 percent of the rural population was uprooted and herded into resettlement camps. The countryside then became a free-fire zone.

Such gross violations of human rights appalled Nicaragua's moderates and earned the Somoza government well-deserved international opprobrium. In January 1977, Nicaragua's Roman Catholic bishops joined in a pastoral letter accusing the National Guard of "humiliating and inhuman treatment ranging from torture and rape to summary execution." Reports by both Amnesty International and the U.S. Department of State confirmed the bishops' charges.

Thus, when the Carter Administration unveiled its new human rights policy in 1977, Nicaragua became one of its principal targets, constituting a near-perfect showcase for the policy. The FSLN, never a serious threat to the Somoza regime, had not been heard from since their Christmas operation. The absence of any apparent security problem in Nicaragua meant that U.S. policy there, unlike policy toward Iran or South Korea, could be safely guided by the moral imperative of human rights undiluted by national security concerns. Reductions in U.S. military assistance to Nicaragua on human rights grounds emboldened Somoza's moderate opponents, who had historically been immobilized by the unflagging U.S. support which the dynasty had enjoyed.

Then, in October 1977, the supposedly defunct FSLN launched a series of small-scale attacks on National Guard garrisons in five cities. Though the attackers were easily driven off, the assaults shattered the myth of Somoza's invulnerability and provided additional fuel to the burgeoning opposition's moderate and radical wings. Coincident with the attacks, 12 prominent Nicaraguan professionals exiled in Costa Rica (*el grupo de los doce*) praised the Sandinistas' "political maturity," and asserted that the FSLN would have to play a role in any permanent solution to Nicaragua's problems.

The willingness of the more progressive moderate forces to open a dialogue with the FSLN was due both to their own exasperation over the ineffectiveness of electoral opposition, and to a significant shift in strategy by elements of the FSLN itself. Ideological differences over the proper strategy for defeating Somoza emerged within the FSLN in 1975, and after the FSLN's founder, Carlos Fonseca Amador, was killed in combat in November 1976, the Sandinistas split into three factions, or "tendencies." The traditional strategy of rural-based guerrilla warfare was upheld by the Prolonged People's War Tendency (*Guerra Popular Prolongada*—GPP), while the Proletarian Tendency (*Tendencia Proletaria*—TP) advocated a shift to political work among the urban proletariat. Both groups agreed, however, that the time was not ripe for major military actions, and both rejected extensive cooperation with "bourgeois elements."

A third group, the Insurrectional Tendency (*Tendencia Insurreccional,* known popularly as the *Terceristas*), shared neither of these views. Believing that opposition to Somoza had become nearly universal, its leaders favored exemplary military action to spark popular insurrection. Most significantly, they also advocated the unity of all opposition forces, whatever their class character, around a program of social reform and democracy. It was the Tercerista faction which carried out the October 1977 attacks, and it was they who set about building links to the moderate opposition through Los Doce. Still, as 1978 began, the FSLN had neither the political nor the military strength to offer a serious challenge to the Somoza regime.

On January 10, 1978, Pedro Joaquín Chamorro was assassinated in Managua, and the nation erupted in a paroxysm of outrage and spontaneous violence. After two weeks of riots in Managua, Nicaragua's business leaders called a general strike with a single demand—Somoza's resignation. The two-week strike was 90 percent effective. Midway through it, the FSLN added its endorsement, and the Terceristas launched military attacks in several cities. But the political initiative clearly lay with the moderate opposition.

For the next six months the country was rocked by sporadic violence, most of it uncoordinated and organized by a widely disparate array of opposition groups. During these crucial months from March to August 1978, the political initiative slipped inexorably from the moderates to the FSLN. The Sandinistas spent those months gathering their forces, stockpiling arms and organizing the urban and rural poor. The moderates spent them waiting for the United States to push Somoza out of power. Unable to bring Somoza down by themselves and afraid of the Sandinistas' radicalism, the moderates expected the United States to act for them. They were encouraged in this belief by the Carter Administration's earlier condemnation of Somoza's human rights record, and by the shared interest in avoiding a Sandinista victory.

As civil violence became endemic, U.S. policy was caught in the pull of opposing imperatives. Should the United States stand by its advocacy of human rights and democratic reform in the face of Somoza's deteriorating political position? Or should human rights be subordinated to the political stability long provided by a brutal but reliable ally? Complicating this choice was the Carter Administration's self-imposed prohibition on interventionism in the Hemisphere and uncertainties as to whether Somoza could, in fact, restore order. To some extent, differing evaluations of the situation tended to be bureaucratically based. The ability of the Administration to devise a coherent policy was further diminished by the potent "Nicaragua lobby" in Congress, and its willingness to hold unrelated legislation hostage to the Administration's actions. This interplay of forces resulted in a policy which was more a product of bureaucratic compromise than of a clear assessment of U.S. interests. In fact, there was hardly a policy at all.

In April 1977, the United States restricted both military and economic aid to Somoza on human rights grounds; in September, the restrictions were relaxed. The government's harsh repression of the January 1978 riots sparked by Chamorro's assassination prompted the United States to impose new restrictions and to call for a "dialogue" between Somoza and the moderate opposition. Six months later, President Carter sent Somoza a letter congratulating him on his improved human rights record.

This last action in particular led much of the moderate opposition to conclude that their strategy of forcing Somoza's resignation with the help of U.S. pressure was untenable. Their only viable option, then, was to join in cooperation with more radical elements. The result was the creation of the Broad Opposition Front (*Frente Amplio Opositor*—FAO), the first coalition uniting the moderate and radical wings of the anti-Somoza opposition.

In August 1978, the FSLN seized the National Palace while the congress was in session, taking 1,500 hostages. The Sandinistas' audacity captured the popular imagination and with it the leadership of the anti-Somoza struggle. As the attackers and 59 newly freed political prisoners drove to the airport for a flight to Panama, thousands of Nicaraguans lined the streets to cheer them. The palace assault was followed swiftly by a new general strike, and in September the FSLN repeated its action of the previous October by attacking the National Guard in several cities. This time, however, the guerrilla actions sparked mass insurrections in Matagalpa, León, Estelí, Chinandega and Granada. To "save" the cities from the rebels, the National Guard was forced to destroy them from the air. It took nearly three weeks and over 3,000 dead before the Guard prevailed. When the Sandinistas withdrew, taking thousands of new recruits with them, the Guard "mopped up" with hundreds of summary executions. After September 1978, no compromise that would retain Somoza in power was possible.

The spectacle of an army waging war against its own citizenry prompted a reevaluation of U.S. policy by convincing officials that Somoza would never be able to restore political stability. Moreover, the FSLN's unexpected strength and support raised the specter of an eventual Sandinista victory unless some sort of "political solution" could successfully replace Somoza with a moderate government. From the fall of 1978 onward, the single goal of U.S. policy was to prevent the succession of an FSLN-dominated government. Under OAS auspices, the United States organized a mediation effort aimed at creating an "interim government" composed of the FAO and Somoza's National Liberal Party; the National Guard would remain intact. The plan envisioned no role for the FSLN, and the guerrillas denounced it as *somocismo* without Somoza.

Such a strategy might have had some chance of success in January 1978. By 1979, it was hopelessly unrealistic. The U.S. mediation effort destroyed what little remained of the moderates' political initiative. By pressuring the FAO to abandon its call for Somoza's immediate resignation and negotiate with the regime, the United States destroyed the moderates' unity and their credibility. When mediation began, the FAO included 16 opposition groups; by the end, fewer than ten remained. As it became increasingly isolated, the FAO could only have recovered if Washington had made up its mind to force Somoza out of office. This it was not willing to do.

Somoza played the mediation masterfully. By stalling for time, he was able to rearm and reinforce the National Guard, demoralize and fragment the moderate opposition, and give the United States the impression that he was negotiating in good faith. When he rejected the final mediation proposal for an internationally supervised plebiscite in January 1979, his position appeared much improved. His gamble, in essence, was that if the United States faced a clear and unequivocal choice between Somoza and the Sandinistas, it would eventually come to his aid. He was only partially mistaken.

Despite U.S. threats that a collapse of the mediation would affect the "whole range" of its relations with Nicaragua, retaliation was largely symbolic. The four-man U.S. military mission was withdrawn, and the embassy staff was cut by half. The surprising mildness of these sanctions derived from a variety of factors. Washington intelligence analysts were predicting that Somoza's National Guard could, through sheer firepower, defeat any feasible FSLN offensive. Thus policymakers may have felt more secure sticking with an unpopular but powerful Somoza than ousting him in favor of the politically divided and isolated moderates. Somoza, at least, would prevent a Sandinista victory. At the same time, Representatives Charles Wilson (D-Tex.) and John Murphy (D-N.Y.) were threatening to torpedo the Panama Canal treaties' implementation legislation if the Administration moved openly against Somoza.

In June 1979, the three factions of the FSLN launched the "final offensive" against the Somoza dynasty. Within weeks, they controlled most of the nation's major cities, virtually all the countryside and half of Managua. The new offensive heightened U.S. fears of an FSLN victory and prompted a retreat from the "noninterventionist" low profile which characterized policy after the collapse of the mediation. Addressing the Organization of American States (OAS) on June 22, Secretary of State Cyrus Vance finally put the United States on record as favoring Somoza's resignation. The rest of his proposal, however, was largely oblivious to political realities in both Nicaragua and the OAS. Making no mention of the Provisional Government for National Reconstruction appointed only days earlier by the FSLN and National Patriotic Front (a more militant coalition group than the FAO), Vance called for a "broad-based representative government," and an OAS peacekeeping force to ensure a ceasefire. Though the peacekeeping force was roundly condemned, the final OAS resolution called for Somoza's departure and legitimated the next phase of U.S. involvement by calling on member states to "facilitate an enduring and peaceful solution" to the civil war.

With all of Nicaragua engulfed in battle and the FSLN forces gaining steadily, the United States began an attempt to construct a constitutionalist solution. Somoza would resign in favor of a constitutional successor who would then appoint a council of prominent independent Nicaraguans and turn power over to them. The council would mediate between Somoza's Liberal Party, the National Guard and the opposition to create an interim government composed of all these forces. That government, with the National Guard still intact, would then prepare elections in 1981.

The unreality of this convoluted scheme is truly astonishing. The only real difference between it and the U.S. position during the earlier mediation was a willingness to force Somoza's resignation. Had the United States been willing to demand that resignation nine months earlier, such a solution might have been feasible. By July, however, even the most conservative opposition groups had already endorsed the provisional government which the United States insisted on studiously ignoring. The constitutionalist plan collapsed when the United States found that none of Nicaragua's moderates would endorse or participate in it.

Finally, with the FSLN on the verge of a military victory, the United States abandoned its attempts to construct a government which would exclude any significant Sandinista participation. The accession of the FSLN-backed provisional government was accepted as inevitable, and the United

States sought simply to negotiate the terms of transition in order to minimize FSLN influence. In this endeavor, it had two levers: Somoza would resign at U.S. direction, and the United States would provide massive economic aid to an acceptable government. In exchange, it wanted the addition of two more moderates to the provisional government's five-member junta, and a guarantee that neither Somoza's Liberal Party nor the National Guard would be dismantled.

Recognizing full well that the United States was negotiating with it only out of necessity following failure to undermine its support, the junta was not disposed to accede to these demands. Nor could it have done so politically. The provisional government derived its authority from the FSLN, which had appointed it and agreed to abide by its authority. Every important action taken by the junta was cleared in advance with FSLN field commanders. If the junta had shattered its own delicate political balance by adding moderates, or if it had agreed to retain the hated National Guard, it would have signed its own death warrant.

Thus despite pressure from the United States and several Latin American countries which had aided the anti-Somoza opposition, the junta would do no more than guarantee the lives of Somocistas and National Guardsmen, and leave open the possibility for "honest" members of the Guard to join the new national army. The battlefield situation, plus the moderation of the provisional government's program and cabinet, finally led the United States to accept the junta's terms.

On July 17, President Anastasio Somoza Debayle went into exile in Miami. With him went the entire senior command of the National Guard, as well as its morale. The Guard proceeded to disintegrate ignominiously, and within 24 hours had ceased to exist. Thus was realized the very eventuality which U.S. policy since January 1978 had sought to avoid—a complete Sandinista military victory.

How could U.S. policy have failed so dismally? Despite bureaucratic conflicts and congressional pressures, the failure cannot be attributed to the lack of a clear policy objective, at least not after Chamorro's assassination. Nor can the failure be fatalistically attributed to the internal dynamics of Nicaraguan politics. There was nothing inevitable about the final outcome in Nicaragua; indeed, when U.S. policy became fully geared to preventing an FSLN victory, the FSLN was by no means the dominant element in the anti-Somoza opposition.

As events unfolded in Nicaragua, the United States consistently tried to fit a square peg of policy into the round hole of reality. By failing to assess accurately the dynamics of Somoza's decline, the United States produced proposals which were invariably six months out of date. When the political initiative lay with the moderate opposition, the United States acted as if it still lay with Somoza. When the initiative shifted to the radicals, the United States acted as if it lay with the moderates. And when, at the last moment, the United States recognized that the radicals held the initiative, it seemed to think it could cajole them into returning it to the moderates.

Such misperception is not explicable merely in terms of an intelligence failure, any more than it was in Iran. The pace of events in Nicaragua was clear to anyone who wished to see it, and many did. A large part of the problem was the selective perception of policymakers who seemed to believe (or hope) that Somoza could restore order long after that became impossible, that the moderates were strong enough to form a post-Somoza regime excluding the radicals, and finally, that the radicals could be induced to surrender their leadership of the opposition on the very threshold of victory.

The source of these misperceptions was the fear of "another Cuba," and the questionable conviction that the radical opposition was intent on creating one. Now that Somoza has departed in "worst-case" fashion as far as U.S. policy was concerned, there is a great danger that policy toward the new regime will be plagued by assumptions and perceptions which are as unrealistic as those of the past two years. If this happens, the goal of preventing another Cuba will end up as did the goal of preventing an FSLN victory.

The New Cold War and the Nicaraguan Revolution: The Case of U.S. "Aid" to Nicaragua*

By Susanne Jonas

The U.S. proposal for an OAS peacekeeping force in Nicaragua in June 1979 was only the opening round of a long-term campaign to contain the regional impact of a victorious Sandinismo. Susanne Jonas analyzes the political battle which took place in the U.S. after July 1979 over the issue of aid to revolutionary Nicaragua. She concludes that neither of the parties to the debate—the softline and the hardline interventionists respectively—was at all interested in genuinely assisting the war-ravaged Nicaraguan people.

Susanne Jonas is a staff member of the Institute for the Study of Labor and Economic Crisis, and an editor of ISLEC's journal, Contemporary Marxism. She is a former staff member of the North American Congress on Latin America and has written extensively on the region for the past 15 years.

The Policy Debate over U.S. "Aid" to Nicaragua

During the year and a half following the victory of the Sandinistas, U.S. policy toward Nicaragua was the subject of intense debate. After having their way for over 40 years, the advocates of overt U.S. military intervention to keep the right-wing Somoza dictatorship in power were temporarily silenced in the summer of 1979—not out of any change of heart by the U.S. ruling class, but rather out of necessity, a necessity imposed by the military victory of the revolutionary Frente Sandinista over the Somoza dictatorship.

---

*Excerpted and abridged from Contemporary Marxism, No. 3, Summer 1981.

These circumstances forced a reappraisal in Washington, and presented the opportunity for a different breed of interventionists to be heard—the soft-line interventionists. These officials, represented most clearly by Assistant Secretary of State for Inter-American Affairs Viron Vaky and his successor, William Bowdler, sought to prevent "another Cuba" in Nicaragua (and "another Nicaragua" in El Salvador) by giving conditioned U.S. economic aid. The goal of soft-line interventionists was the same in all cases: to recoup or at least to minimize the losses of U.S. power. Their principal weapon was not the machine gun but the dollar.

The weapon of the dollar was particularly powerful because at the time of the Sandinista victory, the Nicaraguan economy was in ruins and required massive international aid. Somoza had maintained the country in a state of underdevelopment for years, and waged a brutal war against the Frente Sandinista which left a number of towns utterly destroyed and 70 percent of industry damaged or destroyed. When Somoza fled the country, he left barely $3.5 million in international reserves. Unemployment had reached 35 percent in Managua, higher elsewhere, with an additional 25 percent underemployment. Eight hundred thousand people, more than one fourth of the population, needed daily food handouts.[1]

Clearly, the job of reconstructing a devastated country required massive international aid, and the Nicaraguan government sought $2.5 billion in aid from a wide variety of sources, including the United States.[2] The Carter Administration responded with various small loans and grants, and with a longer-range proposal of $75 million for Nicaragua as part of the overall foreign aid bill for Fiscal Year 1981. This sparked an intense, months-long debate within the Carter Administration and within the U.S. Congress.

Before tracing the details of this debate, let us see briefly who were the main players and what interests they represented. The Carter Administration was itself divided, with a number of State Department officials such as Vaky and Bowdler taking the "accommodationist" view toward Nicaragua, while others in the Pentagon and intelligence agencies took a "hard-line" approach. Behind the "accommodationists," on the one hand, was a significant chunk of transnational banking capital (which, as we shall see, had its own interests in controlling U.S. relations with Nicaragua) backed by major Eastern newspapers (*New York Times, Washington Post,* etc., which carried numerous editorials supporting aid to Nicaragua). Aligned with the hard-liners, on the other hand, was a vocal right-wing bloc in Congress, whose goal was to stop U.S. aid to Nicaragua altogether—or to impose so many conditions as to make U.S. aid unacceptable to the Nicaraguan government. As we shall see, they were able to make great headway toward that latter goal.

Lest the intensity of the debate obscure the underlying unity of objec-

---

[1] See *Miami Herald*, December 11, 1979, and *New York Times*, February 3, 1980. Note: these and most of the newspaper articles cited below were found in Information Services on Latin America (ISLA), a monthly clipping service which follows major English-language newspaper coverage of Latin America (ISLA, 464 19th St., Oakland, CA 94612).

[2] *Financial Times*, December 5, 1979.

tives, let us be clear from the outset: all parties were in agreement that the United States must preserve maximum control over Nicaragua (within the context of declining U.S. power worldwide); the debate was merely about how best to achieve that objective. Because the stakes were high, the tactical debate was intense, but at no time was this underlying objective ever questioned.

From the very beginning, an underlying issue in U.S. policy circles was not simply Nicaragua, but Cuba (and, by extension, the Soviet Union): how to stop Cuban assistance to Nicaragua, how to prevent Nicaragua from following the "Cuban Model," how to counter Cuban training of Frente leadership, "Cuban troops" on Nicaraguan soil, etc., etc. Or at least, so it seemed in the Congressional debate; in fact, the international bankers had other objectives as well.

Thus, when President Carter presented the aid request to Congress in late 1979, the right-wing lost no time in launching a counteroffensive. In response to the dominant position within the Administration that the United States could only keep control over the future of Nicaragua (and keep Nicaragua out of the Cuban/Soviet camp) by giving U.S. aid, the right-wing argued that it was already too late for any real U.S. influence, and U.S. funds would only aid the consolidation of a pro-Cuban, Marxist regime; therefore, the United States must move directly to overthrow that regime, and certainly must send no aid.

After Carter submitted the request for $75 million in U.S. "aid" (of which $70 million were credits to buy U.S. goods, and only $5 million a grant),[3] the Senate Foreign Relations Committee approved the aid package, and the House Foreign Affairs Committee approved it after attaching a condition requiring Carter to cut off aid if Cuban or Soviet combat troops were found in Nicaragua.[4] The bill was approved on the floor of the Senate in January 1980. When it came to the floor of the House in February, the House convened a highly unusual two-hour secret session (for the second time since 1830—the first being in June 1979, also on Cuban influence in Nicaragua) to hear testimony on classified documents as to whether or not Nicaragua had become "Cuba-like." After this unprecedented session, the bill was passed in the House by a thin five-vote margin, and with several onerous conditions attached.[5]

First, the legislation itself contained a stipulation that 60 percent of the aid go to the private business sector—the idea being to strengthen the influence of the private sector in the new regime and in the economy.

Second, the house added a stipulation making the aid conditional on Nicaragua's "overall human rights performance," and on the holding of elections within a "reasonable period of time." This of course could become a ready-made justification for cutting off aid and possibly intervening in the future.

---

[3] *Miami Herald*, December 14, 1979.

[4] *New York Times*, December 2, 1979.

[5] See *Wall Street Journal*, February 29, 1980.

A third condition placed on the $75 million package was that the funds could not be used in facilities with Cuban personnel. This meant that, at a time when the literacy campaign was a principal national priority, no U.S. funds could be used in schools or educational facilities where there were Cuban volunteers or technicians, as would be likely given Cuba's extended experience with such campaigns.

A fourth condition prohibited Nicaraguan involvement with "international terrorism or attempts to subvert other governments," or the presence of Soviet or Cuban combat troops in Nicaragua.[6]

The Nicaraguan government and people reacted angrily to these conditions. On the one hand, they needed approval of the aid—not so much because of the amount (which, as many have pointed out, was almost insignificant compared with Nicaragua's needs)—but because international banking sources were holding up some $500 million in additional international funds for Nicaragua until passage of the aid bill as a "signal of U.S. confidence in the stability of Nicaragua."[7] On the other hand, the conditions imposed amounted to blackmail.

Twenty thousand Nicaraguans marched in the streets to protest the conditions on U.S. aid. The Nicaraguan government indicated that it would study the aid package in its final form before deciding to accept it—and meanwhile negotiated new trade agreements with the Soviet Union[8] and Eastern European countries, as well as with Western Europe, all of which were "absolutely without conditions."

In April, the situation took a new turn with the resignation of businessman and political "moderate" Alfonso Robelo from the government junta. Conservatives in Nicaragua, consulting with the U.S. Ambassador,[9] seized the opportunity to renew their clamor for "pluralism" and representation for the private sector in government. Conservatives in Washington seized upon the Robelo resignation and the Nicaraguan government's agreements with the Soviet Union and Eastern Europe to continue their efforts to stall or kill the U.S. aid bill. Speaker of the U.S. House of Representatives, Tip O'Neill, stated publicly that there was concern about Nicaragua becoming a "Marxist state," and that Congress would not approve the Nicaragua aid bill "unless they have a bipartisan government down there"[10] (meaning unless the private sector representatives were appointed to the government). The State Department declared that Nicaragua's agreements with the Soviet Union "clearly signalled" a Soviet move to expand its influence in Nicaragua. Others went further, pointing to the agreements as evidence of "a Soviet plan to communize Central America and to use that land bridge as a dagger pointing north and south...."[11]

---

[6] *Miami Herald*, March 17, 1980.

[7] *Wall Street Journal*, February 29, 1980.

[8] *Miami Herald*, March 20, 1980.

[9] *Miami Herald*, May 8, 1980.

[10] *Washington Post*, May 21, 1980.

[11] *Los Angeles Times*, May 17, 1980; *New York Times*, May 16, 1980.

The pressures were somewhat relieved when the Sandinista leadership, while denouncing U.S. "blackmail," appointed two new "moderates" to the Junta. In Washington, the Senate accepted the House version of the aid bill with all the new conditions. The House voted to approve the measure after Carter had a top-level Congressional delegation visit Nicaragua; Speaker O'Neill, in his first foreign aid speech in 28 years, and Majority Leader Jim Wright pushed the bill through after 9 hours of debate on the House floor.[12] The final version of the bill required President Carter to report every three months on the "state of Nicaraguan democracy" and to give assurances that Nicaragua was not aiding revolutionary movements in other countries.[13] In signing the authorization measure, Carter declared the U.S. intention to resist "interference" by Cuba "and others."[14]

However, only the first stage of the battle was over, for the funds still had to be appropriated by Congress. New pressures began to build up for the Nicaraguan government to announce a date for "free elections." In July, the Republican Party platform directly attacked the "Marxist Sandinista takeover of Nicaragua," opposed the Carter aid program, and stated support for any movement to overthrow the Sandinista government.[15] In August, there were reports that conservative groups within the Carter Administration (the intelligence agencies and the Pentagon) were trying to stop the appropriation and disbursement of the aid until after the November elections in the United States, when the whole aid package would be cancelled by the Reagan Administration—and that these officials were deliberately leaking information (to the Evans and Novak column, published August 1, 1980), portraying Nicaragua as a "Soviet and Cuban puppet, supplying arms to Communist insurgents in neighboring El Salvador."[16] The Carter Administration compiled the Congressionally required investigation, and on September 12, 1980, reported that the Nicaraguan government was not supporting violence or terrorism in Central America (as opposed to right-wing allegations that Nicaragua was shipping Cuban arms to other countries).[17] The path was finally cleared for Congressional release of the $75 million, and the final agreement for releasing the funds was signed with the Nicaraguan government in October. Thus ended, at least temporarily, the year-long Nicaragua aid debate.

The Hidden Actors: The Transnational Banks

What were the goals of the pro-aid forces, the soft-line interventionists? And who were they, really? Throughout the debate, the dominant force in the Carter Administration argued that U.S. aid must be given to keep Nicaragua out of the Cuban/Soviet camp, and that the long delay in

12 *Washington Post*, June 6, 1980; *New York Times*, June 10, 1980.

13 *New York Times*, June 10, 1980; *Washington Post*, August 8, 1980.

14 *Miami Herald*, June 1, 1980.

15 *Washington Post*, August 8, 1980.

16 *Washington Post*, August 8, 1980; *Miami Herald*, September 6, 1980.

17 *New York Times*, September 13, 1980.

Congressional approval was having a "radicalizing impact" on Nicaragua.[18] On the surface, the goals of the soft-line interventionists in the State Department were:

- to shore up the political role of Nicaragua's "moderates" and businessmen and to assure a future political role for non-Sandinistas;

- to preserve the role of the private sector in the economy and maintain a "mixed economy," rather than follow the "Cuban Model" of socialism;

- to prevent Nicaragua from lining up internationally in the Soviet camp;

- to exert pressure to get Cuban technicians out of Nicaragua.

To be sure, these political goals were important. But there was another hidden force which provides the key to the Carter/Trilateral strategy:

Pressure on the Administration to help Nicaragua has come from a consortium of U.S. banks, which recently negotiated a refinancing of $600 million of Nicaragua's debt.[19]

In fact, Carter released the U.S. aid only after Nicaragua reached an agreement with the private banks.[20]

Here, finally, we find the key to the mystery—the counterforce strong enough to resist the political/military right-wing forces. Just at the time when Carter was presenting the foreign aid bill to Congress, this consortium of the capitalist world's largest transnational banks was beginning a long series of negotiations with the Nicaraguan government to reschedule payment on the staggering foreign debt left by Somoza. All in all, this was a debt of over $1.6 billion. More than $618 million was due by the end of 1979 (more than the total value of Nicaraguan exports), of which $444 million or 70 percent was owed to private foreign banks;[21] 75 percent of the foreign debt was owed to U.S.-based banks.[22] According to the U.N. Economic Commission for Latin America, Somoza had deliberately designed this private debt so that most of it could be drained from Nicaragua, rather than being invested there![23]

Talks between the Nicaraguan government and a steering committee of 13 bankers representing 90 creditor banks began informally in the winter of 1979-80. The meetings continued in March with the Nicaraguan government attempting (a) to obtain a grace period for repayments; and (b) as against the pressures of international bankers, to keep the International Monetary Fund (IMF) out of the picture. As one official stated, "It is not for us to involve the IMF at this stage and to get involved in an austerity program"; in the words of another, "... we consider that the IMF has no role to play in the formation of economic policy."[24] Later in 1980, the issue of the

---

18 *Washington Post*, September 13, 1980.

19 *Financial Times*, September 16, 1980.

20 *New York Times*, September 13, 1980.

21 *New York Times*, November 27, 1979; *Miami Herald*, December 11, 1979.

22 *Financial Times*, December 18, 1979.

23 *Miami Herald*, September 5, 1979.

24 *Financial Times*, March 18, 1980; June 28, 1980.

IMF did block an agreement between the Nicaraguan government and the "Paris Club," which represented Western governments to which Nicaragua owed most of its $250 million bilateral debt: the United States insisted that Nicaragua open discussions with the IMF, and Nicaragua refused to do so under such pressure.[25] After nine months of talks (and a last-minute ploy by Citibank of New York, the largest creditor, to push for annual debt-service payments, beginning in 1980, of more than 30 percent of Nicaragua's export revenues!), an agreement was reached in September, rescheduling the $582 million due in 1980 for repayment at commercial rates over the next 12 years.[26] Nicaragua succeeded in keeping the IMF out of the agreement and gaining a five-year grace period, but the banks had Nicaragua's agreement to repay all of the Somoza regime's debts, at commercial (not concessionary) rates.[27]

Now it is clear why the banks pressured the Carter Administration not to bow to right-wing political pressure to delay U.S. aid until after the November elections:[28] at the moment when they were successfully completing their own negotiations with Nicaragua, the banks had a great stake in not allowing the apple cart of U.S. aid to Nicaragua to be upset.

Why did the transnational banks care so much about their negotiations with Nicaragua? First, they saw the issue as much larger than Nicaragua itself, as kind of a test case: they wanted to establish a clear precedent of a revolutionary government not defaulting (in contrast to Cuba some years earlier), and of agreement to pay the debt at commercial rates, even under the outrageous circumstances of a staggering debt accumulated by Somoza, primarily for his own gain, and on which Somoza had defaulted after the fall of 1978. Such a precedent would serve them well in their negotiations with other countries ranging from Bolivia, Brazil and Jamaica to Poland, Sudan and Turkey. As one banker stated, the Nicaragua settlement "could make it more palatable for other countries to go the rescheduling route."[29]

Second, the banks and their political spokesmen had a strategy for Nicaragua. In a situation in which the Nicaraguan government began with only $3.5 million total in international reserves, whatever paltry reserves could be accumulated through international aid would have to be used for paying off the international banks for loans made to the Somoza regime, rather than for meeting Nicaragua's domestic needs for the coming years—reconstruction of a devastated economy, creation of 90,000 new jobs, stimulation of economic growth, and reduction of inflation from 60 percent to 20 percent. The Nicaraguan government accepted this intolerable burden for one simple reason: without doing so, they would have faced closed

---

[25] New York Times, December 25, 1980; Inforpress Centroamérica (Guatemala), No. 412 (December 4, 1980).

[26] Latin America Regional Reports (Mexico/Central America), August 15, 1980; Latin America Weekly Report, August 15, 1980; Financial Times, September 16, 1980.

[27] New York Times, September 9, 1980; see also Terri Shaw in Washington Post, October 5, 1980; Latin America Weekly Report, September 12, 1980.

[28] Financial Times, September 16, 1980.

[29] New York Times, September 9, 1980.

doors for all short and medium term credit from international banks in the capitalist world. (In fact, the banks did refuse to extend any new credits to the Nicaraguan government until the rescheduling negotiations were concluded.)[30] This would have left no option other than massive aid from the Soviet bloc; and it is questionable whether the Soviet Union would have undertaken such a responsibility for a second time in the Western hemisphere.

This unspeakable situation had political ramifications as well: it meant that the Sandinista government was forced into the position of imposing austerity upon the Nicaraguan people as the price of their liberation; of asking the Nicaraguan people, who had fought and died for a better life, to suffer and sacrifice still more, so that the international banks could be paid off. As soon as the government made its first move in this direction, by limiting the end-of-year bonus for workers to $150 at the end of 1979, the middle class had its golden opportunity to begin its protests against the government. (Now we can see why the Nicaraguans so strongly opposed IMF involvement, which would have meant a formal austerity plan.)

More broadly, and over a longer range, this situation gave the international bankers a lever to exert pressure upon and squeeze the new government—and wait for the discontent bred by the necessary austerity measures to erupt into anti-government demonstrations (along the lines of the middle class women's "March of the Empty Pots" against Allende in Chile) and eventually perhaps a Chile-style counterrevolution.

Thus, transnational capital may be seen to have adopted a strategy which *appeared* less direct than the militarists', but which was every bit as hostile in attempting to undermine and destabilize (and eventually to "moderate" or get rid of) the Sandinista government. The new gnomes of international finance capital are indeed the *patient interventionists,* but not one whit less interventionist than the shrill right-wing Congressmen in Washington. Their concern (and it was clearly communicated to Carter, we may speculate, via the Trilateral Commission) was above all to assure that U.S.-Nicaraguan relations were not interrupted too early, which might prompt the Nicaraguan government to pull out of the debt renegotiations and refuse to repay Somoza's loans.

This, then, was an important source of the policy of the "soft-liners" in Washington, who were arguing publicly that the U.S. must maintain good relations with Nicaragua, aid Nicaragua, etc. Underneath the Carter position lay the determination to get hard cash repayments, and politically, over the long range, to undermine and destabilize the Sandinista government through austerity policies which would turn the middle class against the government.

---

[30] *Journal of Commerce,* May 9, 1980.

A Splendid Little War:
Drawing the Line in El Salvador*
By William M. LeoGrande

The third selection for this chapter, again by William M. LeoGrande, is a wide-ranging analysis and critique of U.S. policy toward El Salvador during both the Carter administration and the first six months of the Reagan presidency. LeoGrande explains that after the Carter people failed solidly to back reform in El Salvador in the wake of the October 1979 coup, rightist forces in the Salvadorean military were able to consolidate power and close off a historic opportunity for progressive change. It is with these forces that the Reagan administration has allied itself in its pursuit of a military victory over the FDR-FMLN in El Salvador. Although he may underestimate the significance of the domino theory for Reagan administration analysts, LeoGrande expertly exposes the Cold War character of Reagan's El Salvador policymaking and thoroughly details its potential international implications. He ends with a proposal for a negotiated solution to the conflict in El Salvador which deserves more attention in Washington than it has thus far received.

In the midst of the presidential campaign, a skeptical reporter asked one of Ronald Reagan's foreign policy advisers whether he and his candidate really believed their own rhetoric about the communist menace in El Salvador. "El Salvador itself doesn't really matter," the adviser replied, "we have to establish credibility because we're in very serious trouble."

The Reagan Administration has moved quickly to establish that credibility by "drawing the line" against "communist aggression" in El Salvador.[1]

During his first two months in the Oval Office, President Reagan fired the Carter Administration's reformist Ambassador to that country; launched a major political offensive in Europe, Latin America, and on Capitol Hill to convince anyone who would listen that the insurgency in El Salvador is "a textbook case of indirect armed aggression by the communist powers"; and moved to more than double both economic and military assistance to the beleaguered Salvadorean government.[2]

A nation of virtually no inherent strategic or economic interest to the United States, El Salvador has suddenly become a symbol—a vehicle through which the Reagan Administration hopes to set the tone, by dint

---

*Excerpted and abridged from *International Security*, Summer 1981 (Vol. 6, No. 1).

[1] The phrase "drawing the line" was first used by Secretary of State Alexander Haig when he briefed the Congressional leadership on the State Department's White Paper, *Communist Interference in El Salvador*, Special Report Number 80, February 23, 1981 (reported in *The New York Times*, February 18, 1981).

[2] *Ibid.*

of example, for its whole foreign policy. Because the war in El Salvador looks like an easy victory, it provides a perfect opportunity for the new administration to demonstrate its willingness to use force in foreign affairs, its intent to de-emphasize human rights, and its resolve to contain the Soviet Union. In short, the conflict in El Salvador is a splendid little war, made to order for an administration determined to repudiate much of its predecessor's foreign policy.

There is no doubt that Ronald Reagan intends to vanquish the incipient regionalism of the Carter Administration's international outlook and restore globalism to its traditional place of pre-eminence in America's strategic thinking. Whether reality will be so amenable is less clear.

Human Rights in Central America: The Reformist Interlude

Jimmy Carter's decision to make the promotion of human rights a major objective of U.S. foreign policy was at once the most celebrated and excoriated of his international initiatives. From the outset, the policy was presented in moral terms—it was an approach to the world as good and decent as the American people themselves.

It was also intended to distance the United States from the brutal excesses of decaying autocracies, rather than wager the prestige and interests of the nation on their doubtful survival. It made more sense, according to Carter's analysts, to adapt U.S. policy to the currents of history than to try vainly to stem the tide. They argued that right-wing dictatorships bent on preserving anachronistic social orders make bad security risks; that the more they rely upon brute force to sustain themselves, the more rapidly they mobilize and radicalize their opponents. For the United States to enlist wholeheartedly in support of right-wing dictatorships would actually endanger national security; ultimately, such regimes would collapse, and an angry populace would bitterly recall—as it did in Iran—that the United States had sided with the tyrants. The Carter Administration believed that the best strategy for preserving national security was to help create pluralist democracies with relatively egalitarian social structures. Such states would tend to be culturally and philosophically closer to the United States than to the Soviet Union and, moreover, would be politically stable.[3]

Despite the complaints of Carter's conservative critics,[4] human rights were never allowed to overshadow immediate national security concerns of a more traditional kind. When crucial allies were involved (e.g., South Korea, the Philippines, the Shah's Iran), the issue of human rights was always muted. But in Latin America, where there appeared to be no immediate security threats in 1977, the human rights policy was applied full force. This was especially true in Central America, where the four nations of the

[3] For an excellent description and evaluation of Carter's human rights policy by one of the participants, see Richard E. Feinberg, "U.S. Human Rights Policy: Latin America," *International Policy Report*, Vol. 6, No. 1 (Center for International Policy), October 1980.
[4] See, for example, Jeane Kirkpatrick, "Dictatorships and Double Standards," *Commentary*, November 1979, pp. 34-35.

northern tier (Nicaragua, Honduras, El Salvador, and Guatemala) were all ruled by military dictatorships notorious for their systematic repression. By reducing or terminating economic and military assistance to these regimes Washington sought to force them to improve their human rights practices.

The Sandinista victory in Nicaragua set in motion a full-scale review of U.S. policy toward Central America—a review aimed at devising a more effective strategy for preventing similar leftist victories in El Salvador, Guatemala, and Honduras. At issue was the question that had not been adequately addressed during the Nicaraguan crisis: how could the Administration reconcile its commitment to human rights with its desire to preserve political stability? Hardliners within the government argued that these objectives were inherently contradictory, and that stability ought to take precedence even at the expense of human rights. They argued for restoring military aid to the region's anti-communists—in essence, a return to the Kissingerian policy of supporting dictators so long as they were "friendly" ones.

Defenders of the human rights policy replied that military aid could not buy stability in the region and that Washington should instead press for progressive social and political reforms. As in the Alliance for Progress, evolutionary change was prescribed as the antidote to revolutionary upheaval. This option won the bureaucratic battle in Washington, and was put into effect almost immediately in an effort to avert the approaching civil war in El Salvador.

Carter and the Search for Order in El Salvador

For generations, the government of El Salvador served as the guardian of the landed oligarchy, suppressing by force of arms any challenge to the nation's rigid social order. The army seized power in 1932 in order to crush a peasant rebellion, which it did successfully at the cost of 30,000 lives. The military's monopoly on political power was retained for the next half century through alternating periods of modernization and entrenchment. But throughout these five decades, two political characteristics held constant: the policies of the regime never threatened the socio-economic foundations of oligarchic power and the military never allowed the political system to become so open that reformist civilians might actually win control of the government.[5]

The process of political polarization in El Salvador began to accelerate in 1972 when the Christian Democrats (PDC) led by Napoleón Duarte won the presidential election, but were cheated out of victory by the military's fraudulent counting of the ballots. In the wake of this electoral fiasco, the armed forces unleashed a wave of repression against the PDC which drove most of its leaders into exile. Despairing of the prospects for peaceful change, many rank and file Christian Democrats began looking to the radical left as the only viable opposition. The mid-1970s witnessed

---

[5] William M. LeoGrande and Carla Anne Robbins, "Oligarchs and Officers: The Crisis in El Salvador," *Foreign Affairs*, Vol. 58, No. 5 (Summer 1980), pp. 1084-1103.

the rapid growth of both the guerrilla left and the "popular organizations"—grass roots community groups of urban and rural poor who enforced their demands for economic reforms by mass demonstrations and civil disobedience.

The rising tide of popular opposition prompted the military government of General Humberto Romero to enact, in 1977, the Public Order Law—a legal license to terrorize the population into silence. The Public Order Law instituted full press censorship, outlawed strikes, banned public meetings, and suspended normal judicial proceedings. Its effect was to demolish the remnants of the centrist political parties, further polarizing the political situation. The clandestine guerrilla organizations proved to be beyond the reach of the security apparatus; the repression served only to bring them new recruits. The oligarchy and its extremist allies within the armed forces were terrified by the growing strength of the left and the government's inability to contain it. They undertook a private solution—the formation of the death squads, which proceeded to wage a campaign of assassination against priests, students, and trade union leaders.

By the summer of 1979, political order in El Salvador was decaying rapidly. Washington, armed with its new reformist strategy for the region, began pressuring General Romero to ease the strictures of his military rule and to initiate social and economic reforms to stem the growing strength of the revolutionary opposition. Romero refused and in October was ousted by progressive military officers who promised the sorts of changes he had resisted. The new junta quickly incorporated civilian leaders from the centrist opposition parties and even suggested its willingness to reach some sort of accord with elements of the radical left. The regime promised to create democratic institutions and to enact social reforms that would break the socio-economic dominance of the landed oligarchy. This government was a seemingly perfect vehicle for Washington's new regional policy of reformism; the Carter Administration quickly pledged to support it.

Unfortunately, the October junta proved to be incapable of carrying out its promises—a failure due largely to the internal politics of the Salvadorean armed forces and to the reticence of the United States to carry its support for reformism to its logical conclusion. While the Salvadorean military had traditionally governed in ways congenial to the oligarchy, it also had a tradition of allowing progressive officers to initiate modernizing reforms as long as they did not threaten the basic structure of the existing social order. The October coup was very much in this tradition, but the reforms it promised were more radical than those of the past. Whenever the progressive officers and their civilian allies proposed reforms of any significance, rightists within the armed forces blocked them as being too extreme. The result was paralysis of the government which could only have been overcome if the progressive officers had been willing to break with their rightist brethren and take full control of the ideologically divided military. This they were unwilling to do—partly because of institutional loyalty and partly because the United States was unwilling to stand behind them. Though Washington favored social reform, it balked at the October junta's willingness to bring elements of the radical left into partnership with the government. The Carter Administration's strategy was to isolate the radical left politically, not to allow it to share power.

The October junta's paralysis demolished any hope of accord with the radical left, which proceeded to escalate its insurrectionary activities. The mere suggestion of real socio-economic change terrified the oligarchy, which in turn escalated its paramilitary terrorism. Amidst this spiral of political violence, the moderate civilians within the government sought a showdown with the officers, demanding that reforms be implemented and that the rightist Defense Minister, General José Guillermo García, be removed. The military refused, the civilians resigned, and the government moved sharply to the right. At this critical juncture, the United States did nothing to preserve the moderate reformist character of the government. In fact, despite this fundamental shift in the balance of political forces within the government, U.S. policy changed not at all. The Carter Administration continued to provide both economic and military aid to the regime, justifying its policy with claims that it was supporting a moderate centrist government under attack from extremists on both the left and the right.

Reform With Repression: Land Reform and the Rightward Shift of the Junta

Since January 1980, the moderation of the Salvadorean government has been more chimerical than real. The key difference between the junta formed in January and its predecessor lies in their strategy for resolving the nation's political crisis. While the October junta sought to create a political opening to the left, the January government has sought to defeat the left militarily. At the insistence of the United States, the government grudgingly undertook some social reforms, the most touted of which has been the agrarian program, but this strategy of "reform with repression," as Archbishop Oscar Romero characterized it, has been considerably more repressive than reformist.

Under the stewardship of Ambassador Robert White, the U.S. pursued four interrelated objectives during 1980:

- to pressure the government into implementing real social reforms designed to undercut the left's popular support;
- to urge the government to reduce the level of official terrorism by reining in its own security forces, even if that required the removal of some rightist officers;
- to protect the government from a coup by the extreme right; and
- to entice the moderate left away from its alliance with the guerrillas, thus opening the way for a negotiated settlement that would leave the radicals isolated on the political periphery.

By year's end, it was apparent that this reformist strategy had failed. The agrarian program, the cornerstone of an otherwise modest package of reforms, was at a standstill. The level of official violence had risen dramatically rather than subsiding, and there was no evidence whatsoever that the government was making any serious effort to curtail it or to bring its perpetrators to justice. The extreme right had not overthrown the government, but the government itself had moved so far to the right that its extremist opposition was quiescent.

Though the Salvadorean land reform has not significantly altered the socio-economic condition of the nation's 2.5 million peasants, it has nevertheless been, in a perverse sense, a success. From the outset, the principal objectives of the reform package were political rather than socio-economic. For the Salvadorean government, it was a way of satisfying U.S. demands for reform without alienating rightist officers like Defense Minister García who hold the real reins of power. For the United States, it was tangible "proof"—indeed, the only proof—that the government of El Salvador was truly as moderate and reformist as the Administration portrayed it. For if the agrarian reform is a sham or a failure, it is difficult to imagine on what grounds the Salvadorean government might qualify as either moderate or reformist. Certainly not in the political sphere. Ambassador White's hope of consolidating the position of the moderates within the government had even less success than the agrarian reform.

The Loosening Grip of the Moderates

The pivotal political issue over the past year has been whether the Christian Democratic civilians and the progressive military officers within the government could muster the influence to win control of the security forces away from the right. Such control would have allowed the moderates to remove extremist officers from command positions, punish those guilty of political murders, crack down on the death squads, and thereby curb the repression which took the lives of some 10,000, 80 percent of which were civilian deaths ascribed to state security forces.[6]

Not only were the moderates unable to restrain the security forces; they were unable even to maintain what little influence they had. The right-wing coup which Ambassador White labored so diligently to prevent occurred slowly, by degrees, not in the streets but in the high councils of the officer corps. As the rightist officers lost patience with reform, they slipped quietly into agreement with their more extremist compatriots, becoming convinced that the only way to meet the challenge of the left is with violence—however much violence that might take.

Over the past year, the rightist officers—the same officers who blocked the reforms of the October 1979 government—have consolidated their hold on power by reducing the Christian Democrats and the progressive officers to impotence. The steady stream of resignations by Christian Democrats over the last twelve months stands as testimony of the rightist character

---

[6] This widely cited estimate of 80 percent originated with the Salvadorean Catholic Church. During the Carter Administration, State Department officials were willing to acknowledge in private that these were the most reliable figures available.

of the regime. Almost without exception, each letter of resignation has cited the intransigence of the rightists and the inability of the moderates to circumvent them.[7] The progressive officers within the government have fared worse than the Christian Democrats. In mid-summer of 1980, the rightist officers began a campaign to systematically strip the progressives of their command positions, demoting or reassigning them to diplomatic posts.[8] Shortly thereafter, several of the most prominent progressives were assassinated by death squads, and in November their leader, Colonel Adolfo Majano, was finally removed from the five-member governing junta. Majano was later arrested and sent into exile. The progressive faction within the officers corps, which was powerful enough in 1979 to overthrow Romero's government, has now ceased to be a significant political force.

Without allies in the armed forces, the Christian Democrats serve at the pleasure of the rightist officers. The appointment last November of Christian Democratic leader Napoleón Duarte as president should not be mistaken for a significant realignment of political forces. The leadership shuffle that placed Duarte in the presidency left the senior military command basically intact, leading one diplomat to describe Duarte as an "adornment."[9]

Duarte may have his own agenda, but he does not have the political power to carry it out. This is apparent by his inability to act in his own interests: for example, Duarte can neither proceed with the agrarian program nor can he dismiss his military opponents. Like the agrarian reform, the restructuring of the government came at the insistence of the United States. The Carter Administration needed it to preserve the centrist image of its client in the wake of the murders of four North American religious women, and the Salvadorean officers acquiesced to it in order to mollify the State Department. But the reorganization has not altered the structure of political power in El Salvador one iota. The government was and remains a rightist military regime with a civilian facade.

Nothing demonstrates this more clearly than the practices of the government itself. The violence of the security forces accelerated in 1980; despite the pleas and promises of the Christian Democrats, the reign of official terror was much worse than under the openly reactionary government of General Humberto Romero. So too, the atrocities committed by the death squads. Not one person has been arrested for the hundreds of murders of Salvadoreans for which the extreme right took "credit" in 1980.[10] Officers on the extreme right who have been caught plotting against the government have not even been punished. Major Robert d'Aubuisson, who led a coup attempt last May, was arrested and then released after the officers corps voted not to place him on trial. The Vice-Minister of Defense,

---

[7] Cynthia Arnson and Delia Miller, "Background Information on El Salvador and U.S. Military Assistance to Central America" (Institute for Policy Studies), June 1980.

[8] The Washington Post, September 5, 1980.

[9] The New York Times, December 14, 1980.

[10] Two Salvadorean rightists were recently arrested, however, for the murders of Rodolfo Viera and his two AIFLD advisors.

also implicated in the plot, was not even removed from his post.[11]

The Opposition of the Left

Despite U.S. efforts to portray the Salvadorean regime as a centrist government beset by both the left and the right, there are really only two sides to the conflict in El Salvador: the rightist government and its leftist opposition, which is no more a "Pol Pot" left than the government is "centrist." The opposition includes a broad, politically heterogeneous array of groups organized under the political rubric of the Revolutionary Democratic Front (FDR), and the military command of the Farabundo Martí Front for National Liberation (FMLN).

The left clearly failed to create an irreversible military situation before Ronald Reagan entered the Oval Office, but the January 1981 offensive was hardly a great victory for government forces either. Though the guerrillas were unable to defend any of their initial territorial gains, they demonstrated their ability to launch coordinated assaults throughout the country and to operate with impunity in many rural areas. Never before had the various guerrilla groups demonstrated such a capacity for coordinated action. Indeed, the threat posed by the January offensive was severe enough to prompt the Carter Administration to radically reverse its own policy. Lethal military aid had been withheld from El Salvador since 1977 on human rights grounds, and $5.7 million in "nonlethal"[12] aid was suspended in November pending the outcome of the investigation into the murders of the North American missionaries. On the very eve of leaving office, the Administration restored the "nonlethal" aid and rushed an additional $5 million in lethal material to the Salvadorean armed forces, though the offensive was thwarted before the aid arrived.

Ironically, the Carter Administration's decision to restore military aid came on the same day as Carter's Farewell Address in which he offered a stirring rhetorical defense of his human rights policy. Nothing could have better symbolized the contradictions of Carter's policy in Central America. Ultimately, the Administration's commitment to social and political reform could not compete with Washington's traditional fear of leftist governments.

The current military situation appears to be one of stalemate: the left does not yet have the capacity to defeat the armed forces, but neither do the armed forces have the capacity to exterminate the guerrillas. The January offensive was by no means the final battle of El Salvador's civil war—more likely, it was only the opening shot fired. The future course of the war could well depend as much upon external factors as upon the domestic principals, and a great deal more than the tranquility of El Salvador may be at stake.

---

[11] Vice-Minister Carranza was eventually transferred in November 1980 as part of the government reorganization in which Duarte became President.

[12] The designation "non-lethal" must be understood in a technical sense rather than literally; it includes transportation and communications equipment essential for counter-insurgency warfare.

Regional/International Alignments

The conflict in El Salvador has never been a purely domestic affair. The long succession of rightist regimes there have always relied upon Washington's military and political support to help cow their opponents. As political strife escalated in 1980, so too did the level of international involvement, and no external actor was more prominent than the United States. In addition to providing nearly $100 million in aid, Washington was intimately involved in the internal politics of both the Salvadorean government and its armed forces.

The United States has not been the only patron of the Salvadorean government; support from Venezuela and Costa Rica has been crucial for maintaining the regional legitimacy of U.S. policy. Venezuelan President Herrera Campins has lobbied hard within the international Christian Democratic movement to gain acceptance for Duarte's government, and Venezuela has provided considerable economic assistance to San Salvador. Venezuelan opposition leaders accuse their government of covertly shipping arms to the Salvadorean security forces, but Herrera Campins denies the charges. Costa Rica's Christian Democratic president, Rodrigo Carazo, has also been supportive of U.S. policy and maintains cordial relations with Duarte's government, though Costa Rica does not have the resources to make any major material contribution to the conflict.[13]

Guatemala and Honduras are allies of the Salvadorean regime, a fact which the U.S. government has been less than eager to spotlight. Both nations are ruled by right-wing military governments which perceive the possibility of a leftist victory in El Salvador as a threat to their own internal security. Over the past year, both have sought closer ties with the rightist officers in the Salvadorean armed forces rather than with the government *per se.* During the left's January 1981 offensive in El Salvador, Honduran and Guatemalan forces were mobilized along the border, ostensibly to prevent the fighting from spilling across the frontiers. In effect, however, they were providing an anvil against which the Salvadorean military hoped to pound guerrillas. There were numerous reports, though unconfirmed, that some Honduran and Guatemalan units crossed the frontier to operate jointly with their Salvadorean allies.

Whether or not such reports are accurate, there is little doubt that the Guatemalans are predisposed to intervene in El Salvador if the left appears to be gaining militarily. The Guatemalan armed forces have a history of coming to the aid of the Salvadorean right in times of crisis (in 1932 and again in 1972), and the Guatemalan government has spoken openly of the need to halt the "communist tide" before it reaches Guatemalan shores. Finally, U.S. intelligence reports reveal that both the Guatemalan and Honduran governments are assisting in the creation of paramilitary groups within their territories, groups composed of former Nicaraguan National

---

[13] *The Washington Post,* January 17, 1981.

Guardsmen and anti-Castro Cubans whose objective is to wage war against communism on a regional scale.[14]

The left, too, has its international allies, among whom Mexico, Nicaragua, and Cuba have been the most vocal. Though Mexico has not formally broken relations with El Salvador, the Mexican government and ruling Institutional Revolutionary Party (PRI) are firm supporters of Salvadorean leftists. Mexico City is the principal base of operations for the FDR's efforts to build diplomatic support.

Mexico and the United States are farther apart on the issue of El Salvador than on any other. Within hours of Reagan's election, President José López Portillo publicly warned the incoming Administration against intervention in Central America. Mexican protests escalated in January when the Carter Administration restored military aid to El Salvador; Foreign Minister Jorge Castañeda warned the United States to let the Salvadoreans "solve their own problems," and PRI President Gustavo Carvajal promised that the party would support any people that "fights for its freedom." That same week, 25,000 Mexicans marched against U.S. intervention in El Salvador—the largest such demonstration in recent years.[15] In February, when General Vernon Walters travelled to Mexico City to present Washington's evidence of Cuban involvement in El Salvador, he was denied an audience with President López Portillo. López Portillo then followed Walters' visit with a speech in which he went out of his way to stress Mexico's close relations with Cuba, calling it the Latin American state "most dear" to Mexico.[16]

Mexican policy is based upon an assessment of Central American reality not so different from that of the Carter Administration. The Mexicans are convinced that the military governments of El Salvador, Guatemala, and Honduras cannot long survive the growing demands of the poor for social change. Stability in the region therefore requires that these narrowly-based dictatorial regimes be replaced with popular governments willing to dismantle the oligarchic land-owning systems and distribute the benefits of development to a broader cross-section of the populace. While the Mexicans have no desire to see pro-Soviet Marxist-Leninist regimes predominate in Central America, they see fundamental change as inevitable and believe that strong international support for social democratic opposition elements offers the best hope for long-term stability. The Mexicans, unlike the Carter Administration, have not been afraid to carry this policy through to its logical conclusion, i.e., supporting the revolutionary oppositions in El Salvador and Guatemala. Based upon their experience of peaceful coexistence

---

[14] This report, entitled "Dissent Paper on El Salvador and Central America," was circulated in Washington D.C. during November 1980. For a synopsis, see *The Boston Globe,* November 28, 1980. The report has a rather mysterious history. The State Department denies that it was an official dissent channel document, but several Department officials have told the author that the paper cites existing intelligence reports accurately. This suggests it was either written by analysts within the government or by someone with access to classified material.

[15] *The Washington Post,* January 25, 1981.

[16] *The New York Times,* February 21, 1981.

with Cuba, the Mexicans are confident that they can live cordially with whatever form of revolutionary government emerges.[17]

Mexico's view is widely shared within the Socialist International, which has provided financial assistance and diplomatic support to the FDR. A number of key European Social Democratic parties, including those in Germany, Sweden, Holland, and Norway, are on record as supporting the FDR and opposing any deeper U.S. military involvement in El Salvador. Sweden's support for the left has been so vocal that the Reagan Administration was moved to lodge a formal protest in February—the first such protest made to a West European nation since the war in Vietnam.

The breadth of the FDR's European support prompted Washington to launch a major diplomatic offensive on the continent in an effort to counter it. Assistant Secretary of State for European Affairs Lawrence Eagleburger was dispatched to Germany, France, Belgium, the Netherlands, and the United Kingdom to convince the allies that Cuban and Soviet arms shipments to the Salvadorean left constituted a "textbook case of indirect armed aggression" requiring a coordinated allied response.[18] He did not meet with stirring success. Most of the Europeans were unwilling to enter in the Administration's crusade against communism in El Salvador until the Administration provided more detail on how it proposed to respond. None of the Europeans were anxious to see the United States escalate its military involvement; all expressed support for a negotiated political settlement rather than a military solution.[19]

The role of socialist and radical states, especially Cuba and Nicaragua, has received great attention because of the State Department's report on "communist interference" in El Salvador. Up until the last few months of 1980, Cuban and Nicaraguan aid to the left was more than military. Both states had openly endorsed the Salvadorean opposition and were routinely providing it with advice. Managua, like Mexico City, served as an important center of diplomatic and political activity for the FDR and FMLN, but U.S. intelligence could discern only a trickle of arms from Nicaragua to El Salvador. As late as September, 1980, Washington certified that the Nicaraguan government was not materially promoting the revolution in El Salvador and therefore in compliance with the Congressionally-imposed condition for the release of $75 million in economic aid.

The Tide Turns: Presidential Transition

In the midst of the guerrillas' January offensive, the Carter Administration reversed itself, claiming that it had "compelling evidence" that Cuba, Vietnam, and the Soviet Union had begun channelling massive arms shipments into El Salvador via Nicaragua.

---

[17] For an excellent report on the Mexican position, see the interview in *The New York Times*, January 4, 1981.

[18] This phase is from the State Department White Paper, "Communist Interference in El Salvador," *op. cit.*

[19] *The New York Times*, February 2, 1981.

This sudden flood of arms, along with the exigency of the guerrilla offensive itself, were cited as justifications for the resumption of U.S. military aid to the Salvadorean armed forces. At the same time, economic aid to Nicaragua was suspended in an effort to force the Nicaraguans to close the arms conduit.

In February, the Reagan Administration released a White Paper documenting the charges initially levelled by Carter. Compiled from a variety of intelligence sources, the report argued that Cuba and the Soviet Union orchestrated the shipment to El Salvador of 200 tons of arms supplied by a number of socialist and radical Arab states.[20] Most of these arms were said to have been shipped through Nicaragua. While the report left little doubt that sizable quantities of arms were in fact provided to the Salvadorean left by the socialist camp, the report was virtually silent about other supply channels, merely acknowledging in passing that they exist.

Whatever its accuracy, the White Paper is a quintessentially political document in that it was designed not so much to clarify the international dimensions of the Salvadorean civil war as to provide a justification for the Reagan Administration's determination to cast the issue of El Salvador in East-West terms.[21] This effort would have been seriously compromised had the Administration detailed the FDR's contacts with foreign social democrats as meticulously as it documented the FDR's travels within the socialist bloc, or if the report had explored the extent of arms shipments to the left from Panama and Mexico as well as from Cuba and Nicaragua. Even if every allegation in the White Paper is accurate, it still provides only a partial view of the complexity of international involvements in the Salvadorean civil war.

The White Paper serves effectively as a justification for the Reagan Administration's decision to escalate U.S. military involvement in El Salvador. Armed with the report, briefing teams were dispatched to Europe, Latin America, and Capitol Hill in a well-orchestrated effort to build domestic and international support for a change in U.S. policy. But the basic thrust of this new policy was determined long before the arms build-up described in the White Paper. Early in the presidential campaign, Reagan and his foreign policy advisors targeted Carter's human rights policy, especially as applied in Central America, as a major focus of attack. The insurgency in El Salvador was portrayed as resulting primarily from Cuban and Soviet subversion rather than domestic social and political conditions,[22] and Carter's

---

[20] Department of State, "Communist Interference in El Salvador," *op. cit.*

[21] In describing the implications of the White Paper, Acting Secretary of State for Latin American Affairs John Bushnell was explicit: "This outside interference dramatically changes the nature of the struggle in El Salvador from a national one to an international one with East-West dimensions." U.S. Congress, House of Representatives, Statement before the Subcommittee on Foreign Operations, House Committee on Appropriations, February 25, 1981.

[22] National Security Advisor Richard Allen, for example, promised that a Reagan Administration would undertake "quick action against Fidel Castro's Soviet-directed, armed, and financed marauders in Central America, specifically in Nicaragua, El Salvador, and Guatemala," *Latin America Weekly Report*, November 14, 1980.

strategy for achieving stability through reform was denounced as idealistic and foolish, merely aiding the cause of international communism.[23]

The Administration's new policy for El Salvador is one of keeping the left from coming to power, whatever the cost. Within days of assuming office, Reagan increased economic aid by 63 percent and began a full review of policy toward the Salvadorean government. Shortly thereafter, Ambassador White, who was closely identified with the Carter Administration's effort (albeit unsuccessful) to promote reform, was fired. He was replaced by Chargé d'Affairs Frederic Chapin, reassigned from the Defense Department where he had been preparing contingency plans for a major increase in U.S. military aid to the Salvadorean armed forces. Secretary of State Alexander Haig's pledge to shift the focus of U.S. policy away from human rights toward the battle against "international terrorism" was quickly followed by an announcement that U.S. aid to El Salvador would no longer be contingent upon either reforms or human rights.[24] The next day, Department of State's William Dyess tried to dispel the impression that the Reagan Administration was indifferent to reforms in El Salvador, but the after-thought served only to reinforce the obviously tertiary nature of the concern.

The likelihood that this new policy will have the effect of curtailing social reform and encouraging the terrorism of the security forces seems beside the point for the Reagan Administration. The parallels between El Salvador and Vietnam are not merely the constructs of the Administration's liberal critics. Reagan himself seems to see the light of victory in Vietnam at the end of the Salvadorean tunnel. The Administration appears to be less interested in El Salvador *per se* than in creating a symbol of U.S. resolve to use military force abroad and to get tough with the Soviet Union.[25] El Salvador provides what appears to be a geopolitically safe testing ground on which the United States can probe the depths of Soviet commitment to national liberation struggles, assess the cooperativeness of the allies, and begin to purge the national psyche of the "Vietnam syndrome" that Reagan has so denounced.

El Salvador and the Lessons of Vietnam

The parallels between El Salvador and Vietnam apply not so much to the military circumstances of the two cases, which are quite different, but to the way in which U.S. policy is unfolding. El Salvador, like Vietnam before it, is being transformed from an internal war into an international test of will between East and West. The domino analogy has been resurrected to characterize the nations of Central America, falling in chain reaction

---

[23] See, for example, Jeane Kirkpatrick, "Dictatorship and Double Standards," *op. cit.*

[24] The delinking of aid from reform issues was announced shortly thereafter by State Department Spokesman William Dyess, quoted in news reports of *The New York Times*, February 18, 1981. Alexander Haig's statement of this shift came in his press conference of January 28, reported in *The New York Times*, January 29, 1981.

[25] *The New York Times* and *The Washington Post*, February 14, 1981.

from El Salvador north to Guatemala and Mexico, south to Costa Rica and Panama. As candidate Reagan warned, "We are the last domino."[26]

Claims of an East-West confrontation distort reality in two ways—by making it sound as if the Salvadorean revolution is a Cuban creation, and as if it is a purely military struggle that can be won merely by countering the flow of arms from abroad. The revolution in El Salvador began long before the first Cuban arms shipments and it will not fade away if those shipments are halted. By failing to focus on the socio-economic causes of political turmoil, the Reagan Administration betrays a narrowly military conception of national security and a preference for using military means to manage political problems. Revolutions spring from deep social and political fissures in the very foundations of a society—problems that cannot be solved by simply throwing guns at them. Though massive fire-power failed to bring about victory in Vietnam, Administration policies reflect a considerable faith in the efficacy of arms.

By declaring El Salvador to be a test of will with international communism, the Reagan Administration is wagering U.S. prestige and credibility on the survival of one of the weakest, most brutal, and least popular governments in the hemisphere. A nation of virtually no inherent strategic or economic interest to the United States is thus cast, like Vietnam before it, onto the world's centerstage, and the success or failure of U.S. policy takes on implications it would never have otherwise. Once begun, the process of investing blood and treasure in this exemplary case provides its own rationale for incremental escalation.

Policymakers in Washington have already been seduced by the view that just a little more aid, a few more advisors, or one additional reorganization of the government will somehow produce success. Since January 1980, the United States has been drawn almost imperceptibly into a position so totally identified with the Salvadorean government that to disassociate from it would be viewed as a radical change in policy.

American aid has not produced a strong, stable government; it has only fostered dependency. The Salvadorean economy is already comatose, surviving solely on the life support system of U.S. largesse. With the munificence of the United States as a crutch, the rightist military regime has no incentive to make the kinds of political concessions and compromises necessary to achieve a lasting peace. Large-scale military aid to the Salvadorean armed forces will not strengthen them; it will only allow them to continue to ignore political reality. The Reagan Administration promises that it will never send American troops to fight in El Salvador. But if, a year from now, the Salvadorean government is on the verge of collapse, as Saigon was in 1965, how will this Administration respond?

One of the clearest parallels between El Salvador and Vietnam is the way in which the Reagan Administration, and the Carter Administration before it, have waged the public relations war at home. The selling of the war began, as in Vietnam, with a natural effort to put the best possible face

---

[26] NBC News, White Paper, *The Castro Connection*, aired in October, 1980.

on U.S. policy. The Salvadorean government was described as "centrist" even as it engaged in repression worse than its "rightist" predecessor; the opposition was labelled a "Pol Pot left," even though it bore closer resemblance to the Sandinistas than to the Cambodians.

In mid-1980, the Carter Administration evolved a conscious policy of attempting to manage U.S. public opinion on El Salvador by encouraging media coverage favorable to the government. The objective, according to a dissent document purportedly prepared by foreign policy analysts within the Administration, was to prevent the creation of a positive image for the Salvadorean left of the sort enjoyed by the Sandinistas.[27] It was then that truth became hostage to policy; the Carter Administration began making public pronouncements sharply at variance with internal reports—on the effectiveness of the agrarian reform, for example.

The Reagan Administration has continued in this vein. Throughout 1980, Carter's State Department acknowledged that the right in El Salvador was responsible for the overwhelming majority of political murders. One official called the mortality statistics gathered by the Salvadorean Catholic Church "the best data we have." Reagan's State Department now claims that the *guerrillas* have been committing most of the atrocities, and the same official who acknowledged the veracity of the church's data in January now solemnly contends that the church's figures are unreliable because it sympathizes with the communists. Truth has indeed become the first casualty.

Despite strenuous efforts, the Reagan Administration's public relations campaign to justify American involvement in the Salvadorean conflict has not met with overwhelming success. Domestic opposition to the war is mounting and is already greater than was opposition to Vietnam at a comparable stage of the war. On May 3, 1981, some 25,000 people marched in Washington in an anti-war demonstration reminiscent of the 1960s. The Reagan Administration appears to recognize that it cannot sustain U.S. military involvement in El Salvador without the support of the U.S. public. What the Administration appears not to recognize is that public support cannot be manufactured by good public relations; it is inextricably tied to the nature of the conflict itself. A massive counterinsurgency effort against a popular insurgency inevitably requires widespread brutality against the civilian populace if it is to succeed. The lesson of Vietnam at home is that the people of the United States will not long tolerate a policy that necessitates such brutality.

The Reagan Administration's narrow military view of the domestic political situation in El Salvador is matched by its narrow geopolitical view of the conflict's international context and the implications of committing massive economic and military resources there. The Administration seems to believe it can confront the Soviet Union in Central America with relatively little risk—that the Soviets will retreat rather than try to match U.S. escalation in a region far from the areas vital to Soviet national inter-

---

[27] See *supra* note 21.

est. All this is true enough, but it by no means follows that a major U.S. economic and military commitment in El Salvador bears no serious cost. On the contrary, its cost is potentially immense.

The U.S.-Latin American Relations Angle

Reagan's policy places the United States on a collision course with Mexico at the very time that Mexico is unveiling a more activist foreign policy that seeks to extend Mexican influence throughout its "area of concern"—Central America and the Caribbean. While Mexico wants to maintain good relations with the United States, President López Portillo has repeatedly warned against the very policy Washington now seems intent on pursuing. A direct American intervention in El Salvador would demolish relations with Mexico just when it has emerged as the most important Latin American nation for the United States.

Even Venezuela and Costa Rica, two principal regional supporters of the United States on the issue of El Salvador, could not suffer U.S. intervention in silence. In both countries, the social democratic oppositions have harshly criticized their ruling Christian Democratic parties for supporting the Salvadorean government. Deeper U.S. involvement will intensify that opposition and could easily lead those governments to begin distancing themselves from American policy. A direct U.S. intervention could cause their support to evaporate immediately. Indeed, the Organization of American States would probably condemn such an intervention with only a few nations dissenting.

Diplomatic Costs of Involvement: Europe and the Third World

The repercussions beyond the hemisphere of escalating U.S. involvement in El Salvador would be no less damaging. The cool reception encountered by emissaries sent to brief the allies on the Cuban and Soviet role in El Salvador suggests that Reagan will find little support for his policy in Europe. Most of the Western European states would probably be content to leave El Salvador to the United States, but if Washington continues to insist that events in El Salvador will determine whether the United States enters into arms limitation talks with the Soviet Union, the issue will cease to be one which the allies can afford to ignore.[28] Given the strength of European social democracy and its support for the Salvadorean opposition, Reagan may well find that his policy exacerbates tensions within the North Atlantic Community rather than forging a new unity and resolve to resist "communist aggression" in the third world.

In the third world, Reagan's policy of deepening U.S. involvement in El Salvador will undo most of the diplomatic gains accruing from Carter's human rights policy. Third world suspicions, focused in recent years upon

---

[28] President Reagan said in February that the Soviet "invasion" of El Salvador would have to be "straightened out" before a resumption of arms control talks would be possible. See *The New York Times* coverage of February 28, 1981.

the Soviet Union because of its interventions in Ethiopia and Afghanistan, would shift back to the United States if Reagan were to intervene directly in El Salvador. The Soviets have had the good sense not to stake their prestige or credibility on the Salvadorean left, so its defeat would damage the Soviet Union not at all. But the sort of commitment by the United States required to defeat the left (if that is possible at all) would damage U.S. relations with the rest of the hemisphere, strain the Western Alliance, erode U.S. prestige in the third world, and prompt a new wave of domestic recriminations in the United States itself. Not incidentally, it would hand the Soviet Union a custom-made sphere of influence argument to justify its policy in Afghanistan and Poland.

The Costs of Military Involvement: Tumbling into War

The military implications of Reagan's policy are even more sobering than the diplomatic ones. By siding with the right in El Salvador and justifying a deeper U.S. military involvement with claims of Cuban intervention, the United States, intentionally or not, lowers the barriers against direct intervention by Honduras and Guatemala. If massive U.S. aid can be justified as merely a necessary response to Cuban subversion, cannot Guatemalan or Honduran intervention be similarly justified? The Guatemalan government is faced with a major guerrilla insurgency of its own, and the Guatemalan left would surely respond to Guatemalan intervention in El Salvador by escalating its activities and extending its cooperation with the Salvadorean left. The Salvadorean war would thus become a transnational war of left against right in which national boundaries would cease to have any practical meaning.

The danger in Honduras is somewhat different since guerrilla forces there still number only a handful. But Honduras borders Nicaragua, and relations between the two states are strained because of attacks launched on Nicaraguan border areas by former National Guardsmen based in Honduras, and clashes between Honduran and Nicaraguan border guards. Guatemalan or Honduran intervention in El Salvador would be viewed by Nicaragua as a clear and present threat to its own internal security. In such an atmosphere, the former Guardsmen might well try to provoke a conflict between Nicaragua and Honduras by launching a major border attack. If they should succeed, the whole northern tier of Central America would be engulfed by war.

Unfortunately, the danger does not end there. Nicaragua at war would be forced to turn to Cuba and the Soviet Union for major infusions of military aid. If the war were to go badly and Nicaragua were to call for Cuban troops to help defend Nicaraguan territory, Cuba would probably provide them, for the scenario would fit exactly the circumstances under which Cuba has in the past deployed combat troops abroad—at the request of a friendly government threatened by external attack. The arrival of Cuban troops amidst war in Central America would surely call forth a response by the United States—most probably a naval blockade. The stage might then be set for a re-enactment of the Cuban Missile crisis, but without the 3 to 1 U.S. nuclear superiority that is thought to have determined the outcome in 1962.[29]

Is There No Exit? Pursuing the "Zimbabwe Solution"

Ironically, all the actors in the Salvadorean drama profess to recognize the need for a political rather than military solution to the civil war. Thus far, the obstacle to negotiations between the government and opposition has been the conviction of each party that the other lacks sincerity. Such suspicions produce negotiating proposals which are so clearly unacceptable that they must be understood as propaganda ploys rather than as serious initiatives. Yet even these spurious overtures serve to place the combatants on record favoring some sort of negotiations, thereby opening the possibility, however remote, that an appropriate coalition of international actors might be able to devise a workable negotiating formula.

There is little doubt that most of the international supporters on both sides in the civil war truly desire a political solution, and several have been actively pursuing a way to get the process started. Social Democrats in Western Europe, led by the Germans and Swedes, have attempted to cast themselves and their Christian Democratic counterparts in Germany and Italy as intermediaries between the Salvadorean government and opposition, thus far to no effect. In Latin America Mexico, Venezuela, Brazil, Costa Rica, and even Nicaragua are also searching for an acceptable mechanism to initiate a dialogue.

Since there is no measure of trust whatsoever between the Salvadorean government and opposition, three necessary conditions must be met before negotiations can begin: 1) each side must be convinced that it has no hope of winning a military victory in the near term; 2) each must be certain that its opponent will not be able to gain military advantage during the negotiations themselves; and 3) each must be assured that the other will have to abide by the outcome of whatever political process emerges from a peace conference. Even then, substantial political pressure will probably have to be exerted by the international allies of both sides to bring them to the bargaining table.

The military stalemate that currently exists in El Salvador provides what may be the last opportunity for arranging a political solution, but it is fleeting. As the Reagan Administration begins to provide massive amounts of economic and military aid to the Salvadorean government, the armed forces there become increasingly convinced that their drive for military victory will be underwritten by Washington. By announcing that aid will no longer be tied to reforms or human rights practices, the Administration is sending the Salvadorean security forces the message, whether intended

---

[29] Indeed, there is even a possibility that the Administration itself might seek to provoke such a superpower confrontation. Several Administration officials have suggested that the United States might act directly against the "source" of subversion in El Salvador, i.e., Cuba. See, for example, White House Chief of Staff Edwin Meese's comments reprinted in *The New York Times*, February 23, 1981

or not, that the United States will tolerate and abet whatever level of violence pacification requires. Instead of providing unconditional military support of the Salvadorean government, the Reagan Administration ought to be cooperating with European and Latin American efforts to convene a peace conference modelled loosely on the Lancaster House negotiations which produced peace in Zimbabwe.

Indeed, the role of the United States is crucial to meeting all the conditions necessary to launch such a conference. As the premier foreign source of material aid to the Salvadorean government, only the United States has the ability to restrain the Salvadorean Army's quest for military victory, to bring the Salvadorean government to the negotiating table, and to assure that it will abide by any agreements reached (on pain of a cutoff of aid). Germany, Mexico, and Nicaragua can probably bring the FDR-FMLN to the bargaining table, just as the "front line states" brought the Patriotic Front to the Lancaster House conference; only the United States can play the role of Britain by assuring the participation of the Salvadorean government.

Unfortunately, the Reagan Administration's determination to make El Salvador a global example of U.S. resolve probably makes negotiations impossible. Indeed, for Washington, they are counterproductive. It would hardly do to "draw the line" against communism in El Salvador and then fail to win a clear victory. The Reagan Administration gives every indication of believing it can "win" in El Salvador, even if it has to destroy the country in order to save it. As Washington maps this initial gambit in its game of global chess with the Soviet Union, it is Salvadorean pawns that stand in the front rank, about to be sacrificed.

The Day of Reckoning is Coming:
An Interview with Robert E. White*
By Jeff Stein

Jeff Stein is a contributing editor of The Progressive.

In February 1981, the Reagan administration removed career Foreign Service officer Robert E. White from his post as U.S. ambassador to El Salvador and forced him to retire from the State Department. That move turned out to be the opening shot in what White now says is a "political purge"—the removal from the department of any officers the administration identifies with the traitorous human rights policies of the Carter administration.

On the day we spoke in his new office, Thomas O. Enders, the State Department's chief of Latin American policy, was delivering a speech across town that advocated a "political solution" to the war but, at the same time,

*Excerpted and abridged from The Progressive, September 1981. Reprinted by permission from The Progressive, 409 East Main Street, Madison, Wisconsin 53703. Copyright (c) 1981, The Progressive, Inc.

seemed to reiterate a stance of no negotiations with declared revolutionary forces in El Salvador. The current Reagan strategy, White declared, cannot help but support the "creeping coup" from El Salvador's rightist and military elements, which are out to eliminate the reformist Christian Democrats as a factor in a peaceful solution to the civil war now raging.

We began our one-hour talk—wedged into White's grueling schedule of writing articles, giving speeches, meeting with delegations from Central America, and preparing for his own trip to the region—with White's reaction to Enders' major speech.

WHITE: In what it says, the speech represents a positive change. It invites other countries to participate in negotiations leading to elections. And although it appears to exclude the revolutionaries of the Left from the negotiations, I believe there may be some flexibility there. But the most important thing about the speech is what it does not say. As you know, [junta president José Napoleón] Duarte and the Christian Democrats have been under attack from the rightist business forces. They have announced their intention to eliminate the Christian Democrats from the government. Logically, therefore, the Enders speech should have contained a ringing affirmation of our support for Duarte and the Christian Democrats. But it said nothing, and I think this seals the fate of the Christian Democrats as an effective reform component in the government of El Salvador.

Therefore, the "creeping coup" is going to continue, and in all probability is going to succeed, because the far Right has a stranglehold on the economy, and they have a deliberate policy of ceasing economic activity until they get their price. And that price is the exit of the Christian Democrats.

JS: *That presents the United States with a fait accompli, right? And then what? Won't we be locked into a succession of Saigon-style governments?*

WHITE: Not necessarily. But what it does lock us into is a traditional combination that has driven El Salvador into the ground over the last fifty years. The day the administration decided to support the government of Guatemala was, in effect, the day it wrote "finish" to any serious reform in the rest of Central America that depends on U.S. support, because the military of El Salvador are perfectly able to catch the nuances in the messages from Washington. If the Guatemalan military can get anything it wants—a government that has to have one of the most repressive policies in the world—then what incentive does the Salvadorean military have to clean up its act?

JS: *At first, the idea that El Salvador was "another Vietnam" didn't quite fit for me, for several reasons. But as I listen to you, and as time passes, it does begin to take shape. Is El Salvador "another Vietnam" to you?*

WHITE: The really crucial place where the analogy fits is the inability of the United States Government to face up to what the reality is and come to grips with it. Instead, what you've got are U.S. domestic forces—the left wing of the Democratic Party and the right wing of the Republican

Party—fighting out their ideological battles with El Salvador as the ploy. And what each is advocating has little relationship to what's going on in El Salvador.

JS: The Right sees the guerrillas as Soviet proxies....

WHITE: Right. And the Left sees the guerrilla forces as just the result of historical injustices and the growing up of a group of dedicated patriots.

That, of course, is closest to reality. But there's a very great potential for those guerrillas, should they win, to bring the Soviet presence into El Salvador. I don't exclude it. At all. And I don't think the national security argument can be dismissed.

You know, in Nicaragua all the people were against Somoza. In El Salvador, what you have had building up is a real class war. Look, Somoza was a liberal compared to the Salvadorean military. Somoza used to tell me, "Those Salvadorean fourteen families give me hell because they say I'm too soft, because I'm too liberal," and I believe he was telling me the truth when he said that. So I think that the class hatred that has admittedly been engendered by the military and the economic elites which have been supported in the past by the United States has created a situation that is really very dangerous.

The far left are just totally dedicated revolutionaries who, if they came into power, would reject the United States. Their program would be to eliminate all U.S. power from the area and counter the United States by bringing in Cuba and perhaps the Soviet Union. I can't be sure, but I think that would be the way they would act.

JS: Well, look, without romanticizing the guerrillas at all ... they just may have earned their revolution at this point, don't you think?

WHITE: I don't think there's any question about that. Mind you—

JS: Who are we after all these years of silent acquiescence to say they can't have it now because they've taken the revolutionary road after other avenues were denied them?

WHITE: It's hard to make that argument stick with anybody who's got a responsibility for administering the national security of the United States.

JS: I agree only to an extent. It's hard to make it stick for a party which wants to keep itself in power.

WHITE: All right. Had the Carter administration been more intelligent a year and a half, two years ago, instead of—but this is what happens when you become captive of a weak, vindictive oligarchy and a brutal military. If we had, at the beginning of 1980, really made a commitment to negotiations and seeking out [Social Democrat Guillermo] Ungo and company, bringing in Mexico, West Germany, Venezuela, and others, we could have brought about some sort of commonsense solution.

I think there was still a chance to salvage something right up until a couple of months ago. There may even still possibly be a chance today, if the Reagan administration would turn on a dime and come out in favor of negotiations.

JS: They seem to have taken exactly the opposite tack.

WHITE: Oh, absolutely. When you advocate sending arms to Guatemala, you doom El Salvador. I mean, when the Guatemalan military can have everything it wants and be nakedly brutal—even take credit for it! No one in the Guatemalan government has even bothered to deny charges that they deliberately target moderate leaders and kill them in order to destroy any possible bridge between the Left and the Center.

JS: The Reagan team seemed to think that El Salvador was an easy hit.

WHITE: They thought it was like rolling a drunk. You know, "There's El Salvador, and we can dramatize the difference between us and the soft-headed Carter administration." And of course, when you're so wildly wrong in your analysis, the chance that you'll hit on the right prescription to bring about a solution is very doubtful.

JS: If there is some blame for that kind of strategy, doesn't the Carter administration share some of it by its decision to ship arms to the junta just before it left office? And can't the Reagan administration claim that it is continuing what Carter began?

WHITE: I agree—and I thought exactly along those lines at the time. But the thing that really licked us was that Nicaragua had permitted its territory to be used to supply the guerrillas for the January "final offensive." There's no doubt about that. So it was impossible to make the argument in Washington that the guerrillas can get their supplies from Nicaragua but the government we're supporting can't get its supplies from the United States. It was tough to fight, but even so, we tried to fight it.

But what happened? At that time, Carter, Mondale and Muskie were totally involved in the Iranian hostage crisis—right through the administration's last three days, and the pressure increased dramatically for the kind of policy that you're now seeing. And career officers—who are vulnerable to political revenge—whether at State, CIA, or the Pentagon, started to say, looking toward the Reagan administration, "Well, we'd better try and burnish our image with the new fellows." The Pentagon never supported the human rights policy anyway, and when the restraining hand of Muskie was gone, you had them gaining increasing power.

JS: One had the feeling here that the Pentagon almost attempted a coup on El Salvador policy in the last days of the Carter administration.

WHITE: They did. No question about it. They tried to take advantage of the confusion during the transition period and have seventy-five U.S. military advisors in place when Reagan came in. I wouldn't accept it. It amounted to a Pentagon takeover of U.S. foreign policy on El Salvador.

JS: What is the effect of the militarization of El Salvador policy now?

WHITE: The second stage of the land reform has been explicitly cancelled with U.S. approval. And the powers that be are refusing to accept the land reform as a *fait accompli*—they want to roll it back.[1]

JS: So where are we now?

WHITE: The United States can now only postpone the inevitable day of reckoning when the Right exacts its price, and that price is either the elimination or the total neutralization of the Christian Democrats. That day is coming. Whether it will be in two months or six months, I don't know.

JS: Will the time ever come when the United States will see it in its own interest to throw in with the other side—the one that we're fighting?

WHITE: Well, I don't think so. I think that—

JS: I mean that, considering that it may be in everyone's best interest in the long run.

WHITE: The best policy for the United States to advocate is negotiations. Duarte and Ungo [who resigned from the junta last winter] have far more in common than Duarte has with Colonel Morán of the Treasury Police, or than Ungo has with the guerrilla leader [Salvador Cayetano] Carpio. Both sides have to face the fact that they've got indigestible, antidemocratic elements of considerable power within their coalitions, and the way to isolate those is to get together. But the United States has taken that option away from Duarte by refusing to permit negotiations.

JS: In January, there was a big splash in the newspapers about Nicaraguans landing in force on an El Salvador beach. That turned out to be false, and it seemed—even at the time—to have been a deliberate attempt to spread a false report and smear Nicaragua. Do you think you were misled?

WHITE: Two members of the Salvadorean government called me the night this was allegedly happening. I trusted these people to tell me the truth. This was the day of the "final offensive," also, and I was quick to use anything I could to demonstrate that Nicaragua was involving itself when it shouldn't, because it was a mistake for Nicaragua to do it. Later, I sent my military attaché down to the area, and he couldn't find anything. And so, whatever happened, there was no big battle, and they never captured one Nicaraguan, and no one could even find evidence of a battle.

JS: What do you think of it all now—was it a plant?

WHITE: I'm suspicious. Perhaps it was an exaggeration by my sources. On the other hand, it is an interesting coincidence that all this happened when it did, and it could have been designed to dramatize the involvement of Nicaragua. So, I'm suspicious.

JS: That leads me to the State Department's White Paper on El Salvador. What's your estimate of the influence of Cuba or the Soviet Union as alleged in its conclusions?

WHITE: Well, if you regard Cuba as a total surrogate of the Soviet Union,

---

[1] Since the March 1982 elections, the entire land reform program has effectively been cancelled. –Ed.

that Cuba's a marionette and the Soviet Union pulls the strings, then you could say that any place that Cuba is involved, the Soviet Union is involved. If you want to make that equation, then indeed the Soviet Union is involved. That Cuba is involved there's no doubt. I *think* they've trained somewhere between 1,000 and 2,000 Salvadorean revolutionaries in Cuba. And they have undoubtedly sent some arms to the Salvadorean revolutionaries. But none of that is proved by the captured documents which served as the basis of the White Paper.

I believe that the documents are genuine if only for the reason that they prove so little. They tend to prove only (1) that [Communist Party chief Shafik] Handal went to Moscow, that he got what you might call a mixed reception there, and that from Moscow he jumped—presumably at Soviet expense—to a number of other countries, such as Vietnam, Libya, and Ethiopia, and that he obtained promises of support from them; (2) that he did obtain some support from them; and (3) that some Cuban and Nicaraguan leaders met with Salvadorean revolutionaries to talk about a common strategy.

That's all you can say the White Paper and the documents prove. So that what it asserts in addition to that is wildly off mark.

JS: What was your reaction when the White Paper was published?

WHITE: To me it was just an inept and hastily thrown together piece of propaganda. I think some of the things the White Paper says are probably true, but there aren't any documents which justify the conclusions.

JS: This was the premier document laying down the rationale for U.S. military intervention and placing El Salvador squarely on the East-West Cold War chessboard, right? Why, if there were people around like yourself drawing these conclusions, did it take one free-lance reporter [John Dinges for Pacific News Service] three months to provoke the rest of the media into taking a critical look at the White Paper?

WHITE: Well, your question really is, why didn't *I* come out and say this was ridiculous. Look, I am—or at least I *was*—a disciplined Foreign Service Officer. I don't go out looking for windmills to joust. And the idea that I'm some sort of martyr—well, I'm not. I just wanted to keep working in the State Department, pursuing my career. Nobody elected me to do anything.

JS: Is there a political purge going on in the State Department right now?

WHITE: There's something very close to it. Very close to it. It's unheard of for assistant secretaries and deputy assistant secretaries not to receive onward assignments as ambassadors. In this administration, the whole front office of the Latin American region has been removed, and none of them has received an ambassadorial assignment. I'm sure it's a purge.

JS: It seems very similar to what happened in the State Department after the Chinese Revolution.

WHITE: Yes, but there's a big difference. In those days, the ideologues of the Right were much more naïve, open, and honest. They were out to get those guys in the State Department because they had "sold out China."

They said so, and they went after them. The present tactic is much more insidious because they're pretending that everything is just normal and going forward routinely, and that no one is being "purged." This purge, though, is even more complete because the number of people at senior levels who know or are involved in Central America are really very few. The Reagan team has gotten rid of all of them, and in a very shameful and vengeful way.

JS: The new metaphor for "losing China" seems to be being in favor of a human rights policy.

WHITE: You're absolutely right.

JS: That is, if you're for human rights you're "soft on communism."

WHITE: They even talk about the "traitorous" Carter administration.

JS: Traitorous?

WHITE: Yeah, that word has been used.

JS: On the seventh floor [Haig's executive offices]?

WHITE: I can't pin it to one person. But in meetings, Reagan people are actually using that phrase. My real argument with the Reagan administration is that they threw away a very useful tool without even applying the pragmatic test of whether the policy was good or bad. If you want to reject morality in foreign affairs, fine, that's one approach. But obviously the human rights policy was a very useful tool in some cases, as I think it was to some extent in El Salvador.

JS: There are reports that Guatemala, Honduras and El Salvador are cooperating in a policy of arrests, detentions, and "disappearances." Can you comment?

WHITE: There was very little of that when I was there. But there is obviously increasing cooperation between Honduran and Salvadorean forces, such as the forcible removal of refugee camps from the Honduran frontier.

JS: Is the Chilean military aiding the Salvadorean military?

WHITE: The Chilean government has always had a team of military advisors in El Salvador, and they are now increasing their numbers. But actually, the Chilean officers are probably a positive element in the sense that they have professional qualifications and they look down their noses in horror at some of the Salvadorean military's barbarous practices, and they talk about Central Americans as—

JS: Chilean military officers look down on Salvadoreans for barbaric practices?

WHITE: You may find that hard to believe, but it's true. They have been shocked by some of the things going on.

JS: There were reports that Venezuela was training Salvadorean police.

WHITE: There was hope for that, but as far as I know it didn't happen. Venezuela's involvement is more Christian Democrat to Christian Democrat.

JS: *Argentine involvement?*

WHITE: Very little. In Guatemala, yes, a lot.

JS: *How about U.S. training of Salvadoreans in the Canal Zone—so-called human rights training? Wasn't that just a bunch of nonsense?*

WHITE: Well, yes, but look: There was increasing pressure from the Pentagon to get into El Salvador with training programs, groups, and so on, and I just resisted, because I didn't think this was the right idea. But the pressure grew very great, so I said to them, "Look, I don't object to your giving them technical training provided they get some really solid training in civilized conduct, you know, that they don't treat citizens as potential people to be killed, but you treat them as citizens, people who are supposed to be respected." In other words, I wanted them to understand who they're supposed to be fighting for. And conditioned on that, we persuaded the Salvadorean military to write and issue a code of conduct for the security forces. It seemed to me that if you first got a theoretical base, then you might start getting some kind of military justice. But I admit that this was a forlorn attempt. You plow with what you've got.

JS: *In thinking about the possible long years of bloodshed ahead, it seems tragic to have missed an opportunity for negotiations.*

WHITE: It really is tragic. I think that under the Carter administration, we had a chance, because we were constantly pushing, every day pushing the Salvadorean military to improve, every day saying, "No, you can't have these goodies until you accomplish this, accomplish that, accomplish the other things." The Reagan administration has rushed in headlong to prove how macho they are. It won't work.

JS: *One last question: Is the Reagan administration trying to overthrow the government of Nicaragua?*

WHITE: Well, I don't know. I know that there are a number of very worrisome reports of activities going on, both in this country and in Honduras, that I think bear looking at. I won't make any accusations. I'd just say that there are some reports that really do concern me about what's taking place.

Honduras: Into the Central American Maelstrom*
By Steven Volk

Though the fact is little publicized in the United States, the Honduran military is today playing a crucial role in the unfolding of Central America's revolutionary crisis. In the following selection Steven Volk of NACLA briefly details how the U.S. government, under both recent administrations, has manipulated domestic Honduran politics in order to create a

---

*This article consists of brief excerpts from "Honduras: On the Border of War," *NACLA Report on the Americas*, Vol. XV, No. 6 (November-December), 1981 (52 pages, illustrated).

"democratic ally" which would collaborate militarily with the U.S. in the rest of Central America. As post-election developments in Honduras have demonstrated, a division of labor has been agreed to there in which domestic economic policy has become the preserve of the civilians while the military establishment, nourished by continuing high levels of U.S. assistance, remains in charge of the country's foreign policy and plays an openly reactionary role in regional affairs.

In a region where the fires of revolution burn white hot, Honduras is a model of stability, a bizarre anomaly. Not only did the ruling military junta allow constituent assembly elections in April 1980 and presidential elections in November 1981, but, to general surprise, these were honest and well attended. Furthermore, while the Honduran Left has spawned at least four guerrilla organizations[1] as well as many popular movements, these cannot compare to the revolutionary armies of Guatemala, the FMLN-FDR of El Salvador or the victorious FSLN in Nicaragua. Above all, the Hondurans seem genuinely anxious to stay out of the regional conflict.

Yet, ironically, it is U.S. policy itself which today presents the greatest threat to Honduras' relative stability. Not content to let well enough alone, U.S. policy-makers are attempting to build Honduras into a regional reactionary powerhouse and a staging base for counterrevolutionary activities in Central America. And, if this policy carries any guarantees at all, it is that before long, Honduras too will be embroiled in the regional conflagration.

Perceptions vs. Policy

Presidents Carter and Reagan have grounded their policies toward the region in different assumptions. Carter's advisors, for example, were much more likely to see the context of Central America's struggles as "that of authoritarian systems eroding under the pressures of demands for reform which they cannot or will not accommodate."[2] Those vying for Reagan's attention, on the other hand, discount internal factors and, instead, blame the Soviet Union. If the premises are different, policy nevertheless has often been the same. Nowhere is this as evident as in the case of Honduras.

Under President Carter, Honduran military leaders were courted, cajoled and showered with loans and grants. Aid levels to the country were the highest in Central America, except for Panama, in 1978, and second to none in 1979.[3] In September 1979, Carter dispatched special envoy William Bowdler to Tegucigalpa to meet with General Policarpo Paz García, who headed that country's governing military junta. Their talks were obviously positive. A few days later, Assistant Secretary Vaky, in a policy address on

---

[1] These are the Cinchoneros Popular Liberation Movement, the Padre Ivan Betancourt Popular Revolutionary Command, the Morazanista Liberation Front of Honduras, and the Lorenzo Zelaya Popular Revolutionary Command.

[2] Viron P. Vaky, "Hemispheric Relations: 'Everything is Part of Everything Else,'" *Foreign Affairs*, Vol. 59, No. 3 (1981), pp. 623-4.

[3] Department of State, *Country Reports on Human Rights Practices* (Washington, D.C.: Government Printing Office), February 2, 1981.

the region, noted that the Administration was "impressed" by democratic progress in Honduras.[4]

Carter's envoy had pushed two themes with Honduran leaders. First, he pressured strenuously for General Paz to keep his pledge of holding elections. The U.S. strategy of encouraging mild reform (particularly in the guise of elections) in order to avoid a revolution had arrived too late in Nicaragua; in Honduras, though, it was not too late. Second, Carter's policy demanded that the Hondurans no longer stand apart from the regional crisis. Honduras, according to Vaky's 1979 policy statement, had a key role to play in preventing "regional conflicts and [the] potential infiltration" of supplies and guerrillas to other struggles.

To consummate his new marriage with Honduras, Jimmy Carter invited Paz García to the White House in March 1980, where the general was again glowingly praised. With the blessings of the President, he was sent off to the hustings, to visit the Council on the Americas (the major organization of multinational corporations investing in Latin America) and the International Monetary Fund, where the general sacrificed his country on the altar of high finance.

Aid and Elections

Paz García kept his part of the agreement when he returned to Honduras. On April 23, 1980, elections were held for a 71-member constituent assembly which would pave the way for a return to civilian rule. To nearly universal amazement, the Liberal Party won a slim victory over the National Party in very heavy voting. Most observers had expected the Nationals to parlay their control over the national electoral tribunal and their historic alliance with the military into an impressive, if fraudulent, victory. That they didn't was an indication both of popular repudiation of military rule and of U.S. pressure for clean elections. But it was not necessarily to be taken as a mandate for progressive government, for the Liberals were often as conservative as their traditional rivals.

Satisfied that Paz García had kept his part of the bargain, Carter actively lobbied for the increased aid for Honduras he had requested. On March 23, 1980, with Paz García still touring the United States, columnist Jack Anderson had written: "The Administration apparently has chosen Honduras to be our new 'Nicaragua'—a dependable satellite bought and paid for by American military and economic largess."[5] In fact, in 1980 the country received $53.1 million in economic aid and $3.9 million in military aid.

Two days after the Anderson column, Assistant Secretary of State John Bushnell asked Congress to grant Honduras the $3.9 million in military aid which Carter had requested. He argued that if Honduras were to play a key geopolitical role in the region by halting the flow of arms into El Salvador, it had to be well equipped. He asked that Congress approve a one-year loan

---

[4] *Latin America Political Report*, Sept. 14, 1979.

[5] *Washington Post*, March 23, 1980.

of ten UH-1H (Huey) gunship helicopters to Honduras to patrol the border with El Salvador.

The Arms Escalation

The Hueys were just one part of a significant arms build-up which began in the late 1970s and continued into the 1980s. Between 1975 and 1979 Honduras was the fourth largest arms importer in the entire Central American-Caribbean region. Its Air Force, long referred to as the best in Central America, boasted Israeli-modified French Super-Mystère jets, Yugoslav-modified Canadian F-86 sabre jet fighters, A-37 combat planes from the United States as well as training and reconnaissance planes from Britain and the United States.[6]

The United States also played a leading role in the training of Honduran officers. Between 1971 and 1980, the United States trained 2,259 military personnel in Honduras and U.S. facilities, double the number of Hondurans trained in the 1951-1970 period.[7] Nearly 100 Honduran officers attended the "Command and General Staff" courses at the U.S. Army School of the Americas in the Canal Zone from 1976-1980, three times more than from any other Latin American country.

And then there were the military advisors. According to a U.S. Embassy spokesperson in Honduras, the United States had 37 military advisors in that neutral, peaceful country in 1980.[8] Under the Reagan Administration, the role of military advisors would expand. While there were only 27 in 1981, they included Green Berets from a Special Forces battalion based in Panama. As opposed to the original team, the 1981 crop patrolled the border with El Salvador, carried M16s and dressed in camouflage.[9]

Into the Fray

Since the 1969 war, Honduran soldiers and their counterparts in El Salvador have shared nothing but enmity. Yet shortly after Paz García's return from Washington, this decade-old wound was suddenly sutured. On October 30, after 11 years of bickering, Honduras and El Salvador penned their acceptance of a peace treaty formally ending the 1969 conflict. What was remarkable about the treaty was the fact that El Salvador dictated the terms at a moment in which it was exceptionally weak in relation to Honduras. The treaty actually resolved few of the outstanding problems between the two countries. But it did allow the Salvadoreans full access to the *bolsones territoriales*, demilitarized zones along the border which had been patrolled by the OAS since the end of the war. The Carter Administration had been pressing hard for a resolution of the conflict which

---

[6] Stockholm International Peace Research Institute (SIPRI), *World Armaments and Disarmament Yearbook, 1980 and 1981* and *Washington Post*, May 5, 1981.

[7] Department of Defense, Security Assistance Agency, *Foreign Military Sales and Military Assistance Facts* (Dec. 1980), pp. 67-8.

[8] *Miami Herald*, Oct. 8, 1980.

[9] *New York Times*, Aug. 19, 1981.

would give Salvadoreans access to the *bolsones* so that they could pursue the guerrillas.

While the Honduran military moved against Salvadorean guerrillas on their southwestern border, they cast a blind eye on the activities of Somoza's former National Guardsmen who were camped on their southeastern border. As a *Washington Post* reporter wrote, ex-National Guardsmen "regularly cross from Honduras into Nicaragua to stage small-scale attacks on Nicaraguan farms and, occasionally, on the army of the Sandinistas."[10]

As Honduras became more involved in the Central American struggles, its military officials also increasingly discussed and developed strategy with the military leaders of El Salvador and Guatemala. According to a number of reliable sources, top brass from the three countries met secretly in Honduras twice in early 1980.[11]

Thus, by the time the Reagan entourage encamped in Washington, Honduras was already guided by a policy which would lead it both to elections and (presumably) legitimation, and to increasing military participation in Central American conflicts. True to form, Reagan seemed more concerned with the latter goal. He reduced the level of economic aid to Honduras from Fiscal Year 1980 levels, but sharply increased military aid, arms sales and the use of military advisors.

If the Carter-Reagan objective of building Honduras into a regional contender carried with it the danger of drawing that country headlong into neighboring wars, by strengthening the Honduran military the United States also ran the risk of undermining its goal of returning civilian rule to that country. For now, the military would be content to exercise its prerogatives from the sidelines. But if the men in olive drab didn't fancy the results of the November 1981 elections, one could be sure that they were equipped to do something about it.

Guatemala: The Coming Danger*

By Marlise Simons

From the perspective of a "new Cold War" imperial strategy, Guatemala— as the site of important American foreign investments and the last domino in the Central American chain—is in many ways the most important country in the region. In this article journalist Marlise Simons analyzes the recent history of U.S. relations with Guatemala, the political situation in the country as it had developed by mid-1981, and the policy perspective and options facing the Reagan administration. She argues (perhaps futilely) that

---

[10] *Washington Post*, May 5, 1981. See also *Le Monde*, May 7, 1981; *Unomásuno* (Mexico), June 30, 1980 and *El Día* (Mexico), April 16 and 17, 1980.

[11] *Proceso* (Mexico), Dec. 8, 1980.

*Excerpted and abridged from *Foreign Policy*, No. 43 (Summer) 1981. Reprinted with permission from Foreign Policy. Copyright 1981.

precisely because the Guatemalan right views Ronald Reagan's administration as its own last hope, an opportunity may exist for U.S. policymakers to pressure the Guatemalans into curbing human rights abuses and carrying out meaningful reforms.

Marlise Simons is a Mexico-based journalist who reports on Latin American affairs for the Washington Post *and other publications.*

The real test of the Reagan administration's Central America policy will come in Guatemala, not El Salvador. The reason is simple: In El Salvador the administration has been able to disguise its raw anticommunism by pointing to the ruling junta's commitment to democracy and social reform.

In Guatemala, terror is institutionalized. The right-wing death squads responsible for more than 3,000 murders last year are directed from the office of President Romeo Lucas García himself, according to Amnesty International. The repression has ignited a civil war, and there is little pretense that any political middle ground exists.

The notion, developed by U.S. Ambassador to the United Nations Jeane Kirkpatrick, that "moderately repressive" allies deserve U.S. support faces a severe test in Guatemala. How far is Washington willing to back a military dictatorship that adamantly opposes reform and is committed, in the name of "fighting communism," to a policy of political assassination?

The Reagan administration indicated in May 1981 that it was inclined to provide military aid to Guatemala. But even months after Secretary of State Alexander Haig, Jr. declared Guatemala the next nation after El Salvador on the "hit list" of Soviet expansionism, the administration still had no coherent Guatemala policy. In many ways Guatemala is more important than El Salvador or any other Central American nation. With 6.9 million people, it has the largest population and economy in the region; it borders on four countries, including Mexico and its vital oil fields. Direct U.S. investment of $221 million—double the amount in El Salvador—is the highest in the region. In the past 25 years, the United States has played a far more important role in Guatemala than anywhere else in Central America.

Whereas the Reagan administration cites outside agitation as the chief cause of the Salvadorean conflict, such claims will be far more difficult to support here. When analyzing the Guatemalan civil war, the history of U.S. policy and of indigenous reform movements is impossible to discount.

The most important U.S. interference in Guatemalan politics occurred in 1954, when the Central Intelligence Agency engineered the overthrow of Guatemala's reform-minded president, Colonel Jacobo Arbenz. A former defense minister, Arbenz had taken office peacefully and punctually, the first president to do so in more than a century. His labor and land reforms were tepid by the standards of what the United States recommended in El Salvador last year. However, when Arbenz began legal proceedings to expropriate 178,000 acres owned by United Fruit Company, offering to pay the company's own book value of the land as compensation, the company skillfully converted a business dispute into an ideological conflict. The U.S.

government and media presented Arbenz's reforms not as populist attempts to move Guatemala from feudalism to modern capitalism, but as militant communism.

No sooner had Arbenz been overthrown than his CIA-picked successor, Carlos Castillo Armas, dismantled the budding labor movement, the literacy campaign, the peasant cooperatives, and revoked all land reform measures. This aggravated the overcrowding of the several million Indians living on tiny plots on the highland plateaus. Anticommunism became the ruling norm, and it still is today.

After the 1959 Cuban revolution, conditions seemed ripe for guerrilla warfare in Guatemala too. Led by dissident army officers, several guerrilla groups appeared in the early 1960s in the eastern region of the country. Guatemalan ruling groups again looked to Washington for help. In 1966 the United States responded with large numbers of military advisers, weapons, and Green Berets to stop the guerrillas. Guerrilla attacks resulted in the deaths of a U.S. and a West German ambassador, and two U.S. military attachés. The counter-insurgency program escalated into "indiscriminate terror," according to a 1980 State Department study. "To eliminate a few hundred guerrillas," the report concluded, "the government killed perhaps 10,000 Guatemalan peasants."

The elections of 1974 marked another lost opportunity and a new turning point. The liberals and leftists who wanted change, not bloodshed, supported a reformist coalition. To accommodate the military, they chose an army officer, the moderately progressive General Efraín Ríos Montt, as their presidential candidate. However, then-President Carlos Arana Osorio decided that the general he favored had to win. The election results were held up just long enough for the military to fix the ballots. U.S. diplomats admitted an "embarrassing" and "counterproductive" fraud had taken place, and several urged Washington to protest. As in El Salvador two years earlier, where a similar reformist coalition had been cheated of victory, Washington did not raise its voice. In both countries, the blatant fraud convinced many young people, who saw all political doors closed, to go underground.

The Army Stands Alone

As Guatemala prepares for elections in March 1982, revolution is brewing once more. Almost every day there are guerrilla actions: an ambush of an army convoy, an attack on a police station, or a takeover of a village to hold political meetings and kill army informants. As in the 1960s, right-wing death lists are circulating, and mysteriously named murder squads have reappeared.

Wiped out completely a decade ago, the left-wing guerrillas have been able to return because of three factors: the radicalization of the Roman Catholic church, the ability of the guerrillas to mobilize the Indians for the first time, and the inevitable demonstration effect of events elsewhere in Central America.

In contrast to the defeated guerrillas of the 1960s, the Guatemalan leftists in the 1970s decided no revolution would be possible without the participation of the country's Indians, who make up 53 per cent of the population. Descendants of the Mayans, the Indians have protected one of the oldest and most coherent cultures in the Americas by rejecting the values of the society imposed by the Spanish conquest. Their tight social organization also protects them against Guatemala's pervasive racism. Divided into 18 language groups, the Indians follow a conservative, contemplative, and deeply religious lifestyle. Despite years of political pressure, they had always remained aloof from right and left.

Undismayed by the challenge, young members of the Guerrilla Army of the Poor (EGP) moved into the El Quiché area in 1975, learned Indian languages, gave the people legal and marketing advice, became involved in cooperatives, and slowly gained their confidence. Catholic priests, many of them foreigners, served effectively as a bridge between the guerrillas and the Indian population by raising the Indians' consciousness and eventually endorsing—thereby legitimating—the revolutionary path.

These efforts found strong popular support. The Kakchikel, Kekchí, and Quiché peoples have long resented "the army of the whites," which forcibly recruits Indian boys. The Guatemalan military has also made a policy of seizing Indian land on behalf of the powerful, particularly in a new oil, nickel, and forestry development area known as the Transversal Zone. The army has also kidnapped, tortured, and killed local leaders, often entire families, in its hunt for subversives.

In the 1970s, the living conditions of the impoverished Indians worsened. Population growth put more pressure on the short supply of land, services, and employment. Illiteracy remained at more than 60 per cent. Light industry and tourism created a boom in Guatemala City. But every year half a million Indians in the countryside are forced to migrate to the cotton, sugar, and coffee plantations along the Pacific coast, where they often work for less than the minimum wage of $3.20 a day.

Official terror and desperation have pushed many Indians to cooperate with the guerrillas or actually to join their ranks. Of the four armed leftist groups in Guatemala, the EGP and the Organization of the People in Arms have the largest Indian following. Although they are kept small for tactical reasons, these groups can now draw on a vast, invisible support network on a terrain that the Indians know intimately and the army does not.

If the Indians are a key to possible change in Guatemala, the military is the key to the status quo. The military's strategy for preserving power is to terrify the villagers and to put the guerrillas in a moral bind by punishing innocent civilians for guerrilla actions. Frequently, after guerrillas have ambushed a military convoy or taken a village for a political meeting, the army or one of the death squads retaliates by raiding the town. They leave maimed bodies lying in public to underline their warning. If at all reported in the press, these raids are described usually as an armed clash between the army and subversives.

Increasingly, the army feels that it stands alone in the way of revolution.

Encouraged by U.S. military support and equipment and dissatisfied with the role of protecting other people's fortunes, the military began to acquire its own wealth in the early 1970s. Modeling themselves after Brazil's powerful military, the officers decided to build economic muscle to increase their independence. The 14,000-man Guatemalan armed forces now own a bank, an investment fund, and have launched industrial projects. Top military leaders own vast stretches of land. They earn extra income selling protection to the large landowners. As in El Salvador, much of the high command is U.S.-trained. Between 1950 and 1977, according to Pentagon statistics, 3,334 Guatemalan officers attended U.S. military academies.

Three years ago, Guatemala rejected U.S. military aid to protest Carter's human rights criticism. Since then, Guatemala has spent more than $89 million on military purchases, mainly in Israel and Argentina.

Guatemala had seemed the sort of country where the Carter administration human rights program might have had some impact. Between 1974 and 1978, fraudulently elected President Kjell Laugerud García proved surprisingly tolerant of the newly emerging trade union and Indian cooperative movements. And there were hopes that his successor, Lucas, and his social democrat civilian running mate, Francisco Villagrán Kramer, would insure continuation of the *apertura* or political opening.

However, relations between Guatemala and Washington deteriorated sharply within months of the Lucas takeover. Lucas believed that Washington's policies in Nicaragua and El Salvador were destabilizing the entire region and encouraging the extreme left. As the Sandinistas gained strength in Nicaragua, the army command decided to end the *apertura* and demobilize the opposition. In its siege mentality, the right began identifying all non-rightists—teachers, union leaders, students, priests, journalists, Christian Democrats, and social democrats—as communist threats. Within two years, repression had become so extreme that even Vice-President Villagrán resigned and fled the country.

The United States was snubbed. The Carter administration's human rights representations were totally ignored. High-ranking State Department envoys to Guatemala were refused audiences with the president, while the local press taunted them as "moderate Marxists." When Washington decided in 1980 to replace meek Ambassador Frank V. Ortíz, Jr. with a more assertive career diplomat, George Landau, it was met with defiance. Guatemala refused to accept Landau. For the past year, the fortress-like U.S. embassy in Guatemala City has been without an ambassador.

The Fascist and the Jackal

Although U.S. officials now hope that a political solution can be shaped around the March 1982 elections, it is difficult to imagine how Guatemala's political direction could change sufficiently in the coming months to make elections remotely credible. The far left abandoned elections as a political tool after the 1974 fraud. The murders of union and peasant leaders have forced popular organizations to go underground, if not to take up arms, at least to provide support for the armed guerrilla forces. Two of the country's most respected and popular opposition leaders have been murdered by the rightist death squads, which enjoy official protection. Former Foreign Minister Alberto Fuentes Mohr, head of a socialist party, was assassinated in early 1979. Manuel Colom Argueta, the popular former mayor of Guatemala City, was shot to death six days after his left-of-center party had been granted registration with the government.

The left-of-center and centrist groups that have survived the assassination campaign find it impossible to operate publicly. Even the Christian Democrats, whose Salvadorean colleagues are allied with the right-wing military there, feel terrorized in Guatemala. Since last summer, 76 party leaders have been murdered, seven of them in one day. The Christian Democrats are threatening to boycott the elections unless the repression eases.

The Reagan administration has quietly started to encourage Christian Democratic leader Vinicio Cerezo to run party candidates next March. Yet Cerezo himself receives frequent death threats and has narrowly escaped three assassination attempts in recent months. And by early May, Washington had done nothing to help create conditions that would make Christian Democratic participation more than an act of political—and actual—suicide.

With the political center virtually extinct, the elections are very likely to be another squabble for power among the rightists. Besides Lucas, two men count in the jockeying for the presidency. One is former Vice-President Mario Sandoval Alarcón, head of the fiercely rightist National Liberation Movement (MLN), who has already announced his candidacy. The MLN calls itself the "party of organized violence" and claims to maintain a 3,000-man paramilitary force. Its party headquarters are painted with images of the sword and the cross, the symbols of the warrior monks of the Middle Ages. Representing Guatemala's powerful land-owning classes, the MLN is perhaps closest to the European fascist parties. Sandoval himself has expressed great admiration for Spain's fascist Falange and Chile's neofascist organization, Patria y Libertad.

Sandoval's primary rival is Arana, who cannot become president again, but is expected to offer his own candidate. As tough as Sandoval, Arana earned the nickname "the Jackal" for his fierce repression of the left. Architect of the economic boom of the past decade, he has a strong following among the military and the conservative but more modern business community, which does not like to be identified with the fanaticism of the MLN.

Although both groups have supported and encouraged repression, they are being hurt by the current instability. Investment has slowed dramatically, and capital flight has been such that the government was forced to impose exchange controls a year ago. Although the nation's reserves stood at $741 million at the end of 1978, better interest rates abroad and political panic at home brought them down to $444 million at the end of 1980. Scared by the left's assassination of government officials and members of their own community, many businessmen have begun to use heavy security for themselves and their property.

The Guatemalan establishment overestimated how willing the Reagan administration would be to provide support once it took office. Reagan's nomination lasc summer had encouraged Guatemalan hostility toward the Carter administration on both official and private levels. Ultraconservative Guatemalan groups made early contact with the Reagan camp and persuaded hard-line congressmen, retired U.S. military officers, and academics to visit Guatemala City. The visitors, in turn, reassured their Guatemalan hosts that U.S. policies in Central America would be radically different under a Reagan presidency. Members of a conservative group called Amigos Del País—represented at the time by the public relations firm of Michael Deaver, now assistant to the president and deputy chief of staff—even boasted that Guatemalan businessmen had made substantial contributions to the Reagan campaign.

Visibly cheered by Reagan's El Salvador policy, the military in Guatemala hoped for similar aid. The government even came up with purported guerrilla documents proving Cuban arms shipments in the hope of panicking Washington. All of this failed to trigger any immediate U.S. policy commitments. The Reagan administration has not yet responded to requests for the spare parts needed to repair Guatemala's grounded, U.S.-made helicopters.

The administration is in a bind. Although sympathetic to Guatemala's anticommunism, Washington cannot afford to ignore its brutal repression. The administration's professed support for reform in El Salvador is likely to be undermined by open support of reaction in Guatemala.

Whereas the administration has good contacts with the Guatemalan elite—Sandoval and Arana mixed with the Reagan inner circle during inauguration week—U.S. influence on the military is minimal. Even the kind of nominal leverage for reform that the United States has in El Salvador does not exist in Guatemala. If the administration were to push the military regime to reform, knowledgeable insiders doubt that there is even a faction of progressive officers willing to support reform-minded policies. In fact, one of the strongest opponents of a more reformist policy would be the ultraconservative U.S. business community in Guatemala City. The local American Chamber of Commerce has become a vocal defender of the Lucas regime, both in Guatemala and in the United States.

Supporting the current government would mean renewed U.S. acquiescence in the senseless brutal policies of the past. The wide-scale political murder—30,000 killings since 1954—has done nothing to resolve Guatemala's true problems. And it has prevented the formulation of reform policies more in harmony with long-term U.S. interests.

Outside communist involvement is no pretext for U.S. involvement in Guatemala. Contrary to recent State Department allegations, Guatemalan rebels were not created by Cuban agents, nor are they challenging the United States. Cuban Premier Fidel Castro reportedly did intervene to help the four guerrilla groups form a unified command, much as he did in

El Salvador. An unknown number of Guatemalan guerrillas have visited Cuba, and some have received Cuban training. U.S. officials say privately they have no evidence of significant arms shipments to Guatemala from Cuba or Cuban-linked sources.

Betting on the 1982 elections as an avenue of meaningful change is wishful thinking. To rebuild the political center is nearly impossible at this late stage. Even among moderates, U.S. credibility is low.

The only way that the Reagan administration can avoid repeating the mistakes of the past is to show that it opposes government-sponsored terrorism. Without extracting significant concessions from the current ruling groups in Guatemala, the United States will not obtain the measures essential to long-term stability there.

The administration should not go ahead with plans to resume military assistance. The Guatemalans are hurting without U.S. aid. In rejecting military support in 1977, the Guatemalans figured that they could ride out the Carter years and gain friendlier treatment from a Republican administration, without having to curtail their human rights violations. An indefinite military cutoff now could induce the armed forces to revise its reactionary policies.

The United States has not halted Agency for International Development support, which in 1979 amounted to $24.7 million. By denying the portion of this aid earmarked for public works projects, Washington would offer evidence of its determination to promote change.

The Reagan administration has the advantage of being known and trusted in Guatemala. Ruling groups know that they will have nowhere else to turn if they alienate a conservative U.S. administration. Given the choice of facing a hostile United States or instituting genuine reforms, Guatemalan leaders might grudgingly accept the latter. But the United States should not pretend that it can accomplish anything easily in Guatemala. Creating an atmosphere for reform will be very difficult; real arm-twisting will have to take place.

In Guatemala, change is inevitable; to live with long-term stability, the United States will have to live with short-term upheaval. The issue in Guatemala is, once again, not how to prevent change, but how to guide it. The problem is that it may be too late for the United States to play a constructive role. "If only we had an Arbenz now," a State Department official lamented recently. "We are going to have to invent one, but all the candidates are dead."

3

Dependent Development
and Economic Imperialism

The common thesis of the articles in this chapter is that a structure of enforced economic dependency and uneven capitalist development provides the frame for understanding the current build-up of popular revolutionary struggle in Central America. This is not to diminish the importance of the political, social and cultural terrain on which these struggles are being waged—terrain which is surveyed in greater detail in the other chapters of this book.

Any attempt to explain the history of dependency in Central America requires investigating the U.S. role in propagating and entrenching an extensive system of export agriculture, of which the principal commodities are coffee, cotton, bananas and meat. The region's forced reliance on an agro-export economy, in turn, has generated a comparative disadvantage in its trade relations with the U.S. This unequal exchange results from the fact that prices for agricultural exports have not kept pace with those for finished products which Central American nations must import. For example, where 160 bags of coffee purchased a tractor in 1960, it took 400 bags to buy the same tractor in 1970. The inability of the region to escape the deteriorating terms of trade locks it into a vicious cycle of ever-deepening debt.

Central America's economic dependency is not simply a by-product of underdevelopment. Since the late 19th century, it has been generated and reinforced through the geopolitical domination of the United States in alliance with the region's military dictators and local oligarchies. Crucial to the continued success of the U.S. in maintaining its domination over Central America's economy have been its protection and sustenance of a dependent local bourgeoisie. This bourgeois class, both allied with U.S. interests and subordinated to them, is a powerful force working to maintain the existing unequal distribution of land and wealth in the area.

Since the end of World War II, however, internal social contradictions have been generated by the growing repression and maldistribution of wealth which attend agro-export economies. Such contradictions have periodically created pressures for social reform as well as calls to re-orient economic development away from excessive reliance on agriculture and toward the fostering of a regional industrial base. The U.S. has responded to these reformist agendas either by repressing or misdirecting them, limit-

135

ing the political and economic options available to the isthmus in its effort to develop a more balanced and internally oriented economy.

Constrained by a U.S.-imposed "free market" straightjacket, the two related modernization strategies designed to lessen the region's abject dependency have failed. The first strategy, import substitution (the local production of formerly imported goods), was also tied to a program of social reforms and was inspired by the U.N. Economic Commission for Latin America (ECLA). ECLA's project was intended to overcome Central America's excessive reliance on a few primary exports by stimulating internal development. It was expected that the rise of a local bourgeoisie would weaken the traditional oligarchies who were tied to the export-import economy. Combined with an agrarian reform program, import substitution would lead to income redistribution and incorporation of the lower classes into the local economy. This, in turn, was expected to widen the market for locally-produced industrial products. Guatemala, from 1944 to 1954, was the only country in Central America to attempt the reforms suggested by ECLA. The Guatemalan reforms were perceived as such a serious threat to U.S. domination of the region, however, that the CIA engineered a military coup in 1954 which overthrew Guatemala's only democratically elected leader, President Jacobo Arbenz, crushed the reform movement, and reinstituted a chain of rule by military regimes that remained virtually unbroken.

The second attempt at import substitution, regional integration, was based on the premise that internal development could proceed without agrarian reform and income redistribution (since these programs were obviously not acceptable to either the U.S. or the traditional oligarchies) by creating sufficient market territories to justify new industries at existing levels of consumption. This required transforming the many small national markets within each Central American country into free trade zones that could function over the whole of Central America—in effect, a Central American Common Market (CACM). Although the CACM plan did not threaten established structures of oligarchic privilege, even this "second best" ECLA plan (as originally formulated) was regarded by the U.S. as anathema. As Susanne Jonas describes in this chapter, the U.S. went to great lengths to subvert the CACM to the corporate agenda of U.S. multinational corporations.

A major dilemma confronting each of these strategies for regional autonomy has been that industrialization requires large quantities of capital and technical expertise which do not exist within the regional economy. Thus, the demand for foreign aid and foreign capital led, by degrees, to increased penetration of Central America by U.S. multinational corporations, at first producing for the newly created regional markets, and later, for re-export to the U.S. As in the rest of Latin America, such penetration and control of markets has increased—and not decreased—the demand for imports and the transfer of capital abroad.

The burgeoning system of national "debt peonage" which accompanies multinational penetration has been fed externally by U.S.-controlled lending institutions such as the International Monetary Fund (IMF) and the U.S. Agency for International Development (USAID). The level of this debt is a telling barometer of the region's economic plight.

Just how serious is the debt problem in Central America? Guatemala, with perhaps the strongest economy, has a public sector debt of $2.9 billion of which $317 million is overdue. The current government needs to negotiate a "certificate of good housekeeping" with the IMF in order to meet its future borrowing needs and will need $4.1 billion over the next four years (1982-1986). The rest of Central America is in similar straits; the public debt of Honduras has more than doubled to $1.5 billion and, given its current status as the least developed of Central American nations, Honduras will have even more trouble than Guatemala in securing further loans. In El Salvador, the economy is in ruins. According to Alberto Benítez Bonilla, president of El Salvador's Central Bank, without nearly $500 million in grants and long-term credits, almost all industries would stop production and El Salvador would experience at least a 20 percent *negative* growth rate. Six years ago, USAID grants to El Salvador were less than $10 million. Costa Rica's public debt rivals that of Guatemala and has the additional burden of an annual inflation rate over 100 percent. Even the Sandinistas in Nicaragua, who in 1979 inherited a $1.5 billion foreign debt from the rapacious Somoza dictatorship, have been forced to more than double their debt (to $3.5 billion) in order to stave off economic collapse.

Although its causes are rooted in the nature of Central America's dependent industrial development since 1960, this vast public debt has been exacerbated, not only by the recurrence of the 1973 oil shock in 1979 (and a world recession which has depressed the value of Central America's export commodities), but also by an alarming increase in capital flight. Fearing the region's volcanic political activity, the bourgeoisie streams daily to the sanctuary of the U.S., draining away scarce capital in the process. Capital flight for 1981 alone, estimated at over $500 million, exceeded the total amount of aid received by the region during the same year.

The grimness of these statistics is overshadowed by an even more staggering set of figures: those which describe the deterioration of already marginal living standards among the majority of Central America's impoverished people (See Chapter 4). Even in Nicaragua, which has labored to redistribute work and wealth in its war-torn and recession-ravaged economy, per capita annual incomes have dropped from about $800 in 1978 to $650 in 1981. These figures for Nicaragua do not, of course, include the dramatic rise in the "social wage," i.e., the increase in health and education services in the reconstruction period. Nevertheless, even while the Sandinista government has sought to restructure past internal inequities in favor of its many poor, the new government has been unable to escape the U.S.-imposed structures of economic dependency which continue to oppress the region as a whole.

The economic picture for the immediate future is not likely to improve. Commodity prices remain low; international interest rates remain high; and due to the Reagan administration's preoccupation with private investment, multilateral aid is unlikely to be made available on the scale or terms required. Finally, given the high levels of political and economic instability, direct private investment in the region will hardly compensate for reduced multilateral assistance. Indeed, the Overseas Private Investment Corporation (OPIC) is virtually closed for business in both El Salvador and Nicaragua and has been increasingly cautious in Guatemala and Costa Rica. Worst of all, the flight of capital from Central America to U.S. banks is certain to accelerate.

In the absence of investor confidence in the region (see Girling and Goldring's article in this chapter), even the investment incentives provided by the Reagan administration's new Caribbean Basin Investment Program will be meaningless. Trade opportunities and investment incentives will not mean much in the face of the regional economic crisis confronting Central America. Ironically, it has been estimated that a soundly managed U.S. economy, experiencing three percent growth and a five percent reduction in interest rates, would generate over $550 million in foreign exchange for Caribbean Basin countries.

The selections in this chapter etch in stark relief the structures of Central America's dependent capitalist development. These readings share a common critical focus: critical of the land-based oligarchies who enforce dependency internally, and critical of the U.S. multinationals and State Department policymakers who reinforce it externally. At the same time, however, each article offers a distinct vantage point from which this critical stance is developed.

Edelberto Torres-Rivas undertakes a historical review of the changes in strategy that accompany and characterize the dependent capitalist model of growth in Central America. In particular, Torres-Rivas argues that Central American nations, in contrast to more rapidly industrializing third world economies, have failed to expand their internal markets. This failure to broaden internal markets is devastatingly portrayed in the social indicators on literacy, malnutrition, and average annual per capita income. In assessing responsibility for this situation, Torres-Rivas refuses to allow the U.S. to wriggle off the hook; explicit in his analysis is page-after-page of argument detailing how the U.S. economy profits at the expense of the Central American people.

Patricia Flynn and Roger Burbach, with the clarity that only a case-study can provide, document how Del Monte, a U.S.-based multinational firm, established an agro-export banana enclave in Guatemala. Their story is interwoven with reports of Del Monte's misdeeds: the use of bribery to acquire plantations, associations with right-wing business executives who promote their interests through Mafia-like tactics, and Del Monte's abuse of economic power to avoid government taxes. This case-study is particularly noteworthy because it documents a persistent pattern of relations between the U.S. and Central America—a pattern which, as the case of Del Monte shows, continues into the present.

Susanne Jonas provides a detailed historical critique of U.S. manipulation of the Central American Common Market. She demonstrates how the

U.S. established a narrow frame for regional integration which guaranteed "free trade zones" for U.S. multinationals and retarded the development of local enterprise. Jonas develops a careful analysis of how and why the U.S. interfered with the autonomy of the CACM, using the "bait" of foreign aid and a U.S.-controlled regional banking system to its own advantage. Ultimately, Jonas exposes the way that the U.S., through its control of the CACM, actually accelerated the forces of uneven intra-regional development which were played out in the late 1960's and led to the collapse of the common market.

Robert Girling and Luin Goldring's concluding essay analyses the several elements which, taken together, comprise the substance of U.S. "national interests" in Central America. They assess the "value" of Central America to the U.S. geopolitically, as an export market, as a source of direct investment revenues, and as a source of strategic raw materials and petroleum. They argue that the importance of Central America for the U.S. can only be understood in terms of its global geopolitical significance and yet, the pursuit of those interests is likely to be far greater in cost than any perceived imperial returns. Girling's conclusions challenge the conventional wisdom that Central America can be won or lost.

These four articles do not develop in a substantial way, either within the context of reform or in the post-revolutionary situation, possibilities for alternative models of development. That question is addressed, at least partially, in Chapter 8 of this book in reference to post-revolutionary Nicaragua. While Costa Rica remains an alternative example of reform—within the confines of dependent capitalist development—its current economic crisis casts considerable doubt on the viability of that route.

The common thread running through all of these articles is the heavy-handed presence of the United States in Central America's political economy. The U.S. has oscillated with respect to Central America between two vectors of imperialist domination—direct military and economic intervention on the one hand, and indirect economic and political manipulation on the other. Seldom in the twentieth century have these five nations been free to establish an independent strategy of economic development. Indeed, the Central American people have been trapped in a structure of dependent development which has simultaneously polarized the population into "haves" and "have nots" and brutally repressed the impulse for reform and political representation essential to a truly stable polity.

—*Craig Richards*

The Central American Model
of Growth: Crisis for Whom?*

By Edelberto Torres-Rivas

Margaret Towner, Translator

Central America as a region has a gross domestic product (GDP) of more than U.S. \$12,000 million (1976), seventh highest in Latin America, and a population of 17.8 million. Central America ranks third in the export of bananas to the North American market. The basic common characteristics of Central American economies are defined by the importance of the agrarian sector (25 percent of GDP and about 70 percent of exports) as a source of social wealth and dividends, by a chronic crisis in agricultural production for the internal market and by the weakness and newness of the industrial structure.

The economic history of Central America has landmarks indicative of similarities and differences among its component parts. Transitory forms of productive organization, most at the extractive level (cochineal, indigo, and cacao), predominated during the colonial period and at the beginning of the Republican era. Even bird feathers and "balsams," used in primitive therapy, were exported on occasion. The region began to define its economic structure when the supply and demand created by the European industrial revolution allowed the consolidation of a primary-export economy and an internal market of manufactured luxury goods. Coffee first and then bananas constituted the basis of this export-oriented economic structure which utilized abundant land and labor. The manner by which the internal economy was established and its links with international commerce conditioned the entire internal social structure, the nature of political power, and cultural life. The export-oriented economy notably retarded national and social integration and contributed to the extreme rigidity of political and social relations.

In Central America, the crises of the 1930s and the effects of the Second World War discredited the model of development based on monoculture and monoexportation exemplified by the relations between the banana enclave and the local economy. The post-war economic, political, and ideological situation weakened the power of the dominant agrarian classes. The numerous social problems and conflicts that had been frozen for the long period that ended with the 1940s provoked crises (in Guatemala, El Salvador, and Costa Rica) or readjustments (in Nicaragua and Honduras). These were inevitable disequilibriums in the traditional political forms of domination provoked by the rise of new forces and groups formed in the previous period as well as by the need to reorganize the whole society on a new basis.

---

*Excerpted and abridged from *Latin American Perspectives*, Vol. VII, No. 25/26, February-March, 1980.

The period that we can refer to in order to understand this vision began in the decade of the 1950s. In Central America it was characterized more by a political than an economic need to find a new basis for the accumulation of capital. It was based on liberal rather than socialist principles: to improve the standard of living of the majority of the population, to adopt a code of law based more on consensus, and to modernize Central American cultural and political life held back by oligarchic domination.

The Process of Industrialization

In the experience of most agrocommercial societies, the initial stage of industrialization was facilitated by certain internal conditions derived from external demand. The constant growth of production and productivity which resulted from the expansion in the international demand for agricultural products created internal purchasing power for manufactured products supplied first through importation and later less sophisticated types of internal industrial production. The size of the internal market, the volume of population, and, obviously, a certain level of capitalist agricultural development were important in determining the growth of the internal market.

The Central American economy, however, evolved in a different direction. Monoproducing specialization and the total absence of other sources of endogenous growth turned the export sector into the motor for economic growth without the long-range effects of encouraging the development of an internal market. Depending exclusively on international demand, the export sector operated with great independence, with little correspondence to the necessities of the social development of these societies.

Monoproducing specialization did not favor the formation of an internal demand linked to a new manufacturing infrastructure. The export sector was unable to establish an internal market nucleus due to the nature of the organization of production and commercialization of the two basic types of exports (coffee and bananas) and to the geographic and demographic dimensions of these countries. This lack of internal demand is related to the high concentration of property, the result of capitalist development through a "landlord path" and, more importantly, the virtual monopoly of the cultivation and commercialization of coffee. The only sector of the population which created a demand for industrial goods was a minority of people closely linked to foreign capital and who received a part of its benefits. At the other end of the scale was an over-abundant labor force with wage levels so low as to seriously limit the formation of an internal market. In this case the "wage-earner" was not a consumer. The concentration of a relatively better-paid workforce in the banana sector did not significantly increase internal demand due to the organization that the enclave gave to its labor force—a partial consumer of imported products. The rest of the economy consisted of peasants locked into a system of subsistence.

The idea of industrialization in Central America was necessarily linked to the project of regional integration. The goal of regional integration was to establish a new stage of economic growth for the region, based on a form of capital accumulation which would take into account relative losses in the export sector. However, the project was never realized for reasons specific to Central America rather than those in other Latin American countries (balance of payments problems, or crisis, or disorder in the international supply of manufactured goods). The following is a summary of the basic characteristics of this industrialization effort.

In the case of Central America, we are talking about an industrial process that took place in the heart of an agrarian society whose traditional exporting structure not only did not weaken but became relatively stronger. Since 1948, agrarian production oriented toward international demand has increased in spite of continual oscillations in prices, arbitrarily determined quotas in buyers' markets, and the internal distortion caused by the indefinite prolongation of ways of life and activity that resisted capitalist modernization. The rate of growth in agriculture was significantly less than that of the industrial or service sectors. However, in relation to the international market, the region preserved the dependent commercial profile that it had when it was first incorporated into the same system more than one hundred years ago. Coffee production has tripled since 1948, banana production has doubled but with many ups and downs and with a redistribution of productive forms; the production of cotton, sugar, meat, and other minor products increased after the 1950s, diversifying supply and the productive structure but further strengthening the external orientation of the economy. The five most important farm products have contributed almost 70 percent of the exports in Central America, a percentage that has been virtually constant for the past fifteen years.[1]

This high volume of earnings from agrarian exports means that industrialization has depended not only on the evolution and basic characteristics of the internal market but also on its capacity to export. The export sector had to rely on foreign capital investment and, above all, the transference of technology and imported forms of business organization, promotion, publicity, and marketing systems.

It is possible to see in this process a fundamental characteristic of dependent capitalism: when internal demand appears in these societies, the mechanism that generates this market does not have a functional relationship with the dynamics of accumulation. In so-called endogenous capitalist economies, the creation and growth of the internal market, the basis of production and consumption of manufactured items, comes to be the counterpart of the levels of accumulation, which means that a correspondence or at least an association exists between the rhythm of accumulation and the growth of demand.

The growth in productivity did not generate accumulation in the export economy in the proportion hoped for; hence, there was no reason why it should transform into corresponding growth in global demand. The fact

---

[1] In 1976, for example, $1000 million of coffee, $282.7 million of cotton, $231.3 million of sugar, $265.4 million of bananas, and $124.4 million of meat were exported.

that the industrial project took place in the context of an export economy that was not in crisis made that project sensitive to and dependent on this economy and, as such, reinforced the tendency—in itself characteristic of export economies—toward the separation between internal production and international circulation. It is a fact that industrial production tends to follow this sequence since the growth of this production depends less on the increased demand provoked by nonaccumulated surplus value than on the relative expansion of the market, stimulated by the creation of a free market zone parallel to the erection of stiff tariff barriers.

The policies of industrial promotion that emerged at the end of the 1950s did not appear in the context of a crisis in the world market. Rather, they emerged as a result of a reorganization of the system dictated by the almost total hegemony of the United States, achieved at the price of the Second World War through the policies of economic reconstruction initiated under U.S. protection.

To use the language currently in vogue—more conventional than conceptual—this industrialization process took place according to the import substitution "model" which is nothing more than the transference of previously imported production to the internal sector, focusing production around consumer goods for immediate consumption. It tried to satisfy a pre-existing demand by substituting some imports for others without significantly diminishing overall imports. The result of this readjustment of the productive apparatus was the emergence of "final touch industries."[2]

This reorientation of supply can only take place with large foreign investments of fixed capital, importation of equipment, technology, and industrial raw materials, which explains the active presence of foreign capital in the process. During this period, the ease of obtaining financing for investment in infrastructure and industrial activities was due to the growing availability of foreign capital resources. The reason for the presence of international capital was to create new sources of accumulation different from and more flexible than the traditional forms of investment in agriculture and services.

Industrial activity was reduced to the processing of local raw materials or the finishing of consumer goods partially processed abroad—all with imported capital. Foreign control over the local process left little opportunity for the assimilation of new technologies and for the rise of entrepreneurial projects utilizing the knowledge of these technological processes. The industrial mentality of the bourgeoisie was reduced, in consequence, to a subordinate condition—that of administrator.

The change in direction of foreign investment in Central America, almost totally North American, is a well-known fact. Although the change would probably have taken place anyway since it reflects a new moment in the growth of international capital, there is no doubt that the stimuli created by the state in the framework of the Common Market project

---

[2] Industries which merely assemble or package imported products under a local label. —Ed.

Table 1
Profits from North American Private Investments
(1977, in millions of U.S. dollars)

Country	Total Invest.	Growth %	Rate of Rtn %	Industrial Invest.	Growth %	Rate of Rtn %
Argentina	1,505	10.2	18.1	930	3.6	7.5
Brazil	5,956	10.0	11.4	3,935	7.1	9.2
Mexico	3,175	6.7	9.2	2,328	5.0	7.0
Chile	187	4.5	8.0	52	6.1	9.6
Colombia	706	8.0	13.0	436	12.4	15.6
Peru	1,409	3.3	5.4	157	6.5	0.0
Central Am.	734	7.9	13.2	248	8.3	17.3
Others	1,063	3.8	13.7	171	23.0	14.6

Source: Business Latin America (1978).

favored this change. North American capital, whether associated with local resources or not, has gained control of almost all the branches of industrial activity, especially those with assured profitability and, in so doing, has confirmed the parasitic character of these types of investments.

The available information about foreign investment is fragmented and out of date. Statistics about the quantity of investments by types of industries, for example, or by industrial branches for each of the countries and for different periods are not available.

Table 1 is a comparative example of only the quantity of foreign investment in Central America, and it shows some of the regrettable extremes of the problem in terms of the rates of return. As can be observed, the region produced the highest rates of profit in Latin America.

In the import-substitution model of growth, the recourse to foreign technology appears as an inevitable fact. Use of this technology does not necessarily result in the substitution of a previous demand but rather in the creation of a supply according to standards of consumption of the most developed countries. What are popular consumer goods in the developed countries become in the underdeveloped structure exclusive objects of an expensive and sophisticated demand. Additionally, this model, as applied in Central America, only resulted in substitution of former imports by newer ones made up of raw materials, partially finished goods, and capital (see Table 2).

The growth of foreign investment and the persistence of a high import coefficient,[3] one of the key problems of economic modernization, expresses itself in the size of the foreign debt. As can be seen from Table 2, the value of imported industrial inputs tended to decline relatively (from 57 to 44 percent) during the period under consideration, that of industrial equipment doubled, and the tendency towards the exportation of utilities, royalties, and services of capital was equally high.

---

[3] The ratio of imported to domestically produced commodities. —Ed.

Table 2
Value of Industrial Production, Importations of Machinery, and Costs by Origin (in millions of U.S. dollars)

	1963	1969
Imported industrial machinery and equipment	45.7	91.5
Imported industrial inputs	220.1	321.1
Industrial inputs produced in Central America	166.3	405.2
% imported inputs	57	44.3
% regional inputs	43	55.7
Gross value of industrial product	1,130.0	1,981.1
Imported inputs, as % of gross value of industrial product	19.5	16.2

Source: Banco Interamericano de Desarollo e Instituto para la Integración de América Latina (BID/INTAL) (1974, IV: Tables 23 and 30).

The debt appears to be related to externally imposed conditions of this type of international accumulation of capital. In the past, the exporting sector dealt with the sphere of consumer goods, facilitating and expanding the possibilities for importation. Today, it deals with capital goods, raw materials, and semi-industrial products, thus increasing more than before the level of debt for the region.

It is notable, for example, how, in spite of the high prices of export products during certain periods (for example, 1977-1978) the balance of payments deficit continues to grow. Between 1974 and 1978, Central America accumulated a deficit that represents approximately 75 percent of the value of extraordinary exports in 1977. This deficit has made it necessary to rely on growing quantities of foreign capital—in 1977 alone, new capital investment amounted to more than U.S. $913 million.

In mono-agricultural exporting situations like those experienced in Central America in the past, an indebtedness such as reflected in Table 3 below would have created a crisis for some Central American countries. The situation is certainly critical, but not sufficient to paralyze economic activity. The current balance of payments deficit did not originate in the export sector, and the crisis has not impeded the advance of industrialization. Apparent independence was achieved because capital, technology, and so-called material elements of capital (constant capital) were not obtained through mere commercial exchange but rather through the mediation of foreign capital in its double role as direct investor and financier of loans. In this manner the highly vulnerable and dependent character of these economies was redefined.

An important characteristic of the process that we have been analyzing is that it has not resulted in increasing the concentration of capital because capital has been highly concentrated from its beginning. This result is based on assumptions that have social and political consequences of primary importance; such concentration would not have been possible without the double complicity of the state and its economic policies and those benefits

Table 3
Foreign Debt of Central America
(December 1976, in millions of U.S. dollars)

Country	Debt	Gross Industrial Product	Debt as % of GIP
Guatemala	551	5,541	10
El Salvador	462	2,567	18
Nicaragua	936	1992	47
Costa Rica	933	2,191	42
Argentina	6,190	44,840	14
Mexico	17,533	63,851	27

Source: Bancos Centrales de las capitales de Centroamérica
Informes Anuales (1977-1978).

which the state derives from the nature of foreign investments.

The economic "policies" of the Central American governments favor industrial investment of any origin by creating privileges which assure profits. Thus, concentration of capital is not only a consequence of the "natural" tendencies of capital but also, in this case, of artificial political tendencies.

A result that has not been studied sufficiently, except in the pristine example of El Salvador, is that the concentration of manufacturing has as its base the concentration and centralization of capital in other productive sectors, especially in agriculture and commerce. The constitution of a petty bourgeoisie that is multifunctional, oligopolistic, and relatively powerful is a result of this multiple monopoly. In other words, not only industrial but social wealth is concentrated, and they condition each other.

Some recent investigations allow us to assess the true dimensions of this concentration or, at least, give us some insight into its tendencies. In one survey of 320 manufacturing sectors,[4] it was found that in 160 of these sectors, one company or enterprise was responsible for more than 50 percent of the production. This monopolistic tendency was most pronounced in the newest sectors and those levels of production utilizing expensive technology, typically intermediate and durable consumer goods.

Now we shall analyze an aspect that is more than a specific characteristic of the process of industrialization; it is a generic feature of the model of development of dependent capitalism. The impossibility of absorbing the labor force and the concentration of income are two of the most negative characteristics of the functioning of an exclusive and polarizing model such as the one that capitalism has generated in this region.

Structural unemployment appears to be inherent in the development of the productive forces in the periphery of the system instead of constituting a stage in which "marginality" appears as a necessarily transitory process.

---

[4] A. Rapoport, "Estructura industrial en Centroamérica," Chapter II in *Beneficios y costos de la integración económica Centroamericana,* Serie Estudios Proyecto SIECA-BROOKINGS, Volume II, Guatemala, 1977.

The concentration of income constitutes, in the same way, a condition for the expansion of capital in relative terms. Thus, we can ask, do both the unemployment and concentration of wealth that appear associated with the new state of industrial development constitute, in the long run, limits to the accumulation of capital? It is worthwhile to examine, briefly, the nature of these problems in the Central American experience.

The rate of growth of the Economically Active Population (EAP) between 1950 and 1970 was 2.4 percent. Even the most superficial comparison of the indicators shows a serious deficiency in the labor market. The 1970 data on open unemployment, utilizing the official technical parameters, are quite conservative: 8.4 percent for the whole region, 12 percent for Guatemala, and 5 percent for Costa Rica. However, a study by the Organización Internacional del Trabajo (OIT) for Costa Rica shows a rate of total unemployment of 15.2 percent,[5] which suggests that behind the former statistics is a hidden and more serious reality.

The previous data reveal a new dimension when separated into rural and urban sectors. The estimated total unemployment for the agricultural sector in 1970—considering employment as equivalent to 280 days per person per year—was 44.4 percent for Central America as a region, reaching as high as 58.5 percent for El Salvador and as low as 14.7 percent for Costa Rica.[6] In order to have maintained the 1970 rates of employment, it would have been necessary to create 874,000 new jobs, and only 175,000 jobs were created (or 20 percent of those needed). In the first five years of the 1970's only one of every five persons entering the labor market obtained work.

The results of almost two decades of encouraging industrial growth reveal a common sense truth—that increases in productivity are incompatible with increases in employment. This demonstrates the incapacity of the industrial sector to absorb even normal demographic increases (assuming that *ceteris paribus*, the countryside was not complying with its fatal job of expelling increasing numbers of workers). Of all the developmentalist theories, the theory that increased industrialization increases employment is one that has most clearly and quickly revealed itself as false.

Closely associated with the previous problem of employment is the problem of the distribution of income and the level of wages (see Table 4). It is not enough to say that the industrialization mechanism in Central America reinforces the exclusive and polarizing characteristics of an agrarian society supposedly on the way to overcoming its problems. The "oligarchic" style that related peons to the masters of the land changes qualitatively only to take on new dimensions in social and political life.

No one doubts that the accumulation of surpluses in the form of surplus labor forms the basis of the functioning of the system. Every economic system that wants to grow will depend on its capacity for accumulation,

---

[5] The recognized unemployment is 5 percent; to that should be added the so-called equivalent unemployment which is 10.2 percent. The latter is composed of visible and invisible underemployment.

[6] In the rest of the countries, the statistics are as follows: Guatemala, 52.3 percent; Honduras, 42.5 percent; and Nicaragua 21.5 percent.

Table 4

Central America: Distribution of Income in Relation
to Total Population (1970, in Central American pesos)

Stratum	Annual income	Strata of income (%)	% of pop.	Total pop. (thousands)
HIGH	17,600	31	5	756
MIDDLE	5,680	30	15	2,268
LOW	246	26	30	4,536
VERY LOW	74	13	50	7,560

Source: SIECA La política de desarollo social de la integración económica
(Guatemala: 1975), p. 18.

but at the same time, it cannot be based indefinitely on the repetition of
the same possibilities of capital realization. In order to avoid this blockage
which would result in the paralysis of growth, the model inevitably requires
the reinforcement of the tendencies towards the concentration of income.
But to what point?

The available data barely allow us to show, on the one hand, that the
tendencies towards the concentration of social wealth (utilizing the income
indicator) have increased in the last few years and that this, on the other
hand, has been seriously weakened as a result of inflation in the present
decade and by the authoritative application of stabilization programs on
the part of the ownership sector and the state. In analyzing this problem
one must inevitably mention the nature of the state and the role it plays,
which is far from that of an impartial arbitrator in the relationship between
capital and labor. State protection appears in order to reduce the costs of
capital, and police repression grows at the same time in order to maintain
low salaries. Though this is generally true, it is less so for Costa Rica and
much more so in the cases of Guatemala and El Salvador.

In analyzing the problem of salaries, it is necessary to consider the
particular characteristics and direction of working-class organizations. It
is this organization that determines, fundamentally, the final conditions of
the sale of labor. Structural analysis hides the fact that objective deter-
minations of the market are not sufficient to explain salary levels; we need
also to know the subjective conditions of organization, class combativity,
and the possibilities of institutional channeling or repression of conflicts.

This truism has special meaning in Central America where the means
for defending the standard of living and income of the popular classes
are impeded by the use of direct noneconomic methods: extreme anti-
union violence. The final logic of repression is not, hence, the danger
of guerrillas but rather the containment of salaries. "Social-democratic"
programs obviously have a political price that owners' groups are not always
willing to pay. In the same way that these social programs have a limit, the
repression of social conflict also has a price, one that the bosses are today
finding themselves obliged to pay.

The Central American Economy and the Crisis of "Regional Integration"

Eighteen years after its signing in 1960, the General Treaty of Central American Economic Integration as a project of economic growth exhibits some symptoms of weakness. Reference is frequently made to the "crisis" of the Common Market, and this same crisis is generally associated with the armed conflict between El Salvador and Honduras and the later separation of Honduras from the Common Market, resulting in the abrupt interruption of commercial traffic between both countries. Since this unfortunate incident in 1969, which is in itself evidence of the irresponsibility of governments and their respective armies, the integrationist project has continued advancing where it has been on track. For this reason it is appropriate to ask what is meant by the reference to crisis: Is it a crisis provoked by economic growth? Or, is it the project itself and its basic conception that is helplessly shipwrecked?

One thing is certain; the argument which singles out fratricidal "war" between El Salvador and Honduras as the cause and beginning of the crisis is inadequate. The self-exclusion of Honduras from the Common Market was something that had been sought and negotiated for some time by the government of Honduras. Intraregional trade was hurt, but it recuperated within twelve months and since then has continued increasing; in fact the value of this trade has almost doubled.[7]

Of a total fixed investment of 456.1 million Central American pesos in the manufacturing sector, corresponding to a sample of 142 important enterprises in 1974, only 139.2 million pesos (30.5 percent) were invested between 1960 and 1969 (i.e., before Honduras' break from the Common Market). After the conflict, between 1969 and 1973, however, 270 million pesos were invested, which corresponds to 59 percent of the total investment in the sample. What is interesting, finally, is that these investments took place in relatively sophisticated sectors of technology.

If the rate of growth of regional trade, apparently for some the only indicator of interest, increases at a slower rate than that of industrial growth, it indicates that regional markets are being displaced by national markets and/or trade is concentrating in one or two countries. From this viewpoint, the most immediate and crucial element contributing to the integrationist process is the growing disequilibrium between those countries which sell a lot and those which buy a lot. Over the years some economies have emerged as selling economies and others as net buyers, and this in itself detracts from the primary goals of the Common Market project.

During the years since 1960, Guatemala has developed as a major supplier of the region, and El Salvador, which until 1974 had always

---

[7] Horacio Bobadilla, "Encustra selectiva de las inversiones de Centroamérica en el subsector manufacturero," Appendix No. 6 in *Beneficios y costos de la integración económica centroamericana*, Serie Estudios Proyectos SIECA-BROOKINGS, Volume II, Guatemala, 1977, p. 5.

produced a surplus in its favor, has begun to have growing deficits relative to Guatemala. Between 1960 and 1977, the total accumulated value of exports from Guatemala and El Salvador to Honduras, Nicaragua, and Costa Rica were U.S. $700 million more than the purchases those two countries made from the rest.[8] Guatemala received over 679 million Central American pesos of this total; the trade deficits were also shared unequally, the greatest part belonging to Nicaragua (40 percent of the total), followed by Honduras (33 percent) and the least amount to Costa Rica (27 percent).

Why does the greatest competition come from the Guatemalan industrial complex? The previous data do not reveal the emergence of an aggressive industrial bourgeoisie of national origin capable of commanding the development of the productive forces in its favor. The rise of the Guatemala/El Salvador axis is the result of preexisting factors that the integrationist program of the Common Market only accentuated. If the indicators of gross capital formation were indirectly related to the volume of accumulation reached, the Salvadorean local bourgeoisie would be the most prepared to divert capital resources toward industrial investment. The high level of concentration of wealth explains the dynamism of the Salvadorean entrepreneurial minority. In Guatemala the volume of accumulation was less, but the manufacturing experience was relatively more important. In both societies the over-supply of labor power is as important as the extreme authoritarian rigidity of the social political relations. Does this last point suggest the hypothesis that the costs of production in both countries may be less than in Nicaragua and Costa Rica because of lower average labor costs? Is the competitiveness of the final product guaranteed by lower salaries rather than greater productivity? It is difficult to respond affirmatively because available data do not permit a valid comparison between real levels of income for the working population of these countries.[9]

The disequilibrium in the economic growth of the region, expressed in the imbalance of intraregional commerce, attracted little attention in the 1960s because the amount was small and because traditional exports seemed to mask the importance of such imbalances. Only Honduras officially recognized its inability to adapt rapidly in the face of the exigencies of the integration process. In the 1970s such problems could no longer go unnoticed because they had also produced a trade deficit in relation to the rest of the world. In reality, Central America always had an unfavorable trade balance throughout the entire period, especially with North America[10]

---

[8] Data from SIECA, based on CIF imports registered by country.

[9] On the other hand, the simple comparison of average salaries in 1970 by economic activity and in Central American pesos gives the following results: Guatemala, 88.3 pesos/month; El Salvador, 64.1; Honduras 63.7; Nicaragua 93.3; Costa Rica, 78.9.

[10] W. Cline, *Beneficios y costos de la integración económica centroamericana*, Serie Estudios Proyecto SIECA-BROOKINGS, Volume II, Guatemala (1977), p. 69, on analyzing the benefits from economic integration in terms of "economic well-being" indicates that Honduras, Nicaragua, and Costa Rica have permanent negative balances in intrazonal commerce "which does not signify that they benefit relatively less." The intraregional deficits, he indicates, are always less than those with the rest of the world so that the deficits with the region are more the result of general deficits with international trade.

All of the above demonstrates that the Common Market project never went beyond the first stage of being a free trade zone, and also failed, as well, in its attempt to achieve productive integration. Instead, it created a highly competitive and noncomplementary productive structure. In this way, with the mechanisms of capital unleashed, to use the language of the Regional Organization for Central America and the Panama Agency for International Development (ROCAP-AID), free enterprise and the free market only resulted in a growing inequality of economic development favoring Guatemala and El Salvador. But it is difficult to point out who the winners and losers are when the enterprises most favored have been of North American origin.

It thus is not possible to maintain an optimistic view even within the technocratic vision. The social costs of the process defy quantification and as such, underemployment and low incomes translate into the perpetuation and even deterioration of truly deplorable living conditions. The real results of integration are found in the rates of infant mortality, malnutrition, the extremely slow decline in illiteracy, the accelerated increase in underemployment, deterioration in housing, lack of opportunities for getting ahead, and last even the actual physical degradation of the population.

It is true that the integrationist model has contributed towards vitalizing and diversifying economic activity, improving distribution and utilization of regional resources, and fomenting Central American cooperation at other levels. However, inasmuch as it has been a model directed and taken advantage of exclusively by North American capital and small entrepreneurial elites (merchants and industrialists), it has converted itself into a capitalist model of growth with no interest in avoiding the evils that "free" enterprise necessarily produces.

Concluding Remarks

What appears to be irreversible because of the nature of the interests that it has generated and strengthened can be corrected only at the cost of these same interests within the framework of capitalist development. To rethink the original project in light of present realities would mean that the monopoly bourgeoisie (national and foreign) would have to end the mostly corporative direction of the process that it has been able to maintain until now and, consequently, the role of the state would have to be strengthened. Economic growth depends on the capacity for accumulation that the society has; the decisive factor is to determine who controls this process in order to understand the forms that accumulation takes. If it is the crisis of integration that is referred to, we must read between the lines to determine that this means the failure of accumulation by means of private enterprise. To strengthen the state would mean to test its capacity to direct capitalist accumulation under new proposals. It would mean political power, for example, capable of returning to the Balanced Regional Industrial Growth project suddenly abandoned, less ideologically than pragmatically, by foreign capital. But it is not just more equal benefits for participant countries that are needed; the classes that live and produce within them must also benefit more equally. All this depends, however, on the character of the national classes, the type of relations and conflicts that they establish, and the political culture that previous history has passed on.

The processes of economic integration are processes of economic growth. Abandoned to the so-called laws of the market, to the anarchic reign of private interests, the results could not be different from those that are presently observed. In fact, the easy substitution of imports and the first increments in intraregional trade cannot serve as a base for social or economic development; nor can they provide any optimism for the future. Thus, whatever causes are sought to explain the problems of economic integration, they always have a final goal which defines them. The larger problem is not the regional disequilibrium that has undoubtedly been caused, but the social disequilibrium that underlies all this reality. Trade disequilibrium, expressed as both positive and negative returns, hides the brutal consequences of a process that has repeated an already known and much warned about experience in other countries in Latin America.

Paradoxically, the country that has the most important trade returns in its favor, Guatemala, is the one that has the highest unemployment and the most unequal distribution of income; nor is it coincidental that Guatemala is the country with the most anti-union violence. Costa Rica, as is known, maintains net deficits in trade, but the social gap is less, and its political structure is more democratic and tolerant.

At the present crossroads, the crisis of the Common Market can only be resolved on the political level. The decisions that have to be made in order to readjust the process to new realities of economic and social development are profoundly political. No one doubts that at such a crossroads there are many routes to be taken. A strengthening of institutions by means of supra-national decisionmaking was one of them. The treaty framework proposed by SIECA was a well-intentioned project but impossible to carry out. The search for industrial exports to the rest of the world, which Costa Rica now attempts, is another alternative. For that, a highly concentrated and specialized structure would be needed in order to compete internationally, for example, an economy completely oriented towards the producing and selling of underwear internationally. There are also those who give more importance than is merited to the development of agroindustries. Furthermore, some governments are irresponsibly open to the complacency of free zones.

No project that forgets the internal market will be able to function. Back in 1960 this amnesia was perhaps understandable and permissible. Given the degree to which economic growth has advanced, any new strategy of growth should, at least partially, attempt to vitalize internal consumption. We all know that the market is composed of solvent consumers and not citizens. Of eighteen million of the latter, only two million have the option of participating in the market. Under these conditions it is possible to advance, but only very slowly, responding to strictly limited stimuli from the natural growth of demand. The boundaries of the market need to be socially broadened. Until now, the axis of capital accumulation has not been based on broadening the sphere of circulation. It has been limited by the secular tendency to remunerate work at lower than, or very close to a subsistence wage. The politics of low salaries and income regression have until today been a condition for the growth of consumption among the higher strata of society, those that "live off of surplus." It is probable that technical progress augments productivity, but it does not broaden demand because at no time has it been translated into a relative decrease in prices. "Produce small expensive quantities in order to earn more," reveals an impeccable but short-term logic. The longer-term project of the bourgeoisie should be an attempt to increase profits through the increase in the rate of surplus value. The crisis of the common market is obviously not a crisis in realizing capital, but the search for expansion through the internal market could improve profits.

Situated as we are outside bourgeois rationality, we can only think about this possibility on the condition that neither imperialist capital nor the local bourgeois continue commanding the process, or at least that their interests not be the only ones that preside. However, in order for this to succeed, it is necessary that new social forces and new political alliances have a presence in the state and, as a part of the state, finally project economic growth with social development and political democracy.

Masterminding the Mini-Market:
U.S. Aid to the Central American Common Market*
By Susanne Jonas

To the average North American or Latin American taxpayer, the nature and workings of U.S. foreign aid programs remain a mystery, conducted behind closed doors. Although we pay for the show, we seldom see it. We must rely on information handed down from the public relations division of the official aid agencies, which projects a humanitarian image of aid as an example of the United States "helping" the "less developed nations." In our daily lives, both in the U.S. and in Latin America, we experience directly or indirectly the effects of U.S. aid but we seldom if ever get to peep through the keyhole of the closed doors to see the U.S. and "international" aid agencies at work. This article is an attempt to peep through that keyhole.

Specifically, this article tells the story of how U.S. aid helped create— and destroy—the Central American Common Market (CACM). At the most obvious level, this is a story of U.S. aid as a means of manipulating people and governments in Central America to suit the particular needs and whims of U.S. corporate interests, and to keep the region safe for U.S. investors. It reveals the workings of the aid agencies, both directly through

*Excerpted and abridged from *North American Congress on Latin America (Empire Report)* Vol. VII, No. 5 (May-June), 1973, pp. 3-21.

manipulation, and indirectly through their allies in Central America.

But this is also a story of contradictions, a demonstration that the mechanisms of capitalism sometimes do break down almost of their own accord, or as a result of conflicts among dominant groups. It reveals how, in the very process of building an institution, U.S. aid simultaneously set in motion the forces that were to destroy it. In this particular case, the contradictions did not remain implicit, but were actually played out in the late 1960s, through the collapse of CACM.

The implications of this story go far beyond Central America, and apply to hundreds of institutions in underdeveloped countries which have felt the heavy hand of the U.S. and "international" aid agencies exerting U.S. control in exchange for a few hundred million dollars.

The Beginnings of the CACM

Since the sixteenth century, capitalist underdevelopment and foreign domination have been more pronounced in Central America than in any other part of the hemisphere. Even after World War II, this situation had not changed. By the 1950s, the region remained economically dependent on a few agricultural exports such as coffee and bananas, whose prices in the world market fluctuated greatly and constantly. Moreover, Central America had not followed the example of the larger Latin American countries which took advantage of the Depression and World War II, and the consequent decline in U.S. trade and investment, to begin industrializing nationally. But the internal and external pressures to industrialize were mounting.

Internally, the only alternative to total dependence on unstable agricultural exports was "import substitution" (industrialization within the region to produce the goods previously imported). But such industrialization required a larger market in the region—to be achieved either through far-reaching social reforms which would bring millions of new consumers into the market, or through a common market which would combine the small markets of the five countries. There were equally important external pressures: specifically, the post-war need of the industrial corporations based in the advanced capitalist nations to expand and open up new markets for investment. For these corporations too, Central America had to develop a larger market in order to be a worthwhile investment.

Related to these economic pressures was an important political consideration: the desire by U.S. interests and Central American elites to avoid "another Guatemala," i.e., another experience with a progressive, nationalist government, such as that of Jacobo Arbenz (1951-1954), which dared to regulate the operations of U.S. corporations in Guatemala and to institute a serious agrarian reform. The Arbenz experience in Guatemala demonstrated that Central America could not necessarily be taken for granted by the Western capitalist powers. If Arbenz' reforms were unacceptable, some alternative would have to be found.

The first to recognize regional economic integration as a strategy for avoiding a general social and economic crisis in Central America—as an alternative to basic change which required no real challenge to capitalism or to existing power relations in the region—was the U.N. Economic Commission for Latin America (Comisión Económica para América Latina, CEPAL). Working in conjunction with certain groups in Central America during the 1950s CEPAL presented economic integration as a necessary complement to import substitution, particularly for countries with tiny domestic consumer markets.

From the beginning, CEPAL viewed regional integration as a way of modernizing the Central American economies within the capitalist system. Consequently, CEPAL understood that such integration would have to be implemented by the elites already in power within each Central American country. The very emphasis on industrialization was evidence of this strategy, since it was the form of "development" which entailed the least possible challenge to vested interests, and which avoided or at least postponed the social upheaval that would necessarily accompany an agrarian reform.[1] Politically, the strategic decision not to require heavy sacrifices from existing private sector elites amounted to a tacit recognition that CEPAL's influence depended on cooperation from those elites. Thus, during the 1950s, CEPAL worked closely with Central American business leaders.

CEPAL's integration strategy was based on certain principles. First, it stressed "gradual" integration, rather than immediate or total trade liberalization among the Central American countries: integration had to be carried out in such a way as to minimize "disturbances" to the national economies (e.g., "disturbances" resulting from suddenly exposing national producers to new competitors, or losing government revenues from import duties). Second, and closely related, was the principle of "reciprocal industrialization," i.e., the effort to assure all of the Central American nations of an equal opportunity to industrialize. Reciprocity and the desire not to benefit some nations at the expense of others implied a third principle, namely that industrial investment should be based on some form of regional planning.

Assurance about "reciprocal benefits" or "balanced development" were necessary because of the historical imbalances within the region. By the 1950s, according to certain general economic indicators, Honduras and Nicaragua were relatively less developed than their neighbors and growing more slowly. Given the general tendency of capitalism toward uneven development, if abandoned to the "free play of market forces," these regional imbalances would be reinforced. Private (especially foreign) investors, for example, have always favored the areas of relatively greater development— in this case, El Salvador and Guatemala.[2] Thus, to be a corrective influence,

---

[1] See Roger Hansen, *Central America: Regional Integration and Economic Development* (Washington: National Planning Association, 1967), p. 66.

[2] Keith Griffin, *Underdevelopment in Spanish America* (London: Allen & Unwin, 1969), p. 272; see also Vincent Cable, "Problems in the Central American Common Market," *BOLSA Review*, June, 1969, pp. 341ff.

according to CEPAL, integration must be based on regional planning and on mechanisms specifically designed to insure a "fair distribution" of the gains from integration among all member countries.

These principles were reflected in the two integration treaties signed in 1958. The Multilateral Treaty established free trade among the five countries for a limited number of products, and provided for the *gradual* expansion of that list over a period of ten years. The Treaty attempted to minimize the "disturbances" and dislocations in the national economies which could result from a more rapid liberalization of trade.

The companion to this Treaty was the Agreement on Integration Industries, often referred to the the "Régimen" ("System") of Integration Industries (RII). This general Agreement was based on the idea that, for certain major industries, the Central American market could sustain only one plant; in these cases, to avoid duplication and encourage efficiency, exclusive free trade privileges would be granted to one plant. In order to assure regional "balance," the location of that plant would be determined by an inter-governmental regulation.[3]

Shortly after the two Treaties were signed, CEPAL's role in Central American integration was reduced—primarily because of sudden display of interest by another party, the government of the United States.

The U.S. Steps In

Throughout the 1950s, the U.S. watched the movement for Central American integration from the sidelines. But the signing of the CEPAL-inspired Treaties in 1958 made clear that the Central Americans were moving ahead with their plans for economic integration and awakened U.S. interest. U.S. officials realized that if they allowed the movement to continue in the same direction, it could produce "undesireable" results; but that if the U.S. redirected it, Central American integration could be perfectly consistent with, and could be used to further, U.S. objectives and interests. What were those objectives?[4]

First, the U.S. was interested in opening up Central America for trade and investment by U.S. corporations. A Central American free trade area, placing no restrictions on investment and offering proper investment incentives, would create a larger market and new opportunities for U.S. corporations, whose interests the U.S. government was committed to protect.

A second U.S. objective was stabilization of the potentially explosive situation in Central America and defense against the "internal Communist

---

[3] Carlos Manuel Castillo, *Growth and Integration in Central America* (New York: Praeger, 1966), pp. 81-3, 144.

[4] This account of U.S. objectives is taken from James Cochrane, *The Politics of Regional Integration: The Central American Case* (New Orleans: Tulane University, 1969), pp. 208ff.; and Cochrane, "U.S. Attitudes toward Central American Economic Integration,"*Inter-American Economic Affairs*, Autumn, 1964, pp. 76ff., based on U.S. Department of State documents; U.S. Senate, Joint Economic Committee, Subcommittee on Inter-American Economic Relationships, *Latin American Development and Western Hemisphere Trade* (Sept. 8-10, 1965) (Washington: GPO, 1965); also interviews and general reading.

threat." One approach was to strengthen the private sector and promote certain necessary, though minor, reforms in order to reduce class conflict and reinforce Central American capitalism. Anti-Communism and a preoccupation with stability had been crucial elements of U.S. policy during the 1950s, culminating in the U.S.-sponsored ouster of Arbenz in 1954. Throughout the 1950s and 1960s, plans for Central American integration were linked with unifying the defense establishments of the five countries.[5] The U.S. was particularly interested in preventing a "security threat" in Central America, because of the region's strategic location as the gateway to the Panama Canal. After the Cuban Revolution in 1958-1959, the U.S. became obsessed with preventing similar revolutions in other countries. Washington was especially concerned about certain social conditions (such as the serious "overpopulation" problem in El Salvador) which might make Central America more susceptible to Communist influence. Hence, the U.S. in the Alliance for Progress era came to support any movement—such as economic integration—which might strengthen the economies and defuse the social pressures in Central America.[6]

Finally, an important reason for its interest at this particular time was the U.S. desire to counter CEPAL's influence in Central America. CEPAL had always been *persona non grata* in official Washington circles. The U.S. had opposed even the creation of CEPAL in 1947; once CEPAL's existence was an accomplished fact, the U.S. remained basically hostile, attempted to squelch all CEPAL-inspired proposals in the inter-American meetings, and regarded CEPAL as a rival and a nuisance because it raised embarrassing questions about U.S.-Latin American relations.[7]

Beyond the competition for power and influence lay a profound philosophical/political dispute between the U.S. and CEPAL. U.S. officials, who espoused free enterprise and free trade as absolute principles, regarded CEPAL's tenet that investment decisions should be based on planning as overly "statist," tending toward "socialism," hence dangerous. The U.S. opposed even the mildest forms of government planning until the "new look" of the Alliance for Progress brought a change of rhetoric in the early 1960s. Even then, the change did not go much beneath the rhetorical surface. U.S. policy also reflected an aversion to the economic nationalism and protectionism inherent within CEPAL's formula for import-substitution, insofar as these violated orthodox notions of free trade.

---

[5] "Integrating the Big Guns," *NACLA* Vol. VII, No. 5, 1973.

[6] Isaac Cohen, *Regional Integration in Central America* (Lexington, Mass: Heath, 1972), pp. 35-6, 40; Robert Denham, "The Role of the U.S. as an External Actor in the Integration of Latin America," *Journal of Common Market Studies*, March, 1969, p. 200; *Hispanic American Report (HAR)* (Stanford, Calif.), March, 1963, pp. 236-6.

[7] Cohen, *op. cit.*, pp. 28-9; Cochrane, *The Politics* . . ., p. 212; Robert Gregg, "The U.N. Regional Economic Commissions and Integration in the Underdeveloped Regions," in Joseph Nye (ed.), *International Regionalism* (Boston: Little Brown, 1968), p. 313; Miguel Wionczek, "Latin American Integration and U.S. Economic Policies," in Robert Gregg (ed.), *International Organization in the Western Hemisphere* (Syracuse, NY: Syracuse University Press, 1968), pp. 94-5.

A New Direction for the CACM

Thus, by the late 1950s, the U.S. recognized that it would have to take an active role in Central American integration in order to prevent it from moving in "undesireable" directions (i.e., too much government planning, too many restrictions on U.S. investment). The first public signs of a more active interest came with the 1958 state visit to the U.S. of El Salvador's President José Maria Lemus. According to one account, Lemus came to Washington seeking U.S. assistance to push ahead with the integration program. The Salvadorean delegation received special attention from Thomas Mann, ex-Ambassador to El Salvador, and by 1959, Assistant Secretary of State for Inter-American Affairs. Hearing that the integration movement was at an impasse and needed support, Mann is said to have proposed a real "Common Market," immediately reducing trade barriers on almost all commodities. The meeting resulted in a joint Lemus-Eisenhower communiqué calling for the "establishment of *an economically sound system* for the integration of the economies of the Central American Republics...."[8]

Shortly thereafter, in March, 1959, the Eisenhower Administration sent two State Department experts, Isaiah Frank and Harry Turkel, on a fact-finding mission to Central America, "to consider prospects for helping the movement advance."[9] It soon became clear that their mandate went beyond fact-finding. In their private conversations with Central American Ministers, Frank and Turkel spelled out the principles underlying the U.S. position—all of which added up to a clear modification of the integration process laid out in the 1958 Treaties and the adoption of a new approach. The U.S. wanted a specific commitment through a treaty to achieve a common market within a very short time (three years); this treaty would establish low external tariffs and complete freedom of movement of goods, capital, and people within the common market, and provision would be made for two funds to finance the integration projects. Clearly, the State Department knew what it wanted. In addition, Frank and Turkel had a concrete incentive for the Central Americans: an offer of $100 million in U.S. assistance funds.[10]

Lured by the $100 million bait, the governments of El Salvador, Honduras, and Guatemala began a series of discussions. In February, 1960,

---

[8] Cited in Cohen *op. cit.*, p. 31 (my emphasis); for an account of these initial steps, see also U.S. Agency for International Development (AID), Regional office for Central America and Panama (ROCAP), "A Report on Central America's Common Market and Its Economic Integration Movement," reprinted in U.S. House of Representatives, Committee on Foreign Affairs, Subcommittee on Inter-American Affairs, *Central America: Some Observations on Its Common Market, Binational Centers, and Housing Programs*, Report of Rep. Roy McVicker, Aug 4, 1966 (Washington: General Printing Office (GPO), 1966); and Phillippe Schmitter, *Autonomy or Dependence as Regional Integration Outcomes: Central America* (Berkeley: University of California, Berkeley, Institute of International Studies, 1972).

[9] ROCAP, *op. cit.*, p. 24.

[10] J. Abraham Bennaton, *El Mercado Común Centroamericano: Su Evolución y Perspectivas* (thesis) (Tegucigalpa: Universidad Nacional Autónoma de Honduras, 1964), p. 101; and interviews.

the three signed the Tripartite Agreement of Economic Association, establishing both the basis for immediate free trade for almost all commodities originating in member nations, and in principle, the free movement of capital and people. The entire process was engineered independently of CEPAL—even "in defiance of it."[11] In addition, the Tripartite Agreement violated the CEPAL-influenced 1958 Treaties by excluding the Agreement on Integration Industries.

CEPAL's exclusion left the way clear for a decisive role by the U.S. The promise of U.S. financial support was a "vital condition" enabling the three nations to move ahead, and determining the new direction of integration (allowing greater freedom for "market forces").[12]

Industrialists in Honduras later charged that "the accelerated pace of economic integration ... was forced upon Central America by U.S. pressure," and that the first copy of the initial declaration among the three countries "was printed in English and had to be translated into Spanish."[13]

From the Tripartite Agreement, it was only a small step to the General Treaty of Economic Integration, signed in December, 1960. This time, Nicaragua was included, and the door was left open to Costa Rica (which finally joined in 1963). Although including CEPAL in the negotiations, the General Treaty followed closely the approach of the Tripartite Agreement, with one major exception: it formally reincorporated the Agreement in Integration Industries.

What did the U.S. hope to achieve through this power play, and how did it force an alteration of the Central American integration process? To summarize briefly: the CEPAL-inspired Treaties of 1958 implied gradual integration, minimizing the "disturbances" to the national economies caused by integration, and, above all, stressed balanced growth among the countries through regional planning and coordination. The U.S.-inspired Treaties of 1960, on the other hand, eliminated the mechanisms for regional planning, and subordinated balanced growth to immediate and unrestricted free trade.

Thus, the treaties of 1960 did not represent, as is generally claimed, an "acceleration" of the integration process; rather, they signified an abrupt shift in its direction. The price of U.S. support for Central American integration was acceptance of that shift in orientation, and exclusion of CEPAL as a primary actor. By promising $100 million, though without spending a cent (yet), the U.S. managed to step in, once the groundwork for Central American integration had been laid, and to impose its own conditions.

---

[11] Cochrane, *The Politics* ..., p. 82.

[12] Cohen, *op. cit.* pp. 33, 84; Nye, "Central American Regional Integration," *International Conciliation*, No. 562, March, 1967, pp. 53-4; Sidney Dell, *A Latin American Common Market?* (London: Oxford University Press, 1966), p. 55.

[13] Meldon Levine, "The Private Sector and the Common Market" (mimeo.) (Princeton: Woodrow Wilson School, Princeton University, 1965), p. 10.

U.S. Penetration of Central American Integration Institutions

Once having got its foot in the door of Central American integration, the U.S. sought to institutionalize its influence in two ways. First, especially during the formative years of the CACM from 1960 to 1963, the U.S. exerted direct control over the CACM by penetrating the principal CACM institutions and by intervening decisively and strategically in the controversy over integration industries. Second, the U.S. employed a subtler long-range strategy of encouraging dependent industrialization (which allowed maximum freedom for U.S. corporations) in Central America and of building a coalition with the most privileged sectors of the local bourgeoisie, who would then act to promote U.S. interests. In short, the U.S. established certain power relations within Central America which would make overt U.S. intervention unnecessary.

In order to exert direct control over the daily operations of the CACM institutions, the U.S. needed an institutional liaison. Thus, a 1961 Task Force Report of the U.S. Agency for International Development (AID) recommended that a new AID office be set up in Central America, with the following functions: to regionalize AID efforts; to coordinate U.S. policies and programs for Central American integration agencies; to channel U.S. technical and financial assistance; to "improve private investment" in Central America; and to make sure that integration did not take a direction detrimental to U.S. interests. By setting up shop in Central America, U.S. officials hoped, moreover, to weaken forever the influence of CEPAL's Mexico office.[14] This Regional Office of AID for Central America and Panama (ROCAP) was established in Guatemala in July, 1962.

The Battle of the Integration Industries

There is no clearer example of decisive U.S. intervention and the direct imposition of U.S. authority in shaping the CACM than the controversy, at times battle, over integration industries.[15] The integration industries scheme (RII) was a CEPAL-inspired mechanism to insure balanced industrialization in Central America. It provided that a plant in certain industries which required access to the entire regional market in order to operate "economically" would be designated an "integration industry" and would enjoy several economic benefits and protections for ten years—the primary benefit being that the products of the designated plant would enjoy free access to the entire market while competing goods would remain

---

[14] ROCAP, op. cit. p. 37; also Cochrane, "U.S. Attitudes . . .," p. 89; Cohen, op. cit. p. 37; and interview with ROCAP functionary.

[15] Most written accounts and U.S. officials (in interview) have distorted the story of this controversy in several ways. First, they minimize the role of the U.S. by acknowledging it as one factor among many which resulted in the failure of the RII as a developmental mechanism. Second, they attribute to the U.S. the mild and seemingly reasonable position of "opposing" integration industries, of discouraging participation of U.S. firms, and of withholding U.S. funds from the program. This description obscures the full extent of U.S. opposition and the lengths to which U.S. officials went to thwart the RII.

subject to national tariffs. A major objective of the scheme was to stimulate the establishment of large-scale, basic industries.

Another objective was to discourage duplication within certain industries. Since each integration industry was to have a major impact on the economy of the host nation, the scheme could be used to prevent further concentration of industry in El Salvador and Guatemala. Specifically, the RII provided that each nation must receive one integration industry before any nation could receive a second one. A final, less overt, objective of the RII was to regulate the extent of foreign capital in these major industries by stipulating a minimum percentage of local capital for each integration industry.

U.S. opposition to the integration industries scheme crystallized early: according to one high ex-CEPAL official, the Guatemalan government came to Tegucigalpa in June, 1958, under pressure from the U.S. not to sign the RII. The Tripartite Treaty of February, 1960, deliberately left out the RII and was incompatible with it. On paper, the General Treaty included the RII, despite U.S. pressure against it. But by granting immediate free trade to nearly all products originating in the region, the General Treaty effectively eliminated any special benefits to integration industries, hence any incentive for using the scheme. Thus, in the very process of incorporating the RII, the General Treaty "virtually nullified" its impact, in the words of a State Department analyst.[16]

Having managed to weaken but not totally destroy the RII through the 1960 Treaties, the U.S. continued its campaign by other means. In order to begin implementing the RII and to elaborate specific projects, the Central American governments called a meeting in Managua for December, 1961. At this meeting, CEPAL officials presented a series of projects, and each of the four delegations present selected one integration industry. U.S. officials were enraged by this meeting, referring to it privately as the "crime of Managua," and deploring the subservience of Central American officials to CEPAL. This December, 1961, meeting prompted an overt power play by the U.S. (as recounted by a high Central American official, who claims to have heard it directly from U.S. representative, Arthur Marget, and as confirmed by others): Marget drafted a communiqué, which the State Department issued to the Central American Embassies in Washington threatening a weakening of overall U.S. aid to the region if the integration industries scheme was pursued any further.[17] A February, 1962, memo from the U.S. Task Force on Central American Integration stated,

> *We therefore welcome wholeheartedly the joint AID/State Instruction sent to the Central American Embassies on integrated industries as a step indispensable in the interest of keeping the industrial development*

---

[16] Joseph Pincus, "Historical Background and Objectives of the CACM," presented to AID Mission Directors, July 6, 1962 (mimeo.) (Tegucigalpa: 1962), p. 18; also Cochrane, "U.S. Attitudes . . .," p. 82.

[17] Marget, a former high functionary of the U.S. Federal Reserve Bank, was a key figure in BCIE's formative months, holding the double title of Regional Representative of AID (before ROCAP existed) and Financial Adviser of BCIE.

of Central America pointed in the right direction; and we recommend strongly that the influence of our government continue to be thrown in that direction in the handling of whatever further consequences may be found to follow from the Managua meeting.[18]

At the March, 1962, Extraordinary Meeting of the Central American Bank for Economic Integration (BCIE) Governors, U.S. representative Marget restated the U.S. position that, in implementing the RII, the meeting in Managua represented a "step backward" from the 1960 Treaty, and that this "retroceso" was becoming an obstacle to U.S. private investment in Central America. Moreover, Marget:

saw a favorable tendency in the U.S. to support Central American integration, but there would also be an interruption of the part of the U.S. government until the Central American governments decided what policy to follow. The total effect of the meeting of Managua has been to delay support which the U.S. could give to integration.[19]

After making this open threat, Marget questioned the validity of Article 17 of the General Treaty (which formally incorporated the RII). The important thing, he concluded, was that they were all in agreement that no definite decisions had been made at the Managua meeting and that discussions were only beginning. In fact, this was not true, since the Central Americans had actually approved several protocols at the meeting; Marget was attempting to force a reversal of these actions.

The effect of this threat was not immediately clear, and when the Central American Ministers of Economy met in January, 1963, to definitively approve and sign the first Protocol implementing the RII (granting the status of two plants), they did not know what to expect from the U.S. Although U.S. officials continued to voice a hard line, at this point it finally became evident that the U.S. would not go so far as to suspend all U.S. aid to Central American integration institutions over the RII issue. But the threat of suspending aid remained clear to Central Americans. Even in October, 1963,

Central American economists feared that the unfavorable reaction reported in the U.S. Congress and press to their [integration] industries ... indicated a curtailment of Alliance for Progress funds in the area.... The Salvadorean daily, El Diario de Hoy, editorialized that U.S. press opinion unfavorable to this economic policy might influence U.S. government agencies to withhold development funds. Apparently the old fear persisted that business interests dictate U.S. foreign policy.[20]

The first and most crisis-ridden stage of the integration industries battle more or less ended with the adoption of the Protocol in January, 1963.

---

[18] U.S. AID, "Summary Report of the Task Force on Central American Integration," in Marget et al., *op. cit., p. 21* (author's emphasis).

[19] BCIE, *Informe de la Primera Reunión Extraodinaria de la Assembleas de Gobernadores*, March 12-13, 1962 (Tegucigalpa: BCIE, 1962).

[20] HAR, Oct., 1963, p. 948.

But even this Protocol implementing the RII contained provisions which further emasculated it.[21] Moreover, the U.S. also continued its campaign against the RII through financial leverage. The U.S. strategy was to cut off all available sources of funding, and thus to undermine the integration industries, which were by definition such large undertakings as to require outside funding. First, the U.S. has consistently refused to allow U.S. AID funds channeled through BCIE to be used for sub-loans to integration industries. Second, the U.S. prevented other international lending agencies from lending directly or indirectly to integration industries. Third, the U.S. pressured BCIE not to finance integration industries, even out of non-U.S. funds.

In the Interest of U.S. Business

Why did the U.S. go to such lengths to thwart the integration industries scheme? The real reasons are difficult to detect, because they are hidden behind a facade of official justifications and rationalizations.[22] The real concern focused on the effects of the scheme on U.S. investors in Central America. In the words of the State Department:

Many private investors ... have hesitated to invest in Central America because they fear possible discrimination under the Regime. No investor can ever be sure that designation of an industry related to his ... will not seriously affect his own business.... The effect of [these problems] on potential investment from abroad is ... serious.[23]

---

[21] Most important, as the price for implementing the RII (which El Salvador had always opposed), El Salvador proposed a "Special System" which was to serve as a substitute for the RII. It would provide special protection for certain industries, but without setting up legal monopolies and without subjecting the plants covered to "rigid" controls. The U.S. also regarded it as a "workable substitute" for the RII. (See Bennaton, *op. cit.*, p. 151; Andrew Wardlaw, *Achievements and Problems of the Central American Common Market* (Washington: Dept. of State, Office of External Research, 1969), p. 33; numerous other sources, including several SIECA studies, have demonstrated that the Special System is not really a "workable substitute" for the RII, in terms of the latter's initial objectives.) This was an early example of how the U.S. was to articulate its interests through its Central American allies.

[22] The explanation most commonly given by U.S. officials focuses on the monopolistic nature of the integration industries, and insists that U.S. funds could not be used to promote a scheme which violated U.S. anti-trust laws. Whatever the legalities of the U.S. position, however, it seems quite plausible that the U.S. really objected more to the consumer protection regulations of the RII than to the existence of a monopoly *per se*. Second, apologists for the U.S. position maintain that the RII was badly designed, full of ambiguity and hence susceptible to political favoritism. See, for example, documents cited in Cochrane, "U.S. Attitudes ...," p. 83, and in Cochrane, *The Politics* ..., pp. 210-211; also Rep. Martha Griffiths, *Economic Policies and Programs in Middle America*, Report for the U.S. Senate, Joint Economic Committee, Subcommittee on Inter-American Economic Relationships (Washington: GPO, 1963), p. 26; for an evaluation, see Dell, *op. cit.*, p. 68, and Dell, *Trade Blocs and Common Markets* (New York: Knopf, 1963), pp. 278-9. Despite the grain of truth in these "technical" arguments, the principal motivations for U.S. policy were not technical, but ideological and political, and responsive to U.S. business interests in Central America.

[23] AID document cited in Cochrane, *The Politics* ... p 210.

Initially, the U.S. was concerned that the RII would be used to exclude, or at least regulate, foreign (U.S.) investment. The 1958 Agreement did provide that a certain proportion of the capital of each integration industry must be of Central American origin. In one of his famous outbursts in a March 1962 meeting, Arthur Marget implied that U.S. corporations were holding back their investment in Central America because of the RII— because the privileges given to integration industries "exclude the possibility of competition by other U.S. firms, and this naturally is not well received in the U.S."[24] The irony of this position is that, of the two existing integration industries, GINSA in Guatemala is now a subsidiary of Goodyear—in direct violation of the 1963 Protocol granting GINSA integration industry status; and the Pennsalt/Hercules complex in Nicaragua is owned by two U.S. firms.

Once it became clear that the RII would not necessarily be used to exclude U.S. corporations, a second problem arose: if a U.S. subsidiary was designated an integration industry, a competing U.S. firm would doubtless exert great pressure on the State Department not to permit such favors to one corporation. Such a situation actually did arise in the mid-1960s, in the dispute between GINSA in Guatemala (which at the time had technical assistance from and minority stock ownership by General Tire) and Firestone in Costa Rica, putting the U.S. in the awkward position of having to balance the pressures from two U.S corporations. A third concern about the RII was that private U.S. investors would never embrace a scheme so full of regulations on price, quality, supply, and especially on the proportion of local capital.[25] In fact, representatives of U.S. business expressed grave concerns about the RII,[26] which influenced and were reflected in the official U.S. position.

Aside from the concrete problems the RII posed for private U.S. investors, the U.S. government opposed the scheme on broader philosophical grounds: any mechanism which limited a corporation's right or opportunities to invest or its freedom of choice on location, or which restricted free trade, represented an undue and unnecessary interference with the "free play of market forces."

This is not to say that the RII could have resolved Central America's problems of underdevelopment. For one thing, the scheme was designed only to preserve a balance among the underdeveloped countries of the region, not to improve living conditions for the lower classes or to alter the relations of power within each country. Second, there were technical

[24] BCIE, *Informe de la Primera Reunión Extraordinaria* . . . .

[25] Ramsett, *op. cit.*, pp. 68ff.; Marc Herold, *Industrial Development in the Central American Common Market* (manuscript) (Berkeley: Univ. of Calif., Grad. School of Business Administration, 1970), pp. 151ff.; J. Alan Brewster, "The Central American Program for Integrated Industrial Development," *Public and International Affairs*, Spring, 1966, pp. 26-9.———

[26] See, for example, statement by Emilio Collado, Vice President and Director, Standard Oil of New Jersey, in U.S. Senate, Joint Economic Committee, *Latin American Development and . . . Trade*, p. 33-4; also Cochrane, "U.S. Attitudes . . .," p. 85; Wionczek, "Latin American Integration . . .," p. 127.

deficiencies with the scheme, which have been pointed out by "development-alist" critics as well as by apologists for U.S. policy. But these problems were not due to the basic premise of industrial planning (as U.S. officials charged), but to imperfections in its application; and these problems were compounded by the fierce U.S. campaign against the RII. Third, there was no agreement about the scheme within Central America; particularly those sectors which opposed governmental or inter-governmental planning and which stood to gain from unbalanced development (e.g., the government and the private sector of El Salvador) opposed the RII. But this was part of the alliance being built up by the U.S. with Central Americans whose interests coincided with U.S. interests in the region. Thus, the fact remains that U.S. policy created a contest in which the RII could not be used toward its original objectives of planned industrialization and balanced development within the capitalist framework.

U.S. Strategy for Dependent Industrialization

By winning on the RII issue, the U.S. achieved a strategic victory over CEPAL and the CEPAL approach of planned industrialization. Equally important, by 1963, the U.S. had helped establish the dominance of those groups within Central America whose interests coincided with those of the U.S. on most issues—specifically, the business community and those governments (El Salvador and Guatemala) representing the most privileged business groups. In short, having strengthened the position of its allies the U.S. could subsequently achieve its policy aims without resorting to the overt manipulation characteristic of the early years; henceforth the U.S. employed a subtler long range strategy of allowing the process of dependent industrialization set in motion in 1963 to play itself out.

In its steadfast opposition to the integration industries scheme, the U.S. nonetheless insisted that it was committed to "balanced development," to be achieved through different mechanisms. But the measures advocated by the U.S. have proven grossly inadequate. Rather than avoiding intra-CACM imbalances, the U.S. strategy amounted to letting them grow, then correcting them through a special fund (which became the BCIE), through which the U.S. would channel its aid and which would give preferential treatment to the less developed nations. To the U.S., then, balance was desirable—so long as it could be achieved without upsetting the free play of market forces and the freedom of firms to choose their investment location. In short, balanced development was a *secondary* objective. Most observers conclude that the U.S. approach has not worked in practice.[27]

The CACM in (Permanent) Crisis

Although it was only one manifestation of Central American under-

---

[27] For example, Castillo, *op. cit.*, p. 143; Herold, *op. cit.*, p. 59; Hansen, *op. cit.* pp. 60-61; Dell, *A Latin American Common Market?*, p. 66; Stuart Fagan, *Central American Economic Integration: The Politics of Unequal Benefits* (Berkeley: University of California Institute of International Studies, 1970), p. 8.

development, the issue of regional imbalance became the main impetus propelling the CACM toward its dissolution. Without assurances about equal distribution of the benefits of integration, it would be difficult to convince the relatively less developed nations, Honduras and Nicaragua, that the CACM was worth the sacrifices it entailed.

Since 1964, Honduras had expressed dissatisfaction with the CACM on the grounds that it was less developed than its neighbors and that, since entering the CACM, the nation's economic position had further declined:

> Its regional trade balance had become unfavorable, its regional terms of trade were deteriorating, its consumer prices were rising, and the number of its unemployed artisans was growing as a result of industrial competition from the other Common Market members. Finally ... Honduras was suffering from diminished fiscal revenues as a result of the exportation by the more developed members of the CACM of their pseudo-Central American products to Honduras exempt from tariffs; Honduras was in effect subsidizing the industrial development of the other Central American States....[28]

In order to correct these imbalances, Honduras needed preferential treatment and special privileges. In a 1966 meeting of the CACM Economic Council, Honduras secured passage of a few measures granting preferential treatment.

Meanwhile, pressures were building up from other directions. By the mid-1960s, all of the Central American countries were feeling the effects of a generalized balance of payments crisis, rooted primarily in the worsening position of the region's exports to the world market. To make matters worse, the governments could no longer meet balance of payments problems by limiting non-essential imports because an increasing percent of these items were being imported from the rest of Central America and were therefore not subject to these restrictions. These difficulties were compounded by the unregulated proliferation of assembly industries which generated large, inflexible import requirements. As a result, the region's balance of payments deficit with the rest of the world more than doubled between 1963 and 1968.[29]

By early 1967, the balance of payments situation became critical, especially in Costa Rica and Nicaragua. The crisis stimulated regional discussions during 1967 and 1968, which resulted in the adoption of the San José Protocol. This Protocol would impose an economic stabilization tax in the form of a 30 percent duty surcharge on all imports from third world countries and a recommended sales tax on luxury goods. The business communities voiced strong opposition to it, with the result that only Nicaragua ratified it immediately. Throughout 1968 and early 1969, the Nicaraguan government attempted to force its partners to ratify it by imposing taxes

---

[28] Fagan, op. cit. p. 24.

[29] See, Business Latin America (BLA), July 4, 1968, p. 209; CEPAL, The Central American Common Market and Its Recent Problems (Santiago: CEPAL, 1971) (E/CN.12 /855), pp. 10ff.; Cable, op. cit., pp. 336-9; Fagan, op. cit., p. 19.

on imports from the other countries; the others retaliated with measures against Nicaraguan products.[30] Finally, in the spring of 1969 both sides backed down and the five Ministers of Economy agreed to begin discussions to reform the CACM and to prevent similar crises in the future. But the underlying problems were left unresolved.

Soccer and Underdevelopment

If any doubts remained as to the serious problems in the CACM, they were dispelled by the sequence of events beginning in June, 1969. The triggering event was a series of soccer games between Honduras and El Salvador which led to riots in Honduras and the expulsion of 11,000 of the 300,000 Salvadoreans living in Honduras. In the following weeks, diplomatic relations were broken off, both governments geared up their armed forces, and the tension level rose. Salvadorean troops invaded Honduras on July 14, and only withdrew by the end of July in the face of heavy pressure from the Organization of American States (OAS), which was attempting to mediate the conflict. Aside from the 1-2,000 casualties and 100,000 refugees, the war caused a total disruption of CACM trade, particularly since Honduras closed its portion of the Pan American Highway to Salvadorean goods. Border incidents continued sporadically throughout 1970 and 1971; trade and diplomatic relations had not been totally normalized even by the end of 1972.

Underlying the war were the same factors that had caused earlier CACM crises. The ruling class in each country had attempted to use the integration movement as a way of dealing with basic problems without making the necessary social reforms. The clearest example was the Salvadorean "population problem." With a population growth rate of 3.8 percent a year, El Salvador has 3.3 million persons squeezed into 8,000 square miles. El Salvador's population density in 1969 was over 380 persons per square mile, as compared with 57 persons per square mile in Honduras. Rather than undertaking an agrarian reform to provide the people with land and jobs, the Salvadorean ruling class (particularly the 1 percent of the population that owns 40 percent of the nation's arable land) has insisted that El Salvador needs an escape valve, an outlet for the large mass of landless rural and urban unemployed, i.e., through migration to neighboring countries, especially Honduras.[31] And when this escape valve was closed off—that is, when Honduras refused to permit its land to be used as Salvadorean *lebensraum* and threatened to expel Salvadorean migrants—the Salvadorean ruling class resorted to war to preserve this outlet.

In response to similar social tensions, in order to relieve pressure for land, the Honduran ruling class, in turn, evicted the Salvadorean migrants. In a sense, then, the war was the result of class-based cross pressures—both from dominant business groups and from the landless, unemployed

[30] Fagan, *op. cit.*, pp. 37-52; Schmitter, "Central American Integration: Spill-over, Spill-around, or Encapsulation?," *Journal Common Market Studies*, Sept. 1970, pp. 26-7.

[31] These statistics are taken from: *Christian Science Monitor* July 24, 1969; *BLA*, July 17, 1969; *New York Times*, July 22, 1969.

masses—within each country. It was an excuse for each ruling class to fortify itself militarily, to consolidate its power against political opposition, and to stave off profound class conflict.[32]

But in addition to the class conflicts, the war was also caused by imbalances within the CACM. As the Honduran Minister of Economy stated in 1969, integration had brought Honduras fewer benefits and greater sacrifices than the other partners. Certainly the facts substantiated this assertion.[33] The serious disparities revealed that Honduras had been adversely affected by the very policies—promoted by the U.S.—which benefited the private sector in El Salvador and Guatemala. In addition, Honduras was subsidizing industrial development in these countries, at great cost to all sectors in Honduras (i.e., higher prices and lower quality for Honduran consumers, negative trade balances, loss of government revenues, and industrial unemployment).[34] Worst of all, Honduras charged, the industries being subsidized were not really regional insofar as a high proportion were assembly industries (usually U.S.-owned) using Guatemala, El Salvador, or Costa Rica as a base for putting together components imported duty-free from abroad.

Banana Republic Splits

In the aftermath of the war, Honduras used this opportunity to insist on a general restructuring of the CACM. At their December 1969 meeting, the five Foreign Ministers established a commission to study the total reorganization of the CACM and a forum for the Ministers of Economy to discuss a *modus operandi*—a temporary basis for holding the CACM together until a more permanent restructuring could be agreed on. The modus operandi discussions began seriously, after a six-month delay, in July, 1970, and continued until December, 1970, amid increasing pressures and hopes for a successful outcome.

The negotiations broke down abruptly in December, 1970, just as they were apparently closest to reaching a successful conclusion; the government of El Salvador, under intense pressure from the Salvadorean private sector,

---

[32] See Marco Virgilio Carías, "Análisis sobre el conflicto Honduras-El Salvador," in Marco Virgilio Carías and Daniel Slutzky (eds.), *La Guerra Inutil* (San Jose, CR: EDUCA, 1971), esp. pp. 13-14; Roque Dalton, "Notas sobre el Sistema Imperialista de Dominación y Explotación en Centroamérica," OCLAE (Cuba) No. 66, June 1972, pp. 16-19.

[33] In terms of both new industrial investment and trade creation, the overwhelming bulk of the gains had gone to El Salvador and Guatemala, and Honduras' disadvantage was getting worse. By 1968, Guatemala contributed 34.2 percent of regional value added in manufacturing and El Salvador 23.8 percent as compared with Honduras' 7.7 percent. By 1968, Honduras and Nicaragua were accumulating substantial trade deficits with their CACM partners. In the first half of 1969, Honduras suffered a trade deficit of nearly $5 million with El Salvador alone, and its imports from El Salvador amounted to 168 percent of its exports there. These facts come from: Carías, *op. cit.*, p. 54; World Bank, *op. cit.*, Tables 8,17; SIECA, *El desarrollo integrado de centroamérica en la presente decada* (Guatemala: SIECA, 1972) (SIECA/72-VII-6/36), p. 33, Tables 5,13; *El Gráfico* (Guatemala), Feb. 20, 1970.

[34] Acosta speech, reprinted in Carías, *op. cit.*, p. 113; SIECA, *El Desarrollo Integrado . . .*, p. 31; Hansen, *op. cit.*, p. 83.

refused to sign, claiming the agreements would give away too much to Honduras. In response, during the next couple of weeks, Honduras repeatedly threatened to pull out of CACM, but few believed it could afford to do so. But on December 31, 1970, Honduras issued Decree 97. This decree abrogated all regional agreements on trade and taxation, by reimposing duties on merchandise imported from other Central American countries, with exceptions for "essential" or "basic" items. This measure, which Honduras justified as a way of correcting its severe economic problems caused by the CACM, amounted to a withdrawal from the CACM.

The Modus Operandi

Because the modus operandi (m.o.) negotiations touched on all the exposed nerves of the ten-year-old integration process in Central America, it is worth mentioning briefly a few of the main substantive issues and the dynamics of the negotiations. Among the most important issues were the following:[35]

- *San José Protocol*: Final implementation of the Protocol (see above) had to be negotiated, specifically the stipulation of which industries would be exempt from the 30 percent import duty surcharge.

- *Origin of Products*: In response to complaints by the less industrialized countries, especially Honduras, that they were being forced to subsidize industrialization in Guatemala and El Salvador and that this industrialization was not even legitimately "Central American," the five governments drew up an agreement to help determine the origin of goods "produced in Central America," and hence to enjoy full free trade privileges, a product would have to contribute a certain minimum "regional value incorporated" or comply with certain standards of "minimum processing" in Central America.

- *Regional Industrial Policy*: In a quasi-revival of the integration industries scheme, this industrial policy would promote certain basic industries and would simultaneously further balanced development, by permitting only one plant in these industries and having the CACM Economic Council determine its location (giving preference to Honduras). The least acceptable aspect of this proposal to the region's industrialists was that it would curtail the freedom of private investors and allow the inter-governmental Economic Council to make decisions without consulting the private sector.

- *Fund for Agricultural and Industrial Development*: As a final gesture toward correcting imbalances within the CACM, the governments resolved to create a new Fund, which would provide loans on easy terms, giving preference to enterprises in the relatively less developed countries.

---

[35] The longer version of this article contains an extensive analysis of the m.o. Sources for this section include: ROCAP memos, Sept. 11, 1970, and Dec. 11, 1970, on m.o.; all the SIECA *Actas* (minutes) of the meetings of the Ministers of Economy during the second half of 1970, and the working papers prepared for those meetings.

Contributions to the Fund would also be proportional, with the countries enjoying the greatest benefits from the CACM paying a larger share. The need for this Fund, with its objective of promoting balanced development, evidenced the failure of BCIE, whose Charter had stated the same objective ten years earlier, and which had, in fact, allocated a higher proportion of its funds to Honduras and Nicaragua.

What was the significance of the modus operandi? First, it revealed the problems inherent within Central American "development" during the 1960s—the problems of unequal benefits for some countries, of subsidies to private (mainly foreign) investors at high cost to consumers and state treasuries, of imported technology and raw materials, of industrialization based on the merging of five tiny upper- and middle-class markets. The very need for a serious restructuring such as was discussed during the m.o. was proof of the failures of the past.

Second, even if it had been signed, the m.o. would not have resolved the fundamental conflicts between a tiny ruling class and the great majority of Central Americans, whose interests had never been considered at all. On every issue, important concessions were made to privileged business interests which had benefited from integration during the 1960s and wanted to preserve the *status quo*. Moreover, the m.o. really represented a series of stopgap measures, of non-structural responses to structural problems. In regard to the serious budget problems plaguing all the governments, for example, the San José Protocol was an emergency measure, a substitute for, rather than a stimulus to, direct taxation and serious tax reform.[36]

Nevertheless, although the measures under discussion were vastly inadequate to the basic problems, the m.o. did represent a clear acknowledgement of those problems—perhaps the first large-scale honest appraisal of the the costs of Central American integration. The very fact that the m.o. negotiations broke down in the end was a kind of back-handed tribute to those limited advances, an indication that someone's interests were being threatened. The negotiations broke down because a coalition of powerful interests that had benefited from Central American integration during the first ten years insisted on preserving those privileges and refused to allow even the mildest reforms.

The Hard Liners Carry the Day

Specifically which interests were responsible for torpedoing the negotiations? First and most obvious, the breakdown of the m.o. resulted from the determination of the Salvadorean private sector and the government it controlled not to make any concessions to Honduras, such as would have been implied by the Fund. But even more important, the Salvadorean government and business community never accepted the overall objectives of achieving balanced development through restrictions on private investment (such as the restrictions implicit in the industrial policy) or of restruc-

---

[36] Fagan, *op. cit.*, pp. 19, 37ff.; Hansen, *op. cit.*, pp. 81-4; Cable, "The Football War and the CACM," *International Affairs*, Oct. 1969, p. 669.

turing the CACM along the lines demanded by Honduras. Thus, El Salvador's decision not to sign the m.o. was not made at the last minute; in reality according to observers with reliable inside information, El Salvador never had any intention of signing the m.o. agreements, and hoped to get Guatemala to go along with that position.[37]

If El Salvador openly took a hard line, Guatemala played a double game during the negotiations. All along, Guatemala posed as the champion of CACM unity; and indeed, as the main beneficiary of the soccer war and the subsequent disruption of trade between Honduras and El Salvador,[38] Guatemala did have good reason to hold the CACM together and especially to keep Honduras in the CACM. But despite the outward appearance of good will, there is substantial evidence that the Guatemalan government covertly shared the positions being voiced publicly by El Salvador. Although Guatemala never stated openly that it would not go along with the Fund or the industrial policy, throughout the negotiations Guatemala and El Salvador were in agreement on all the major issues, including the view that the m.o. was designed to normalize, not to restructure, the CACM.[39] Moreover, Guatemala actually supported El Salvador at crucial moments during the negotiations, particularly at the end. Even if there was no explicit agreement between the two countries about not signing the m.o., in practice, strong support from Guatemala enabled El Salvador not to sign; conversely, El Salvador's willingness to say "no" openly enabled the Guatemalan government to achieve its aims without looking like a spoiler.

Another force strongly backing the Salvadorean position was the business community in Central America (minus that of Honduras), particularly the organization of industrialists FECAICA. Aside from the feeling that the private sector should be consulted on *all* CACM decisions and regarding as illegitimate any decision made without its approval, FECAICA held positions similar to those voiced by El Salvador.[40] Industrialists, at least in Guatemala and El Salvador, pressured their governments not to sign the m.o.—even if this meant losing the Honduran market.

The Role of the U.S.

Finally, what was the role of the U.S.? During the m.o. negotiations the U.S. maintained a low profile, stating only its willingness to respond to initiatives from the Central Americans. From the sketchy evidence available (*not* including clear policy statements, of which there were none), it seems that the U.S. hoped for a favorable outcome of the m.o. discussions in order

---

[37] This conclusion is based on interviews with participants and newspaper accounts; see also SIECA, *Acta Final de la Tercera Reunión de Ministros de Economía de Centroamérica*, Dec. 8-11, 1970 (Guatemala: SIECA, 1970).

[38] *BLA*, Aug. 14, 1969, p. 257 and Jan. 8, 1970, p. 16; interviews; CEPAL, *Economic Survey of Latin America 1970*, Part I (Santiago: CEPAL, 1971) (E/CN.12/868), p. 47 and CEPAL, *The CACM and Its Recent Problems*, p. 67.

[39] Statement by Guatemalan Minister of Economy, *El Gráfico*, Dec. 15, 1970.

[40] FECAICA statements, July 1970 and October 1970; interviews; *El Gráfico*, Nov. 5, 1970, and Nov. 18, 1970; Fagan, *op. cit.* p. 33.

to preserve the CACM. Recognizing that U.S. interests would be adversely affected by a collapse of the CACM, the U.S.—unlike its allies in Central America—apparently was willing to accept certain limited reforms to avoid such a collapse. Nevertheless, the U.S. did not use its influence to pressure El Salvador to sign the m.o. agreements.

During the soccer war too, the U.S. had projected a low-profile image. This did not mean, however, that the U.S. had no policy:

> It is understood—from very well informed Washington sources—that the U.S. was well aware of the coming armed clash. Since no Communist or Castroist threat was apparent on either side, the U.S. is reported to have decided on a hands-off attitude.[41]

The U.S. had good reason for wanting to preserve peace and stability in Central America and, after the war, to normalize the situation in each country and between the two. But despite the public stance of deploring the war, and washing its hands of all responsibility, the U.S position was not so simple. For one thing, as was pointed out by Senator J. William Fullbright, U.S. military assistance had increased the influence of the military in both countries.[42] Second, despite protestations of neutrality, the U.S. supported El Salvador, both directly and indirectly. Hondurans and other observers doubt that El Salvador would have launched the war without a green light from Washington. Moreover, as an outgrowth of its concern since the early 1960s about the explosive potential of El Salvador's "population problem," some charge, the U.S. allowed the Salvadorean ruling class to wage this war, in order to preserve the escape valve of Salvadorean migration to Honduras.[43]

More important, ever since the earliest days of the CACM, the U.S. has aligned itself with a coalition of forces in Central America, in which the Salvadorean government and bourgeoisie were key. This coalition included: U.S. investors, most of the Central American private sector (minus that of Honduras), and the governments of El Salvador and Guatemala. These were the privileged sectors, which benefited the most and sacrificed the least for integration, and which refused to give up their privileges. In all the decisive debates in the early stages of the CACM (the Tripartite Treaty, integration industries, etc.), Washington voiced its positions indirectly through El Salvador, as well as directly. Throughout the first ten years of the CACM, the U.S. supported and advocated independently the positions taken by this coalition of privileged groups.

Thus, despite the low U.S. profile during the events of 1969-70, we cannot accept the view that the U.S. had nothing to do with these events. To the extent that the breakdown of the m.o. and the withdrawal of Honduras from the CACM was a result of the failure to resolve the problems

---

[41] Wionczek, "The Rise . . .," p. 57.

[42] Fullbright, quoted in New York Times, July 24, 1969.

[43] Carías, op. cit., pp. 102-5, 13-14; on the above assertion, see also Cable, "The Football War . . .," p. 661; Los Angeles Times, July 23, 1972; New York Times, Dec. 3, 1969; and interviews.

of unbalanced development, the U.S. had a clear responsibility for those outcomes. By late 1970, it hardly mattered that the U.S. had set into motion and nourished those forces which finally destroyed the CACM. In this sense, the Central Americans are now reaping the harvest of U.S. policy and U.S. "aid" in the formative stage of the CACM.

The Contradictions of Dependent Capitalist Integration

Once the eleventh-hour salvage operation—the modus operandi—failed and Honduras pulled out of the CACM, it proved impossible to repair the damage or to prevent a further deterioration. The steady deepening of the crisis during 1971 and 1972 revealed the fragility of the whole common market structure, and even the new initiatives for re-unification by the end of 1972 appeared highly tentative. If any temporary resolution should be reached, there is little reason to believe it would last.

CEPAL's Alternative: Balanced Underdevelopment

This collapse was the logical outcome of the contradictions within the integration strategy imposed by the U.S.; acceptance of that strategy had been the price for U.S. aid to the CACM. But was there any alternative route for Central American integration under capitalism? This question brings us directly to an evaluation of the role of CEPAL. For if the U.S. was the leader of a coalition of the most privileged interests in Central America, CEPAL headed an opposing coalition. This coalition included many technocrats in integration institutions, the Nicaraguan government (particularly in the early stages), the government and private sector of Honduras after the mid-1960s, and nationalistic individuals in the other governments—sectors of the bourgeoisie whose interests brought them temporarily in conflict with U.S. policy. But CEPAL's commitment to planning should not obscure certain realities about CEPAL and its strategy.

First, most CEPAL functionaries and CEPAL as an institution did not stick to their original principles as forcefully as would have been necessary to pose a serious alternative to the U.S. strategy. In the process of cooperating with the U.S. after 1960 and adjusting to U.S. hegemony, CEPAL officials "gave up their role as agents of change and became agents of the *status quo*."[44] By the end of the 1960s CEPAL had lost its potential function as an outside critic or "conscience" of the CACM, and never seriously challenged the strategy imposed by the U.S. and its allies.

Second, even if CEPAL had retained its original stand, and even if that strategy had prevailed, it too contained fundamental contradictions. If CEPAL had really wanted to follow through on its principles of planning and balance, it would have had to challenge the power of the capitalist class within Central America, since this class would never accept intergovernmental planning (e.g., through the integration industries scheme) unless its survival as a class was threatened. In addition, CEPAL would have had to

---

[44] Cohen, *op. cit.*, p. 85.

make a total break with the U.S., and thus to reject U.S. investment and aid (both of which CEPAL accepted as necessary). It would have had to push for a redistribution of resources within each country. In short, CEPAL would have had to address not only the intraregional disparities, but also the disparities stemming from the *class* structure of dependent capitalism. But CEPAL was not prepared to do this. Thus, we may speculate, if the original CEPAL strategy had prevailed, the crisis and collapse of the CACM might have been postponed, since the regional imbalances would not have escalated so rapidly to the critical point. But the class inequalities would not have been resolved.

Thus, CEPAL offered no serious alternative to the CACM. The only real alternative would have been a common market based on *thorough structural reforms within each country and a radical change in the class basis of power*, leading to a large-scale redistribution of income and a broad market incorporating the lower classes in each country. CEPAL, by contrast, did not insist on these changes, and hence was willing to settle for *balanced underdevelopment* in Central America. From this perspective, the struggle between the U.S. and CEPAL, and between the two coalitions they represented, was a struggle within the dominant groups, a struggle between two different strategies for preserving the dependent capitalist system in Central America.

Contradictions of the U.S. Strategy

But the attempt to preserve the dependent capitalist system is inherently contradictory. These contradictions become concrete if we briefly recapitulate the two principal U.S. objectives: first, to promote the interests of U.S. business, especially U.S. investors in Central America; and second, to stabilize the potentially explosive situation in the region, defend it against the internal "Communist" threat, and reduce class conflict, thereby strengthening capitalism.

With regard to the first, we have seen that the specific contours of the CACM were shaped in accordance with the changing needs of U.S. corporations; as a result, U.S. and other foreign corporations have been the main beneficiaries of Central American integration. But the strategy of dependent industrialization, which made the CACM a virtual playground of the U.S. corporations, was contradictory. Because they were dependent— because they were controlled by foreign corporations and adapted to imported, capital-intensive technology—industrialization and integration did not alleviate urban unemployment. Meanwhile, the lack of an agrarian reform has created increasing impoverishment in the countryside. Those social classes which were to have been incorporated within the national market have been marginalized. This has limited the expansion of the domestic market, which is necessary for increased foreign investment in Central America. Moreover, this kind of industrialization has led directly to the withdrawal of Honduras in 1970 and the collapse of the CACM as a free-trade area.[45] Thus, the multinational corporations, with official U.S. support, have created conditions which in the long run limited their own expansion in Central America.

With regard to the second U.S. objective the contradictions are even clearer. Somehow, it seems the U.S. hoped to stabilize the socio-economic system in Central America, but without making the necessary reforms. This brought two results. First, the class structure of Central America remained that of dependent capitalism. The only significant shift in class structure during the 1960s was the incorporation of new groups, mainly industrialists, into the ruling class,[46] solidifying the alliance with foreign capital. The function of the Central American state, and of the intergovernmental integration institutions, meanwhile, has been "reduced ... to the creation of favorable conditions for private enterprises and the protection of a process of dependent industrialization."[47] As a result, socio-economic conditions within each country for the majority of the population have worsened. This, in turn, has sharpened[48] social tensions. No one who has visited Central America in the late 1960s or early 1970s could seriously argue that the "threat" of internal revolution or class conflict has declined since 1960!

Second, and closely related, the CACM structure has suffered because the response of each member to its deepening internal problems has been to project these onto the Central American stage, to avoid dealing with them nationally. For example, El Salvador has done this with regard to its

---

[45] It is clear that U.S. companies, as well as the Central American economies, were hurt by the collapse of CACM. As a result of the disruption of trade, new foreign investment in the region has fallen off markedly since the end of 1970; in addition, several U.S. companies closed down their Central American operations. See, for example, *BLA*, April 1, 1971, pp. 98-9, June 10, 1971, pp. 177-9, Aug 5, 1971, p. 244; U.S. AID, "Guatemala's Trade with Honduras" (Guatemala: AID, May 1971.)

[46] The best class analyses include: Edelberto Torres Rivas and Vinicio Gonzalez, "Naturaleza y crisis del poder en Centroamérica," *Estudios Sociales Centroamericanos* (Costa Rica) No. 3, Sept-Dec. 1972; Torres Rivas, *Interpretación del Desarrollo Social Centroamericano* (San José, CR: EDUCA, 1971): Miguel Murillo, "El Nucieo de Contradicciones del Proceso Integracionista Centroamericano," *Estudios Sociales Centroamericanos* No. 1, Jan-April 1972; Dalton, *op. cit.*; Carías and Slutzky (eds.), *op. cit.*; and Guillermo Molina Chocano, *Integración Centroamericana y Dominación Internacional* (San José, CR: EDUCA, 1971).

[47] Molina Chocano, "Interdependence or Dependence," *CERES* (FAO), no. 26, March-April 1972, p. 52; also Molina Chocano, *Integración Centroamericana . . .*, pp. 71 ff.

[48] While the population grew at a rate of 3.2 percent a year and higher in the cities, urban unemployment and underemployment have risen, and industrial employment has declined as a percent of total employment. The gaps in income distribution have widened steadily. The "benefits" from integration have all gone to the upper class, particularly the industrialists; meanwhile, the costs of integration (e.g., the regressive sales taxes, to compensate for the governments' increasing fiscal problems) have been borne by the lower income groups. Moreover, the structure of the Central American economies has barely changed. For all the emphasis on industrialization, the region has remained essentially dependent on a few traditional agricultural exports to the world market. And the reliance on imports has increased (despite the shift in the composition of those imports), creating serious balance of payments and fiscal problems. Sources include: Torres Rivas, *Interpretación . . .*, pp. 285, 291-2; SEICA, *Desarrollo Integrado . . .*, p. 25; Molina Chocano, *Integración Centroamericana.*

"population problem," Honduras with its fiscal problems, and Costa Rica with its balance of payments problems. In this way too, the CACM has been used as a substitute for structural reform. The result has been to aggravate inter-country tensions and hasten the collapse of the CACM.

Finally, the U.S. could not have achieved its second objective, the stabilization of Central America, precisely because it was in contradiction with the first and narrower U.S. objective, the protection of U.S. corporations investing in the region. That same narrow definition of U.S. interests that made the U.S. perceive CEPAL as a threat also gave the U.S. a very shallow approach to preserving social stability. The U.S. was not able to distinguish between CEPAL's challenge to the narrow interests of U.S. corporations and a broader threat to the interests of the capitalist system, which CEPAL did *not* present. Similarly, if the U.S. had been less concerned about protecting the absolute freedom of U.S. investors, it could have accepted a degree of planning; this would have permitted greater balance within Central America, hence a more stable CACM, and more effective stop-gap reforms within each country. In short, the commitment of U.S. policy-makers to specific U.S. economic interests crippled the U.S. effort at regional pacification. This was the essential irrationality of the U.S. strategy for Central American integration.

What does this story mean to the majority of Central Americans who have been paying the bill, but who have not benefited from the hundreds of millions of dollars of U.S. aid to the CACM? To the lives of these people, the ups and downs of the CACM have made little apparent difference. But in fact, the integration process *has* changed the conditions of their struggle for survival—and for liberation. Just as the ties binding Central America to the capitalist system have shifted from the national to the regional level, so too, the resistance is being regionalized. It is for this reason that U.S. aid, designed to make direct military intervention in Central America unnecessary, may well fail to do so.

A New "Banana Republic": Del Monte in Guatemala*
By Roger Burbach and Patricia Flynn

Roger Burbach and Patricia Flynn are currently working at the Center for the Study of the Americas (CENSA) in Berkeley, California. Their forthcoming book (1983) published by Monthly Review Press is entitled The Politics of Intervention: The United States in Central America.

Talking to a reporter from *Forbes* magazine, Del Monte's chairman Alfred Eames mused, banana trees "are like money trees. I wish I had more of them."[1] Unlikely as it may seem, eight short years ago Del Monte did not own a single banana tree. But today, the corporation owns or controls an estimated 38,000 acres of banana plantations in Costa Rica, Guatemala, and the Phillipines.[2] It is one of the three U.S.-based multinationals that dominate the world banana economy: Del Monte, Castle & Cooke, and United Brands together account for 70 percent of the world's $2.5 billion banana trade. Because of this dominance, the companies also exercise considerable influence on the economic life of the banana producing countries, many of which depend on banana exports as a principal source of foreign exchange.

The kingpin of Del Monte's banana empire is its plantation in Guatemala, which was purchased from the old and infamous United Fruit Company in 1972. When Del Monte took over from United Fruit, it stepped into the shoes of a company that had long been the symbol of U. S. imperialism in Central America, particularly in Guatemala. As Guatemala's largest landowner and major foreign investor, United Fruit had dominated the country's economy, exploiting its natural resources and workers and consistently opposing organized labor, and it was the leading force in pushing for the CIA-engineered overthrow of the progressive government of Jacobo Arbenz in 1954.[3]

By the time Del Monte entered the picture, United Fruit had lowered its political and economic profile in Guatemala and the rest of Central America as part of a sophisticated strategy to rationalize its operations and undercut nationalistic resentments. But beneath this facade, Del Monte continues the old tradition of the United Fruit Company in Guatemala. It still operates as though it were above the law; it is allied with the most reactionary elements within the Guatemalan bourgeoisie; it manipulates its workers to

---

*Chapter 11 of *Agribusiness in the Americas*, (New York: Monthly Review Press/North American Congress on Latin America, 1980), copyright 1980 by Roger Burbach and and Patricia Flynn.

[1] *Forbes*, Dec. 15, 1970.

[2] UNCTAD, *The Marketing and Distribution System for Bananas* (Geneva: UNCTAD, 1974).

[3] For a comprehensive history of Guatemala, including U.S. political and corporate involvement, see *Guatemala* (Berkeley: NACLA, 1974).

avoid labor unrest; and along with the other banana companies, it has tried to torpedo efforts by Central American governments to gain greater control over their natural resources. Like the United Fruit Company, Del Monte reinforces economic underdevelopment and political reaction in Guatemala and acts as a formidable obstacle to change.

The Guatemalan plantations that Del Monte took over from United Fruit in 1972 are the most productive in Central America, assuring Del Monte's position as a major force in the world banana trade. For United Fruit the acquisition meant the further erosion of its dominance, unchallenged before the 1960s when it controlled 75 percent of the world trade.

Ironically, the original impetus for Del Monte's entry into the banana business in 1968 came from the United Fruit Company itself. In an apparent bid to take over the food processing company, United Fruit purchased a large chunk of Del Monte's stock. To thwart the takeover attempt Del Monte went out and bought a banana company—the one line of business United Fruit was legally blocked from acquiring. A 1958 antitrust ruling had found United Fruit guilty of monopolizing the banana trade, and in fact the company was under court orders to sell off about 10 percent of its banana operations. With the purchase of the Miami-based West Indies Fruit Company and its Costa Rican subsidiary, the Banana Development Corporation (known as BANDECO), Del Monte was able to make its first inroads into the U.S. banana market.

The banana business proved highly profitable, and Del Monte began looking for ways to expand its Central American holdings. Again United Fruit provided the opportunity. The final deadline for United Fruit's required divestiture was approaching, and the company still had no buyers when Del Monte approached United Brands (which had purchased United Fruit in 1970) with a purchase offer for its Guatemalan plantations. By the end of 1970 the two companies agreed that Del Monte would purchase United Fruit's holdings in Guatemala for about $10 million, provided the Guatemalan government agreed.

For Del Monte, Guatemala was the ideal place for expansion. Not only would the plantations there double the company's banana production, but just as important, fifteen years of U.S. sponsored counterrevolution since 1954 had made the country safe for U.S. investors, providing the kind of "stable" political climate Del Monte demands wherever it operates. However, Del Monte had one formidable obstacle to overcome—a provision of the Guatemalan constitution that prohibits the sale of border lands (as United Fruit's lands were defined) to foreign interests. To complicate matters further, several purchase offers were put forward by Guatemalan nationals, including two entrepreneurs who had even lined up bank loans.[4] But in the best tradition of U.S. multinationals overseas, Del Monte did not let ethics or legal technicalities stand in its way.

Despite personal lobbying visits by Del Monte executives to then president Carlos Arana and several cabinet officers, in late 1971 the govern-

---

[4] *El Gráfico*, July 14, 1975; and *Diario de la Tarde*, July 16, 1975.

ment denied permission for the purchase.[5] Not to be deterred, company officials simply dipped deep enough into corporate coffers to change the Guatemalan government's decision. Following the advice of then ambassador to Guatemala, Nathaniel Davis, to retain a local "consultant," in the summer of 1972 Del Monte hired Domingo Moreira, a Cuban-born Guatemalan entrepreneur. Moreira agreed to help swing the deal in return for a half million dollar "consultant's fee." He soon proved his political clout. Even before the Guatemalan government officially reversed its position, Del Monte received the go-ahead from the government to conclude the deal with United Brands. One month later, in September 1972, Arana formally issued a decree approving the sale.[6]

Del Monte, of course, claimed that there was no bribe involved, since the corporation did not make any direct payment to a government official. But the truth of the matter is that Del Monte was carefully covering its tracks. The half million dollar fee was paid through several of the company's Panamanian shipping subsidiaries and charged to general and administrative expenses. Thus, Del Monte managed to stay within the formal limits of the law by satisfying Securities and Exchange requirements that accurate records be kept, and no secret slush funds be used to channel funds abroad. Del Monte also went to great lengths to conceal the transaction with Moreira. No company record was ever made of his name, and Del Monte promised never to reveal his identity.

In spite of Moreira's disclaimers that no bribery was involved, in Guatemala the universally accepted assumption is that Moreira handed over a good-sized chunk of his "fee" to then President Arana. Some sources in the Guatemalan bourgeoisie even claim to have personal knowledge of the transaction.[7]

But more important than the question of the impropriety of the payment is what the Moreira connection reveals about Del Monte's ties with the most reactionary and corrupt elements of the Guatemalan bourgeoisie. Moreira is a fast-dealing entrepreneur whose holdings have expanded greatly since he came to Guatemala from Cuba. He is a well-known backer of conservative political forces in Guatemala and has close ties with a group of right-wing business executives who promote their political and personal gain through Mafia-like tactics. In Nicaragua he had business links with former dictator Anastasio Somoza.[8]

Plantation Enclave

The United Fruit plantations Del Monte took over lie in the hot tropical lowlands of northeastern Guatemala, not far from the Atlantic coast ports which face the markets of Europe and the United States. The most notable

---

[5] See *Wall Street Journal*, July 14, 1975.

[6] *Wall Street Journal*, July 14, 1975; and *Guatemala and Central America Report*, October 1972 and July 1975.

[7] Interview in Guatemala, 1976.

[8] *Inforpress*, Nos. 60, 64, and 151; *El Gráfico*, February 10,1972; "Nicaragua," NACLA *Report on the Americas*, February 1976, p. 16; and interviews in Guatemala.

change at the plantation since Del Monte's takeover are the new signs on company buildings. They now read BANDEGUA, for Banana Development Corporation of Guatemala, the subsidiary that runs Del Monte's operations there. Recognizing that the plantation system developed over the years by United Fruit serves its interests well, Del Monte has made few basic changes. In fact, several of the workers interviewed by NACLA wondered whether the company had really changed ownership.

For the $20.5 million Del Monte finally paid to United Brands in 1972, the company acquired 55,000 acres of prime agricultural land, plus an agro-industrial complex that stretches from plantation to port. It also inherited a position of privilege and influence that had long characterized United Fruit's operations.

Though no longer the major representative of monopoly capital in Guatemala, where U.S. multinationals now have sizeable industrial investments, Del Monte is still a formidable economic and political power. It is the country's largest single private employer and totally monopolizes the export of bananas, one of the top five sources of foreign exchange for Guatemala. Del Monte continues to run the plantations like an independent enclave within the Guatemalan state, where government officials are barely tolerated. It is Del Monte, not Guatemalan officials, that supplies official export statistics on bananas. Del Monte pays no tax on its land, and has only 9,000 acres under cultivation. The remaining 48,000 acres are grazed by 7,000 head of company cattle—not to produce meat, but, as a company official explained, as a tactic designed both to keep squatters off the property and to prevent the government from expropriating it as idle land.[9]

While Del Monte does not dominate the country's key transportation networks as United Fruit once did, it still benefits from special privileges. When its port facilities at Puerto Barrios on the Atlantic were destroyed by the earthquake in 1975, the company was immediately able to relocate to choice facilities at the nearby government port of Santo Tomás. The corporation also enjoys a special relationship with the government-run national railway, Ferrocarril de Guatemala (FEGUA). Del Monte is one of FEGUA's creditors and also repairs the company's rail cars at its plantation machine shop.[10]

The first thing that strikes a visitor to the town of Bananera, where the plantation headquarters are located, is the highly stratified social system typical of plantations everywhere. On one side of the railroad tracks, behind fences and guard posts, is the company compound. Amidst country club surroundings, a few North American executives and their Guatemalan aides oversee Del Monte's vast lands and its 4,500-person workforce. The compound's manicured lawns, spacious tropical mansions, its pool and tennis courts, stand in sharp contrast to the dusty company town on the other side of the rail tracks. The evident poverty of the town, which exists

---

[9] Interview with Del Monte official in Guatemala, 1976.
[10] *El Gráfico*, July 25, 1975.

mainly as an adjunct to the plantation, belies Del Monte's claim that its presence has a beneficial effect on the surrounding economy.

Most of Del Monte's workers and their families live on the plantation itself, isolated even from the small town of Bananera. The company-owned housing camps are conveniently clustered around the banana farms where the men work, along the edges of the railway line. The workers' housing is spartan and barely adequate, a far cry from the luxurious company compound. Since there are no roads going into the plantation, the only access to the outside world is the company operated rail wagon, which runs only twice daily—at the beginning and end of each work day. No one, neither workers, their families, nor company executives, is allowed to board the train without a special pass given out daily by a company office. To further assure "law and order," there is a Guatemalan army post in the middle of the plantation, staffed by armed Guatemalan soldiers. A company executive explained to NACLA interviewers that the soldiers take care of any disturbances which occur on the plantation. He also recalled the original reason for the post: in the late 1960s guerrillas were active in the area, and a United Fruit pilot was killed. Given the social unrest in the Guatemalan countryside, Del Monte is clearly not taking any chances.

Plantation Workforce

Many of the workers at the BANDEGUA plantation were once peasant farmers from the neighboring provinces who were either forced off the land, or were unable to survive by farming. Now, with their sole source of sustenance the salary they receive, the plantation workers have become part of the Guatemalan proletariat. However, with salaries averaging about $780 a year, and with benefits such as free housing, water, electricity, and medical facilities, Del Monte's employees are better off than the bulk of the Guatemalan working class.[11]

Although the policy of maintaining a *relatively* well-off workforce was originally pioneered by United Fruit, today it has become an integral part of the strategy of all the multinational banana companies. Like other monopolistic corporations, they recognize their own self-interest in ensuring labor peace by paying high salaries—something their hefty profit rates allow them to do. For the banana industry, however, a docile and cooperative labor force is a special imperative. Bananas are a highly perishable commodity, and time is critical in the marketing process. A plantation or port work stoppage of even a day can mean the loss of hundreds of thousands of dollars in overripe bananas. Thus, harvesting at BANDEGUA's plantation is carefully timed to coincide with the arrival of Del Monte's ships at Puerto Barrios. Within one day, the bananas are cut, washed, packed, and sent by train to the nearby port. There they are immediately loaded onto specially refrigerated ships which will transport them to the U.S. and

---

[11] Carlos Figueroa Ibarra, *El proletariado rural en el agro guatemalteco* (Guatemala: Instituto de Investigaciones Económicas y Sociales del la Universidad de San Carlos, 1976), p. 187.

European markets. The whole process must be regulated like clockwork, and delays avoided at any cost. In this context, it is possible to understand why Del Monte is willing to pay its dockworkers, who are the key to the whole marketing process, up to $600 a month on a piecerate basis.

Work conditions on the plantation are also extremely difficult. Banana production is highly labor intensive, and requires continual painstaking work of weeding, trimming, marking plants, and spraying with insecticides. Under the hot tropical sun, crews of workers roam among the banana trees under the constant supervision of the BANDEGUA foremen. When one of Del Monte's ships is in port, workers often do the grueling job of harvesting for twelve or thirteen hours at a time—one man cutting down the banana stem with his machete, and another carrying the stem (which can weigh up to 150 pounds) in a sack slung across his back. As one of the U.S. executives on the plantation told NACLA, "It's backbreaking work, and you couldn't get a single person in California to do it, especially for $2.80 a day.... I wouldn't do it for any money." But, as he explained, cheap labor is key to the company's profits. "If you can pay a worker 35 cents an hour, why buy an $8000 tractor?"

The main device the company uses to extract the maximum value from the workers' labor is payment on a piecerate basis. While this gives the banana workers the possibility of earning more, it also means a higher level of exploitation. Workers drive themselves to the limit, often with disastrous long-range consequences for their health. This system also makes the workers extremely productive. For the company, this productivity translates into a higher rate of profits, far out of proportion to the meager wage increases.

As Del Monte realizes, in spite of its "enlightened" labor policies designed to coopt the workers, there is always an underlying danger of labor unrest. Historically, the banana workers in Guatemala have a strong tradition of struggle. During the years when Jacobo Arbenz was president (1950-1954) the United Fruit workers' union was one of the most militant and progressive unions in Guatemala. It was only as a result of the massive repression unleashed against the labor movement after the 1954 coup—when banana union leaders were especially targeted to be jailed, killed, or exiled—that the militancy of banana workers was quelled in Guatemala.[12]

Recently, in other Central American countries, there have been renewed signs of militancy among banana workers. In Honduras, 18,000 workers at United Brands' subsidiary voted in 1975 to oust the conservative, pro-U.S. union leadership, installed twenty years ago in a U.S.-engineered effort to undercut the then progressive leadership. In May 1976, Del Monte was itself the target of a strike at its Costa Rica subsidiary, where workers were demanding higher wages, recognition of their union, and reinstatement of 54 fired workers.[13] Like other corporations, Del Monte attempts to

---

[12] Guatemala, p. 75.

[13] Inforpress, No. 191, and Guatemala and Central America Report (Berkeley), February 1976.

prevent worker discontent from bursting into open conflict by identifying and weeding out the most outspoken and militant workers—a tactic one of the company's plantation supervisors admitted using.

To further control its labor force, Del Monte relies on the union itself—*Sindicato de Trabajadores de BANDEGUA* or SITRABI—which is known in Guatemala as a "sindicato blanco," or a sell-out union. In a pattern familiar in the United States, the union performs the function of the loyal opposition—it may oppose the company on bread-and-butter issues, but promotes an ideology of cooperation and common interest with the company, rather than one of anticorporate class interest.

The BANDEGUA union has cooperative relations with the American Institute for Free Labor Development (AIFLD), an organization funded by AID, supported by the AFL-CIO and U.S. corporations, and often used by the CIA to undercut genuine progressive unionism in Latin America. Every year a handful of chosen BANDEGUA workers spend months at AIFLD-sponsored courses in Guatemala City learning U.S.-style unionism, and some are sent to AIFLD schools in Honduras and Colombia. Many of these AIFLD graduates become union officials or are given supervisory jobs on the plantation.[14]

The Banana War

The most serious challenge Del Monte has faced in Guatemala has come not from labor, however, but from rising third world nationalism. Barely a year after the company took over the plantations in Guatemala, Latin America's major banana exporting countries—Guatemala, Costa Rica, Panama, Honduras, Columbia, Nicaragua, and Ecuador—proposed forming a producers' organization, the Union of Banana Exporting Countries, or UBEC. Like the oil producers who formed OPEC, those who controlled the governments of banana producing countries were rebelling against the disadvantages raw material producers face in world trade. For most of these countries, bananas constitute a major source of foreign exchange, yet the world market price of bananas remained unchanged for twenty years while the cost of their manufactured imports skyrocketed. Whereas in 1960 a tractor cost three tons of bananas, in 1970 the same tractor cost eleven tons of bananas.[15] Instead of the mere 11.5 cents of every dollar of banana sales staying in producing countries,[16] UBEC governments

---

[14] When NACLA researchers visited BANDEGUA, the union office was being used for a three-month course sponsored by the International Federation of Plantation, Agricultural and Allied Workers, an international secretariat that has worked in the past with the CIA, according to Phillip Agee. As one of the instructors, a Colombian, explained, the purpose of the course was to train potential leaders in "social problem solving." The other course instructor was a BANDEGUA office employee, a graduate of AIFLD courses with extensive travel experience in Central America and the U.S. Besides workers from the plantation, there were five Salvadoreans and twenty local peasant farmers recruited for the course.

[15] UNCTAD, *The Marketing and Distribution System*, p.11.

[16] Frederick F. Clairmonte, "Bananas: A Commodity Case History," in Cheryl Payer, ed., *Commodity Trade of the Third World* (New York: McGraw Hill, 1975).

set out to capture a larger share of the banana dollar. Their chief target was the multinationals like Del Monte who reap the lion's share of profit from the banana dollar.

When in 1974 UBEC proposed a $1 tax on each box of bananas exported, the banana companies moved quickly to confront the challenge. Documents submitted to the U.S. Senate Committee on Multinationals allege that the three companies met in Costa Rica in early 1974 to coordinate a strategy for confronting the UBEC challenge.[17] The Costa Rican foreign minister also charged that the companies had set up a secret fund to "destabilize" the UBEC member governments in order to prevent them from levying the banana tax.[18] The companies of course denied the charges, but they all proceeded to move against the UBEC countries.

Castle & Cooke took the lead by cutting back on exports and destroying 145,000 boxes of bananas rather than pay any tax. United Brands, it was later revealed, bribed Honduran government officials $1.25 million to reduce their tax, a scandal that eventually led to the suicide of the company's president, Eli Black, and the removal of the president of Honduras.

By comparison, Del Monte was careful to keep a relatively low profile in its campaign against UBEC. In Costa Rica, the company agreed under protest to pay the tax but began judicial proceedings to challenge the government.[19] By 1975 the Guatemalan government had not yet levied the tax, arguing in effect that the company was above the law. Its case rested on the grounds that it assumed all the rights and privileges granted United Fruit in its contract with the government, namely, that the export tax could not be raised above 2 cents per stem until the contract expired in 1981. Del Monte found its strongest allies in extreme right-wing members of the Guatemalan congress, who blocked attempts to impose the tax.[20]

When the new government of General Kjell Laugerud responded to public pressure and announced it would support the tax, Del Monte countered with a new public campaign aimed at intimidating the government. In a full-page advertisement in the Guatemala City papers, the company brazenly threatened that it would reconsider expansion or even cut back operations if the tax passed, leaving Guatemala with even less foreign exchange earnings than previously.[21] When another attempt to pass the tax was defeated, there were once again rumors that Del Monte had resorted to bribery.[22]

When the tax was finally pushed through the Guatemalan Congress in late 1975, the company showed that it was indeed above the law. That year Del Monte managed to pay no tax at all on its banana exports by declaring a volume of over three million boxes lower than the year before. The

---

17 *La Nación*, April 18, 1974.

18 *New York Times*, May 21, 1975.

19 *San Francisco Examiner*, May 21, 1975.

20 *Inforpress*, No. 114.

21 *Diario La Hora*, September 10, 1975.

22 *Central America Report* (Guatemala), November 24, 1975.

company's export figures were suspiciously low given that the area of land under production remained the same and there were no adverse weather conditions to affect productivity.[23] However, without an independent count of the number of boxes exported, the Guatemalan government had no way of knowing whether the company had manipulated export figures. So hefty were Del Monte's profits in 1975 that the Guatemalan minister of the economy predicted the company would recoup its entire investment in Guatemala in three years.[24]

The outcome of the so-called banana war highlighted the limits of the brand of nationalism that led to UBEC. First, whatever monetary gains the ruling elite who control the Guatemalan government reaped had no effect on the well-being of the majority of Guatemalans. Moreover, producers of nonstrategic raw materials like bananas have very little leverage vis-a-vis global corporations like Del Monte who wield decisive power because of their control over marketing and distribution channels. A clear sign of the success of the banana companies' intimidation campaign was the failure of a single member government of UBEC to impose the full $1 tax. Even when a smaller tax was levied it was the multinationals who came out on top by jacking up prices. Just after the tax was first imposed, the box price of bananas in the United States shot up from $2.50 to $5.20, an increase way out of proportion to the tax. This gave the companies a profit more than four times the profit rate company spokespeople usually call reasonable.[25]

Hedging Bets

This is not to say that Del Monte and the other banana companies are immune to pressures from reformists and nationalists. In fact, the threat of land expropriations has forced the banana companies to modify their investment strategies significantly—a necessary adaptation which they have turned to their own advantage.

Instead of relying solely on their own lands, the companies now purchase a significant amount of bananas from "associate producers"—local growers who contract to sell their production to the companies. This associate producer program, first pioneered by United Fruit in Guatemala in the 1960s in response to the land reform attempts of the previous decade, has allowed the companies to lower their profiles without cutting into their profits.[26] The companies also use the associates to buffer themselves against fluctuations in the world market. When demand for bananas is strong, the companies turn to associates for increased supplies. On the other hand, when there is an oversupply and the danger of falling prices, the companies simply purchase less fruit from associates by raising their quality

---

[23] Information from Frank Ellis.

[24] *Inforpress, No. 165.*

[25] *La Nación*, May 23, 1974; *Inforpress*, Nos. 93, 101.

[26] See *Guatemala*, pp. 122-131 for an article on the United Fruit Company's changing strategy.

specifications.[27]

The companies also use the associate producer system as a public relations ploy to demonstrate their beneficial impact in helping local farmers. But in reality, those who are helped are usually large and wealthy landowners—those who have the capital and technological sophistication required to produce the uniformly high quality fruit demanded by the multinationals.

Del Monte's associates are a prime example. In Costa Rica, about two-thirds of Del Monte's bananas come from the company's thirteen associate producers, each of whom has an average plantation of 612 acres.[28] In Guatemala, where United Fruit never set up an extensive associate program, Del Monte obtains nearly all of its contract production from one business group, headed by Spanish-born Julian Presa. Presa and his family contract about 3,000 acres to Del Monte, partly through a joint venture with a Florida-based U.S. company, Taylor Enterprise of Guatemala. Such associates provide the multinationals with important political allies within the local bourgeoisie. Del Monte's associates, for example, were prominent in arguing the company's case against the imposition of the UBEC tax.

Although the associate producer scheme has given the companies some security that their profits could survive a new wave of land expropriations, the multinationals still have a strong vested interest in maintaining the status quo. Del Monte's plantation lands are the most productive in Central America, and for all of the banana multinationals, profit margins are significantly higher on their own plantations, which are able to produce quality fruit more cheaply and efficiently than are the associates.

Given this, Del Monte and the banana multinationals will remain a highly conservative force in the third world, in spite of their image of flexibility. They are likely to oppose progressive changes like land reforms, and will certainly be a major obstacle to the basic social changes necessary to meet people's needs.

U.S. Strategic Interests in Central America:
The Economics and Geopolitics of Empire*

By Robert Henriques Girling
with Luin Goldring

Robert Henriques Girling is Associate Professor in the Department of Management Studies, Sonoma State University. Luin Goldring is with the Department of Anthropology, Sonoma State University.

Traditional views of U.S. strategic interests in Central America emphasize an inventory of national security, economic and geopolitical interests.

---

[27] Information from Frank Ellis.

[28] Estimated acreage in UNCTAD, *The Marketing and Distribution System*, p. 24.

*From the Latin American Studies Association Meeting, Washington D.C., March 1982.

Protection of these vital interests has been justification for U.S. intervention in the domestic affairs of countries located within the region on more than one occasion. Indeed, the current phase of U.S. interventionism, in which Central America has become a major theater of East-West tensions, is justified by recourse to traditional articulation of U.S. strategic interests.

Addressing the Subcommittee of Inter-American Affairs of the House of Representatives, M. Peter McPhereson, Administrator of the Agency for International Development recently reiterated these views:

> The geographic proximity of Latin America and the Caribbean has a direct bearing on our national security. Our vital concerns in the region include unimpeded use of the sea lanes adjacent to North America and the Panama Canal, and continued access to oil from Venezuela, Mexico and other exporters in the hemisphere.[1]

Moreover, McPhereson cited the economic significance of the Latin American region in purchasing "nearly $39 billion of U.S. exports, making them the second largest market for our products, topped only by Western Europe." He went on to say that "Seventy-seven percent of all U.S. foreign direct and financial investment in the developing world is in Latin America and the Caribbean.... We depend on the region for significant shares of several important raw materials and other commodities such as bauxite and alumina, coffee, sugar and petroleum." Central America is seen as vital to the integrity of the entire Caribbean Basin which stretches from the island economies of the Caribbean through Mexico to Venezuela and Colombia.

Strategic interests include U.S. security interests in the region, the strategic military corridor through which one-half of U.S. oil imports pass, and the economic mineral resources—petroleum, aluminum and nickel—that are situated in the region, resources which generate four dollars for every one dollar of invested capital. To protect these assets, the traditional views of U.S. interests have stressed one overriding concern—innoculation of the region against any regime potentially hostile to the U.S. or U.S. business interests.

An alternative view of U.S. interests in the region questions the security and economic value of the region. U.S. security interests were seriously questioned by Abraham Lowenthal, Director of the Latin American Program at the Woodrow Wilson Center in Washington, D.C., in recent testimony before the Subcommittee on Inter-American Affairs.

> If we are really honest about the situation and think about the contingencies in which the use of U.S. military force might be a possibility in the Western Hemisphere, they would not be to protect against threats to vital U.S. security assets, (but) rather to shore up beleaguered regimes, such as we see now in Central America ... as (to) strategic and other materials, Latin America's relative importance as a source for the United States has dropped for most products as the country's international links have multiplied, and as synthetics have increasingly come to be used

---

[1] M. Peter McPhereson, Testimony before Committee on Foreign Affairs, Subcommittee on Inter-American Affairs, House of Representatives, December 15, 1981.

... the United States no longer depends on Latin America for any commodity, as it does on South Africa and the Soviet Union for chrome and platinum, for example.[2]

Moreover, the direct economic significance of Latin America and the Caribbean has been declining in terms of direct foreign investment and political support. Clearly there are some assets of considerable value to the U.S. located in Central America. The Panama Canal is a vital commercial and military link to Latin America and Europe. The Mexican oil fields are located in close proximity to Central America. Strategic analysts argue that any adverse course of events in the region could have detrimental consequences upon these vital assets.

As Harry Magdoff in his study of imperialism and foreign policy points out, "Small Latin American countries that produce relatively little profit are important in United States policy making because control over all of Latin America is important."[3] Since U.S. economic and strategic interests are global, it is important that the entire globe remain open to U.S. trade and investment. In viewing the assets of the region, policymakers are likely to ask themselves what sorts of strategies to protect U.S. interests are viable and what are the economic and political costs associated with different strategies. Naturally policymakers who hold differing views will be inclined to view the alternatives and their associated costs quite differently.

The question which arises then is "what is the relationship between the costs and benefits associated with U.S. interests and strategies for their defense?" In this respect it is worthwhile to consider some implications of current economic interests and the methods for securing these assets both in Central America and Latin America. There are two basic approaches for dealing with that problem: they may be simply stated as confrontation and accomodation.

The present strategy of the Reagan Administration is a strategy of confrontation. Meanwhile, the overriding concern of U.S. business with respect to the area is stability. In order to protect these economic interests in Latin America and to ensure their effective use, stability must be fostered and maintained. As John Purcell of New York–based Banker's Trust observes in his recent study of the perceptions and interests of U.S. business in Central America, some business respondents "fear that Reagan's policy would polarize Central American society and make lasting stability impossible."[4] This fear seems to be borne out in part by recent data on country risk in El Salvador which places a 70 percent probability on a major investment loss due to the political instability. *Business Latin America*, an industry newsletter, reports that the capital flight from the region has had a serious and destabilizing effect on export sales and general business conditions.

---

[2] Abraham Lowenthal testimony, *U.S. National Interest in Latin America*, Hearing before Subcommittee on Inter-American Affairs, March 1981.

[3] *The Age of Imperialism*, Monthly Review Press, 1966, p. 14.

[4] John Purcell, "The Interests and Perceptions of U.S. Business in Relation to the Political Crisis in Central America," Mimeo, April 1981, p. 24.

Resident U.S. business interests in Guatemala and El Salvador have resisted efforts for moderate alternatives to the current extremist regimes. While these views reflect business interests which have the most to lose, all U.S. business and labor will pay for an ill-conceived policy. Nevertheless, *Business International* reports that "nearly all (executives) believe that the U.S.'s traditional hegemony in Central America has been irretrievably lost."[5] This attitude, however, appears to some to be unconsidered in view of changing political realities. As one executive declared, he is worried by "the simplistic analogy with the World Series and the idea that the U.S. would 'win' or 'lose' in Central America."[6]

This brings us to the other alternative: accomodation. This was the policy that was waveringly pursued under the Carter Administration. A number of business executives and policy makers regarded these policies as fuel to an already unstable situation. Accomodation calls for negotiated solutions which recognize the need for the U.S. to extract itself from the role of the region's gendarme. As *Business International* asserts, "dissatisfaction with the U.S.'s traditional duty as hemispheric policeman has prompted Latin American governments to assume a more forceful role in ensuring regional stability."[7]

This approach calls for increased reliance on two regional powers, Mexico and Venezuela, to take the lead in stabilizing the region. In the words of a senior Bank of America official, it recognizes a basic truism: "Repression works in the short run; but it doesn't work in the long-run. Our interests and concerns are matters of the long-run. What we want is long-term stability."

Yet current U.S. strategy seems likely to accentuate political instability by ruling out options for negotiated settlement. Central America clearly has a symbolic value that is much greater than its economic value. Under President Reagan, Central America has become a symbol of U.S. determination to stand firm against further loss of political influence. And there is an apparent willingness to pay a high price. Thus, while the strategic interests in the region might not be worth much, the strategic significance of the region as part of a growing East-West confrontation is evident.

Identification and Measurement of Strategic Interests

Few would argue over the assertion that the U.S. economy is strategically dependent on its economic relationships with the world as sources of raw materials, critical minerals, as well as cheap labor and markets for its export products. Recent economic data amply demonstrate U.S. economic reliance on trade to garner resources. Presently the U.S. is dependent on imports for more than half of its consumption of 13 strategic minerals. U.S.-based multinational corporations produce over 80 percent of their output overseas, and production by U.S. corporations overseas is four times the

---

[5] *Business International,* April 11, 1980.
[6] Purcell, *op. cit.,* p.24.
[7] *Ibid.*

level of U.S. exports. The nations of the Third World play a large part as suppliers and consumers of U.S. products. Over one-third of U.S. exports are sold to the Third World. The Third World in general and Latin America specifically are major purchasers of U.S. agricultural products.

The penetration of U.S. corporations overseas and in the Third World has benefited the U.S. economy. Some 20 percent of all earnings of U.S. multinational corporations comes from the developing world. Recently, loans by financial institutions to the Third World have been a source of great profit.

In response to these issues let us turn to consider specific U.S. interests in Central America in detail. In what follows we will be examining a rather large amount of economic data. It is not our intention to confuse the reader with charts and tables. Nevertheless, it is important that such information be incorporated as evidence in support of our arguments. We will therefore make every effort to present our information clearly, without an excessive reliance on economic jargon, and to explain terms wherever they may be unclear.

Any attempt to sort out the issues and the facts will necessarily begin with some definitions. U.S. interests may be seen as comprising two general types: geopolitical and economic interests. On the one hand, geopolitical interests are those aspects of Central America's location which impinge upon or potentially affect events beyond the region. Economic interests, on the other hand, concern the quality and quantity of trade investment and financial interests within the region; for example, the level of profitability of U.S. investments and loans, the availability of raw materials, and the current as well as future market potentials.

Yet in this network of strategic U.S. dependence, just how important is Central America? Is it in fact true that oil from Guatemala will one day rival the Mexican oil fields? Just how likely is it that the Central American Common Market will become a major market for U.S. industry and a significant source of inexpensive products?

Is there any economic asset at stake in Latin America and the Caribbean that may have led to the increasing commitment of military, political and ultimately economic resources in Central America? Is the area generally vital to the survival of U.S. economic power? Or is the region merely part of an area of declining significance and in economic terms not worth the extensive commitments being made and that will be further necessary in order to defend it? Just what is the value of Central America?

We will begin first with geopolitical interests, then proceed to analyze economic interests in terms of raw materials, foreign trade and finally financial interests.

Geopolitical Interests

Economically, U.S. geopolitical interests are centered not in the Western Hemisphere but in the Persian Gulf, the principal source of U.S. petroleum imports. Other areas include South Africa, the source of a host of critical minerals, and Japan, a key trading partner, and in the postwar period, the linchpin of U.S. Asian policy.

In contrast, the geopolitical significance of Central America derives from its proximity to the U.S., its proximity to key areas of security concern—Mexico and Brazil, and the potential political, economic and military capabilities of the region's nations.

U.S. concerns in the area center around the sea lanes of communication, military weaponry and commercial shipping in the Caribbean Basin, of which Central America forms the western flank. Within the Basin are located military listening posts for monitoring ship and submarine activities in the Caribbean and Atlantic, military training facilities in Panama, Puerto Rico and Cuba, and the Navy's Atlantic Underseas Testing and Evaluation Center, a focus of antisubmarine warfare testing.[8]

Economically, the region is central to interoceanic and hemispheric trade which passes through the Panama Canal. Additionally, petroleum refineries located in the Caribbean process some 50 percent of U.S. petroleum imports from Africa and the Middle East. Finally, the region contains numerous raw materials, with Mexico as the second most important supplier of raw materials to the U.S., Venezuela a source of 23 percent of U.S. petroleum products, and Jamaica supplier of 25 percent of U.S. bauxite.[9]

The Panama Canal is the *sine qua non* in the realm of Caribbean geopolitics. Through its gates and locks pass over 100 million tons of cargo annually. Each year over 12,000 ships from 64 nations pass through the Canal. Some 12 percent of U.S. seaborne commerce traverses the isthmus. The cargo includes a third of corn and phosphate exports, approximately one quarter of U.S. coal exports, and 15 percent of grain exports. The gross investment value of the canal, excluding defense investments, is $1.9 billion; but some $1.2 billion has been recovered, leaving $700 million outstanding.[10]

There can be little doubt that the Canal is an important facility for interoceanic and hemispheric trade. Militarily the Canal is considered to be essential to the defense of Europe in the event of a prolonged war. Its proximity to the U.S. and the importance of the Canal to the U.S. as a military training site cannot be discounted. Nevertheless, despite these facts, the economic importance of the Canal has been on the wane since the 1960s.

World Business Weekly recently pointed to the emerging obsolescence of the Panama Canal. "Built in 1914, the present Canal can accomodate ships of up to 56,000 deadweight tons. It is now more economical, however, to use larger ships—up to 250,000 dwt—even if it means going around Cape

---

[8] Margaret Daley Hayes, "United States Security Interests in Central America in Global Perspective," in *Central America: International Dimensions of the Crisis* (New York: Holmes and Meier, 1982).

[9] *Ibid.*

[10] U.S. Congress, House Merchant Marine and Fisheries Committee, *U.S. Interests in the Panama Canal Hearings* 95-1, July 25-27, 1977, p. 7ff.

Horn, according to the international shipping industry."[11]

Two new competitors to the Canal are on the scene. An oil pipeline in Panama will carry Alaskan oil, which accounts for one seventh of the Canal's cargo, opening in 1983. And Mexico has just begun rail and road container shipment across the Isthmus of Tehuantepec. While there is still talk of building a new canal, the enormous cost, $15 billion, is all but certain to preclude its feasibility.

In the past decade there have been several studies on the economic value of the Canal. A 1966 study by Arthur D. Little measured the value of the Canal in relation to tolls collected, while in 1971 the United Nations Economic Commission of Latin America (ECLA) studied the Canal revenues and estimated the savings to users. And in 1974 the Maritime Administration (MARAD) presented estimates of the effect the Canal's closure would have upon U.S. exports and imports. The range of estimates from these studies varies from $57.9 million for the Arthur D. Little study to $805 million for the ECLA study. According to the House Merchant Marine and Fisheries Committee, the most reliable and thorough study was done by the Stanford, California, based International Research Associates in 1973. That study looked at the value of the Canal in terms of alternatives that would be employed were the Canal to be closed and incorporated commodity traffic forecasts as well as estimates of alternative shipping costs. The result of this study estimated a $117 million sustainable user surplus, an estimate of the economic value of the Canal following the one year transition period to find new shipping routes, of which approximately $39 million would rebound to the U.S. This is equal to less than two hundredths of one percent of the value of U.S. exports.

Raw Materials and U.S. Strategic Interests

Historically the quest for raw materials has been a major spur to the establishment of colonies. In Central America, discoveries of silver and gold fueled Spanish colonization. And today, U.S. concern with supplies of critical minerals is a major policy consideration in U.S. international relations. For while the U.S. would no doubt wish to be completely independent of raw material imports, studies have served to demonstrate again and again the physical impossibility or economic prohibitiveness of this ambition.

In the early 1970s a study by the National Commission on Materials Policy (NCMP) advocated diversifying supply sources as protection from disruptions, developing new ties with more reliable sources, and developing substitutes. This Commission rejected self-sufficiency in materials, because this option was, and still is, considered uneconomic for some materials and impossible in the case of others. In 1976 the National Commission on Supplies and Shortages (NCSS) concluded that "Resource exhaustion is not a serious possibility within the foreseeable future,"[12] and advocated the

---

[11] "A New Way Around the Old Canal," *World Business Weekly*, October 5, 1981, p. 8.
[12] Eckes, p. 245.

use of government stockpiles to guard against economic problems caused by supply disruptions.

From the point of view of U.S. policy makers, four problems are seen as potentially critical with regard to materials supplies during the 1980s: danger of materials shortages due to the inability of production and supply to meet demand; temporary supply disruptions resulting from wars, revolutions, or cartel action; large price increases; and competition with the Soviet Union.[13]

In order to assess the economic and geopolitical significance of Central America's minerals, metals and petroleum to the United States, it is necessary to examine the availability of these materials in the region, and to present data on U.S. investments in mining and petroleum and on imports of these materials from the region.

Central America as a region remains largely unexplored for potential resources. Lack of technology and funds, as well as geographic and environmental factors, have contributed to this, but some exploration operations are underway. While the area is known to contain deposits of a number of ores and minerals, not all of them are mined. Recent petroleum finds in Guatemala and Honduras have drawn attention to the region's potential role as an oil supplier.

Clearly Central America contains a variety of mineral resources. The main minerals obtained from Central America include iron, lead, zinc, antimony, nickel, silver, gold and petroleum.

Perhaps more important from the perspective of analyzing the strategic importance of these minerals to the U.S. economy is the proportion of U.S. imports supplied by the Central American economies. As Table 1 demonstrates, Central America supplies a very limited share of the strategic minerals indicated. The portions range from a low of three hundredths of a percent for petroleum to 10.2 percent for lead imports. If these are in turn calculated as a share proportion of U.S. consumption the figures fall even further to a bare one-hundredth of a percent for petroleum to 2.8 percent for zinc consumption.

Just how important are these resources to the health of the U.S. economy? The regional specialist at the Bureau of Mines, when asked about the impact of a potential halt to the flow of these resources to the U.S., replied that the effect would be from "negligible to minimal."

The reasons for this are not hard to find. There are numerous and ready alternative sources of supply for each and every one of these resources.

But what is most important is that in no case does it appear that interruption of the Central American supplies would have any significant effect on strategic activity (i.e. military production) in the U.S. The current mineral resource imports from Central America appear insignificant to the health of the U.S. economy or to any sector of industrial activity.

---

[13] *Fortune*, July 1980, pp. 43-44.

Table 1

U.S. Net Import Reliance on Selected Materials
and Per Cent Supplied by Imports from Central America

Material	Net Import Reliance %	% Imports from Central America
Mica	100	–
Manganese	97	–
Bauxite	94	25.5
Tin	84	0.0001
Nickel	73	–
Cadmium	62	–
Zinc	58	4.6
Tungsten	54	–
Antimony	53	1.1
Mercury	49	–
Oil	38	0.03
Gold	28	3.8
Iron Ore	22	–
Copper	14	–
Iron and Steel	13	0.0004
Sulfur	13	*
Salt	8	*
Lime	2	0.006
Aluminum	**	0.0001
Silver	**	0.19
Lead	**	
(Lead ores and concentrates)		10.8
(Lead and alloys)		0.009
Iron and Steel	**	2

*not gathered.
**net exporter.
– not imported from the region.

Source: Mineral Commodity Surveys, 1981. These 1980 N.I.R. figures are estimates. Figures on imports from Central America were derived from data in "U.S. Foreign Trade: General Imports," Schedule A. 1981.

Guatemalan Oil

There has been an inordinate degree of speculation regarding the potential significance of recent discoveries of oil in Guatemala. Guatemalan oil exports to the U.S. began in 1980, making the country the first Central American oil exporter.[14] Oil discoveries in Guatemala have drawn considerable attention in the U.S. media, among businessmen and politicians anxious about dependence on high-priced foreign oil. The discoveries have prompted one geologist to call Guatemala "the Saudi Arabia of Central America." In relation to the rest of Latin America, however, Guatemala's

---

[14] Wall Street Journal, "Guatemala's Oil Attracts Attention," May 28, 1981; and Guatemala Newsletter, "Oil Exports Launch Guatemala into a New Era of Prosperity," October 1980.

oil is of minor significance to the U.S. In 1980 crude oil imports from Mexico accounted for 9.5 percent of the value of all U.S. crude imports and crude imports from Venezuela accounted for 2.7 percent, compared with 0.03 percent from Guatemala.[15] It is also worthwhile to note that oil companies tend to overestimate reserves in order to obtain more favorable contract terms.[16] The government received 51 percent of the revenues as a tax under the old petroleum code, which has since been revised upward to require 55 percent. The new petroleum code also provides for government specifications as to the number of wells a company may drill, places limits on oil extraction, and requires companies to make infrastructure investments and provide technical training. The new code has generated some conflict between the government and oil companies who consider that 55 percent cut too high. Some observers believe the code has limited the number of bids received by the government for concessions.

Even so, estimates of Guatemalan reserves vary widely. Some analysts estimate that Guatemala will produce as much as one million barrels per day (bpd) within three or four years, making it third among Latin American producers, behind Mexico and Venezuela. Yet more realistic estimates place production at about 30,000 bpd.

Arthur D. Warner, Petroleum Geologist in the International Affairs Division of the U.S. Department of Energy and an analyst for over 25 years, regards the company estimates of Guatemalan reserves which run as high as 3 to 6 billion barrels (still far less than Mexico's 60-65 billion barrels) to be highly exaggerated. In any event, the extent of Guatemalan oil reserves would be of minimal value to the U.S. economy. Even were production in Guatemala to reach the maximum levels predicted, which are by all accounts highly exaggerated, they would provide only about 2 percent of 1985 oil imports.[17]

The data on U.S. imports of minerals, metals, and petroleum from Central America and the Caribbean demonstrate that the area is not a significant supplier of these materials to the United States, with the following exceptions: bauxite and alumina from Jamaica accounted for 25.5 percent of the value of all bauxite and alumina imported by the U.S. in 1980, and lead ore and concentrates from Honduras accounted for 10.8 percent.[18]

The fact that the United States imports a major proportion of its minerals, metals and petroleum from South Africa, Canada, Brazil, Mexico, Zambia, Zaire, and OPEC nations, coupled with the insignificance of U.S. investment in Central American mining and petroleum sectors, leads to the conclusion that the area does not represent an important resource

---

[15] "U.S. Foreign Trade: General Imports," Schedule A. 1981.

[16] The first shipment, consisting of 120,000 barrels of crude extracted over a one month period, was sold for $3.5 million ($29.20/barrel).

[17] This is calculated using U.S. Department of Energy data on 1985 consumption supplied by the International Affairs office of the DOE.

[18] Jamaica has been included in this discussion because of its importance as a producer of bauxite and alumina, and because of its active role in the International Bauxite Association (IBA).

supply or income source to the United States, and therefore, that present involvement in Central America is not based on such short-term economic considerations. Long-term considerations of potential reserves may possibly affect U.S. interests in the region, but as stated, reserve projections differ, and it is therefore difficult to assess their significance.

U.S. Trade Interests in Central America

In the quarter century following World War II the United States was able to sustain a comfortable trade surplus. But during the early 1970s the trade surplus had narrowed and by 1976 had turned into a substantial deficit. This fact accentuated U.S. concern with the impact of trade on the health of the U.S. economy.

Foreign investment and foreign trade are complementary. While foreign investment provides the access to sources of raw materials which enter the U.S. economy as imports, U.S. exports of machinery and equipment provide the factories and equipment used in the production of bauxite, bananas and cotton that multinational corporations import. Profits earned overseas by these corporations yield investment income, which benefits the U.S. economy.

Recently, the acceleration of overseas production has highlighted the exploitation of cheap foreign labor as a means by which corporations reduce their production costs. Hourly wages for manual workers employed in manufacturing ranged from 62 to 99 cents per hour in Central America, a fraction of U.S. labor costs.[19]

Foreign trade provides additional markets for products, potentially reducing per unit production costs at home and generating additional growth for a wide range of industrial sectors. Exports to the developing world are becoming increasingly important to the health of the advanced capitalist nations. Currently more than one-third of U.S.-manufactured exports is destined for the Third World, up from 17 percent in the sixties. Latin America is assuming increasing importance in this equation, causing one analyst to argue that "The United States counts especially on expanding its exports to Latin America to help pay for its increasingly expensive energy imports."[20] And the Central American Common Market has been an additional element in the strategy to promote U.S. trade with Latin America.

A recent study commissioned by former President Carter elucidated the increasingly vital role which exports play in the U.S. economy. Titled "The Export Imperative," the report pointed to some 14 reasons behind the urgency of U.S. export expansion. Among the factors identified were (a) the need to pay for "increasingly expensive oil imports and other essential raw materials;" (b) "to reduce ... unsustainable trade deficits;" (c) "to strengthen the dollar as the world's reserve currency;" (d) "to bring in

---

[19] Business International, "Indicators of Market Size for Latin American Countries." Data is for 1978.

[20] Lowenthal, op. cit., 1981.

Table 2
U.S. Imports from Central American Common Market

Product*	Percent from CACM
Beef	13
Shrimps	13
Bananas	63
Plantain	28
Sugar and Molasses	11
Coffee	16
Cigars	22
Lead	10
Oil Seed	20
Cotton	18
Variable Resistors	14
Fixed Capacitors	17
Men's Pajamas	11
Undergarments	92
Brassieres	21
Corsets	12
Automotive Voltage Regulators	27

*Only items accounting for more than 10 percent are included.

foreign source income to bolster our rate of capital investment;" (e) "to provide industry with greater economies of scale, border markets;" (f) "to provide additional funds for national defense;" and (g) "to help restore U.S. economic, military and diplomatic credibility...." This list says in words which are unequivocal and far-reaching why foreign trade is strategically important to the U.S. economy.

A superficial examination of U.S. trade data might convince one to the contrary. In 1980 U.S. exports accounted for only 14.4 percent of GNP in contrast with 23.7 percent for Japan and over 40 percent for West Germany, Italy and the United Kingdom. Imports were about 20 percent of GNP, also far below the European countries. Nevertheless, closer examination reveals that the U.S. economy is heavily dependent upon foreign markets for crucial industries—e.g. aircraft and power generating equipment—as well as being reliant upon foreign sources for imports of strategic minerals.

These imported raw materials are vital to the smooth operation of manufacturing industries and defense. Zinc imported from Central America is important to U.S. steel production, while cotton imports are the basis of the textile industry. The high standard of living of U.S. consumers is in part attributable to imported coffee, cocoa, sugar and bananas from abroad. (See Table 2, *U.S. Imports from Central America*.) But in order to obtain these imports it is essential to export, since exports make the imports possible. In addition, exports are an important means for the disposal of surplus products in industries where U.S. production exceeds domestic consumption. And exports generate employment. In 1976 an estimated 11.3 percent of U.S. manufacturing jobs were dependent upon exports.

The role that exports play in the health of the U.S. economy has grown during the last decade, while previously reliable trade surpluses narrowed and turned into chronic deficits. By 1976 a perennial surplus turned into a $7.7 billion deficit, and this was followed by successively larger deficits in each following year. As the President's Export Council noted with a sense of heightened urgency:

> The United States finds itself in a deteriorating position in the competition for world markets. We need more exports to pay for the large increases in the price of our oil imports, but it is more than an oil problem. Foreign competitors are cutting into the U.S. market share of foreign markets for manufactured goods—at a time when foreign sales have been vitally important to many U.S. workers and U.S. companies.[21]

Between 1970 and 1979 the U.S. share of world exports slipped from 15.4 to 12.1 percent. This may be attributable to several causes. Postwar U.S. exports have been dominated by manufacturers, particularly of transport equipment. The contraction of the international auto market and the rise of new assembly plants in newly industrializing nations of the Third World has undercut U.S. exports. Structurally, the Third World has become increasingly important both as suppliers and consumers of U.S. products. Imports from developing nations have increased from 26 to 45 percent of imports, while exports have risen from 29 to 35 percent.

The Composition of U.S. Imports from Central America

In spite of its historical decline, U.S. trade with Central America remains the key element in the region's external trade. Central America's dependence on U.S. markets and U.S. technology transfer cannot be eradicated in a short period without very high costs. Furthermore, this dependence is an important tool in the portfolio of U.S. policymakers. (As we have recently observed in the case of the U.S. cutoff of wheat to Nicaragua, it is a tool to which the Reagan Administration has already had recourse.)

The overwhelming portion of U.S. imports from Central America consists, not unexpectedly, of agricultural commodities. In 1980, these commodities accounted for 80 percent of total U.S. imports from the region. Imports are dominated by coffee, bananas, sugar, and meat comprising 16, 63, 11 and 13 percent respectively. The only other agricultural commodities which are relatively important in U.S. imports are cigars (22 percent of the total U.S. cigar imports) and shrimp.

The next largest category of U.S. imports from the CACM is miscellaneous manufactured goods, which is dominated by several specific types of clothing. The most important of these are men's and boys' underwear, brassieres, pajamas, slacks, and rainwear. On the whole, these imports could be readily replaced by other foreign sources. Others include wood furniture and some specialized electrical instruments. The wood furniture imports reflect the growing timber and wood-working industries in Central America,

---

[21] *The Export Imperative*, Vol. 1, 1980, p. 13.

in particular Honduras and Costa Rica. Under the specialized electrical instrument category, two items bear notation. El Salvador accounts for 27 percent of U.S. imports of automatic voltage current regulators for low voltage batteries and for approximately 10 percent of U.S. imports of artificial respiration apparatus.

The third largest category of U.S. imports is machinery. This is composed mainly of integrated circuits, calculators, resistors, capacitors, and insulated electrical cable. El Salvador is the largest foreign supplier of monolithic, bipolar integrated circuits to the U.S. (9 percent of total U.S. imports). El Salvador also supplies 4 percent of handheld calculator imports, reflective of Texas Instruments' presence there. Other significant imports include non-wirewound variable resistors (14 percent) and ceramic fixed capacitors (17 percent of total U.S. imports).

The final category of Central American exports of any significance to the United States is crude materials. As mentioned above, the most important items in this category are lead, zinc, oil seeds, silver and lumber. Honduras supplies over 10 percent of U.S. imports of lead and lead ore and 5 percent of zinc ore, both metals being on the Department of Defense's list of strategic metals to stockpile. Central America also accounts for 5 percent of silver ore imports, with Honduras being the main regional supplier.

CACM nations also supply 20 percent of U.S. imports of oil seeds and oil nuts. Honduras and Guatemala also make marginal contributions to imports of lumber. In summary, the region's contribution to strategic materials imported by the U.S. is minimal, save for Honduras' lead and zinc.

Thus, while U.S. imports from Central America are dominated by agricultural commodities, it is also apparent that the importance of this region's exports are not limited to these items. Honduras' metals and El Salvador's small but growing specialized electronics export sector are significant factors in the import categories. However, it seems clear that on the whole the imports from Central America are not of vital importance to the United States.

Composition of U.S. Exports to Central America

Central America's general imports are dominated by manufactures. Therefore it should not be surprising to find that manufactures constitute the bulk of U.S. exports to the region. Basic manufactures, machines and transport equipment and miscellaneous manufactures account for the majority of U.S. exports. Other significant U.S. exports are chemicals and food. Capital goods and machinery are perhaps the most important U.S. exports. In many categories of capital machinery, the U.S. supplies 50 percent of total Central American imports. This situation makes Central America highly dependent on U.S. technology and also implies a dependence on the United States for replacement parts for this machinery. One obvious implication of this dependency is that the U.S. could easily make economic life more difficult for any of the Central American nations.

Table 3

Indicators of Market Potential:

Latin America and Central America

	A. Latin America	B. Central America	B/A %
Population 1979 (millions)	305.5	20.0	6.7
1990 forecast	409.8	27.8	6.8
Gross Domestic Product ($ million)	553.2	10.8	2.0
Average GDP increase (past five years)	26%	18%	69.2
National Income (per capita $)	1,669	472	28.3
Total Imports (1979) ($ million)	64,407	5,169	8.0
Private Consumption Expenditure ($ billion)	302.6	11.9	3.9

Source: *Business International* "Indicators of Market Size for Latin American Countries," 1979.

Other important U.S. exports of manufactures to the region include textile fibers and clothing, of which the U.S. supplies 41 and 49 percent respectively. The U.S. also supplies 3/4 of the region's paperboard imports. Its role as a major supplier of road motor vehicles has been weakened by declining demand, continued competition (especially from Japan and West Germany), and the development of a growing auto assembly industry in Costa Rica. The U.S. also supplies 50 percent of Central America's chemical imports.

The foregoing raise certain questions regarding the importance of Central American trade to the U.S. economy. It is possible that another less tangible and more long-term factor may be of greater importance—the market potential of the region.

Market Potential

Table 3 presents a range of indicators of market potential. These indicators reflect the size of the market and the income available for purchase of commodities in each market, and the current level of imports, an indicator of the industrial demand for inputs into the manufacturing sector.

Relative to the Latin American market, the Central American market is a poor cousin. The population of the CACM is about 6.5 percent of Latin America, but in terms of total output it is only 1.9 percent. Moreover, the growth of GDP for Latin America during the past five years, as good an indication as any of the likely future performance, was an average of 26 percent for the eleven Latin American countries and only 18 percent for CACM.

Turning to the per capita level of income, for Latin America it was

$1669 while for Central America the figure was $472. This means that the average level in Central America was only 28 percent of the average in Latin America. Total consumer expenditure was 3.9 percent of the Latin American total.

What this all adds up to is a market of generally limited potential in comparison with the Latin American market.

Financial Interests

U.S. financial interests in Central America comprise two main components: one is real investment or direct foreign investment, and the other is monetary investment. The latter is in the form of loans to governmental institutions, private banks and corporations by U.S. banking institutions, and is frequently referred to as the "exposure" of the banks.

Both of these concepts require interpretation and definition; and both are difficult to measure. The value of foreign investment is composed of the accumulated value of past investments as well as reinvested profits of U.S. corporations and subsidiaries. Bank loans comprise a variety of different types ranging from short-term credits of less than a year to loans with a maturity of ten years or more.

A major interest of the investors is the profitability of their investments relative to other opportunities in other areas of the world. The size of the market is also a major consideration in foreign investments, as it tends to affect the future opportunity for earnings. And political and economic stability is of such import that many firms are hiring political analysts to apprise them of the political risks involved in their investments: an issue of particular moment in the case of Central American investments.

For the banks, their main and overriding concern is timely repayment of their loans. Losses result when repayment is delayed or when it is on terms more lenient than those originally specified in the loan agreement. An issue of overarching concern at this moment is the fear that any renegotiation of outstanding debt or, worse yet, repudiation of past debts, would set a dangerous precedent with potentially catastrophic consequences at the international level. The current outstanding debt of the underdeveloped countries is an estimated $530 billion, the highest in history.[22] Costa Rica is on the verge of default, and Honduras may not be far behind.

Nicaragua's debt was renegotiated following the Sandinista Revolution. This was acceptable to U.S. banks only because the level of exposure was small and the uniqueness of the situation considered exceptional and not precedent-setting. Nevertheless, any further debt renegotiation in the region is unlikely to be considered in this vein.[23]

Moreover, a similar situation is unlikely to occur in El Salvador, since the banks have been systematically reducing their exposure. This can be demonstrated by some revealing data on the lending exposure of the eight

---

[22] *Wall Street Journal,* "Third World's Debts Totalling $500 Billion May Pose Big Dangers," January 28, 1981.

[23] Purcell, *op. cit.,* pp. 10, 12ff.

Table 4
U.S. Balance of Payments with Central America, 1980

	Net Trade Balance	Investment Income	Direct Economic Assistance
Costa Rica	137	na	13.7
El Salvador	159	na	68.1
Guatemala	113	na	11.5
Honduras	45	na	60.6
Nicaragua	36	na	37.0
Total	82	144	190.9

Sources: *Quarterly Economic Review, Survey of Current Business,* Foreign Assistance Legislation for Fiscal Year 1982, Hearings and Mark-up.

largest U.S. banks in Central America. While between 1978 and 1980 the exposure of these banks, which account for 75 percent of U.S. lending, increased by some 35 percent in the Western Hemisphere, their exposure in Central America as a percentage of Western Hemisphere lending was very small, totaling 4.1 percent in 1978 and 2.3 percent in 1980. Yet despite these low levels of exposure, the region accounted for an alarming proportion of U.S. world-wide bad debt write-offs: $37.4 million or 17.5 percent of all write-offs between 1975 and 1979.[24] These figures indicate that the region is no longer a profitable zone for the banks.

Within these trends the interests and policies of particular financial institutions vary. In general, the banks are attempting to shift their lending to short-term loans. One large bank is reducing all loans to Central American countries, while another is continuing business as usual. Yet several small banks with regional offices in Guatemala have moved operations to Panama. In view of the recent nationalization of Citibank in El Salvador and Bank of America in Nicaragua, the banks are understandably cautious.

To summarize, the interests of financial institutions are small and insignificant and have been further reduced as the banks have sought to minimize their exposure in the region.

Likewise direct foreign investment in Central America is marginal when compared with other areas of the world. The proportion of U.S. investment in the Central American region is a mere four-tenths of one percent of the world total. The net income generated by U.S. investments in 1980 was $144 million, correspondingly only four-tenths of one percent.

While earnings from Latin America totaled some 20 percent of all foreign profits, the CACM region accounted for a small share. Despite the fact that investment in the region was slightly more profitable than the average, virtually no additional investment is planned for the region.

What this seems to indicate is that exposure of United States firms and banks in Central America and the earnings of U.S. business in general are

---

[24] Arturo C. Porzecanski, "The International Financial Role of U.S. Commercial Banks: Past and Future," *Journal of Banking and Finance,* March, 1981, p. 1.

Table 5

Summary: The U.S. Economic Stake in
Central America, 1980 (millions $)

1. Trade
Exports	$1,847
Imports (Mineral Imports)	$1,931

2. Investment
Fixed Capital	$1,033
Income from Investment	$144

3. Finance
Private Lending Expense*	$1,232
Public Loans Outstanding	$629

4. Panama Canal
Net Annual Return	$31-47
Fixed Capital	$752

*Eight largest U.S. banks.

very limited. Doubtless, some specific firms have substantial investments in the region. For example, United Fruit Company has sizeable holdings of banana plantations. Loss of these assets which affect particular companies would not have a significant effect on the U.S. balance of payments or on any other significant economic variable.[25]

Balance of Payments

As noted in the initial section, an issue of some importance to the U.S. is the contribution of each country to the U.S. balance of payments, which has been in deficit largely due to rising oil prices. To what extent does the Central American region contribute to U.S. foreign exchange earnings?

Table 4 provides a partial summary of the net effect of the Central American Common Market area on the U.S. balance of payments for 1980. In that year there was a net gain from trade of $82 million and a net earning from investment of $144 million. There were additional earnings beyond this level from shipping and other minor contributants to U.S. earnings, but these data are not available. During the same period a total of $190 million returned to the area in the form of direct economic assistance. In addition to this sum an estimated $600 million was made available from multinational lending agencies, the World Bank, IMF and Inter-American Development Bank, in which there is a sizeable U.S. component.

---

[25] Perhaps more interesting, if the experience of U.S. business operating in Nicaragua may be taken as a bellwether, the economic condition of firms operating in the post-revolutionary environment indicates that the losses attributable to the change to a socialist government have in many cases not been as disastrous as anticipated. In fact, several U.S. firms reported improved labor relations since the Revolution. In Nicaragua, among the firms which remained following the Sandinista Revolution, according to an August 1981 survey by *Business International*, most report that "their relations with the government vary little from experiences in other developing countries. . . . Corporate life under the Nicaragua's Sandinista's (sic) is not the nightmare most companies had anticipated." *Business International*, August 14, 1981, p. 264.

What does this data indicate? One way of interpreting these figures is to say that in order to earn a net trade balance and income on investments of approximately $299 million, some $190 million was made available in economic assistance and an additional $650 million in military assistance and indirect economic assistance. In addition, with the impending bankruptcy of Costa Rica and El Salvador, the specter of vastly increased economic assistance is apparent. Clearly, this raises questions about the nature of the regional contribution to the U.S. balance of payments. It would not be unreasonable to argue that the region contributes to U.S. balance of payments deficit.

U.S. Economic and Geopolitical Interests: Summary

An accounting of the U.S. economic stake in Central America indicates that it is rather limited in strict dollar terms. Table 5 shows that trade with the region in 1980 amounted to $1,847 million in exports and $1,931 in imports, less than 1 percent of total U.S. exports and imports. The region is a supplier of zinc, lead, antimony and some other minerals.

In respect to overseas investments and the value of U.S. property, fixed capital was just over $1 billion and generated an income of $144 million in 1980. This was the equivalent of less than 1/2 of one percent of U.S. investments on income overseas.

Meanwhile the estimated financial exposure in the region by U.S. public and private agencies was some $1.9 billion. This represents about six-tenths of a percent of global exposure. These sums are not particularly large. Yet they may be important in that any repudiation of these debts, no matter how small, could have a potentially serious impact throughout the entire capitalist world. This of course is the crucial element in understanding the U.S. economic interests in the region—they go far beyond the region itself.

The significance of Central America has to be seen in terms of its global geopolitical significance. For starters, the region is seen as important to the defense of Mexico and Brazil, two enormously important countries, by an administration that views the world as standing and falling dominoes caught in a simplistic bipolar rivalry. Within this context, Central America is strategically important due to its *symbolic* value, in showing the world "that the United States has stopped abandoning even its pockmarked friends."[26]

Yet there is an underlying contradiction. The costs to U.S. taxpayers and long-term business interests of pursuing such a policy are certain to be far greater than they are perceived to be; they are likely to be far in excess of any perceived imperial returns.

The costs are likely to be both economic and diplomatic. On the one hand a policy which anticipates restoration of international authority through use of military power will require significant military expenditure in addition to economic security assistance. As the region's economies

---

[26] W. Scott Thompson, "Choosing to Win," *Foreign Policy*, Summer 1981, p. 83.

continue to deteriorate, and they will with the militarization of the region, aid disbursements will have to rise to several times the current annual level, estimated at $850 million.

World Bank forecasts estimate that Costa Rica alone will require nearly $4 billion in public and private finance between 1982 and 1985, even assuming that the economy is stabilized and returns to a 4 percent growth path, a most optimistic assumption. For the five nations of the CACM an inflow of approximately $13 billion will be required. If these estimates are correct, the costs of maintaining traditional U.S. dominance in the region will become increasingly burdensome.

The present course of U.S. foreign policy in the region presumes that a resumption of a Cold-War, Soviet-U.S. rivalry can restructure world politics, inspire unruly allies and fence-sitting nations to see merit in American policy. Yet Michael Harrison, Professor of European Studies at Johns Hopkins School of Advanced Social Sciences, argues that the present attempt to reassert U.S. global authority in response to the relative decline of U.S. power is not only anachronistic but will damage U.S. interests.

... No foreign policy of global leadership based on the resumption of a pervasive Soviet-U.S. rivalry can restructure world politics into the simple, sometimes appealing, but anachronistic hierarchy of the Cold War. Such a misreading of international trends threatens the potential benefits of a more realistic approach to the Soviet Union and offer the unsettling prospect of damaging U.S. economic and security interest in key regions of the Third World. Moreover, it may inflict further damage on the U.S.-West European alliance which although continually frayed, now seems especially fragile.[27]

There seems little doubt that once again, U.S. policy in Central America seems but poised to demonstrate the sagacity of Samuel Johnson's wit:

"Extended empire, like expanded gold, exchanges solid strength for feeble splendor."

---

[27] Michael Harrison, "Reagan's World," *Foreign Policy*, Summer 1981, p. 8.

4

Heritage of Hunger:
Population, Land and Survival

For Central Americans, as for most people in agrarian-based Third World societies, the probability of survival and the quality of life are directly related to access to land and the resources with which to work it. An irony of the last two decades' economic growth and industrialization is that this relationship has grown more, rather than less, crisis-ridden. The explanations favored by mainstream social scientists in the developed capitalist countries—the neo-Malthusians' "too many people exploiting a fixed amount of land and resources" and the modernizers' "swollen traditional farming sector employing inefficient production methods"—simply do not stand up when confronted with the facts. It is no wonder, then, that they have failed to elicit viable solutions to Central America's spreading poverty.

Mainstream views of the persistence of poverty in the Third World tend to ignore a crucial fact: underdevelopment is a dynamic historical process, not the residue of a history that has ceased to evolve. The historical dynamism of underdeveloped societies springs from a fundamental inequality of power and wealth. On the one hand, there are those social sectors which have been able to maintain and expand their political and economic domination; on the other are those whose virtual exclusion ("marginalization") from economic and political power has been correspondingly perpetuated. Generally speaking, the achievement of development by the one sector is predicated on the underdevelopment of the other, to the point where underdevelopment becomes the other side of the coin of development. This contradiction has persisted over time both internally and in the international relationships between underdeveloped countries and the "developed" world.

The current status of life and land in Central America attests to the contradictory nature of development/underdevelopment. Worsening living conditions for the majority of the population and growing inequities in the distribution of income and wealth have long existed side by side with relatively rapid rates of GDP growth. Control over natural resources and the means of production and decisions about the composition and distribution of GDP are the exclusive prerogative of a small class of people. As a result, domestic production of staple items, particularly food, is not oriented to the needs of the majority of the population and indeed falls far short of satisfying them. The elite minority's compulsion to maximize and maintain profits has rarely coincided with improvements in the standard of living or distribution of the fruits of economic growth among the marginalized majority. For the latter group, the consolidation of economic and political power in the hands of a few has meant a continual shrinking of opportunities to achieve economic self-sufficiency, beginning with ever more restricted access to land.

An extensive study by Durham of conditions leading to the 1969 "Soccer War" between El Salvador and Honduras analyzes in detail the causes of resource scarcity in the two countries. The evidence uncovered, particularly for El Salvador, in the author's words, "confirms Ernest Feder's general observation ... that in Latin America 'land is a scarce resource only for the small holders.'"[1] Durham estimates an 1892 land base of 7.41 hectares per farmer available to the 50.8% of Salvadorean agriculturalists occupying farms less than 2 hectares in size; by 1971 this land base had shrunk to an average of 0.38 hectares—5 percent of the 1892 figure. The analysis shows that increasingly unequal land distribution over this period had a greater effect on land scarcity than did rapid population growth. This finding is a particularly important challenge to the neo-Malthusians because El Salvador has many of the surface manifestations of the "population-resource race:" rapid population growth, the highest demographic density and land utilization ratio in Latin America, and increasing landlessness and food shortages. In fact, El Salvador's well-kept agricultural census data reveal that, beginning in the 19th century, the success of large farmers in expanding their extensive holdings and shifting land out of basic food crops into more lucrative export crops such as coffee, cotton and sugar directly resulted in a reduction in the amount of land available to small farmers. This process lay behind the increased landlessness and food shortages; by the mid-1920s, and for the first time in its history, El Salvador was importing large quantities of basic grains such as corn, beans and rice.

The articles in this chapter reach a conclusion similar to that of the Durham study: institutional and structural factors, rather than the pressure of population growth against a constant resource base, are primarily responsible for the deepening and widening of poverty in Central America. Their methodology is based on a historical approach which asks the following questions: (1) What sorts of institutional arrangements currently govern the survival prospects of different social groups, and how did they evolve? (2) What kinds of institutional changes are likely to result in an improvement and equalization of those prospects?

Focusing on the first of these questions, Peter Dorner and Rodolfo Quiros analyze data on the size distribution of farms, land tenure arrangements, and market orientation (production for export versus production for

---

[1] William H. Durham, *Scarcity and Survival in Central America: Ecological Origins of the Soccer War* (Stanford, California: Stanford University Press, 1979), p. 52, citing Ernest Feder, *The Rape of the Peasantry: Latin America's Landholding System* (Garden City, New York: Doubleday, 1971), p. 30.

domestic consumption) in the five Central American countries. What they find is a dual agricultural structure with roots extending back to the period of Spanish colonialism. This system pits small farmers producing largely for domestic consumption in an unfair competition against large farmers producing mainly for export. Moreover, it displays a tenacious capacity for perpetuating itself, through phases of export expansion as well as export contraction, with the result that ever larger sectors of the agrarian population are pushed to the margin of economic survival and political power.

The second article included in this chapter, "Land of the Few" by Andrea Brown, analyzes a similar pattern of development in Guatemala. There, as in the other countries of Central America, increased landlessness has brought about a growing proletarianization of the rural labor force. In other words, wage labor has become the exclusive source of income for growing numbers of rural dwellers. This situation is particularly acute among indigenous peoples who have been progressively dispossessed of their ancestral lands. A powerful agrarian-based bourgeoisie, backed by the brute force of military governments in active collaboration with foreign (especially U.S.) capital, has thus succeeded in incorporating the rural majority into "modern" capitalist agriculture. Below-subsistence wages, enforced indebtedness, denial of access to sufficient land to satisfy minimal needs, and job insecurity caused by the seasonal nature of employment and the lack of alternative opportunities, translate into high social costs— hunger, homelessness and disease—for rural workers. Conversely, such factors translate into low costs and high profits for agricultural capitalists. For the dispossessed majority, the need for agrarian reform is dramatic; for the prosperous minority entrenched in privilege, the prospect of reform is terrifying. The unrelenting violence of official and semi-official repression since the U.S.-backed overthrow of the Arbenz government in 1954 has attempted to silence the call for reform; ironically, it has convinced more and more Guatemalans of the need for a genuine social, political and economic revolution.

Throughout Central America, with the notable exceptions of Costa Rica and post-Somoza Nicaragua, dominant political and economic groups continue to resist popular pressure for reform, hoping in this way to squelch the possibility of revolution. (The historical record of the elite's intransigence is discussed at greater length in Chapter 1 of this book.) Nevertheless, from time to time the opposite tack has been taken: experiments with reform have been permitted in the hope that they would serve to stave off revolution. Because they have typically proven to be reforms in name only, in reality these experiments cannot even be qualified as reformist. In the third article included in this chapter, Philip Wheaton offers a detailed analysis of such a "reform" in El Salvador. Once the reform's counterinsurgency apparatus was in place, its tragic consequences could hardly be hidden from the masses of Salvadoreans it ostensibly was meant to help. That it failed to dampen the revolutionary enthusiasm of those seeking real structural change is therefore not surprising. More surprising is the failure of the reform's U.S. architects and government financial backers to keep it, or at least its reformist appearance, around for long: as one of the first major acts of El Salvador's newly elected Constituent Assembly, the reform program was for all intents and purposes scuttled in May 1982. Once again, land reform—even a version that is essentially capitalist and seeks only to modernize an inefficient market system of agriculture—has proven too revolutionary a demand for Central America's elites.

Unbending oligarchic opposition and U.S. intervention notwithstanding, the need for a revolutionary transformation of institutional arrangements—the social relations of production—in Central America is growing more urgent by the day. In the preceding discussion we have referred to the distorted economic relationships which constrain the survival prospects of Central America's marginalized majority. In the next few pages we investigate the resulting deterioration of living conditions which serves as incontrovertible evidence of the need for revolutionary change.

Survival and the Quality of Life: Socioeconomic Indicators

Living Standards: Nutrition, Mortality and Health Care

Nutritional status is one of the simplest and most direct indicators of social well-being in underdeveloped countries. Table 1 presents the dismal statistics on protein-calorie malnutrition[2] among children under 5 in Central America. As shown, three Central American countries—El Salvador, Guatemala, and Honduras—are well above the Latin American average for percentage of malnourished children in the 0-5 age group.

Equally as disquieting as this cross-country snapshot is the trend in malnutrition depicted in Table 2. In every country except Costa Rica, malnutrition prevalence[3] among children age 0 to 5 increased from 1965 to 1975. For the region as a whole, there was a 65 percent increase in the number of malnourished children. One study of El Salvador by Puffer and Serrano[4] found that nutritional deficiency was a major underlying or associated cause of mortality in children under 5 years of age. Over the period 1968-1970, 37.2 percent of these deaths in San Salvador and 46.9 percent in the *municipios* were related to nutritional deficiency. But malnutrition is not confined to children. Taking the population as a whole, the majority of Central Americans suffer from chronic malnutrition. According to Valverde *et al.*, chronic protein-calorie malnutrition "is one of the principal health problems of Central America and possibly an important factor limiting the social and economic development of the area."[5]

---

[2] "Protein-calorie intake is generally considered the most consistent and convenient criterion for comparing the nutritional status of groups within countries, among countries and over time." Inter-American Development Bank (IDB), *Economic and Social Progress in Latin America, 1978 Report* (Washington, D.C: IDB, 1978), p. 137.

[3] Malnutrition prevalence refers to the absolute number of persons suffering from malnutrition in a given age group.

[4] R. R. Puffer and Carlos V. Serrano, *Patterns of Mortality in Childhood*, Pan-American Health Organization, Washington, D.C., 1973, p. 165.

[5] Victor Valverde *et al.*, "Relationship between Family Land Availability and Nutritional Status," *Ecology of Food and Nutrition*, Vol. 6, 1977, pp. 1-7.

Table 1

Protein-Calorie Malnutrition in Children Ages 0-5,
Various Years, 1971-75, Central America

	Total	Percentage Malnourished*		
		Grade I	Grade II	Grade III
El Salvador	74.5	48.5	22.9	3.1
Guatemala	81.4	49.0	26.5	5.9
Honduras	72.5	43.0	27.2	2.3
Nicaragua	56.8	41.8	13.2	1.8
Costa Rica	57.4	43.7	12.2	1.5
Latin America (except Cuba)	61.4	42.5	16.4	2.5

*Gómez classification (Grade I = mild, can be corrected by an increase in nutrients; Grade II = moderate, requires nutrients plus medical care; Grade III = severe, requires nutrients, medical care and in-patient care).

Source: Inter-American Development Bank (IDB), Economic and Social Progress in Latin America, 1978 Report (Washington, D.C.: IDB, 1978), p. 138. Adapted from Políticas nacionales de alimentación y nutrición, Pan-American Health Organization, Publication No. 328, Washington, D.C., 1976, p. 34.

Challenging the view that the increase in malnutrition prevalence in Central America is mainly the result of excessive population growth, Teller et al.[6] conclude that a policy directed at reducing malnutrition prevalence by 30 percent would have a much greater positive impact than would a one percentage point decrease in the population growth rate. According to the authors' estimates, the nutritional policy would result in an increase of only 3 percent in malnutrition prevalence over the 10 year period 1975-85, while lowering the population growth rate from 3.5 to 2.5 percent per annum would result in a 28 percent increase in malnutrition prevalence.

In their study of the relationship between child nutritional status and family land availability in four Guatemalan villages, Valverde et al. find ample evidence to support their claim that "The fundamental causes of malnutrition are of a social nature. Due to a lack of and/or inefficient use of resources, the majority of the Central American population is unable to achieve good health and nutritional status."[7] Of the farmers comprising their sample, 25.2 percent had access to (owned or rented) less than 2 manzanas (1 manzana = 0.7 hectares), 50.3 percent had access to between 2 and 5 manzanas, and 24.5 percent had access to more than 5 manzanas. Significant differences in the risk of child malnutrition were found between these family farm-size categories: the two- and three-year-old children of families with access to less than 2 manzanas were 2.3 times more likely to have moderate malnutrition than their counterparts in families with access to more than 5 manzanas.

[6] Charles Teller et al., "Population and Nutrition: Implications of Sociodemographic Trends and Differentials for Food and Nutrition Policy in Central America and Panama," Ecology of Food and Nutrition, Vol. 8, 1979, pp. 95-109.

[7] Valverde et al., op. cit.

Table 2
Change in Numbers of Malnourished Children
Age 0-5, Central America, 1965-67 and 1974-76.

	1965-67		1974-76		Numerical and % increase 1965-76	
	% of age group	(1000s)	% of age group	(1000s)	(1000s)	%
El Salvador	26.0	148	38.0	277	129	87.0
Guatemala	32.4	281	38.1	421	141	50.1
Honduras	29.5	124	38.0	224	99	79.9
Nicaragua	15.0	50	22.6	102	52	105.2
Costa Rica	13.7	38	12.3	33	-5	-13.2
Central America	–	641	–	1052	416	64.9

Source: IDB, op. cit., p. 141. Based on Vigilancia epidemiológica de la desnutrición, Pan-American Health Organization, 1978, p. 8.

With an average of well over half of the population residing in rural areas[8] and about half of the labor force engaged in agriculture,[9] most Central Americans derive the bulk of their income from the land. It follows that income distribution should affect nutritional status in much the same way as does land availability. Recent surveys have found evidence of just such a relationship. In Guatemala, the lowest 50 percent of income recipients are able to meet only 61 percent of the minimum required caloric intake. In Costa Rica, which boasts the highest standard of living in Central America, the lowest 50 percent are able to obtain 92 percent. With respect to protein intake, the lowest 50 percent of Salvadorean income recipients are able to obtain only 50 percent of the minimum requirement; the corresponding figure for Costa Ricans is 87 percent.[10] The high and growing degree of landlessness among rural families[11] implies a precarious income situation and poor nutritional prognosis unlikely to improve in the near future.

The trend in per capita beef consumption among the general population is consistent with the apparent decline in nutritional status among children. As shown in Table 3, between 1960-64 and 1970-74 there was an average drop of 20 percent in per capita beef consumption in Central America

[8] World Bank, World Economic and Social Indicators, Report No. 700/79/04 (Washington, D.C.: The World Bank, October 1979). The figures are: Costa Rica, 59%; El Salvador, 60%; Guatemala, 63%; Honduras, 68%; and Nicaragua, 50%.

[9] World Bank, August 1980. The figures are: Costa Rica, 29%; El Salvador, 52%; Guatemala, 57%; Honduras, 64%; and Nicaragua, 44%.

[10] Teller et al., op. cit., p. 97.

[11] In El Salvador, for example, the proportion of rural families who were landless increased from 11.8 percent in 1961 to 29.1 percent in 1971. See Gerald E. Karush, "Plantations, Population, and Poverty: The Roots of the Demographic Crisis in El Salvador" in Studies in Comparative International Development, Vol. XII, No. 3, Fall 1978, p. 61. By 1975, the figure had reached 40 percent and was expected to climb to 60 percent by 1980. See L. Simon and J. Stephens, "El Salvador Land Reform, 1980-81, Impact Audit" (Boston: OXFAM America, 1981, mimeo), p. 5.

Table 3
Per Capita Beef Consumption for
Central America, 1960-64, 1970-74, (kg/year)*

	1960-64	1970-74	% change
El Salvador	8	5	-37.5
Guatemala	8	7	-12.5
Honduras	7	7	–
Nicaragua	16	14	-12.5
Costa Rica	17	10	-41.2
Central America	10	8	-20.0

*Apparent consumption = output + (imports – exports).

Source: IDB, op. cit., p. 143. Based on Alberto Valdés and Gustavo Nores, Growth Potential of the Beef Sector in Latin America, International Food Policy Research Institute, Washington, D.C., 1978, p. 26, and IDB calculations.

overall. Ironically, over this period there was a simultaneous increase in beef exports from Central America, particularly to the United States.[12] The drop in beef consumption was accompanied by a decline in consumption of dairy products, as big ranchers throughout the region increasingly shifted from dairy to beef cattle, sending milk prices far beyond the reach of most families.

As suggested by the Puffer and Serrano study, malnutrition and undernutrition bear a direct relation to Central America's unusually high mortality rates, particularly among small children. Table 4 compares statistics on life expectancy, infant mortality and the child death rate for the countries of Central America with those for Cuba and the United States. These indicators have improved considerably since 1960 in most Central American countries, with the introduction of immunization and other simple medical advances, yet the infant mortality rate is still up to 8 times as high and the life expectancy 10 to 15 years shorter than in countries with widespread availability of health care and basic social services.

Indirect evidence of the disparity in child mortality rates among different social classes and between urban and rural areas is provided in Tables 5 and 6. The number of years of schooling received by the mother is used as an approximate indicator of social status in the comparison of mortality rates among children 0 to 2 years of age. Considered on this basis, the effect of social class on infant mortality in Central America is dramatic: a 4- to 5-fold differential between children of illiterate mothers and children of mothers with 10 or more years of schooling. In fact, as can be seen in Table 5, the social class differential is far more dramatic than the sizeable differential observed when rural and urban areas are compared.

As a counter-example to the infant mortality rates for Central America, Cuba stands out due to its policy of providing universal medical care

[12] Inter-American Development Bank (IDB), Economic and Social Progress in Latin America, 1978 Report (Washington, D.C., 1978), pp. 143-144.

Table 4
Mortality Statistics for Central America,
Cuba, and the United States (1960 and 1978)

	Life Expectancy at Birth		Infant Mortality Ages 0-1 (per 1000 births)		Child Death Rate, Ages 1-4 (per 1000)	
	1960	1978	1960	1978	1960	1978
El Salvador	50	63	–	60	24	8
Guatemala	47	57	–	77	31	15
Honduras	46	57	*130*	*118*	30	14
Nicaragua	47	55	–	*37*	30	17
Costa Rica	62	70	80	*28*	10	3
Cuba	64	72	35	*25*	8	1
United States	70	73	26	*14*	1	1

Numbers in italics are for years other than those specified.

Source: World Bank, *World Development Report, 1980* (Washington, D.C.: The World Bank, August 1980).

Table 5
Probability of Death during the First Two Years of Life
(per 1000 Births) by Education of Mother, 1966-1970

	Total	Years of Schooling				
		0	1-3	4-6	7-9	10+
El Salvador	145	158	142	111	58	30
Guatemala	149	169	135	85	58	44
Honduras	140	171	129	99	60	35
Nicaragua	149	168	142	115	73	48
Costa Rica	81	125	98	70	51	33
Cuba	41	46	45	34	29	–

Source: H. Behm and D. Primante, "Mortalidad en los primeros años de vida en la América Latina," *Notas de Población,* Año 6, No. 16, 1978.

regardless of an individual's ability to pay for it. Thus infant mortality rates for Cuba are both significantly lower in absolute terms (about 1/3 the Central American average), and far more equal across different social groups.

As with the statistics on mortality, the official figures on health care, expressed as population averages, mask enormous differences between social classes within each country. In addition to statistics on population per doctor, Table 7 gives figures on the distribution of doctors per person indicating that there are between 3 and 6 times as many doctors per person in the cities as in the countryside. A fuller picture of this problem is given by examining the clientele typically served by these doctors:

> One indication of a nation's probable health is the proportion of physi- cians in its population. This standard alone indicates a health problem in Central America—its six nations have fewer physicians than the state

Table 6

Rural-Urban Differentials in Mortality of Children Age 0-2,
Central America, 1966-1970, (deaths per 1000 births)

	Metropolitan	Rest of Urban	Rural
El Salvador	113	143	148
Guatemala	72	142	161
Honduras	97	122	150
Nicaragua	126	157	152
Costa Rica	53	69	92

Source: H. Behm and D. Primante, "Mortalidad en los primeros años de vida en la América Latina," Notas de Población, Año 6, No. 16, 1978.

of Tennessee. It is bad enough to have so few physicians; what is much worse is that the doctors huddle together in a few cities with the same concern for private patients and specialization that characterizes the physician on Park Avenue.

The first important fact about Honduran physicians is that one in every ten of them is not there. Of the 675 doctors registered in the Medical Association, 74 are out of the country—an indication of the brain drain and the pursuit of exotic specialties. Next, of those who are in Honduras, over two-thirds are in Tegucigalpa, San Pedro Sula, and La Ceiba, cities which account for only 16 percent of the population. In Honduras' eight poorest departments, which contain 550,000 people—over a fifth of the population—there are exactly 28 physicians, half of whom are young interns putting in their government service.[13]

The situation is even worse in Guatemala, the country with the most unequal and inadequate distribution of health care services in Central America, as shown in Table 7. Close to 80 precent of the medical and paramedical personnel are concentrated in Guatemala City alone, leaving the vast majority of the population without access to medical care.[14]

The foregoing discussion confirms the importance of structural and institutional factors in creating and perpetuating poverty in Central America. Land availability, income, social class and urban or rural residence were identified as determinants of three social indicators: nutritional status, mortality and access to health care. Clearly, improvements in the level and distribution of these indicators can only come from a restructuring of their determinants. Just how profound a restructuring is required is suggested in the following pages, through a closer look at four factors influencing survival and the quality of life.

Economic Barriers: Land, Income, Employment and Education

As mentioned previously, agriculture is the major source of income

[13] Mayone Stycos, Margin of Life: Population and Poverty in the Americas (New York: Grossman, 1974), p. 85.

[14] IDB, op. cit., p. 271.

Table 7
Health Care Statistics for Central America

	Population per physician		Distribution of physicians*
	1960	1977	1968-71
El Salvador	5660	3600	3.7
Guatemala	4410	2490	5.8
Honduras	12610	3420	4.3
Nicaragua	2740	1670	3.1
Costa Rica	2600	1390	2.1

Numbers in italics are for years other than those specified.

*Distribution of physicians is the ratio of physicians per person in cities with population over 100,000 divided by physicians per person in all other parts of the country. The higher the ratio, the greater the discrepancy in the availability of physicians between more urbanized areas and less urbanized ones.

Source: World Bank, *World Development Report, 1980* (Washington, D.C.: The World Bank, August 1980); and James W. Wilkie and Stephen Haber, eds., *Statistical Abstract of Latin America, Volume 21* (Los Angeles: UCLA Latin American Center Publications, University of California, 1981), p. 7.

for most Central Americans. Large numbers—in some countries, the majority—of small farmers are renters; their livelihood is therefore constantly threatened by the possibility of eviction. For landless rural workers (those without access to land, either owned or rented), economic survival is even more uncertain. In an economy marked by high degrees of under-utilization of labor, they must opt between agricultural wage employment and migration to urban areas in search of jobs. Few among them have access to the alternative route to survival available to some (though by no means most) propertyless urban dwellers: formal education. Denied even the rudiments of schooling, the landless are both forced to the margin of economic survival and deprived of the fundamental tools necessary for demanding and seizing political power.

While the landless rural workers would therefore appear to be the most disadvantaged social group, in fact the majority of Central Americans, urban as well as rural, face profound economic barriers to obtaining a decent standard of living. Barriers of access to land, income, employment and education are among the most serious. Table 8 provides a portrait of the extreme inequality in the distribution of farmland. Summing up for each country, in El Salvador we find the 1.5 percent of farms in the largest size categories (50+ hectares) controlling 59.5 percent of the total land in farms, while 86.9 percent of farms are of less than 5 hectares in size and control only 19.6 percent of total farmland.[15] The Guatemalan picture is

---

[15] It is therefore not surprising that 60 percent of El Salvador's rural families have been estimated to earn less than the minimum income required for subsistence. See Carmen Diana Deere, "A Comparative Analysis of Agrarian Reform in El Salvador and Nicaragua 1979-81" in *Development and Change*, Vol. 13, 1982, p. 37.

Table 8
Size Distribution of Agricultural Landholdings, Central America, Various Years
(% of total no. of holdings, % of total hectares in farms)

Hectares		El Salvador (1971)	Guatemala (1964)	Honduras (1966)	Nicaragua (1963)	Costa Rica (1963)
under 1	% of holdings	48.8	*	*	*	5.7
	% of hectares	4.8	*	*	*	0.1
1-5	% of holdings	38.1	87.4	67.5	50.8	30.3
	% of hectares	14.8	18.7	12.4	3.5	1.8
5-10	% of holdings	5.8	*	15.2	13.0	16.7
	% of hectares	7.7	*	10.4	3.2	2.9
10-20	% of holdings	3.3	8.9	*	*	14.2
	% of hectares	8.7	13.0	*	*	5.1
20-50	% of holdings	2 5	1.6	14.8	25.1	*
	% of hectares	14.5	5.9	29.4	20.5	*
50-100	% of holdings	0.8	*	1.4	6.2	26.6
	% of hectares	10.6	*	9.4	14.1	27.8
100+	% of holdings	0.7	2.1	1.0	5.0	6.6
	% of hectares	48.9	62.5	38.6	58.8	52.7

*Combined with next largest category.

Source: Wilkie and Haber, op. cit., p. 58.

similar: 2.1 percent of farms control 62.5 percent of total farmland, while 87.4 percent control only 18.7 percent. In Honduras, 2.4 percent of farms control 48.0 percent of total farmland, while 67.5 percent eke out their subsistence on 12.4 percent. In Nicaragua, in 1963, 5 percent of farms controlled 58.8 percent of farmland, while 50.8 percent of farm families subsisted on 3.5 percent of the total farmland.[16] Even Costa Rica, the country with the least unequal distribution of wealth and income, evidences a high degree of inequality: 6.6 percent of farms control 52.7 percent of total farmland, while at the other extreme 36.0 percent occupy only 1.9 percent.

A similar pattern of concentration characterizes the distribution of income. The data presented in Table 9 are a conservative reflection of actual income disparity, since they refer to income from labor only; hence income from land and capital is excluded.

High rates of unemployment and underemployment throughout Central America have served to depress the economic and political bargaining power of workers. In the rural sector, the combination of land scarcity and lack of year-round wage employment opportunities makes it possible for employers to pay below-subsistence wages. The cost of the employment crisis is

---

[16] The 1971 Nicaraguan census shows that medium and large landowners, constituting 3.5 percent of the agricultural labor force, received 63.1 percent of agricultural income, while wage workers, who made up 51 percent of the agricultural labor force, received only 7.5 percent. Cited in Deere, op. cit., p. 37.

Table 9
Income Distribution: Central America

Income received by:	El Sal- vador[a]	Guate- mala[a]	Hondu- ras[b]	Nicara- gua[c]	Costa Rica[b]
Lowest 20 percent	5.8	5.0	2.3	*	3.3
Highest 20 percent	*	*	67.8	60.0	54.8
Highest 10 percent	*	*	50.0	*	39.5
Highest 5 percent	21.4	35.0	*	28.0	*

*No data available.

[a]Source: World Bank, *World Economic and Social Indicators*, Report No. 700/79/04 (Washington, D.C.: The World Bank, October 1979).

[b]Source: World Bank *World Development Report 1980* (Washington, D.C.: World Bank, August 1980).

[c]Source: UN/ECLA, "Nicaragua: Economic Repercussions of Recent Political Events" (Note by the Secretariat), mimeo, September 1979, p. 15. Figures are for 1977. The lowest 50 percent of income earners received just 15 percent of total income.

therefore shifted onto workers, who pay a high price in the manner discussed earlier in this paper: through nutritional deprivation, poor health and early mortality. The urban employment situation is not much better. The United Nations Economic Commission for Latin America estimated open unemployment rates in 1973-74 at the national level for three countries, as follows: El Salvador, 13.1 percent; Honduras, 10-12 percent; Costa Rica, 7.1 percent.[17] ECLA obtained unemployment data separately for Nicaragua, showing a rate of 8.7 percent in 1976 and 1977, climbing to 14.5 percent in 1978 and an estimated 33.3 percent in 1979.[18] Returning to the rural sector, ECLA has also obtained figures on total underutilization of labor—the sum of the open unemployment, underemployment and disguised unemployment rates—in agriculture which reveal the magnitude of the employment crisis, as follows: El Salvador, 58 percent; Guatemala, 62 percent; Honduras, 43 percent; Costa Rica, 15 percent; and pre-war Nicaragua, 15 percent.[19]

To what extent can education contribute to an improvement in the economic well-being of Central Americans? The data in Table 10 permit an appraisal of Central America's dramatic educational deficit. Of the five republics, to date only Nicaragua has undertaken a major commitment to wipe out illiteracy and improve the level and distribution of educational services.[20] El Salvador, Guatemala and Honduras continue to maintain the majority of their population under the shadow of functional illiteracy,

[17] UN/ECLA, *Estudio económico de América Latina, 1976*, Vol. 1 (Santiago de Chile).

[18] UN/ECLA, "Nicaragua: Economic Repercussions of Recent Political Events" (Note by the Secretariat), mimeo, September 1979, pp. 62ff. The radical reduction of these rates is a top priority of Sandinista reconstruction plans.

[19] UN/ECLA, *Estudio económico de América Latina, 1976*, Vol. 1 (Santiago de Chile).

[20] For a detailed account of Nicaragua's literacy campaign, see the article by Cardenal and Miller in Chapter 8, this volume.

Table 10
Levels of Illiteracy and Schooling,
Central America, 1970-75 (% of population)

	El Sal-vador	Guate-mala	Hondu-ras	Nicara-gua	Costa Rica
Illiteracy (1970)[a]	42.9	53.8	40.5	42.1	11.6
Functional illiteracy (1975)[b]	70.2	46.1*	69.8	67.7	35.2
Levels of schooling (1970)[a]					
None	48.5	63.1	41.0	50.4	13.6
Primary	43.9	30.4	51.6	22.0	69.0
Secondary	6.9	4.4	6.4	21.4	13.7
Post-secondary	0.6	1.0	0.7	3.4	3.7

Illiteracy = cannot sign own name.
Functional illiteracy = lacks level of literacy necessary to function normally and efficiently in society.

*Accuracy of this figure is in doubt since Guatemala's illiteracy rate (percentage of population who cannot sign their own name) is higher than the functional illiteracy rate and was the highest in Central America in 1970, as shown. Also note that Guatemala has the highest percentage of population with no schooling.

[a]Source: UN/ECLA, Statistical Yearbook for Latin America 1979 (New York: UN/ECLA, 1981). Figures on illiteracy are for population age 15 and over. Figures on levels of schooling refer variously to population age 6 and over (El Salvador and Nicaragua), 7 and over (Guatemala) and 10 and over (Honduras).

[b]Source: Charles Teller et al., op. cit. Figures are for population age 10 and over and are taken from population censuses.

with only a tiny elite able to go beyond primary school.[21] On the one hand, for these societies overall, it seems obvious that raising literacy rates and average educational levels can only have a positive effect on production, and hence income. On the other hand, from the viewpoint of individuals, even if education were made more widely available, its potential for improving income is constrained by the limited access to land, capital and employment. Beyond a certain point, these limits could render additional schooling of little economic value. Meanwhile, education, like land, capital and employment, remains such a scarce resource that it plays little, if any, role in enhancing the economic prospects of most Central Americans. This is a specially enforced scarcity, necessitated by the unique threat which mass education would pose to Central America's elite: the potential for disseminating fundamental tools for building popular awareness of current inequities. But it is precisely in this capacity that education holds out the greatest hope for improving the living conditions of Central America's poor.

---

[21] On average, levels of literacy and schooling among the labor force are only slightly higher than among the population at large. See UN/ECLA, Statistical Yearbook for Latin America 1979 (New York: UN/ECLA, 1981), pp. 444-445.

Conclusion

What then are the prospects for improving living conditions in Central America? Even for believers in trickle-down theories of development, the statistical facts of the last 5 years' economic crisis leave little ground for optimism. Declining and/or negative rates of GDP growth per capita and falling real wages are the trend in each of the republics.[22] Given their propensity to deteriorate even in periods of robust GDP growth, living standards can hardly escape the effects of such a generalized economic disaster. (See Chapter 3 for a discussion of the roots of the crisis.) But insofar as conditions deteriorate beyond the limits of popular tolerance, disaster may yet pave the way for progress: the emergence of a popular consciousness and political power capable of overturning the institutional structures which benefit so few and oppress so many.

—*María Angela Leal*

---

[22] See UN/ECLA, *Economic Survey of Latin America, 1979* (Santiago de Chile: UN/ECLA, 1981).

Institutional Dualism in Central America's Agricultural Development*

By Peter Dorner and Rodolfo Quiros

The five nations of the Central American Common Market (Costa Rica, El Salvador, Guatemala, Honduras and Nicaragua) have all the characteristics generally associated with less developed countries—largely agrarian economies, great dependence on agricultural exports for foreign exchange earnings, rapid population growth, widespread illiteracy, and low per capita incomes. Their economies display the dual structure found in many of the less developed countries, but the most significant duality is not industrial-agricultural but rather one within the agricultural sector itself. This sector is divided into large farms producing mainly (though not exclusively) for export, and small farms producing largely those commodities used for internal, domestic consumption. These two sub-sectors are also quite distinct in terms of the factor proportions employed in production processes.

When measured by the rather restricted criterion of economic growth, the performance of the Central American economies has been quite impressive. Since 1950, industrial output and agricultural production for export have increased substantially. Intra-regional trade, as well as trade with the rest of the world, has expanded rapidly. However, performance is not so impressive in terms of the more inclusive criteria of economic development—a reduction of mass poverty and unemployment and a more equal distribution of income. Per capita averages fail to show the widening gap between rich and poor, between those who have secure access to a share in the growing output and those who do not. The institutional structures which today often hinder the achievement of such broad development objectives in the agricultural sector had their beginnings in the system established under Spanish colonialism and evolved to their present forms under the influence of nineteenth-century liberalism.

In the present article, we will concentrate on the institutional dualism within the agricultural sector. In the first section, land tenure patterns, farm size and market orientation (export or domestic production) of the two sub-sectors are discussed. The next three sections analyze the interaction between the two sub-sectors and the way in which public policy often favors the large farm, export-producing sub-sector while it discriminates against the small farm, domestic food-producing sub-sector. The final two sections analyze the interaction between these two sub-sectors during a period of rapid export expansion on the one hand, and a period of export contraction on the other.

*Excerpted and abridged from *Journal of Latin American Studies*, Vol. 5, No. 2 (1973), pp. 217-232.

Table 1
Land/Man Ratios in Central America by Farm Size Category:
Manzanas per Agricultural Worker*

Country	Subfamily	Family	Multi-family (Excluding Landless Workers)	(Including Landless Workers)
Guatemala (1950)	1.6	13.9	324.5	32.2
El Salvador (1961)	1.5	17.0	165.6	15.6
Honduras (1952)	2.3	12.8	122.2	18.0
Nicaragua (1963)	1.9	11.7	111.2	35.9
Costa Rica (1963)	2.5	13.7	129.6	29.8
Central America	1.7	13.4	146.0	27.1

*One manzana=0.70 hectares.

Source: Based on information in CIDA/CAIS, "Características generales de la utilización y distribución de la tierra en Centroamérica," Preliminary Report (Mexico, 1969).

Land Tenure, Farm Size, and Market Orientation

In Central Amerca, land ownership by a relatively small segment of the population has led to concentration of income and of economic and political power. These conditions have greatly reduced access to production and market opportunities for the vast majority of the rural poulation. In these still largely agrarian countries, land tenure institutions are crucial in determining investments, type of technology adopted, and levels of employment, as well as income distribution. Less than half of the farmers (44.8 percent) own land, while 48.8 percent are renters or *de facto* occupants. The remaining 6.4 percent of farmers have mixed tenure arrangements. More than three-fourths (78 percent) of all farm units are sub-family sized farms, not large enough to provide either adequate income or full employment for the families living on them. Although sub-family units represent 78 percent of all farms and account for 60 percent of the rural labor force, they occupy only 11 percent of the farm land. At the other extreme, 6 percent of all farm units are multi-family units. They control 72 percent of the farm land but employ only 28 percent of the rural labor force (even assuming that all landless workers are employed on these units).[1]

Land concentration for the region as a whole is such that the land/man ratio on multi-family farms is more than ten times that on the family units and over eighty times that on sub-family farms. Even if landless workers are included in computing the land/man ratios for multi-family farms, land per worker on these farms is twice that of family farms and sixteen times that of sub-family farms. Table 1 shows these ratios for the

[1] CIDA/CAIS, "Características generales de la utilización y distribución de la tierra en Centroamérica," Preliminary Report (Mexico, 1969); and Agricultural Census for individual countries for the 1950s and 1960s.

Table 2

Structure of Production of Basic Grains and
Three Major Export Crops by Size of Farm Categories
(Percentages)

Size of Farm Category	Basic Grains*			Export Crops**		
	No. Farms	Area	Production	No. Farms	Area	Production
Sub-family	75.3	51.5	51.3	57.0	9.0	8.5
Family	16.8	23.4	23.3	27.9	15.2	14.2
Medium Multi-family	5.9	12.8	12.7	11.5	19.0	16.2
Large Multi-family	2.0	12.3	12.7	3.6	56.8	61.1
All Categories	100.0	100.0	100.0	100.0	100.0	100.0

* Includes corn, rice, beans and sorghum.
** Includes coffee, cotton, and sugar cane.
Source: Agricultural Census: Guatemala (1950); El Salvador (1961); Honduras (1962); Costa Rica and Nicaragua (1963).

several countries by farm size group. The high concentration of population in the sub-family farm sector, together with this population's low average productivity, largely explains the low output per worker in Central American agriculture.

Although statistical sources do not permit a complete breakdown for all countries and commodities, data in Tables 2 and 3 show the heavy emphasis on export production by the large farms and the concentration of production for domestic consumption by the small farms. These data support the assertion that the economic organization of agriculture in Central America exhibits a dual structure characterized by export and domestic market sub-sectors. Multi-family farms producing for the domestic market are mainly livestock operations or those combining livestock with a few selected crops. Large farms account for 85 percent of all pasture land. Since beef is becoming increasingly important as an export commodity—now the fourth largest export earner after coffee, cotton and bananas—the generalization that the export sector is dominated by production from the large properties is further substantiated.[2]

The competition for land among the large producers of the different export commodities is quite limited. Coffee, cotton, bananas, sugar cane and livestock have quite distinct soil, climatic and other ecological requirements. The competition for land has always been, and continues to be, between the large export producers and the small farm sector producing mainly for the domestic markets. For example, in the intercensal period (1950-1960/64), 72 percent of the total increase in the number of farms was in the sub-family class, but it incorporated only 8 percent of the increase of land in farms. At the other extreme, 73 percent of the new land in farms

[2] In 1969, almost half of the beef produced in the region was exported; 97 percent of these exports went to the United States.

Table 3
Distribution of Land Use for Export and Domestic Market Production by Size of Farm Category in Three Central American Countries* (Percentages)

Size of Farm	Domestic Market Production	Export Production	Total
Sub-family	80.5	19.5	100.0
Family	58.7	41.3	100.0
Medium Multi-family	42.7	57.3	100.0
Large Multi-family	25.4	74.6	100.0
All categories	48.1	51.9	100.0

*Data for Costa Rica, Nicaragua and El Salvador.

Source: Based on information in CIDA/CAIS, "Características Generales."

was incorporated by the large farms whose numbers increased by less than 9 percent.[3] The export sector grew by almost 700,000 hectares between 1950 and 1966/68. Meanwhile, land/man ratios in small farm areas often declined. For example, in the major cotton producing departments of El Salvador, the number of farms 10 hectares or smaller increased by 72 percent from 1950-61, but average farm size in this category declined by 54 percent. The major cotton producing departments in Nicaragua likewise showed an average decline of farm size of 38 and 20 percent (1952-64) for holdings in the 1-9.9 and the 10-49.9 manzana size classes.

Interdependence in the Labor Market

Although Central America's agricultural economies are dichotomized in both tenure structure and market orientation, there are many interdependencies, particularly in the functioning of the labor market. Historically, the export sector recruited its *permanent* labor force from the traditional small farm sector, but in modern times the role of the small farm sector as a pool of *seasonal* labor has become far more important. The fundamental factor in this change has been the use of labor-saving technologies in certain seasonal tasks, with a continued dependence on labor-intensive methods for other operations. Families on small farms often rely on large farms for temporary employment to supplement annual family incomes, while large-scale enterprises depend on the small farm sector to provide labor at peak seasons of the agricultural cycle. One study showed that in the Guatemalan highlands, for example, sub-family farms utilize 66 percent of their available labor time for, and derive 57 percent of their annual family incomes from, temporary employment on large farms and plantations.[4] In a more recent

---

[3] From Agricultural Census Reports for the individual countries.

[4] Sergio Maturana, *Las relaciones entre la tenencia de la tierra y el uso de los recursos agrícolas de Centroamérica* (Proyecto de Tenencia de la Tierra y las Condiciones del Trabajo Agrícola en Centroamérica. Unpublished report, San José, Costa Rica, 1962), pp. 204, 215.

Guatemalan study, Schmid found that laborers engaging in seasonal work averaged 52 percent of their annual incomes from it. Seasonal labor on cotton farms averaged 74 days per year; that on sugar and coffee plantations averaged 99 and 136 days of work per year, respectively.[5]

In the Usulután region of El Salvador, small farm owners derive 38 percent of their annual income from seasonal work on cotton plantations and other large farms, while for tenant farmers these sources account for nearly two-thirds of their annual income.[6] It is estimated that 97 percent of the agricultural labor force in El Salvador is employed during the harvest season of the principal export crops; during slack seasons, employment falls as low as 32 percent of the available labor force.[7]

This labor market relationship between small and large producers arises from both structural and technical characteristics. Shortage of land compels small producers (and the landless) to seek seasonal employment to supplement earnings. Large producers can save on overhead costs while meeting their labor needs in peak seasons, especially during harvest, by hiring labor only seasonally. On the technical side (except for bananas, in which harvesting occurs throughout the year), the harvest of the main export crops corresponds roughly to the dry season; most domestic market crops such as basic grains, on the other hand, are produced during the rainy season. The low availability of labor during the rainy season is one reason why large-scale production of rice, a recent phenomenon, has been highly mechanized.

As with land, export producers do not usually compete among themselves for labor. Tenure institutions, fortuitous technical aspects regarding the sequential nature of peak labor requirements for the major export crops, and low productivity and low incomes in the traditional domestic sector facilitate the labor transfer process. Although both sectors have something to gain, the large producers have most of the advantages.

Credit Allocations within Agriculture

In some instances, because of technical factors which limit their access to regular credit channels, small producers also depend on large farm enterprises for their credit needs. In the case of small producers of export crops, the large-scale enterprises often act as financial intermediaries between these small producers and the banking system. In so doing, they not only guarantee a certain supply of raw materials (especially in the case of coffee and sugar processors), but also increase their operating income through commission fees and interest rate differentials. Although the existence of this function is well-known, a lack of research makes it impossible to quantify its importance.

---

[5] Lester J. Schmid, "The Role of Migratory Labor in the Economic Development of Guatemala," *Land Tenure Center Research Paper No. 22*, University of Wisconsin, 1967.

[6] Maturana, *op. cit.*, p. 148.

[7] Banco Hipotecario de El Salvador, *El crédito agrícola en El Salvador*, Vol. 1 (San Salvador, 1966), p. 18.

There is, however, less uncertainty with respect to the allocation of credit through the banking system. Producers of major export crops receive over half, in some countries nearly three-fourths, of the institutional credit. It would seem reasonable to include livestock in the export category too, since nine-tenths of the livestock loans are allocated to enterprises raising beef cattle, a major export commodity.

Marketing, Services, and Technology in the Two Sub-sectors

Small farm producers of export crops are dependent on large-scale processors to process and market their entire output. Where large-scale operations combine production with processing facilities, the output from small farms can be an important source of raw material. For example, 55 percent of all sugar cane milled in El Salvador is purchased from independent producers (large and small). In Costa Rica, only 5 percent of the existing coffee processors handle their own crop exclusively. Thus a product market relationship has developed from the mutual need for market outlets on the one hand, and raw materials on the other.

Road and railway facilities—a crucial support system for a modern agriculture—are to this day designed to connect the main export crop production areas and principal cities (except Tegucigalpa) with exit ports. Not until the creation of the Central American Common Market was transport infrastructure purposefully designed to integrate domestic markets of a given country to those of other member nations. Until the completion of the Interamerican Highway in the 1950s, the Central American nations did not have any interconnecting system of all-weather roads. In Honduras, the capital city of Tegucigalpa was not connected with its principal ports on the Atlantic Coast by an all-weather road until 1969, although the coastal banana producing area has had considerable infrastructure since early in this century.

Research and extension services, which might compensate to some extent for the many disadvantages of the small farm sector, are generally weak. In 1968-69, only 355 extension agents and 332 agricultural researchers served the needs of 1.8 million farm families (less than one extension worker per 5,000 families). To the extent that these services operate successfully, they appear to be oriented to the problems and needs of export agriculture.

During the 1950-67 period, output growth rates of major export crops averaged 4.7 percent annually. In contrast, the corresponding growth rates for domestic market crops averaged only 2.9 percent. Furthermore, during 1950-59, when export expansion gained momentum, output of domestic market crops was virtually stagnant. Domestic crop output did increase considerably during 1960-67, but the 5.4 percent annual growth rate remained below the 6.2 percent rate of export crops.

This acceleration in growth rates may have been influenced by the emergence of a large-scale and technologically modern segment in the production of basic grains. In the 1960-67 period, the annual growth rates in yields of corn and rice were considerably higher than those for beans and sorghum, the production of which remains largely in the domain of the traditional small farm sector. Prior to the development of large-scale enterprises in corn and rice production (1950-59), declining rates in average yields of basic grains coincided with the most rapid gains in yields of the major export crops. As with output, growth rates in yields—the fruits of technical progress—have been rather consistently higher in the export sector.

During the recent rapid expansion in both area and output of export crops, total employment in this sector increased, but at a decreasing rate. The slowing rate results from increased use of capital-intensive, labor-saving technology in the export sector. In coffee production, for example, the use of herbicides reduces the need for permanent labor (in some instances by 50 percent or more), but increases the use of strictly seasonal labor for the coffee harvest. The displacement of permanent workers often leads to out-migration and a subsequent shortage of available workers during the peak requirements of the harvest season.

Relatively labor-extensive developments in coffee production are reflected in the aggregate statistics for Guatemala. Between 1950 and 1964, Guatemalan coffee acreage increased by 85 percent while output increased by 157 percent. Total employment in coffee production during this period (including field, mill, clerical and managerial) increased by only 6.6 percent.[8] Increased labor efficiency would, indeed, be welcome if alternative work of equal or higher productivity were available for those not finding employment in export production. In the absence of such alternatives, however, the inequities within the dualistic system increase.

This trend toward relatively capital intensive production methods in export agriculture is not limited to coffee. Many of the small farmers, mostly basic grain producers, displaced by the cotton boom in Nicaragua, moved to other regions. Labor shortages and rising wages became such a serious problem during the cotton harvest that during the four years following 1963 the number of mechanical cotton pickers rose from 13 to 200. By 1967 an estimated 20 percent of Nicaragua's cotton crop was harvested with mechanical pickers.[9]

The labor saving nature of technological developments in sugar cane production is similar to that in cotton and coffee. Data from El Salvador show a consistent inverse relationship between the size of plantation and the use of labor; the smaller plantations use two to three times as much labor per unit of land as the larger ones. This relationship holds for both permanent and seasonal labor, including field and processing plant workers.[10]

---

[8] Dirección General de Estadística, *Censo cafetalero 1950* (Guatemala, C.A., agosto-octubre 1953); and Banco de Guatemala, Official Statistics (unpublished).

[9] Justin Gutknecht, "El proceso de demote de algodón en Nicaragua" (Managua, 1960) cited in Comisión Nacional de Algodón, *La economía nacional y el algodón* (Managua, Nicaragua, 1968).

[10] Calculated from statistics in Ministerio de Agricultura y Ganadería, *Anuario de estadísticas agropecuarias contínuas, 1967-1968* (San Salvador, octubre de 1968).

Even though banana production utilizes considerable amounts of labor—mostly on a permanent basis—it has not escaped the labor saving trends. Aerial application of fertilizers and insecticides and the use of cable and belt conveyors have reduced the labor requirements of modern production and handling, and labor requirements in established banana plantations have declined from 3.0 to 0.8 laborers per hectare from the 1930s to the present.[11] Incremental rates of 2.2 workers per hectare are reported for establishing new plantations.

The development of export agriculture along capital intensive lines is reducing the capacity of this sector to absorb labor. While capital intensity has reduced the need for permanent labor, increased yields and the present limited mechanization of most harvesting operations have intensified the need for seasonal labor. The increasing importance of temporary (as against permanent) labor represents a significant change in the nature of the labor market. Its overall impact is to reduce incomes and employment security of farm workers. Furthermore, increased capital requirements are likely to result in further concentration and polarization of resources, both within the export sector and in this sector relative to the small farm sub-sector producing largely for domestic markets.

Historically, the establishment of the export sector was achieved by claiming resources, particularly land and labor, from the traditional sector of agriculture. Except for the new technological developments, this process takes place even today in an institutional context that is not too different from the historical one. A number of case studies will illustrate that context, the nature of this process, and the effects on the traditional sector.

Interaction between the Two Sub-sectors in the Export Expansion Phase

The expansion of Central America's banana production in the 1960s has occurred primarily in Costa Rica's Atlantic lowlands which accounted for over two-thirds of the region's expansion in the 1963-67 period. Total banana exports from the region averaged 981 thousand tons during 1963-67, but increased to 1.5 million tons in 1968 and surpassed the 2 million mark in 1969.[12] Meanwhile, banana plantations in these lowlands expanded from 5,400 to 17,500 hectares between 1963 and 1967. Local entrepreneurs under purchasing contracts with major banana companies account for 87 percent of the total increment in area planted and hold almost half of the banana land in Costa Rica.

Since there is much underutilized land in this Atlantic region, the rise in banana production did not require that significant amounts of land be claimed from the traditional sector. Furthermore, the discovery of varieties resistant to Panama disease allowed replanting of land previously used for

---

[11] Based on information in Charles M. Wilson, *Empire in Green and Gold* (New York, Henry Holt and Company, 1947) and SIECA, *Informe sobre el banano en Centroamérica*, Guatemala, unpublished preliminary report, 1969.

[12] From SIECA, *op. cit.*

bananas. But this expansion did require a great deal of labor which was available only from the traditional sector. This labor drain has caused the virtual disappearance of small farm agriculture in the area. Since corn was the traditional crop on these small farms, corn purchases by the National Production Council (CNP), the main buyer and marketing agent in the area, are an appropriate indicator of the production changes that occurred. Before the banana expansion, the CNP purchased an average of 5,323 metric tons of corn per year; by 1966 the figure had declined to 3,462 metric tons. Between 1967 and 1969, CNP corn purchases declined from 2,924 to 718 metric tons.

This displacement of small-scale agriculture by the expanding banana industry is consistent with the opportunity cost of labor. A typical family on a small farm could increase its earnings substantially by working in a banana plantation rather than cultivating its own land. In addition to some company fringe benefits, workers also become eligible for benefits from the nation's Social Security System and enjoy other services and amenities not readily available to them as independent farmers. As long as the banana industry does not decline as it did in the 1940s and 1950s, the major negative effect on the Costa Rican economy is the growing corn deficit which must be met by imports (annual corn imports increased from 2,913 metric tons in 1960-64 to 6,352 metric tons in 1965-68). These deficits, however, demonstrate the inability of the economy, or of economic policies, to increase output in other producing regions to offset the reduced supplies coming from the Atlantic region.

Another case, the cotton expansion in Nicaragua, has far more serious economic implications. Nicaragua has become the region's largest producer of cotton, with 44 percent of the area in cotton and 46 percent of Central America's total cotton exports in the 1965-68 period. Less than 6 percent of the farms in Nicaragua, all with more than 200 manzanas in cotton, accounted for over 50 percent of the country's crop.

Cotton is best adapted to the ecological conditions prevailing in the Pacific coastal areas. Before the coming of cotton, immigrants from the highlands, unable to find land or employment there, were employed in the coastal livestock haciendas as tenants and sharecroppers. Under these tenure arrangements, haciendas became mixed enterprises producing both beef and grains. The advent of cotton upset this system. Tenure institutions made it simple to divest campesinos of land and make room for large-scale production of cotton, often by a new class of entrepreneurs who rented the land from the hacienda owners. In fact, 52 percent of the land in cotton, in both Nicaragua and El Salvador, is rented. Rental arrangements also simplified severing of any ties or claims which may have existed between previous landlords and their sharecroppers. Many independent small farmers, lacking financial resources or technical know-how, rented out their land or joined the cotton expansion on a modest scale.

The end result was a massive displacement of small farmers and a sharp decline in basic grain production from these traditional grain producing areas. In Nicaragua, the displacement of small farmers (many migrated to other regions of the country) was of such magnitude that as early as 1964, an estimated 5 percent of the cotton crop was lost because of regional labor shortages, motivating the use of mechanical pickers (noted earlier) first in the major cotton departments and later in other parts of the country as well. In this case, as in some others, there exists the seemingly paradoxical situation of (regional) labor shortages amidst widespread (national) unemployment and underemployment.

Guatemala and El Salvador have not resorted to the same degree of mechanization as Nicaragua. Guatemala, with its overpopulated highlands, has relied on migratory workers to meet the highly seasonal labor requirements of the cotton harvest. In heavily populated El Salvador, which lacks an agricultural frontier, the traditional sector had to absorb a large proportion of those displaced by the cotton expansion. Others migrated, mostly illegally, to neighboring Honduras, and this influx of landless workers, largely generated by the cotton expansion, was perhaps the single most important underlying factor in the armed conflict between these two countries in 1969.

In addition to labor displacement, Nicaragua suffered a major decline in basic grain production which was not offset by increased production in other areas. From 1952-1967, land planted in cotton increased steadily from 13,600 to 61,100 manzanas, while the area in basic grains and sesame declined from 78,100 to 31,900 manzanas during the same period. Cotton acreage expanded almost exclusively at the expense of the area in basic grain production. Nicaragua shifted from a net exporter to a net importer of grains, with a total of 39,700 metric tons exported over the period 1953-57, but a net of 70,300 metric tons imported in 1963-67.[13]

The export sector has always expanded at the expense of the weaker, traditional sector. Addition or expansion of an export crop has seldom resulted in a permanent opportunity for the traditional sector to enhance its development alternatives. Furthermore, the institutional constraints faced by the traditional sector within the present system prevent it from compensating for the production which has been displaced. Expansion of the export sector has frequently been accompanied by deficits in food crops which have created inflationary pressures and subsequently led to increased food imports.

The impact of the growth of the export sector on variables such as employment, income and general welfare depends greatly on the particular crop in question. For example, banana expansion may have resulted in net gains (in addition to any gains in the trade balance) because of the transfer of labor from a low productivity occupation to one of higher productivity and income. This, however, was not likely the case in cotton expansion which resulted in massive small farmer displacement, migration, and additional overcrowding in the remaining areas of peasant agriculture.

---

[13] Aggregate figures for the periods mentioned computed from: Ministerio de Economía, *Memoria de recaudación de aduanas* (Yearbooks 1953-5); Dirección General de Estadística, *Anuario de comercio exterior* (Yearbooks 1956-63); and SIECA, *Anuario estadístico centroamericano de comercio exterior* (Yearbooks 1964-7).

Moreover, given the seasonality of labor requirements and low wage rates, it is likely that total employment and labor income declined, and that income distribution became even more skewed as a result of the cotton boom.

Irreversibility in the Export Contraction Phase

Thus far, the dynamic changes which occur in the expansionary phase of the export sector have been emphasized. Available evidence from both historical and current records indicates that the disruptive effects on traditional agriculture are not reversed in times of contraction in the export sector. For permanent crops such as coffee and bananas, adverse technical or price conditions may reduce total output, but the area under cultivation remains rather stable because of the heavy investments that established plantations represent. Moreover, in times of financial crises, public policy operates to relax the rules governing credit, to grant fiscal exemptions, or to freeze legal wages.

The banana industry is dominated by corporations managing banana acreage in various countries. In sustaining the overall volume of operations, a high degree of vertical integration acts as a buffer for declining revenues. When the international market is weak, however, such monopsonistic powers over the industry frequently result in reduced purchases from independent producers. The recent horizontal diversification of the major banana corporations has caused a shift of new lands, or those previously used in banana production, into new uses. Since the formation of the Central American Common Market, the United Fruit Company has made major investments in the oils and fat industry. These investments have made it profitable to diversify its commercial production with African palm, beef cattle, and even some basic grains for the regional market as well as other products such as pineapples.[14]

In short, contraction in that part of the export sector producing permanent crops does not normally lead to a restructuring of opportunities for the traditional sector. On the contrary, it may even contribute to further concentration either through diversification or through special fiscal and monetary policy measures designed to protect the industry from external conditions. The contraction in cotton production in El Salvador will illustrate the process in the case of an annual export crop. Beginning in 1964, a convergence of rising costs and declining cotton prices in international markets induced producers to shift large amounts of land out of cotton production. A total of 99,400 manzanas were taken out of cotton production between 1964 and 1967; 46,671 manzanas were taken out during the crop year of 1965/66-1966/67. Of the latter, 47.3 percent was planted to corn, 33.7 percent was converted to pasture, and 7.6 percent was planted to rice (the remaining lands were planted to kenaf, sorghum and other crops). Of the 15,700 manzanas converted to pastures, only 1,470

---

[14] For an interesting study of changes in use patterns of ex-banana lands, see Pierre A. Stouse, Jr., *Cambios en el uso de la tierra en regiones ex-bananeras de Costa Rica*, Instituto Geográfico de Costa Rica (San José, 1967).

were actually planted to improved pastures.[15] In fact, much of the land, which was largely rented to investors on a yearly basis, was left idle when it reverted to its owners. In other words, over 30 percent of the former cotton land reverted to a much less intensive use regardless of social or private opportunity costs. Rather than being returned to small farm agriculture under some new tenure arrangement, land was used for extensive livestock grazing in a country with about one hectare of land per worker in the small farm sector.

Nor did the cotton land planted to rice and corn revert to *campesino* operation. It was used by its owners mainly for large-scale production of these grains using machine methods and other technology not available to the small farmer. In fact, if yields on the land diverted to corn equalled those obtainable with high-yielding inputs, the additional output would amount to almost 37,000 metric tons, equivalent to more than half of the increase in corn production in El Salvador for the 1966-67 crop year. Under the same assumption, the 4,056 metric tons of rice produced on this ex-cotton land would represent over 40 percent of the increase in rice production for the same year. During the period in question, El Salvador increased its shipments of rice to other countries in the region and approached self-sufficiency in corn.

This case illustrates that the contraction of an annual export crop is also unlikely to result in a restructuring of opportunities for the small farm sector. It seems that in cyclical movements in export production, particularly when products are competing for land and/or labor, the traditional sector is sacrificed. This case also exemplifies a more general process under way in Central America. This is the increased polarization in the production structure of basic grains caused by the emergence of large-scale, technologically advanced firms in a market traditionally dominated by *campesino* producers. Several factors are contributing to these developments. On the supply side, price support policies have kept prices of basic grains high in the Central American countries. This together with depressed or declining prices of traditional export products has made relative prices more favorable for the production of these staple crops. On the demand side, a rapid increase in domestic needs induced by high rates of population growth and urbanization has been accompanied by the development of the animal foodstuff industry. Small farmers, constrained as they are within this dual system, have not been able to increase production at rates or magnitudes required by domestic demand, thus creating incentives for large-scale producers to enter the industry. Moreover, enlargement of the market under the Central American Common Market agreements has reduced some of the risk of adverse price effects that might result from large increments in output.

---

[15] Ministerio de Agricultura, Dirección General de Economía Agropecuaria, *Estudio económico agrícola del cultivo de algodón, 1966-67* (San Salvador, April 1968), Table 1.

Conclusions

Although the gains from agricultural production for export seem impressive, hidden costs must also be evaluated. If the total benefits from the expansion of export production are balanced against the social costs of disruption in the small farm sector and its consequences on production, imports, employment, and income distribution, the net benefits are much reduced. If foreign firms are involved, any repatriation of profits is a further deduction to be made in order to arrive at net benefits.

Within the present economic organization of agriculture, economic and institutional forces combine to induce patterns of growth where the market mechanism intensifies the existing duality and concentrates further the claims to resources, market opportunities, and income. These patterns in turn contribute to the economic, social, and political isolation of the majority of the farm population. In this setting, serious doubts arise about the net benefits of export-led economic growth when its total benefits are weighed against the less obvious but all-pervasive social costs.

Land of the Few:
Rural Land Ownership in Guatemala*
By Andrea Brown

"Land tenure or land ownership is the basic social problem of Guatemala, and portends to be such until some sort of revolution can completely reverse the present patterns of ownership." [1]

Guatemala's land story can be summarized in two simple striking facts: 2.1 percent of landowners own 62 percent of the arable land, and 87 percent of landowners own 19 percent of the arable land. [2]

The 2.1 percent are rich agro-export barons, owning large haciendas, called latifundia or *fincas,* that grow crops and ship them to the United States, Europe, or Japan. The latifundia generally use the most fertile lands in the country, such as those on the Pacific coast producing cotton and cattle, and the Pacific mountain slopes yielding Guatemala's major export crop, coffee.

The 87 percent are subsistence farmers, many of them Indians crowded into the Western Highlands (*Altiplano*) situated above the coffee fincas. On tiny, steeply inclined, depleted plots, or minifundia, they grow corn which

---

*Excerpted and abridged from *Guatemala* (North American Congress on Latin America, 1974).

[1] Thomas and Marjorie Melville, *Guatemala: The Politics of Land Ownership* (New York: Free Press, 1971), p. xi.

[2] Lehman B. Fletcher, Eric Graber, William C. Merrill, Erik Thorbecke, *Guatemala's Economic Development: The Role of Agriculture* (Ames: The Iowa State University Press, 1970), p. 59.

does not provide enough food or purchasing power to allow them to survive. Thus the Indians, in addition to working their own plots, are forced to seek seasonal work on the fincas.

This latifundia-minifundia system has a clearly defined purpose: to bring the greatest income to the large landowners at the lowest possible cost. In a capitalist economy based on land, labor power is needed to extract wealth and profits from the land. Yet labor is a costly input, and unlike machines it has a tendency to make demands or even revolt if not treated decently. Since the bulk of labor power is needed only at harvest time, a particular problem is what to do with the workers the rest of the year. If they are employed for the entire year they cost too much. Yet if they are unemployed for a large part of the year they either require a welfare system that costs money, or they starve and thereby are unavailable to work the following year.

The ideal solution is the latifundia-minifundia system. This provides the labor force with tiny bits of land, with space to live on and with enough produce to keep the workers barely alive throughout the year. Yet it is not enough land that the workers will decline to do work on the coffee and cotton fincas at harvest time. In this way, the large landowners are guaranteed a workforce when they need it, yet are not responsible for this workforce during the off-season.

The latifundia-minifundia system, then, is a slave system without true slavery. It depends on a high level of exploitation of a large number of Guatemalans. And it does not tolerate reform: if the peasant masses received enough land to survive without going to work on the fincas, then there would not be a cheap labor force to pick the profitable export crops.

Because agriculture is the basis of the economy, those who have the land in Guatemala have the power. Thus, despite pressure from the majority of the population for a more equal distribution of resources, the Guatemalan government and the landowners have resisted any type of change. This gross inequality provided fuel for a strong guerrilla movement in the 1960s. It has also resulted in a high level of spontaneous violence in the countryside. The Pacific Coast is the scene of frequent armed incidents between landowners, managers and police on the one hand, and peasants on the other. Kidnappings and murders are daily occurrences. Landlords are legally empowered to carry guns, whereas peasants are not; many peasants are armed anyway. Many landowners have become afraid to live on their own land, and some areas are completely controlled by the military.

In the words of Christian Democratic Congressman (and Social Christian labor union leader) Julio Celso de León Flores,

> *The current conditions of distribution of resources in the agricultural sector have accentuated an unjust duality.... While great plantations have mechanization, credit, corporate facilities, and above all great extensions of land, so that 82 percent of the agricultural land is held by a few exporters, the rest of the people, 90 percent of the population, live a subsistence economy, with only 6 percent of the agricultural capital and*

no necessary social and economic infrastructures. . . . The violence is in the system, which denies the majority of Guatemalans access to power, wealth and culture.[3]

Current Conditions

Guatemala's total land area is 108,889 square kilometers (equals 42,042 square miles, or about the size of Tennessee), of which half is mountainous. [Mountain ranges] split the country into a number of distinct geographical entities with a variety of climates and soils. This makes Guatemala extremely suitable for agricultural production, with a capacity to produce many crops at some time or another during the yearly cycle. Only 31.6 percent of the land is currently used, 13.3 percent for agriculture, 9.6 percent for cattle grazing and 8.7 percent for forests; and only 9 million acres more can be incorporated into production.[4] The population of Guatemala is largely rural—75.1 percent in 1964—and 82 percent of the rural population is illiterate.

Most of the minifunda in the country are located in the Altiplano, where the land is scarcest, poorest and most eroded. This area is the most densely populated in the country and is extremely mountainous, with the incline of cultivated land sometimes reaching 60 degrees. There is little unused land; it is common to see people farming up to the mountain peaks.

As described by Eduardo Galeano:

> [The Indians] are at the center of national economic life; in a continuous annual cycle they leave their "sacred lands"—high lands where each small farm is the size of a corpse—to contribute 200,000 pairs of hands to the harvesting of coffee, cattle, and sugar in the lowlands. They are transported in trucks like cattle.[5]

It has been estimated that a campesino with 0.5 to 2.5 hectares of land is employed 50 to 70 days a year on his own land. Harvest time on the Altiplano complements harvest time on the coast.[6] Schmidt has shown that the income earned by migrant workers on the large fincas is an essential supplement to their subsistence earnings. The annual per capita income of the migrant worker is significantly higher than that of the non-migrant, about $60 a month compared to $43.[7] This income earned by migrating is crucial for survival.

This seasonal migration is increasing every year. Usually the entire family is involved, and children start working at the age of seven, just to be

---

[3] Quoted in *Guatemala Report*, No. 3.

[4] Julio Segura, *La situación rural de Guatemala* (Guatemala: Asociación Nacional de Municipalidades, II Censo Agropecuario, 1964), p. 5.

[5] Eduardo Galeano, *Open Veins of Latin America* (New York and London: Monthly Review Press, 1973), pp. 61, 62.

[6] Fletcher, *op. cit.* p. 50.

[7] Lester Schmid, *Migratory Labor in the Economic Development of Guatemala* (unpublished Ph.D. dissertation, University of Wisconsin, 1967), cited in Fletcher, *op. cit.*, p. 50.

able to meet their quota and pay off the landowner, or *contratista*. (Indian families usually have to get advance payment of wages to make it through the year.) Conditions are terrible—once on the finca they are all crowded into a huge empty building and must buy their food from the landowner. Wages are extremely low (estimated $1.25 average daily on cotton farms, $1 for coffee, and $0.93 for sugar plantations). It is estimated that over one million people in a nation of under six million are affected by this practice. Furthermore, the number of landless peasants who migrate in permanent search of work is increasing. They become *colonos* (resident laborers on fincas who receive small plots on the finca for subsistence production), agricultural workers, or they join the growing ranks of the unemployed. This large supply of cheap labor gives the *finqueros* a free rein in setting wages. Conventional forms of organizing for improved working conditions are outlawed; any protestor is immediately fired or jailed—and occasionally shot on the spot as a warning to his fellow workers.[8]

Because of the maldistribution of land, the majority of the population suffers from malnutrition. The Institute of Nutrition for Central America and Panama (INCAP) has estimated that as a result of the low income of the vast majority of the population in Guatemala, 80 percent of the caloric food intake is based on corn. This creates a deficiency in high-grade plant and animal protein, accounting for a high mortality before the age of five. Seventy-five percent of the children under five are malnourished, according to an INCAP study, and it is believed that malnutrition during the early years impairs mental development of the future adult.[9]

Meat is a luxury that few can afford, since the minimum cost of meat is $.35 a pound. Small children do not drink milk after being weaned from the breast. Corn and a few beans are the daily diet. The highland areas often have corn shortages due to the high population density, and corn and beans must actually be imported into Guatemala. The average family of five in the highlands needs approximately 100 pounds of corn a week. Over two hectares are needed to produce this much corn,[10] and many families have far less than two hectares. Corn costs about $.07 a pound to buy.

One oft-cited justification for the maldistribution of land in Guatemala is that large holdings are more efficient. This simply is not true. Farms of less than one hectare utilize close to 90 percent of their land, whereas latifundia use 45 percent, with the largest category of farm using only 30 percent.[11] Studies have shown that large holdings in Guatemala produce only one-fourth the yield per hectare produced by small farms.[12]

Because the land in the minifundia is used so intensively, with such primitive methods of farming, production has declined in the highlands and

[8] *Ibid.*

[9] U.S. House of Representatives, Committee on Banking and Currency, *A Report on Agricultural Development in Latin America* (February 8, 1967), pp. 132, 133.

[10] Melville and Melville, *op. cit.*, p. 298.

[11] Segura, *op. cit.*, p. 298.

[12] Edelberto Torres Rivas, *Interpretación del desarrollo social centroamericano* (San José, Costa Rica: Editorial Universitaria Centroamericana, 1971), p. 313.

other subsistence sectors. Total corn production fell from 102,856 metric tons in 1950-52 to 88,826 in 1965-66.[13] At the same time, production of export crops has risen at 6 percent per year. Coffee, cotton and bananas account for 90 percent of agricultural exports, and the net contribution of agriculture to the trade balance was 81 percent in 1966.[14] Cattle is becoming a big business. In spite of attempts at industrialization, the country's dependence on export crops has been growing.

The maldistribution of land increased between 1950 and 1964. Twenty percent more small farms are listed in the later census, and their average size decreased. In the region containing the Altiplano, the average size of the small farm declined by almost 50 percent.[15] This trend represents the subdivision of existing farms into a larger number of smaller units. Each generation gives part of its plot to its children, thereby creating the continuing subdivision process. Population growth promises more pressure to subdivide holdings. According to one study,

All the data that have been reviewed on production, yields, farm size, income and employment indicate that the income position of small farmers has deteriorated considerably since 1950.[16]

History

To understand the present landholding structure and the importance of the "land question" in Guatemala, we must examine its historical development. This history can be divided into six main areas, according to the major changes in land tenure and social organization of labor. These are: the pre-Hispanic era, the Spanish conquest, the colonial period, the liberal period, the 1944-1954 Revolution, and 1954 to the present. Except for the brief, arrested 1944-54 Revolution, the history of Guatemala has meant a progressive concentration of the land in a few hands at the expense of the Indian population, and an increased exploitation of the natives. A parallel development has been Guatemala's dependence on agricultural exports and integration into the world capitalist market.

Pre-Conquest

The social structure of the Mayan Indians before the arrival of the Spaniards in the early 1500s was complex, basically organized around agriculture. They were ruled by priests and military *caciques* (chiefs). During the period between 200 B.C. and 875 A.D., the ruling elites in the cities had ultimate rights over the land. During the militaristic period (875 B.C. to 1500 A.D.), members of a family inherited rights of *use* of land (rather than ownership), which they distributed according to need and capacity to

[13] Fletcher, *op. cit.*, p. 43.
[14] *Ibid.*, p. 47.
[15] *Ibid.*, p. 61.
[16] *Ibid.*, p. 196.

work it. Although the concept of "private property" was alien,[17] individual holdings and concentrations of land existed along with communal holdings, which were worked communally or parceled out to individuals.[18]

The land was considered sacred, and the ultimate owners were said to be the gods:

> *Religious rites were directly related to agriculture; the periods of sowing, cultivating, and harvesting were all times of official solemnity, and the acts themselves of production constituted a rite.*[19]

The Mayans paid religious taxes to the priests-bureaucrats for the use of the land. Thus Mayan society was basically dominated by a privileged elite which supported itself through the labor and tribute of the peasant masses.

However, at no time before the conquest did the Indians suffer the deprivation that they have suffered since 1524; malnutrition and starvation, which have become endemic, were practically unknown. Their diet consisted mainly of corn, supplemented by beans, vegetables, fruits, roots, cacao and occasionally meat. According to Moisés Behar, a noted expert on nutrition, compared with the diet of the average European of the era the Mayan ate well; in general, despite occasional severe famine due to drought, the pre-Hispanic Indians did not have serious nutritional problems. The main reason was the population's access to sufficient land for cultivation of food—unlike today's Indians, who are forced to buy even staple foods, since they have no land.[20]

Conquest

The effect of the Spanish Conquest in 1524 was catastrophic—according to Eric Wolf, two-thirds of the population was killed between 1519 and 1610; other sources put the figure as high as five-sixths of the population.[21]

Guatemala was viewed not as a country to be developed, but as a source of wealth for foreign interests. The army, sent by the Spanish Crown, came in search of wealth, mainly gold. Finding none in Guatemala, they had to base their fortunes on land—and, more important, on the cheap labor to make the land produce. Thus the first act of the conquerors was to

---

[17] The Indians' tradition of private property differed radically from the individualistic ladino and Spanish conceptions. They have no exact and universal method of recording and measuring the extension of individual plots of land. They are also unfamiliar with Western concepts of law, so that even now unrecorded plots of land can easily be stolen from them by ladinos.

[18] Thomas and Marjorie Melville, unpublished article, 1973.

[19] René de León Schlotter, *Estudio histórico y jurídico de la tenencia de la tierra en Guatemala en relación con el minifundio*, cited in Klaus Oehler, *Los minifundios en Guatemala* (Guatemala: IDESAC, 1971), p. 30.

[20] Moisés Behar, "Food Nutrition of the Maya before the Conquest and at the Present Time," *Biomedical Challenges Presented by the American Indians*, Proceedings of the special session during the 7th meeting of the Pan American Health Organization Advisory Committee on Medical Research (Washington: PAHQ, September 1968).

[21] Eric Wolf, *Sons of the Shaking Earth* (Chicago: University of Chicago Press, 1959), pp. 31, 195.

appropriate Mayan lands, and to institutionalize forms of exploiting the Indian labor.

The Spaniards controlled all but subsistence farming. The land was divided into large haciendas which were organized for commercial production of a large export crop for profit—first cacao, then indigo (blue dye) and cochineal (red dye). These haciendas involved vast expanses of unused land: while the Indians had cultivated the land intensively, the Spaniards, who had brought sheep and cattle with them, used the land extensively, for pasture. Land meant prestige and power, and to a certain extent was coveted for itself. The Spaniards were greedy for land, yet inefficient, and always produced below capacity. To produce a cash crop they farmed only a small portion of the land. As Eric Wolf describes it,

> [The hacienda] needed and wanted more land, not to raise more crops, but to take the land from the Indians in order to force them to leave their holdings and to become dependent on the hacienda for land and work.... Like the slave plantation [it] was a system designed to produce goods by marshalling human beings regardless of their qualities and involvements as persons.[22]

Once a *criollo* (resident of Spanish descent) acquired the land, he eagerly rented it out to Indians, who in exchange had to work a certain number of days on a cash crop. The reliance on cheap Indian labor obviated the need for introducing more efficient and productive methods of agriculture, and allowed the continuing use of antiquated methods of farming.[23]

Through advance payment of wages the Indians were forced to descend from the highlands to the lowlands to work, where many became sick and died. Cut off from their land, many of them died from starvation and malnutrition. The massive destruction of the Indian population during this period forced the Spaniards to import black slaves. The need to preserve Indian laborers became so desperate that the Spanish Crown finally intervened, making the Indians its direct subjects, independent of the landlords, and taxing them directly. The *encomiendas* and other forms of slavery were abolished, but the Indians were forced into *reducciones* or special communities controlled by the Church[24] for the benefit of the landlords and the Crown. This was hardly an improvement as the Indians were heavily taxed; the new communities proved to be a more efficient means of controlling the Indian population.

Aside from the criollos and Indians, the Conquest gave rise to a new group of people, the *ladinos*, who were basically the product of racial mixture; the term also refers to Indians who had left their communities

---

[22] *Ibid.*, pp. 205, 207.

[23] Melville and Melville, *op. cit.*, p. 16.

[24] The Church was the first big moneylender in Guatemala—and a sizeable landowner. By 1700 the Church owned 5 of the 8 large sugar mills. It served as the "right arm" of the ruling class, and provided the institutional and ideological underpinning for the pacification of the Indians. See Susanne Jonas, "Guatemala, Land of Eternal Struggle," in Ronald Chilcote and Joel Edelstein (eds.), *Latin America: The Struggle with Dependency* (Cambridge: Schenkman, 1974), p. 111.

for the town and adopted western ways. Economically, the ladinos were neither slaves (like the Indians), nor property owners; they were landless free laborers, who often led a miserable existence. They worked on the haciendas for a salary or rented land, and did not have to pay taxes as did the Indians.

Independence from Spain

By 1820 the basic structure of capitalist underdevelopment—mono-export, and concentration of land in a few hands—had been established. Guatemala's economy was determined by external events. Following an economic boom, in which Guatemala was the main producer of indigo, in the last years of the 17th century, and after 1800, production declined (due to inadequate port and transportation facilities, plus heavy Spanish taxation which made Guatemalan producers unable to compete with British colonies). A large sector of criollo latifundistas (especially indigo growers) began to see that independence from Spain was the only way of eliminating impediments such as regulations on the treatment of Indian labor, burdensome taxes, and state monopoly on trade. They were spurred on by British and French agents, who wanted to eliminate Spanish control over the colony.

The Indians were also revolting against the royal tribute, and there were several violent uprisings in different parts of the country. Although the Indians were not motivated by a desire for independence from Spain, their rebellions fed into the movement. The merchants were the last to support it; but faced with the possibility of large-scale Indian uprising, they allied themselves with the growers and the rest of the criollos, and in 1821 proclaimed their independence from Spain, basically without a struggle.

Despite "independence," the colonial structure remained intact. The first major attempts to change this structure came with the "liberal" regime of Mariano Gálvez, from 1831 to 1838. He attempted to modernize the economy by incorporating more land into production. This was done through legislation to expropriate lands formerly held by the Church. Large latifundia, however, were left intact. Once again, the main group to suffer from the legislation were the Indians, as Indian communities were legally deprived of their communal holdings. The main beneficiaries were the previously small ladino landowners and foreign interests. Guatemala's dependence on Spain was quickly supplanted by dependence on Britain. Under various colonization programs and land concessions, British interests gained access to vast amounts of land, and took the best lumber. The main crops during this period, cochineal, indigo and cotton, were transported on British ships.

Gálvez was overthrown in 1838, and was followed by 30 years of conservative rulers, who reversed most of his legislation, except that affecting the Indians. The "Liberals" were finally able to get into power in 1871, first with Miguel García Granados, who was followed by Justo Rufino Barrios.

The Liberal Era

By 1860 the colonial economy had taken on new forms but remained basically the same. However, developments in the international economy forced changes in Guatemala. The invention of cheap chemical dyes in 1850 brought an end to the cochineal industry. This stimulated an interest in diversification of crops—mainly sugar, cotton and coffee. Finally, the increasing demand for coffee, the industrial revolution in Western Europe, and the rise of the United States as a world power affected the economy of Guatemala, and made necessary some changes during this period.

The spread of coffee as the main crop required widespread changes in the division of land and labor, and this implied a change in Guatemala's power structure. Indigo and cochineal had been grown on relatively small plots of land. Coffee required more land, and capital in the form of credit; new transport and port facilities had to be created. The criollo ruling class was forced to expand to include a new group of people, the ladino upper class, which found in coffee the basis for its rise to power.[25]

This was the context for what has been termed the "Liberal reforms" of Justo Rufino Barrios. In order to incorporate more land for coffee production, Barrios moved to nationalize all lands belonging to the Church and monasteries. Small landholdings and ejidos (communal lands) were also nationalized for incorporation into large latifundia. Uncultivated state holdings were divided up and sold cheaply. Land ownership registry and property inheritance laws were enacted. Most important, communal holdings in Indian villages were absorbed. Unlike indigo or cochineal, coffee could be grown at much higher altitudes. Thus Indian lands which had been safe because of their mountain locations were taken over. State legislation requiring titles to private property legitimated the appropriation of municipal and Indian communal holdings.

Thus the situation of the Indians, which had already been desperate, became intolerable. To give one example, Lisandro Barillas received the following declaration from the Highland Nahualá in the 1890s:

> You have ordered us to leave our lands so that coffee can be grown.... In exchange you have offered us 600 caballerías on the coast. We know how to grow coffee—we do this for the landowners in their fincas—but we want our fathers' land for corn. They have always been ours.[26]

The liberal governments intensified the latifundia-minifundia system. Through various new laws, these governments guaranteed a permanent supply of cheap labor required by coffee growers and foreign investors. Even more than after the Conquest, the Indians were dispossessed of their lands, and forced to depend on the plantations for work. Indian villages left over from the colonial period were shattered, and Indians were forced to migrate from the highlands to pick coffee. The land was concentrated in fewer

---

[25] *Ibid.*, p. 131.

[26] Adrián Recinos, *Monografía de Huehuetenango* (Guatemala: Ministerio de Educación Pública), p. 217, cited in Melville and Melville, *op. cit.*, p. 12.

hands. By 1926, only 7.3 percent of the Guatemalan population owned land. Forced labor was officially instituted through legislation—debt slaves became *colonos*—peons tied to the haciendas through hereditary debts to the landowners. Under the *habilitación* system, designed to recruit seasonal labor under contract, agents of fincas went to villages to lend money, thus indebting the Indians and forcing them to work during the harvest. Local officials maintained a list of Indians available to work at the request of the landowners. Vagrancy laws passed in 1934 required all Indians to work at least 150 days a year and to carry a card showing the number of days they had worked. Those who resisted were jailed. These measures were considered necessary for "modernization." Thus in effect, the government was no more than a police force for the landowners.

The 1929 economic crash had a serious effect on the price of coffee, and on the Guatemalan economy in general. Jorge Ubico's power base was the coffee growers' oligarchy; instead of diversifying the economy, Ubico sought to strengthen the existing system. He was overthrown in 1944 by a coalition of middle class intellectuals and petty bourgeoisie, who were attempting to break the power of the landed oligarchy and institute certain reforms in order to modernize the country. This was the beginning of the decline of the power of the *cafeteleros*.

The "Revolution"

A few months after the ouster of Ubico, Juan José Arévalo won the Presidency in what has been termed the "freest" election Guatemala ever had. The Constitution adopted in 1945, a few days before he took office, abolished the 1934 vagrancy laws and all forms of forced labor, and laid the foundations for labor legislation. At least 95 percent of the labor force in Guatemala was rural at this time, consisting mainly of unorganized, unprotected Indian coffee pickers. The only organized rural force were the 15,000 workers on the two United Fruit plantations. Wages for agricultural workers were as low as $2 a week.[27] The 1947 Labor Code included compulsory labor-management contracts, minimum wages, the right to strike, and to organize unions—for the first time in Guatemalan history.

The situation of the peasants, however, was not basically changed. Rural wages were hardly affected. The 1947 Code made no provisions for unionization on the large plantations employing less than 500 workers. Peasant unions were required to have at least 50 initial members, two thirds of whom had to be literate.

Despite pressure from the main rural labor confederation, Arévalo was not prepared to make the basic structural change required to reverse centuries of inequality and underdevelopment: a radical land reform which would have affected the power of the latifundistas. He instead contented himself with creating a "climate" for land reform.

Arévalo did attempt to modernize the economy, and to promote what was officially called the "industry of agriculture." One of the main efforts

---

[27] Jonas, *op. cit.*, p. 153.

was decree No. 712, the 1948-9 Law of Forced Rental. This law was designed to force latifundistas (who, for fear of expropriation, had stopped renting lands to their tenants) to continue renting these lands. Meanwhile, a new agency, *Instituto de Fomento de la Producción* (INFOP), and the new state bank, *Banco de Guatemala,* provided credit for agricultural diversification. Most of the former German plantations, expropriated during the War, remained under government administration as *fincas nacionales* (national farms) to be rented out to individuals, cooperatives or joint stock companies. But basically, the agrarian structure which had evolved since 1860 remained the same, and the power of the landlords remained untouched.

Arbenz succeeded Arévalo in 1951 with the announced intention of carrying out a true and complete land reform. Upon taking office, Arbenz stated that his goal was to modernize the nation's economy, to raise the living standard of the masses and to transform Guatemala's semifeudal basis of production to a more modern or "capitalist" form. This was a necessity if Guatemala was to industrialize, as the purchasing power of the majority of the population had to be expanded. Arbenz meant to create national independent capitalism; the prerequisite was an agrarian reform.

Thus in 1952 Arbenz promulgated Decree No. 900, the Agrarian Reform Law. The stated purpose of this law was to:

> *eliminate all feudal type property in rural areas, abolish antiquated relations of production, especially work-servitude and the remnants of slavery, such as* encomiendas, *to give land to the agricultural workers who do not possess such or who possess very little, facilitate technical assistance, expand agricultural credit for the benefit of all who work the land.*[28]

This law was aimed at large fincas with unused lands, not at plantations which were using the land productively. Although it affected large, private holdings, it in no way threatened the principle of private property.

The law provided for expropriations of holdings over 223 acres, particularly idle lands. Peasants would receive land in lots up to 42.5 acres in ownership or in use for life; they would pay for it at a rate of 3 percent or 5 percent annual production. Compensation to former owners would be made through 25-year government bonds at 3 percent interest, value of the land to be determined by the owners' own declarations for taxes in 1952. The law was to be implemented by agrarian committees, representing mostly peasants; this was the most explosive aspect of Arbenz' legislation, as for the first time in history peasants had power.

In 1952, 107 (state-owned) *fincas nacionales* were distributed, many of them to peasant cooperatives. Expropriations began in 1953. By June, 1954, 1002 plantations covering 2.7 million acres had been affected (although only 55% of that was actually expropriated, constituting 16.3 percent of the available privately-owned idle lands), worth $8,345,554 in indemnization bonds. One hundred thousand peasant families received land,

---

[28] Melville and Melville (unpublished article).

as well as credit and technical assistance from new state agencies.[29]

The landowners objected vehemently to the new legislation, often with violent retaliations against the peasants, who sometimes rushed and occupied lands before the legal formalities were completed. Moreover, the peasants did not discriminate between latifundistas and small landowners, and this increased the violence in the countryside.

The United Fruit Company was still the largest landowner in the country. Of its over 555,000 acres, it was using only 15 percent (the Company claimed to need the large reserves because of banana diseases). In several decrees the government expropriated from UFCo a total of 387,000 acres, offering $1,185,115 in compensation, based on the company's tax declaration. This represented almost 14 percent of the total land taken from private owners. The Company, backed by the U.S. State Department, claimed the property and damages were worth nearly $16 million. This issue brought the struggle between the Arbenz government and the United States to a head.

The rest is history. In 1954, Castillo Armas overthrew Arbenz in a coup inspired, organized and financed by the CIA. This marked the end of the period of the "national bourgeoisie," and the end of all possibilities of land reform through constitutional means.

Basically the Revolution had aimed to modernize and stabilize capitalism by eliminating the "feudal" remnants; not to eliminate the existing capitalist structures, and certainly not to institute socialism. The 1952 agrarian reform law was basically capitalist, and it in no way provided for the other necessary structural changes. One thing the Revolution had done, however, through its various diversification programs, was to create a new class. This class, which can be considered a more "modern" bourgeoisie (as contrasted with the coffee growers), had investments in cotton, banking and industry. Originally they were oriented towards the Guatemalan market, and supported Arbenz' moves to modernize the economy. However, when faced with the possibility of real mass mobilizations, they began to withdraw support from the Arbenz government, and did not defend the Revolution; and after 1954, they became bulwarks of the Counterrevolution.[30]

Counterrevolution

Castillo Armas immediately proceeded to reverse all changes made in the previous ten years, and to eliminate all new organizations and traces of progressive political consciousness which had developed. Special targets were UFCo union organizers and Indian village leaders. Peasants accused of being involved in the agrarian committees, or of benefiting from the agrarian reform programs, were jailed, exiled, or killed. For example, peasants on the agrarian committees in Villanueva, Morán, Ipal and Morales

---

[29] For more details see Melville and Melville, *Guatemala.*

[30] *Ibid.*, Jonas, *op. cit.*, p. 77.

were executed without trial.[31] Peasant unions were disbanded, and many of their members jailed.

At the same time, all progressive legislation was reversed. Decree No. 35 ordered the suspension of all expropriation decrees. The Law of Forced Rentals and the Agrarian Reform Law were repealed. By January 1956, 99.6 percent of all land expropriated under the law was returned to its former owners, including the UFCo. (In a public relations gesture, the Company then returned 108,000 of it back to the government.)[32] Almost all the beneficiaries of the agrarian reform law were dispossessed, and all cooperatives were dissolved.

Another change since 1954 has been increased government participation in promoting agricultural production through large-scale credit and other incentives, and increased involvement of U.S. government agencies in Guatemalan agriculture. The result has been a "modernization" but not a basic change in the existing structures. Every government since 1954 has been caught in a contradiction: on the one hand, there is a need to increase the purchasing power of the majority of the population, and to respond to their pressure for land; on the other hand, because of the increased dependence on agricultural exports, the latifundistas need more and more land. Moreover, given the current tax rates (the lowest in Central America),[33] the Guatemalan government has not had the resources to create the infrastructure needed to incorporate inaccessible or underdeveloped land in Guatemala. During the 1960s, following the Cuban Revolution, particularly during the Alliance for Progress, there was much talk of agrarian reform, and funds were given for different agrarian programs.[34] However, in practice there has been no possibility of any real land reform since 1954. Aside from other legal impediments to an agrarian reform, the 1965 Constitution specifically prohibits the use of government bonds for expropriation.

Colonization Programs

Under the influence of his U.S. advisers,[35] Castillo Armas introduced the concept of "colonization" with Decree No. 559 in 1956. He created a General Office of Agrarian Affairs to oversee the colonizers. By 1957 when he was assassinated, his government had given out land to 15,494 families. Of these, only 2,814 were family-sized farms in the newly created Agrarian Development Zones. Most of the land distributed was land which had been donated by UFCo.[36] The Law of Agrarian Transformation, decreed in 1962 by the next president, Miguel Ydígoras Fuentes, became the basis for all future colonization schemes. Ydígoras only distributed 2,451 farms, mainly land donated by UFCo.

---

[31] Alvaro López, "La crisis política y la violencia en Guatemala" in *10 años de insurrección en América Latina* (Chile: Ediciones Prensa Latinoamericana, 1971), pp. 85, 86.

[32] Melville and Melville, *Guatemala*.

[33] Jonas, *op. cit.*, p. 193.

[34] U.S. House, *op. cit.*, p. 132.

[35] Jonas, *op. cit.*, p. 185.

[36] Melville and Melville (unpublished article).

A more "ambitious" colonization scheme was devised under President Julio César Méndez Montenegro who was elected on a reform platform in 1966. A new piece of legislation, called the Adjudication Law of Petén, called for the distribution of land to landless peasants in the northernmost department of Petén, up until then almost totally uncultivated.[37] The director of FYDEP, the new government agency charged with developing the Petén, declared: "To believe that up there (in Petén) there is a field for an agrarian reform constitutes a national crime. We have nothing to reform, nothing to remake; rather everything to construct, everything to form."[38]

Although the law is supposed to help poor peasants, large cattle ranchers from the South coast had already begun to move to Petén, and they benefited immediately from the new law. They received extensive properties (2500 acres each) for little more than the price of fencing the lands. Legally they could obtain up to 11,000 acres by forming a cooperative and listing 15 people as members (they could be from the same family). As a result

petitions for lands made by lawyers, doctors, Aviateca (the national airline) pilots—and permit us to say—the members of a certain political party, were resolved favorably almost immediately.[39]

Many military men obtained land during this period. Most of the ranches were dedicated to cattle, some to rubber and chicle.

The Petén program has been a failure for the peasants, as the area is almost totally lacking in basic services, transportation and marketing facilities. The program has benefited the new latifundistas who have been able to acquire already cleared land cheaply, and have a ready supply of cheap labor. Méndez also initiated a series of "agrarian reform" programs, under which peasants who were already farming state-owned lands were forced to buy land or get off it.

A more sophisticated version of "colonization" (i.e. more obviously designed by international agencies) can be found in President Carlos Arana Osorio's heavily publicized National Plan for Rural Development—1971-75. This plan was written at the request of the Méndez government, with heavy assistance from several international agencies, including BID and AID, and designed to be implemented by whoever won the elections in 1970. It makes clear that a true agrarian reform would be incompatible with the existing legal system.

Altogether the amount of land distributed through the various colonization programs has been miniscule, despite the high cost—as noted even

---

[37] Actually, the "frontier myth" dates back to the 19th century. The Petén is a tropical jungle area constituting 1/3 of the national territory. The Food and Agriculture Organization made a study of the chemical and organic composition of the Petén Lands in 1965-68 to determine what extensions could be used. It was found that due to poor soil quality, very little land could be used for agriculture, and that a high percentage, but not an excessive one, could be used for cattle raising.

[38] Melville and Melville (unpublished article).

[39] *Ibid.*

by AID consultants.[40] Even the weak laws have been full of loopholes and mechanisms for the defense of latifundistas. Even though agricultural credit institutions were established, by 1967, 90 percent of all credit had been monopolized by big growers.[41] Another important factor has been the lack of services provided by the main institutions created by the plan—BANDESA, DIGESA, INDECA as well as INTA.

According to one source, for the period of 1955-56, an average of less than 500 families were settled each year, and in Petén less than 500 private farms and 14 cooperatives by 1968. Between 1961-67 under the Alliance for Progress, only 7 percent of the rural population was resettled. Even according to official figures, by 1967 only 22,000 families had received 400,000-500,000 acres of land—as compared with 100,000 peasants who had received 1.5 million acres in less than 2 years under Arbenz.[42]

Thus, as shown by the 1964 census, the land tenure situation hardly changed from 1950, before the Arbenz reforms. And thus, diversification of production, and the agricultural promotion programs of the past 20 years have benefited and enlarged the agricultural bourgeoisie, and have created a small agricultural petty bourgeoisie through land grants. However, the situation of the majority of the population has steadily deteriorated.

Conclusion

The prospects for the campesino seem bleak as the population increases and the amount of available land to subdivide decreases. Trends towards mechanization of cotton, the decline of coffee prices, and the introduction of cattle as the main export crop are lessening the need for human labor. This will force more people into the cities in search of work, but in the cities there is little work, as most industries require few workers and the country does not have a sufficient consumer base for further industrialization.

Thus the latifundia-minifundia system that has worked for 400 years is breaking down. Furthermore the dislocation involved in large scale migration is having a radicalizing effect—especially as Indians see their centuries-old way of life organized around their land disappear. On the fincas the contrast between owners' wealth and workers' poverty is stark; and the peasants-turned-workers are forced into a direct exploitative relationship with the landowners. Furthermore the Indians come into contact with poor ladino workers who are in the same situation. This contact may finally break down the cultural and ethnic barriers which have divided the work force for 500 years.

Colonization is clearly not the answer to the increasing pressure for land. Once conceived of as a stopgap to revolution, these programs are increasing the contradictions for the ruling class: they create expectations for land, and yet, through their failure, they further reveal the government's inability or unwillingness to meet its promises to the campesinos.

---

[40] Fletcher, *op. cit.*, p. 138.

[41] Jonas, *op. cit.*, p. 186.

[42] *Ibid.*, p. 186.

Furthermore, as the situation of the peasants in the colonization program deteriorates, and they often lose their new land, they will become even more radicalized—this time with nothing to lose. (The Petén was the scene of much of the guerrilla activity in the early 1970s).

Clearly, under the present system, Guatemala's ruling class will continue to block significant changes in land distribution, as it had in the past. But the pressure from peasants for land is constant and is increasing. The growing militancy and spontaneous violence in the countryside—and the government's emphasis on rural counterinsurgency and military control—underscore the fact that land distribution remains the principal problem in Guatemala. The problem will only be resolved when a significant mass of the population is sufficiently mobilized and organized to overthrow the system.

Agrarian Reform in El Salvador:
A Program of Rural Pacification*
By Philip Wheaton

Philip Wheaton is the Director of the Ecumenical Program for Inter-American Communication and Action (EPICA). He has lived and worked in Central America and has written extensively on the region.

On October 15, 1979, the Carter administration was informed that younger officers in El Salvador were planning a coup and did nothing to challenge them.[1] Almost immediately after the new junta took power, promising "major reforms," the U.S. government announced its support. Yet no such reforms were implemented during the fall months of the first junta. Since the first junta ended in failure and represented the last hope for a peaceful implementation of reform, analyzing this inaction is critical.

One reason for inaction on the reforms was the opposition of the oligarchy. A "palace coup" had occurred but the old structures of power were still very much in place. One Salvadorean peasant leader explained: "It is the same military, the same National Police and National Guard, the same wealthy oligarchs entrenched on their massive haciendas. Not very much has changed. A small group of progressive military men rid the country of their corrupt superiors. That's it."[2]

A second reason for the fall inaction on reforms revolved around the fact that the United States did not want the first junta to carry out changes because its make-up was not to the liking of the U.S. The U.S. embassy distrusted the civilian center of the junta precisely because they were committed to improving the lot of the Salvadorean peasants while

*Excerpted from *Agrarian Reform in El Salvador: A Program of Rural Pacification* published by the EPICA Task Force, Washington, D.C., November, 1980.

[1] *Washington Star*, October 18, 1979.

[2] Carolyn Forche, "The Rainy Season," unpublished, May 1980.

the United States envisioned reforms that were more cosmetic.[3] Basically, it involved a choice by the Carter administration to back a conservative military over against progressive civilians; since both were part of the same junta, the problem was resolved by doing nothing *vis-à-vis* reform.

Younger Officers' versus a Reactionary Military Structure

The weakness of the younger officers' position was precisely their own ingenuousness and lack of hegemony among their own ranks. While supporting generic slogans about reform, they had developed no concrete programs for change. More importantly, while they reflected some genuine pro-populist concerns—having entered the military, in many cases, from the working and peasant classes—they also deferred to the United States. Thus, when they chose Col. René Guerra y Guerra as their second representative on the junta, the U.S. embassy opposed the selection, proposing instead Col. José García and Col. Jaime Gutiérrez. When the younger officers were asked why they acceded to this foreign pressure, they responded: "We needed American support, and we agreed to this."[4] This acquiescence to the State Department was decisive in the early weeks of the coup in terms of the younger officers' inevitable loss of power.

Although some 20 high-level pro-oligarchic officers were removed from the armed forces by the coup, many others of a reactionary orientation remained in power. In fact, the so-called overthrow of Romero had been worked out ahead of time with Romero agreeing to it; i.e., a palace coup. His exit left behind a rightist power structure which had been carefully set up the previous January, an organization called ANSESAL. Created by the pro-oligarchic tendency within the military, ANSESAL was a double command, integrated and coordinated within the Armed Forces with control over the intelligence services, G-2 and S-2, and with the power to make high-level decisions behind the backs of whoever was in the Supreme Command. Besides having its own officers in key positions, ANSESAL also had under its authority the territorial patrols and the rightist terrorist groups, ORDEN, Unión Guerrera Blanca (UGB) and FALANGE. Furthermore, under the leadership of Roberto Hill, Regalado Dueñas and other professional oligarchs, ANSESAL could count on civilian support mechanisms—both financial and technical—to service its operations outside the military structure. Two key former officers in the Romero high command who operated within ANSESAL were Col. "Chele" Medrano, head of ORDEN, and Major Roberto d'Aubuisson, head of the UGB. This pro-oligarchic sector of the military never lost control of the armed forces despite changes in command during the fall months, and during the spring of 1980 openly defied the leadership of Col. Majano, the leader of the younger officers. The opposition of Medrano and d'Aubuisson to any kind of agrarian reform is public knowledge.

---

[3] Robert Armstrong, "El Salvador: A Revolution Brews," *NACLA*, July-August 1980, p. 8.

[4] Forche, *op. cit.*, p. 10.

U.S. Reform Strategy: Reorient the Oligarchy and Control the Countryside

The overall goal of the U.S. reform strategy in El Salvador was to prevent another Nicaragua, i.e., to prevent another progressive popular movement from taking power in Central America. This geopolitical preoccupation completely overshadowed any genuine reform intention, including its hopes to reform the Salvadorean oligarchy. Since U.S. support of *somocismo* had led to disaster from the standpoint of its imperialist influence over the region, a more sophisticated strategy was called for in the case of El Salvador. This strategy included reorienting the Salvadorean oligarchy and confining or destroying the progressive forces. These goals were to be accomplished by:

- Re-direction of the landed aristocracy away from the land and into the mainstream of modern capitalism, by removing it from its rural stronghold and taking control of the country's banking system.

- Using the model of agrarian "pacification" developed in Vietnam to control the countryside, by having the military take over the large haciendas and use them as military enclaves, or resettle them with selected peasants who were either apolitical or supportive of the government.

The first half of the U.S. strategy, involving the reorientation of the oligarchy, implied the forcible removal of the landowners from their estates and plantations. The plan would affect, however, only those latifundista holdings of 500 hectares or over which were the worst symbols of rural power. It would not include the coffee *fincas*—belonging to the wealthiest sector of the oligarchy—since their farms were relatively smaller (50 to 150 hectares). While the United States recognized that the expropriation would incur the wrath of some, it was apparently hoped that the exclusion of the coffee barons would win some tacit cooperation from the oligarchy. Next, the strategy involved "modernizing the rural oligarchy by paying the disenfranchised landholders 25 percent in cash for their land while the remaining 75 percent would be repaid in bonds redeemable only through investment in the commercial or industrial sector."[5] The hope was that this would keep the bulk of this landed wealth in the country. Finally, the reorientation would involve the nationalization of the banks, since these were controlled by the oligarchy and used to enhance their power. It was, in effect, a strategy for modernizing the capital of the reactionary oligarchic sector.

The second element in the strategy involved "pacifying" the countryside. The military would occupy the plantations and large haciendas, expel any dissident peasants, and set up new cooperatives among the *colonos*. On tracts where outside peasants had to be brought in, these would be screened by AIFLD through its organization, the Unión Comunal Salvadoreña (UCS), making UCS the main clearinghouse through which campesinos would have

---

[5] Decree No. 153, Basic Law of Agrarian Reform, Revolutionary Junta of the Government, March 5, 1980, Chapter IV, Art. 14, p. 3.

to pass to become eligible for receiving land. The goal in this case was to create small independent farmers who were sympathetic to the government. This implied AIFLD's regaining control over the UCS which had become quite independent, even hostile, towards AIFLD during the years of its absence from El Salvador.

The main weakness of this strategy lay in the countryside with the exploited, landless and poverty-stricken peasantry. The danger was two-fold from the standpoint of the United States: first, that the left—such as the Revolutionary Popular Bloc (BPR)—which already had a strong foothold among the campesinos, would further politicize the peasants against the goals of the reform and use them as their base of rural support in challenging the armed forces. Second, there was a less radical but equally dangerous threat of allowing the peasants to have their own voice in the reform process, especially through their independent cooperatives, even if their demands were only economic in nature. This double "threat" led the Unites States early on to decide that any reform had to be imposed from the top-down and could not include creative dialogue or cooperation with the peasantry.

This raises the issue of the nature of the Salvadorean peasant. There are today in El Salvador basically three categories of peasants. The first, the *colono*, is a poor wage earner living on a large hacienda or plantation who, while he has no rights to organize, is usually given a small plot of land on which to grow subsistence crops for his own family: beans, corn, and sorghum. Second, there is the mini-tenant farmer or small property-holder possessing 1 to 5 hectares of land (2.5 to 12 acres) whose property is heavily mortgaged or who pays high rent and ekes out a living exposed to all the risks of climate, pests and marketing with limited or no access to extension loans for seed, fertilizer or equipment. Third, there is the large mass of squatter peasants who have no land and who hire out as seasonal workers on coffee, cotton or sugar plantations during the harvest season.

Under the existing military-oligarchic domination, the only form of collective organizing allowed in El Salvador was the cooperative. Thus, cooperativism was the main hope of the poor peasant in the pre-revolutionary situation. The bottom line for most campesinos is land and their control over it. Few peasants have any faith in government projects or promises of reform. These are seen by the peasants as a means to their ends—in particular the end of owning a plot of land. The cooperative—a peasant-controlled instrument in most cases—is viewed as the only collective protection or guarantee for the peasant's private plot, and his ability to make it produce and to sell his products once they are harvested. Therefore, when the reform of March 6, 1980 was instituted, the colonos were offered the chance to organize their own cooperatives while the military set about to systematically eliminate all independent cooperatives by killing off their leaders. In other words, cooperatives were used as a tool to reinforce a reform that would be imposed from the top-down while all real power was to rest in the hands of the military and the government.

The Agrarian Reform as a U.S. Counterinsurgency Strategy

The State Department and the U.S. embassy imposed the decision to proceed with an agrarian reform on the rightists within the Supreme Command by convincing them that only through it could the armed forces guarantee their victory over the popular-revolutionary movement which was spreading and deepening. Although it implied a counter-revolutionary role in the reform process for the Salvadorean military, this "imposed argument" had the effect of "coalescing and unifying the two sectors of the army by satisfying the reform project and the quasi-historical nature of one sector of the military leadership."[6] The model to be imposed would be that of agrarian pacification which the United States had developed in Vietnam using the argument of Dr. Hans Morgenthau: "the real problem facing American foreign policy ... is not how to preserve stability before an imminent revolution, but how to create stability outside of the revolution."[7] There were five elements to the U.S. argument.

1) Control the Countryside by Imposing a State of Siege

A key factor in limiting the growing power of the popular forces would be the army's ability to justify acts of institutionalized violence while at the same time rejecting any social demand or adverse public opinion through instituting a state of siege. That is, by suspending all constitutional guarantees and militarily occupying the entire country, freedom of the press and of speech, the right to public assembly, and the rules of habeas corpus for all cases of arrest or disappearance would automatically be eliminated. Thus, on the evening before the reform decree:

> The army carried out a military occupation not only of the large haciendas of 500 hectares (and larger) but of the whole national territory. Hours later, together with the agrarian reform decree, a decree announcing the suspension of constitutional rights was declared, known as a State of Siege. From then until the present, this military occupation and suspension of guarantees has continued in effect, terrorizing the Salvadorean population.[8]

This State of Siege Decree No. 155 was enacted the day after the Agrarian Reform on March 7, 1980, justifying itself on the basis of a potential threat by certain persons who might try to create "a state of agitation or social unrest."[9] It should be noted that the U.S. model of reform in Vietnam was similarly accompanied by a decree calling for a state of siege.

---

[6] Alberto Arene, *Sin censura*, Fall 1980.

[7] John A. Bushnell, Sub-Committee on Foreign Relations, U.S. Congress, March 25, 1980.

[8] Alberto Arene, *op. cit.*

[9] *ECA*, Decree No. 155, State of Siege, March-April, 1980, San Salvador, p. 390.

2) The Reform Would Unify the Army for Its All-Out Offensive

In order for the armed forces—whose goal was the annihilation of all progressive forces—to carry out its offensive against the left, military unity was essential. During the fall of 1979 a strategy of marginalizing the younger officers was successful, but the weakening of the Majano tendency did not imply unity and in fact the Majano forces continued to challenge the rightists until May 1980. But de facto unity was created through the Agrarian Reform, thereby sweetening the relationships between the liberals and the hard-liners:

> On March 3rd, the representative of the reformist sector of the army within the government junta, Col. Adolfo Majano, stated: "Since the coup of October 15, the government has been very soft on its enemies, but now the party is over." After announcing the imminent appearance of the Agrarian Reform, Majano guaranteed that the moment would mark a new stage in the Salvadorean process to be characterized by a "strong hand" against the enemies of Salvadorean democracy.[10]

Thus, notwithstanding the moral or tactical differences between Majano and d'Aubuisson over repression, the unity which the army needed to proceed with its offensive had been achieved.

3) The Reform Would Serve to Justify U.S. Military Assistance

Behind this military unity stood the U.S. guarantee of military assistance. Even though much more aid comes directly from the Pentagon or indirectly through "unstructured" funds (i.e., unspecified in terms of use) from multilateral lending agencies that do not require Congressional approval, selling a military aid package to Congress is politically and psychologically crucial since it tends to legitimize the administration's support of a given regime. In the case of El Salvador, however, there had been many reports of violence by the armed forces, and in late March the assassination of Archbishop Romero made it more difficult to get Congressional approval. Therefore, it had to be rationalized under another rubric. The basis of the administration's argument was that there was a centrist government in El Salvador trying hard to carry out a beneficial agrarian reform which needed the backing of the military:

> The principal obstacle to the reform, however, is that the extremists both from the left and the right are intent on dividing the Government and preventing the consolidation of a powerful moderate coalition which it will attract to its program if it is allowed to prosper ... I want to emphasize that contrary to a common misconception, our proposals for security assistance are not disconnected nor contrary to our support for reform in El Salvador. The redistribution of land would not be possible if it weren't for the protection and security provided by the Salvadorean Army to the new property holders and the civilian technicians and agents

---

[10] EFE, San Salvador, March 3, 1980.

who are helping them. ... Although (these proposals) are modest, they are also expenses that cannot be delayed for future years without losing unique opportunities to change the political balance in our favor.[11]

While the agrarian reform idea did not please the "hawks" in Congress, it fulfilled a far more important function: *it immobilized the liberals* and thus allowed the military appropriations bill to pass.

4) The Reform Justifies Christian Democratic Participation

A purely military government in El Salvador, without any civilian component, would open itself to the charge of dictatorship. This accounts for the United States' intense struggle to keep the Christian Democrats in the second junta. Now just as the Agrarian Reform was being implemented, the PDC liberals were all resigning, creating another crisis; this time a crisis of image. The right wing of the PDC—led by Morales Erlich and Napoleón Duarte—had to be convinced to join the third junta. Their pre-condition was the implementation of an agrarian reform:

On March 10 of this year (four days after the Agrarian Reform decree and the takeovers of the large estates by the military), during the national convention (of the PDC) but before the progressive sector of the party had resigned from the government, the right-wing of the party leadership shouted: "For 20 years we have been fighting for the day when an agrarian reform would be carried out that would take power from the oligarchy and give it back to the people. Now we have accomplished the beginning of this democratic and anti-oligarchic revolution, so it is our duty not to leave but to continue in this government and make our historic project a reality."[12]

5) The Reform Will Strengthen the Government's International Image

The inclusion of the Christian Democrats in the third junta was only part of the task of strengthening the international image of the Salvadorean government; it needed the progressive guarantee represented by the agrarian reform. This was particularly important in terms of building up support for the junta among European countries and in the United States, in addition to holding on to its tenuous support in Venezuela and Costa Rica where Christian Democratic regimes were in power. Thus:

Three days before the Agrarian Reform was decreed, Col. Jaime Gutiérrez declared that the consolidation of the External Front has been the primary concern of the military who assumed power on October 15, adding that "a coup by the right would politically isolate us from the rest of the American nations," and reminding his audience that the overthrow of Gen. Anastasio Somoza in Nicaragua was preceded by the

---

[11] John A. Bushnell, Address to the the House Foreign Relations Sub-Committee, U.S. Congressional Hearings, March 25, 1980.

[12] Alberto Arene, *op. cit.*

*decision of the American nations not to recognize the legitimacy of his
government.*[13]

With these arguments, the State Department convinced the reactionary officers in the Salvadorean armed forces to go along with the agrarian reform, a drastic step for years considered totally antithetical to the interests of the Salvadorean oligarchy.

Implementing the Reform: Issues of Urgency, Private Property and Propaganda

The speed with which the Agrarian Reform was passed amazed everyone. On March 3rd there was still no official word of an agrarian reform; on March 4th, the Institute for Agrarian Transformation (ISTA)—which was to administer the reform—was reconstituted; on March 5th, the oligarchy first became aware that the reform would become a reality; and on March 6, 1980 the Agrarian Reform became law. Clearly, everything had been prepared so that the reform could be put into motion whenever it was politically expedient. With a threatened coup the last week in February, that moment had arrived. There was a related reason for urgency: the reform had to be "successful" quickly if it was to turn the tide against the growing unity of the democratic and revolutionary forces. As Roy Prosterman subsequently predicted, "If the reforms are carried out successfully here, the armed movement of the left will be effectively eliminated by the end of 1980."[14]

One non-political argument used for getting on with the process as quickly as possible was that the reform should not interrupt the normal cycle of planting and harvesting. In this argument the reform managers revealed the top-down nature of their plan:

*It is clear that the coming crucial stages in the beginning of the agrarian
productivity cycle make it necessary on the one hand to proceed with
the execution of the structural reforms precisely on time; and on the
other hand not to delay their development by discussing very general
questions which would require for their implementation and consolidation a very long period of time, which contradicts the goal of accelerating
the transformations that will benefit the immense rural population.*[15]

Yet it is these "very general questions" having to do with the "distribution of some human, physical and monetary resources" (according to the same document) which are precisely the matters that most concern both the campesinos and the landlords. Obviously, dialogue and participation were not priority matters for the government. The emphasis was on speed,

---

[13] AFP, San Salvador, March 3, 1980.

[14] Inter Press Service, San Salvador, "Overview Latin America," Cambridge, Massachusetts, July 25, 1980.

[15] "Proposals for the Organization and Functioning of the Public *Agropecuario* Sector for the Agencies Affected and the Operational Directives for Training the Beneficiaries in the Context of the Agrarian Reform," San Salvador, March 5, 1980, p. 1.

not substance, so that "we can confront these problems during this calendar year." [16]

A second concern in the implementation of the Agrarian Reform was the issue of public reaction to the question of private property raised by the expropriation of land. Because the Reform had the dual goals of eliminating the landed aristocracy while at the same time preventing the peasantry from joining the popular forces, the Reform could not be a charade nor restrict itself to a pilot project. The stakes were too high. Thus the Reform would have to carry out the expropriation of significant tracts of land, which in turn raised the question of how far the military might go. On the one hand, the drafters of the Agrarian Decree did not wish to deny the philosophy of private property and thus stated from the outset: "Private property is recognized and guaranteed as a social function." [17] On the other hand, the Decree had to make it quite clear that the latifundia system was to be replaced:

> *For purposes of the present law, we understand by agrarian reform the transformation of the agrarian structure of the country and the incorporation of the rural population into the economic, social and political development of the nation, through a just system of property tenancy and exploitation of the land, based on an equitable distribution thereof.*[18]

This double thrust of the Decree—an apparent contradiction: pro-private property/anti-big private property—caused concern among the middle and ruling classes. Would the army stop their expropriations with the takeover of the large haciendas, or would it also take the middle-sized farms? Thus one of the stated concerns of the government planning the Reform was, "to minimize the inevitable fear, particularly because of the presence of the Army in this process." [19] The only reassurance it could give these two classes, however, was that the military would implement the Reform through "clear leadership and unity of purpose." Part of the contradiction was that the military, traditionally the servant of the ruling class, was now clearly effecting the policy of a foreign patron.

A third element in this implementation process involved selling the Reform to the mass public. Because the Reform had been thrust upon the society so suddenly, there was widespread ignorance and skepticism about the process. Therefore the government developed an extensive media barrage to allay the fears which such a change naturally evoked. The overall slogan was: "The Reform is for everyone." However, the campaign had to be carried out with great care, and therefore all radio and TV station operators were warned that *the urgency, importance and confidentiality of this (Reform) process do not permit:*

- Any prior investigation of the topics included;

---

[16] *Ibid.*, p. 2.

[17] Decree No. 153, Basic Law of Agrarian Reform, Chapter 1, Art. 1.

[18] *Ibid.*, Chapter 1, Art. 2.

[19] *Reforma Agraria: Comunicación inicial por medios masivos*, March 1980, San Salvador, p. 5.

- Any actual testing of public opinion;

- Any creative investigation;

- Any detailed plan of action or argument for it.[20]

The primary concern was about the reaction of the peasant population for which a slogan never before allowed in El Salvador suddenly became official language: "It is the campesino who has historically initiated this process and it is he who will make it a reality and who will defend it."[21] The media operators were also warned that they had to speak to the campesino in his own language and therefore:

> The Reform should be presented in a "simple, serious, tranquil and professional tone" in order to diminish completely any note of fear. The format should avoid at all cost any martial music and should instead employ "traditional Mexican songs, tropical boleros and classical music." Most importantly, announcers should avoid any form of paternalism, such as the terms "Papa government or Papa MAG" (Ministry of Agriculture).[22]

The most instructive aspect of this media campaign, however, was that it lasted only two days, suggesting that the planners felt either that the Salvadorean people could only take a small dose of such heavy medicine, or that ongoing communication of the issue could lead to the very dialogue and questioning which the government wished to avoid. Thus the Reform was injected into the public consciousness as a "quick fix," a political narcotic meant to both excite and calm, to leave the Salvadorean people officially informed but totally marginalized from the process.

Agrarian Reform in El Salvador: Theory versus Practice

The land reform initially decreed on March 6, 1980, was divided into two parts. Phase I affected all properties over 500 hectares, which according to the original announcement numbered 376 tracts covering approximately 15 percent of the country's agricultural land. Phase II was to affect all properties between 100 or 150 (depending on the quality of the soil) and 500 hectares, covering 1723 tracts and involving 340,000 hectares or 23 percent of the land area.[23] The government began to implement Phase I immediately; Phase II has been postponed indefinitely. On April 29, the military junta announced that Phase III would begin, aimed at the "institutionalization" of the minifundia system. The fruits of this phase are equally tenuous.

Phase I: A number of factors seriously compromised the impact of the initial phase of the land reform. Although it is stated that Phase I affects most of the nation's best agricultural land, in fact 69 percent of the

---

[20] Ibid., p. 1.

[21] Ibid., Estrategia de Radio (For Internal Use Only), March 1980, p. 3.

[22] Ibid.

[23] Figures from 1971 Agricultural Census, San Salvador.

land affected by Phase I is used for grazing cattle, not cultivated in any way. Furthermore, only 9 percent of the nation's coffee land is affected by Phase I since most of the coffee farms are less than 500 hectares in size. Coffee is El Salvador's major export crop and represents the backbone of the oligarchy's power. The failure to implement Phase II is particularly significant in this regard since it would have cut deeply into the oligarchy's power by expropriating 30 percent of the coffee lands.

A further limitation on Phase I is a provision in the law which allows a landlord to withhold 100 to 150 hectares from the reform process as his "right of reserve;" he may add an additional 20 percent to this reserve if he makes improvements in the quality of the land. This loophole in the law drastically reduces the impact of the reform if the landlords in fact make their claims. Landlords have found other ways of subverting the reform, both legal and illegal, with and without government cooperation. The most significant subversion of Phase I has occurred through landlord removal of the equipment and machinery from farms, as well as the slaughter of cattle prior to the takeover in order to liquidate their assets. No reliable estimates exist on how much equipment has been removed, but it is believed to be significant. It was not until May of this year that the government passed a law (Decree 220) prohibiting the removal of assets from farms, giving landlords ample time to drive their tractors to Guatemala, slaughter cattle, and even to remove barbed-wire fences.

Many landlords have not contested Phase I, being satisfied with the generous compensation that the government offers—25 percent in cash and 75 percent in bonds. This group generally has interests in other sectors of the economy, such as agro-industry, where profits are more secure than in actual agricultural production, while still others from this group have left El Salvador for the safety of Guatemala or Miami. For those who remain, however, informed sources who worked within the Ministry of Agriculture state that as many as 45 estates have been returned to the landlords through a "Plan of Devolution." Although there is no provision in the law for this devolution, such "sweetheart deals" between the military and the oligarchy have long been commonplace in El Salvador, especially since the Committee of Devolution—set up shortly after the reform was enacted—included such people as Col. Casilio Torres from the Ministry of Defense.

Perhaps the most important factor in limiting peasant participation in Phase I of the reform is the widespread fear and atmosphere of violence that has characterized the reform process. It has been the very military who are occupying the farms and giving "protection" to the peasants who have carried out much of the repression. As a result, only the permanent workers on the large estates (colonos) haved joined the new agricultural coopera-tives, while the bulk of the rural population of temporary workers has been completely excluded. Members of the local paramilitary organizations, along with government collaborators, count heavily among the beneficiaries of the expropriated lands.

The net effect of these flaws—both in design and execution of Phase I—has been to seriously reduce its impact in terms of acreage and number of beneficiaries, making an effective reform impossible. The original claims for Phase I in terms of numbers of peasants affected and the amount of land transferred have been grossly exaggerated. These claims have served the crucial function, however, of giving the impression that the reform would fundamentally change the agrarian structure and thus the power relations in El Salvador.

Phase II: In a press conference held in San Salvador on May 14 Col. Gutiérrez announced that there would be no more reforms carried out beyond Phase I (except for Decree 207, described below), thereby effectively cancelling what had been announced as Phase II in the initial reform statement on March 6.[24] Although this announcement received no media coverage—unlike the original March 6th declaration—it is perhaps of even greater significance since it reduces by more than 50 percent the initially proposed extent of the reform. Phase II would have affected, furthermore, lands where major crops are produced: coffee, cotton, and sugar cane. Specifically, four times the amount of coffee land was scheduled for expropriation under Phase II than under Phase I.

Whether the government ever intended to implement Phase II is unknown. What is clear is that Phase I, despite all its limitations, was widely opposed by the Salvadorean oligarchy and hardline military, so that Phase II would have deepened this opposition even further. The government needed the support of the landlords who would have fallen under the Phase II conditions; thus the postponement helped cement relations between the medium-sized landlord and the shaky regime of the junta. Furthermore, the administration of Phase I reforms had stretched El Salvador's meager technical resources to their limit, so that the government simply lacked the personnel to carry out Phase II.

The initial report on the reform from the *New York Times* stated that "El Salvador's military-civilian junta expropriated about 60 percent of the country's best farmland."[25] In fact, all the potential land available under Phase I and II combined amounted to only 38 percent of the nation's farmland. On March 8, the same newspaper reported that 300,000 hectares were to be expropriated under Phase I and then two days later, staff writer Alan Riding reduced his figures to "224,000 hectares, approximately 25 percent of the cultivable land."[26] Furthermore, if we exclude the 69 percent of pasture, wooded or other unutilized land from Phase I and speak only of cultivated land, we find that the supposedly sweeping reforms have expropriated less than 5 percent of the best agricultural land. This does not include the estates that have been returned to their owners, nor the land claimed by landlords as their "right of reserve," nor those lands that still have not been expropriated.

Phase III was the "Land-to-the-Tiller" program. The agrarian reform program prepared by the first junta in the fall of 1979 included a plan to

---

[24] *Central American Report*, Guatemala City, Vol. VII, May 19, 1980, p. 146.

[25] *New York Times*, March 7, 1980.

[26] *New York Times*, March 10, 1980.

promote collectivization of small farms and the formation of cooperatives in order to increase efficiency and break down the traditional system of minifundia which is dominant among small farmers in El Salvador. Over 70 percent of all farms are under two hectares in size and, according to the U.S. AID, these farms receive almost no help: "The small farmer in El Salvador is essentially without access to agricultural credit."[27] The problems of getting credit and other services out to some 200,000 small farms are legion, and thus the original plan of the Ministry of Agriculture was to try to introduce some form of collectivization.

On April 29, however, the junta announced that Phase III of the reform would not include any effort to collectivize farms but instead would institutionalize the minifundia system by converting all peasant tenant farmers into owners of the plots they were farming. Previous owners would be compensated, but the junta announced that the law, Decree 207, would "immediately convert 150,000 families into small owners." As one AID official put it, "There is no one more conservative than a small farmer. We're going to be breeding capitalists like rabbits."[28] However, this law does not affect those who already own their own lands and it places a ceiling of 7 hectares on the size of plot that any one individual can claim.

To gain some insight into the origin of the Land-to-the-Tiller aspect of the reform, we quote the following U.S. AID memorandum:

> It is closely identified in El Salvador with the U.S. government and the American Institute for Free Labor Development (AIFLD). Phase III presents the most confusing aspect of the reform program, and it could prove to be especially troublesome for the United States because it was decreed without advance discussion, except in very limited circles, and, we are told, it is considered by key Salvadorean officials as a misguided and U.S.-imposed initiative.[29]

Beyond the fact that Decree 207 lacks Salvadorean support, it has already fallen prey to a host of technical and administrative problems and has proven inappropriate for El Salvador's agricultural reality. While the program was billed by its supporters (chiefly AIFLD and the AFL-CIO) as being "self-executing," nothing could be further from the truth. Implementation of Decree 207 has been minimal because renters are reluctant to claim their land under the law. Many small farmers rent land from relatives or neighbors who are almost as poor as they are, and so they are not inclined to dispossess these acquaintances. In addition, the reaction of landowners of larger tracts to Land-to-the-Tiller claimants has generally been hostile. The same AID memorandum states that landlords have forcibly evicted tenants or have forced tenants to sign legal documents removing their claim to the land, thereby evading the law. Fear of reprisals by landlords has kept others from participating in the program.

---

[27] Darnes and Steen, U.S. AID Agricultural Sector Assessment, 1977, Washington, D.C., p. 35.

[28] *New York Times,* March 11, 1980.

[29] U.S. AID Memorandum, Washington, D.C., August 8, 1980.

Despite being listed as official beneficiaries, the land deeded to those who do participate in this program will be of questionable benefit. Participants must purchase the land by making yearly payments, but without access to credit and without any organized political power in El Salvador, the peasant—be he renter or owner—will remain as indebted and powerless as ever. Yet despite all evidence to the contrary, the U.S. press continues to make grandiose claims for this aspect of the land reform program. In a September 28, *New York Times* article, Alan Riding reports that "the junta's land reforms have benefited nearly one million peasants ..." which by October 25, according to the same writer, had been mysteriously reduced to "tens of thousands." Most skeptical estimates from El Salvador suggest that only a few thousand peasants have actually received land under Land-to-the-Tiller. Furthermore, with genocidal repression in whole departments, and fighting and disruption of services throughout the country, even well-established farmers are having trouble harvesting and marketing their crops.

In summary, the U.S. agrarian reform program in El Salvador—viewed simply as an agrarian model—is a failure, regardless of propaganda to the contrary.

The Anti-Communist Role of AIFLD and Rejection of the Reform by the UCS

As the State Department's William Bowdler announced, "Since the new junta was founded on October 15, 1979, the only project funded by AID to provide assistance to the Government of El Salvador has been for planning a land reform project."[30] This primary focus on agrarian reform has been funnelled almost exclusively through AIFLD with credits of $1 million to assist with the land tenancy program, using the *Unión Comunal Salvadoreña* (UCS) as AIFLD's justification for being in the country. However, AIFLD has not limited its work to training UCS leadership.

Under the conditions of the contract loan, AIFLD separately contracts the services of Prof. Roy Prosterman, a recognized expert in land reform who helped draw up the legal document for the Phoenix pacification program in Vietnam as a consultant. Prosterman quickly moved from this "adviser" role into a top leadership function, coordinating decisions of the U.S. embassy in San Salvador and the Salvadorean Institute for Agrarian Transformation (ISTA) with the Supreme Command of the armed forces. AIFLD also contracted the services of Mary Temple—Prosterman's friend—for advisory services to ISTA. Temple is the Executive Director for an organization called "Land Council for Rural Progress in Developing Countries," based in New York and apparently paying Prosterman's salary.

The common link between AIFLD and Prosterman is anti-communism—AIFLD was created by the Alliance for Progress in collaboration with the AFL-CIO precisely to counteract leftist political organizing among trade

---

[30] Bowdler, *Congressional Record*, No. 99, Part II, Washington, D.C., June 17, 1980.

unionists and peasants throughout Latin America. Prosterman once wrote an article for *Foreign Affairs* entitled "Land Reform as Foreign Aid"[31] in which he described how countering the exploitation of rural populations was the basis of the success of the Russian, Chinese, and Cuban revolutions. His alternative was Thieu's pacification program ("Land to the Tiller") in Vietnam, which he claims almost rescued that revolution from the left. William Bowdler described the State Department's similar concern about the situation in El Salvador:

> We are convinced that if the Government doesn't move drastically to undercut the popular attractiveness of the Radical Marxist solutions to the grave economic and social problems in El Salvador through means of a significant program of reforms, the result will almost certainly be a bloody civil war with a subsequent victory of the radical left.[32]

The coordination role played by AIFLD and Prosterman was directly responsible for drafting Decree 207 ("Affecting the Transfer of Agricultural Lands to Those Cultivating the Land"), a law which was approved by the Supreme Command and the third junta without ever being seen by the Ministries of Agriculture and Planning prior to passage. The goal of Decree 207 was propagandistic: to prove that Salvadorean peasants were becoming landowners. Yet the real lesson emerging from Decree 207 is the incredible influence a supposedly private institution like AIFLD had acquired within El Salvador, confirming its linkages to the highest levels of decision-making with the U.S. government and the Salvadorean military.

The creation of the UCS by AIFLD leadership has led to legitimate questions and criticism of the role of the UCS in El Salvador, especially since October 15. Furthermore, because UCS is a potpourri of elements from the whole political spectrum, including strong influences from ORDEN and its generally anti-progressive economic and political orientation, the popular-revolutionary forces have always seen the UCS as a collaborator with the oligarchy. But the peasant side of the UCS history is equally legitimate: its gradual withdrawal from AIFLD influence between 1973-79; UCS peasant skepticism about government reforms following the oligarchy's rejection of the 1976 reform plan and its repression of rural leadership; and UCS peasant participation in the March 6 reform not as "believers," but simply as a means to obtain land they believed to be the right of the Salvadorean campesino. That is to say, the UCS had a life of its own at the local village and departmental level which was not involved in the AIFLD manipulations through its national office; and in the countryside, UCS generally identified itself with the plight of the Salvadorean peasantry.

The indiscriminate repression that became an expanding reality in the countryside during the months of April and May finally fell upon the UCS as well. On May 30, at 3:30 a.m., uniformed members of the National Guard appeared at the San Francisco Guaiovo Cooperative in the department of Santa Ana and forced the male members of the cooperative from

---

[31] Roy Prosterman, "Land Reform as Foreign Aid," *Foreign Affairs*, Spring, 1972.
[32] Bowdler, *op. cit.*

their homes, subsequently assassinating 12 of their number, including three workers who were employees of ISTA. These UCS peasants had supported the agrarian reform and had received lands under the new Decree 207. As a result of this atrocity, the Executive Councils of eight UCS departmental organizations signed a protest on June 5, stating their opposition to the Agrarian Reform:

> Given all this, we feel that we cannot continue supporting the Agrarian Reform which up to now we have been doing because it seemed to benefit us campesinos. And if they don't cease these acts (of repression) against us, we will be obliged to take other steps in defense of our organization. At the very moment when our dream of having land is becoming a reality, we find ourselves facing a situation in which they are eliminating the very campesino who has finally taken hold of the land. We have called our compañeros in the Unión Comunal to be prepared for whatever decision that may be taken under these difficult circumstances in which some of our compañeros have had to pay with their lives for the very accomplishments of our organization and our people.[33]

This UCS rejection of the agrarian reform—which AIFLD not only supports but helped design—undercuts AIFLD's only grassroots justification for being in the country and receiving assistance from AID. Similarly, the congressional lobbying by the AFL-CIO and Roy Prosterman in behalf of the agrarian reform in El Salvador, which AIFLD attempted to legitimize through its relationship with UCS is, since June 5, 1980, no longer valid.

Pacification in El Salvador: The Vietnam Model

While land reform programs have the reputation of being progressive attempts at a basic restructuring of a country's economic system, in fact, the term "land reform" has often been invoked by a given oligarchy, dictatorship or foreign power to reinforce the existing power structure. This is particularly true when the ruling regime feels itself threatened by popular organizations which are mobilizing a dissatisfied peasantry. When such popular movements turn to guerrilla warfare against the ruling regime, a program of reforms is often a necessary technique employed to guarantee its continued control of the state; repression and violence against the popular groups and the peasantry in general is an additional requirement.

This is essentially the scenario that has been followed by the United States in a number of primarily agrarian countries around the world where it felt its interests threatened: Vietnam, the Philippines and now El Salvador. The history of land reform and "rural pacification" in Vietnam provides some key insights into the present U.S. strategy in El Salvador. Conceptually, according to Robert Komer, the first head of the pacification program in Vietnam before he was succeeded by former CIA director William Colby, the program had two goals:

---

[33] *Comunicado de la Unión Comunal Salvadoreña al Pueblo Salvadoreño,* San Salvador, June 5, 1980, signed by the Executive Councils from eight departments.

1) sustained protection of the rural population from the insurgents, which also helps to deprive the insurgency of its rural popular base, and

2) generating rural support for the Saigon regime via programs meeting rural needs and cementing the rural areas politically and administratively to the center.[34]

In the Vietnam case, the "protection of the rural population" was carried out by the Phoenix program under which some 30,000 Vietnamese peasants were killed for being alleged Viet Cong guerrillas or their sympathizers. The "generating rural support" aspect of the program was carried out through a proposed land reform called "Land-to-the-Tiller."[35] A key aspect of the whole process of rural pacification was the combination of civil and military operations under one unified management. The military counterinsurgency and the civilian land reform were part and parcel of a united strategy aimed at defeating the enemy.

If the comparison between Vietnam and El Salvador seems far-fetched, consider the following. First, the name of the El Salvador program is also "Land to the Tiller." Second, one of the key advisors to the Vietnamese land reform, Dr. Roy Prosterman, is now the chief advisor to the El Salvador junta. Third, the U.S. has brought the land reform program under the control of the armed forces in El Salvador to facilitate a much more effective counter-insurgency activity.

Let us explore these points one by one. The name, "Land to the Tiller," is self-explanatory; it is an effective mechanism for attracting the peasant to the program and has been invoked in U.S.-imposed programs from the time of the Allied occupation of Japan after World War II to the present day. Ironically, the term was first coined by Lenin during the Bolshevik revolution in Russia and gained him the support of the peasantry.

The Prosterman connection to Vietnam, the Philippines and El Salvador is similarly instructive. Prosterman, a law professor at the University of Washington, drafted the 1966 land reform law in South Vietnam and was also intimately linked to the agrarian reform in the Philippines.[36] Interestingly, in the Philippines as in El Salvador, the day the Agrarian Reform law was decreed, martial law was also invoked. Prosterman claimed that, "If the reforms are successfully carried out here [in El Salvador], the armed leftist onslaught will be effectively eliminated by the end of 1980."[37] Whether the government expects to eliminate the left via the land reform or via the violence of the military and paramilitary forces, Prosterman did not say.

Part of Prosterman's expenses for his work in El Salvador are being paid for by the American Institute for Free Labor Development (AIFLD), a

---

[34] Robert W. Komer, "Impact of Pacification on Insurgency in South Vietnam," reprinted Government Operations Subcommittee Hearings, July 15–August 2, 1971, p. 282.

[35] William Colby, Testimony before House Subcommittee on the Committee on Government Operations, July 19, 1971, p. 178.

[36] Inter Press Service, "El Salvador: Land Reform as a Counter-Insurgency Programme like the CIA's Phoenix Operation in Vietnam," July 25, 1980.

[37] *El Salvador Gazette,* May 5, 1980.

known conduit for CIA funds.[38] Prosterman also receives funds through the Land Council, a private, New York-based organization. In a 1972 article in *Foreign Policy,* he proudly refers to the Vietnamese land reform as "probably the most ambitious and progressive non-Communist land reform of the twentieth century."[39] Now, in 1980, Prosterman terms the El Salvador land reform "the most complete agrarian reform in the history of Latin America."[40] Such hyperbole during the Vietnam period covered up the enormous proportions of the U.S. counter-insurgency program that cost 30,000 lives. Today in El Salvador, it is having exactly the same effect.

Finally, let us consider the relationship between the land reform program and the military and paramilitary counter-insurgency strategy. The U.S. government has carefully tried to separate the two in the public mind by saying that the Salvadorean junta should be supported because of its sincere desire to carry out reforms which are thwarted by extremist violence caused by the left and the right. In a letter to the *New York Times,* Assistant Secretary of State for Inter-American Affairs William G. Bowdler stated, "The current military-civilian junta in El Salvador is attempting to carry out fundamental socio-economic reforms in the face of violent opposition from the extreme left and the extreme right."[41] Thus, the reasoning follows: massive economic assistance and limited military assistance are needed to increase the "professionalism" of the armed forces.

Bearing in mind that U.S. military assistance is now flowing into El Salvador, consider the type of "protection and security" being provided by the Salvadorean armed forces in its implementation of the land reform presently under way:

A technician with the government's Institute for Agrarian Transformation (ISTA) tells this story: The troops came and told the workers the land was theirs now. They could elect their own leaders and run the co-ops. The peasants couldn't believe their ears, but they held elections that very night. The next morning the troops came back and I watched as they shot every one of the elected leaders.[42]

This is but one example of the massive campaign by government security forces and paramilitary groups such as ORDEN to wipe out any popular organizations—such as cooperatives—and kill and terrorize the peasantry into complete submission. Numerous sources have also reported that government troops are burning crops and peasants' homes before evacuating entire areas of all civilians and then coming in with helicopter gunships to "eliminate" all remaining persons in hopes of destroying any guerrilla forces. This scorched earth practice was one of the most common

---

[38] *NACLA,* July-August, 1980, p. 18.

[39] Prosterman, *op. cit.,* citing *New York Times* editorial, April 9, 1970.

[40] Roy Prosterman and Mary Temple, "Agrarian Reform in El Salvador," AFL-CIO *Bulletin,* July, 1980.

[41] *New York Times,* April 29, 1980.

[42] *NACLA,* July-August, 1980, p. 17, referring to NACLA interview with an ISTA technician on June 2, 1980.

procedures of the Phoenix program in Vietnam.

In showing the parallels between rural pacification in Vietnam and the present U.S. policy towards El Salvador, one must recognize the implications of such a charge. Operation Phoenix in Vietnam remains as one of the tragic legacies of U.S. involvement in Southeast Asia.

Thus reform and repression in El Salvador are two complementary parts of a single U.S. strategy to defeat the popular and revolutionary forces and to retain U.S. control over that country through a ruling junta. Reform and repression are not, as the Carter administration would have us believe, two opposing forces: one to be supported and the other lamented. Rather, they are both essential parts of a single design for El Salvador.

Selling the Reform: The U.S. Propaganda Campaign

The U.S. government has never been thought of as a proponent of land reform, but rather as an unfailing defender of the vested interests of North American private multinational corporations and the entrepreneurial class in foreign countries which operate in concert with international capital. Except for its abortive attempts at reform during the early years of the Alliance for Progress, it has only recently adopted the Vietnam pacification model—applying it to Thailand, the Philippines and now El Salvador— as a means of modernizing backward agrarian societies, particularly those threatened by popular revolution. This is the context for the present land reform in El Salvador.

In order to sell this reform in the United States, the State Department has enlisted as a key ally, the AFL-CIO. In its July, 1980, *Bulletin,* the AFL-CIO published a front-page article on this land reform program, hailing it as "the most complete agrarian reform in the history of Latin America."[43] The AFL-CIO's key agents in this sales campaign are none other than AIFLD's director for Central America, Michael Hammer, and Prof. Roy Prosterman, AIFLD's consultant in El Salvador; both have made numerous trips to Washington and specifically to key Congressmen to convince them of the merits of the reform program.

In addition, the U.S. government has been able to count on the media establishment to faithfully follow Washington's line in El Salvador. Thus it came as no surprise when the *New York Times* endorsed the administration's program in an editorial entitled "Gambling on the Center in El Salvador," in which it states that the Salvadorean government's "ambitious program of land redistribution cuts at the very heart of oligarchic power."[44]

A similar editorial from the *Washington Post* states, "the United States has found it politically more feasible and ideologically less objectionable to support reform, even reform soiled by some repression, than to condone revolution, especially revolution stained by nihilism."[45] Similar media support, reflecting neither hard evidence nor close examination of the facts,

---

[43] Prosterman and Temple, *op. cit.*
[44] *New York Times,* March 15, 1980.
[45] *Washington Post,* July 23, 1980.

has appeared in the *Wall Street Journal*, the *Christian Science Monitor*, and *The Washington Star*.[46]

Within El Salvador, the job of allaying the fears of the Salvadorean oligarchy and business community was also given to Roy Prosterman, who was asked by U.S. Ambassador Robert White to address them at a luncheon in San Salvador on May 5th.[47] In his talk he emphasized that: a) they would be generously reimbursed for what land they lost—monies for which would come from the United States; b) the benefits of increased production from the land would largely accrue to the processors, middlemen and export companies—all activities firmly controlled by the wealthy elite; and c) the destruction of the left to be achieved by the land reform would increase business fortunes as El Salvador became a safe haven for foreign investment. Despite these promises, the more reactionary elements of the oligarchy are still opposed to any reform and view the Carter policy as overly conciliatory to the left.[48]

What this selling campaign masks, however, is the internal debate within the State Department and U.S. AID about the advisability and effectiveness of the reforms. The State Department has, therefore, been extremely reluctant to openly discuss the nature of the land reform program, for they secretly acknowledge that it—like its predecessors in Vietnam and the Philippines—is a "failing program."[49]

Conclusion

In searching for an indirect form of intervention and method of controlling the revolutionary process in El Salvador, the Carter administration decided to apply its rural pacification model developed initially in Vietnam. It did so in the face of the opposition of the Salvadorean oligarchy and its military supporters. Therefore, it had to convince the right-wing which was in control of the armed forces of the benefits of such an agrarian reform *as a strategy of counter-insurgency, ultimately beneficial to the ruling class.* The U.S. goal in carrying out this reform was primarily propagandistic in nature while the actual success of the reform was incidental. By gaining the military's backing the Carter administration was able to both unleash the fury of the armed forces to carry out untold acts of terror and genocide in their attempts to destroy the left, while appearing to support a moderate government supposedly trying to control the *extreme* right and left.

The failure of the reform was therefore predictable, both as an agrarian model of change and in terms of its true goal, the destruction of the

---

[46] *Wall Street Journal*, April 29, 1980; *Christian Science Monitor*, May 1, 1980; *Washington Star*, Spring 1980.

[47] *El Salvador Gazette*, May 5, 1980.

[48] *Washington Post*, Paid advertisement: El Salvador Freedom Foundation, Oct. 7, 1980.

[49] Gerald Hickey and John Wilkerson, "Agrarian Reform in the Philippines," Rand Corporation, Washington, D.C., 1978, p. 1. Although Hickey and Wilkerson are describing the Philippine land reform as a failing program, their criticism is equally applicable to El Salvador: lack of government will to implement the program, landlord opposition, and lack of peasant participation.

popular revolutionary struggle. Just as the pseudo-attempt at reform in the fall failed to materialize, so—by the summer of 1980—the agrarian reform had failed even though the U.S. media continued to claim success. If the U.S. government really believed that the reform might help win the Salvadorean peasantry away from the left and back to supporting the junta, this hope was dashed precisely because the peasants recognized—through the repression—that the reform was a hoax, neither truly in their interest nor one which involved them in any decision-making. Thus the reform failed first and foremost among its basic constituency: the Salvadorean peasantry.

The issue for the American public and the world at large is not merely a question about the viability of the agrarian reform *as a model*—one which now has even been questioned by AID officials. The real issue involves, rather, the question of duplicity—of using the high ideal of agrarian reform as an instrument of counter-insurgency towards the self-interested goal of continued U.S. control over the region in terms of its imperialist interests.

At this moment—just after Jimmy Carter has lost the election—it would be easy to blame his administration while arguing, as some will, that a different strategy might have fared better. Rather, the point is to understand that the struggle of the Salvadorean people to free themselves from the domination of the oligarchy and military is an absolutely legitimate one, while any U.S. strategy—sophisticated or crude—which tries to prop up that domination is illegitimate. The Salvadorean peasantry is ultimately seeking not merely land but land-with-justice, and this cannot be accomplished as long as the oligarchy or any foreign power dominates their country. Because the peasants understand this they are increasingly joining the revolutionary process as the only means to accomplish their objectives.

5

Violations of Human Rights:
The Price of Stability

- A twenty-four year old leader of a textile plant trade union disappears after having been arrested by Guatemalan authorities for handing out leaflets at the Guatemala City airport.
- A farmer from El Quiché province is arrested after taking part in the occupation of the Spanish Embassy in Guatemala City in protest against abuses committed by the army in El Quiché. Three days later his tortured body is discovered.
- A Christian Democrat *campesino* in El Salvador is detained by the National Guard near San Vicente, tortured by electric shock in the local Guard headquarters, and then taken with other prisoners to the shore of the Pacific, where he is hacked nearly to death and thrown into the sea. The other prisoners are beheaded; their bodies later wash ashore at a nearby beach resort.
- Hundreds of Salvadorean refugees, mostly women and children, are gunned down by both Salvadorean and Honduran armed forces as they flee across the Sumpul River, which divides the two countries. They are victims of a massacre which the responsible authorities have declined even to acknowledge.

And the list goes on: 32,000 noncombatants murdered in El Salvador; 25,000 in Guatemala; 35,000 in prerevolutionary Nicaragua. The vast majority of these murders committed either by government troops or by death squads closely linked to the government.

Personal testimonies of torture abound: electric shocks administered to the genitals, heads covered with rubber hoods soaked in acid, prisoners submerged in water. Such techniques are a part of deliberate government tactics designed to terrorize the citizenry into total submission. According to Amnesty International, the victims of the security forces have not generally been people engaged in armed insurrection. Amnesty further states that most victims have been killed after being abducted from their homes or work places, and while they were completely defenseless.

Per capita, Central America's human rights record is the worst in the world. A closer look at the shattered human lives that lie behind the monumental torture and death statistics reveals a common pattern: students, teachers, trade unionists, journalists, clergy, and—above all—peasants are the prime targets. Given these stark facts, it is simply ludicrous to speak of government-guaranteed human rights in Central America (with the notable exception of post-Somoza Nicaragua). A government that systematically brutalizes its own people cannot, despite the Reagan Administration's lofty rhetoric, be seen as moving toward democracy.

Further probing of the above statistics leads to yet a more chilling revelation: these repressive regimes are subsidized through U.S. military and economic assistance. The connection between these two facts—internal repression and external aid—provides the organizational framework for this chapter. The recognition of this link is crucial to an understanding of the sources of human rights violations in Central America.

The thesis that emerges from this chapter is that much of the violence imposed on the people of Central America by their governments is a product of U.S. policy—a product financed by U.S. taxpayers. Simply put, the U.S. is exporting repression to Central America. Interspersed among grisly accounts of personal suffering are some startling statistics: fifty-six million dollars supplied to Latin American governments between 1961 and 1973 under the "Public Safety Program"; over 3000 Latin American military personnel trained at the U.S. Army School of the Americas in the Panama Canal Zone between 1976 and 1980 at a cost of millions more; over 5000 gas grenades and projectiles sold to Guatemala and over 6,000 rifles, carbines, and submachine guns sold to Somoza's Nicaragua between 1976 and 1979.

As the preceding statistics indicate, there is ample documentation of the U.S. role in subsidizing repression in Latin America. Even under President Carter, who purportedly predicated aid on a good human rights record, there was a strong positive correlation in the region between U.S. military aid and human rights violations. In his article "U.S. Foreign Policy and Human Rights Violations in Latin America," Lars Schoultz demonstrates that the Carter Administration lavished aid on repressive regimes (such as Brazil and El Salvador) while giving the Latin American countries with the best human rights records practically nothing. Needless to say, this trend has become much more pronounced under President Reagan, particularly in Central America.

Schoultz's assessment of U.S. policy towards human rights violators is confirmed by research carried out by the Institute for Policy Studies (IPS). This research shows not only that the Carter Administration provided 2.3 billion dollars in military aid and arms credit to ten of the governments with the worst human rights records (one third of all aid awarded in the period), but also that this aid was used for internal "control," i.e., repression, rather than for defense against external enemies, the purpose often alleged. Utilizing the Freedom of Information Act, IPS discovered that U.S. firms and agencies are providing guns, equipment, training, and technical support to the police and paramilitary forces most directly involved in the torture and assassination of civilians. IPS concludes that the United States stands at the supply end of a pipeline which funnels repressive technology to practically all the world's most repressive right-wing regimes.

What emerges from the research done by Schoultz and IPS is a clear pattern of U.S. support for anti-democratic regimes throughout the world— a pattern especially pronounced in Latin America and, at the moment, even more particularly in Central America. The U.S. government is pouring into Central America amounts of aid entirely out of proportion to that region's diminutive size. The question of *why* the U.S. government consistently pursues such a policy will not be addressed directly in this section (although one article does attempt to provide an analytical framework for understanding the political-economic roots of some of the Guatemalan authorities' atrocities). This question is addressed in other chapters of this book. What the reader will find in this section is extensive, at times almost cruelly detailed and objective documentation of the horror that most people in Central America daily endure.

In a sense, the question of why U.S. foreign policy has taken the position delineated above is moot. What should be clear to any American of common sense is that the policy is wrong, not only from a moral perspective, but from a practical one as well. The systematic denial of fundamental human rights always nurtures the very thing it is intended to prevent: armed rebellion. The course of America's own revolution, which involved much less government brutality than the current fighting in Central America, illustrates this fact. Wholesale government repression can, it is true, wipe out revolutionary movements while they are still in their early stages, but this constitutes only a very short-lived triumph. In any case, the time when this was possible has long passed in El Salvador and Guatemala, not to mention Nicaragua.

The ultimate irony of the current U.S. policy on human rights in Central America is that it defeats the very goal it is designed to achieve: regional stability. Genuine stability is possible only under regimes which are prepared to respect the human rights of all social classes. Instead of encouraging or at least permitting the emergence of such regimes, U.S. administrations have generally done everything in their power to crush all indigenous movements toward democracy—and to subvert the only democratic government in the region, that of Sandinista Nicaragua. Only when U.S. officials realize and rectify their mistake will the stability they desire become a possibility; and only then will the Central American people's long agony come to an end.

—*Diann Richards and Steve Babb*

U.S. Foreign Policy and Human Rights Violations in Latin America: A Comparative Analysis of Foreign Aid Distributions*

By Lars Schoultz

The following article by Lars Schoultz is one of the few factual pieces of research that explores the relationship between United States economic and military assistance to Latin America and recipient governments' repression of fundamental human rights. Schoultz specifically researched whether U.S. foreign assistance under Jimmy Carter, a president who purportedly linked aid to a good human rights record, demonstrated a positive correlation with Latin American governments which respected the human rights of their citizens. Schoultz uses as an independent variable records of U.S. foreign assistance to Latin America for fiscal years 1962 to 1978, focusing in particular on the Carter years 1976, 1977 and 1978.

The dependent variable in Schoultz' article is the mean evaluation of the level of human rights violations by each Latin American government in 1976 provided by 91 human rights experts. From among the 87 Third World countries which received U.S. foreign aid between 1962 and 1976, the 91 respondents to Schoultz' questionnaire were asked to rank only those nations whose human rights records they were familiar with. The nations were ranked on a scale from 1 to 4 of ascending violations, using as a time frame the calendar year 1976 (See Table 1).

This then is the procedure Schoultz used to obtain part of his data. Schoultz makes it very clear that the results of his analysis only document the correlation between U.S. foreign aid and human rights records in Latin America. He makes no attempt in this paper to address the issue of the function of foreign assistance or to answer the question of why the U.S. pursues certain foreign policies.

The purpose of this paper is to explore the relationship between United States economic and military assistance to Latin America and recipient governments' repression of certain fundamental human rights. The emphasis of this study is upon the human rights to life, liberty, and the integrity of the person in the sense that they cannot be denied without the impartial application of due process of law. Thus, the human rights violations upon which this study will focus are torture and other forms of cruel, inhuman or degrading treatment, including prolonged detention without trial. The selection of certain human rights and the exclusion of others is by no means meant to imply that one group has a status superior to others; nor is it an arbitrary focus. Rather it reflects the fact that during the 1970s the U.S. government formulated its human rights policy primarily in terms

---

*Excerpted and abridged from *Comparative Politics*, January 1981. Copyright (c) 1981 by The City University of New York. All rights reserved.

Table 1
Level of Human Rights Violations,
Latin America, 1976

Rank Order*	Country	Mean Expert Assessment (N=38)
1	Costa Rica	1.00
2	Trinidad and Tobago	1.13
3	Surinam	1.36
4	Jamaica	1.43
5	Venezuela	1.48
6	Colombia	1.52
7	Guyana	1.56
8	Mexico	1.85
9	Ecuador	2.05
10	Panama	2.05
11	Peru	2.13
12	Honduras	2.19
13	El Salvador	2.35
14	Dominican Republic	2.43
15	Bolivia	2.61
16	Nicaragua	2.95
17	Guatemala	3.00
18	Haiti	3.33
19	Brazil	3.35
20	Paraguay	3.44
21	Uruguay	3.44
22	Argentina	3.59
23	Chile	3.79

*Ordered from least offensive to most offensive

of what have come to be known as "antitorture" rights. This paper is an analysis of the implementation of that policy, not a discussion of what one might wish the policy contained.

The results presented here are for both absolute and relative levels of foreign assistance. *Absolute assistance* is defined as the gross dollar amount of aid provided each Latin American government. Because the twenty-three nations of Latin America vary so widely, particularly in their population size, a focus upon the absolute volume of aid distorts some aspects of the aid/human rights relationship. *Relative (per capita) assistance* recognizes these enormous population differences. The examination of absolute and relative aid levels is complementary, describing from two perspectives United States aid programs in Latin America.

Absolute Levels of Foreign Assistance

Total U.S. Assistance. The correlations between the absolute level of U.S. assistance to Latin America and human rights violations by recipient governments are presented in Table 2. These correlations are uniformly positive, indicating that aid has tended to flow disproportionately to Latin

Table 2
Pearson Correlations between Absolute Levels of U.S. Aid and Level of Human Rights Violations, Latin America, 1975-77*

Fiscal Years	Total Economic & Military Assistance	Total Economic Assistance	A.I.D.	Food for Peace	Total Military Assistance	Foreign Military Sales
1975	.68	.46	.50	.34	.57	.53
1976	.50	.26	.24	.30	.28	**
1977	.49	.29	.37	.31	.34	.27

*$N = 23$
** Too few cases available for analysis.

Source: Data on foreign assistance provided by the Bureau for Program Policy and Coordination, Agency for International Development.

American governments which torture their citizens. In addition, the correlations are relatively strong: 8 of the 18 coefficients in Table 2 are +.40 or greater.[1]

Given the low number of cases (twenty-three countries) and the gross character of a single correlation coefficient, scatterplots provide a clearer description of the relationship between aid and human rights violations. In Figure 1, the dollar magnitude of the 1975 foreign assistance program is plotted against the experts' evaluation of human rights violations. There are two major clusters of Latin American countries. One group of seven countries received little aid and maintained a relatively high level of respect for human rights, while a second cluster of the remaining sixteen countries received comparatively large amounts of assistance and had a low level of respect for human rights. Colombia is the only major deviation from this pattern.

Figure 2 is a scatterplot relating U.S. aid and human rights violations in 1976. Since data on the level of human rights violations are the same in both Figures 1 and 2, between 1975 and 1976 changes in aid distributions caused the aid/human rights correlation to drop from +.68 to +.50. In Figure 2 the two clusters have largely disappeared, and several cases stand isolated on the scatterplot. In plain English, the two scatterplots indicate that, while the human rights/foreign aid relationship is far from perfect, in both 1975 and 1976, United States aid tended to flow disproportionately to the hemisphere's relatively egregious violators of fundamental human rights.

Figure 3 is a scatterplot relating U.S. aid in FY 1977 and the level of human rights violations in 1976. While the correlation remains high (+.49), it is obvious from Figure 3 that this simple summary statistic masks

---

[1] Since these correlations reflect findings from the universe rather than a sample of Latin American countries, significance tests are not used. For a contrary position see Robert F. Winch and Donald T. Campbell, "Proof? No. Evidence? Yes. The significance of Tests of Significance," American Sociologist, 4 (May 1969), p. 143.

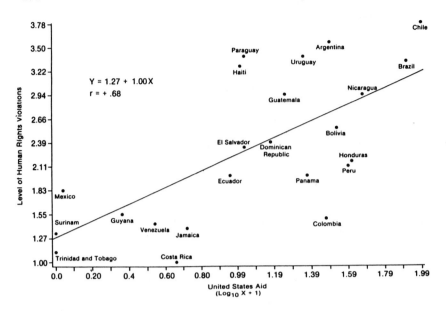

Figure 1: Scatterplot of Relationship between U.S. Aid to Latin America in 1975 and Level of Human Rights Violations by Recipient Governments, 1976.

several significant changes. Between 1976 and 1977 two countries with very repressive governments (Argentina and Brazil) experienced major aid reductions, and three relatively nonrepressive governments (Costa Rica, Guyana, Jamaica) obtained major aid increases. By 1977 the clear pattern in Figure 1 had disappeared, making the standard error of the regression equation so large that it would be inappropriate to draw a regression line. Nonetheless, the placement of Chile, Bolivia, Guatemala, and Haiti in Figure 3 confirms the allegation of critics that human rights criteria did not determine several major decisions on the distribution of aid to Latin America. With the single exception of Chile, however, it is instructive to note that of the countries ruled by repressive governments, by 1977 only the neediest (Bolivia, Guatemala, Haiti) remained major aid recipients. Unlike 1975, by 1977 aid to countries with repressive governments *and* relatively few needy people (especially Argentina and Uruguay) had been severely restricted. As the discussion below will indicate, this is because the issue of basic needs became a major part of the aid/human rights debates of the late 1970s.

Economic Aid. One of the two major components of the total U.S. foreign aid program is economic aid which in turn is composed primarily of funds from the Agency for International Development and the Food for Peace program. The relatively strong correlations between economic aid and human rights violation (see Table 2) suggest that in FY 1975-FY 1977 the international protection of human rights was not a central

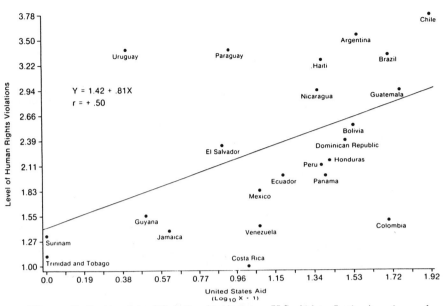

Figure 2: Scatterplot of Relationship between U.S. Aid to Latin America and Level of Human Rights Violations by Recipient Governments, 1976.

concern of economic assistance decision making. But it should also be recognized that one of these correlations is not strong and that others tend to fluctuate dramatically over short periods of time. Between 1975 and 1976, for example, the correlation between AID disbursements and human rights violations dropped from +.50 to +.24. Most of this change occurred through major declines in aid to Brazil and Uruguay, and through a substantial boost in aid to Costa Rica. On the other hand, during 1976, the repressive governments of Chile, earthquake-torn Guatemala, Haiti, and Nicaragua continued to receive relatively large amounts of assistance.

   Between 1976 and 1977 the correlation between AID disbursements and human rights violations rose from +.24 to +.37. Given the low number of cases from which these correlations were computed, a change of this magnitude should not be considered highly significant. It is worth noting, however, that the correlation did not rise in response to a clear pattern. In FY 1977 AID reduced its assistance to very repressive (Chile, the Dominican Republic), moderately repressive (Panama), and nonrepressive (Colombia, Costa Rica) countries. Similarly, AID increased funding to both repressive Haiti and to nonrepressive Jamaica. The inspection of these individual cases reveals no perfect pattern of AID assistance being directed toward repressive governments. When considering all Latin American countries, however, during FY 1975-FY 1977 AID's funds tended to be directed toward countries with repressive governments. Given the finding in Table 2, it cannot be argued that respect for human rights was a major criterion in AID decision making.

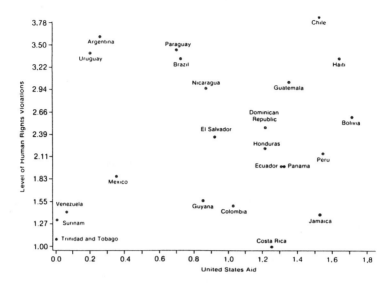

Figure 3: Scatterplot of Relationship between U.S. Aid to Latin America in FY 1977 and Level of Human Rights Violations by Recipient Governments, 1976.

No major changes occurred in the proportional distribution of Food for Peace credits and grants between 1975 and 1977. As a result, the correlations between this second major form of economic aid and human rights violations remained roughly unchanged. Persons familiar with the Food for Peace program to Latin America are already aware that the positive correlations in Table 2 are almost entirely the result of a truly massive food aid program to Chile, the country with the most repressive government in Latin America. With only 3 percent of Latin America's population and probably no more than its proportional share of undernourished people, Chile received an extraordinarily large amount of PL480 assistance.[2] Under similar circumstances, critics of the Food for Peace program have charged the U.S. government with financing food imports so that repressive governments can use their foreign exchange for arms purchases which are essential to the continued repression of their citizens. Responding to this perceived abuse, Congress in 1977 added a human rights clause to the existing PL480 authorization.[3]

---

[2] In 1975, 49 percent of all PL480 aid to Latin America went to Chile: in 1976 the percentage dropped slightly to 43 percent; in 1977 it decreased further to 34 percent. Had Chile received no food aid in 1976, the correlation between the Food for Peace Program and the level of human rights violations would have been +.13 instead of +.30.

[3] Milton Leitenberg, "Notes on the Diversion of Resources for Military Purposes in Developing Nations," *Journal of Peace Research*, 13 (1976), p. 113; Hubert H. Humphrey, "Economic Disengagement from Vietnam," *New York Times*, 5 June 1974; Emma Rothschild, "Is It Time to End Food for Peace?" *New York Times Magazine*, 13 March 1977, p. 44.

Military Aid. The second major component of the total U.S. aid program is military assistance which, in turn, is composed of Military Assistance Program (MAP) and International Military Education and Training (IMET) grants, excess defense stocks transfers, and Foreign Military Sales (FMS) credits. In Table 2, the "Total Military Assistance" column reflects all military aid from these four categories. By far the largest portion of U.S. military aid to Latin America—89 percent in FY 1975 through FY 1977—is in the form of FMS credits.

Each of the military aid/human rights correlations in Table 2 is positive; most are stronger than those generated by U.S. economic assistance programs. As in the case of economic aid, however, major fluctuations occur over short periods of time. This instability is most evident in the substantial one-year decline from +.57 (1975) to +.28 (1976) in the correlation between human rights violations and total military aid. In 1975 the most repressive governments fared unequally in their receipt of U.S. military aid. Three of the six most repressive governments (Argentina, Brazil, and Uruguay) received a substantial proportion—69 percent—of total military aid to the region, while the other three (Chile, Haiti, and Paraguay) together received less than 2 percent. The positive correlation between military aid and human rights violations existed not only because the United States favored three repressive regimes, but also because the nonrepressive governments of Latin America received almost no military aid. Excluding Haiti (which obtained military aid to train three students and to import navigational equipment for air and sea rescue units), not one of the ten least-repressive Latin American governments was granted more military aid than any of the ten most-repressive governments.

In 1976 the human rights military aid correlation dropped to +.28, half the size it had been a year earlier. The reduction was accomplished simply by cutting aid to repressive Uruguay from $9.2 million in 1975 to $1.0 million in 1976, and by dramatically increasing aid to nonrepressive Colombia ($700,000 in 1975 to $20.3 million in 1976). Military aid to two of the hemisphere's most repressive governments, Argentina and Brazil, remained high. In 1976 these two governments received 56 percent of all military aid to Latin America.

In 1977 the correlation between military assistance and human rights violations rose slightly to +.34. Although several substantial changes occurred in the distribution of military aid between 1976 and 1977, the rise primarily reflected a major (36 percent) increase in aid to Brazil and an even more dramatic decrease (99 percent) in aid to Venezuela. As in previous years, Argentina and Brazil continued to receive slightly more than half of all U.S. military aid to Latin America.

Relative Levels of Foreign Assistance

The correlations between relative (per capita) United States aid to Latin American countries and human rights violations by recipient governments are presented in Table 3. As in the case of absolute aid levels, these correla-

Table 3
Pearson Correlations between Relative (Per Capita) Levels of U.S. Aid and Level of Human Rights Violations, Latin America, 1975-77*

Fiscal Years	Total Economic & Military Assistance	Total Economic Assistance	A.I.D.	Food for Peace	Total Military Assistance	Foreign Military Sales
1975	.45	.31	.38	.28	.51	.49
1976	.29	.22	.13	.35	.27	**
1977	.35	.26	.25	.30	.15	.20

*$N = 23$
** Too few cases available for analysis.

Source: Bureau for Program Policy and Coordination, Agency for International Development.

tions are uniformly positive. Thus, even when the remarkable diversity of population size among Latin American countries is considered, the findings suggest that the United States has directed its foreign assistance to governments which torture their citizens. When compared with the correlations between human rights and absolute aid levels (Table 2), about half of the correlations in Table 3 are of equal strength and the remainder are slightly lower. In no case is a relative aid/human rights correlation stronger than an equivalent absolute aid/human rights correlation.

In considering per capita rather than absolute aid, the most striking change is a precipitous decline in the prominence of Argentina and Brazil. In 1976, for example, Argentina ranked fifth in absolute aid but sixteenth in relative aid, while Brazil was third in absolute terms yet twentieth in per capita aid. Since both the Argentine and Brazilian governments are ranked as extremely repressive, the relative aid/human rights correlation would have declined somewhat had not Nicaragua been the third major change in the ranking, moving up from twelfth in absolute aid to second in relative aid. The remaining twenty nations are ranked roughly the same on both absolute and relative scales. In 1976 Chile was first in absolute aid and third in relative aid; Guatemala was second in absolute aid and fourth in relative aid; Bolivia was sixth by either calculation. Because most of the other differences are minor, nearly everything written regarding human rights and absolute aid levels applies as well to the relationship between aid per capita and the level of human rights violations by recipient governments. In neither case is it possible to find a negative correlation which would indicate that U.S. aid programs favored nonrepressive governments.

While the correlations between various types of aid and human rights violations are far from perfect, these findings for FY 1975-FY 1977 reveal not isolated instances, but rather a clear pattern of aid distributions that favored Latin American governments which abused their citizens' human rights. During this period, aid officials regularly denied the existence of a positive correlation between the level of assistance and the violation of human rights.[4] In those individual cases where the linkage was evident beyond doubt, officials insisted that other equally important foreign policy concerns required that human rights considerations be minimized in aid decision making. Even in the era of relatively intense governmental interest in human rights during the Carter administration, only in isolated instances were human rights factors permitted to become the principal determinant of aid distributions. Aid officials perceived other legitimate reasons for the granting of foreign assistance.

Conclusion

These data and common sense suggest that there is no simple answer to the dilemma facing aid officials who must weigh multiple criteria in reaching their decisions. Few studies of aid decision making, including this one, would wish to underestimate the difficulties these officials face. What the findings from the data presented here clearly demonstrate, however, is that during the mid-1970s United States aid was clearly distributed disproportionately to countries with repressive governments, that this distribution represented a *pattern* and not merely one or a few isolated cases, and that human need was not responsible for the positive correlations between aid and human rights violations.

Now that these three facts have been established, researchers can turn to the more intriguing question of *why* in the mid-1970s the United States tended to award relatively large amounts of aid to Latin American governments which repressed their citizens' human rights. It is tempting to begin such a discussion here, for certain features of the scatterplots, particularly the unusually strong anticommunism of several major aid recipients and, later, the emphasis on aid to Latin America's poorest countries, are so evident that they should at least be mentioned. But the conclusion to a paper on one subject—the identification of positive concomitant variation between aid disbursements and human rights violations—is not the proper place to begin another—the reasons for the variation. The data presented in this paper are not able to address the reasons underlying any type of aid distribution. What they confirm is the validity of the concerns of a broad variety of citizens, interest-group activists, and members of Congress, who in the early and mid-1970s insisted that the United States aid program was serving to identify their government with unusually repressive Latin American regimes, and that there was no obvious humanitarian justification for such a policy.

---

[4] Examples of implicit or explicit denials include State Department testimony in the following: *International Protection of Human Rights*, fn. 8, pp. 819-820; *Political Prisoners in South Vietnam and the Philippines*, fn. 8, pp. 87-89; and U.S. Congress, Senate Committee on Appropriations, *Foreign Assistance Appropriations*, 1965, 89th Cong., 2d Sess., 1964, p. 82.

Guatemala: A Government Program
of Political Murder*
By Amnesty International

Amnesty International is a nonpartisan human rights organization. Among its many honors, Amnesty International won the Nobel Peace Prize in 1977.

Guatemala Today

Nearly 5,000 Guatemalans have been seized without warrant and killed since General Lucas García became President of Guatemala in 1978. The bodies of the victims have been found piled up in ravines, dumped at roadsides or buried in mass graves. Thousands bore the scars of torture, and death had come to most by strangling with a garotte, by being suffocated in rubber hoods or by being shot in the head.

In the same three year period several hundred other Guatemalans have been assassinated after being denounced as "subversives." At least 615 people who are reported to have been seized by the security services remain unaccounted for.

In spite of these murders and "disappearances" the Government of Guatemala has denied making a single political arrest or holding a single political prisoner. (But in February 1980 Vice-President Francisco Villagrán Kramer put the position like this: "There are no political prisoners in Guatemala—only political murders." He has since resigned and gone into exile.)

The government does not deny that people it considers to be "subversives" or "criminals" are seized and murdered daily in Guatemala—but it lays the whole blame on independent, anti-communist "death squads."

According to a distinction drawn by the government under President Lucas García, "criminals" are those people who have been seized and killed by what the authorities call the *Escuadrón de la Muerte* (Death Squad) and "subversives" those killed by the *Ejército Secreto Anti-comunista* (ESA)—Secret Anticommunist Army. The authorities have issued regular statistics on the killings and on occasion have come out with death tolls higher than those independently recorded by Amnesty International.

What the Government of Guatemala Says

National Police spokesmen told the local press in 1979 that the *Escuadrón de la Muerte* had killed 1,224 "criminals" ("1,142 men and 82 women") from January to June 1979 and that the ESA had killed 3,252 "subversives" in the first ten months of 1979. Although no similar statistics have been issued for 1980, government spokesmen have continued to report on the

---

*Excerpted and abridged from a report published by Amnesty International, 1981.

latest victims of "anti-criminal" and "anti-communist," but allegedly independent and non-governmental, "security measures."

Amnesty International believes that abuses attributed by the Government of Guatemala to independent "death squads" are perpetuated by the regular forces of the civil and military security services. No evidence has been found to support government claims that "death squads" exist that are independent of the regular security services. Where the captors or assassins of alleged "subversives" and "criminals" have been identified, as in the cases cited in this report, the perpetrators have been members of the regular security services.

The Victims

During 1980 the security forces of the Government of Guatemala were reported to have been involved in unexplained detentions and murders of people generally considered as leaders of public opinion: members of the clergy, educators and students, lawyers, doctors, trade unionists, journalists and community workers. But the vast majority of the victims of such violent action by the authorities' forces had little or no social status; they came from the urban poor and the peasantry and their personal political activities were either insignificant or wholly imagined by their captors.

The precarious balance for the poor in Guatemala between life and death at the hands of the security services is illustrated by the testimonies in this report. The former soldier describes house to house searches in which the discovery of certain "papers"—leaflets or circulars—was sufficient reason to wipe out an entire family. The prisoner, who was brutally tortured and escaped only the day before he was scheduled to be executed at Huehuetenango army base, believes that a neighbor denounced him as a "subversive" because of a dispute over the village basketball court—a good enough reason, as far as officers of the Guatemalan army were concerned, for him to be tortured and put to death.

At first glance most of the victims of political repression in Guatemala appear to have been singled out indiscriminately from among the poor; but the secret detentions, "disappearances" and killings are not entirely random; they follow denunciations by neighbors, employers or local security officials, and the evidence available to Amnesty International reveals a pattern of selective and considered official action. By far the majority of the victims were chosen after they had become associated—or were thought to be associated—with social, religious, community or labor organizations, or after they had been in contact with organizers of national political parties. In other words, Amnesty International's evidence is that the targets for extreme governmental violence tend to be selected from grassroots organizations outside official control.

A more elaborate pattern is followed for dealing with Guatemalans of higher social or economic status, such as business people and professionals—doctors, lawyers, educators—or with leaders of legal political parties. Where people in these groups are suspected of "subversive" activity, past or present, the discretionary powers of security service agents do not appear to be unrestricted. Such cases are thought to require consideration by high-ranking government officials before individuals can be seized or murdered; the system appears to function hierarchically, with the official level at which a decision may be taken corresponding to the status of the suspect.

In 1980 a number of occupational groups which, in recent years, had largely escaped being particular targets of political repression were singled out for violent attacks, resulting in numerous "disappearances" and deaths; they included priests, educators and journalists.

The President's "Special Agency"

The evidence compiled and published by Amnesty International in recent years indicates that routine assassinations, secret detentions and summary executions are part of a clearly defined program of the Guatemalan government. New information in the possession of Amnesty International bears this out. It shows that the task of coordinating civil and military security operations in the political sphere is carried out by a specialized agency under the direct supervision of President Lucas García.

The presidential agency is situated in the Presidential Guard annex to the National Palace, near the offices of the President and his principal ministers, and next to the Presidential Residence, the *Casa Presidencial*. Known until recently as the *Centro Regional de Telecomunicaciones* (Regional Telecommunications Center), the agency is situated under two rooftop telecommunications masts on the block-long building.

The telecommunications center in the palace annex is a key installation in Guatemala's security network. For years informed sources in the country referred to the organization working from there as the *Policía Regional* (Regional Police)—although the authorities repeatedly denied the existence of such a body. In 1978 a former mayor of Guatemala City, Manuel Colom Argueta, denounced the *Policía Regional* as a "death squad." On 23 March 1979 he was assassinated in the city center as a police helicopter hovered overhead.

The center was previously called the *Agencia de Inteligencia de la Presidencia* (Presidential Intelligence Agency); in a speech in 1966 Colonel Enrique Peralta Azurdia, head of state from 1963 to 1966, described its founding in the National Palace complex in 1964.

During 1980 sources in Guatemala City reported that the name had been changed again, to the *Servicios Especiales de Comunicaciones de la Presidencia* (Presidential Special Services for Communications); an alternative title was said to be the *Servicios de Apoyo de la Presidencia* (Presidential Support Services).

It is this presidential agency, situated in the palace complex and known by various names, which Amnesty International believes to be coordinating the government of Guatemala's extensive secret and extralegal security operations.

In 1974 a document from the records of a United States assistance program described the *Centro Regional de Telecomunicaciones* as Guatemala's principal presidential-level security agency, working with a "high level security/administrative network" linking "the principal officials of the National Police, Treasury Police, Detective Corps, Ministry of Government (*Gobernación;* alternately translated as "Interior"), the Presidential House (*Palace)*, and the Guatemalan Military Communications Center." (The document, which was declassified, came from the United States Agency for International Development, *Termination Phase-Out Study, Public Safety Project: Guatemala,* July 1974.)

The National Palace complex makes it possible for the security services to centralize their communications and also to have access to the central files of the army intelligence division, which are reported to be housed in the Presidential Residence itself. The files are believed to include dossiers on people who were political suspects even at the time of the overthrow of the government of Colonel Jacobo Arbenz in 1954—they include Colonel Arbenz' active supporters in the left-wing political parties of the time.

Files of political suspects were established by law in Guatemala first in the wake of the 1954 coup and more recently under the auspices of Military Intelligence in 1963, when they were incorporated into a "National Security Archive" (Decree Law 9, 1963, *Ley de defensa de las instituciones democráticas.)* It is believed that outdated files are still used as a basis for political persecution.

In many cases on record with Amnesty International, political activities during the 1940s and 1950s appear to have been the sole motive for a detention followed by "disappearance" or by a "death squad" killing. For instance, the submachine-gun attack in September 1980 on Professor Lucila Rodas De Villagrán, 60-year-old head of a girls' school, was widely attributed to her active membership in her youth in the *Partido Acción Revolucionaria* (Revolutionary Action Party), which ceased to exist more than 25 years ago.

Reliable sources in Guatemala say that the presidential intelligence agency is directed by the joint head of the Presidential General Staff *(Estado Mayor Presidencial)* and military intelligence. Policy decisions and the selection of who is to "disappear" and be killed are said to be made after consultations between the top officials of the Ministries of Defense and the Interior, and the Army General Staff, who command the forces responsible for the abuses.

Much of the information included in this section is general knowledge among informed Guatemalans of many political orientations. It is widely accepted that the Presidential Guard annex of the National Palace houses the headquarters for the secret operations of the security services. Entry to the center is guarded by heavily armed soldiers, with close-circuit television cameras mounted on the corners of the building. Unmarked cars without license plates, or with foreign plates, are usually parked outside the center.

Details of the presidential coordinating agency's operations are not known—for example, Amnesty International had not been able to confirm allegations by some Guatemalans that the agency holds prisoners inside the

A Program of Pacification

The "death squads" of Guatemala are part of a "program of pacification" carried out by the Guatemalan security services, according to a former Ministry of the Interior who resigned on 3 September 1980.

Elías Barahona y Barahona, who had been the ministry's press representative since 1976, described his job there as that of carrying out a press policy to explain governmental violence in terms of fighting between "clandestine groups of the extreme right and left." He said that blank letter-head stationary of the alleged "death squads," *Ejército Secreto Anticomunista* and *Escuadrón de la Muerte*, was stored in the office of the Minister of the Interior, who is responsible for internal security.

According to Elías Barahona lists of people to be eliminated were prepared from the records of Military Intelligence and the National Police. They included the names of "trade union leaders and *campesinos* (peasants) provided by the Department of Trade Unions of the Ministry of Labor and by a sector of private enterprise."

Citing as his authority an officer of Military Intelligence, he said that the "defensive lists" were prepared "in a dependency of the army called 'military transmissions' (*transmisiones militares*), on the fourth floor of the National Palace, and were approved at meetings held there attended by the Ministers of Defense and the Interior, and the Chief of the General Staff of the Army."

The former press official said the Chief of the Presidential Staff and of Military Intelligence Archive (*Archivo de la Inteligencia Militar*) were responsible for coordinating operations. Decisions were carried out by "the principal army and police headquarters of the republic," he said.

Elías Barahona fled to Panama after his defection and later declared his membership in the Guatemalan guerrilla organization *Ejército Guerrillero de los Pobres* (Guerrilla Army of the Poor).

Presidential Guard annex—but that the agency exists and that it serves as the center of the Guatemalan Government's program of "disappearance" and political murder seem, on the evidence, difficult to dispute.

Testimony of a Survivor[1]

Who captured you?

Well, at first I didn't know they were soldiers because they were dressed like civilians, well-armed, in a van.

How did they capture you?

---

[1]The following is an excerpt from an interview with the only known prisoner to have escaped from a Guatemalan jail in 1980.

Well, they tricked me. They came to my house asking for someone else who doesn't even exist, and since I didn't know anything, I went out of the house, and then they said, come along with us, the minute I stepped outside—just like that they got me in the van and off it went; the engine was already running.

Where were you taken?

At first I had no idea they were taking me to Huehuetenango military base, but the next morning they locked me in a very small room and I heard the sound of bugles, and I heard marching and military commands, and running and shouting and that's when I got the idea that I was at the military base.

Could you tell us what the place you were kept was like?

There was a big room; there was a toilet and another very small room. It had two troughs of water, two doors, one opening out on to the interior of the base and the other opening towards the old highway. The place they kept me in is the slaughterhouse which will be used for butchering cattle, but they haven't opened it yet, as that base is still being built.

How many people were being held prisoner there?

When I got there the next day I realized there were nine.

Was anyone you knew there? What was his name? Did they kill him?

Yes, there was one person from my town who had disappeared from there a year ago and we thought he had gone to Mexico to work. They killed him. I don't know when they killed him, but they showed me his body, with six others.

What kind of treatment did they give you, as regards food and sleep?

They didn't have a fixed time for giving us food. They brought us a big piece of bread and a glass of water and when they remembered in the afternoon they brought us a bit of rice and another glass of water. As for sleeping, we slept really badly because we were handcuffed to the legs of some concrete tables.

What torture did you see them inflict on the others?

Several. Electric shock between the water troughs. They put a hood on one of them with quicklime in it. They pulled one up by his testicles and an officer slashed his jaw in two with his knife; and he cut his wrists to the bone; but I suppose although the boy screamed at first he stopped later because he'd fainted. I saw another boy they had handcuffed with his hands behind his back; they also locked his feet together then lifted him up between the two of them and dropped him. I saw his teeth drop out and gushes of blood—that's how they break your ribs—from the way you fall—and that's when they give you the worst kicks. That's what they did to me—that is, they didn't lift me up but they kicked me in the ribs, the mouth, the stomach until I passed out.

How did they torture you?

They pulled me up by my testicles; and they hooded me with quicklime; that means they put a bit of quicklime inside the inner tube of a truck tire, then they put it over your nose and then they roll it onto you and you feel like death itself until you pass out, or, well, you tell some lies or the truth if you don't know. [sic]

What did they accuse you of?

They accused me of being a guerrilla and said that I should tell them where the camps were, who were the leaders, who were my friends and what ideology they taught us. Well, that's what they accused me of, and that I should tell them these things but as far as I can tell they had only one reason for capturing me. The only problem I had had in my town was having got involved in a sports committee, because you see there were two other authorized committees, and so we were always at loggerheads with them, and there's no doubt, at least so it seems to us, that they must have sent some kind of anonymous letter to the [military] base, accusing me of being a guerrilla, to get me out of their hair. And really, what I had opposed was these two committees using the basketball court for dances! I would never have been against that if it had been for the benefit of our sport, but they just kept the profits. Some of those people on the committee ended up with fine houses and that's why the rest of us began to notice what was going on and tried to stop it; and that's how the problems began.

Did they kill anyone in your presence? If so, how?

Yes, before my very eyes they killed three people; they strangled them. The way they killed them was with a piece of rope, a kind of noose, which they put around the neck and then used a stick to tighten it like a tourniquet from behind—handcuffed, and with their heads held down in the trough. When they came out, their eyes were open; they'd already turned purple. It took at most three minutes in the water. I also saw that one of these three, a boy, when they threw him on the floor with his clothes wet, was still moving and one of the officers ordered them to put the tourniquet on him again until he stopped moving. They just showed me the other six bodies and said the same thing would happen to me if I tried to lie to them.

You saw the bodies? How many?

I saw nine, including the three who were killed in front of me.

As far as you know, did they let anyone go?

No. In a conversation I heard them having—the ones who were guarding us—people who land up there never leave; but even so, well, we had some hope of being freed since, well, they told us that we would be handed over to the courts, civil or military, depending on whether you were a soldier or deserter, or something like that.

You had some hope of being released?

No. After seeing those corpses I imagined that they would not want any witnesses at large. I had already made up my mind that they were going to kill me.

How did you manage to escape?

I escaped for the simple reason that I saw how they killed the other prisoners there and I thought that that sort of death was just too horrible. So I decided it was better to die from a bullet or possibly win my freedom; only God helped me. The way I escaped was first by pretending I was sick. I told the guard on watch that I had to go to the toilet but he abused me, and asked why, seeing the next day I wasn't going to need anything anymore.

Because already, earlier on the officers had told me my turn was coming the next day. That was when I became completely desperate, praying, asking God to help me, until I got the idea of breaking out. I pretended I was sick, that I had diarrhea, and I told the guard I had to go to the toilet. Finally he gave in a bit and unlocked the handcuff chaining me to the post to fix it on my other hand while I went to the toilet. That was my opportunity. I hit him, not really hard, but hard enough to leave him stunned for a minute; then I grabbed his submachine gun and hit him with it several times on the nape of the neck. The guard didn't shout; I just saw blood coming out of his nose and mouth and thought he might be dead. I opened the door—it opened from the inside—and took the submachine gun with me. I left by the route I knew and I didn't see anybody. There were two guards; I saw them but they were quite far away so I went out very slowly. I didn't run because I didn't want to look suspicious. When the lights on the base weren't on me any more, I ran until I reached the old highway.

Did they pursue you? If so who? Did you hear the steps they took to recapture you?

Yes, there was a tremendous uproar throughout the province. All the villages near the base were searched the next day; the soldiers came through as if they were looking for illegal liquor stills. There were several truckloads of soldiers at the guardposts outside the towns, and the passengers from buses and trucks had to get out and show their wrists, as they knew my hands had marks from the handcuffs and were infected.

How long were you in that place?

Eleven days.

Who tortured you? Soldiers?

Well the officers themselves did the torturing, and so did the people there they used as killers—some men with long hair. They didn't look like especially bad people.

Testimony of a Conscript[2]

How long did you serve in the army?

Well, when I joined, they didn't tell us anything but when they seized us, they just seized us without letting us, well, talk to our families—what did it matter to them? That's what they told us then, but when they got us there they said that it was three years, because that's the service that you have to do.

So you have been in the army three years?

Only two years; I was in the army two years.

It is the military commissioners (comisionados militares), isn't it, men in plainclothes but armed, who hunt down the men for the army?

Yes, well, here the commissioners are like that, civilians, they don't carry weapons, just their machetes, but actually clubs too—big ones.

---

[2]The following is an excerpt from an interview with a Guatemalan soldier who defected from the army in 1980.

Does this military commissioner do his work alone, or is he helped by other soldiers or civilians?

Yes, well before they used to seize people, well more peacefully. They didn't beat them, not a lot that is, but now they do.

Why now?

Because now, now they aren't the only ones who seize the young men for the barracks; the military police do too. They go around with a truck, and anyone they find ... they don't tell them even where they are being taken; if you are carrying some of your things, something like a pack or something, they don't care, if there is room in the truck then they take it in. If they don't like you, they throw it in the street.

So, now it isn't just the military commissioners but also the military itself?

Yes. What happens now is that the military commissioners are afraid because really the peasants now know what's going on and what they do now is get together in crowds and if the commissioner dares to seize one of their group, what they do is beat them up, so now this means that the commissioners are all afraid.

The boys attack the military commissioners?

Yes, this is happening, because as they already know—just as we do who have already left—we tell them that the army isn't any good because, because, well because I've finally discovered the army is nothing, nothing but a school of murderers, so that's what you are dragged into, nothing better than that.

Weren't you afraid that one day an officer might have ordered you to kill someone?

I wasn't afraid. At that time I was full of the ideas they filled me with. I wasn't afraid they might tell me to kill someone. I used to do it because my mentality by then had changed completely—that's what had happened to me.

You could kill people without any problems?

Yes, without problems. Once they saw that I was really keen and understood the things they had taught me, they took me out of my unit with two others. Afterwards, we didn't stay in the same unit but were instructed separately. They didn't discipline us much then; we had already suffered enough, so they didn't discipline us so much, although the men in the unit did get disciplined. Then they gave us a little black *"galil"* that had only just arrived.

Is that a weapon?

Yes, "galil."

It's very sophisticated isn't it?

Yes, it's very new. They said Israel sent them to Guatemala, because it owed Guatemala something and other arms arrived. This one can fire a maximum of 350 shots a minute.

So they gave us this weapon and we were happier because we were better equipped. When these weapons arrived they gave us one each, then stopped giving us the M-1 rifles. They collected these and stored them.

When they gave us this weapon, they took me out of the unit but the others stayed on.

Then they sent the three of us to the office of the S-2, where we met officers. They stopped cropping our hair, instead they let us look really good. They told us: "Now you have been selected; you were chosen; you aren't just simple soldiers anymore, like those in the unit. If you've got guts you might even become officers."

They told you that you were better than the others?

Yes, better than the others.

Then, they had already brainwashed you?

Yes, that's what I'm saying, they had already brainwashed me; they had already filled my head with their own ideology, so I felt superior to my fellow soldiers.... What I thought then was that I was superior to everyone because I had managed to reach this position. They gave us separate training and each of us was given a .45 and left full of enthusiasm.

.45, what's that?

It's a weapon only officers use, with eight shots. They gave us one and we went out in civilian clothes. They told us: "You are going to get orders. You are going out now." They sent us out on the street in an army car.

That's how we used to go out, as civilians, but to keep an eye on things, especially to control the students, because there [in S-2] we went to different classes where they told us that the students could be guerrillas and that they were the people that caused the disorder on the streets, and that according to the law in the army's constitution, you've got to kill all of these people.

That's what they told us, then we went out in twos and threes to drive around the capital and control things.

Did you have permission to kill anyone?

Only suspicious characters. And they gave us orders of the day. And we also had classes—we were students just like the suspects! And we could kill them.

And they gave us special identity cards so that if there were any police around, even if there were more of them than us and we did certain things we could just show them these, so they wouldn't seize us and we could get away. That's what they told us. They gave us cards, so that if we made some great mistake—we could kill someone, just like that, and then escape, and the police wouldn't have the power to seize us; we could just show them the cards.

And the police don't do anything?

They don't do anything, nothing. So I realized that the army is a school for murderers, it's as simple as that. They said to me, if you discover your father is in subversive movements—I didn't understand the word— "subversive," they said, is whatever is against the government and is what causes disorder in Guatemala—if your father is involved in groups like that, kill him, because if you don't he'll try and kill us....

Could you kill your father or your mother or your sister?

Anyone who turned up, if I were ordered to. I could have done it then, that's how I used to feel, I'd do anything the army told me to. I remember how, when I was in it and we set off to bring in two students—I say they were students—I didn't think of fighting or anything; there was nothing in my mind. So we went to get these students, and we went to get another man who was also a student, at about two in the morning.

And there were others as well as us; there were others who got the job of seeing what time they left school, what· time they got back, where they ate, how they dressed and so on. That's what other people did.

But aren't there officers who tell you to investigate what these people do? Do you get the names from officers?

Yes, the officers give us this information—the names and the places.

And you have to check them out?

Yes, that was my job. We went out to find things out; we even talked to a lot of people.

To learn more?

Actually, to watch them; see who they were, and where they were. That was the job we had to do in the streets. We would stay there, and there were always officers travelling around in private cars too, with radios. There might be one in the central park in zone 1, another could be in zone 6, or in zone 7, who were in contact—they could talk directly to each other.

And they wore the uniforms of judicial police? G-2?—all these people?

Well, they were in plainclothes, in civilian clothes or in actual army uniform. When they set out to attack that man I was telling you about, he said he was just out having a lemonade. I asked the boy about it; he was very young; they brought him in all tied up, they had him well and truly tied up and blindfolded. Only his mouth was uncovered so he could talk. His arms were tied. We were going to move him, they had him....

You had to transfer him—did you have to capture this boy?

We had our job to do, but there were other people who had actually to do that job. We just set out to move him from where they had him.

And where did you have to go to see these people?

We took him to the Brigada Mariscal Zavala to hand him over.

An army base [un cuartel]?

Yes, the base. But not actually the barracks; but in Guatemala City in the base there are cells; let's see, there's one cell they call "the powder magazine," "*el polvorín,*" there's another cell they call "the olive," "*la aceituna,*" that is where we put him in a locked room. We arrived about two in the morning. They had him all tied up then; his mouth was gagged, and he had a bullet wound here—he couldn't talk. Then they did whatever they wanted to with him, and later, when we arrived, we just picked him up as if he was an animal, then threw him into the car and that was that. We took him there, sat him down, untied his feet, sat him up again, and the next day an officer arrived. He brought a tape-recorder and began to ask: "What is you're profession?" "What work do you do?" "Where do you work?" "Where do you study?" and so on, questioning him.

Were you there all the time?

Yes, because it was my job to be. I was there and so I knew what they did.

Had they tortured this boy?

Well, yes.

Beaten him?

Yes, sure.

Was electrical apparatus also used?

Yes, it was.

You saw it?

Yes, I have seen it—some things the Model Platoon [*Pelotón Modelo*] carry about with them which they call "canes" *"bastones,"* with electric batteries—no, they're called "batons" *"batones."* If they touch you with these things, you fall down, you're electrocuted, they, that's what they have.

I mean, I knew this man didn't want to say whether he belonged to a secret organization, or was "subversive" as they put it, and they began to beat him savagely.

How did you feel then?

When I was there, I felt sorry when I watched them hitting him.

Did you think the boy was a guerrilla?

Yes, yes I did. But I felt sorry for him when they beat him, and he didn't want to say he was one. He said he was accused of being a guerrilla— but no, what he said was: "They have accused me of being a guerrilla, but why should they?—if I was a guerrilla I wouldn't be here." "Talk," they said, and began to beat him.

Where did you have to beat this boy?

No, it wasn't me....

You just watched?

Yes, I watched. They were from G-2; they were the people who beat him, plainclothes army agents.

Are they from the secret service of the army?

Yes, they were. I stood back when they were beating him, because I didn't want to be drawn into it—I didn't want to join in beating him up. I kept out of the way when I saw they were beating him. Three more men arrived, all trussed up. They tape recorded everything these men said and as there were a lot of names on that list—there were countless names on the "black list," that's what we call it. The people on the list are—that's the order they gave us—wherever we find them we just ask their names and if it's them, we kill them.

Did they kill that boy too?

Yes, what they said to him was, if you don't talk, we'll kill you.

But was he killed?

No, I didn't kill him.

But did the others kill this boy?

Oh yes, definitely; he confessed: "I confess everything, everything" that he wasn't a guerrilla or anything, but, in any case, they began to beat him, that is to torture him, and they even tried to knock out one of his teeth like this, with a hammer. They hit him with a hammer like this. He screamed.

They even smashed his finger. They put it on a piece of iron to make him talk; but he didn't say anything; and so the next day, at about 12 o'clock at night—though I'm not sure of this—if it was the judicial police, or the G-2 who turned up—there is such a bunch of them, so you couldn't figure out who was who—who am I for example? If I'm from G-2, you wouldn't tell me anything and I wouldn't tell you anything because this is a security precaution to stop enemies getting control of us. They tell us not to identify ourselves but we have the same idea, the same work. Then at midnight they took those men who were there; they just went and grabbed them by the hair and feet and threw them into a car and took them away—took them who knows where.

They went off to kill them and leave them somewhere?

Must have. That's how it's done. Because at that time of night ... if they were going to set them free they would have done it in the daytime. Why drag them out at that hour of night? So they would have killed them on the road and left them just thrown down anywhere.

Do they always take the people they capture out at nighttime?

Yes, they go out....

Always at night?

Yes.

Never in daylight?

No, only at night, at the quietest time of night.

In official or private cars?

Private ... what they use mostly are those cars—vans—like station-wagons, with darkened windows—cars you'd never imagine had killers in them—though they can be in any car.

But where do they capture and kill the people? In the countryside? In the towns?

In the towns. Like the students that "disappear." It's definitely them that do it and they come and take them away at night, they seize them at night and kill them just like that; then they turn up just dumped anywhere.

But what have you done in the little towns and in the countryside? Have you gone out in trucks? And did you have to do house-to-house searches, or what?

Yes, when we were there, it was pretty much like that. We'd go off in a truck; we'd get to the place we had to search, yes, search and so forth; I mean if there were any people there who were, well, suspicious characters. What we kept an eye on was mostly the organizations where a lot of people get together—and there are guerrillas there too. So that's what we would go off to deal with. They'd take us in a truck. In the villages which cars can't get to, we'd walk and then search the houses just like that. Simple.

You searched from house to house?

In ... where they killed ... where we went, about 20 of us went through all the houses to see if we couldn't find any papers, the ones they'd told us about.

When we found a paper in a house, we took the family out, and if there was just one person we killed him. And that's what happened. We arrived in a car, left it far away and then walked on. And they told us not to be afraid and if we found the papers to kill those people, and that's the way it was—but we didn't find any papers, so we didn't do anything. . . .

You could have killed anyone?

Anyone who was a suspicious character.

And has your unit killed too?

Well, yes—the others did.

Yes, the people you find when you search like that you kill. And if they are not killed then, you just leave them and note things down. You get to know them really well, and in order not to commit these crimes at that moment, you jot down the name of the house and such like, so that they can secretly order another commission to "bring them to justice" [*ajusticiar*]. That's what you do, that's what we all do—I mean, get the name of the young man, the father and so on; find out what work he does, where he works etc. The reports these commissions make are sent into the offices, such and such an office, circulated in such and such a way. The people there are in charge of finding a commission and secretly giving it its orders. Only they know where it's gone and what it's going to do. This is all done by army G-2—that's the way they work.

And the reason I'm telling you this is because I was there. These killers come from the actual army. They told us I wasn't guilty of anything, because they told us: "You yourselves are going out to kill and because you've got your cards, you can kill the people on your list. If a policeman turns up, show him your gun like this and your card in this hand, then they won't seize you"—that's what they said.

So what I mean is, you kill, then you return; you get dressed. You've maybe committed these crimes in army uniform; if so, they tell you to get out of those clothes fast and put on civilian clothes or police clothes then go out and look for whoever killed the person.

But how are we supposed to find them if it was us that did it in the first place? How can we go out and find them? They have this fantastic idea [*idea mágica*] and—this is what's going on right now today in Guatemala.

They say "unknown persons" killed the student and that today they are being sought by the police; but how can they find them if the people who did it are the people going out to do the searching? This is what the army is up to.

The soldiers can kill people when they have orders to, but can they kill people without orders, just because someone is a suspicious character?

Yes, certainly, any of us can be ordered to kill any man like that, who is a suspicious character. Yes, we have got the right to kill him, and even more so if we have been given strict orders to. Yes, we have the right to commit these offences.

What did the officers say?

Well, they say that if we don't carry out all the orders that they give us, if we disobey, instead of them dying, they will kill us, so you have to be very careful about all this.

Background Information on Guatemala, Human Rights, and U.S. Military Assistance*

By Flora Montealegre and Cynthia Arnson

Flora Montealegre and Cynthia Arnson are both researchers with the Institute for Policy Studies and have written extensively on Central American issues.

Introduction

In the early morning hours of March 23, 1982, troops and tanks of the Guatemalan Army surrounded the Presidential Palace in Guatemala City. Within hours high-ranking officers had negotiated the departure of President Romeo Lucas García and declared a new junta led by General Efraín Ríos Montt. A statement broadcast over national radio that same day said that the officers had staged the coup to restore "authentic democracy" to Guatemala and to prevent the installation of General Aníbal Guevara as president on July 1, 1982.[1] The next day, a military triumvirate composed of Ríos Montt, Colonel Francisco Luís Gordillo and General Horacio Maldonado Schaad suspended the constitution, dissolved Congress, and announced rule by decree. They said they took power because of "disorder and corruption" in the government.[2]

The immediate justification for the coup was alleged fraud in the national presidential, congressional and municipal elections held on March 7. The election for president was won by Defense Minister General Aníbal Guevara, who ran with the backing of the Army and two right-wing parties, the Institutional Democratic Party and the Revolutionary Party. In both 1974 and 1978, the military imposed its candidate amidst widespread charges of fraud.

Besides Guevara, three civilian candidates from a narrow spectrum of conservative and centrist parties campaigned for president: Mario Sandoval Alarcón (National Liberation Movement—MLN), Alejandro Maldonado Aguirre (Guatemalan Christian Democratic Party—DCG, and National Renovating Party—PNR), and Gustavo Anzueto Vielman (Authentic Nationalist Central—CAN).[3] Voting in Guatemala is compulsory for literate adults, but in 1978 only about 35% of the registered electorate voted.[4] According to the Central Elections Council in Guatemala City, 48% of the electorate of 2.3 million voted in the 1982 elections.[5]

---

*From a report by the Institute for Policy Studies, July 1982.

[1] New York Times, March 24, 1982.

[2] Washington Post, March 25, 1982.

[3] New York Times, Dec. 6, 1981, and March 6, 1982.

[4] New York Times, Dec. 6, 1981.

[5] Washington Post, March 11, 1982.

On March 9 the Central Elections Council declared General Guevara the winner with 37% of the total vote. Opposition representatives charged that the results were manipulated, especially after early returns showed Guevara losing in the capital.[6] The three losing candidates were detained by riot police on March 9 when they sought to present documents at the Presidential Palace which they said proved their charges of fraud. Battle-dressed government troops and secret police with automatic rifles dispersed demonstrators in the capital who defied a government ban to protest the election results.[7]

While electoral fraud provided the context for the military coup on March 23, discontent within the officers corps centered fundamentally on three issues:[8]

- Human rights violations, resulting from what Amnesty International called in 1981 a "government campaign of political murder," seriously eroded the government's image abroad, making it more difficult for Guatemala to obtain foreign aid and credits for both economic and military purposes.

- Political and administrative corruption by senior Army officers contributed to problems of military discipline, morale, and hierarchy, as well as to disorder and inefficiency in the economy. In one incident reported by junior officers, eight leading generals ran an arms-buying racket which overvalued the cost of weapons acquisitions. The difference was placed in private bank accounts in the Cayman Islands. In another incident, five officers who wanted to expose Army involvement in the rape and murder of a university student were murdered, allegedly on the orders of the high command.

- The war against the guerrillas was intensifying, with the brunt of the casualties being borne by the junior officers. At least 57 officers (captains and lieutenants) were killed in combat in 1981, and about 1000 soldiers and officers were killed in the first half of 1981 alone. The younger officers viewed the harsh counterinsurgency tactics advocated by Army Chief of Staff Benedicto Lucas García (brother of the deposed president) as counterproductive, and claimed that there were about 6000 guerrillas in Guatemala as opposed to the State Department's estimate of about 2000.

The Evolving Government

The coup set in motion a variety of struggles over the shape and program of the new government. The younger officers had formulated a three-point plan calling for elections within sixty days, the ineligibility

---

[6] *New York Times,* March 9, 1982.

[7] *Washington Post,* March 10, 1982.

[8] See Washington Office on Latin America, "The Military Coup in Guatemala," Update No. 1, March 30, 1982; *Latin America Weekly Report,* July 31, 1982; *Washington Post,* April 18, 1982.

of military candidates for office, and an end to government corruption.[9] General Ríos Montt, ignored this agenda as he relegated the junior officers to the role of advisers, and stressed the need to maintain military hierarchy and unity.[10] Ríos Montt removed several government officials identified with repression during the Lucas García regime, including Chief of Police Ruiz, and replaced them with officers loyal to him. In many instances, officers brought into new positions had been identified in the past with human rights violations (The new Minister of the Interior, Ricardo Méndez Ruiz, for example, was chief of security for General Lucas García when he was campaigning for the presidency in 1978.). In the immediate post-coup period, however, violence in the cities declined markedly.

The reformist nature of the coup was immediately called into question, however, as the ultra-rightist National Liberation Movement announced its backing for the coup. On March 23 MLN Vice-President Leonel Sisniega Otero seized a radio station and read a statement saying that the uprising was prompted by "corruption following a fraudulent election."[11] Sisniega told reporters that he had been approached by the young officers to "sound out" Army generals about the plan to oust Lucas García and to rally the support of civilian opponents of the regime.[12] Sources close to the young officers, however, denied MLN participation in the coup, noting that Sisniega's son was a second lieutenant who informed his father of the coming events.[13]

Following the coup, civilian parties which previously had been bitterly at odds with one another began to articulate common demands. The Christian Democrats and the MLN announced agreement on several political demands including (1) elections in six months, (2) a declaration by the junta that military rule was transitional, (3) the creation of a new national electoral commission with equal representation from each party, and (4) the revision of electoral laws.[14] In a press conference in Washington, D.C. in early April 1982, DCG leader Vinicio Cerezo repeated that the Christian Democrats would not join the post-coup government, and would press for elections and an investigation into the violations of human rights.

The Response of the Left

The left opposition, including left-of-center parties, trade and peasant unions, university professors and students, and other professionals, boycotted the March 1982 elections, maintaining that the history of electoral fraud by the military, as well as government repression, precluded the possibility of broad participation and open campaigning. In 1979 two prominent opposition leaders—former mayor of Guatemala City and leader of the

---

[9] *Washington Post*, March 25, 1982.
[10] *Washington Post*, March 28, 1982.
[11] Quoted in *New York Times*, March 24, 1982.
[12] *Washington Post*, March 28, 1982.
[13] Interview, Guatemalan politician, Washington, D.C., April 6, 1982.
[14] *Washington Post*, March 26, 1982.

United Revolutionary Front (FUR) Manuel Colóm Argueta, and Social Democratic Party (PSD) leader Alberto Fuentes Mohr—were assassinated in the capital. It had been widely believed that they would present a joint ticket in the 1982 elections.

The period prior to the March elections witnessed a growing consolidation of left opposition forces. In February 1982 four guerrilla groups—the People's Revolutionary Army (EGP), Rebel Armed Forces (FAR), Organization of People in Arms (ORPA) and Guatemalan Labor Party (PGT)—announced the formation of the Guatemalan National Revolutionary Unity (URNG), a joint political and military directorate. The URNG released a five-point program calling for an end "to repression against the people," to "cultural oppression and discrimination," and to "economic and political domination of the repressive local and foreign wealthy class," and promising to establish a representative government and to adopt a non-aligned foreign policy.[15] The statement made an appeal to both small- and medium-sized landowners and businessmen, and to military officers not identified with official corruption and repression, to join in the fight against the government.

Several days after the formation of the URNG, prominent Guatemalan exiles led by writer Luis Cardoza y Aragón announced the creation of the Guatemalan Patriotic Unity Committee (CGUP) to coordinate the international political work of the Guatemalan left. The CGUP, with over fifty leaders from opposition parties, unions, and professional organizations, hopes to build unity among opposition sectors represented in the Democratic Front Against Repression (FDCR) and the Popular Front—31st of January (FP-31).[16] The FDCR and FP-31 are coalitions of close to 200 peasant and labor unions, student, teacher, and professional groups, as well as opposition parties including the Social Democrats.

Both the URNG and CGUP denounced the March 7 elections as a "fraud." Later the URNG called the Ríos Montt coup a mere "change in the facade" of the government, and vowed to continue armed struggle against the regime.[17]

The United Front of the Revolution (FUR) has joined neither the CGUP in denouncing the current regime nor the emerging coalition of moderate and right-wing parties in jockeying for a role in the evolving situation. The FUR reportedly remains deeply divided, with many members in exile extremely critical of the new government and others inside Guatemala seeking to define some role for the party in the changed circumstances.[18]

The Government Program

The military junta formed after the March 23 coup dissolved on June 9,

---

[15] *Foreign Broadcast Information Service* (hereinafter cited as *FBIS*), Feb. 10 and March 19, 1982.

[16] Interview, member of CGUP, Washington, D.C., June 28, 1982.

[17] Quoted in *New York Times*, March 6 and March 28, 1982.

[18] Interviews, U.S. Department of State, June 25, 1982, and Guatemalan politician, April 6, 1982, Washington, D.C.

1982, when Ríos Montt deposed General Schaad and Colonel Gordillo and appointed himself President of Guatemala. Earlier, however, the government had elaborated a general 14-point program to serve as the basis for governing as long as the 1965 Constitution remained suspended. The platform promised:[19]

- To achieve individual security and happiness on the basis of absolute respect for human rights.

- To lay the foundations for the participation and integration of the different ethnic groups that make up our nationality.

- To achieve the recovery of the national economy.

- To eliminate administrative corruption and to promote a true spirit of public service among government workers.

- To improve the people's living standards.

- To reorganize the electoral system.

- To reestablish constitutionality within a brief period of time.

Ríos Montt also announced his intention to improve diplomatic relations with Cuba and Nicaragua, while Foreign Ministry officials stated that Guatemala would join the Central American Democratic Community composed of Honduras, Costa Rica and El Salvador.[20]

Within several weeks of the March 23 coup the government began to prosecute officials charged with administrative corruption. At least twenty officials were arrested in late March, and on April 21 the 8th Criminal Court issued indictments against several government personnel, including the former attorney general, the former prison director, Finance Ministry officials, and the security chief of the Guatemalan Telecommunications Enterprise. They were accused of "abusing their authority, embezzlement, extortion, and continuous fraud."[21]

Under the provisions of a general amnesty proclaimed on May 31, however, members of the Army and security forces charged with committing human rights abuses would be pardoned if the acts were committed while "fulfilling their duties in anti-subversive actions."[22] On the first day of the amnesty, Ríos Montt declared that reported human rights violations were actions undertaken to confront communism and said that any violations were to prevent the Soviets "from raising their hammer and sickle" over Guatemala.[23] The amnesty was also extended "to all subversives" if they turned in their guns and ammunition at Army outposts or to the Guatemalan Red Cross by June 30. The rebels officially rejected the amnesty offer.[24]

---

[19] *FBIS*, April 7, 1982.
[20] UPI, April 1, 1982, and *FBIS*, April 27, 1982.
[21] *FBIS*, March 31 and April 23, 1982.
[22] *Washington Post*, May 26, 1982.
[23] UPI, June 1, 1982.
[24] *FBIS*, June 1, 1982.

According to Guatemalan military authorities, 430 guerrillas took advantage of the amnesty during the 30-day period in which it was in effect.[25] Following the expiration of the amnesty, Ríos Montt declared a state of siege and said that the death penalty would be applied to anyone caught with large quantities of weapons, or engaged in "terrorist acts" such as burning buses or planting bombs. He said that special tribunals would be convoked to judge rebel suspects.[26]

Ríos Montt also proposed, in mid-June, a high-level dialogue with guerrilla leaders, an initiative effectively overridden by the imposition of the state of siege. At the time of the proposal the Christian Democrats expressed "many doubts about its potential efficacy."[27] CGUP leader Luis Cardoza rejected the dialogue idea, as did the FDCR, which claimed that "the Ríos Montt proposal is a cynical mockery because the campaign of terror continues, as do the kidnappings, killings and repression."[28]

General Efraín Ríos Montt

Guatemala's President, Brigadier General Efraín Ríos Montt,[29] joined the Guatemalan Army in 1943. He graduated from Guatemala's Polytechnical Institute and later served as its director.

During the regime of Carlos Arana Osorio (1970-1974), Ríos Montt served as Army Chief of Staff. Opposition leaders have charged him with conducting the massacre in 1973 of more than 100 peasants in the village of Sansirisay, in eastern Guatemala. During the latter part of the Arana Osorio administration, Ríos Montt served as director of studies for the Inter-American Defense College, a Washington-based organization set up under the Rio Treaty for purposes of joint hemispheric defense.

In 1974, Ríos Montt ran for the presidency of Guatemala as the candidate of the National Opposition Front. Although Ríos Montt and his Christian Democratic supporters claimed electoral victory, the government declared General Kjell Laugerud García, the military's candidate, the victor. After denouncing the elections as fraudulent, Ríos Montt accepted a position as Military Attache with the Guatemalan Embassy in Spain.

In 1978, Ríos Montt returned to Guatemala as chief of the National Military Reserves, and soon thereafter joined the charismatic Church of the Complete Word, a mission of the Gospel Outreach of Eureka, California. Under the rule of General Lucas García, Ríos Montt reportedly appeared in several public events, particularly of a military nature, but he was not linked with any kind of political activity on behalf of or against Lucas García.

---

[25] *Diario Las Américas*, June 30, 1982.

[26] *Diario de Las Américas*, July 2, 1982.

[27] *FBIS*, June 18, 1982.

[28] *FBIS*, June 21, 1982.

[29] Information on General Ríos Montt has been compiled from: *New York Times*, March 25, 1982; *FBIS*, March 26, 1982; *Mesoamérica* (Costa Rica), April 1982.

Human Rights: Continuing Violence in the Countryside

According to reports from the U.S. Embassy in Guatemala, political murders ran 250 to 300 monthly in 1981, and rose to over 400 in January and February 1982.[30] By most accounts, the killing was sharply reduced immediately after the March 23 coup. Kidnappings and assassinations in the cities declined dramatically, as did attacks on politicians, foreign journalists, and Roman Catholic priests. However, recent reports from Congressional staff members, religious leaders, refugees, and many other Guatemalans indicated that the levels of violence in the countryside have reached, and exceeded, the levels of the last days of the Lucas García regime.[31]

During a House Foreign Affairs Committee meeting in May 1981, Human Rights Subcommittee Chairman Rep. Don Bonker (D-Washington) stated that his office continued to receive reports of human rights violations in Guatemala, particularly in the countryside.[32] Upon their return from a visit to Guatemala one year later, several Congressional staff members reported that large numbers of people were still being killed in the rural areas. They recommended that the House Foreign Affairs Committee turn down the Reagan Administration's renewed military aid request.[33]

In May 1982, the *Comité de Unidad Campesina* (CUC), one of the largest peasant organizations in Guatemala, claimed that 3,000 peasants, mostly Indians, had been killed by security forces since the March 23 coup. The CUC also charged the Guatemalan army with seeking to decimate the Indian population by employing a new tactic—starvation. Using scorched-earth tactics apparently similar to those employed by the Indonesian military in East Timor, the Guatemalan army has been destroying the forests where large numbers of peasants have sought refuge from political violence. The CUC fears that those who remain hidden in their mountain refuges will die of starvation, while those who come out into the open will be killed by the army.[34]

To assist in counterinsurgency operations in the countryside, the government has begun recruitment of 30,000 to 50,000 peasants for a "civilian militia"[35] promoted in the fall of 1981 by then-Guatemalan Army Chief of Staff Benedicto Lucas García. In early April 1982, the Guatemalan government equipped the civil defense patrols with automatic weapons, including

---

[30] *Washington Post*, April 18, 1982.

[31] See *New York Times*, May 20, 1982; Washington Office on Latin America, *Latin America Update*, May/June 1982, p. 3; and Shelton H. Davis and Julie Hodson, *Witnesses to Political Violence in Guatemala: The Suppression of a Rural Development Movement* (Boston: Oxfam America, 1982), p. vi.

[32] Washington Office on Latin America, *Latin America Update*, May/June 1982.

[33] "Central America Watch," *Nation*, June 26, 1982, p.786.

[34] Comité de Unidad Campesina (CUC), "The Military Junta's Army Continues the Massacres of Our Communities," May 12, 1982.

[35] *New York Times*, May 5, 1982; *Diario de Las Américas*, April 20, 1982.

M-1 rifles.[36] According to some reports, the newly recruited civilian militias have already been utilized in military operations in the central highlands. Between April 24 and 29 alone, massacres were reported in five peasant villages, with at least 150 men, women and children killed.[37] The civilian militias appear analogous to ORDEN in El Salvador, a paramilitary group operating in close collaboration with government forces as well as carrying out its own acts of repression and harrassment.

In addition, the National Police established on April 20, 1982, a new "Special Operations Commando" headquartered in Guatemala City. According to the unit's commander, "we are going to cooperate and to strengthen police work in the departments of the republic."[38]

Displaced Persons and Refugees

Little is known about the exact dimensions of the problem of Guatemalan refugees and displaced persons. A recent investigation conducted by Oxfam-America concludes that "political violence is destroying the very fabric of Guatemalan rural society," and forcing thousands of indigenous peoples to abandon their village communities. Many have sought refuge with the guerrillas in the mountains; others have fled to Guatemala City where they have joined the unemployed and the slum dwellers. At least 200,000 have been driven out of Guatemala and into neighboring Central American nations.[39] Of these, an estimated 50,000 have crossed the border into Mexico, while some 20,000 have reached the United States.[40]

An April 1982 report by Roman Catholic bishops in Guatemala estimates that over one million Guatemalans have been forced to abandon "their homes and small plots of land" as a consequence of the widespread terror.[41] With the persistence in the post-coup period of high levels of rural violence, the number of displaced persons and refugees will undoubtedly continue to increase.

Refugees in the Mexican state of Chiapas, which borders Guatemala, have accused the Ríos Montt government of conducting systematic raids on Indian villages in northern Guatemala. Accounts by the refugees tell of decapitations, torture, the random killing of women and children, disappearances, rape, and the burning of entire families in their homes.[42]

According to Mexican Bishop Samuel Ruiz, Guatemalan military and paramilitary forces have also embarked on a campaign of terror against refugees who have fled to southern Mexico, and against Mexican peasants and religious groups who give refuge to the Guatemalans. Large numbers of

---

[36] *FBIS*, April 13, 1982.

[37] *Latin America Weekly Report*, May 7, 1982.

[38] *FBIS*, April 22, 1982.

[39] Davis and Hodson, *Witnesses to Political Violence*, p. 26.

[40] Washington Office on Latin America, "The Military coup in Guatemala," Update No. 6, June 6, 1982.

[41] *New York Times*, April 18, 1982.

[42] *San Diego Union*, May 5, 1982.

Guatemalan troops reportedly have crossed the Mexican border in pursuit of fleeing refugees. Bishop Ruiz has also charged the Guatemalan military with seeking to create a free-fire zone in a six-mile-wide strip along the Mexican border.[43]

Church authorities in Mexico have also denounced their government's treatment of the Guatemalan refugees, and its policy of forced repatriation.[44] Last year, some 1,800 Guatemalans were reportedly driven back across the border by the Mexican army. Other reports, however, claim that Mexican immigration authorities have adopted a more humane policy and are granting "border resident permits" to the Guatemalan refugees. These permits allow the holder to cross into Mexico repeatedly for three years, but restrict travel to no more than 50 kilometers from the border.[45]

Persecution of the Church

From 1978 to 1982, according to Amnesty International, foreign priests and missionaries, and outspoken members of religious orders and of the Guatemalan Justice and Peace Committee, were subjected to threats of violence and government-sponsored campaigns of defamation and repression. Many foreign priests were expelled by the government; others were hampered by severe restrictions on visas. In 1981, Father Stan Rother, a Roman Catholic diocesan priest from the United States, and Father Marco Tulio Maruzzo, an Italian-born Franciscan missionary, were assassinated. Numerous cases of "disappearances" were also documented, such as that of Father Luis Eduardo Pellecer, a Jesuit priest kidnapped on June 9, 1981.[46]

Recent U.S. Policy and U.S. Military Assistance

Since 1977 U.S. policy toward Guatemala has been constrained by the continuing reports of serious human rights violations by the Guatemalan government. This has led the U.S. Congress to reject administration requests for military assistance, even at a time when concern over the country's mounting guerrilla insurgency was increasing. In Fiscal Years 1978, 1979, 1981, and 1982, the Pentagon requested no new military aid for Guatemala. Small amounts of cash and commercial sales were, however, approved. In Fiscal Year 1980, a modest request for $250,000 in military training was overturned by the House Foreign Affairs Committee.

During the debate over military aid in Fiscal Year 1982 (a budget prepared by the Carter Administration but authorized in the first year of the Reagan Administration), Representatives Michael Barnes (D-MD) and Stephen Solarz (D-NY) agreed not to introduce formal legislation banning

---

[43] National Catholic Reporter, May 21, 1982.

[44] Ibid.

[45] San Diego Union, May 6, 1982.

[46] Prepared Statement of Amnesty International-USA, in U.S. Congress, House Committee on Foreign Affairs, Human Rights in Guatemala, Hearings before the Subcommittee on Human Rights and International Organizations and on Inter-American Affairs, 97th Cong., 1st sess., 1981, pp. 142-145.

military aid to Guatemala in exchange for administration assurances that no military sales, grants, or training would be provided without prior consultation with and approval by the House Foreign Affairs Committee.

In Fiscal Year 1983, the administration asked Congress for $250,000 in International Military Education and Training (IMET) grants in a program designed "to help the Guatemalans defend themselves against the leftist guerrillas, and to control the spread of violence of all kinds."[47] The Defense Department also indicated that Guatemala would be permitted to purchase modest amounts of equipment for cash through the Foreign Military Sales program. The request, made prior to the Ríos Montt coup of March 1982, noted that:

> Guatemala is facing a Cuban-supported Marxist insurgency that seeks to overthrow the government. If it succeeds, neither our objectives nor those of the Guatemalan people will survive. The challenge Guatemala faces is to respond effectively to the guerrilla threat, without engaging in the indiscriminate violence to which some elements of the Guatemalan security forces have resorted.[48]

As of this writing, Congress had not finally approved the Fiscal Year 1983 foreign aid bill. However, both the Senate Foreign Relations Committee and the House Foreign Affairs Committee approved the inclusion of $250,000 in IMET funds for Guatemala. The House Foreign Affairs Committee nevertheless reiterated its expectation that "its understanding with the executive branch with respect to military assistance, military training, and foreign military sales will continue in effect for the remainder of fiscal year 1982 and fiscal year 1983; that is, that no such assistance will be provided to Guatemala without the approval of the Committee on Foreign Affairs."[49]

After the Ríos Montt coup, Assistant Secretary of State for Inter-American Affairs Thomas Enders told a House Subcommittee that "a promising evolution may have begun" in Guatemala, and that "concrete measures have been taken against corruption.... All political forces have been called to join in national reconciliation. We hope that the new government of Guatemala will continue to make progress in these areas and that we in turn will be able to establish a closer, more collaborative relationship with this key country."[50]

Accordingly, the administration began consulting with members of the House Foreign Affairs Committee about a sale of $3.5 million in spare parts, mostly for helicopters crucial to the counterinsurgency war, as well as a "re-programming" of $50,000 in military training funds. A delegation of congressional aides who visited Guatemala City in May 1982, however, was told by Ríos Montt that his government had not requested military

---

[47] U.S. Department of Defense, *Congressional Presentation*, p. 461.
[48] *Ibid.*
[49] U.S., Congress, House, Committee on Foreign Affairs, *International Security and Development Cooperation Act of 1982*, No. 97-547, 97th Cong., 1st sess., 1982, p. 13.
[50] Quoted in *Washington Post*, April 22, 1982.

Table 1
U.S. Commercial Sales to Guatemala:*
October 1, 1978 to July 27, 1981

Year	Item	Quantity	$ Value
1978	Pistols and Revolvers	564	75,690
	Rifles	550	36,007
	Small Arms Spare Parts	—	158
	Military Vehicle Spares	—	36,053
	Cartridges up through 20 mm	1,060,000	29,293
	Riot Control Agent/Herbicide	—	85,500
	Ammunition Raw Materials	—	2,037
	Disapproved/No Action**	4	—
1979	Pistols and Revolvers	1,299	206,296
	Rifles and Carbines	571	54,808
	Submachine Guns	10	4,800
	Shotguns	97	13,682
	Small Arms Spare Parts	—	1,780
	Cartridges up through 20 mm	1,335,116	112,678
	Propellants	—	80,500
	Ammunition Raw Materials	—	272
	Armored Vests	60	12,750
	TF-76 Taser	22	3,750
	Taser Spares	—	1,019
	Tank Spare Parts	—	106,939
	Disapproved/No Action	9	—
1980	Pistols and Revolvers	416	65,416
	Rifles	259	32,281
	Shotguns	40	4,198
	Small Arms Spare Parts	—	1,204
	Cartridges up through 20 mm	1,028,000	32,205
	Misc. Military Vehicles	—	80,490
	Speech Scramble P-11	4	767
	Propellants	—	175
	Explosives	—	80,833
	Protective Personal Equipment	—	584
	Auxiliary Military Equip. Spares	—	600
	Disapproved/No Action	69	—
1981	Speech Scramble P-11	2	403
	Auxiliary Military Equip. Spares	—	3,600
	Disapproved/No Action	16	—

*Commercial Sales are sales of military equipment by private U.S. companies and are licensed by the U.S. Department of State's Office of Munitions Control.

**Disapproved/No action refers to applications for licenses which were turned down or withdrawn from consideration.

Source: Table compiled by Cynthia Arnson from data in "Additional Material Submitted by the Department of State in Response to July 22 Letter from Representatives Barnes and Bonker," in U.S. Congress, House Subcommittees on Human Rights and International Organizations and on Inter-American Affairs, Hearings, Human Rights in Guatemala, 97th Cong., 1st sess. (U.S. Government Printing Office, Washington, D.C., 1981), pp. 41-50.

Table 2
Sales of Non-Military Equipment to Guatemala
Licensed by the U.S. Department of Commerce*
July 1, 1978—July 28, 1981

Year	Item	$ Value
1978	Shotguns	9,885
	Shotgun Parts	63
	Crime Investigation Equipment	410
	Handcuffs	4,400
	Truck Parts	668,854
1979	Shotguns	17,957
	Surveillance Camera	60,000
	Trucks	3,023,060
	Truck Parts	18,663
1980	Shotguns	270
	Psychological Stress Analyzer	11,150
	Truck Parts	541,234
	Trucks and Trailers	2,714,542
	2 L-100-20 Aircraft	23,897,000
1981	Trucks	3,035,000
	Truck Parts	150,000
	Protective Vests	1,700
	Kevlar Fabric	7,323

*In some cases a sale might not have resulted from the issuance of a license.

Source: See Table 1, "Additional Material Submitted . . .," in *Human Rights in Guatemala*, p. 52.

aid, and discovered that the administration's proposal for spare parts had originated with the Lucas García government.[51] Shortly after the aides returned, Deputy Assistant Secretary of State Stephen Bosworth visited Guatemala. Following meetings with government leaders, then-junta member Colonel Francisco Gordillo announced that Guatemala needed economic and military aid from the United States.[52]

As of early July 1982, the reaction of members of the House Foreign Affairs Committee to the spare parts and reprogramming requests was that no military aid be given pending a demonstration by the Ríos Montt government that it would make good on its pledge to curb human rights abuses.

Commerce Department Sales

Since at least mid-1981, the Guatemalan government has purchased significant amounts of equipment for military use through the Department of Commerce. These items, while not appearing on the U.S. Munitions List detailing all equipment designated for military use, are nevertheless used

---

[51] Interview, congressional staff aide, May 25, 1982.

[52] *Diario de Las Américas*, June 3, 1982.

by the armed forces for military purposes. One such sale which stirred considerable controversy involved Guatemala's purchase of 50 2 1/2 ton trucks and 100 jeeps in June 1981. The Commerce Department removed the trucks and jeeps from the "Crime Control and Detection" list, which contains prohibitions on sales to countries which violate human rights, and placed them in a new category of "Control for Regional Stability."

Fifty-four members of the House of Representatives wrote to then-Secretary of State Alexander Haig protesting the sale, on the grounds that it would support "terrorist elements within the Guatemalan military and [appeared] to reflect a conscious effort to undermine the human rights provisions of our arms export laws."[53]

In 1980 and 1981 the Guatemalan government also spent about $10.5 million on three Bell 212 and six Bell 412 helicopters sold through the Commerce Department. According to early reports, at least two of the helicopters had been mounted with .30 caliber machine guns.[54] The Bell 212 is a civilian version of the Bell UH-1N; the two have basically the same configuration but different electronics and mission kits. The 212 carries a pilot and 14 passengers. The 412 is a four-blade variant of the 212, but has a more stable flight.[55] Photos appearing in the Guatemalan press also identified the Bell 212 as a "military helicopter on a patrol mission flying over the zone of San José Poaquil."[56]

Under the consultation agreement worked out between the Reagan Administration and the House Foreign Affairs Committee, Commerce Department sales do not necessarily have to be presented for review. Indeed, given the licensing procedures in the Commerce Department, members of the State Department often are not aware that a sale is being processed.

Arms Sales by Non-U.S. Suppliers

Over the past decade Israel, France, Switzerland, Taiwan, Italy, Belgium, and Yugoslavia have also supplied arms to Guatemala. Many of these sales are reported by international research organizations such as the Stockholm Peace Research Institute (SIPRI) and the International Institute for Strategic Studies (IISS). Sales of small arms, electronics, and personal equipment, however, often escape detection. Based on our own research and press accounts, we have been able to piece together the following information:[57]

- Junior officers in the Guatemalan Army have claimed that since 1975 Guatemala has spent $175 million on Italian, Belgian, Israeli, and Yugo-

---

53 *Washington Post*, June 25, 1982.

54 *Washington Post*, Jan. 23, 1981.

55 John W. R. Taylor, ed., *Jane's All the World's Aircraft*, 1976-1977 and 1981-1982 editions (London: Jane's Publishers, 1976 and 1981), p. 231 and p. 299.

56 *El Gráfico* (Guatemala City), 1981 (exact date unknown).

57 *Latin America Weekly Report*, July 31, 1981; *Washington Post*, Jan. 23, 1982; *FBIS*, July 27, 1981, and Aug. 10, 1981; *El Gráfico* (Guatemala City), Nov. 4, 1981; *Latin America Working Group*, *Latin American and Caribbean Labor Report*, Toronto, May 1980.

slav weapons. Senior officers reportedly declared their value to be $425 million and pocketed the difference.

■ Israeli machine guns and personal equipment are now standard issue to Guatemalan troops. In 1980, however, the Israeli labor federation *Histadrut* wrote Israeli Prime Minister Menachem Begin asking that all arms sales to Guatemala be stopped. The letter called human rights violations in Guatemala "an affront to all humanity and civilization."

■ In July 1981 the Chairman of the Taiwan Joint Chiefs of Staff, Admiral Chang Chi-Soong, visited Guatemala City and offered "to continue technical military aid" against leftist guerrillas. For at least a decade, numerous Central American officers have received training in Taiwan.

■ In August 1981 then-Defense Minister Aníbal Guevara sent to the Guatemalan Congress a bill providing for the domestic manufacture of small arms and ammunition. The legislation was designed to reduce Guatemala's dependence on foreign suppliers. The status of the legislation is unclear given the dissolution of the legislature, but many observers believe that Guatemala will soon have its own arms-producing capacity.

■ In November 1981, Generals Romeo and Benedicto Lucas García inaugurated in Guatemala City the Army Electronics and Transmissions School (*Escuela de Transmisiones y Electrónica del Ejército*) built with Israeli assistance and technology. During the ceremonies, attended by the Israeli ambassador to Guatemala, President Lucas García stated that "thanks to the assistance and transfer of electronic technology provided by the State of Israel to Guatemala" the Guatemalan Army has enhanced its ability to stay on top of the latest technological developments.

The Massacre at Panzós
and Capitalist Development in Guatemala*
By Gabriel Aguilera P.

Gabriel Aguilera P. is a professor of political science and history at the University of San Carlos of Guatemala, and advisor to the planning commission of the University of San Carlos. The translation is by Cedric Belfrage.

On May 29, 1978, the town of Panzós, capital of the municipality of that name in the department of Alta Verapaz, Guatemala, was the scene of a peasant massacre described by Amnesty International as the year's worst act of violence—a judgement formed before the great massacres in Iran which began in July of that year. More than 100 Indian peasants were

*From *Monthly Review*, December 1979, pp. 13-23.

machine-gunned in Panzós' main square, survivors finished off, and the wounded pursued into nearby mountains. The perpetrators were regular troops and armed farm owners of the region.

This bloodbath will take its place in the long list of massacres of workers on our continent committed in this century by Latin America's dominant classes and by imperialism. Panzós has become a new symbol of the prodigious social cost of reproducing the capitalist system in the Americas—along with the notorious "incidents" in Chile (Santa María de Iquique miners in 1907, the comuneros in the 1930s), Argentina (rural workers in the 1920s), Colombia (banana plantation workers in 1928), El Salvador (poor peasants and Indians in 1932), and Mexico (students in Tlatelolco, Mexico City in 1968).

Various accounts of the Panzós massacre have been published, but we must continue to press for a deeper analysis of its causes: first, to help impress it on the collective consciousness of the Latin American peoples in their struggle for liberation and second, to shed more light on the mechanisms whereby the dominant classes exercise their violence and terror. This essay should then be seen as a contribution to the debate already begun by social scientists seeking to explain the Panzós massacre.

Panzós and the "Northern Transverse Strip"

As we know, reproduction of the capitalist mode of production in Guatemala has been conditioned by the Guatemalan state's dependency relationship with the central capitalist countries, particularly the United States. That relationship has also conditioned the development of our country's dominant class and consequently impresses special characteristics upon the country's class struggle.

Hence it is appropriate to recall briefly the modalities of imperialist penetration in the country, a theme which has undergone sufficient scientific analysis to be a valid point of departure. That penetration was systematized in the second half of the nineteenth century when the accelerated development of productive forces in the United States propelled capitalist reproduction there into its monopoly imperialist phase. Monopoly capital, in accordance with the economic characteristics of that phase, penetrated Guatemala in the form of investment in agro-industrial production of food products for export; thus the banana enclaves came into being. U.S. investment was at the same time directed toward the service sector as reinforcement of the main productive activity and as a source of profits. This took the form of appropriation by foreign concerns of the essential means of communication and energy—railroads, docks, and electric power.

Of concern to us in the period under study are the consequences of imperialist penetration with respect to the dominant class and the state.

The agrarian oligarchy that was then the dominant class depended, by its agro-export nature, on foreign markets to sell its product and realize surplus value, and was hence unable to allow the development of a basic contradiction vis-a-vis foreign capital, to which it was structurally subordinated. This explains why the coffee-plantation state of the period facilitated penetration and development of the enclave by the United Fruit Co., the International Railroad of Central America, and Electric Bond & Share. The grim banana dictators running the state apparatus made these concessions under circumstances in which class domination needed to be imposed by physical force.

We must next consider the period after the Russian Revolution, characterized by accelerated changes in the capitalist system after the Second World War and the rise of socialism on a world scale—a period of transition and accommodation for dependent capitalist countries. In that situation the collapse of the Ubico tyranny in Guatemala (1944) marked the beginning of a process in which the petty bourgeoisie allied itself with the embryo of what looked like becoming a nationally-based industrial bourgeoisie, and with the meager organized sectors of the working class. The logic of this populist alliance would have been to accommodate the Guatemalan state to the above-mentioned changes in world capitalism. But the class-struggle dynamic, reflected in the growth, organization, and rising class consciousness of rural and urban wage-earners, radicalized the process, so that part of the state apparatus began to be used against the interests of the oligarchic sector of the bourgeoisie (agrarian reform) and imperial interests (President Arbenz' triple nationalist program: roads, ports, hydroelectric installations). And this led to the notorious outcome in which imperialism and the dominant class, allied with a petty bourgeoisie that feared the popular advance, resolved the situation in their favor by using the state apparatus' most important branch from the viewpoint of social struggles— the armed forces.

The third period to consider is the restoration of a dominant class modified by development in capitalism, in which industrial and financial elements of the bourgeoisie gain ever more weight; but the "*comprador*" character of this bourgeoisie remains unchanged, since industrial growth without reforms was linked to the Central American Common Market at the same time that foreign capital investment (with the United States still predominating) takes on two characteristics: the enclave loses importance, and the foreign capital is directed toward the production of manufactured articles in countries of the periphery. This is a phase of development in which monopoly capital is becoming internationalized in the framework of a transformation of the capitalist mode of production not yet completed and not even totally perceived.

Consequently the industrial and financial bourgeoisie, which strives for hegemony, exists and reproduces itself to the extent that its ties with imperialism are maintained and fortified. There is no way, if there ever was, to develop a sector of the dominant class in fundamental contradiction with imperialism. That is, the objective circumstances of capitalist reproduction in Central America make a national element impossible.

It is pertinent to add that the collapse of the Central American Common Market at the end of the 1960s and global acceleration of the process of capital internationalization are reflected in new forms of imperialist presence in the country. On the one hand, a new type of foreign investment penetrates Guatemala, originating in the southern United States and linked to the activities of small investors, including Cuban-Americans. This is directed toward branches of agro-industry (cattle), horticulture (fruits and vegetables) and floriculture for export to the United States and toward services (tourist industry). On the other hand, big internationalized monopoly capital in the form of multinational corporations enters Guatemala for the extraction of minerals and hydrocarbons (e.g., the exploitation of nickel by the Canadian multinational, INCO, and of oil by, amongst others, Basic Resources), materials of high strategic value and great importance for world capitalist development.

We are concerned to broaden the analysis of changes in the state in this third period of our survey. Ever since 1954, successive governments have sought to transform the Guatemalan state in accordance with the changing needs of capitalist reproduction in the area. Planning efforts under Castillo Armas, industrial expansion and integration legislation under Ydígoras Fuentes, the mine and hydrocarbon legislation and administrative and financial modernizations under Peralta Azurdia, massive efforts under Méndez Montenegro, Arana Osorio, and Laugerud García for planned development of communications, hydroelectric power, and technical education (along with intensified state repression, as we will see); all this is closely correlated with the new modalities of imperialist penetration of the country and the consequent changes of relations in the local dominant class.

The change undergone by the state repressive apparatus is also significant. Beginning with the military regime of 1963-1966, the armed forces outstripped other elements of the bureaucracy in their potential for generating and using power. At the same time there was a drastic change in the situation of the officer corps and its position in the social hierarchy, so that today we see an integration of general officers with the bourgeoisie's most advanced elements, those most directly linked with transnational interests. This process of change must not be considered as an example of "Bonapartism" in the sense of military men occupying a power vacuum; rather in our view, it must be seen as a consequence of the qualitative growth of the class struggle into its armed stage during the same period. Thus that state sector which in the last instance can preserve class domination—the armed forces—takes on proportionately greater weight.

Finally, we must note that Panzós lies precisely in the area of one of the most—if not the most—significant projects for capitalist reproduction in Guatemala: the north-central region comprising the north of Izábal, Alta Verapaz, Quiché, and Huehuetenango departments, and the southwest and northwest of Petén department. There are located the Petén and Alta Verapaz oil exploration/exploitation zones (multinationals include Basic Resources, Centram-Zamora, Hispano Oil, Getty Oil); the Izábal nickel exploitation zone (Exmibal, an International Nickel affiliate); the antimony and tungsten mines exploited by Minas de Guatemala, S.A.; the copper exploited by Transmetales, Ltda. in Ixtahuacán, Huehuetenango and Oxec, Alta Verapaz; and the pipeline under construction to bring oil from the

Basic camps in Rubelsanto to the Atlantic port of Barrios.

The Guatemalan state is making every effort to develop this area, where exploitation of Guatemalan resources for the benefit of international monopoly capital is concentrated, by providing the multinationals with necessary infrastructure. This includes construction of the Chixoy hydroelectric installation in Alta Verapaz, designed to produce 300,000 kilowatt-hours by the end of 1981, and the complex known as the "Northern Transverse Strip," covering the far north of Izábal, Alta Verapaz and Quiché departments and a small part of Huehuetenango. The "Strip" extends over 8,106.41 square kilometers and has five sectors: Ixcán, Lachná, Sebol, Modesto Méndez, and Livingston.

Originally the "Strip" was a project to open a "virgin soil" area for cultivation, to settle landless *campesinos,* and at the same time to increase the country's production of basic grains. Project studies began appearing in the mid-1960s in the framework of National Agrarian Transformation Institute (INTA) plans; and colonization of the area began, such as that of the Maryknoll Fathers who from 1966 on brought 1,600 campesino families from Huehuetenango and El Quiché to form agricultural cooperatives in the Ixcán area.

Large-scale colonization is now on the agenda: INTA has concentrated all of its activity in the "Strip" with a view to eventually settling 70,224 families in cooperative enterprises over a 573,256-hectare area. To facilitate this, INTA and the army engineer corps are building a transverse highway from Modesto Méndez in Petén to Barillas in Huehuetenango, with AID financing.

This highway is a key part of the infrastructure development mentioned above, since it will give access to oil exploitation and construction of the pipeline. As for the INTA colonization scheme, it also fits into the capitalist project, since only 42 percent of the area is identified as agricultural, and massive peasant mobilization there rouses fears for the economic viability of the scheme and for the conversion of the region's natural resources. However, the presence of a poor peasant mass may be necessary to provide cheap and abundant labor for the various capitalist enterprises to be established. In any case, what the "Strip" project means for the system in Guatemala is indicated by the appointment of an army general to head it up.

Another project for the "Strip" area, important not only for Guatemala's capitalist development but for the United States as well, is the inter-ocean pipeline which will take Alaskan oil from Champerico (or possibly some other port) on the Pacific to Puerto Barrios on the Atlantic en route to East Coast U.S. refineries. Since the rise of OPEC, the Central American capitalist countries have stepped up exploitation of oil resources in their own territories, and Alaskan production is supposed to supply 10 percent of total U.S. consumption. The Guatemalan pipeline project, backed by the bourgeois sector that is decisive in determining state policies, will further deepen Guatemala's integration into the world capitalist system.

Panzós and Guatemalan Social Struggles

All this goes on in an area that has been relatively isolated, with an economy traditionally based on the most backward kind of coffee plantation, and with day laborers and impoverished small farmers predominating in the exploited class. Concentration of modern mining and oil centers in such an area, together with the creation of an accompanying infrastructure, have speeded changes in the economic base and in relations of production. Today it is an area with concentrations of wage-workers in modern industrial enterprises where real estate is valued in terms of mineral possibilities, not agricultural production. Thus the big property owners, including military and political bigwigs, tend to link themselves to the interests of internationalized monopoly capital rather than to the traditional oligarchy. Hence the class struggle in the area takes on qualitatively higher forms. Some of the biggest worker mobilizations of the past have been brought about by labor conflicts in this area. Among these have been:

■ *Miners of San Ildefonso Ixtahuacán, Huehuetenango.* This conflict involved a confrontation between the miners' union and Minas de Guatemala, S.A., which sought to break the union by closing the mine. It was won by the workers who organized the famous "Ixtahuacán miners' march" in November 1977. As part of a national mobilization sponsored by the National Trade Union Unity Committee (CNUS), 80 miners marched 300 kilometers to the capital. They reached Guatemala City at the same time as another column of workers from the Pantaleón de Escuintla sugarmill. The two columns marched in on November 19 accompanied by a crowd estimated, at one point, at 100,000 persons.

◘ *Workers of Oxec-Chixoy.* Two labor conflicts broke out simultaneously in April 1978. One involved workers in the Oxec mine in Cahabón, Alta Verapaz, owned by the Guatemala Mining Corporation operating under the name of Transmetales—part of the multinational Basic Resources, which also exploits oilfields around Rubelsanto. The other was at the Chixoy hydroelectric installation built by various firms, among them the Italian Cogefar and the German Hochtief. Both conflicts arose from wage demands and included a march to the city of Cobán which also evoked big local and national demonstrations of solidarity. Both were finally won by the workers.

While the workers fought for their demands, campesino struggles erupted in the "Strip" area arising from conflicts over land. Such struggles generally break out when latifundists resort to legal maneuvers, especially what is known as "supplementary entitlement," to appropriate lands of small peasant owners whose titles to them are often defective or unproveable. As a sociologist specializing in the subject has pointed out, this type of robbery occurs in areas where land is being reassessed, due either to the expansion of agro-industry (as on the south coast) or to penetration by multinationals as in the case in point.

When conflicts of this sort arise the state security forces are apt to intervene more speedily than in urban areas to resolve the problem in the oligarchy's favor. They are equally quick on the draw in other rural confrontations such as those stemming from attempts by the agrarian exploited class to organize unions. The state's generally lower "tolerance" in the countryside than in the city, which one notes in analyzing the dynamic of the class struggle and the terror in Guatemala, is of course not accidental. It responds to the fact that while urban manufacturing workers are a small minority of the proletariat, rural wage-workers are the great majority of the exploited class, giving the countryside an enormous but yet undeveloped revolutionary potential. This explains the state's creation in 1964 of an armed force with the main original function of rural repression: the Policía Militar Ambulante.

The area under study has, however, been the scene not only of "normal" rural repression but of more extensive terror operations. Highly specialized army units participate in these, in addition to police and irregular and paramilitary groups. In the past four years such incidents of massive violence have occurred in municipalities of northern Quiché, particularly Chajul, San Juan Cotzal, and Nebaj, inhabited by the Ixil people: a partial count identified 28 kidnapped inhabitants of San Juan Cotzal in three years. Some of the most violent repression occurred in villages of the Fray Bartolomé de las Casas settlement in Ixcán Grande, in the "Strip" area.[1]

It is from this perspective that the Panzós massacre must be seen. The immediate background was a clash between impoverished campesinos cultivating plots of vacant land in Panzós municipality and big farmers of the area who sought to dislodge them. But in what had seemed to be just another episode of the daily struggle for land in Guatemala, an extraordinary degree of terror was unleashed. The "normal" thing would have been the kidnapping, torture, and murder of a few leaders by "unidentified armed men." Instead, there was a generalized massacre in full light of day and in the presence of dozens of surviving witnesses. Asking ourselves what the logic of such super-terror could have been, we offer the following hypothesis.

We have analyzed the importance of this region for the country's capitalist development, and seen that the state's "contribution" is to create suitable local conditions. This "creation" of conditions involves not only infrastructural works, labor mobilization, etc., but also creation of the necessary "social peace," i.e., preventing the development and mobilization of popular organizations which could hamper the project of capitalist development. It was thus as a response to the growth of combative trade unionism that the student leader and trade unionist Mario Mujia Córdoba was assassinated in June 1978 in the departmental capital in Huehuetenango. And when "Guerrilla Army of the Poor" units began operations in the area—attacking oil camps and killing the well-known latifundist José Luis Arenas

---

[1] Roger Plant, *Guatemala: Unnatural Disaster* (London: Latin America Bureau, 1978).

Barrera—the response took the form of military operations and a terror campaign against the population. The great Panzós massacre was a logical culmination of this campaign to terrorize the people into withholding support from the insurgents and to suffocate the cries for land.

This hypothesis suggests that Panzós was no isolated or accidental event. Big public massacres come within the tactics of terror, despite their political disadvantages for the terror machine, in that the usual denials of state participation are ruled out and consequent national and international accusations have to be confronted. On the other hand they multiply a hundred times, as far as the public at large is concerned, the intimidating effect which is the name of the terror game. By this logic, the massacre of 115 campesinos bears a clear if unarticulated message: social struggles, including struggles for land, must stop, in the "Strip" area, on pain of death.

Amnesty International
Report on El Salvador, 1981*

Amnesty International is a nonpartisan human rights organization. Among its many honors, Amnesty International won the Nobel Peace Prize in 1977.

Amnesty International has been concerned about reports that people from all sectors of Salvadorean society have been detained without warrant, have "disappeared" or have been murdered. Although conflict between guerrilla groups and the authorities has escalated and human rights violations by non-government forces have been reported, Amnesty International believes that the majority of the reported violations were inflicted by all branches of the security forces on people not involved in guerrilla activities.

The year has also been characterized by continuing instability in government. Following the overthrow of President General Carlos Humberto Romero in October 1979 by a civilian-military junta, the new government announced an amnesty for political prisoners, the restoration of human rights and the implementation of agrarian reform. However, in the ensuing months the civilian members of the first junta withdrew from the government in protest as the agrarian reform stalled and the repression continued; most went into exile. They had particularly objected to the failure of the authorities either to disband the rural paramilitary group ORDEN (now operating under another name) as recommended in the 1978 Inter-American Commission on Human Rights *Report on the Situation of Human Rights in El Salvador*, or to initiate proceedings against officers implicated in human rights violations. Christian Democrat José Napoleón Duarte joined the government in December 1980 as its civilian President.

*Excerpted and abridged from *Amnesty International Report 1981* (London: Amnesty International Publications, 1981).

Colonel Adolfo Majano led the coup which overthrew General Romero in 1979 and had continued to press for land and social reforms. An attempt on his life in November 1980 failed and in December 1980 he was made to leave the junta. When he then accused the government of condoning right-wing "death squads" a warrant was issued for his arrest and he was detained in February 1981. Released on 20 March 1981, he reportedly left the country.

Those now in control have implemented what appears to be a systematic and brutal policy of intimidation and repression. When challenged about arbitrary detention, "disappearances" and extra-judicial killings, President Duarte repeatedly responded that his government was under attack from extremist groups of the right and the left who were responsible for many of the abuses. Asked about killings of peasants in strategically important areas where guerrillas were believed to be operating, the government held that many were killed in confrontations with the security forces. In those areas the government appeared to be implementing a counter-insurgency policy that presumed that all civilians were supporters or potential supporters of the armed opposition.

Additional emergency legislation, which contravenes regional and international standards for the protection of human rights, has been passed to legitimize such practices. Decree Law 507, which came into force on 1 January 1981, defines unlawful groups broadly, and under Article 11 statements in the news media that a person belongs to such a group will be sufficient proof. Article 7 permits a secret six-month period of investigation at the pre-trial stage, starting when the detainee is transferred to the custody of the examining judge, and appears to allow at least six months' incommunicado detention. It could be construed as an attempt to legitimize "disappearances."

Many of the "disappeared" and killed were young people apparently assumed to be sympathetic to the opposition simply on grounds of age. Amnesty International has a photographic record of two arrests on 3 October 1980. Two young men were pictured being arrested by the National Guard who were then shown binding and tying the young suspects before turning them over to men in plain clothes. Five days later their corpses were found showing clear marks of torture.

On 1 November 1980 Gloria del Rosario Rivera, aged 15; Alfonso Román Hernández, aged 22; and 60 others, aged between 14 and 22, were detained in the Colonia Amatepec and Ciudad Credisa in Soyapango, to the east of the capital, by members of the army and security services on a house-to-house search. All were taken away in an armored lorry. Two days later 15 of their bodies were found in Ilopango. On the same day the bodies of the others were found on the road to Mil Cumbres. All showed signs of torture.

In January 1981, as the guerrillas began their unsuccessful "final offensive," indiscriminate repression against the young intensified. On 10 January troops took 22 teenagers from Mejicanos; all were found tortured and dead. The faces of five of the young women had been obliterated.

On 9 April 1981 Amnesty International publicly urged the authorities to investigate the massacre which allegedly occurred during the week of 7 April. More than 20 people, including many youths, were killed in the Soyapango suburb of the capital, San Salvador. Unusually, Salvadorean officials, the United States Embassy in El Salvador and the State Department had reportedly acknowledged that an official security unit, the Treasury Police, was involved.

Amnesty International also recorded many abuses directed against children too young to have had any involvement with opposition groups. On 9 July 1980, 31 members of a peasant family by the name of Mojica Santos were reportedly killed by ORDEN members with the complicity of the National Army and the National Police. Those murdered included 15 children under the age of 10. One was only two weeks old.

The children of "displaced persons" fleeing areas of fighting to seek shelter in church-run reception centers in San Salvador and elsewhere have suffered abuses, as have the children of refugees who have sought asylum abroad. Persistent rumors have been received of Salvadorean troops entering Honduras unmolested to pursue refugees, and a number of incidents have been reported in which Salvadorean refugees have been detained with the aid of Honduran troops, been taken back across the border into El Salvador, and "disappeared."

A combined military action was reported in May 1980, when hundreds of people, mainly women and children, were killed by Salvadorean troops as they tried to cross the Sumpul River into Honduras, while Honduran troops blocked their way. Both governments initially denied the incident, but a denunciation of the killings by local priests was supported by the Honduran Bishops Council and confirmed by Salvadorean and Honduran human rights groups and eye-witnesses. Later the Salvadorean authorities did state that there had been a confrontation between government forces and guerrillas in the area.

Peasants who survived the massacre later described to visiting foreign delegations of inquiry how Salvadorean soldiers and ORDEN members gathered children and babies together, threw them into the air and slashed them to death with machetes. Some infants were reportedly decapitated and their bodies slit into pieces and thrown to the dogs; other children were reported to have drowned after Salvadorean soldiers threw them into the water.

Similar incidents, involving Salvadorean and Honduran armed forces as well as members of ORDEN, reportedly occurred in March and April of 1981. Amnesty International presented information it had received regarding human rights abuses directed at Salvadorean refugees to international and regional organizations.

Internal refugees or displaced persons fleeing areas where the government's agrarian reform program had been violently imposed and confiscated lands handed over to ORDEN supporters have been removed from church-run relief centers and summarily executed. A government "pacification" program of massive bombings intended to force civilians out of areas controlled by opposition forces had also driven many peasants from their homes.

Clergy, both Salvadorean and foreign, who have denounced such atrocities have themselves been repressed, and Amnesty International has repeatedly called for inquiries into the murder and "disappearance" of priests and lay workers including Father Marcial Serrano, parish priest of Olocuilta, kidnapped by the National Guard on 28 November 1980 and still missing.

The assassination of Archbishop Romero, an outspoken defender of human rights, provoked an international outcry. In March 1980, shortly after he had written to President Carter asking the U.S. not to provide military assistance to El Salvador which could be used to perpetuate human rights violations, he was killed while saying mass. Since then there have been reports that the authorities have refused to act upon information about the identities of those behind the Archbishop's assassination.

Slow progress has been made in investigating the murders of four American women whose partially-clothed bullet-ridden bodies were found near Santiago Nonualco, a small town southeast of the capital, on 4 December 1980. All bore marks of strangulation and other physical abuse. A mission of inquiry led by former U.S. Undersecretary of State William Rogers found that there was circumstantial evidence to implicate local security forces. It also found indications that highly-placed Salvadorean officials had obstructed efforts to investigate the disappearance and deaths of the four women. The magistrate of the department where the bodies were initially held asked for official protection so that he could give information to the U.S. Ambassador and was reportedly murdered two days later.

After the mission the U.S. suspended assistance to El Salvador until the government clarified the circumstances of the deaths. When the U.S. resumed its military aid program in January 1981, no charges had been brought nor any criminal proceedings initiated in connection with this incident.

Amnesty International wrote to the U.S. administration of President Jimmy Carter to express its concern at the alleged involvement in human rights violations of official security agencies which could be presumed to be likely beneficiaries of U.S. military aid. In May 1980 the U.S. State Department replied that its assistance was intended to enhance the professionalism of the armed forces.

Following further correspondence with the Carter Administration on the subject, Amnesty International welcomed public statements by the new administration of President Reagan when it assumed power in January 1981 that it would continue to be U.S. policy to endeavor to protect human rights in El Salvador, but noted that Amnesty International shared the concern expressed in December 1980 by the United Nations which called upon governments "to refrain from the supply of arms and other military assistance in the current circumstances." After indications that the new administration intended to increase military assistance to El Salvador significantly, Amnesty International announced its intention to urge the new Secretary of State, General Alexander Haig, to review the effects of U.S. assistance programs upon the human rights situation in El Salvador, and to make public the findings of that review.

Academics have been subjected to many abuses. On 10 February 1981 troops burst into a regular meeting of the *Consejo Superior Universitario*, the Supreme University Council, of the National University of El Salvador. Twenty people were detained including the Deans of six faculties and the interim Rector of the National University, Lic. Miguel Parada. Parada's predecessor, Felix Ulloa Martínez, President of the Geneva-based World University Service, died in October 1980 after a machine-gun attack in San Salvador. Ulloa's name had previously appeared on several anonymous death lists. Fourteen of the University Council members detained on 10 February were released shortly afterwards, but there were fears for the safety of the others. However, a journalist eventually located and interviewed them in Santa Tecla prison in the capital.

They described their arrests as the final step in a government campaign to destroy the university, and stated that hundreds of students and professors had been assassinated and the university assaulted by troops on several occasions. The last assault occurred on 26 June 1980, when the institution was completely occupied by troops supported by tanks and helicopters. Students, professors, university administrators and staff, as well as members of left-wing organizations and 15 foreign journalists, were taken into custody. At least 22 were reported killed.

Following the publication of their names in the international press, the University Council members were released on 1 April 1981, but approximately 117 other political prisoners remained in Santa Tecla. Many testified that they had been physically and psychologically tortured while in custody. Electric shocks, beatings and the use of hallucinogenic drugs were alleged in attempts to extort confessions of guerrilla involvement. A young teacher, Rafael Caruas Flores, displayed large areas of burnt flesh on his arms, legs, body and face, where he said interrogators had thrown sulfuric acid. He also claimed to have been indecently assaulted, and to have had acid poured on his testicles. His two-year-old son was arrested at the same time and has not been located. Four prisoners were reportedly removed from Santa Tecla in September 1980 in reprisal for a hunger strike calling for a general amnesty and an end to human rights violations and remained missing.

Others held in Santa Tecla included members of the *Sindicato de Trabajadores Empresa Comisión Ejecutiva Hidroeléctrica*, the Hydroelectric Workers Union, which represents workers in the privately-owned electricity-supply industry. They had been jailed after a strike in August 1980. The strike was in protest at a government ruling that the union was unconstitutional under Decree 296 prohibiting trade unions from discussing politics. The discussions in question had dealt with the killings in front of their families of 10 trade unionists who had held meetings to protest against dangerous working conditions.

Also found in Santa Tecla prison was journalist Francisco Ramírez Avelar, who when arrested on 15 January 1981 had been writing for the newspaper *El Independiente, The Independent,* later forced to close. The whereabouts of eight other staff members detained at the same time remained unknown. Ramírez stated that he had not yet appeared before a court, though he had been brought blindfolded and handcuffed before a military judge for questioning, and guns had been jabbed into his chest. He was charged with having served as a link between the news media and the opposition, but he said he had been imprisoned because he had written about the authorities' involvement in political killings. The persecution of *El Independiente* had included several violent attacks on the newspaper's offices, three unsuccessful attempts on the life of its editor, Jorge Pinto, and two failed attempts to arrest him. The only other newspaper that had refused to practice self-censorship, *La Crónica del Pueblo,* the *People's Chronicle,* closed down in the summer of 1980 after its managing editor and a photographer were abducted. Their bodies were found the next day hacked to death.

Foreign journalists have also suffered. In December 1980 American journalist John Sullivan disappeared from his hotel and has not been heard from since. Nina Bundgaard, writing for the Danish monthly magazine *Politisk Revy,* survived detention by the Treasury Police. Arrested on 25 November 1980, blindfolded and interrogated at both Air Force and National Guard Headquarters, the 22-year-old reporter was threatened with death on several occasions and was eventually expelled on 30 November 1980 after intervention by the Danish authorities. Her Salvadorean husband had been killed two days earlier; another friend was kidnapped at his funeral and her dead body later found with torture marks. Mauricio Gamero, a young Salvadorean arrested at the same time as Nina Bundgaard, remained missing. One month later Venezuelan film director Nelson Arrieti was abducted from his hotel by 18 heavily armed members of the security forces in plain clothes. After his release on 18 January 1981 Nelson Arrieti stated that he had been beaten and drugged at the military barracks where he was interrogated.

Salvadorean human rights groups which have tried to inform the international public about human rights abuses have also been decimated by murder and enforced exile. In early October 1980 María Magdalena Enríquez, press secretary of the Human Rights Commission of El Salvador, was abducted and found dead in a shallow grave about 35 kilometers from the capital. Another of its representatives, Ramón Vaddadares Pérez, was killed on 26 October 1980. The offices of the commission have been bombed frequently since then, and its information and administration secretary, Victor Medrano, was abducted in January 1981 and held by the National Police until 11 February. Attacks have also been mounted against the *Socorro Jurídico,* another body which monitors human rights abuses and which also offers legal assistance to the poor. In mid-December the offices were forced to close temporarily, having been raided 17 times in one week by the National Police, and many of its personnel have been forced into hiding or exile. In early April, a number of *Socorro Jurídico* workers were named on a list issued by the press office of the army as "traitors to their country."

Amnesty International issued a press release which expressed regret that the army had published such a list which suggested that official sanction was being given to people wishing to eliminate those who denounced violations of human rights by the security forces. Amnesty International called upon the authorities to protect those named on the list.

Teachers were another profession to suffer repression. From January to October 1980 at least 90 were murdered by uniformed and plainclothes members of the security forces, and at least 19 primary and secondary schools were raided by the security forces. A further 22 teachers were killed in the period 1 January to 1 May 1981, while others have been detained and "disappeared." Many have gone into exile; 85 percent of the schools in the west of the country have reportedly been closed.

The attacks on teachers appeared to be an attempt to destroy the teachers' union *Asociación Nacional de Educadores de El Salvador* (ANDES), the National Association of Salvadorean Educators. This union was a member of one of the largest opposition bodies, the *Bloque Popular Revolucionario* (BPR), the Popular Revolutionary Bloc, which united unions of peasants, teachers, students and shanty town dwellers and was in turn a member of the coalition of opposition parties, the *Frente Democrático Revolucionario* (FDR), the Democratic Revolutionary Front, formed in April 1980.

In November 1980 six FDR leaders, including Secretary General and former Minister of Agriculture under the first post-Romero government, Enrique Alvarez, were kidnapped as they were about to hold a news conference. An estimated 200 men in army and National Police uniforms surrounded the area while men in plain clothes arrested the six along with approximately 25 others. The bullet-riddled bodies of the six were later found at a lake near the international airport, showing signs of torture, dismemberment and strangulation.

In December 1980 Amnesty International sent messages to the United Nations, pointing to the overwhelming evidence that Salvadorean troops had been responsible for the killings, and urging member states to condemn these actions which "outraged the minimum standards of government conduct."

A previous submission by Amnesty International to the United Nations Working Group on Enforced or Involuntary Disappearances included the case of teacher Leonel Meléndez, an ANDES leader. Shot and wounded in May 1980, Meléndez was abducted from the operating theater of the Rosales Hospital in San Salvador when the hospital was surrounded by vehicles belonging to the National Guard and agents of the National Police.

Throughout the year Amnesty International received similar reports of individuals, in some instances incontestably non-combatants, being removed from hospitals and killed, apparently merely because they had sought medical attention after being wounded in civil conflict. Medical personnel have also been abducted and murdered, apparently for giving treatment to the wounded, including non-combatants. First aid workers have also reportedly been abducted as they tried to transport medical supplies.

In June 1980 and March 1981 Amnesty International launched a campaign to mobilize doctors throughout the world to urge the Salvadorean authorities to protect the health services and bring those who violated their neutrality to justice.

In April 1981 the British charitable agency Oxfam reported that 17 Salvadoreans who worked on Oxfam-supported projects in El Salvador had been killed by the army or government-controlled paramilitary forces in the last year. More than 300 people less directly involved in the projects had been killed.

Such atrocities prompted Amnesty International to submit information about the detained and "disappeared" in El Salvador to regional and international organizations. Amnesty International made an oral statement to the UN Commission on Human Rights in March 1981 in which it estimated that 12,000 people had been killed during 1980 and noted that evidence it had collated from hundreds of individual cases of human rights abuses clearly indicated the responsibility of the regular security forces for the majority. The commission later decided to appoint a special representative to investigate the reported violations. Submissions were also presented to UNESCO and the Inter-American Commission on Human Rights of the Organization of American States. A statement on El Salvador was presented to the Tenth Regular Session of the General Assembly of the Organization of American States, held in November 1980, in which Amnesty International expressed hope that given the continuing gravity of the human rights situation there, the Inter-American Commission on Human Rights would carry out an *in situ* investigation and seek effective means of checking abuses. In March 1981 Amnesty International advised the U.S. section of Amnesty International, who testified before the Sub-Committee on Inter-American Affairs to the United States House of Representatives on human rights violations in El Salvador, and urged the sub-committee to uphold human rights considerations as fundamental guidelines in the development of U.S. policy towards El Salvador. In other testimony to the House a former military doctor in the Salvadorean Army stated that it was the high command of the armed forces and the directors of the security forces who wielded the power in El Salvador; that the *Escuadrones de la Muerte*, "death squads," were made up of members of the security forces; and that acts of terrorism ascribed to those squads—such as political assassinations, kidnappings and indiscriminate murder—were in fact planned by high-ranking military officers and carried out by members of the security forces.

During the year, Amnesty International launched 58 appeals on behalf of 472 people believed to have been detained or "disappeared."

Abuses of Medical Neutrality*

Committee for Health Rights in El Salvador

Recurrent reports of violations of the neutrality of medical institutions and of the rights of health workers, including the killings of doctors and patients, made imperative a prompt, on-the-spot inquiry by a respected group of health experts. Such a Public Health Commission of Inquiry was organized by the Committee for Health Rights in El Salvador with the support of the American Public Health Association, The Physicians Forum and the American Friends Service Committee. The Commission consisted of three physicians, a professor of public health and a teacher of community health and social medicine. It visited San Salvador July 14 to 17, 1980.

The five members of the Commission were: **Sally Guttmacher**, PhD, Assistant Professor, Columbia University School of Public Health, and Chairperson of the APHA Task Force on International Human Rights; **Frances Hubbard**, BS, Associate Director, field education, Sophie Davis School of Biomedical Education at City College of the City University of New York (CUNY), and former vice president, National Union of Hospital and Health Care Employees, District 1199; **Walter Lear**, MD, public health physician, President of The Physicians Forum, and President, Institute of Social Medicine and Community Health; **Leonard Sagan**, MD, researcher in occupational health, internist, and fellow of the American College of Physicians; and **Arthur Warner**, MD, pediatrician, fellow of APHA, and representative of the American Friends Service Committee.

While in San Salvador, the Commission interviewed almost 50 individuals in the health and relief fields representing many organizations and a spectrum of political beliefs. Among those interviewed were the Minister of Health and a member of the ruling Junta who is a physician. Many hours were spent with representatives of the major national doctor, nurse and health worker organizations. The principal conclusions of the Commission are:

- Since the coup of October 15, 1979, the traditional protection conferred on doctors and other health workers has been increasingly ignored as military and paramilitary gangs have assassinated, tortured and threatened doctors, nurses and medical students.

- Military and paramilitary personnel have flagrantly entered hospitals and shot down patients in cold blood.

- There is no instance in which the Salvadorean Government has punished, prosecuted or even identified those responsible for these killings.

Since the signing of the Geneva Convention in 1864, nations have pledged to regard doctors and nurses as well as the sick and wounded as neutrals during military conflict. These principles are being recklessly

---

*Excerpts from a report by the Committee for Health Rights in El Salvador, 66 West 87 St., N.Y., N.Y. 10024.

disregarded in El Salvador today. On the basis of these and other findings, detailed in the body of this report, the Commission urgently calls upon the following bodies to undertake these recommendations:

The Government of El Salvador to

- take vigorous action to stop violations of medical neutrality, and to insure that all health personnel can treat persons in need of care without fear of reprisal;
- reopen the Medical School, as well as other branches of the university, under democratic, civilian leadership and without a military or paramilitary presence;
- guarantee the safety of personnel working in rural health services, and replace the mobile health units destroyed during the conflict;
- lift any import restrictions on medicinals and medical supplies designated for relief agencies.

The International Committee of the Red Cross to

- immediately appoint a permanent medical representative to assess the current situation;
- establish a presence in all hospitals to insure neutrality;
- organize modern blood-banking facilities accessible to all Salvadoreans;
- set up safe facilities for the treatment of the wounded.

International relief organizations to

- send medicinals and other medical supplies to refugee camps and health facilities, to be distributed through appropriate private relief organizations.

The United Nations to

- dispatch a High Commission to promptly evaluate the needs of displaced persons for food, shelter, clothing and medical services.

The Organization of American States to

- investigate violations of the neutrality of hospital and health services.

Professional organizations to

- visit El Salvador to continue the assessment of the situation in the health field and in other areas of society.

Violence to Health Workers

From the time of the October 1979 coup, death squads and uniformed forces have repeatedly entered hospitals and clinics and shot down patients, doctors, nurses and medical students in cold blood. These assassinations are frequently preceded by the cruelest forms of dismemberment and brutality. At least 9 physicians, 7 medical students and 1 nurse have been killed since the coup. Many other health personnel have also been victims of violence and harrassment. Two episodes are presented here:

- On May 15th, Drs. Miguel Angel García and Carlos Ernesto Alfaro Rodriguez were kidnapped by armed men from a hospital in Cojutepeque where they were performing an operation. Both doctors were later found with clear evidence of torture. One corpse had multiple lacerations, a depressed skull fracture and evidence of strangulation. The other victim suffered a penetrating wound of the neck cutting the spinal cord at a high cervical level. He was found alive but never regained consciousness. Their deaths precipitated a work stoppage by health workers across the nation.

- A health worker told this Commission of a slaughter which occurred in late June in the vicinity of Santa Ana. While conducting a routine, sweeping search for "oppositionists," military forces entered the home of Dr. Montes and his wife, a nurse. Two medical students (one named Tonativ Ramos) and two relatives were visiting the Montes at the time the military appeared. Hearing a commotion, another young physician who lived nearby, Dr. Matamoros, went to the house, too. Four hours later and after the soldiers had departed, our informant felt it safe to enter the house. He found all seven killed by shots in the head, apparently with a high-power weapon. "They had their heads nearly blown away," he reported. The reason for the massacre was that an ordinary examining table and small amount of anesthesia material had been found. The military presumed that they had discovered a clandestine clinic for the treatment of guerrillas.

The brutality involved in the killings of health workers and patients and the accompanying torture suggest that this is a deliberate tactic aimed at striking terror into the hearts of others. Victims have been decapitated, emasculated or found with the initials "EM," which stands for *Escuadrón de la Muerte* (Death Squad), in their flesh. Official forensic medical reports document these atrocities.

The outcome—no doubt intended—of this pattern of killings and torture on the part of military and paramilitary groups is that health workers are afraid to render services to patients who are, or could conceivably be considered, "oppositionist," even if this means merely being a member of one of the numerous *legal* popular organizations. The risk of swift, brutal and fatal reprisal means that most health care professionals will necessarily have second thoughts about which patients they will treat. They are, moreover, aware that the government has not taken effective steps to identify or prosecute the killers. Not even the Minister of Health or Dr. José Ramón Avalos, a physician member of the Junta, could promise that the culprits would be apprehended and punished. This intimidation makes it inevitable that some patients needing surgical or medical attention will not receive it.

The murders of health personnel were acknowledged by all groupings on the political scene including the Government. Nor was it alleged that these acts of violence were the consequence of political activity on the part of health workers. The Commission concluded that violence was directed against physicians and other health personnel simply because they were fulfilling their ethical responsibility to treat the sick and wounded.

In addition, the Commission heard reports of intimidation against members of the medical profession. Newspapers and television publicized the names of the leaders of the National Committee for the Defense of Patients, Workers and Health Institutions at the time of the doctors' work stoppage in an obvious bid to bring retaliations against them. The Board of the National Medical Association (Colegio Médico) resigned as a group to protest the threats made against Board members when it voted to support the medical strike action.

These threats and the generally high level of violence and political turmoil have proved demoralizing to physicians and have led to the exodus of many highly qualified and otherwise devoted health professionals. A former official of the Medical Society said that most of his medical school graduating class had fled the country. After receiving threats against the lives of his family and himself, former Minister of Health Dr. Robert Badilla, emigrated, as did Dr. Hector Silva, former Director of the Eastern Health Region. A country as small and poor as El Salvador can ill afford this loss of experienced professionals.

Violations of the Neutrality of Health Institutions

There is a reign of terror in the health facilities of El Salvador. The Commission was told that there is virtually no hospital or clinic which has escaped the intrusions of armed men. The following are some typical examples:

- At San Vicente Hospital, members of the armed forces in civilian clothes continually appear and fire their weapons, endangering patients and health workers.

- At the out-patient clinic in Ciudad Barrios in late May, the line of patients awaiting care was machine-gunned, leaving three patients dead.

- On May 23rd, army troops searched the medical care center of the SSI (Social Service Institute). Two days later, soldiers invaded the Central Hospital of the SSI.

The Commission was told that spies are posted in hospitals who pass information concerning admissions and ward assignments to military and paramilitary groups. Later the hospitals are invaded and selected patients are assassinated on the spot or kidnapped and later found dead. Usually the motives for these killings and the identities of the assassins are not known but the National Guard has been clearly identified on occasion. Patients who enter hospitals with bullet wounds are especially vulnerable—even if they were wounded by chance and are politically uninvolved. A medical student working for the El Salvador National Red Cross ambulance service revealed that they were specifically told not to transport persons with bullet wounds because it was too dangerous for the ambulance personnel.

In sum, testimony from all sources indicated that almost every government hospital has experienced armed invasion and the violation of neutrality normally accorded medical facilities.

Aside from government officials and the U.S. Ambassador, all sources vigorously urged that U.S. military aid be stopped forthwith. It was the strongly-held belief of health and relief workers that U.S. military aid finds its way into the hands of those who invade hospitals and terrorize displaced persons, and that this aid aggravates rather than alleviates repression in health institutions.

Medical Supplies and Blood

The Government of El Salvador maintains strict vigilance over the importation of medicines, surgical equipment and other supplies. As a consequence, relief organizations have expressed concern about obtaining necessary medicinals. Some health practitioners are unable to obtain ordinary equipment and supplies. Thus the Government's restrictions aggravate the deterioration of the health care delivery system.

Like many under-developed countries, El Salvador does not have a modern blood bank or community-wide blood donation system. When patients need blood, they must depend on donations from family and friends at the time of need. Recently the little extra blood collected in the central hospitals of San Salvador has been taken to, and stored in, the military hospital on the outskirts of the city. This hospital is administered directly by the Defense Ministry rather than the Ministry of Health. Release of the stored blood is under the control of the military hospital authorities. There is, under the present political circumstances, considerable reluctance on the part of civilian facilities to request this blood.

There is, moreover, considerable hesitancy on the part of potential donors to identify themselves as relatives of, or in any way associated with, any wounded person. In effect, the Government maintains a stranglehold on blood availability. Many of the wounded therefore do not have access to blood when a transfusion is necessary.

In the Commission's discussion with representatives of the International Red Cross, the Minister of Health, Dr. José Ramón Avalos of the Junta, and the U.S. Ambassador, there was a difference of opinion as to whether a new building is needed to house blood facilities but no disagreement that El Salvador needs to increase its capacity to collect, process, store and transport blood. The International Red Cross would consider acting as a coordinating agency only if absolute neutrality is guaranteed.

The Closing of the Medical School

On June 19th governmental troops entered the grounds and buildings of the El Salvador National University and closed the university. This entailed the closing of El Salvador's only medical school. From the standpoint of health care delivery, this has disastrous immediate and long-range effects as virtually all physicians in the rural areas are drawn from medical practitioners in their eighth or final "social service year." Moreover, the Medical School is the only training site for most non-physician health workers. There are 4,500 students at the Medical School of whom approximately 40% are working for degrees other than the M.D.

The 1972 military intervention in the El Salvador National University had an important impact on the Medical School. The military forced out many of the most scientifically able and dedicated faculty in its effort to weed out political progressives. These physicians emigrated to Venezuela, Costa Rica, the U.S.A. and Great Britain. For example, Salvador Enrique-Moncada, who is currently the Research Director of the Welcome Foundation in London and a Nobel Prize nominee, was forced to leave El Salvador after the government's take-over of the Medical School. After the take-over, faculty spent less time in teaching students, public health was diminished as a curriculum area, and the quality of education deteriorated. Because of this historical precedent, the present closing of the University is viewed with alarm; it is feared that the quality of medical education will suffer further setbacks when the school is eventually re-opened.

Health in Rural Areas

Although this Commission spent all its time in San Salvador because of security considerations, it gathered information from health professionals who worked in rural areas and refugees who recently had fled the countryside. Small health centers and mobile units, under governmental auspices, represent the only health resources in most rural areas. As noted above, the closing of the Medical School meant the withdrawal of "social service year" practitioners who provide the bulk of care. Many other physicians providing rural care have left their posts because of threats and kidnappings. Mobile health units have been destroyed and drugs stolen. The Minister of Health, who is responsible for rural medicine, acknowledged the demoralization of his medical personnel. Some services have had to be closed down. He held the Left responsible for this situation and saw it as part of the Left's effort to discredit the Government's agrarian reform program.

The endemic violence in the nation coupled with the closing down of the Medical School have seriously undermined health care for El Salvador's predominantly rural civilian population. Even prior to the current civil strife, undernourishment was widely considered the leading health problem facing El Salvador. It was estimated that 75 percent of children less than 5 years of age suffer malnutrition. Crop burnings have intensified the food shortages. Thus the curtailment of medical services in the countryside could not have happened at a worse time. A rise in rates of infant mortality, childhood infections and parasitic disease can be anticipated.

Refugees

Although governmental officials were loath to acknowledge the existence of refugees, the Commission was readily able to visit a refugee camp on church grounds within the capital city which contained over 1,000 persons. It was said to be one of five or six such camps in San Salvador. The refugees are peasants who fled the shootings and burnings in the countryside. The refugees in this camp were predominantly very young children and women.

In the refugee site visited by the Commission, food, water, bedding and medical care were in critically short supply. Outbreaks of diarrhea, especially in the children, were compounded by inadequate water supplies and sanitary facilities. Children with distended bellies and lice were seen. The refugees slept in an open yard exposed to the elements, or beneath a veranda.

The fear and grief of the refugees were palpable. Their movements were slowed down. Even as they struggled to meet their minimal survival needs, they dared not leave the sites provided by the churches for fear of further retaliation by military forces. They were therefore unable to seek out needed medical services. And so the violence which plagues El Salvador once again interfered with access to health care.

Background Information on El Salvador and U.S. Military Assistance to Central America*

By Cynthia Arnson

Cynthia Arnson is a researcher for IPS and has written many papers on the connection between U.S. economic and military aid to Central America and the repression that results from that aid. The following article, while not focusing exclusively on human rights violations, describes ways in which the U.S. directly and indirectly helps to export repression to the region.

Introduction

On December 15, 1981, Under Secretary of Defense Fred Iklé announced a significant increase in U.S. military assistance to El Salvador. Claiming that "the news is bad, the hour is late," with respect to "the Soviet-Cuban effort presently underway to further expand the reach of Soviet imperialism," Iklé informed the Senate Foreign Relations Committee that the United States would soon begin training 1600 Salvadorean soldiers—500-600 officers and a light infantry battalion of 1000—at U.S. bases.[1] Iklé also indicated that the Reagan Administration would "need the support of Congress" in meeting the costs of Salvadorean military requirements—costs which exceeded the $26 million approved for El Salvador in Fiscal Year 1982.

---

*From a report by the Institute for Policy Studies, March 1982.

[1] Testimony of Deputy Secretary of Defense Fred Iklé before the Senate Foreign Relations Committee, Dec. 14, 1981, p. 10.

Elsewhere in his testimony, Iklé stated that a team of U.S. experts had spent two months in El Salvador assisting in the development of a national military strategy (see section on U.S. military personnel in El Salvador), and that "other concerned Latin American countries" had begun helping in the effort to break the external supply lines to the Salvadorean guerrillas.

Hardly had Iklé spoken and the first contingents of Salvadorean soldiers arrived for training (see below) than Salvadorean rebels staged a surprise attack on the largest air base in El Salvador. In a pre-dawn raid on the Ilopango Air Force Base on January 27, 1982, guerrillas destroyed or severely damaged 18 aircraft, including 6 Bell UH-1H helicopters, 5 Douglas C-47 transports, 6 Dassault Ouragan fighters, and 1 Fouga Magister jet trainer.[2] At least 28 Salvadorean soldiers stationed at the base were detained for questioning about their possible collaboration in the attack.[3]

The Administration responded immediately by announcing on February 1 the provision of an additional $55 million in emergency military assistance (see below) that did not require Congressional approval. It was the second time within a year that President Reagan had invoked special executive authority to send such aid to El Salvador, bringing the total amount of emergency assistance alone to $75 million since March 1981.

The new aid was provided against a backdrop of increasing skepticism about the capacity of Salvadorean government troops to defeat guerrillas of the Farabundo Marti National Liberation Front. In early September 1981, head of the U.S. Southern Command Lt. Gen. Wallace Nutting declared that the military situation in El Salvador was a "stalemate," and that "in that kind of war, if you're not winning, you're losing."[4] On November 5, 1981, the *New York Times* reported that "a consensus had developed in the Reagan Administration that the civil war in El Salvador has reached a stalemate that will eventually cause the defeat of the government unless the United States takes decisive action soon."[5] During a February 1982 visit to San Salvador, furthermore, Lt. Gen. Nutting stated that he had "absolutely no idea" how much aid might be needed to defeat the guerrillas, but that if he had to "pick a winner or loser," he would say that "the [Salvadorean] government was winning."[6]

The Presidential Certification—Human Rights in El Salvador

Immediately after President Reagan authorized $55 million in emergency military assistance, his Administration confronted a hostile Congress. The foreign aid bill for Fiscal Year 1982 had stipulated that $26 million in military aid to El Salvador could be provided only after the President certified that six conditions were being met: greater respect for human rights, greater civilian control over the armed forces, continued progress on

---

[2] *Aviation Week and Space Technology*, Feb. 8, 1982.
[3] *The New York Times*, Feb. 7, 1982.
[4] Quoted in *Time*, Sept. 7, 1981.
[5] *The New York Times*, Nov. 5, 1981.
[6] Quoted in *The Washington Post*, Feb. 19, 1982.

economic reforms, progress in the investigation into the deaths of six U.S. citizens, commitment to the holding of free elections, and a willingness to enter into discussions with major parties to the conflict.

On January 28, 1982, President Reagan certified to Congress that "the Government of El Salvador is making a concerted and significant effort to comply with internationally recognized human rights," and is "achieving substantial control over all elements of the armed forces so as to bring to an end the indiscriminate torture and murder of Salvadorean citizens." The certification concluded that "there can be no doubt that much more must be done in these areas, but significant initial steps have been taken in this short timeframe. Progress is apparent and we have every reason to believe it will continue."[7]

The claims made by the Reagan Administration clashed with those of most other independent observers, such as the United Nations Human Rights Commission, the American Civil Liberties Union, and the Salvadorean Catholic Church, whose figures showed an increase in politically motivated deaths and violence at the hands of government troops between 1980 and 1981. Amnesty International, moreover, stated that "the pattern of abduction, torture and murder reported in the *Amnesty International Report 1981* was unchanged."[8]

Chairman of the House Inter-American Affairs Subcommittee of the Committee on Foreign Affairs Michael Barnes opened hearings on the certification by stating that "I am disappointed that the President of the United States would put his name to this document."[9] Chairman of the Foreign Affairs Subcommittee on Human Rights and International Organizations Don Bonker declared that "I, for one, am not and will not be satisfied with the Administration's attempts to conceal, excuse, or justify a consistent pattern of gross violations of internationally-recognized human rights in El Salvador. Any such certification is an affront to this Committee and the Congress, and a contravention of the spirit and the letter of the law."[10]

The Administration used the occasion of the certification hearings to raise the intensity of its language around El Salvador policy. Assistant Secretary of State for Inter-American Affairs Thomas Enders declared before a House Appropriations Subcommittee on February 1 that "the decisive battle for Central America"[11] was underway in El Salvador. Secretary of State Alexander Haig told the Senate Foreign Relations Committee the next day that the United States would do "whatever is necessary"[12] to defeat

---

[7] The White House, "Determination to Authorize Continued Assistance to El Salvador," Presidential Determination 82-4, Jan. 28, 1982.

[8] Amnesty International, "Press Release," Feb. 9, 1982.

[9] Opening statement of Rep. Michael Barnes, Hearings, House Foreign Affairs Subcommittees on Inter-American Affairs and on Human Rights and International Organizations, Feb. 2, 1982.

[10] Testimony of Rep. Don Bonker, *Ibid.*, p. 2.

[11] Testimony of Assistant Secretary of State for Inter-American Affairs Thomas Enders before the House Foreign Operations Subcommittee, Feb. 1, 1982, p. 3.

[12] Quoted in *The New York Times*, Feb. 3, 1982.

the Salvadorean insurgents. Responding to public fears that the United States was contemplating direct military involvement in El Salvador, Haig affirmed the following week that "there are no current plans for the use of American forces" in Central America.[13]

U.S. Military Aid to El Salvador and Central America

Emergency Funds to El Salvador

The content of the $55 million in emergency aid announced on February 1, 1982, represents a shift in the sophistication and kind of military support provided to El Salvador. Administration officials, in describing the aid to members of Congress, claimed that $25 million for aircraft was to replace equipment damaged during the guerrilla raid on the Ilopango Air Force Base. This is only partially true. The planes provided will give the Salvadorean Army a new air assault capability as yet unforeseen in the war, as well as the ability to coordinate ground and air attacks involving a large number of troops, especially from El Salvador's quick-reaction battalions.

The content of the $55 million in emergency aid is as follows:[14]

12 UH-1H Bell "Huey" helicopters
8 Cessna A-37B "Dragonfly" counterinsurgency jet fighters
4 C-123K troop transports
4 Cessna O-2A "Skymaster" forward air control spotter planes

	$25.0 million
Improve ground force capability (equip two quick reaction battalions; replace G-3 rifles with M-16s)	13.5
Establish and equip military intelligence school	1.0
Decentralize command and control and enhance capability (improve communications networks)	2.0
Security and illumination systems (night vision devices, flares, airfield security, etc.)	1.0
Spare parts, administrative and logistics costs	7.5
Training related to above equipment	5.0
Total	$55.0 million

A description of the aircraft provided to El Salvador is as follows:

Bell UH-1H "Huey" helicopter—standard Army transport helicopter with room for a pilot and 11-14 troops; can be armed with door-mounted machine gunships and rocket pods.[15]

Cessna A-37B "Dragonfly"—intended for armed counterinsurgency operations from short, unimproved airstrips; each wing has four underwing

---

[13] Quoted in *The New York Times*, Feb. 8, 1982.

[14] Interview, U.S. Defense Security Assistance Agency, Feb., 1982.

[15] John W.R. Taylor, ed., *Jane's All the World's Aircraft 1976-77*, London: Jane's Yearbooks, p. 227.

pylon stations: two inner ones can carry 870 lb. bombs, next one can carry 600 lb. bomb, outermost one can carry 500 lb. bomb; has a 7.62 mm minigun established in the forward fuselage.[16]

C-123K transports—jet transport plane no longer used by the U.S. Army; can carry 58 fully equipped troops or 54,000 lbs. of cargo.

Cessna O-2A "Skymaster"—equipped for forward air controller missions, including visual reconnaissance, target identification, target marking, ground-to-air coordination, and damage assessment; four underwing pylons carry rockets, flares, or other light ordinance such as a 7.62 mm. minigun; seats 4-6.[17]

The Caribbean Basin Initiative

In addition to the $55 million in emergency funds for El Salvador, the Reagan Administration is requesting an additional $35 million in military aid and $128 million in economic aid as part of its Caribbean Basin development initiative. A preliminary list of the military aid for El Salvador includes:[18]

Improve ground force capability	$12 million
Expand and develop command and control (communications, intelligence, etc.)	3
Ammunition	5
Logistics—management, repair, storage of weapons	4
Improve naval capability (boats, radar, communications, etc.)	8
Upgrade support units (engineers, maintenance, communications units, etc.)	3
Total	$35.0 million

Honduras is also slated to receive $17 million in military aid as part of the Caribbean Basin Initiative. This aid will include communications gear, trucks, jeeps, and other vehicles, UH-1H helicopters, transport aircraft, spare parts, personal equipment (uniforms, boots, etc.), training, and the overhaul of patrol boats.[19]

Fiscal Year 1983—Administration Requests

In Fiscal Year 1983, the Administration is asking Congress to approve another $61.3 million in military aid to El Salvador, as well as $164.9 million in economic aid. This brings to a total of $202.3 million the amount of military aid approved or requested for El Salvador by the Reagan Administration, as opposed to $16.5 million approved by Presient Carter.

---

[16] *Ibid.*, p. 266.

[17] *Ibid.*, p. 267.

[18] Defense Security Assistance Agency, March 11, 1982.

[19] *Ibid.*

Military aid requests for other countries in Central America in Fiscal Year 1983 include:

Honduras—$14.5 million in Foreign Military Sales credits and $800,000 in training grants (International Military Education and Training Program);

Costa Rica—$150,000 in training grants;

Guatemala—$250,000 in training grants;

Panama—$5 million in Foreign Military Sales credits and $500,000 in training grants.[20]

U.S. Military Personnel in El Salvador and Honduras

El Salvador. As of March 3, 1982, forty-seven U.S. military personnel were stationed in El Salvador for the following purposes:[21]

5—staff of the U.S. Military Group at the U.S. Embassy

2—communications maintenance and repair

25—small unit training teams to train additional recruits for the Atlacatl rapid reaction battalion and support companies

1—medical technician

5—helicopter maintenance

2—electronics maintenance (repair of radar, helicopter avionics, etc.)

4—logistics, communications, and maintenance to establish depots and maintenance centers at the national level

3—engineer training (repair of bridges, roads, etc.)

47—total

Beginning in September 1981 the United States also had one three-man tactical intelligence team to assist in the setting up of the Salvadorean Tactical Intelligence Center. In November 1981 U.S. personnel began intensive training of Salvadoreans in the gathering and analysis of military intelligence.[22]

Honduras. On March 19 State Department spokesman Dean Fischer announced that approximately 100 U.S. military personnel were stationed in Honduras "training the Honduran military in such technical areas as helicopter maintenance, air base security, patrol boat maintenance, and communications."[23] Pentagon spokesmen in Washington also indicated that the trainers included members of the U.S. Special Forces (Green Berets) providing training in small unit tactics and border patrol. The spokesmen

---

[20] U.S. Department of Defense, request to Congress for Fiscal Year 1983 military aid, Appendix A, p. 3.

[21] Interview, U.S. Department of Defense, March 7, 1982.

[22] U.S. Department of State, Reports on U.S. Military Personnel in El Salvador, Jan. and Feb., 1982.

[23] Quoted in *The New York Times*, March 20, 1982.

added that because the number of U.S. personnel "change too frequently for us to keep tabs," a specific breakdown of the U.S. trainers and their function was unavailable.[24]

A spokesman at the U.S. Embassy in Honduras said that the purpose of the training was to help Honduras improve the defensive capacity of the Honduran armed forces as well as to assist the Hondurans in blocking arms shipments through Honduras to El Salvador.[25] However, *The Washington Post*, in a March 1982 series on U.S. covert activities directed against Nicaragua, reported that

> As a separate part of the U.S. strategy in the region, the U.S. military currently is engaged in two operations in neighboring Honduras to indirectly support anti-Nicaragua efforts, informed administration officials said.[26]

In early February 1982, several U.S. military officers began visiting the Honduran Army command post in Puerto Lempira near the Nicaraguan border, an area populated largely by Miskitu Indians. Nicaraguan exile groups are known to have provided military training for Miskitu refugees camped near Puerto Lempira. The Honduran Army has sent a battalion to the port and has requested communications equipment from the United States for use in the area.[27]

The number of U.S. military personnel in Honduras is a dramatic increase from last summer, when the State Department announced that there were 21 U.S. military personnel in Honduras. U.S. trainers first arrived in early 1980 to provide assistance in border security operations and training in urban counter-guerrilla techniques. After March 1980, when the United States provided Honduras with 10 Bell UH-1H helicopters under a no-cost lease program, other trainers arrived to provide pilot and maintenance training.[28]

U.S. Training of Salvadorean Soldiers

The training of 1600 Salvadorean officers announced by Deputy Secretary of Defense Fred Iklé on December 15, 1981, began on January 9, 1982. Sixty officers and sergeants arrived at Fort Bragg, North Carolina, to begin one month of training in military leadership before the arrival of a 1000-troop battalion in mid-February. According to U.S. Colonel Edward Richards, commander of the 7th Special Forces, the 1000-man quick reaction battalion would be trained in basic and advanced individual and unit skills, such as the use of weapons (M-16 rifles, 60 mm. mortars, 90 mm. recoilless rifles, M-79 grenade launchers, etc.), day and night land

---

[24] Interview, U.S. Department of Defense, March 26, 1982.

[25] *The Washington Post*, March 20, 1982.

[26] *The Washington Post*, March 10, 1982.

[27] *The New York Times*, Feb. 21, 1982.

[28] Documents received by the author under the Freedom of Information Act; see also "Update No. 5, Background Information on Honduras and El Salvador and U.S. Military Assistance to Central America," Institute for Policy Studies *Resource*, Aug., 1981.

navigation, medical combat support, and leadership.[29] Fort Bragg is the home of the U.S. Special Forces (Green Berets) and the 82nd Airborne. The last contingent of Salvadorean officers arrived at Fort Bragg on February 13.

In addition, the entire student body of the Salvadorean military academy arrived at Fort Benning, Georgia from mid-January to mid-February 1982. The officers were to be trained in leadership, tactics, maintenance, and "troop leading procedures."[30] The Salvadorean Army has been plagued by a critical lack of trained officers to meet its expansion to a size of over 12,000 men.

The United States has undertaken three major efforts to train Salvadorean recruits for quick-reaction counterinsurgency battalions:

- in March 1981 when 15 Green Berets formed part of the contingent of U.S. trainers dispatched to El Salvador by President Reagan;

- in January 1982 when soldiers began arriving at Fort Bragg to be trained as an entire unit;

- in the first months of 1982 as 25 U.S. Green Berets in El Salvador continued training for a steady stream of recruits for the rapid-reaction and support units.

Although Pentagon sources would not confirm the precise content of the training at Fort Bragg and Fort Benning, the kind of equipment recently provided to El Salvador, as well as the fact that entire units are being trained at one time, suggest that U.S. and Salvadorean officers aim to create an air-mobile battalion, in which troops are transported to points of conflict in coordination with other ground units and the strike missions of counterinsurgency aircraft.

Intelligence Gathering

On February 24, 1982, Defense Department officials said that U.S. surveillance ships had been stationed for the last two months in the Gulf of Fonseca bordering El Salvador, Nicaragua, and Honduras. One intelligence vessel, the *Deyo*, was replaced by the *Caron* on February 24; both are Spruance-class destroyers fitted with sophisticated electronic surveillance devices. Defense Department officials stated that the ships were stationed in international waters, outside the three-mile zone of territorial waters claimed by each country.[31] President José Napoleón Duarte of El Salvador, however, indicated that the U.S. vessels entered the portion of the Gulf of Fonseca corresponding to El Salvador, and that the decision to allow the ship to enter the Gulf was made by the Salvadorean armed forces.[32]

According to Pentagon sources, sensitive eavesdropping gear aboard the ships can intercept high frequency radio transmissions and other com-

---

[29] *Montclair Star Ledger*, Jan. 10, 1982.

[30] AP, Dec. 24, 1981.

[31] *The Washington Post*, Feb. 24, 1982; *The New York Times*, Feb. 25, 1982.

[32] *Foreign Broadcast Information Service*, March 1, 1982.

munications ashore; these sources add that the intelligence gathered can enable officials to pinpoint guerrilla positions inside El Salvador, as well as to locate the source of command and control. The devices are also capable of monitoring other government communications in Nicaragua and El Salvador.[33] The State Department's special report on "Nicaraguan Support for the Salvadorean Insurgency" claimed that Salvadorean guerrillas' military, communications, and propaganda headquarters were outside the Nicaraguan capital of Managua.

Base Rights

As part of its effort to increase intelligence-gathering and military capabilities in Central America and the Caribbean, the Reagan Administration is also considering re-opening parts of a U.S. Navy air, sea, and submarine base at Key West, Florida.[34] Recently, the Navy has stationed several fast hydrofoil patrol boats carrying Harpoon anti-ship missiles at the base, and is considering re-opening the 76-acre Truman Annex to accommodate up to six destroyers. According to the Pentagon, the destroyer group would serve to enhance anti-submarine warfare capabilities against threats from Cuba.

In early March 1982, Secretary of Defense Caspar Weinberger told two House subcommittees that the United States was conducting conversations with Latin American countries over the use by the United States of regional military facilities in case of an emergency. The State Department confirmed on March 3 that two countries were specifically Honduras and Colombia. State Department spokesman Dean Fischer told reporters that the United States would seek permission to improve airfields in Honduras and Colombia and use them for training, search and rescue, relief flights, "and for such other activities as agreed upon by the two countries."[35] The Defense Department's Fiscal Year 1983 military construction budget calls for $21 million for "airfield improvements in the Western Caribbean area."[36]

---

[33] Interviews, U.S. Department of Defense and Department of State, Feb.26-March 7, 1982.

[34] The Washington Post, Feb. 13, 1982.

[35] The New York Times, March 4, 1982.

[36] Ibid.

Victims of the Massacre
that the World Ignored*

By David Blundy

Lolita Guardado was awoken at about 4 a.m. by a strange noise. There was the usual sound of the persistent drizzle pouring through the roof of closely packed palm leaves and through the walls of mud sticks.

But outside, across the Sumpul river, she could hear men shouting. Groups of peasants gathered anxiously in the grey dawn to watch as Honduran soldiers formed a line on the far bank and ran to and fro, carrying stones from the riverbed. They built a low wall. Only later that day, after her family, friends and neighbors had been slaughtered did she fully understand why they were there.

Lolita, her husband Genaro and their eight children are Salvadorean peasants. They lived, along with about 1,500 others, in Las Aradas, a settlement which lies a few yards inside the Salvadorean border on the banks of the Sumpul, the frontier with Honduras.

There were few comforts. Lolita was considered fortunate because at least she had a hut. Most of the others lived under trees, with sheets of plastic to protect them from the rain. There was no electricity, no clean water, no medicine, barely enough food and no road. But Las Aradas, they believed, had one virtue. It was so remote that they were safe from the violence between the left and the right that wracks El Salvador. They had fled from their houses and land—away from the soldiers, the national guard, the secret police, the right-wing death squads and left-wing guerrillas to this haven.

That morning a group of 300 peasant refugees, mostly women and children, had arrived after a three-day trek through the Salvadorean mountains. Few of them would survive the day.

As Margarita López, a bright and pretty 16-year-old was preparing tortillas for the new refugees, 300 Salvadorean soldiers from Chalatenango army base were already taking up position behind the nearest hills. Beside them, merging into the forest, were two olive-green helicopter gunships, each with machine guns and bombs. On the other side of the Sumpul, 150 Honduran soldiers stood behind their stone wall.

El Salvador and Honduras, although technically still at war after 11 years, were about to carry out their first joint military venture. The Salvadoreans call it an "operación de limpieza"—a cleaning operation.

The decision to carry out the attack was made, according to Honduran sources, at a joint meeting between Honduran and Salvadorean military commanders at El Poy, a town on the border about 13 miles from Las Aradas.

---

*This news article originally appeared in the *Sunday Times of London*, February 22, 1981. David Blundy is a reporter for the *London Times*.

The motive was clear. In the border area are the camps of the left-wing guerrillas, against whom the Salvadorean ruling junta has been fighting a bloody civil war. It is also one of the main channels for arms shipments from Nicaragua and Cuba. The Hondurans were keen to help because they feared both the war spilling over into their territory and their neighbor falling into communist hands.

The only flaw in the plan was that Las Aradas was not a guerrilla base. It seems not a shot was fired in defense by the people there. But for the Salvadorean military mind, the distinction between peasant and guerrilla is academic: they are, indeed, often one and the same.

Also, the guerrillas need peasant support if they are to achieve popular insurrection, and more immediately they need the peasants to provide food and shelter when necessary. For the Salvadoreans this made the peasants a fair military target.

The "cleaning" began at about 10 am on May 14 last year. Margarita remembers a deafening explosion of gunfire which would continue for the next six hours: "the bullets came in fistfuls. They went through the walls of houses, people were falling and cattle were dying. The bullets were everywhere."

Genaro Guardado heard the thud of bombs falling outside his hut. With his 17-year-old daughter, Ernestina, he grabbed five children, all under 12, who were standing outside, and ran; Rosabel Sibrían, a 22-year-old, saw the gunships buzzing low over the trees and heard the rattle of their machine guns. Then he saw soldiers standing round his friend, Amanda Rodríguez: "She begged them not to kill her. They all opened fire. They shot her 11-year-old son."

The troops had surrounded the settlement. The obvious escape route was across the river into Honduras—that was when the peasants learnt the function of the Honduran solders.

The peasants "ran to the river in flocks," said Genaro. It was the beginning of the rainy season and the river was flowing deep and fast. Margarita ran into the water and found it came up to her neck: "Children were drowning. The Salvadorean soldiers stood on the bank and fired at us. My two friends were killed next to me."

As Genaro jumped into the water with about 70 people, his daughter Ernestina was shot dead in the back of the head. First he walked, pulling the five children, across to the other bank. He left them there and went back for Ernestina's body. Then, carrying the body, he walked up the bank towards the Honduran soldiers: "They grabbed Ernestina and threw her into the river. Then they pushed us back into the river. We pleaded with them. Begged them. They just pushed us. They didn't fire their rifles, but they wouldn't let us through."

He returned to the Salvadorean side, to face the guns. "The Salvadoreans fired from the hip and kept their guns low. I suppose they didn't want to shoot the Honduran soldiers. But they fired into the river." Those who survived the crossing were herded together by the Salvadorean soldiers, who tied their hands and made them lie face down on the ground. "They beat us with their rifle butts. They kept asking, 'Where do you keep the guns? Who are the guerrillas?' "

"They took groups to one side and machine-gunned them. I had my children with me. Then a soldier cut my bonds. I don't know why he did that. But I ran with my children. Only three others survived."

Rosabel Sibrían, who hid between some rocks, says the main slaughter took place on the river bank, near Las Aradas: "There were 50 soldiers and they gathered a big group together. Then they shot them. The people were screaming. Those who would not die were beaten on the heads with rifle butts."

He says, and this is corroborated by other eye-witnesses, that the soldiers were aided by members of Orden, a paramilitary right-wing group, distinctive in their black shirts with skull-and-crossbones insignia. "Some soldiers and Orden people gathered children and babies together," said Sibrían. "I saw them throw children into the air and then slash them with long machetes. They cut their heads off and slit their bodies in two." One soldier told the mother of a child: "We are killing the children of subversion."

Sibrían tried to run downstream, carrying his baby son. Soldiers chased him and a bullet smashed into Sibrían's leg: "I couldn't run with my baby any more. I left him beside a small ditch, then rolled away and crawled through the bushes. I thought the soldiers would kill him." But, in one of the few acts of humanity carried out by the Salvadorean army that day, they did not. "They picked him up very gently and carried him away. Later I heard they bought him milk in a local town. I think he is in a children's camp. I am trying to find him," said Sibrían.

Lolita was not so fortunate. Just after the first bombs dropped at 10 am, she had lost sight of her husband. So, with her brother-in-law, Angel, and three of her children, she made her way slowly upstream, hiding for long periods in the bushes until soldiers and paramilitary men had passed. She went for a mile along the Sumpul until the cordon of Honduran soldiers on the opposite bank had ended. Then at about 4 pm she started to cross the river.

She walked over the rocks and had just reached the water when she heard rapid firing behind her and felt "a burning pain" all over her body. She fell backwards into the Sumpul. Her body lay in the water, her head resting on a rock. She had been hit by 15 bullets, in an arc from her thigh across the small of her back. One bullet passed through her hand. Two of her children lay dying in the water beside her. One died quickly—a bullet had passed through his armpit into his chest: the other, shot in the testicles, did not. "He lasted half an hour," said Lolita. "I couldn't move. I couldn't comfort him." Her brother-in-law was dead, too. She lay with her surviving child three-year-old Ovidio, clasped to her breast. He had been hit in the leg and the scalp.

"Ovidio kept crying and shouting. He called out 'Uncle Angel, Uncle Angel! Come. Come see my mother. Her leg is bleeding into the water.' He kept talking to his two brothers long after they were dead. He shouted at them: 'Why don't you talk to me?' "

After dark, Lolita says that occasionally soldiers walked along the bank. She tried to hold Ovidio still and keep him quiet: "The baby cried with pain, but I told him to be silent. I heard a soldier say: 'Hit them. Hit them again.' But another soldier said: 'I have hit them already. Let's not shoot again. They will just die.'

"I had a terrible thirst. The water was full of blood. It was the blood of my children. But I kept drinking water, drinking water."

That night she felt an object bump against her in the river. Then it floated off downstream. It was, she says, the head of a child. The next morning a Honduran fisherman pulled in his nets. They contained the bodies of three dismembered children.

Lolita lay in the river until after dawn, when a group of four Honduran men saw Ovidio moving. They crossed the river and put Lolita in a hammock, then carried her to a Honduran's home. It was another 15 days before she received hospital treatment.

For the peasants, the behavior of the army at Las Aradas was not new, just a little more extreme than usual. The Salvadorean soldiers have a single tactic to discourage peasant support for guerrillas—terror. Lolita and her husband had fled to Las Aradas after soldiers had decapitated some of their neighbors. The heads had been left neatly by the side of the road to ram the lesson home. Most refugees have stories of such appalling brutality it is difficult to believe that it became almost a way of life.

Officially they were all victims of a massacre that never happened. The government of El Salvador has denied that any killings took place at the Sumpul river on May 14. On June 25, the military leader of Honduras, President Policarpo Paz García, said on national radio that the massacre did not happen. One of his army chiefs, however, Colonel Rubén Montoya, head of the third military region, denied that the Honduran army had taken part, while admitting that the incident took place: "The Honduran troops did not help in killings of civilians."

At first the American embassy in Tegucigalpa, the Honduran capital, told reporters that there was no evidence to support claims of a massacre. But like the government, the Americans later changed their line, admitting "something happened" at the Sumpul river that day.

At noon the day after the massacre, a Roman Catholic priest from the Capuchin order walked over the hills towards the Sumpul. If he had not, then the massacre might have become just peasant folklore. Father Earl Gallagher, 35, comes from Brooklyn, New York City. He has worked in Honduras for four years. Because of his prematurely grey hair and prowess at climbing the hills, he is known by the peasants as "the old billy goat."

He noticed that the river banks looked strangely black. When he got closer he saw why. They were covered in a thick carpet of buzzards. In the village of Talquinta he met his first survivor, a 10-year-old boy with bullet wounds in his mouth, thigh and shoulder.

"I heard that Salvadorean troops were coming back to kill the survivors," said Gallagher. "I felt I had to make it public and perhaps that would help them." It did not help the little boy. A month later he fled from the Honduran army back to El Salvador, where he was killed.

Gallagher returned with a camera and tape-recorder and took down the stories of dozens of survivors. He could not visit the Sumpul itself because it was still patrolled by members of Orden, who shot intruders. Meanwhile, dogs and buzzards picked the bodies clean.

On June 24, Gallagher's report condemning the massacre and the role of the soldiers of both El Salvador and Honduras was published as a joint declaration by the priests of Santa Rosa de Copán.

Gallagher immediately received death threats over El Salvador Radio. He was threatened with expulsion and condemned by the Honduran government. The then minister of foreign affairs, Eliseo Pérez Cadalso, said on July 1: "The church declaration responds to a well-orchestrated campaign with the purpose of destabilising the convivial and highly democratic climate in which the people of Honduras live."

Gallagher's report reached Washington, where the only person who paid attention was Senator Edward Kennedy. He had it placed on the congressional record on September 24, and said: "I am deeply concerned by reports of increasing hardship and often death that face innocent men, women and children who try to escape the escalating violence in El Salvador."

But the world paid scant attention, inured perhaps by the daily stories of violence in Latin America. The Sumpul massacre was mentioned in a few newspapers which ran part of Gallagher's report. It was almost completely ignored by the American press at the time. "Our thing was: it happened. Come and have a look. And nobody did," said Gallagher.

The misery for the Sumpul survivors and the 29,000 refugees who have fled El Salvador for Honduras did not end on May 14.

"They live in fear," Gallagher said last week. "Their only hope is international attention."

He and other priests have compiled a list of incidents against refugees since the massacre. It runs into several pages, a litany of murder, rape and cruelty.

Hundreds of refugees have been handed to Salvadorean troops to face certain death. In the Honduran town of Santa Rosa last week an 18-year-old girl described her life in El Salvador. She lived near the Honduran border with her husband until soldiers took him away and shot him. She moved in with her four brothers. Last year, Salvadorean national guards took them out of the house and sprayed them with liquid from cans they carried. "Their skin went black. Their eyes melted;" she said. Her brothers were pushed into a cornfield and killed with machetes.

Last week we spoke to Lolita, who now lives with her husband and five remaining children in an adobe hut deep in the Honduran hills. Life for her is not convivial. She is afraid, and for good reason. The Honduran government has refused, at the urging of El Salvador, to grant Lolita or the other refugees "refugee status." This means their movements are tightly restricted and they cannot find work. They are constantly threatened with expulsion.

There are also signs that the Honduran government is growing more repressive. A week ago a colleague of Gallagher's, Father Fausto Milla, was arrested by security men. He was blindfolded and interrogated for three days. He had just returned from a human rights conference in Mexico City where he presented the testimony of Lolita and other Sumpul survivors.

The day we saw Lolita, she had been visited by a Honduran security man, who threatened her with expulsion back to El Salvador. "They may as well kill me here," she said. "It's easier."

Human Rights in Nicaragua, 1982*

Americas Watch Committee

In sharp contrast to the Guatemalan and Salvadorean governments' systematic repression, the Sandinista government of Nicaragua has compiled a very good record on human rights, as the report excerpted below documents. After conducting a detailed investigation, the nonpartisan human rights monitoring group Americas Watch concluded that torture and "disappearance" (i.e., kidnap and murder by security forces) are practically nonexistent in Nicaragua. The investigators find fault with the way the government carried out the relocation of the Miskitu Indians, but feel that it had reasonable grounds for believing that they had to be moved from the border area. While the authors of the report express certain reservations, their overall tone is a positive one.

[On torture]

We found widespread agreement, even among the Government's strongest critics, that physical torture is not practiced in Nicaragua today. The physical treatment of prisoners is not ideal and is, in some respects, unsatisfactory; nevertheless, we were advised by virtually all persons with whom we met that, to the best of their knowledge, those forms of torture routinely practiced in some Latin American countries—severe beatings, electric shock, intentional near drowning, and the like—have been effectively eliminated by the Nicaraguan Government. Not one person with whom we spoke reported having been tortured, and those of our sources who observed the operations of Nicaragua's police, security and prison services told us that torture simply is not practiced or sanctioned by the Government.

[On "disappearances"]

"Disappearances"—illegal and unacknowledged abductions—are not common in Nicaragua, as they have been in Argentina and El Salvador in recent years. Indeed, we found no credible evidence—or reports—of

---

*Excerpted and abridged from a report by Americas Watch.

either the use or tolerance of widespread disappearances on the part of the Government or of any real fear of such acts by those opposed to the present government.

We believe that the Nicaraguan Government does not maintain or condone a policy of forced disappearances of political dissidents or other Nicaraguan citizens. There is, to the best of our knowledge, no systematic use of unacknowledged arrests by Governmental bodies to suppress dissent, to shield themselves from judicial or other inquiries, to facilitate interrogation or to dispose of victims without risking criminal punishment. Nor does there appear to be a Governmental practice to use clandestine detention centers or to conduct secret, extra-legal arrests.

[On the relocation of the Miskitus][1]

Nicaragua has experienced a series of border attacks across the Rio Coco during the past six months, resulting in casulties to the Nicaraguan armed forces and some destruction of Government property. Particularly in the context of continuing military threats against its Government, Nicaragua is plainly entitled to defend its territorial integrity and to take those reasonable actions which it believes are necessary for that purpose. In our view, this right may, at least where a nation's security is threatened, include the power to evacuate civilians within a reasonably defined border area. Under the circumstances present in Nicaragua today, we are not able to say that the Government was unreasonable in determining that such an evacuation was necessary in order to defend the Rio Coco border region.

[As a prerequisite to returning the Miskitus to their native villages,] Nicaragua will undoubtedly wish assurances from Honduras and the United States, as well as from the Miskitu leadership, that the repopulated areas will not be used for border raids or guerrilla activities against the Government. By furnishing such assurances, the United States and Honduras could contribute significantly to the welfare of the Miskitus. By suspending military, financial and other aid to those engaged in guerrilla activities against the Nicaraguan Government, the United States and Honduras can assist in reestablishing the full measure of freedom rightfully belonging to the Miskitus. Conversely, continuing support for such operations by the United States or Honduras must ultimately require those states to bear a measure of responsibility, together with Nicaragua, for the inability of the Miskitu people to return to their former homes and villages.

---

[1]This is excerpted from a long section which includes some strong criticisms of the way in which the Sandinista government carried out this project.—Ed.

6

The Church and Liberation

Over the past two decades, the Catholic Church in Latin America has sought to resolve a crisis which reverberates all the way back to the Vatican. Already by the late 1950s, growing difficulties in clerical recruitment and the decline in lay participation indicated something was amiss. The swelling ranks of the poor and the sharpening of social inequities had created conditions ripe for social upheaval, but the Church appeared dangerously removed from the vast majority of its constituents—the poor and the destitute. In his encyclicals, Pope John XXIII astutely redirected the Church's attention to the world's poor, setting the stage for Vatican II during his papacy. An outgrowth of Vatican II, the 1968 Latin American Bishops' Conference in Medellín, Colombia, inspired many within the Church to focus their energy on alleviating injustice and oppression. Nowhere was the need for action more urgent than in Central America.

This chapter examines that segment of the Church which has made a clear and uncompromising commitment to the indigent majority in Central America. This progressive faction, like the population at large, is dominated by Catholics, but also includes the participation of some Protestants. Together, they lead a new religious movement that is deeply committed to the process of liberation, and can be credited with both the new dynamism kindling within the Church and the visible resurgence of lay participation.

For religious workers, siding with the poor and oppressed in Central America has involved the acceptance of conflict as a way of life, and the adoption of a secular posture with revolutionary overtones. In light of the significance which revolution and social transformation bear, it is understandable that the growing popularity of this stance should have fomented intraecclesial division.

Radicalizing Effects

Living and experiencing the daily hardships of the poor forced many religious people in Central America to reevaluate their personal commitment to the values and ideals of Christianity. For many, this exposure led to a radicalization of their social outlook. The late archbishop of El Salvador, Monsignor Oscar Arnulfo Romero, underwent a profound transformation in his views as he witnessed the needs and hopes of the poor dashed by the violence of those who serve the privileged classes. He became

344

the "voice of the voiceless" in El Salvador, and his Sunday homilies evoked a clear, constant denunciation of injustice. Pleading with soldiers not to kill their "brothers and sisters," he spoke of the role Christians should assume: "A Christian who does not wish to live this commitment of solidarity with the poor is not worthy of the name Christian ... we are incarnated in the poor, we want a Church that is shoulder-to-shoulder with the poor of El Salvador." Because of its revolutionary overtones, this interpretation of Christianity was, and remains, totally unacceptable to the privileged classes in El Salvador. On March 24, 1980, Monsignor Romero was gunned down by the same death squads he had denounced in his sermons.

A Legacy of Power

Until this century, the interests of the Catholic Church in Latin America were tightly interwoven with the wealthy and politically powerful sectors of society. Early in the conquest of Latin America, colonial administrators received ecclesiastical authority when the papacy gave the Castilian monarchy full supervision over the religious establishment in return for the conversion of Native Americans and the maintenance of the Church. Thus, the Curia legitimized hierarchy, subordination and control by the state over the population. The ecclesiastical establishment financed and administered schools, hospitals and charities, which encouraged abiding loyalty to the state.

However, the Church's functions were even more extensive than this. Religious endowments in convents, monasteries and other church facilities in fact supplied investment funds to mineowners, merchants and landlords. From Church funds in America flowed income to maintain ecclesiastical offices and establishments in Spain, Portugal, and ultimately the Vatican. In return, colonial churchmen contributed to the stability of the colonial state and society by exhorting parishioners to be faithful to the monarchy and its local representatives. Although it is important to realize there were a handful of clergymen who opposed this arrangement, they had little voice in deciding Church affairs. In sum, the interpenetration of church and state kept the Church allied to the powerful, and nourished a spirit of conservatism among the Church hierarchy.

Centuries of colonialism and global capitalist expansion saw transformations of the social class structure and concomitant shifting of Church-class alliances. Ideologically, some segments of the Church have evidenced little change since colonial times; yet other segments have experienced a sharp break from their colonial past and today ally themselves with the marginalized mass of Christians whose needs have so long been neglected. These ideological divisions within the Church have become an important characteristic of the Latin American polity.

The conservatives, for example, prefer the role of colonial Christianity, and they reject all modifications of the hierarchical structure. Although their strength has waned since the 1950s, the traditionalists' ideology survives in small, reactionary groups. The more moderate current, which is highly identified with recent papacies, opts for internal renewal of the Church and a clear distinction between the religious and political spheres. The moderate current can be credited with bringing about the Medellín Conference which, in turn, enabled the Church to house yet a more progressive current, the revolutionary Christians. This movement consolidated itself in the 1960s, but also reclaimed the heritage of "social protest" of some priests of the colonial era. It disengages itself from reformist views, moves beyond the separation of the religious and the political, and emphasizes the concept of "praxis"—integrating theory and practice. The theory is referred to as liberation theology; it translates into practice as grass-roots Christianity and the formation of Christian base communities.

Revolutionary Christianity

In its essence, the theological concept of liberation is biblical. But liberation theology in Latin America did not derive solely from the biblical themes of liberation, i.e. salvation, redemption, etc. Rather, it was born of the experience of oppression and biblical reflection in the worldly context of dependence and domination. In his renowned book, *A Theology of Liberation*, Gustavo Gutiérrez describes the liberation process at three levels:

1) liberation expresses the aspirations of oppressed peoples and social classes; this emphasizes the economic, social and political process which puts the poor at odds with the wealthy nations and oppressive classes;

2) at a deeper level, liberation can be applied to an understanding of history; man makes himself throughout history, and the gradual attainment of true freedom creates a new man and a qualitatively different society;

3) finally, in the Bible, Christ is presented as the Savior who liberates man from sin. Sin is the ultimate root of all disruption of friendship, injustice and oppression in both its individual and social dimensions. This liberation is the gift which Christ offers people: communion with God and other people.

For the progressive faction of the Church, an integral part of the process of liberation is the establishment of grass-roots communities, better known as Christian base communities (*comunidades eclesiales de base*) or CEB's. They have been instrumental in providing communal activities and services in rural areas and working-class neighborhoods in Central America. The work of the CEB's has also been conducive to raising the consciousness of those who were never given the opportunity to question the misery in which they live. The CEB's have become incorporated in pastoral work throughout many regions of Latin America. Leonardo Boff, a Brazilian theologian deeply involved in the CEB's, explains that "the Christian base community is the place where the theological essence of the Church is realized and, at the same time, the practice of liberation of the poor by the poor themselves." More specifically, the rural communities or working-class neighborhoods *become* the Church, and the Church becomes the catalyst for cooperative living and communal spirit.

What is key to the concept of the CEB's and what goes against the traditionalists' thinking is the decentralized or "horizontal" nature of the relationship between the Church and its constituency. The progressives feel that the only way the Church can become important to the lives of the poor, the needy, and the oppressed is if the poor themselves determine the relevancy of the Church and Christ's teachings to their own reality. With limited guidance from the clergy, the direct expression, communication and biblical reflection carried out in the CEB's can be conducive to forming a collective consciousness and revolutionary spirit.

A famous example of this type of community in Central America was Solentiname, which was formed on the islands of Lake Nicaragua during the Somoza dictatorship. Father Ernesto Cardenal, most recently the Minister of Culture in the Sandinista government, was instrumental in organizing this peasant community. Much has been written about the special qualities of Solentiname by visitors from all corners of the world. From Germany: "Solentiname is everywhere; it is the beginning of a more human world. It is Christian life—not just waiting for a better world, but working for their neighbors' peace, for peace with nature, for peace within the community." From Venezuela: "Solentiname is something so God-like and so much of this world that it is a place where poetry, painting, and the harvest do not divide people into poets and farmers, but constitute the solidarity of one life." The truth is that Solentiname was a revolutionary community whose members labored together and shared their reflections in a collective spirit. In addition to their artwork and handicrafts, they worked on the formation of producer-cooperatives. But repression by Somoza's National Guard resulted in the destruction of the community in October 1977. Shortly thereafter, Father Cardenal announced his incorporation into the FSLN guerrilla movement.

Concluding Remarks

The readings in this chapter suggest that the Church's progressive faction has become an inextricable component in the process of social change in Central America. The Church is so paramount in the beliefs and mores of most Central Americans that one cannot imagine a successful revolution without its active support and involvement. This is not to suggest that liberation is imminent. A deep ideological chasm persists between much of the clergy and the hierarchy, giving rise to equally profound divisions among the laity. Furthermore, there is the problem of mistrust in relations between believing and non-believing revolutionaries. Is their alliance only tactical and temporary, or will it lead to a long-lasting fraternity that will form the basis of a new society?

On the one hand, the Church has to make a conscious and visible effort to alter its legacy of being used as an instrument of counter-revolution. On the other, all revolutionaries must accept the importance of solidarity with a Church that nurtures the pursuit of liberation.

If there is a glimmer of hope in the series of Central America's endless tragedies, it is the example being set by Nicaragua. The participation by the clergy in the struggle to overthrow the Somoza dictatorship has carried over into an active role in the revolutionary Sandinista government.[1] While this has yet to resolve many lingering ideological tensions—within the clerical establishment, between revolutionary and non-revolutionary Christians, and between believing and non-believing revolutionaries—it has nevertheless impressed upon grass-roots Christians the importance of their contribution to the revolutionary process. Indeed, the experience of Christians in Nicaragua has given practical meaning to the words of Father Miguel d'Escoto: "Communion in liberation and hope is lived and celebrated in a Church born from the struggle of the people."

—John Althoff

The Church and Revolutionary Struggle in Central America*
By Blase Bonpane

Blase Bonpane is a professor of sociology at California State University, Northridge, and previously served as a Maryknoll priest in Guatemala.

The Cursillos de Capacitación Social (1962-1967)

The arrival of Pope John XXIII took many traditional churchmen by surprise. During his office, there was a new concern for primitive Christian values. The very pillars of rigidity, formalism, legalism, and triumphalism were under attack. The encyclical letters *Mater et magistra* and *Pacem in terris* identified the real devils as malnutrition, ignorance, and disease.[1] In the early 1960s the impact of the Vatican Council II was felt in Latin America. In Venezuela an enthusiastic program was started called *Los Cursillos de Capacitación Social* (Social Training Classes). At its inception the movement was simply a Catholic response to alleged communist infiltration in the university. As an anticommunist movement the cursillos sought the objective of Christian revolution in Latin America. The cursillos were developed throughout Central America by the Jesuits and the Maryknoll Fathers and Sisters working very closely with university and high school students. To the surprise of its founders, instead of their stated objectives,

---

[1] Father Miguel d'Escoto is Minister of International Relations; Father Edgar Parrales is Minister of Social Welfare; Father Ernesto Cardenal is Minister of Culture; and Father Fernando Cardenal is Director of the National Literacy Campaign and leader of the July 19 Sandinista Youth Movement.

*Excerpted from *Latin American Perspectives,* Issues 25/26, Spring/Summer 1980, Vol. VII, Nos. 2 and 3.

[1] Pope John XXIII, *Mater et magistra* (Washington, D.C.: National Catholic Welfare Conference, 1961).

the cursillos became an effective instrument of actual Marxist-Christian dialogue both in study and in action.[2]

By 1965 the cursillos were operating in a Central America where (except for Costa Rica) anything to the left of the Christian Democratic Party was under attack physically, and where thousands of the best educated citizens of Nicaragua, El Salvador, and Guatemala were being slaughtered in a vast institutional drive for political illiteracy.[3]

The cursillo leadership was saying that its objective for Central America was to create a Christian enterprise which was neither capitalist nor socialist, a society in which the profits of its owners would be shared by all the workers. The emphasis was on revolution: "We cannot Christianize capitalism with paternalistic patches. We will lose many of our privileges for the greater general betterment. There will be opposition, and armed resistance will be called for if necessary."[4]

The Cursillos de Capacitación Social were brought to the rural sectors of Central America by an experienced student vanguard together with priests and sisters who had been their mentors. The expropriation of unused lands was called for on behalf of the common good, and peasant leagues were fostered as essential to the obtainment of campesino justice.[5]

At an international convention of Cursillos de Capacitación Social in Costa Rica in January of 1967, a growing militancy was obvious. Many members had determined that philosophical Marxism had a deep rapport with Christianity. The *Populorum Progressio* of Pope Paul VI was observed as having a series of Marxist deviations. In the new encyclical, papal opposition to violent revolution was stated with such clear qualification in section 31 that many Central Americans considered the qualification to be a mandate for the support of their liberation armies:

We know, however, that a revolutionary uprising—save where there is manifest, long-standing tyranny which would do great damage to fundamental personal rights and dangerous harm to the common good of the country—produces new injustices, throws more elements out of balance and brings on new disasters.

Central American members of the cursillos were delighted with section 81 of the same encyclical letter:

It belongs to laymen, without waiting passively for orders and directives, to take the initiative freely and infuse a Christian spirit into the mentality, customs, laws and structures of the community in which they live.

Encouraged by what they considered a new papal directive, changes were made in the cursillo programs. Six-week literacy training programs

---

[2] Manuel Aguirre, and Jesús Rodríguez Jalón, *Cursillos de Capacitación Social* (Panama: Centro de Capacitación Social, 1965).

[3] Thomas and Marjorie Melville, *Guatemala: The Politics of Land Ownership* (New York: The Free Press, 1971).

[4] Centro de Capacitación Social, *Archivos*, Guatemala, 1966.

[5] *Ibid.*

were formed as well as day-long programs on hygiene, and meetings with peasants interested in forming leagues were organized. This constant exposure to the rural sector led to a better understanding of the guerrilla position. By 1967 armed rebels would appear unannounced at cursillo programs. They would speak privately and informally with participants and occasionally they would address the entire group. They often expressed admiration for the cursillo system but warned that as the movement grew it would be stopped. They urged the students to understand the importance of armed resistance. The deeply academic background of the guerrilla leadership together with their courage left the students with a sense of respect and admiration.[6]

In 1967 cursillos were stopped. This author was exiled from Guatemala and categorized by the Cardinal Archbishop of Guatemala as a "communist anti-Christ." Syndicated columnists from the United States began an investigative journalistic coverage of the Centro de Capacitación Social. News of "the Guerrillas of Peace" spread throughout the United States and Latin America, and the journalists correctly reported the mission of the Cursillos de Capacitación Social as one of the last effective non-violent programs in Central America. The reporting made it clear that the cursillos were more than a "paper" organization and that the movement represented a dynamic instrument of social and political awareness. A visible integration was taking place between urban students and Indian peasants, between Marxist humanists and Christian humanists.[7] The Central American Church would never be the same.

Observing the crisis in the cursillos, the leadership of the guerrilla organization Fuerzas Armadas Rebeldes (FAR) approached the former church group with a proposal for the leadership of both organizations to meet and discuss the future of the Central American revolution. At a farm house near Esquintla members of FAR and the cursillos reached a consensus that a Christian Revolutionary Front would bring different strata and classes of Central Americans together. Such a front would in no way oppose existing guerrilla groups but it would be a revolutionary call to the Christian Indian community. At this point Cursillos de Capacitación Social in Central America evolved from an anti-communist Catholic organization into an integrated movement toward social and political revolution.[8]

Hence the Cursillos de Capacitación Social represent at least one reason for the politicization of the Central American clergy in recent decades. It was an experience of a disciplined movement in complete communion with the people which led to a rapid raising of social and political consciousness.[9] "Communist" clergy have been branded as the enemy in El Salvador, Honduras, and Guatemala. Many church people have been arrested and some have been executed in the struggle for justice. The Church today

---

[6] *Ibid.*

[7] Blase A. Bonpane, "Priest on Guatemala," *The Washington Post*, February 2, 1968.

[8] Jeffrey M. Paige, *Agrarian Revolution* (New York: The Free Press, 1973), p. 120ff.

[9] Susanne Jonas and David Tobis, *Guatemala* (New York: North American Congress on Latin America, 1974).

can fortunately no longer be trusted as a stabilizing element in Central American dictatorial settings. Members of the Cursillos de Capacitación Social are participants in the formation of the Revolutionary Government of Nicaragua.

Conclusion

The Latin American Bishops Conference at Medellín, Colombia, in 1968 only gave added support to the priests and sisters involved in revolutionary change in Central America. Among those already deeply involved was Father Ernesto Cardenal, one of Latin America's best known poets, who organized the community of Solentiname on an island in Lake Nicaragua. The Gospel in Solentiname was primitive, clear, and revolutionary. It was not surprising, then, that Somoza's Guardia Nacional arrived on the island and destroyed the community. Father Cardenal, currently the Minister of Culture in the Revolutionary Junta of Nicaragua, responded with the following message:

> The government of Nicaragua has accused me of illicit association with the National Liberation Front of Sandino. Now (1978) is the moment which I declare publicly that I do belong to the FSLN and this is an honor.
>
> I consider it my duty as a poet and as a priest to belong to this movement. In these Latin American countries which are fighting for their liberation, the poet cannot be alien to the struggle of the people and much less can a priest. I belong to the FSLN above all because of my fidelity to the gospel. It is because I want a radical and profound change, a new and fraternal society in accord with the teachings of the gospels. It is because I consider this a priestly struggle as Camilo Torres said (Letter of Ernesto Cardenal, December 1968).

Opposition to repressive regimes in Central America is developing a church that is less visible, more ecumenical, less impacted with religiosity, and more bent on service. The concern for ritual correctness fades as the pursuit of justice becomes the focal point. Enemies of justice are no longer comfortable as members. Archbishop Miguel Obando y Bravo of Managua allowed his episcopal office to be used as a center for the Broad Front of Opposition during the revolutionary struggle in Nicaragua. The Archbishop recently issued a pastoral letter entitled, "A Christian Obligation for a New Nicaragua." It states in part:

> If socialism means, as it should, that the interests of the majority of Nicaraguans are paramount and if it includes a model of an economic system planned with the national interests in mind, that is in solidarity with and provides for increased participation by the people, we have no objections. Any social program that guarantees to use the country's wealth and resources for the common good, and that improves the quality of human life by satisfying the basic needs of all the people, seems to us to be a just program.

If socialism means that the injustice and traditional inequalities between the cities and the country, and between remuneration for intellectual and manual labor, will be progressively reduced, and if it means the participation of the worker in the fruit of his labor overcoming economic alienation, then there is nothing in Christianity that is at odds with this process.

If socialism implies that power is to be exercised by the majority and increasingly shared by the organized community so that power is actually transferred to the popular classes, then it should meet nothing in our Faith but encouragement and support. If socialism leads to cultural processes that awaken the dignity of the masses and give them the courage to assume responsibility and demand their rights, then it promotes the same type of human dignity proclaimed by our Faith (Carta Pastoral, 1979).

In many ways the impetus toward conversion and purification of the Central American Church has come from the forces outside the clergy. Students eager and willing to sacrifice their lives for the poor have challenged the Church hierarchy and have won some of them over to the struggle for justice. Many priests realize that their work for liberation includes the risk of losing their "good standing" in the institutional church, as was the case with Fathers Hidalgo and Morelos in Mexico. In any case, an irreversible dynamic has been released; it is the very catalyst of the hemispheric revolution and its potential was observed by Ernesto "Che" Guevara just prior to his death in 1967 when he stated:

Christians must definitely choose the revolution, and especially on our continent where the Christian faith is so important among the masses. When Christians begin to give an integral revolutionary witness, the Latin American revolution will be invincible. Until now, Christians have permitted their doctrines to be manipulated by reactionaries.[10]

Archbishop Romero: Martyr of Salvador*

By Plácido Erdozaín

Plácido Erdozaín is an Augustan priest who worked with Archbishop Romero in the Archdiocese of San Salvador.

Meetings continued with the priests, the Christian communities, and the Mass Revolutionary Coordinating Committee. At the University of Louvain, Belgium, our bishop received an honorary doctorate. He received this kind of recognition a number of times. He always wondered if responding to

---

[10] Hugo Assman, *Habla Fidel Castro sobre los cristianos revolucionarios* (Montevideo: Tierra Nueva, 1972) p. 7.

*Excerpted from *Archbishop Romero: Martyr of El Salvador*, translated by John McFadden and Ruth Warner (Maryknoll, N.Y: Orbis Books, 1980).

public awards really benefited the people or not. When he was nominated as a candidate for the Nobel Peace Prize, he said it was something like being nominated in the Miss Universe contest, but that if it gave some kind of protection to the people he would go through with it. He knew that he had to speak in strong terms, but because the truth was not getting out. He made his speech at Louvain perfectly clear. It was February 2, 1980:

> *The course taken by the Church has always had political repercussions. The problem is how to direct the influence so that it will be in accordance with the faith.*

> *The world that the Church must serve is the world of the poor, and the poor are the ones who decide what it means for the Church to really live in the world.*

He made it clear that the Church does not have a political program of its own, but rather that its role is to keep alive the hope that the people have in their own historical march forward:

> *The hope that the Church fosters is a call ... to the poor, the vast majority, that they take responsibility for their own future, that they conscientize themselves, that they organize; ... the call is one of support for their just causes and demands.*

> *It is the poor who force us to understand what is really taking place.... The persecution of the Church is a result of defending the poor. Our persecution is nothing more nor less than sharing in the destiny of the poor.*

> *The poor are the body of Christ today. Through them he lives on in history.*

He expanded on the situation of the poor in El Salvador with words that came close to poetry:

> *The Church has committed itself to the world of the poor.... The words of the prophets of Israel still hold true for us: there are those who would sell a just man for money, and a poor man for a pair of sandals. There are those who fill their houses with violence, fill their houses with what they have stolen. There are those who crush the poor ... while lying on beds of the most exquisite marble. There are those who take over house after house, field after field, until they own the whole territory and are the only ones in it.*

What hurt Bishop Romero the most was to see the intrinsic evil of the economic system, which revealed its deadly consequences most clearly in dependent countries such as El Salvador. On one occasion when the cathedral was surrounded by soldiers, he preached once again, "How evil this system must be to pit the poor against the poor; the peasant in the army uniform against the worker peasant." But he was even more anguished to see the faith being manipulated to serve the goals of oppression. In an interview given to *Prensa Latina* at the same time, he said, "The situation of injustice is so bad that the faith itself has been perverted; the faith is being used to defend the financial interests of the oligarchy."

This was the reason for his urgent pleas to the Christians involved in the revolutionary organizations that they maintain their Christian identity within the struggle and that they find a new way to make it explicit:

> *Those who are involved in the process of liberation in our country can be assured that the Church will continue to accompany them—with the authentic voice of the gospel.*

> *Christians who belong to ecclesial base communities ... the Church challenges you to reach out to a goal that will be politically valid. Christians, in this difficult hour, our country needs liberators who are morally good and a liberation that is socially authentic.*

Preparing to Die

During the final days of February 1980, we celebrated the annual priests' retreat. All of the priests from the archdiocese participated in this week of reflection and spiritual encounter. That year it had a special meaning. Like Jesus at the last supper, Bishop Romero felt the walls closing in on him. After the retreat he said in an interview with the Mexican newspaper *Excelsior*:

> *My life has been threatened many times. I have to confess that, as a Christian, I don't believe in death without resurrection. If they kill me, I will rise again in the Salvadorean people. I'm not boasting, or saying this out of pride, but rather as humbly as I can.*

> *As a shepherd, I am obliged by divine law to give my life for those I love, for the entire Salvadorean people, including those Salvadoreans who threaten to assassinate me. If they should go so far as to carry out their threats, I want you to know that I now offer my blood to God for justice and the resurrection of El Salvador.*

It is in the light of his personal beliefs, his commitment to and solidarity with the poor, and his dialogue with the Mass Revolutionary Coordinating Committee—representing the poor—that we should understand the clarity with which Bishop Romero identified the people's enemies. Our bishop felt his death coming closer day by day. On February 18 a bomb had destroyed the YSAX offices, the radio station of the archdiocese, the "stronghold of truth" as he called it that very day. Then on March 9, a suitcase filled with dynamite had been placed in the church where he was to celebrate Mass for Mario Zamora, another assassination victim.

At Louvain he had already said, "I have warned the oligarchy time and time again to open their hands, give away their fancy rings, because if they don't, the time will come when they will be cut off."

In the famous interview with *Prensa Latina* he was much more explicit:

> *The cause of the evil here is the oligarchy, a small nucleus of families who don't care about the hunger of people. ... To maintain and increase their margin of profits, they repress the people.*

The assassinated priests—martyrs of the God of the poor, martyrs of the poor of God—helped him see the truth clearly:

Those exemplary priests deserve great admiration.... They were victims of the effort to maintain an unjust system.... Neto Barrera, Rutilio Grande, Alfonso Navarro, Octavio Ortíz, and the others had great insight; they grasped reality with great clarity and saw that the common enemy of our people is the oligarchy.

Letter to President Carter, February 17, 1980

Your Excellency,
President of the United
    States of America,
Mr. Jimmy Carter

Mr. President:

In recent days a news item has appeared in the national press that causes me great concern. According to the newspapers, your government is studying the possibility of supporting, by economic and military aid, the junta that is presently governing El Salvador.

Because you are a Christian and have spoken of your desire to defend human rights, I should like to express my pastoral point of view regarding what I have read and make a concrete request.

I am very worried by the news that the United States is studying a way of encouraging El Salvador's arms race by sending military equipment and advisors to "train three Salvadorean battalions in logistics, communications, and intelligence." If this newspaper report is correct, your government's contribution, instead of favoring the cause of justice and peace in El Salvador, will surely increase injustice here and sharpen the repression that has been unleashed against the people's organizations fighting to defend their most fundamental human rights.

The present junta government, and especially the army and security forces, unfortunately have not shown themselves capable of solving the country's problems, either by political moves or by creating adequate structures. In general they have only resorted to repressive violence, amassing a total of dead and wounded far higher than in the previous military regimes, whose systematic violation of human rights was denounced by the Interamerican Human Rights Commission.

Recently, members of the security forces dragged out and killed persons who had occupied the Christian Democratic Party headquarters. Neither the junta nor the party had authorized any such steps to be taken. This is proof enough that neither the junta nor the Christian Democrats govern the country. Political power is in the hands of the armed forces. They use their power unscrupulously. They know only how to repress the people and defend the interests of the Salvadorean oligarchy.

Is it true that last November "six Americans were in El Salvador ... supplying $200,000 worth of gasmasks and bulletproof vests, and giving classes on riot control"? You must be informed that since then the security forces, with their increased personal protection and efficiency, have been repressing the people even more violently. They do not hesitate to use their weapons and they shoot to kill.

As a Salvadorean and as archbishop of San Salvador, I have the obligation of seeing to it that faith and justice reign in my country. Therefore, assuming you truly want to defend human rights, I ask that you do two things:

- Prohibit all military assistance to the Salvadorean government.

- Guarantee that your government will not intervene, directly or indirectly, by means of military, economic, diplomatic, or other pressures, to influence the direction of the destiny of the Salvadorean people.

We are living through a serious economic and political crisis in our country at this time, but it is beyond doubt that increasingly it is the people themselves that are becoming conscientized and organized, and thereby preparing itself to take the initiative and shoulder the responsibility for the future of El Salvador. The people's organizations are the only social force capable of resolving the crisis.

It would be totally wrong and deplorable if the Salvadorean people were to be frustrated, repressed, or in any way impeded from deciding for itself the economic and political future of our country by intervention on the part of a foreign power. It would also violate a right defended by the Church. The bishops of Latin America, in our meeting in Puebla, publicly recognized "the legitimate right to self-determination by our peoples, which permits them to organize as they wish, set their own historical direction, and participate in a new international order" (Puebla, 505).

I hope that your religious sentiments and your desire for the defense of human rights will move you to accept my petition and thereby avoid any intensification of bloodshed in this tormented country.

Sincerely,

Oscar A. Romero
Archbishop

Disobedience in the Service of a Higher Law

And finally Bishop Romero made a call to civil disobedience by soldiers, the "uniformed peasants." It was a decision that put him outside the bounds of legality and outside the established order. And he knew it. But our bishop had understood a fundamental, revolutionary truth of the Christian way of life: the duty to obey God before human beings.

He had already called the people to meet despite the state of siege that prohibited it. He had buried his murdered priests in church services with no other permission than the support of the local communities. He had denounced the government, the president of the republic, and the armed forces, thereby disobeying constitutional law, which prohibits such denunciations from the pulpit.

He always spoke as a free man:

Without the support of the people no government can be effective. Much less can it be so if it tries to impose itself by the force of blood and suffering.

I want to make a special appeal to soldiers, national guardsmen, and policemen: Brothers, each one of you is one of us. We are the same people. The campesinos you kill are your brothers and sisters.

When you hear the words of a man telling you to kill, remember instead the words of God, "Thou shalt not kill." God's law must prevail. No soldier is obliged to obey an order contrary to the law of God. It is time that you come to your senses and obey your conscience rather than follow out a sinful command.

The Church, defender of the rights of God, and the dignity of each human being, cannot remain silent in the presence of such abominations.

We should like the government to take seriously the fact that reforms dyed by so much blood are worth nothing. In the name of God, in the name of our tormented people who have suffered so much and whose laments cry out to heaven, I beseech you, I beg you, I order you in the name of God, stop the repression!

Source of Hope: The People's Organizations

At the same time that he called attention to oppression and its agents, he also pointed out reasons for hope. On January 11, 1980, the formation of the Mass Revolutionary Coordinating Committee (CRM) had been announced. In his sermon Bishop Romero said:

This week we have seen the first steps toward unity among the people's organizations. A national coordinating committee has has been formed and it is inviting all progressive forces in the country to joint participation.

I am pleased that they are finally breaking away from sectarian and partisan interests and managing to find broader unity. I will always encourage this.

In the interview with *Prensa Latina* on February 15, 1980, he repeated that the organizations are the best hope for liberation:

I believe in the mass organizations, I believe in the need for the Salvadorean people to become organized.... The organizations are the social force that will promote, and pursue, and be able to create an authentic society.... Organization is necessary to be able to struggle effectively.... Because I am convinced that organization is important, I am very pleased to see this new spirit of unity.

In his last sermon, on the eve of his death, he again insisted on the same point: "Of course the Coordinating Committee has its faults ... but it will be the solution to the problem if it matures and if it is able to truly comprehend the wishes of the people."

The Right to Insurrectional Violence

As Bishop Romero's thought evolved, insurrectional violence has been one of the problems that was dealt with in his give-and-take relationship with the people. In his last two pastoral letters he had explained the right that a people has to insurrection and under what conditions. And with each passing day, he saw that possibility coming closer and closer to being a concrete reality and, therefore, he insisted:

Christians are not afraid of combat; they know how to fight, but they prefer the language of peace. However, when a dictatorship seriously violates human rights and attacks the common good of the nation, when it becomes unbearable and closes all channels of dialogue, of understanding, of rationality—when this happens, the Church speaks of the legitimate right of insurrectional violence.

They Had to Kill Him

They had to do it. This completely free and holy man, this man of God at the service of the historical movement forward of the poor, was costing them more alive than dead. They coldly entered into a sort of economic cost-benefit analysis and planned his death.

Of course they would have preferred to find some other solution. They sent one person after another to talk to him. They sent North American diplomats: Todman, Devine, Vaky, Bowdler. And they promised him that certain things would be done, that there were solutions within the system.

They had recourse to Rome; "apostolic visitors" came, as well as neighboring papal nuncios on "unofficial" visits. But Bishop Romero continued making the point that the laws of God are above human laws. On Sunday, the eve of his assassination, the American ambassador was seen at Bishop Romero's Mass. And the next day the same ambassador stated, as if it were the official line, that the assassination had been the work of an expert and that it could have been done by the extreme right or the extreme left. And there *he* was in the middle, washing his hands.

They assassinated him. It was as simple as that. On March 24, at six-thirty in the evening. And he rose again, as he had promised.

Prophecy and Denunciation

The Christian communities, the people of God, publicly denounced the assassins of Romero: imperialism, the rich, and the instruments they use to control the country—the Christian Democratic Party, the junta, and the military tyranny.

The same communities also denounced the complicity of the ecclesiastical hierarchs who had either abandoned or fought against Romero, and they excommunicated them from his funeral. A huge banner at the door of the cathedral prohibited entrance to the papal nuncio and to Bishops Aparicio, Alvarez, and Revelo. Never before had anyone heard of such a prophetic act. It came from the kind of church that is borne from the committed faith of the people.

Of the Salvadorean hierarchy, only Bishop Rivera y Damas of Santiago de María attended the funeral. Bishops from other countries came, to be in solidarity with our people and our church.

All the people's organizations joined the protest and repudiated the despicable assassination of Arnulfo Romero. They promised to redouble their efforts to attain the definitive liberation announced by the bishop who gave his life for that cause.

Aftermath

Bishop Romero's death caused a problem for the Vatican. Bureaucratic interests within the institutional church wanted to regain control of his diocese and turn it once again into the center of tranquility and episcopal unity that it had been before Romero became a prophet of the people's church. But they could not appoint just anyone. The people had already rejected all but one bishop. He was Bishop Arturo Rivera y Damas, and the Vatican's solution was to name him apostolic administrator of the archdiocese of San Salvador.

The task assigned to Bishop Rivera was clear: to try to rebuild the outward unity of the Church around its hierarchy and smooth out the differences among the bishops who had been divided over the words, the example, and the life of Bishop Romero.

Bishop Rivera took on the task—which meant that he started to yield ground that had been won by Bishop Romero. He tried to reconcile the irreconcilable. He kept Bishop Revelo, who had been Romero's auxiliary bishop. He signed letters that he was not totally in agreement with, but he felt he had to sign them because of his mandate. He tried to find a non-existent middle ground. He was trying to be a prophet to two opposed camps at the same time. He denounced the structural sins of the junta, made up of Christian Democrats and members of the military. But he also coolly denounced errors made by the people's organizations, instead of helping to correct them through appropriate channels and personal contact.

Bishop Rivera also began to use a false analysis of the Salvadorean socio-political makeup—the same interpretation made and promulgated by the oligarchy. The analysis was, basically, that in El Salvador there are two extremes—the military and the government—and the people were caught in the middle. In Rivera's thinking, the Church, inasmuch as it should be with the people, should be like the central upright of a balance, identified with the people, with the two ends of its crossbeam representing the military and the government.

That was during the first months after Bishop Romero's death—but the junta systematically continued its massacre of the people. Bishop Rivera began to see that he would have to change his position. He had to be faithful to the people. By September 1980 he accepted the analysis that had been adopted by Bishop Romero, and he took up Romero's prophetic stance. He began to explain the real situation in El Salvador in terms of the confrontation of a people with the tyranny fomented by the military and the government—instigated and manipulated by the oligarchy.

The public denunciations by Bishop Rivera, his return to a truly prophetic stance, unleashed the forces of repression against the Church once again. And the repression escalated. First there were the bombs that destroyed the bishop's chancery office, the dynamite that silenced the "stronghold of truth," YSAX, two bombs in the Jesuit house, and the bombing of the residence of the Belgian priests. And the violent entry of soldiers into churches, killing more than sixty Christians who were there to call attention to the repression of the people by the government.

Then the death of a Christian leader, Magdalena, in charge of the Human Rights Commission, the break-ins at several parishes in the north of the country where the communion hosts were profaned, and the soldiers demonstrated even more their rage and irrationality. They defecated inside the churches in order to show their contempt. After many other threats were made, they capped it all with the killing of yet another priest, Manuel Reyes.

CONIP

The unity of the Church in and around the historical movement forward of the poor found expression in the founding of CONIP (*Coordinadora Nacional de la Iglesia Popular*), National Coordinating Committee of the People's Church. The Salvadorean church had formed several unifying organizations. When Bishop Romero became the archbishop of San Salvador there was already an organization called the National Council of Peasant Christian Communities. During the period of his service to the Church of San Salvador the Coordinating Committee for Urban Christian Communities came into existence. Through participation in the struggles of the people, unity between those two organizations grew and in August 1980 they formed CONIP. It took up the work left unfinished by Romero and made it possible for the Church to become ever more deeply committed to the struggle of our people, and to become an example for the Church in all Latin America.

"Saint Romero of the Americas"

Despite silence on the part of the institutional church and the Latin American Episcopal Conference, and their nonrecognition of Bishop Romero as someone important in the history of the Latin American Church, he is by no means forgotten. The people know how to identify the people of God in their history, and throughout Latin America the image of Bishop Romero is recalled, eulogized, and kept alive. Songs and poems dedicated to him are flourishing; a beautiful anthology could be made of them. Books are being published of his sermons, his theological contributions, his pastoral letters, his example. His life is being studied in search for something very valuable: the key to keeping the Church at the heart of the people's struggle.

And solidarity grows. Christian groups in solidarity with the Salvadorean people's struggle emerge throughout all of Latin America—and beyond—and name themselves after Bishop Romero.

Within El Salvador, where the people are preparing for a definitive liberation battle, Bishop Romero's dream is becoming a reality—the unity of all the poor so that they can create a society of justice and equality. The people have forged a unity in the Farabundo Martí Front for National Liberation. Five million individuals trying to become a people are a people of God on pilgrimage.

And we see clearly the truth of the words of Bishop Pedro Casaldáliga of São Félix, Brazil, in a poem that he dedicated to the memory of Archbishop Romero: "Saint Romero of the Americas, no one will ever silence your last sermon."

Social and Religious Context
of the Theology of Liberation*

By T. Howland Sanks, S.J.
and Brian H. Smith, S.J.

The theology-of-liberation literature was conditioned both by the social upheaval and turmoil that characterized Latin America at the end of the 1960s and by the search within the Church to respond more authentically to the hope and agony that this rapid change involved.

By the late 60s the social context of the Latin American world had changed dramatically from what it had been at the beginning of the decade. In the early 1960s the Alliance for Progress, the Kennedy administration, and the rise of reformist democratic movements in several countries of the continent—notably in Chile, Brazil, Venezuela, Peru, and Colombia—all signalled a new era of hope for peaceful but steady economic and social reform in Latin America. By the end of the 1960s, however, much of this optimism in the possibility of democratic reform was on the wane. Reformist efforts in Brazil and Peru by civilian governments had been curtailed by military interventions, and in other countries where they had not yet been started (Bolivia, Argentina, Uruguay) they were pre-empted by military coups. In Chile, where the Christian democratic administration had been the "showcase" of the Alliance for Progress in Latin America and had received more per capita U.S. foreign aid than all other Latin American countries combined, the reform efforts had not produced the results as quickly as expected. Many student groups and young intellectuals in the country were turning to Marxist analysis and movements as solutions to what they considered a stagnant economy, chronic maldistribution of income, and a lack of genuine participation of the urban and rural poor

*Excerpted from "Liberation Ecclesiology: Praxis, Theory, Praxis" in *Theological Studies*, Vol. 38, No. 1 (March, 1977).

in public decision-making. Hence the reactionary positions of those on the Right were stimulating a corresponding increase of interest in radical solutions offered by the Left among the most idealistic elements in Latin American society.

The religious context of the continent was also undergoing significant transformation as a result of the rapidly changing social and economic situation and was stimulated as well by events occurring both in the universal Church and within Latin America itself. The fathers of the Second Vatican Council had urged all Catholics to scrutinize "the signs of the times" and share in the agonies of modern man so as to make the Gospel credible to the people of our day, especially to the suffering and oppressed. They had described the Church as the sacrament of mankind's unity, consciously pointing to the Spirit's actions, which go far beyond the institutional framework of the Church itself.[1] Hence the ecclesiological principles of Vatican II were clearly oriented to service of the world and its struggles for justice and dignity.

Furthermore, the major social encyclicals of Pope John XXIII and Pope Paul VI, *Pacem in terris* (1963) and *Populorum progressio* (1967), broke away from earlier papal emphases on corporatist solutions to social problems and moved cautiously towards more socialist proposals such as the need for increased state planning and public ownership of key natural resources, limitations on private property (which was not to be treated as an absolute), more equitable distribution of world resources to favor the developing nations, and the right to use violence under certain repressive situations.

In Latin America itself many Christians were no longer seeking Christian solutions to social and economic problems but were joining forces with secular elites and Marxists to find more just solutions to societal problems and thereby rediscover the meaning of Christian symbols from within a revolutionary praxis. The Colombian priest Camilo Torres, who put aside his sacramental ministry and joined in the guerrilla movement in order to establish the structural conditions of justice necessary to make celebration of Eucharist and true reconciliation possible, epitomizes the growing disillusionment with Christian reformist strategies and the preference for "blurred boundaries" between Church and world which later became the normative model in liberation ecclesiology.

Much of this frustration and exploration on the part of Latin American Catholics culminated at the Second General Conference of Latin American bishops held in Medellín, Colombia, in August 1968, when 150 bishops from every country on the continent met to discuss the response of the Church to the new challenges presented in the 1960s. Drawing upon some of the new structural emphases in the encyclicals of Popes John and Paul, as well as upon neo-Marxist categories current in the literature generated by Latin American social scientists in the late 1960s, the bishops denounced the

---

[1] *Gaudium et spes*, Nos. 1 and 4; *Lumen gentium*, No. 1; *The Document of Vatican II*, ed. Walter M. Abbott, S.J. (New York: America Press, 1966), pp. 199-201, 15.

"institutionalized violence" of the *status quo* and placed responsibility for injustice squarely on those with the "greater share of wealth, culture, and power" who "jealously retain their privileges," thus "provoking 'explosive revolutions of despair.'" They demanded "urgent and profoundly renovating transformations" in their respective societies and in the world economic order.[2]

As a fitting Church response to this social and economic crisis, the bishops proposed a new strategy for evangelization which clearly paralleled the ecclesiological principles later to be incorporated into the theology-of-liberation literature. They placed in the forefront of pastoral priorities the necessity for Church leaders to "awaken in individuals and communities ... a living awareness of justice." To achieve this, the Church should promote "small basic communities" so as to evangelize the marginal poor more effectively. The Church was also to stimulate a more heightened "political consciousness" among the faithful, and through its educational ministry of conscientization urge Christians "to consider their participation in the political life of the nation as a matter of conscience." The pastoral scope of Church activities was also to include encouraging the "efforts of the people to create and develop their own grassroots organizations for the redress and consolidation of their rights and the search for justice."[3]

Finally, the bishops took upon themselves as pastors of the Church the duty to "defend the rights of the poor and the oppressed ... urging ... governments and upper classes to eliminate anything which might destroy social peace: injustice, inertia, venality, insensibility." Each national episcopal conference was to take effective steps to present "the Church as a catalyst in the temporal realm in an authentic attitude of service."[4]

Hence the theology-of-liberation literature emerged in the context of a rapidly polarizing social and economic situation in Latin America where democratic processes were breaking down, the economic gap between the rich and poor was widening, and extremist political movements on Right and Left were gaining in prominence. It was also part of an overall response in Rome and Latin America to identify the Church more profoundly with the problems of the poor, to develop new pastoral strategies serving both spiritual and social needs of the people, and to make the Church an effective prophetic force against chronic injustices and repressive regimes.

---

[2] Latin American Episcopal Council (CELAM), *The Church in the Present Day Transformation of Latin America in Light of the Council 2* (Bogota: General Secretariat of CELAM, 1970), pp. 78-79.

[3] *Ibid.*, pp. 81, 66, 65.

[4] *Ibid.*, pp. 81, 67.

The Church in the Process of Liberation*
By Gustavo Gutiérrez

Gustavo Gutiérrez is a Peruvian priest.

The new theological thinking now occurring in Latin America comes more from the Christian groups committed to the liberation of their people than from the traditional centers for the teaching of theology. The fruitfulness of reflection will depend on the quality of these commitments.

The process is complex and things are changing before our very eyes. Here we focus our attention on participation in the process of liberation and thus do not concern ourselves with other aspects of the life of the Church. It will be helpful to point out some of the highlights which characterize the new situation now being created.

Laymen

The ever more revolutionary political options of Christian groups—especially students, workers, and peasants—have frequently been responsible for conflicts between the lay apostolic movements and the hierarchy. These options have likewise caused the movement members to question their place in the Church and have been responsible for the severe crises experienced by some of them.[1]

Moreover, many have discovered in these movements evangelical demands for an ever more resolute commitment to the oppressed peoples of this exploited continent. But the inadequacy of the theologico-pastoral plans which until recently were considered viable by these movements, the perception of the close ties which unite the Church to the very social order which the movements wish to change, the urgent albeit ambiguous demands of social action—all these factors have caused many gradually to substitute working for the Kingdom with working for the social revolution—or, more precisely perhaps, the lines between the two have become blurred.

In the concrete, all this has often meant a commitment to revolutionary political groups. The political situation in Latin America together with the subversion of the status quo advocated by these groups force them to become at least partially clandestine. Moreover, as awareness of existing legalized violence grows, the problem of counterviolence is no longer an abstract ethical concern. It now becomes very important on the level of political efficacy. Perhaps more accurately, it is on this latter level that the question of man himself is concretely considered. Under these conditions, the political activity of Christians takes on new dimensions which have

---

*From *A Theology of Liberation: History, Politics and Salvation* (Maryknoll, N.Y: Orbis Books, 1973).

[1] Literature on this problem is abundant but not easily accessible. See, however, a good panoramic view of the university apostolic movements in Gilberto Giménez, *Introducción a una pedagogía de la pastoral universitaria,* MIEC-JECI, Servicio de Documentación (Montevideo), Series 1, Doc. 19, 1968.

caught by surprise not only the ecclesial structures but also the most advanced pedagogical methods of the lay apostolic movements. On this continent, the oppressed and those who seek to identify with them face ever more resolutely a common adversary, and therefore, the relationship between Marxists and Christians takes on characteristics different from those in other places.[2]

A profound renewal or renaissance of various lay apostolic movements is nevertheless apparent. After the initial impact of a radical politicization for which they were inadequately prepared theologically, pedagogically, and spiritually, everything seems to indicate that they are beginning to find new approaches. There are also arising new kinds of groups.[3] A clear option in favor of the oppressed and their liberation leads to basic changes in outlook; there emerges a new vision of the fruitfulness and originality of Christianity and the Christian community's role in this liberation. This is not a matter merely of reaffirmation of a choice but also of concrete experiences of how to witness to the Gospel in Latin America today. But many questions remain unanswered. The new vitality that can be foreseen does not have before it a completely clear path.

Priests and Religious

A clearer perception of the tragic realities of the continent, the clear options which political polarization demands, the climate of more active participation in the life of the Church created by Vatican II, and the impulse provided by the Latin American Bishops' Conference at Medellín—all these factors have made priests and religious today one of the most dynamic and restless groups in the Latin American Church. Priests and religious in ever increasing proportions seek to participate more actively in the pastoral decisions of the Church. But, above all, they want the Church to break its ties with an unjust order, and they want it—with renewed fidelity to the Lord who calls it and to the Gospel which it preaches—to cast its lot with those who suffer from misery and deprivation.

These concerns, as well as other factors, have led in many cases to friction with local bishops and apostolic nuncios.[4] We can say that unless deep changes take place this conflictual situation will spread and become more serious in the immediate future.

Moreover, there are many priests who consider it a duty to adopt clear and committed personal positions in the political arena. Some participate

---

[2] Fidel Castro's statement regarding Camilo Torres is interesting in this regard: "Camilo Torres is the case of a priest who went to die for those struggling to liberate their people. This is why he has become a symbol of the revolutionary unity of the people of Latin America." (Speech delivered January 4, 1969, quoted in Aldo Buntig, *"Iglesia en Cuba,"* p. 40).

[3] See Gustavo Pérez Ramírez, "Theology of Liberation: Bogotá, 1970" in *IDOC-NA*, No. 14 (November 28, 1970), pp. 66-78.

[4] These clashes have taken place in almost all Latin American countries, the most serious perhaps in Brazil, Argentina, and Guatemala. In this regard see the documents reproduced by SEDOC (Petrópolis, Brazil), CIDOC (Cuernavaca, México), and NADOC (Lima, Perú).

actively in politics,[5] often in connection with revolutionary groups. As a matter of fact, this participation is not essentially new. In many ways the clergy have played and still play a direct role in political life (barely veiled in some cases under pretexts of a religious nature). The new dimension is that many priests clearly admit the need and obligation to make such a commitment and above all that their options in one way or another place them in a relationship of subversion regarding the existing social order.

There are other factors: for example, the effects of a certain weariness caused by the intensity of the resistance that must be overcome within the Church; and then there is the disenchantment caused by the apparent futility of work regarded as purely "religious," which has little contact with the reality and social demands of the continent. We are facing an "identity crisis." For some this means a reassessment of the current life-style of the clergy; and for others it means even a reevaluation of the meaning of the priesthood itself. On the other hand, the numbers are growing of those who have found renewed meaning for their priesthood or religious life in the commitment to the oppressed and their struggle for liberation.

Bishops

The new and serious problems which face the Latin American Church and which shape the conflictual and changing reality find many bishops ill-prepared for their function. There is among them, nevertheless, an awakening to the social dimension of the presence of the Church and a corresponding rediscovery of its prophetic mission.

The bishops of the most poverty-stricken and exploited areas are the ones who have denounced most energetically the injustices they witness. But in exposing the deep causes of these injustices, they have had to confront the great economic and political forces of their countries. They naturally leave themselves open to being accused of meddling in affairs outside their competence and even of being friendly to Marxist ideas. Often this accusation is made, and vigorously, in conservative sectors, both Catholic and non-Catholic. Some of these bishops have become almost political personalities in their respective countries. The consequence has been tightened police vigilance and in some cases death threats on the part of groups of the extreme right.

But it is not just a question of isolated personalities. It is often entire conferences of bishops who openly take a position in this arena. We should also mention the efforts of many bishops to make changes—of varying degrees of radicalness—in Church structures. The results are still much below what is desired and necessary. The first steps do appear to have been taken, but the danger of retreat has not been eliminated, and, above all, there is much yet to be done.

---

[5] The instance of Camilo Torres is well known. See his collected works in *Camilo Torres, Revolutionary Writings* (New York: Herder and Herder, 1969); see also *Revolutionary Priest: The Complete Writings & Messages of Camilo Torres*, ed. John Gerassi (New York: Vintage Books, 1971).

In the majority of cases, options at the episcopal level regarding social transformation have been expressed in written statements, but there have also been cases in which these declarations have been accompanied by very concrete actions: direct intervention in workers' strikes, participation in public demonstrations, etc.[6]

Towards a Transformation of the Latin American Reality

One unifying theme which is present throughout these documents and which reflects a general attitude of the Church is the acknowledgement of the *solidarity of the Church* with the Latin American reality. The Church avoids placing itself above this reality, but rather attempts to assume its responsibility for the injustice which it has supported both by its links with the established order as well as by its silence regarding the evils this order implies. "We recognize that we Christians, for want of fidelity to the Gospel, have contributed to the present unjust situation through our words and attitudes, our silence and inaction," claim the Peruvian bishops.[7] More than 200 laymen, priests, and bishops of El Salvador assert that "our Church has not been effective in liberating and bettering Salvadorean man. This failure is due in part to the above-mentioned incomplete concept of the salvation of man and the mission of the Church and in part to the fear of losing privileges or suffering persecution."[8]

As for the bishops' vision of reality, they describe the misery and the exploitation of man by man in Latin America as "a situation of injustice that can be called institutionalized violence;"[9] it is responsible for the death of thousands of innocent victims. This view allows for a study of the complex problems of counterviolence without falling into the pitfalls of a double standard which assumes the violence is acceptable when the oppressor uses it to maintain "order" and is bad when the oppressed invoke it to change this "order." Institutionalized violence violates fundamental rights so patently that the Latin American bishops warn that "one should not abuse the patience of a people that for years has borne a situation that would not be acceptable to any one with any degree of awareness of human rights."[10] An important part of the Latin American clergy request,

---

[6] Norman Gall recounts some of these instances in "La reforma católica," in *Mundo Nuevo*, June 1970, pp. 20-43; see also Norman Gall, "Latin America: The Church Militant," *Commentary*, April 1970, pp. 25-37.

[7] "Closing Statement of the Thirty-sixth Peruvian Episcopal Conference," 1969, in *Between Honesty and Hope: Documents from and about the Church in Latin America*, Issued at Lima by the Peruvian Bishop's Commission for Social Action, trans. John Drury (Maryknoll, New York: Maryknoll Publications, 1970), p. 230.

[8] Conclusions of the first week of joint pastoral planning in El Salvador, June 1970, in *NADOC*, No. 174, p. 2.

[9] "Peace," No. 16, *The Church in the Present-Day Transformation of Latin America in the Light of the Council*, Documents of the Second General Conference of Latin American Bishops, Medellín, Colombia, August-September 1968 (Bogotá: General Secretariat of CELAM, 1970), hereafter cited as *Medellín*. We must emphasize that this is not merely a phrase mentioned in passing; the whole document is constructed around this focus.

[10] *Ibid.*, No. 16.

moreover, that "in considering the problem of violence in Latin America, let us by all means avoid equating the *unjust violence* of the oppressors (who maintain this despicable system) with the *just violence* of the oppressed (who feel obliged to use it to achieve their liberation)."[11] Theologically, this situation of injustice and oppression is characterized as a "sinful situation" because "where this social peace does not exist, there we will find social, political, economic, and cultural inequalities, there we will find the rejection of the Lord Himself."[12]

Indeed, in texts of the Latin American Church of varying origins and degrees of authority, in the last few years there has been a significant although perhaps not completely coherent replacement of the theme of *development*[13] by the theme of *liberation*.[14] Both the term and the idea express the aspirations to be free from a situation of dependence; the "Message of the Bishops of the Third World" states that "an irresistible impulse drives these people on to better themselves and to free themselves from the forces of oppression."[15] In the words of 120 Bolivian priests: "We observe in our people a desire for liberation and a movement of struggle for justice, not only to obtain a better standard of living, but also to be able to participate in the socio-economic resources and the decision-making process of the country."[16] The deeper meaning of these expressions is the insistence on the need for the oppressed peoples of Latin America to control their own destiny. Quoting *Populorum progressio* Medellín advocates, therefore, a "liberating education."

The Church wishes to share in this aspiration of the Latin American peoples; the bishops at Medellín think of themselves as belonging to a people who are "beginning to discover their proper self-awareness and their task in the consort of nations."[17] "We are vitally aware of the social revolution now in progress. We identify with it."[18]

For some, participation in this process of liberation means not allowing themselves to be intimidated by the accusation of being "communist."[19] On

---

[11] "Continent of Violence," in *Between Honesty and Hope*, p. 84.

[12] "Peace," No. 14, in *Medellín*.

[13] *Presencia activa de la Iglesia en el desarrollo y la integración de América Latina*, Conclusions of the Episcopal Conference of CELAM, Mar del Plata, 1966, Documentos CELAM, No. 1 (Bogotá: CELAM, 1967).

[14] This substitution has been very well treated by Héctor Borrat in "El gran impulso," *Víspera*, No. 7 (October 1968), p. 9.

[15] "Letter to the Peoples of the Third World," in *Between Honesty and Hope*, p. 3.

[16] "Carta de 120 sacerdotes de Bolivia a su Conferencia Episcopal," 1970, in *NADOC*, No. 148, p. 2.

[17] Cardinal Landazuri Ricketts, "Closing Address at Medellín Episcopal Conference," in *Between Honesty and Hope*, p. 223.

[18] Cardinal Landazuri Ricketts, "Servants to Society," baccalaureate address at the University of Notre Dame, 1966, in *Between Honesty and Hope*, p. 60.

[19] "It is easy to hurl the charge of communism at all those who, lacking any ties with the party or the ideology, dare to point out the materialistic roots of capitalism; at all those who dare to point out that, strictly speaking, we do not yet have one uniform socialism or capitalism, but a variety of socialisms and capitalisms" (Helder Câmara, in *Between Honesty and Hope*, p. 35).

the positive side it can even mean taking the path of *socialism*. A group of Colombian priests affirmed, "We forthrightly denounce neo-colonial capitalism, since it is incapable of solving the acute problems that confront our people. We are led to direct our efforts and actions toward the building of a Socialist type of society that would allow us to eliminate all forms of man's exploitation of his fellow man, and that fits in with the historical tendencies of our time and the distinctive character of Colombians."[20] According to the Argentinian Priests for the Third World, this socialism will be a "Latin American socialism that will promote the advent of the New Man."[21]

In a speech which has been bitterly debated and attacked, one of the most influential figures of the Mexican Church, Don Sergio Méndez Arceo, asserted: "Only socialism can enable Latin America to achieve true development.... I believe that a socialist system is more in accord with the Christian principles of true brotherhood, justice, and peace.... I do not know what kind of socialism, but this is the direction Latin America should go. For myself, I believe it should be a democratic socialism."[22] Old prejudices, inevitable ideological elements, and also the ambivalence of the term *socialism* require the use of cautious language and careful distinctions. There is always the risk that the statements in this regard may be interpreted differently by different people. It is therefore important to link this subject to another which enables us at least under one aspect to clarify what we mean. We refer to the progressive radicalization of the debate concerning private property. The subordination of private property to the social goods has been stressed often.[23] But difficulties in reconciling justice and private ownership have led many to the conviction that "private ownership of capital leads to the dichotomy of capital and labor, to the superiority of the capitalist over the laborer, to the exploitation of man by man.... The history of private ownership of the means of production makes evident the necessity of its reduction or suppression for the welfare of society. We must hence *opt for social ownership of the means of production*."[24]

The process of liberation requires the *active participation of the oppressed*; this certainly is one of the most important themes running through the writings of the Latin American Church. Based on the evidence of the usually frustrated aspirations of the popular classes to participate in decisions which affect all of society, the realization emerges that it is the poor

---

[20] "Underdevelopment in Colombia," in *Beyond Honesty and Hope*, p. 90.

[21] "Coincidencias básicas," in *Sacerdotes para el Tercer Mundo* (Buenos Aires: Ed. del Movimiento, 1970), p. 69.

[22] "Proyección y transformación de la Iglesia en Latinoamérica," an address delivered July 17, 1970, in "Confrontación de dos obispos mexicanos," *CIP Documenta* (Cuernavaca, Mexico), No. 7 (September 1970), p. 4.

[23] The Archbishop of La Paz, Bolivia, advocates a new Christian ethic which ought to "recognize that work is more important than property in the use of material goods.... Thus every system of property ought to be evaluated according to its ability to humanize life and the labor of the working man." ("Enfoque de la nueva ética cristiana," pastoral letter in *CIDOC*, No. 224, 1970, p. 4).

[24] "Private Property," statement of ONIS, *IDOC-NA*, No. 16, pp. 94-95. See also the ONIS statement "La Iglesia ante la reforma agraria," in *Iglesia Latinoamericana*, pp. 335-36.

who must be the protagonists of their own liberation: "It is primarily up to the poor nations and the poor of the other nations to effect their own betterment." [25]

However, existing structures block popular participation and marginalize the great majorities, depriving them of channels for expression of their demands. Consequently, the Church feels compelled to address itself directly to the oppressed—instead of appealing to the oppressors—calling on them to assume control of their own destiny, committing itself to support their demands, giving them an opportunity to express these demands, and even articulating them itself. At Medellín a pastoral approach was approved which encourages and favors "the efforts of the people to create and develop their own grass-roots organizations for the redress and consolidation of their rights and the search for true justice." [26]

A New Presence of the Church in Latin America

(a) The denunciation of social injustices is certainly the prevailing theme in the texts of the Latin American Church. The denunciation of injustice implies the rejection of the use of Christianity to legitimize the established order. It likewise implies, in fact, that the Church has entered into conflict with those who wield power. And finally it leads to acknowledging the need for the separation of Church and state because "this is of primary importance in liberating the Church from temporal ties and from the image projected by its bonds with the powerful. This separation will free the Church from compromising commitments and make it more able to speak out." [27]

(b) A second thematic line in the texts we have examined is the urgent need for a *concienticizing evangelization.* "To us, the Pastors of the Church, belongs the duty to educate the Christian conscience, to inspire, stimulate, and help orient all of the initiatives that contribute to the formation of man," asserted the bishops at Medellín.[28] This awareness of being oppressed but nevertheless of being masters of their own destiny is nothing other than a consequence of a well-understood evangelization.

(c) *Poverty* is, indeed, one of the most frequent and pressing demands placed on the Latin American Church. Vatican II asserts that the Church ought to carry out its mission as Christ did "in poverty and under oppression" (*Lumen gentium,* no. 8). This is not the image given by the Latin American Christian community as a whole.[29] Rather, poverty is an area in which countersigns are rampant: "Instead of talking about the Church of the poor, we must be a poor Church. And we flaunt this commitment

---

[25] "Letter to Peoples of the Third World," in *Between Honesty and Hope,* p. 9.

[26] "Peace," no. 27, in *Medellín.*

[27] "Clero peruano a la Asamblea episcopal," in *Iglesia latinoamericana,* pp. 314-15.

[28] "Peace," No. 20, in *Medellín.*

[29] There are few serious studies regarding the wealth of the Church in Latin America. Some bishops are beginning to be concerned with the problem. See, for example, "Statement of Peruvian Episcopal Conference," in *Between Honesty and Hope,* p. 232.

with our real estate, our rectories and other buildings, and our whole style of life."[30] At Medellín it was made clear that poverty expresses solidarity with the oppressed and a protest against oppression. Suggested ways of implementing this poverty in the Church are the evangelization of the poor, the denunciation of injustice, a simple life-style, a spirit of service, and freedom from temporal ties, intrigue, or ambiguous prestige.[31]

(d) The demands placed on the Church by prophetic denunciation, by the concienticizing evangelization of the oppressed, and by poverty sharply reveal the *inadequacy of the structures of the Church* for the world in which it lives. These structures appear obsolete and lacking in dynamism before the new and serious challenges. She does not have the right to talk against others when she herself is a cause of scandal in her interpersonal relations and her internal structures. There arises, therefore, the urgent need for a profound renewal of the present ecclesial structures.

(e) "The need to change the current *life-style of the clergy*[32] is to be considered in this light, especially regarding the commitment to the creation of a new society. Although the denunciation of injustice has political overtones, we feel that if we did not denounce it we would be responsible for and accessory to the injustices being committed. The exercise of our ministry inevitably leads us to commitment and solidarity."[33] There is need for change also with regard to ways of earning a living: "New ways must be found to support the clergy. Those who do not wish to live on stipends or from teaching religion should be allowed to experiment.... A secular job could be very healthy: it would lessen the temptation to servility on the part of those who depend totally on the clerical institution; it would likewise diminish the financial problems of the institutional Church."[34] Changes are also urged regarding greater participation of lay people, religious, and priests in the pastoral decisions of the Church.

The issues discussed are markedly different from those being dealt with up to a short time ago.[35] Moreover, in the approach to the problems there is apparent a *growing radicalization*. Although there is still a long road ahead, positions are being taken which are no longer so ambiguous or naive. There is a new attitude—ever more lucid and demanding—suggestive of a qualitatively different society and of basically new forms of the Church's presence in it.

---

[30] See the clear, extensive statement of the Conferencia Latinoamericana de Religiosas (CLAR), *Pobreza y vida religiosa en América Latina* (Bogotá, 1970).

[31] "Poverty of the Church," nos. 8-18, in *Medellín*.

[32] See for example *La pastoral en las misiones de América Latina* (Bogotá: Departamento de Misiones del CELAM, 1968), pp. 38-39.

[33] "Carta de sacerdotes tucumanos," in *Iglesia latinoamericana*, p. 137.

[34] "Clero peruano," in *Iglesia latinoamericana*, p. 318.

[35] The change of tone—and origin—can be easily seen by consulting, for example, *Recent Church Documents from Latin America*, CIF Monograph (Cuernavaca, Mexico: CIF, 1963), where episcopal documents of 1962-63 are reproduced.

The Other War in Central America:
U.S. Fundamentalists Battle Liberation Theology
for El Salvador's Refugees*

By Frank Viviano

As the Salvadorean military mounted a new offensive in its eastern provinces in the Spring of 1981, another kind of war was being fought across the border in Honduras. It pitted Latin America's activist priests and nuns directly against deeply conservative U.S. Christian fundamentalists, who had been encouraged to work in Central America in an apparent government effort to defuse liberation theology. At the center of the struggle were tens of thousands of Salvadorean refugees pushed into the region by the Salvadorean army, which briefly invaded Honduras on July 17, 1981, in an attempt to stifle activism along the border by more forceful means. Pacific News Service editor Frank Viviano filed this account from the refugee camp at La Virtud, 12 miles from the Salvadorean invasion point. The camp was later forcibly evacuated by the Honduran Army.

LEMPIRA PROVINCE, HONDURAS—While the Salvadorean civil war rages on just miles beyond the Sumpul and Lempa rivers, a different, but related battle has been joined in this remote Honduran countryside. It involves tens of thousands of Salvadorean refugees, several international relief agencies, and a bitter conflict over what relief and religious humanitarianism are meant to accomplish.

Here in the hot, overcrowded refugee camps of Lempira, deeply conservative U.S. Christian fundamentalism has come head up against the Roman Catholic theology of liberation. The stakes include the refugees and, ultimately, the very shaping of this region's future. At the center of the controversy are CARITAS, a Swiss-based Catholic humanitarian agency; World Vision, a fundamentalist Christian relief organization operating out of Monrovia, California; and CEDEN, a mainstream Protestant Evangelical committee which is presently the Honduran government-selected representative of the United Nations High Command for Refugees on the Salvadorean frontier.

The differences between these organizations are extensive, and touch directly on the crucial role of the Catholic Church in Latin American social change over the past decade, as well as what appears to be a deliberate effort by Central American governments to defuse that role with the assistance of conservative religious groups. At the two extremes lie CARITAS and World Vision. One represents the growing force of liberation theology, which was born in Latin America and has since attracted followers both Catholic and Protestant, all over the world. The other represents a religious point of view held most widely in the United States, which emphasizes uncompromising

---

*From a special report for Pacific News Service, July 21, 1981.

anti-communism and a dependence on faith, rather than political action, to bring about needed changes.

The basic thrust of liberation theology is clearly apparent in the life of the largest CARITAS camp near La Virtud, a small village five kilometers from the Lempa river. Although the 17,000 people here have experienced severe hardships, there are surprisingly few signs of despair. The refugees have formed their own governing committees to work out camp security procedures, refugee men have planted the surrounding hillsides with corn and beans to counter the food shortage, schools have been established and families assigned makeshift homes under open truck tarps which dot the landscape alongside a small stream.

Some 300 kilometers away at the airport in Tegucigalpa, the capital city of Honduras, brochures are passed out to waiting passengers which seem directed precisely against the union of social activism and religious exercise evident at La Virtud. The brochures come from the Miami-based International Evangelical Church, and they express a chief tenet of the large influx of North American fundamentalist missionaries who have been encouraged to work in Honduras and El Salvador since political troubles began to heat up in the mid-Seventies. "Creemos que el ministro no debe mezclarse en politica," the brochures read: "We believe that a clergyman must not meddle in politics." In fact, despite the overwhelming Catholicism of the Honduran population, the only literature sold at the government-controlled Tegucigalpa airport bookstore is fundamentalist Protestant material from the United States, translated into Spanish. The shelves display several books by Tim LaHaye, a close associate of Jerry Falwell and chairman of a powerful U.S. conservative political advisory group.

Catholic and mainstream Protestant relief officials here and in the United States say that the government effort to stifle dissent with a mixture of fundamentalist Christianity, conservative American ideology, and an open assault on the theology of liberation, is well suited to the philosophy of World Vision. "World Vision has helped sensitize Americans to the fact that there are terrible problems in other countries," said Hugh Wire, director of the West Coast office of the U.S. Protestant Church World Service, another relief agency. "But they bring in a strictly American version of what the problems are, and what to do about them. It's a terribly imperialistic approach, devoid of any understanding of local conditions."

That approach becomes particularly damaging, say World Vision's critics, when "local conditions" involve what fundamentalist Americans view as a confrontation with communism. On June 30, spokesmen claiming to represent more than 100,000 Salvadorean refugees in Honduras and Guatemala issued a statement alleging that World Vision collaborated with the military of all three countries in a political counter-insurgency campaign directed at the refugees. Spokesman Father Fausto Milla, pastor of the border-area parish of Corquín, said that the organization's staff members "landed helicopters in places where there were large concentrations of refugees, and told them 'communism is your enemy and it has ruined everything in Honduras.'" Since arriving in Central America, Milla said, World Vision has constantly "preached to the refugees against 'communist religious workers and priests,'" and exerted pressure to obtain denunciations against them.

Sister Irma, a Franciscan nun in Santa Rosa de Copán responsible for coordinating CARITAS programs along the border, insisted that World Vision also employs staff members who have worked for the Honduran Department of Investigative Police (DNI). "Our conflict is not religious, it is political," she says of the CARITAS-World Vision split. "It is a question of the theology of liberation against the theology of repression."

Perhaps the most severe charge against World Vision—and one which is raised constantly by relief workers here—is that the group allows troops from the Salvadorean armed forces and the paramilitary organization OR-DEN to enter its camps in search of suspected guerrillas. Similar reports have reached the Catholic-affiliated Washington Office on Latin America and other U.S.-based religious humanitarian organizations. The reports are based on interviews with refugees who have managed without authorization to leave the La Guarita settlement, 40 kilometers from La Virtud, where World Vision is in control of approximately 2,400 Salvadoreans. Outsiders—and journalists in particular—have not been allowed into the camps to determine the validity of these charges.

This is not the first time that such charges have been levelled against World Vision. During the Vietnam War, it was criticized for allegedly passing intelligence information on to U.S. military personnel, who were not allowed to enter refugee camps. In Cambodia, according to a 1979 article in *Christian Century*, at least "75 percent of (World Vision's) operation was funded by the USAID. American military trucks and helicopters were always available for World Vision programs, and the CIA used information obtained from the group's field workers as part of its normal intelligence function."

Since the organization's founding in 1950, it has expanded to mount operations in 85 countries, most notably those where refugee populations have grown in the wake of political revolution. Its major projects currently involve Cambodians and Laotians in Thailand, Vietnamese boat people and Somalian refugees, says World Vision spokesman Jim Jewell. Jewell categorically denies that the organization has acted in collaboration with the military, stating that "these are old, oft-repeated charges dating back to the 1960s" which have never been verified.

Caught in the middle of the fierce controversy between World Vision and CARITAS is CEDEN, a mainstream Protestant Evangelical committee staffed largely by Hondurans. Although sympathetic to the orientation of CARITAS, CEDEN is hamstrung in practice by its official administrative status. "We must coordinate our activities with the military chiefs of the region," admits Mario Argenal, coordinator and administrator of the refugee program for the border country. "It is clear that these people are fleeing from repression; we have no doubt of that. But we must keep in mind the worries of our own government about security."

The Church Born of
the People in Nicaragua*
By Miguel d'Escoto, M.M.

Miguel d'Escoto is a Maryknoll Priest and Minister of International Relations for Nicaragua.

It is impossible to sum up in a few short phrases the richness of the life experience of an entire people, an experience marked by the special character of a process, a movement, a historical breakthrough. Nevertheless, permit me to underline a few points that seem to me to be interesting with respect to our topic.

Forgers of History

Throughout its history the poor of Nicaragua, like the people of Latin America, have been robbed not only of the fruit of their work, but also of their lives, their freedom, and their homeland. But in this history we also find important breaks, ruptures in events where the oppressed reveal themselves and demand their rights. In Nicaragua nothing better expresses this protest than the example of the extraordinary figure of the General of Free People: Augusto César Sandino. Sandino and others, such as Carlos Fonseca Amador, opened deep furrows in the history of my country and sowed a seed that the tyranny of Somoza tried to destroy. However, this was buried in fertile soil, nourished by the blood of the poor. It took root and began to live. It developed, and today we are reaping the fruits. An entire people repeated the cry of its vanguard, the Sandinista Front: "Free Homeland or Death." They achieved this freedom by giving their lives. For the first time in history this people felt that it was the master of its own destiny, not because anyone conceded it, but because they knew how to win it for themselves, with gun in hand and with hope in the heart.

If the proclamation of the Christian message does not take into account this increasing maturity, it will be reduced to the restricted area of a private concern. It will remain on the fringe of history. Let us speak frankly. The Church does not really feel comfortable in relation to these efforts to achieve national liberation. Its ties to the world against which the poor are struggling are stronger than it thinks. This makes the Church feel out of place, foreign, vacillating and at times even hostile to such historical processes. We are aware of concrete cases in which the church, and here I speak of those who represent it in an institutional way, has had and continues to have the same reflexes as the dominant sectors of society and has contributed to the defense of their interests. There are cases in which the church echoes all the fears and lamentations of the bourgeoisie as their

*Excerpted from *The Challenge of Basic Christian Communities* (Maryknoll, N.Y: Orbis Books, 1981).

privileges are affected by the victorious popular processes. The bourgeoisie considers these privileges as rights, as if one could have the right to exploit, to cheat, and to despoil the poor.

Solidarity in the Struggle

The oppressors try to divide and fragment the poor, to make them believe that they are merely individuals, isolated from one another, and not a social class, a culture, a race. They try to make them believe that each one can and should overcome their situation of poverty individually, even by stepping on their brothers and sisters of the same class or race. The individualist mentality is the hallmark of the dominant class, or the bourgeoisie. It does not recognize friends; it only wants tactical allies in order to maintain its privileges.

One of the most impressive aspects of the Nicaraguan revolution is the increase of solidarity and unity—unity of the people; unity of the workers, campesinos, village people, and students; unity of the masses forged by the "People United Movement"; unity of the people with the vanguard, the FSLN; unity of all the tendencies within the front; unity of the people whose power was able to touch even important sectors of the anti-Somoza bourgeoisie; unity that integrated large groups of young people into the mainstream of the popular movement; unity in which women played an exceptional part; unity that generated international solidarity and that made even the OAS and regional groups on the continent tremble. Nicaragua was able, at the peak moment of the struggle, to unify the majority of the Latin American countries against Somoza, and in this way isolate North American imperialism.

This unity and solidarity constituted the dynamic force of the revolutionary process that has made a people of Nicaraguans; a people who have decided to make themselves present in history, in that very history from which the oppressor tried to make them disappear; people proud of their own values.

Here I would like to cite the text of the important pastoral letter of the Nicaraguan bishops, written in November 1979:

> Today we are in our country facing an exceptional occasion to witness and announce the kingdom of God. It would be a serious act of infidelity to let this moment pass by because of fears and anxieties, because of the insecurity that every radical process of social change creates in some people, because of the defense of small or large individual interests—this demanding moment in which this preferential option for the poor can be concretized. It is precisely this option which Pope John Paul II and Puebla call us to make.

And they add an evident consequence of this for the life of the Church:

> This option has presupposed the giving up of old ways of thinking and acting, the profound conversion of all of us as Church. In effect, the day that the Church fails to present itself to the world as poor and as an ally of the poor, it will betray its divine founder and also the proclamation

of the kingdom of God. Now more than ever before in the Nicaraguan situation, it is urgent to ratify convincingly this preferential option for the poor.

Conclusion

Our communion in liberation and our hope, lived and celebrated in a church born from the struggles of the people under the impulse of the Holy Spirit, must nevertheless be translated into concrete terms. We have defeated Somoza, but we have still not completely defeated *somocismo*. Furthermore, the reconstruction of our homeland, destroyed by the forces of tyranny, remains as a challenge ahead of us. This is a gigantic task, even more difficult than winning the war. North American imperialism is just waiting for the chance to destroy us. We need the solidarity of all the Latin American peoples—economic and political solidarity, solidarity to combat the counter-revolution, solidarity to break the blockade and the isolation that they want to impose on us. We have complete confidence in the solidarity of the poor and the exploited, and we believe that the action of committed Christians will be decisive in the bringing about of this broad movement of continental solidarity. From these struggles, we Christians up and down the continent are proclaiming our faith and hope in the God who liberates.

The victory of July 19, 1979, is only the beginning. I want to make an appeal to all of you: that each one in his or her own place of struggle and all together at the continental level finish our process of liberation—today in Nicaragua and, sooner or later, in our great Latin American homeland! Free Homeland or Death!

The Salt of the Earth
and the Light of the World*

By Ernesto Cardenal

Many of the biblical reflection sessions at Solentiname were taped and compiled into a fascinating book by Ernesto Cardenal. The following is an excerpt of a dialogue between two young men discussing the following passage from the Bible and comparing it to their reality.

You are the light of the world.
A city that is on a hilltop cannot be hidden. (Matthew 5:14)

Félix Mayorga: "Maybe the light is the good people, who practice love. Everyone that has a good spirit and loves others, he is the light of the world. They set the example and the people will follow them, as someone follows a

---

*Excerpted from *The Gospel In Solentiname*, Vol. I, translated by Donald D. Walsh (Maryknoll, N.Y: Orbis Books, 1976).

person that carries a lamp to light up the darkness. Or let's suppose we're lost in the dark, and there's a light. The guy that's lost looks for the light."

Marcelino: "A lit up city that's on top of a hill can be seen from far away, as we can see the lights of San Miguelito from very far when we're rowing at night on the lake. A city is a great union of people, and as there are a lot of houses together we can see a lot of light. And that's the way our community will be. It will be seen lighted from far away, if it is united by love, even though we don't have the city houses, just huts like the ones we have now, scattered here and there. But this union will shine and it's going to be seen from San Miguelito, from Papaturro, from San Carlos. And we may even get to be a city, too, because then we won't be in scattered huts the way we are now, and we'll have electric light, and when somebody goes by in a boat he'll see those lights of our union. But the thing that will shine most, and that's what Christ is talking about, is love."

7

Women and Revolution

One of the most remarkable aspects of Central American revolutionary movements is the high degree of active participation by women, who have appeared in liberation struggles in numbers and with responsibilities unprecedented in revolutionary history. This phenomenon is important on two counts: first, the incorporation of women into the revolutionary struggle is crucial during both the period of insurrection and the subsequent process of building a socialist society.[1] Secondly, the active participation of women prepares the conditions for a transformation of the oppressive gender relations that exist in Central America as well as in most other societies.

The reasons for the significant revolutionary role of women can be best understood in the context of the economic, social, and historical roots of women's oppression in Central America. Women *in general* constitute an oppressed group, since the patriarchal family structure cuts across all classes (with perhaps the exception of some Indian populations). In addition, working-class and peasant women experience another form of exploitation deriving from their class position; this exploitation interacts with their subordinate status as women to produce a complex set of oppressive relations. Thus, while bourgeois women are oppressed as women, at the same time, as a result of class privilege, they can be indirectly exploiting other women as workers. Therefore, an analysis of gender relations must take place within the context of prevailing class antagonisms, differentiating the forms of exploitation and subordination experienced by women of different classes. As the majority of women in Central America belong to the peasantry and the working class, it is the struggle of these women that will be the main focus of the articles in this section.

Class differences notwithstanding, the dominant patriarchal ideology assigns to all women the roles of wife and mother, defining the domestic sphere as the only domain where women are allowed some degree of autonomy. While women are idealized as faithful wives, sheltered nurturers of children and pious churchgoers, the structural reality of Central America negates these ideal images. Poverty requires that most working-class women labor outside their homes; a high percentage are deserted by their mates, and their class position makes them vulnerable to sexual exploitation by males from the dominant classes. It is not uncommon, for example, for

---

[1] One of the mistakes of the Allende government in Chile was the failure to incorporate women fully into the Chilean path to socialism. See Norma Chinchilla, "Women in Revolutionary Movements: The Case of Nicaragua," in this chapter.

domestic servants to be sexually harassed by their male employers, only to be subsequently condemned as "immoral." Female workers in the industrial and agricultural sectors are also subjected to this harassment.

The majority of Central America's population lives in the countryside, engaged in some aspect of agricultural production. Life in rural areas is especially difficult for women, most of whom perform full days of agricultural labor in addition to their arduous domestic responsibilities. The dispossession of small landholders by the agro-export sector has created a class of migrant workers whose insecure and poorly-paid jobs cannot adequately support a family. Abandonment of women and their families by male partners, due to low wages and seasonal demand for migratory labor, has led to a high percentage of female-headed households (33% in prerevolutionary Nicaragua). As a result, many Central American women are the sole providers and socializers for their large families.[2]

For those women who migrate to the cities, the opportunities for employment, although better than in the countryside, are still very limited. The path of capitalist development in Central America has created a situation in which women are mostly employed in the marginalized sectors of the economy, as domestic servants and "penny capitalist" street vendors. In prerevolutionary Managua, for example, the women employed in industry constituted less than 20% of the economically active female population.[3]

The majority of the people, whether living in urban centers or rural areas, have little or no access to health care, education or stable employment; in these respects, conditions for women are even worse than for their male counterparts. Even that small percentage of Central American women who have access to training and education for white-collar and professional work is largely concentrated in traditional service occupations—teaching, nursing, and clerical work. As in other capitalist countries, women in most sectors receive lower compensation than men for the same work, although wage differentials are less pronounced in the agricultural sector. This indicates all the more clearly the level of poverty for women in view of the fact that Central American wages in general are at or below subsistence level for men as well. For instance, 62% of the women workers in the most important factories of San Salvador earned less than 80 cents per day in 1969, well below the minimum wage of $1.28;[4] in 1972, wages for women in urban Honduras averaged 58% of men's wages.[5]

---

[2] Central American birth rates are the highest in Latin America. Crude birth rates (live births per 1000 people) in the 1970s were: Honduras, 49; Nicaragua, 46; Guatemala, 42.6; and El Salvador, 39.8. The average for Latin America was 36.7, while the figure for the U.S. was 18.2. Source: Elise Boulding, Shirley A. Nuss, Dorothy Lee Carson, and Michael A. Greenstein, *Handbook of International Data on Women* (New York: Halsted Press, 1976), pp. 196-198.

[3] Susan Ramirez-Horton, "The Role of Women in the Nicaraguan Revolution" in *Nicaragua in Revolution*, Thomas W. Walker, ed. (New York: Praeger, 1982) p. 148.

[4] CAMINO, *El Salvador: Background to the Crisis* (Cambridge, Massachusetts: CAMINO, 1982), p. 55.

[5] USAID, *Estudio sobre la participación de la mujer en el desarrollo económico y social de Honduras* (Tegucigalpa, mimeo, 1977) pp. 116-117; Table 27.

The challenge to the subordinate status of women in Central American societies has not come from an identifiable "feminist" movement as it has in the U.S. and Western Europe. Rather, the struggle against women's oppression has been realized as an integral part of popular revolutionary movements. As the following articles reveal, those who are struggling against women's oppression in Central America view the emancipation of women as inseparable from the larger struggle against the economic and political inequalities inherent in the capitalist system.

At the same time that the most promising challenge to the oppression of women comes within the context of a revolution, many of the more economically privileged women, acting in accordance with their class interests, have allied themselves with the dominant ideology, which ironically also serves to oppress them as women.[6] Nevertheless some middle-class women, who have perceived the relationship between the capitalist system and the exploitative, oppressive structures that such a system creates, have identified themselves with the oppressed.[7]

The participation of women in the revolutionary struggle has assumed an organized and conscious character through the formation of mass organizations that are specifically women's organizations or are dominated by women. In one of the most exemplary cases, Nicaraguan women of varied class backgrounds united in 1977 to form a mass organization under the name "Association of Women Confronting the National Problem" (AMPRONAC).[8] AMPRONAC defined its objectives in the following way:

> *Our organization began its activities on 29th September 1977 with a broad character. Its members are free to adopt different political ideologies but their participation in AMPRONAC must be determined by the following objectives: (1) to encourage the participation of women in the resolution of the problems of the country; (2) to defend the rights of Nicaraguan women in all sectors and in all aspects–economic, social and political; (3) to defend human rights in general.[9]*

AMPRONAC played a very direct role in the Sandinista victory of July 1979 in Nicaragua. A high percentage of the Nicaraguan popular guerrilla forces was made up of women; among them, Dora María Tellez gained prominence as "Comandante Dos" during the Sandinista takeover of the National Palace in August 1978.

After the victory in Nicaragua, AMPRONAC became AMNLAE, the "Association of Nicaraguan Women, 'Luisa Amanda Espinoza,' " named after the first woman militant of the FSLN to be killed in battle. AMNLAE

---

[6] Carolina Castillo, "The Situation of Women in El Salvador," in *Women and War: El Salvador,* (New York, n.d.), p. 6; see also "Fiesta, Fatigue, Fear and Fascism," in *NACLA Report on the Americas,* Vol. XVI, No. 2, (March/April) 1982, p. 17.

[7] Norma Chinchilla notes that more women than men of middle class background have joined the Sandinista revolution; see "Women in Revolutionary Movements" this chapter.

[8] Nicaraguan women's participation is discussed in more detail by Norma Chinchilla in "Women in Revolutionary Movements" and Patricia Flynn in "Women Challenge the Myth," both in this chapter.

[9] *Women in Nicaragua* (London: Nicaraguan Solidarity Campaign, 1981), p. 11.

holds one seat on the Council of State and conducts various activities ranging from editing *La Voz de la Mujer* (*Woman's Voice*), a women's newspaper, broadcasting radio and television programs, and organizing child development centers, to changing the oppressive legal structure.

The experience of Salvadorean women in the struggle for liberation has paralleled that of their Nicaraguan sisters. One of the most important mass organizations in El Salvador is the National Association of Salvadorean Educators (ANDES), which was formed in 1969, and today has a membership which is 80% female. ANDES has played and continues to play an important role in the Salvadorean revolutionary struggle. In 1979 the Association of Salvadorean Women (AMES) was formed to further the integration of women into the revolutionary struggle.

As was the case in Nicaragua, women in El Salvador are participating at every level of the liberation movement. They not only play an important role in building popular organizations and providing logistical support for the guerrillas; but they also engage in combat activity. In El Salvador one third of the FMLN forces are reported to be made up of women. Among the women who are in leadership positions in the FMLN/FDR are Dr. Mélida Anaya Montes ("Ana María"), second in command of the Popular Liberation Forces and a member of the FMLN's Unified Revolutionary Directorate; and Ana Guadalupe Martínez, a leader of the People's Revolutionary Army (EGP) and member of the FDR/FMLN's seven person political-diplomatic commission.[10]

In Guatemala, as well, testimonies document the incorporation of women into revolutionary organizations in large numbers, particularly among indigenous people. However, it appears that no organization has yet arisen specifically intended to mobilize women.

It must be noted that neither Nicaragua's AMNLAE nor El Salvador's AMES is a narrowly defined "feminist" organization; in general this is true of most women's organizations in the Third World. In fact, many members of mass women's movements in the Third World see feminism as yet another divisive manifestation of imperialism that pits women and men against each other, detracting from a unified fight against imperialism and capitalism.[11] While many issues raised by "western feminists" are of universal interest (e.g., the oppressive nature of the nuclear family structure), feminism in industrialized countries by and large reflects conditions peculiar to those societies and cannot be automatically applied to the very different social and economic environments of the Third World.[12] One cannot say, however, that organizations like AMNLAE or AMES are less concerned with equality between men and women than are feminists. As noted

---

[10] An excerpt from Martínez' book *Secret Prisons of El Salvador* is included in this chapter.

[11] For an articulation of this position, see Domitila de Chungara, *Let Me Speak* (New York: Monthly Review Press, 1978).

[12] The term "western feminist" is used to refer to feminists from developed capitalist countries. There are important distinctions, however, among "western feminists," whose approach to feminism ranges from a reformist, bourgeois framework to a Marxist one.

earlier, these organizations view the struggle of women as inseparable from the larger political struggle, and they define their own field of action to be the whole social sphere, not just those aspects of society that are typically defined as women's domain (such as child care). This is not to argue that gender relations are easily transformed within a revolutionary framework. On the contrary, oppressive ideological structures persist for a long time, and women, particularly in Nicaragua and El Salvador, are acutely aware of the necessity to continue their struggle to change these structures. This awareness, a product of experience in struggle, is eloquently articulated by AMES:

> *In our country, as in Nicaragua, new procedures are being developed not only in revolutionary organization and leadership, but also in the transformation of human relations.... We think that in a revolutionary organization there can be no contradictions between professed ideas and behavior. There must be consistency between the choices made, the values affirmed, and daily life—with no exceptions, no ambiguity.*
>
> *Keeping clearly in mind that the struggle for women's liberation must be immersed in the struggle for the liberation of our peoples, it is also necessary to point out that we women are a group defined by our own conditions and specific demands and that we cannot wait for socialism or a change of structures to solve tomorrow the very problems that are today the source of our limitations, of our backwardness as integral human beings, as agents of change....*
>
> *A woman's conscious decision to join in organized struggle implies a transition much longer and more arduous than that of men, inasmuch as we must overcome an endless number of hurdles. If we evaluate these hurdles, we see that, qualitatively speaking, a dual leap has been taken. Obviously this does not mean that we have solved our specific problems of "being a woman," nor is organized participation a panacea that will permit us to achieve our full identity. However, we think that the hallmark of revolutionary feminism is that it locates itself within a context of total transformation of society. We also know that the liberation of women requires a level of generalized collective consciousness which is the result of a development of a new ideology. And that new ideology must be the result of a project for a new structuring of society—a society without private property and without exploitation of one human being by another.*[13]

* * *

The articles in this chapter were selected with two purposes in mind. The first was to provide an insight into the lives of Central American women

---

[13] This quotation is taken from a paper presented by a representative of AMES (Association of Salvadorean Women) at the First Latin American Research Seminar on Women, in San José, Costa Rica, in November 1981. For the complete text, see AMES, "Participation of Latin American Women in Social and Political Organizations: Reflections of Salvadorean Women," in *Monthly Review*, Vol. 34, No. 2 (June, 1982), pp. 11-23.

through their own testimonies. Secondly, we have selected articles that are of an analytical nature, going beyond individual situations to present more general conclusions about the status of women in Central American societies and the reasons for their participation in revolutionary struggle.

Needless to say, the articles included do not address all the important aspects of "the woman question" in Central America. This is due in part to limitations of space, but more importantly it is because women, in particular Third World women, have not been a subject of serious inquiry and analysis until recently. This neglect of scholarship on women is reflected in our chapter by the inadequate treatment given to a number of important questions, among them: the conditions of women among indigenous and minority populations; the situation of Honduran women; the relationship between women and the Church; and the status of middle and upper class women. In addition, space did not permit us to include a comprehensive historical background of gender relations in Central America.

We hope that this chapter will serve as a stimulus for further research on gender relations in Central America, for such research is crucial to an understanding of the oppressive structures that the revolutionary struggles in Central America aim to destroy. More importantly, we hope that the experiences of Central American women, who through their revolutionary practice have advanced the liberation of women and men in different aspects of social life, will be a source of inspiration to all those struggling to build truly liberated societies.

—*Fatma N. Çağatay and Jo-Anne Scott*

Industrialization, Monopoly Capitalism, and Women's Work in Guatemala*

By Norma Stoltz Chinchilla

Norma S. Chinchilla is Professor of Social Relations at the University of California, Irvine, and a coordinating editor of Latin American Perspectives. She has written extensively on Latin America and women in Latin America. In this article, she explores the changes in Guatemalan women's economic status brought about by capital-intensive industrialization. She finds that, in this context, industrial growth has created a disproportionate demand for male labor, leaving women "locked into the most traditional and backward sectors of the economy."

For different reasons, Marxists, feminists, and developmentalists have called attention to the alarming numbers of women in Third World countries who can neither depend on a "family wage" nor find employment in economies in

---

*Excerpted and abridged from *Signs, Journal of Women in Culture and Society*, Vol. 3, No. 1 (Autumn), 1977.

which cash income is becoming increasingly necessary.[1] Surprisingly, very little is really understood about the political economy of women's work, the factors which determine when and where women are employed, and the social and political consequences of particular configurations of "women's work."

Industrialization almost universally destroys or weakens artisan industries, which are usually in the hands of women. But whether industrialization then absorbs the women displaced from productive roles in the home or traditional precapitalist economy into manufacturing depends on the total political-economic context in which it occurs. The fate of women depends, in the final analysis, not so much on the policies of their governments or the "enlightenment" of the men around them as on the function that the economy of which they are a part serves in the world system.

Guatemala is a case of rapid recent industrial growth in which, unlike industrialization in late nineteenth-century Mexico and early twentieth-century Argentina, women have not been pushed into manufacturing industries in large numbers and have even declined proportionally in industries considered "female."[2] Although more women are working than ever before, the proportion of women officially classified as working has changed very little. Those who work remain largely in the most backward sectors of the economy, except for the rapidly expanding clerical, sales, and professional strata. Industrial growth is mostly capital intensive, based on foreign monopoly capital, and exploitative of a cheap labor force. This industrialization, rather than destroying the large agricultural sector, has held intact a sector which produces cash crops for export but which relies on traditional, labor-intensive methods of production, including a large seasonally employed work force. This study is designed to explore, within Guatemala's particular historical context, the changes in occupational structure, demand for labor, division of labor by sex, and inequality of employment by sex during industrial expansion.

Foreign Capital, Industry, and Women's Work in Guatemala before 1944

Capitalist relations of production came late to Guatemala. Before World War II the proportion of the population that was working for wages

---

[1] See, e.g., Frederick Engels, *Origin of the Family, the State, and Private Property* (New York: International Publishers, 1972); and Charlotte Perkins Gilman, *The Home: Its Work and Influence* (New York: Maclure, Phillips & Co., 1903). Two authors who make reference to the connection between decreased fertility and women working outside the home are Nadia Haggag Youssef, *Women and Work in Developing Societies*, Population Monograph Series, No. 15 (Berkeley: University of California, 1974), p. 2; and Nora Scott Kinzer, "Priests, Machos, and Babies: Or Latin American Women and the Manichaean Heresy," *Journal of Marriage and the Family* 35, No. 2 (1973), pp. 300-312.

[2] See Margaret Towner, "Monopoly Capitalism and Women's Work During the Porfiriato," and Nancy Caro Hollander, "Women Workers and the Class Struggle: The Case of Argentina," both in *Latin American Perspectives* 4 (Winter 1977), pp. 90-105 and 180-93, respectively.

was very small. However, foreign control of the Guatemalan economy was established very early and was not successfully challenged, and even then in a limited way, until the revolution of 1944. Manufacturing and modern forms of industrial organization began after the liberal reforms of the 1880s and were made possible by the establishment of public education, communications, a banking system, and new roads and ports.

Lured by concessions offered by the dictator Cabrera, three large U.S. companies—the United Fruit Company, Electric Bond and Share, and International Railways of Central America—entered Guatemala and were able to dominate its economy and politics until 1944. Among them, they had the power to enthrone and dethrone presidents and to exploit local labor.[3]

In the context of a largely agricultural economy in which most of the population worked under precapitalist relations of production, it is not surprising that female suffrage was never seriously considered in the package of reforms that characterize the Liberal period. One of the leading intellectuals opined that there was no point in introducing political equality for women in Guatemala since it clearly had "not worked" in the countries where it had been tried: "The right of suffrage ought not to be granted to the woman for nature created her for the home and she is only fitted to be occupied with the multitudinous and difficult family cares, in feeding and educating the children, in teaching them morals and to know the rights and duties which they will later have as citizens. The destiny of the mother does not permit her to busy herself with politics."[4]

Yet contrary to this idealized image, the contribution of women to social production in an economy in which the boundaries between home and work were still unclear must have been great. Women undoubtedly raised food for family consumption or exchange and made clothing, pottery, candles, and cooking utensils. When forced labor was reinstituted in the last quarter of the nineteenth century, rural women must have shared, if not assumed completely, the responsibility for cultivation while the men were away. The 1921 census records that women made up more than half (58 percent) of the nonagricultural labor force and 18 percent of the total number of workers.[5] Furthermore, women were employed in the sectors of the economy with the largest numbers of workers: 45 percent of those in food; 20 percent of the public employees (including teachers, nurses, and nuns); 10 percent of those in "electricity"; 9 percent of those in "specialized arts and industries" (musicians, office workers, typesetters, fireworks makers); and 0.8 percent of those in "furs and skins." The largest number of female employees, then as now, were domestic workers—63 percent. Even when this figure is removed from the statistics, women still made up 26 percent of all nonagricultural, nondomestic workers, a proportion which has declined with

---

[3] Jaime Díaz Rozzotto, *El carácter de la revolución democrátic burguesa carriente* (México: Ediciones Revista "Horizonte" Costa Amic, 1958).

[4] Rafael Montufar, cited by Chester Lloyd Jones, *Guatemala: Past and Present* (Minneapolis: University of Minnesota Press, 1940), p. 105.

[5] Dirección General de Estadística, *Censo de población* (Guatemala: Tipografía Nacional, 1921).

industrialization. The contribution of women to nondomestic production prior to industrialization was great. Evidence suggests that Guatemalan women had an economic role not unlike that of women in preindustrial, precapitalist Mexico, Argentina, and the United States—an important and varied one.

Nationalist Capitalist Industrialization, 1944-54

By 1944 the repressed demands for industrial expansion and agrarian reform had exploded into the "revolution of 1944," based on a multiclass movement in which urban women, especially teachers, played an important role.[6] The early reforms extended bourgeois democracy and legal protections for workers. Programs included expansion of education, establishment of rural schools, creation of social security for workers, encouragement of unions, indemnification for dismissed workers, regulation of exploitative working conditions (especially for women), guaranteed maternity leave, recognition of "illegitimate" children, and political equality.[7] The government strategy for industrial growth reflected the dual goals of the multiclass movement: "social justice" for workers and peasants and competitive opportunities for national "progressive" capitalists interested in producing for the expanding internal market. Foreign investors were to be welcomed as long as they obeyed indigenous labor laws. The Guatemalan state was to assume a larger role in planning, directing, and regulating investment.

Although landlord and foreign capitalist opposition to agrarian reform and regulation of foreign investment created uncertainty and hindered industrial expansion, the index of manufacturing increased a healthy 13.1 percent in four years (1946-50), due to growth in the tobacco, chemical, nonmetallic mineral, and food industries. Output declined slightly in textiles, clothing, and wood. Industries appeared in new areas of production, including cement, food processing, clothing, and transformation of raw materials.[8] At the beginning of the period, the largest concentrations of workers were still in traditional industries: food, clothing, footwear, and textiles. These, in addition to chemicals (especially fireworks and matchmaking), were also the highest categories of female employment. Although we lack reliable data on the number of new workers who entered the work force during this period, it seems likely that more women were drawn into industrial employment at the same time that women's wages in manufacturing increased.

---

[6] The teachers founded a permanent national association, the STEG, on January 15, 1945, which became second only to the railway workers' union in political importance; see Díaz Rozzotto; and Edwin Bishop, "The Guatemalan Labor Movement, 1944-1959" (Ph.D. dissertation, University of Wisconsin, 1959).

[7] Díaz Rozzotto; and Susanne Jonas, "The Democracy That Gave Way: The Guatemalan Revolution of 1944-54," in *Guatemala*, Suzanne Jonas and David Tobis, eds. (Berkeley, Calif.: North American Congress on Latin America, 1974), pp. 44-56.

[8] Mario Monteforte Toledo, *Centro América: subdesarrollo y dependencia* (México: Universidad Nacional Autónoma de México, 1972), 1, p. 274.

Industrialization without Redistribution, 1954 to Present

The revolution of 1944 was overturned ten years later and with it the "soft line" on industrialization. Counterrevolution and the "hard line" on industrialization took its place. The "soft line" policy had been characterized by agrarian reform, increased consumption, improvement of the standard of living, alleviation of gross inequities, regulation of foreign investment, and policies favoring public investment and the middle class. "Hard line" industrial strategy seemed the only means to contain class struggle (in the short run) and leave existing dominant groups intact. Such a strategy depended on the establishment of the Central American Common Market in order to expand demand without internal redistribution.[9] Generous incentives were given through it to industries which developed new exports (cattle, flowers, seeds, and nonessential oils) and those which assembled products previously imported (drugs, cosmetics, etc.). National investors were guaranteed no tax reforms and minimal state interferences, while foreign investors were promised free repatriation of profits.[10]

The hard line industrial strategy has yielded increased output, but the benefits of increased production have accrued to a very few. The market remains very small, and the jobs created few. As a result, the number of people working in agriculture and the service sector remains high, and both foreign investors and large landowners have a vested interest in keeping it that way.

Land and Rural Labor

In the two decades since agrarian reforms were abolished, agricultural land ownership has reconcentrated. Severe repression of union activities and the existence of few alternatives for employment assure low wages, which are clearly beneficial to landlords and foreign investors.

Although agricultural production has become large and modern, working conditions are almost as harsh as they were under forced labor. Seasonal workers, recruited on large *fincas*, often work as a family unit to pay off loans incurred earlier in the year. Their hours are long, their rations meager, their housing sparse. Women and children risk transportation in open trucks and often die in accidents or of carbon monoxide fumes. They live primitively, with as many as 500 workers in large open-air dormitories that have dirt floors and laminated roofs, no sanitary facilities, electricity, or potable water. They sleep on the ground, in hammocks, or on straw mats. They are given about twelve to fourteen pounds of corn per week,

---

[9] Susanne Jonas, "Master-minding the Mini-Market: U.S. Aid to the Central American Common Market," also in abridged form in Chapter 3 of this reader. –Ed.

[10] As much as 66 percent of all direct investments came from the United States in 1969, an increase of 128.8 percent over 1950, as compared to an increase of 37 percent during the 1950s (see Gert Rosenthal, "The Development of the Central American Common Market" [Ph.D. thesis, Guatemala, 1971], chap. 3, pp. 4, 5, 10, cited by David Tobis, "The U.S. Investment Bubble in Guatemala," in Jonas and Tobis, p. 132, n. 3).

one to two pounds of beans, and occasionally some sugar and rice. Children receive half rations and women none if they do not work because of their young children. Sickness among workers who migrate from the highlands to the coastal lowlands is common. Insecticide poisoning is frequent, and the amount of DDT in mother's milk has been found to be dangerously high. Women earn the same wages as men and are an important part of the rural labor force, although only 7 percent are officially registered as agricultural workers. Even with all of its members working, however, an entire family earned an average of $1.00 a day in 1966, and about half of that was actually taken back after the migration.[11] Only food from the sub-family plot and occasional cash income from the sales of handicrafts and wood can help rural families survive on the low wages of seasonal labor.

Employment and Industrialization

Agriculture remains the most important sector of the economy in terms of foreign exchange and employment; in 1973 it employed 65.5 percent of all male workers. Nevertheless, agriculture as a source of *new* employment has fallen behind. On the other hand, manufacturing and construction have attracted large amounts of new investment and have increased the absolute number of jobs. The number of new occupational specialties has created a demand for new labor which men have filled in much greater proportion than women, even in industries, such as textiles and tobacco, that have traditionally hired women.

It would appear to be the destruction of independent artisan industries, without an increased demand for factory labor, that has seriously affected the employment of women in the manufacturing sector. Moreover, the industrial censuses of 1946 and 1965 report a decline in female workers from 22 to 18 percent. The largest declines are in tobacco, textiles, chemicals, rubber, foods, and paper. For male workers, on the other hand, employment is rapidly increasing in the areas of chemicals, paper, rubber, and metal products, as well as electrical appliances, transportation, and furniture, which first appear in the 1965 census. Thus, not only have new industries created a disproportionate demand for male labor, but men are replacing women in some industries.

Since the population continues to increase, and agriculture and manufacturing absorb relatively little labor, the residual category, that is, the tertiary sector, composed of commerce, transportation, communication, and services, must act as the "sponge" for the remaining labor. This sector now employs 22.4 percent of all workers, as compared to 16.9 percent in 1950 and 19.9 percent in 1964. The increases are not as dramatic for women, who have been concentrated in this sector since the 1921 census as

---

[11] Lester J. Schmid, "El papel de la mano de obra migratoria en el desarrollo económico de Guatemala," *Economía* 15 (1968), pp. 68-70; and Escuela Facultativa de C. C. Económicas de Occidente y Comité Interamericano de Desarrollo Agrícola, *Tenencia de la tierra y desarrollo socio-económico del sector agrícola en Guatemala* (Guatemala: Editorial Universitaria, 1971).

domestic servants or teachers. While two out of three women worked in the tertiary sector in 1973, the majority were not employed in commerce, transportation, or communications (as were 44 percent of male workers), but in domestic service; 64 percent of all female tertiary sector workers are classified as maids. Thus, while industrial growth has created new employment areas for men and women—clerical, sales, and professional— the proportion of all women who are domestics has not dropped below 40 percent, and the absolute number of women in this category has actually increased by 28.9 percent since 1964.

Industrialization and Occupational Structure

The continuing concentrations of workers in domestic service and agriculture conceal some important transformations in the occupational structure which have resulted from the type of industrial growth Guatemala has experienced in recent years. Large corporations with world-wide markets, banks involved in world-wide transactions, and even landowners who read daily computer printouts require a corps of technical experts and office workers. Moreover, expanded commercial activity requires clerks and salespeople.

Women are in fact desirable as "white collar" workers in Guatemala, as in the United States, because they can dress to "sell" the product or service, they have education and skill (facility in several languages, for example), and will accept low pay with little possibility of advancement when there is a large reserve of women who can replace them. The proportion of women in clerical work rose to 34 percent in Guatemala in 1973, although they were concentrated in secretarial rather than in skilled or unskilled office work categories. It is unlikely, however, that women will dominate this category of employment in Guatemala, as they do elsewhere, since it is one of the few expanding sources of employment for male high school graduates who are expected to support their families.

While the administrative, owner, manager category of employment has declined sharply for both men and women in the recent period of foreign penetration—by 77 percent for males and 99 percent for women since 1964—the demand for professionals and technicians has risen dramatically and created a new stratum of employment for those few women with technical and professional training, which is reflected in census statistics. To what extent this trend will continue is difficult to predict, since the fiscal crisis of the Guatemalan state makes expansion of services virtually impossible without major reforms, and professional and technical employment depends on state employment, especially for women. Moreover, although one of every three "technical or professional" workers is a female, and the percentage of all women workers in this area rose to 11 percent in 1973, the proportion of women to men is declining as the category expands, and the degree of sex segregation within the category may be increasing overall. Indeed, the large proportion of "professional" women obscures their concentration in three sectors of employment—teaching, nursing, and social work—which require no university degrees and are poorly paid. Three out of every four professional women are actually teachers, the majority in public schools. If nonuniversity teaching were treated separately, professional work would clearly constitute a male sector of employment.

Inequality by Sex

While it is true that women have entered the labor force at a faster *rate* than men since 1950, because of a lower base, it is also true that the occupational structure has become increasingly segregated by sex, except for the expanding areas of sales and commerce. The ratio of male to female workers has actually increased from 1.93 to 2.29. The increased segregation by sex has been high among artisans and operatives, unskilled laborers, and transportation workers—those categories most directly affected by expanded industrial output. Only in services do women outnumber men, by a slightly declining margin. Although the wages of women relative to men in manufacturing are slightly more equal in the skilled category and considerably more equal in the unskilled category, the wages of everyone are depressed to such an extent that it makes little difference. Industrial growth has meant increasing inequality of wealth and opportunity overall and greater inequality of employment by sex.

Under conditions of competitive capitalism (in the developed countries) and early national (dependent) capitalist development (in Latin America), the demand for labor in a previously agricultural economy was great. In the United States, Argentina, Mexico, and perhaps elsewhere, large numbers of women workers were drawn into the first factories, where they were at the center of the most militant political and economic struggles of their day. To a lesser extent this was also true of the nationalist phase of industrial growth in Guatemala, where the expansion of the market and the promise of agrarian reform put a premium on the labor of women willing to work for wages.

Yet under industrial growth conditioned by the needs of monopoly capitalism, the period of a large industrial work force composed in large part of women is skipped. Thus in Guatemala the dramatic increases in industrial production are accompanied by only modest increases in employment, hardly sufficient to cover the number of traditional jobs eliminated or the increase in population. The level of unemployment is high; advocating, as government policy, incentives for employing females would only extend their superexploitation. Most workers, male and female—but especially female—remain locked into the most traditional and backward sectors of the economy (subsistence agriculture and domestic service). Lacking adequate employment outside the home and lacking sufficient income coming into the home, the role of women in the daily reproduction of labor power becomes more important than ever for survival.

Industrial growth, once the liberal panacea to poverty and backward ideas about "women's place," becomes linked to increased poverty and feudal patriarchy. Modernity and backwardness in employment and in the status of women arrive in the same package. The solution is not more of the same, that is, more industrialization, more modernity within the same framework, but the necessity for a new framework in which industrialization has the truly liberating effect on backbreaking labor and the control of women as property that it was meant to have.

Industrial growth under imperialism thus generates and accentuates many of the contradictions it was supposed to solve and in so doing creates its own opposition. Women as consumers, direct producers in the countryside, and urban workers increasingly become part of this opposition to unemployment, rising food prices, and increased repression. It is not surprising that in Guatemala, in the absence of a large female industrial work force, the mobilizations of professional and semiprofessional women (such as teachers, nurses, and social workers) in alliance with other social groups have had strategic importance. While their participation so far has been directed toward political and economic demands on behalf of classes, rather than social and cultural demands that speak to the special oppression of women, it is not inconceivable that at some point in the struggle "women's consciousness" and "class consciousness" might intersect. In the meantime, however, the struggle of women is inseparable from the struggle of the majority of the population for survival.

Testimonies of Guatemalan Women*
By Luz Alicia Herrera
Translated by Maria Alice Jacob

The interviewer is a Guatemalan woman who is also involved in the struggles of the mass movement. These interviews serve to illustrate the personal dimension of the analysis developed in the previous selection by Norma Chinchilla.

Introduction

As a contribution to the knowledge of Guatemalan social reality, I offer the following statements as they were told to me by the women themselves. Each is selected for a reason. Through the statement of the first woman, we discover thousands of Guatemalan women: poor peasants, agricultural workers, maids, industrial workers, unmarried mothers, and the women who are active in the struggle of popular organizations. Through the statement of the second woman, we see an example of a person from a wealthy background who opts for the interests of the great oppressed majority of Guatemalans. We present this second interview, knowing full well that it may generate the common psychological interpretation that this serious process of transformation is actually a manifestation of "social resentment."

*Excerpted and abridged from *Latin American Perspectives,* Issues 25 and 26, Spring and Summer 1980, Vol. VII, Nos. 2 and 3.

With such an explanation the bourgeoisie tries to dismiss the choice of those who side with the majority of the people.

First Woman's Testimony

I was born in a little village on the southeast coast. I was fifteen when we moved to a parcel of land far away, still on the same south coast. My mother was a widow. There were four children, three girls and a boy. In the new place where we went to live, my mother established a little restaurant. We cooked for thirty people. We also picked cotton. My mother, my thirteen-year-old sister, and I would get up at one in the morning to do the household chores: cook corn, make tortillas, prepare food and clean the house. At 6 o'clock all was ready, and at 7 a.m. we would take the bus to the cotton fields. I used to go with my sister to a plantation that employed between 150 and 200 cotton pickers, men and women.

On the plantation, an active picker would pick 100 to 150 pounds of cotton. My sister and I would pick 100 pounds between us and be paid one cent per pound. We would take our own food with us. When it rained, we would work from 8 a.m. in the morning to 3 p.m. in the afternoon. If the weather was very humid, we would work from 12 noon to 3 p.m. in the afternoon.

It is hard work under the hot sun on a cotton plantation. The women wore hats to protect their heads from the sun. There would be many of us women with the sack of cotton tied to our waists. The foreman and the labor contractors made sure that the workers kept their attention on the picking and tried to keep them from establishing contact with their fellow workers.

Sometimes, when we were picking cotton, the airplane would fly over us, spraying insecticide, and the majority of the workers would get poisoned. We had to hide the water and food so that the poison wouldn't get to them.

The foremen were rough and would make the women use the plough by themselves if they left some cotton behind. They treated us badly and humiliated us. The indigenous workers were treated even worse than other workers. They were given only tortillas and beans to eat. Indigenous workers were forced to weigh their cotton on a different scale, undoubtedly to pay them less. The indigenous workers came with their whole families to work—wives and children. The children were only five years old when they began to pick cotton.

Working on the plantation, I was angry about earning so little. Working under the hot sun all day and for so little pay! The foreman and the labor contractors who took advantage of us thought they were kings. A man from the village—a contractor—hired the rest of the workers from the village to do the picking. The foremen were also exploited people but they chose to be on the side of the bosses. We would get home from work at 6 or 7 p.m. and after that feed the other workers—about thirty people outside of our family. Then we would do the dishes and start to cook corn all over again. We would cook 25 pounds of corn a day.

"Serious work. Get up, get up, it's time." That's how my mother would wake us up. So short was the night! We would go to bed at 10 p.m. the evening before and get up at 1 a.m. in the morning. At that time, I was fifteen years old and my sister was thirteen; since we were the eldest, we were made to do the hardest work. We also worked on the little plot of land that was given to my mother. On it, we would plant corn, *maicillo* (millet), and chile for everyday use. Sometimes we would sell the little bit that was left. For us, there were no Sundays, no good times. Only weeks of work.

In 1963, through a friend, I got a job working as a babysitter and maid in Escuintla. I worked there for five years. The first six months they paid me seven *quetzales* a month[1] to take care of a little girl from 7 a.m. in the morning to noon when the woman of the house, who was a secretary in an office, would get home.

After this job I returned to my mother's place in the village. The three of us sisters separated from my mother because she was with a man who didn't like us. We rented a tiny house. With a little money that my mother gave us we started a store, and, there in the house, my sister (since she is a dressmaker) had her sewing machine, and we continued with the little restaurant, just we three. There we had thirty mobile military police and the people who passed by on their way to the *fincas* (ranches) for customers. The three of us lived happily. We earned very little, just enough to eat, more or less dress, and shoe ourselves.

After that, I came once again to work in Escuintla, in a soft-drink stand. There I worked only for room and board. During this time I had the stupidity to run off with a boyfriend. He studied in the capital and his parents paid for him to stay in a boarding house. From the soft-drink stand, I went with him to the capital. I lived a year and a half with him. We lived on what his parents sent us in a small room that didn't have a place to cook so we bought our meals. I put up with this difficult situation for a year and a half. I went to work in a clothing factory. I was a seam-gatherer. It was my job to gather and trim. I earned four quetzales and twelve cents weekly. I didn't know how to sew on the electric machines. There were times when I worked extra hours and then I would earn twenty quetzales a month. But I didn't continue in this factory because he didn't like me to work. At the same time, what we had didn't cover anything. I became so desperate that I went home to my mother in the village, once again.

My boyfriend fought with me a lot because I didn't get pregnant. "You'll never have a child; heaven knows what things you do" [he would say]. Well, it was just my bad luck that the month I left him I was already pregnant, but neither of us knew it then. Once when I was with my mother, I noticed how I was, and I told my sister and she told my mother. And my mother caused a big uproar. My mother did not like the boy and she was angry at me. My mother threw me out of the house on my own. I went to

---

[1] One quetzal is the equivalent of U.S. $1.

a friend's, the one with the soft-drink stand and told her my problem, and I worked with her for room and board.

After two months, my mother arrived to look for me and took me back to the house. I returned to the house and in the state I was in, no one would give me work. An uncle told me, "You can't work in a bar anymore." I told the problem to a neighbor who had a *nixtamal* (the dough used for tortillas) mill. She let me go there and grind for one quetzal a day. I felt very tired and worn-out working there. Everyday my belly grew larger. My friend found some women who would buy tortillas from me each day and she ground my corn without charging me a cent. Daily, I ground twenty pounds of corn, made and sold the corn. After that, I washed clothes for people, did embroidery and needlework, and bought small clothing to sell with the earnings of the needlework. My stepfather would say: "I will not maintain someone else's children," and my mother would get angry with me.

I sent a message to my boyfriend about my pregnancy, and the response he gave was that the child I was about to have was no child of his, and he wouldn't pass me one cent—at least until the child was born. My son was three months old when my boyfriend came to see him with his mother. They came with the idea of taking him away from me but, like the majority of mothers who struggle to keep their children, I wouldn't give him up.

My ex-boyfriend had married another girl and he wanted to keep me as his lover. He only arrived to see his child when he was drunk and never even brought him candy. One time he even arrived with a revolver, threatening us from the window. My sister and I threw him out and punched him. Not until my son was three years old did I manage to convince his father to recognize him. I did it because children need to carry their father's name.

My son didn't like his father. Because he is not with us, he would say. He would notice that other fathers would bring their little children home from school. I've told him everything, and he doesn't like his father. "Because he was bad with us, because of that, I only love you," the child would say to me.

I began working for the revolution some time ago. My stepfather was from a peasant organization. Aside from the fact that he was bad with us, sometimes, when he was in good humor, he gave us advice and we began to collaborate with the organization in the countryside. I, working as a babysitter, already collaborated.

He did not think like me.[2] He is a teacher but he doesn't understand the necessity of organizing the workers. He didn't know that I had those ideas and when he realized it, he told me not to get involved in anything, that this was bad for me. I told him that as long as I lived, I would continue struggling for an organization wherever I was and that there were no limits on where my commitment might take me. "You believe in a struggle that will never triumph, one that won't ever even end," he would say. I went to work in a factory again, and there, convinced that I should stay, joined a

---

[2] Here she seems to be referring back to her ex-boyfriend (rather than her stepfather).

union. I have girlfriends who say I am crazy, that I shouldn't get involved in these things, that all I am going to get in return is unemployment or death. But I feel even braver when they tell me that I am going to end up dead. Also, it makes me want to know things I haven't known before.

I have had a lot of serious problems, but I have never been afraid. They have taken away my job.... I think about my son. But he tells me: "If my mother dies, I will stay with the *compañeros* (comrades)..." The compañeros are from the *sindicato* (union). Therefore, thinking about the welfare of my child has not kept me from organizing. Sooner or later we all have to die. It might be in some accident. My little boy already is aware of everything and I have taught him how one survives here. He already pays attention to the movements of the police... and advises us of them.

Second Woman's Testimony

What motivated you to join the struggle to transform Guatemalan society?

I am going to answer you with what may seem to be a contradiction but it was, precisely, because of my nonproletarian class background. I come from what could be called the agro-export bourgeoisie. As a child, I customarily spent my end-of-the-year vacation at the *finca*. This vacation coincided with cutting and harvesting. It was there where the answers that were given to my innumerable questions didn't satisfy my childhood curiosity about the conditions I confronted daily.

My father considered the Indian a species half-way between human and animal. I noticed this in a number of incidents. For example, one day, seeing hundreds of men, women, and children descend from the mountains bathed in sweat, carrying enormous loads, I had an enormous feeling of pain and anguish. My father must have noticed it because he explained that Indians were born to do such work, that they were incapable of doing any other, that they were dumb, lazy, drunken, that they had no desire to better themselves, and that they lacked our intelligence—those of us who were descendants of Spaniards. (He never referred to us as *ladinos;* he considered us to be located at the top of the social stratification among whites, and the term *ladino* was applied to the *mestizo* or white who did not possess a powerful name).

At harvest time, the labor of *mozos colonos* (resident tenants) or *rancheros* (ranch hands) who live on the finca is not sufficient, and day laborers are contracted from more arid regions where from necessity they migrate to the fincas to supplement their precarious family income. They would arrive in trucks, piled up like animals, dragging along with them their misery and disease. They were put up in enormous *galeras* (sheds) which only had a few posts, a roof, and no walls. There, each family gathered around a fireplace previously placed, was given a *comal* (a piece of clay on which corn tortillas are cooked), an empty tin can of milk or whatever other product in which the corn could be cooked, a grinding stone, and naturally, tools. There wouldn't even be a cloth dividing one family from another.

I was strictly prohibited from entering these sheds because the Indians were said to have fleas, were dirty, and some were sick. One night, I remember, a child in one of the sheds began to cough. The next day, there were about five children coughing; the next week, all of the children had whooping cough. The sheds were almost in front of the house of the finca, and during the night you could hear the coughing of the little children as though it were part of a bad dream. A certain fear overcame me and I ran to my father's room to tell my father that these children were going to die, that they were suffocating, and that we had to do something. My father took my hand and walked me back to my room, put me to bed, covered me up and said sweetly, "Don't worry, they're not children, they're Indians."

Thus, I later saw, lined up in front of the house, some little caskets, painted white, accompanied only by the fathers, mothers, and others who were most likely relatives. The rest of their fellow workers were missing because the harvest had to continue. At night, much larger groups of people climbed up to the cemetery; many Indians, lighting the way with candles, lanterns of wood and paper, moving in silence or with low voices, speaking in low voices in dialect, carrying out their rituals. My father pointed out to me "these pagans who worship idols and get drunk and weep and wail in the cemetery."

"You see?" he would say, "they don't even care that their children have died; the only thing that interests them is the *guaro* (liquor); they are not like us."

My questions were endless. Innocently, I asked why shoes weren't bought for them, why they weren't given food, why the children had inflated stomachs, why they never laughed, why they spoke differently, why doctors weren't called for them. Why? Why? Until one day, my father, tired of so much questioning, said, "Because they are Indians, understand? I don't want to hear another word about the matter again."

I began to ask questions again and I received a beating. I learned, then, "not to stick your nose in matters that don't concern you," and I opted for silence. For several years I lived these experiences, always painful.

I remember that in order to reach the finca, two jeeps were necessary, one for us and one for the baggage and food. One would suppose that these were marvelous vacations; our friends and my father's friends would arrive at the ranch, I would entertain myself and almost grow accustomed to the situation. But as I grew to adolescence, I began to judge my parents and their friends; now it was no longer necessary to ask questions. I knew by then; there was injustice and exploitation but not at the level of reason. I just felt it.

One of the last times I was there at the finca, there was a storm, rains that wouldn't stop. The rivers grew and we had to return to the capital. The jeeps couldn't pass to the other side. Up on their shoulders, I saw my mother and brothers and sisters who went ahead. All on the shoulders of Indians, dirty and sweaty. I swore I would never return, and so I never did.

I had a turbulent adolescence. I lived in a world of total frivolity. Sex presented itself in a very natural manner. I had a group of friends who often got together to have fun. There were parties with everything—food, alcohol, even drugs. Accustomed as I was to not asking questions, I only observed. Inside me I had a lot of doubts: why was it necessary for us to have stimulants in order to be happy? I saw this decadence, this rottenness, this promiscuity as natural, but I didn't stop thinking. I was always looking for another path, another way out, another life.

My parents didn't stop worrying about me. They thought it wasn't normal for me to be worried about such things. To them, it was irrational for me to be sad at seeing a beggar or kids who sleep on the streets covered with newspapers or drunkards lying on the streets. I was crazy! They sent me to a psychologist. Laziness was my problem. They registered me at the university so I would "do something." It wasn't the national university, of course, but the Catholic one (Universidad de Rafael Landiver). I wasn't enthusiastic about it at first, but to my surprise, I met young men and women from the same background as my own, with the same concerns. We started to look together for solutions, read books, make hypotheses, and try to change the world. We were a group of seven people. Five of them have died, victims of repression.

How was your political education after that?

This group of seven who shared the same ideas, not yet clearly defined, fell apart. I returned to being alone. I took a trip to Europe where I met an old militant who lived in political exile. He started telling me his personal experiences, answering my many doubts, lecturing to me, showing me the way. Back in Guatemala, I immediately tried to get involved in practice. That's when I acquired my real education. A new conception of the world and of life. A well-defined objective: contribute to the continuation of the revolution that was stopped in Guatemala in 1954, a revolution that Guatemala still needs.

Studying and practicing Marxism resolved the doubts of my childhood and adolescence. Now I know what the Indian is, what my father and other landlords like him are, what we—myself included—the salaried middle sectors are, what the urban and agricultural proletariat is.

In what way have you been affected by political repression in Guatemala?

Before responding to this question, I'd like to relate what I know of the repression: in the houses of the bourgeoisie, particularly in that of my parents, there is economic aid to repressive groups. Fortunately, at the time when these right-wing paramilitary groups appeared, I already had a political formation, and I knew how to take advantage of all occasions. I knew many people in "La Mano" (National Organized Anti-Communist Movement), made up of groups of assassins who massacred thousands of peasants in the eastern part of the country under the orders of ex-President Arana Osorio. Many times I have had to bite my tongue. I would hear these men speak of us, vainglorious about their exploits, telling how they personally fight against the guerrillas, mentioning forms of tortures that Cuban exiles in Guatemala would provide them. I knew of their assaults and their links. All of this we studied and interpreted with the compañeros;

they never said more in my house than what they wanted me to hear, but they always revealed more than they thought they did.

I remember, for example, that in an assault on the Bank of Guatemala, they dressed up as priests. I knew, likewise, that it was the priest of a certain Church who gave them the cassocks. I saw them dressed up as women on one occasion (for purposes of disguise, they said). I saw my mother dye the hair of one of them. In short, I had them very close and and what I most remember about them was the death outlined in their eyes. Such hard looks behind friendly smiles. Since they were dealing with paid groups, little by little they began to degenerate into common delinquents, and in doing so entered into conflict with their "papa" Arana who took responsibility for eliminating them one by one after the supposed "pacification" of the eastern part of the country.

These events were clear manifestations of the union between the Church and the dominant classes. "The faithful, above all the poor and the miserable, should be humble and accept the Christian dogma along with exploitation because God knows what he does. Some were born to be poor and some to be rich. It is the law of God."

I, personally, have not been a victim of repression. Nevertheless, many compañeros in the struggle, which is much broader than the popular organization to which I belong, have been its victims. With so many of these Guatemalans (men and women) who have been captured or have died I feel solidarity!

What has been your relation with your compañeros?

I had to pass several difficult tests and demonstrate my loyalty to the revolutionary struggle. Revolutionary discipline demands of us a behavior worthy of someone who struggles with the oppressed of Guatemala, our brothers and sisters. In this struggle, men and women have equal rights and obligations such that I can say that my relationship with both is very good.

What has been the historic participation of Guatemalan women in social change?

Definitely the participation of women throughout the long history of Guatemala is undeniable. At the moment, I can think of the example of Maria Chinchilla who died struggling for changes in the schools and the working conditions of teachers. Women within the dominant classes play a role too; remember, for example, the participation of women in the 1954 campaign to overthrow President Arbenz.

In your opinion, what do women need to do to achieve their liberation?

In this case, let me speak concretely of the revolutionary woman. The fundamental tasks that are necessary to achieve her liberation cannot be separated from the political emancipation of the population. To speak of personal liberation doesn't make sense for us. Men and women linked to the revolutionary struggle work together for the liberation from dependency, underdevelopment, and the ignorance that typifies us as a backward country, by means of a permanent struggle that will allow us to construct a society free of exploitation of man by man. It is only possible to speak of liberation in a society not divided in classes.

Within all of the groups that struggle for the interests of the great majority of oppressed people, there are remnants of typical bourgeois *machismo*, and there, fundamentally, the revolutionary woman has a well-defined task. These particular cases have to be eliminated through study, dialogue, criticism and self-criticism.

Is there some particular experience you would like to share?

Yes, there is one. After several years in this struggle—ones dedicated exclusively to the study of Marxism, education of young people and theoretical work—I became anxious to go out to the countryside. One nice day in the month of July, two compañeros and I went out destined for a place in one of the departments (provinces). During the day, we rested a little but at night we walked all the time in order to finally arrive at different little towns, intersections, and fincas where we would meet with agrarian workers to talk about their struggle. There for the first time since I had first seen Indians in the service of my father, we talked together as equals, as comrades.

Women in El Salvador*
By Toye Helena Brewer

The story of the women of El Salvador, while inseparable from the larger context of the crisis in Salvadorean society, must also be understood in its own right. This article is devoted to the specific conditions of the majority of women's lives, the 80% who form the poor, the landless and the powerless.

Women in Rural Areas

Land distribution in El Salvador is extremely skewed; of all rural Salvadorean families, 40.9% are classified as landless and must depend on wage labor to meet their subsistence needs. Wage work supplies only 51.6% of their income owing to extremely low wages and extremely high rates of seasonal unemployment and underemployment. Landless rural families derive the other 50% of their subsistence income from the cultivation of small garden plots, petty commerce, crafts, animal husbandry and fishing, among other things. Additionally, families with less than 2 hectares can rely on their crops for only 1/3 or less of their income and similarly must

---

*This selection is an abridged version of chapter six of *El Salvador: Background to the Crisis* (Cambridge, Massachusetts: Central America Information Office, 1982).

engage in wage labor and a wide range of other subsistence activities.[1] These figures reveal that among the landless, as well as the *minifundistas*, 90% of rural Salvadorean families, women's work is essential to family income and subsistence. While men migrate to look for wage labor opportunities on large plantations, women engage in subsistence activities such as gardening, craftsmaking, raising animals for sale, and finding any other odd jobs that may be available. At harvest time, it is common for an entire rural family to migrate for 2-3 months to a plantation in order to pick coffee beans to supplement their income.[2] The domestic unit, therefore, supplements the wage, which does not meet subsistence requirements, and also provides labor during the harvest when large numbers of workers are needed.

According to official figures from the Salvadorean Planning Ministry, women, who form 31% of the labor force nationally, form only 22% of the rural labor force.[3] These figures understate women's role in productive activities. First, productive activities in the home such as raising animals and cultivating gardens are considered "housework." Second, women tend to work in agriculture at the time of the harvest, when the official census counts are not usually taken. Third, when families live on plantations as resident workers (*colonos*) only the male head of the family is officially employed, although the entire family works.[4] Lastly, many women in informal service, such as washing and ironing clothes, sewing and cooking, and commercial activities, are not likely to report their activities to avoid the burden of licensing and taxation.[5] The Ministry of Planning data does reveal that women form 66% of the rural commerce (marketplace) work force, 48% of the rural service work force, 10% of the agricultural labor force, and 50% of the rural industrial work force.[6] The central role of women at work is critical whether reported or not.

Before 1965, women and children worked on coffee farms throughout the year. When in 1965 the Rivera regime instituted the minimum wage, requiring women to receive salaries 7/9ths of those received by men, coffee

---

[1] Melvin Burke, "El sistema de plantación y la proletarización del trabajo agrícola en El Salvador," *Estudios Centroamericanos*, Nos. 335-336 (septiembre/octubre, 1976), pp. 476, 479; Carlos Samaniego, "Movimiento campesino o lucha del proletariado rural en El Salvador?" in *Estudios Sociales Centroamericanos*, 1980, No. 25, p. 139; and USAID *Agricultural Sector Assessment: El Salvador* (Washington, 1977), p. 45.

[2] Bill Durham, *Scarcity and Survival in Central America: Ecological Origins of the Soccer War* (Stanford, 1980), pp. 74-75; Richard N. Adams, *Cultural Surveys of Panama—Nicaragua—Guatemala—El Salvador—Honduras* (Detroit, 1957), pp. 442-443; Alistair White, *El Salvador* (New York, 1973), p. 140.; and Mac Chapin, "A Few Comments on Land Tenure and the Course of Agrarian Reform in El Salvador," mimeo ms., 1980, p. 7.

[3] Ministerio de Planificación de El Salvador (MINPLAN), *Indicadores económicos y sociales, enero-junio 1980*, p. 174.

[4] Carolina Castillo "The Situation of Women in El Salvador" in *Women and War: El Salvador*, Women's International Research Exchange (New York, n.d.), p. 5.

[5] Castillo, *op. cit.*, p. 6; and Johannes Linn, *Policies for Efficient and Equitable Growth of Cities in Developing Countries*, Working Paper No. 342 (Washington, 1979), p. 63.

[6] MINPLAN, *op. cit.*, p. 174.

planters stopped hiring women. The planters did not believe women were worth so "high" a wage. "Apart from the harvest, the only work on the coffee plantation now usually given to women is manuring." Harvesting coffee beans does not require the strength needed for crops like sugar cane, but requires care and technique. As a result, women and children are considered perfectly fit for this type of work.[7] Another ironic effect of the minimum wage law was to displace large numbers of resident plantation families (*colonos*), increasing the number of families without access to land.[8]

When rural women are not involved in wage labor, they engage in a wide variety of subsistence activities at home. One way to supplement their cash income is to raise chickens in order to sell eggs and meat. Because of the relatively high value of these foods, peasant women rarely use them for their families' consumption. According to White, women act as marketers of grains; they also sell the fruits and vegetables that they grow in their gardens.[9]

Women's home industries have traditionally been important sources of income for the rural poor. In the late 1950s Adams reported several regional specializations, although some, like weaving in Izalco and Pachimalco, were on the verge of extinction, owing to the availability of cheap industrial substitutes. Women in Nahuzicalco were still using leaves and wicker to produce baskets, fans and mats, which were sold throughout the country and in Honduras. Indigenous Salvadoreans and ladinos, both men and women, of the Cacopera area made string products from henequen fiber. The major proportion of the country's pottery needs was supplied by the handmade products women in small towns and rural areas produced. In other areas such as Tonacatepeque and Nueva Guadalupe, women specialized in sewing men's pants, which the men took to sell in other towns.

In the early 1970s basketry and mats were still produced wherever the necessary cane was found, but the pottery industry was declining because of competition from industrial substitutes.

One home industry which has been able to adapt to changes in technology is that of palm braiding to make hats. In Tenancingo, up to the 1890s palm-woven hats were produced in almost every household. After the sewing machine was introduced into the production of these hats, finishing work was transferred to Texas, leaving behind a palm-braiding industry alone.[10] Women and children still make palm braids (*trenzas*) to be assembled into hats and it is still an extremely important economic activity for the poor.

The introduction of industries had other effects as well. The introduction of electric grinding machines for grains in many areas affected women in a mixed way. While women with small amounts of cash and proximity to the electric mills were freed from the time-consuming work of grinding

---

[7] Claude Bataillon and Ivon Lebot, "Migración interna y empleo agrícola temporal en Guatemala" in *Estudios Sociales Centroamericanos*, Año V, no. 13, 1976, p. 55.

[8] Chapin, *op. cit.*, p. 3.

[9] Samaniego, *op. cit.*, pp. 136-137.

[10] Durham, *op. cit.*, pp. 74-75.

maize by hand, women who worked on the haciendas preparing the workers' meals were often dismissed as unnecessary. As the monopolization of land increased, leaving more and more families landless or with extremely small plots, home crafts were facing increasing competition from industrial substitutes, and minimum wage laws were making women less desirable as workers on haciendas. This resulted in increased female migration to urban areas.

Women in Urban Areas

Women in El Salvador have tended to migrate to urban areas to find employment while, until recently, men tended to migrate to Honduras.[11] Young women are attracted to towns where employment in domestic service and the informal sector is readily available. Salvadorean Ministry of Planning data confirm that of the 43% of the urban work-age female population that is economically active, 74% work in commerce and services,[12] areas dominated by the informal sector. The 1/3 of the female labor force that USAID reports as self-employed[13] is largely composed of these informal sector workers.[14] In addition, women form 21% of the urban industrial workforce.[15]

Informal sector jobs can generally be thought of as those with easy entry and requiring little capital.[16] Some have argued that those informal activities created by the worker are a form of "self-help job creation program."[17] These jobs, with very few exceptions, offer marginal wages (hence the informal sector is often known as the marginal sector) and little security of income. A World Bank study states "self-employed and domestics, the two main groups of the informal sector, were usually below the earning poverty line for 1975."[18] Nonetheless, women enter the informal sector because of the ease of finding work and the flexible hours which allow them to care for their children at the same time.

According to Jung,[19] between 1961 and 1975 the number of non-agricultural wage earners in El Salvador increased by one third, while the

---

[11] Edelberto Torres Rivas, "Familia y juventud en El Salvador" in Adolfo Gurrieri, E. Torres Rivas, Janette González and Elio de Vega, *Estudios sobre la juventud marginal latinoamericana* (México, 1971), p. 211; Isabel Nieves, "Household Arrangements and Multiple Jobs in San Salvador," in *Signs*, Vol. 5, No. 1 (May, 1979), p. 139; and White, p. 146.

[12] MINPLAN, *op. cit.*, p. 174.

[13] USAID, *op. cit.*, p. 27.

[14] World Bank, *Cuestiones y perspectivas demográficas* (Washington, 1979), p. 9.

[15] MINPLAN, *loc. cit.*

[16] See ILO (International Labor Organization), "The Urban Informal Sector," in Gerald M. Meier, ed., *Leading Issues in Economic Development* (New York, 1976), p. 215.

[17] Lisa Peattie, " 'Tertiarization' and Urban Poverty in Latin America," in Cornelius and Trueblood, eds. *Latin American Urban Research*, Vol. 5 (Beverly Hills: Sage, 1975), p. 109.

[18] World Bank, *op. cit.*, p. 9.

[19] Harald Jung, "Class Struggles in El Salvador," *New Left Review* (July-August, 1980), p. 8.

number of self-employed increased almost three-fold. This increase was due in large measure to the growth of the informal sector, as more and more men and women were unable to find satisfactory work in the "regular" employment sector.

Informal sector workers are invariably under-counted in urban areas for the same reason they are under-counted in rural areas: licensing, permits and tax regulations make it desirable to go unreported. However, the dominance of women in this sector is evident. In 1977 when Fedecrédito, a Salvadorean official credit agency, and the World Bank began a program to give small loans to informal sector workers, they expected that women would form a large proportion of those requesting loans. However, one report states, "it is surprising that this figure exceeds 80%. Two reasons for this are the large number of female heads of household in low-income neighborhoods and the need for self-employment."[20] While women do need self-employment for its "compatibility" with child-caring, this compatibility is only relative. Speaking of street vendors, Castillo states,

> These compañeras must take their children with them on the streets, even tiny infants, whose cradles are cardboard cartons. Since they have no place to set up stalls, and must either find space on the street or walk all day, these women and their children are forced to endure bad weather as it comes ... the women street vendors must also suffer the repression of the municipal police, who hunt them down, beat them, confiscate their merchandise, take them to jail, and fine them.[21]

In El Salvador, women commonly work in informal commerce as walking vendors of candies, lottery tickets, and foods, or in fixed locations selling utensils, combs, and magazines. In informal service, women work washing and ironing clothes or sewing, and many are forced to resort to prostitution.[22]

The other important source of work in the informal sector is domestic service. Girls twelve years of age, and even younger, frequently go to towns to work as private servants. Twenty percent of the women in the Salvadorean labor force work in domestic service.[23]

Table 1 shows the importance of vending and domestic service as a source of employment for poor women.

In El Salvador, it is common for domestic servants to work from 6 a.m. to 10 p.m. every day. A World Bank study confirms that 76% of domestic servants in El Salvador work over 60 hours a week, as do 31% of all informal sector workers.[24] The relationship of domestic servants to employers is frequently referred to as a master-slave relationship. They receive a nominal wage, as room and board is considered in calculating their pay, have no rights to organize, to medical care or to severance pay.

---

[20] *The Urban Edge*, June 1980, pp. 3, 6.
[21] Castillo, *op. cit.*, p. 6.
[22] Torres Rivas, *op. cit.*, pp. 222, 224.
[23] USAID, *op. cit.*, p. 27.
[24] World Bank, *op. cit.*, p. 11.

Table 1
Occupations of a Sample of Mothers
in San Salvador Slums

Mother's occupation	Female head of household	Male head of household
Market or walking vendor	35.6%	22.9%
Domestic servant	14.9%	11.0%
Worker or craftworker	25.3%	20.2%
Housewife	24.1%	45.8%
Total	100.0%	100.0%

Source: Torres Rivas, *op. cit.,* p. 244.

Needless to say, this work is very difficult for women with families, as they are usually required to live in and work at least six days per week.[25]

The 21% of economically active women employed in industry are paid less than men—women earn an average of 82% of men's wages. Outside of San Salvador wages can be considerably lower. Moreover, as Torres Rivas points out, in 1967, 79% of women in industry were earning less than the minimum wage. "In the most important factories of San Salvador," he states, "62% of the women workers earned less than 80 cents per day, well below the minimum wage of $1.28."[26] Unfortunately, data for more recent years are not available.

Women are also very significant in agro-industry, where most jobs are closely related to the types of work women have traditionally performed, that is, they are related to the production of food, clothing, textiles, and drinks.

Marriage and the Family

Researchers have reported two outstanding characteristics with regard to marriage and the family in El Salvador. The first is the high rate of free, or non-legalized, marriage unions, which are estimated to encompass about 50% of all unions.[27] Free unions are more characteristic of urban areas and among the poor, who have the highest birth rates and no need to legalize their unions to protect property inheritance.

The second important characteristic of Salvadorean families is not unrelated to the first. This is a very high level of households with female heads. In the late 1950's it was estimated that one third of urban and one fifth of rural households were headed by females. AID data for 1970[28] confirms that such households were more frequent in urban areas, but as the

---

[25] María, "What We Are Fighting For," as told to Debbie Farson in Women's International Resource Exchange, *op. cit.,* p. 11; and Castillo, *loc. cit.*

[26] Torres Rivas, *op. cit.,* p. 218.

[27] Stephen Webre, *José Napoleón Duarte and the Christian Democratic Party in Salvadorean Politics: 1960-1974,* (Baton Rouge, 1979), p. 64; and White, *op. cit.,* p. 246.

[28] USAID, *op. cit.,* p. 24.

data is expressed as the proportion of economically active females who head households (14.7% in urban areas, 9.2% in rural areas), it does not reveal the proportion of families affected. However, the 1978 FUNDUSAL survey of the urban poor in San Salvador revealed that 39.5% of the households were female-headed.[29]

In rural areas, the fact that men often migrate away from home helps to explain this phenomenon. If the man must constantly be searching for wage labor, his contact with the household is minimized, leaving the family effectively without his presence. This instability, along with the lack of inheritable property to pass on and the lack of social pressures to marry, also contributes to the frequency of free unions.

In urban areas where free unions and female-headed households are even more frequent, the relative ease with which women can find certain types of work, for example in domestic service and industry, means that

> A woman can earn a living for herself, even if encumbered by children, not much poorer than a husband can give her, unless he has a regular job; and the independence which this position gives them is valued by some women who don't want to form permanent unions.... With underemployment and widespread alcoholism, many of the men who do live together with their wives are more of a hindrance than a help.[30]

These types of households, with women at the head and men who come and go, make women the central figure in the structure of the family of the poor. Even though at the time of a marriage union a new residence is formed by the couple, "the subsequent departure of the man of the family leaves it a domestic establishment based on the fact the woman lives there. It is ... matrilocality-by-default."[31] In rural areas it is not at all uncommon for a daughter's husband to move in with her family.[32] The mother is therefore the stabilizing family figure.

"Illegitimate" children, known by the Salvadorean people as "natural" children (hijos naturales), follow their mother's descent line, taking her last name. The mother, of course, has the primary responsibility in socializing children as well. The triviality of "legitimacy" in childbirth among the poor and rural folk is expressed by Salvadoreans in their rejection of the term. Even if a mother has children born both within and out of wedlock, no social or legal distinctions are made between them, and it is common to find men living with women who have children from other unions, raising them as their own.[33]

In addition to the specific conditions that confront Salvadorean women, they are confronted by problems general to all Third World women. Sal-

---

[29] Fundación Salvadoreña de Desarollo y Vivienda Mínima (FUNDUSAL), "Análisis del proceso evaluativo y las soluciones autónomas en proyectos de lotes y servicios," Tomo 2 (San Salvador, 1979), Table 4.

[30] White, op. cit., pp. 245-246.

[31] Adams, op. cit., pp. 460-461.

[32] USAID, op. cit., p. 25

[33] White, op. cit., p. 246; Adams, op. cit., p. 461; Torres Rivas, op. cit., pp. 238-239, 241-242.

vadorean women, like women elsewhere, are subjected to the now well-known infant formula campaign[34] as multinationals seek to make profits at the cost of children's lives. In addition, the abuse of sterilization techniques in El Salvador was documented in the 1976 Congressional hearings on human rights. According to Dr. René de León Schlotter, who testified at these hearings, "They are imposing birth control without the consent of the people involved. This is not family planning. This is a policy of the government against the population."[35]

Conclusion

Salvadorean women, as peasants and workers, have suffered enormously in a society that has torn apart the social fabric of the family in order to ensure cheap labor. Thus it is not surprising that women have played a crucial part in the movement to transform Salvadorean society. As early as the 1920s market women were organizing and protesting repressive measures,[36] and the efforts of women in organizing and struggling against repression have continued and grown. Salvadorean mothers have recently organized to gain information about the whereabouts of their children who have "disappeared."[37] Forty percent of the Revolutionary Council of the FDR is composed of women[38] and the second in command of the FMLN is "Ana Maria," a fifty-five year old educator.[39] Ana Guadelupe Martínez, a member of the FMLN/FDR Diplomatic Mission, is an ex-political prisoner and author of the book *Clandestine Jails of El Salvador*.[40] More and more women, fully aware of the brutal consequences they will suffer if captured by the security forces, join the revolutionary forces in search of a tomorrow without misery, hunger, violence and exploitation.

---

[34] Amanda Claiborne, "Women in El Salvador," in *Resist Newsletter* no. 141, June-July 1981, pp. 4-5.

[35] U.S. House of Representatives, Subcommittee on International Organizations of the Committee on International Relations, *Human Rights in Nicaragua, Guatemala, and El Salvador: Implications for U.S. Policy, Hearings, June 8-9, 1976*, p. 74.

[36] Castillo, *op. cit.*, p. 9.

[37] Christine Dugas, "El Salvador's Mothers of Intervention," in *Worldview*, Vol. 25 No. 5, May 1981.

[38] Katherine Pettus, "Sorrow and Shared Purpose: Salvadorean Women," in *Sojourner*, vol. 6 no. 9, May 1980; p. 5.

[39] *The Guardian*, "El Salvador Supplement," Spring 1981, p. s-5.

[40] A chapter of this book appears as a selection in this chapter. –Ed.

The Secret Prisons of
El Salvador: An Excerpt*

By Ana Guadalupe Martínez
Julie Pearl, Translator

Ana Guadalupe Martínez was born in 1952 in Metapán, El Salvador. She joined the high school student movement in 1968 at the time of the first national teachers' strike. An activist in the university student movement, she participated in the general strike of Arcos Communes in 1969-70. In 1974 she joined the Revolutionary Army of the People (ERP). In 1975 she was given the responsibility of chief of the ERP's armed forces in the Eastern Zone. At the time of her capture by the National Guard in 1976, she was a member of the Central Committee of her party. The book from which this excerpt is taken (Las cárceles clandestinas de El Salvador) was written by her in 1978, after her release from prison, and was a finalist for the Casa de las Américas award for testimony in 1979. Currently she is a member of the Political and Diplomatic Commission of the Farabundo Martí National Liberation Front (FMLN) and of the Democratic Revolutionary Front (FDR), the organizations that direct the people's struggle in El Salvador.[1]

"This is Josefina, my commander."

Before me stands a man in his thirties, dressed in civilian attire. He has a rugged complexion, which smells strongly of lotion. He seems pale, sweaty, and agitated as he looks at me and commands:

"Blindfold her and tie up her hands and feet."

Since they don't have any cotton or sticking plaster with them, a private goes to fetch some. Meanwhile, the commander and his side-kick observe me. The latter, about 40 years old, short and thin, with a sickly, yellowish face, approaches me. He pulls my hair and forces me to turn my head to look at him. His face has a terribly sinister look.

Then he lets go of my hair and the private comes in with the blindfolds. The soldier puts a big piece of cotton over each of my eyes, around which another starts to wind sticking plaster. When they wrap the tape over my nose, I can barely breathe, so I automatically raise my hands (not yet bound) and pull at the tape a bit. This infuriates one of them, who hits me in the face and says:

"Leave it like that, bitch! Men, make it tighter!"

Then they pull my hands behind my back to handcuff me. They also put cuffs around one of my ankles, but leave the other one free so I can

---

*This excerpt is a translation of Chapter 9 of *Las cárceles clandestinas de El Salvador*.
[1] Introduction from WIRE (Women's International Resource Exchange) "Women and War: El Salvador," New York, n.d., p. 26.

walk down the stairs. They start bolting down the staircase, pushing me along, whereupon I fall down, since I can't see anything. I am yanked up and then punched by someone. With every step I take, the ankle-cuff flies up and hits my other ankle, producing a sharp pain which makes walking any further extremely difficult.

I am taken to a place on the second floor—maybe a dining room or a sleeping quarter of the barracks. There I am pushed to the floor and a voice screams at me:

"Look, Josefina, we've already figured you out here. Now we're telling you that nobody leaves here without talking. We've made the men talk, and the same thing goes for you women. So that you can get a taste of what's waiting for you, here comes the first one."

They stand me up, put two ice-cold objects on my hips, and activate the electric current. The shock is overwhelming; my every muscle is jolted, especially those of my extremities, to the extent that I fall to the floor against my will. I'm lying there on my side, keeled over with pain, when the supposed commander says:

"Show her how you're going to lift her up every time she stays lying down."

Instantly, the soldier closest to me grabs my hair, which is too short for him to lift me up with, so he pulls me up by my collar and punches me in the abdomen. He gives me a harsh blow, but it is not nearly as painful as the electric torture. Once back on my feet, the interrogator continues:

"This is the principle. From here on in whether or not we finish the interrogation quickly depends on you. Now, tell me—where are Chon and Choco?"

"I don't know."

"Ah, you don't know, eh? Let's help her remember where these bastards are! Give her a long one."

This one is much worse than the first and I hit the floor again. I try to rise, but the current is still running through my legs, leaving them immobile. I faintly hear the commander say, "Enough." Then the electric shock stops, but the sensation lingers. Once again, they lift me up with kicks and punches.

"Well, do you remember yet where they are?"

I remain silent.

"We have to keep helping her. Give her an even longer one—that ought to refresh her memory!"

And another. *The passing of the current through the body is so penetrating and excruciating that one feels as if she is being burned alive.*

"O.K. We'll capture those two, anyway, with or without your help. We've got them under control. But we know that you went when they killed one of the guardsmen at the Alvarez Meza in Santa Ana. You were there, weren't you?"

"No."

"Ah! But we know very well that you went. There's no use trying to deny it. Remind her of when she marched down to Santa Ana to kill guardsmen."

Another discharge. Just when I thought this one was over, a few more followed.

"You mustn't dare to touch the National Guardsmen. Here you'll learn to never bother them again. Good, enough of that."

They were unleashing their rage against the guerrillas; their frustration and humiliation over every repressive body that had fallen. They become savage beasts of vengeance, wanting to annihilate those whom they consider enemies to the death: the organizations that were rising up in arms against the tyrannic government that these soldiers served.

The interrogation continues. This time they want me to tell them where the arms are kept.

"I don't know."

"Son of a bitch! This whore doesn't know anything, but we already know all about these bastards. Put an electrode on her tits." They place it over my left breast.

Each current jolted me more fiercely than the last, and every breath of air scorched my throat like dry ice. I was clenching my fists to restrain any groans of pain in front of these perverse sadists.

The discharges continue, as do the questions. They want to know where to find the money and the suspected insurgent bases in Oriente.

There is a pause and the one who keeps interrogating says, "Aren't you thirsty? We know you must be thirsty. If you want a glass of water you have to earn it. Here nobody gets anything without giving us something first."

He was right about my extreme thirst. These prison guards know their work perfectly.

"Let's see if you want water. Tell us who and where Baltazar is."

"I do not know him."

"Well, I guess this one doesn't want water, then. Put another one in her vagina."

This time two men approach me. One of them undoes my pants and pulls them down, then the other puts something in me that I can't describe, not having seen it, but the iciness feels like that of metal or something similar. The jolt makes me double over in pain—but it is more than just pain; it's like burning coal, an overall shock which blazes through the innermost muscular fiber.

I'm still lying flat on the floor, suffocating, since the tape blocks my nasal passages and when I try to breathe through my mouth, my already parched throat dries out even more. They no longer await responses to their accusations; they just go on naming incidents and taunting me with remarks and electric discharges. When they see that I'm nearly unconscious, that I can no longer speak nor move, they stop the treatment. They lift me up, and I fall to the floor the instant they let go of me. My mouth and nose are all smashed up and bloody by now—well, my flesh and bones have been pounded against the floor many times.

They know just how far they can go if they want to keep their victims alive. I am left alone in the room. At least three hours have passed, throughout which the radio has been turned up to full blast. They always do this when they want to drown the shouts of the tortured. *How many times, in between the musical interludes have those other, terrifying sounds reached our cells—the shouts of some patriot who is suffering unfathomable torment in the hands of the very ones who at that moment were torturing me?*

Two men manage to drag me to my cell, where they uncuff me so that they can take off my clothes. Even in the awful state I'm in, these pitiful creatures take advantage of the opportunity to paw me. They lock my feet and hands in cuffs again, then pick me up and throw me to the middle of the cell, from where I hear them lock me in. I have been made into a worn and crumpled cleaning rag, tossed onto the ground. My muscles are all cramping and I have an urge to both defecate and vomit. The electric treatment has afflicted even the involuntary muscles, like those of the stomach and intestines. I try to move to look for the pit, but am unable. So I stay until I fall asleep—or perhaps I have fainted—I'm not sure which.

A few hours have gone by when I sense that someone is opening the gate. Lieutenant Castillo comes in and tells me to get up.

I don't move. When he sees this, he says, "What's wrong?" Feigning genuine concern, he bends down and looks at me up close. "What is it? Have they tortured you?" he asks, cynically.

The lieutenant calls in Sergeant Palomo and some other soldiers. "What have they done to this woman? Who came for her?" One of them responds. "They were from the police."

Addressing me again, Castillo says, "And how do you feel? Do you want to go take a bath so that what you're feeling goes away faster?" Then he shouts to the men, "Go to the infirmary to get aspirin. Sergeant Palomo! Bring back some aspirin and water!"

He turns back toward me. "Look, they came to take you out and torture you without my permission. I wasn't here.... I was in Oriente."

Palomo comes in with the water and aspirin.

"Help her take them!" I swallow them only to throw them up later.

"Look, Palomo, how they've left this woman. They sure are a bunch of assholes."

The truth is that they had his full consent. I later recognized his soldiers as the very ones who had tormented me. The so-called commander was Sergeant Claros, I learned, who aspires to be promoted to Major. Apparently he is a specialist in torture, primarily in electric shock treatment. Surely he is to be one of the future heads of Section II of the National Guard.

I was very weak for a few days, still feeling the shocks and spasms all over my body. Anything I ate, I regurgitated. Since my cell was cold and damp, I was constantly shivering, yet the internal flames continued blazing from head to toe. The only external signs of the burns were little brownish drops that collectively formed bigger marks on the parts of my body where the electrodes had been placed.

The physical sign—the testimony of so much suffering—is barely perceivable. What can these little marks say about the electric discharges transmitted through these spots into the human body? What sophistication they've achieved to leave only a few insignificant dots to show for such a horrifying, scathing method of torture!

On August 15, they raided the San Miguel headquarters and found them empty. A week later, they searched the little hotel room we had, which had also been abandoned.

I knew that these locations had already been evacuated, that the *compañeros* had taken the necessary precautions, and thought perhaps it was O.K. to give the interrogators these addresses. Even so, I knew that I'd been weakened and that I had to boost up my morale in order not to fall again. Above all, my comrades had entrusted me with many other party secrets, and it was my obligation to protect them.

Whatever piece of information, no matter how small or insignificant it may seem, should never be passed on to the enemy, because aside from aiding their investigative processes in that one tip may lead them to another trail, this act implies that they have succeeded in breaking down the prisoner's principles and sense of dignity, these being the revolutionary's only weapons in the face of the enemy's torture and harassment.

The fact that a certain "tip" is useless to them does not justify revealing it. Whoever speaks, collaborates, and this constitutes a strong break in the moral fiber of the captive. The resistance of the revolutionary lies not in her physical endurance—this will be exhausted just in surviving the enemy's prison conditions and all—but as long as one retains her morale and sense of conviction, there is neither drug nor torment which can defeat her.

My duty was to keep quiet and direct my thoughts toward all those who had fallen in the attempt to construct a new nation. When faced with my captors' torture, I had to remember that the life-long suffering of my countrymen and women is infinitely more painful than that to which I was then subjected. And anything I confessed would only serve to delay this process of liberation that is burgeoning in the breast of our people.

On top of all this, I was plagued with the idea of a possible pregnancy, since a few days earlier, Sergeant Mario Rosales, one of our most despised butchers, came to my cell at around four in the morning. These arrivals were becoming so common that his did not surprise me. But this time, he came with two men, opened the cell and said, "Get up and take off your clothes." In those days, they often got their kicks from ordering me to strip.

"What for?" I asked. "Your men came in just a bit ago for that. Besides, I'm coughing a lot and the cold floor makes it worse."

"Take off your clothes, I command you!" he shouted. "Or would you rather have these two men do it by force?"

It was always this guy Rosales who ordered them to leave me naked. This degenerate enjoyed seeing my embarrassment when I began to undress myself, which I did to avoid being manhandled by his soldiers.

I started unbuttoning my shirt slowly, trying to conceal my humiliation from them and to ignore their obscene comments. When I'd taken off almost all my clothes and asked if that was good enough, Rosales shouted, "All your clothes! You are to remain with nothing!" I finished undressing. What an abominable sensation I had! Feeling outraged and impotent at the same time, I stood there fully exposed. Then the two soldiers approached me and one held my hands behind my back while the other bound them together.

"Leave," Rosales commanded them, and immediately he pounced on me like a tiger upon its prey, knocking me onto the floor. When I fell, my head hit hard against the concrete floor, and I sort of blacked out for a moment, seeing only those little, blinding stars. He took advantage of the opportunity to stay on top of me, 'till I came to and understood what it had come to. In spite of being handcuffed, I resisted him, struggling to get him off in any way I could. Then he snarled at me, "There's no use in screaming because I'm in charge here all week and nobody will come without my ordering them to do so."

My shouts were drowned by the cell walls, and my voice soon gave out. I was still fighting him when he called in a private to hold down my legs. Two others came in and stood watch by the door. They were heavily intoxicated and the stench that filled the cell was revolting.

Then I thought that Rosales' little assistant was going to take his turn, but fortunately, the phone rang, and since they were on duty, they had to go downstairs to answer it. They closed the door.

I remained sprawled out on the floor, totally shattered, though I'd been aware that this could happen any day there. I crawled to the corner where they had thrown my clothes, and immediately covered myself up the best I could. Then I lay awake, shuddering at every sound I heard, certain that they would return. They never came back that night.

This same Sergeant was the one who had repeatedly barged into Mireya's cell when she was here so they could all rape her. In spite of all their intents, they had never succeeded in doing the same to me ... until then. I have never felt so demoralized in all my life. And from there on in, added to my worries would be that of his filthy seed being planted in me.

About a week later, when I was expecting my period, I grew more and more frantic as each day passed and I still hadn't begun menstruating. This was surely the most wicked and ultimately base form of torture they could ever inflict upon their female enemy. It tormented me so fiercely that I had only one idea: to abort if I were indeed pregnant. Just thinking about it provoked in me an unfathomable despair.

Women Challenge the Myth*

By Patricia Flynn

Patricia Flynn is co-author with Roger Burbach of Agribusiness in the Americas, *from which an excerpt appears in Chapter 3 of this book. Flynn is currently with the Center for the Study of the Americas. She has done research and travelled extensively in Central America. In "Women Challenge the Myth," she presents the "unprecedented revolutionary model" of Nicaraguan women's participation in the transformation of their society.*

Approaches and Perspectives

Today, what can loosely be called the women's movement consists of a diversity of individuals and small groups whose political orientations span the spectrum from bourgeois to Marxist feminist. Some work within the framework of the existing system to achieve juridical and political reforms—from the right to vote to the right to hold office. Others have organized specific constituencies to grapple with the most concrete issues of their daily lives—as housewives, peasants and workers, students, feminists and, particularly in recent years, as the most vocal combatants against dictatorial repression.

What Marxists call the "woman question" presents very difficult theoretical and political questions that are still being hotly debated.[1] Among the most fundamental of these are the origin of women's oppression and, thus, the relationship between it and class oppression. It is not surprising, therefore, that even the most experienced groups in Latin America have not clearly formulated a strategy and tactics for women's liberation, and are still experimenting with organizational forms and alliances.

One key element shared by a number of organizations in Latin America is that the starting point must be an analysis of the broader social and political context. Mexico's leading feminist journal, *Fem*, illuminated the clear congruence between many of the demands of the women's movement and those of broader struggles for political freedom and economic justice:

> *It is not enough to struggle for voluntary maternity—i.e., access to contraceptives and abortion—but also against the forced sterilization and birth control plans adopted by many governments due to North American pressure. It is not enough to fight for such services as daycare centers, laundromats, etc., but also for such basic community provisions as water, electricity, housing, and medical and sanitation services. The issue of the double day takes on another dimension here as well: the demand for wages for housework is inappropriate as long as the broader*

---

*This article consists of brief excerpts from *NACLA Report on the Americas*, Vol. XIV, No. 5 (September-October), 1980 (52 pages, illustrated).

[1] See Lise Vogel, "Questions on the Woman Question," *Monthly Review* (June 1979).

struggle remains focused on issues of high unemployment, exploitation of the heads of household and starvation wages. Women should have the right not to work under such existing conditions. Finally, it is not enough to fight against the consumerism of one group in society, but against the impoverishment of the majority, and the impossibility of their being able to consume anything at all.[2]

The conclusion of this analysis is that the struggle for women's liberation must ultimately be linked to the struggle for a revolutionary transformation of society. In the words of a Peruvian group, the Flora Tristan Women's Center:

The woman question, far from being an issue isolated from the rest of society, is in itself a political issue, with economic, social and ideological determinants. While each of these aspects can be confronted separately, only partial—though not unimportant—gains can be made, since only within the context of a radical transformation of social structures can the woman question be addressed directly. Thus, to regard the woman question as a political issue means to place it within the dynamic of class struggle, here and now, to view it as a demand for the democratic rights of a specific sector of the population—an integral component of the demands which must be advocated by any group or party attempting to change the present society and move toward socialism."[3]

Marta Lamas, a journalist and member of the MLM,[4] addresses those threatened by questions both of autonomy and of immediacy advocated by most women's groups:

The name 'women's liberation movement' does not imply that it pretends only to liberate women, or that women must oppose themselves to men, but that they must start with their own interests, uniting with all other oppressed sectors which are also seeking a revolutionary change for all.[5]

Nicaragua: Women Making Changes

What in Mexico is still a hope has in Nicaragua become an unprecedented revolutionary model that will be watched and examined carefully by women around the world in coming years.

Anyone visiting Nicaragua in the past year cannot but be struck by the visible examples of women's changing status there. Women in olive drab carrying machine guns are everywhere—making up a quarter of the new Popular Sandinista Army and almost half of the police force. They hold

---

[2] Sara Sefchovich, "América Latina: la mujer en lucha," *Fem* (January-February 1980), p. 11.

[3] From an internal document, "Fundamentación del Centro de la Mujer Peruana Flora Tristán," excerpted in "Perú: las mujeres salen a la calle," *Fem* (January-February 1980).

[4] "Movement for the Liberation of Women," Mexico's major socialist-feminist organization. –Ed.

[5] Marta Lamas, "The Women's Liberation Movement," *El Universal*, November 29, 1977, p. 5.

positions of responsibility and often leadership in almost every government office and ministry. While no women are in the National Directorate of the Sandinista National Liberation Front (FSLN), women are in charge of two of its five Secretariats (those of mass organizations and external relations) and a woman directs the Front's political work in Managua. And on International Women's Day, the mass women's organization, AMNLAE, mobilized 35,000 women for the largest celebration Latin America has ever seen outside of Cuba.

Women's participation in the new mass organizations is not limited to AMNLAE (Association of Nicaraguan Women, named for Luisa Amanda Espinoza, in 1970 the first Sandinista woman to fall in combat). Women also play a central role in the Sandinista Defense Committees, the politically crucial national network of neighborhood organizations. And a majority of the members of the FSLN committees in the provinces are women, as are almost all the political cadre in those committees.[6]

Women were not just given this new role by the Sandinista leadership, although women's emancipation has been one of the FSLN's programmatic points since the founding of the organization in 1961, according to AMNLAE leader, Gloria Carrión. It is hard to find anyone in Nicaragua today who will not acknowledge that women "earned the right to their new roles in the revolution in the streets and at the barricades." Women participated in the struggle against Somoza in numbers unprecedented in Latin America and in every task imaginable. Some were in guerrilla cells in the mountains for many years, fighting in the front lines as well as working as medics or carrying out other tasks of their organization. Many who joined the struggle early on had followed in the footsteps of brothers; others were recruited through the Sandinista-connected student association.

As the brutal repression by the Somoza forces intensified, women saw sons and daughters being imprisoned, tortured or killed. Initially motivated by the desire to defend their families, many of these women also became integrated into the struggle.[7]

By the final offensive against Somoza in mid-1979, women made up an estimated 30% of the Sandinista army and held important leadership positions, commanding everything from small units to full battalions. In the crucial final battle of León, four out of seven commanders of that military front were women.

A key factor facilitating women's participation was the decision of the FSLN to actively encourage and recruit women into the struggle. In 1977,

---

[6] Interview with Margaret Randall, "*FSLN: Women Make History,*" printed in *The Guardian*, February 20, 1980.

[7] The account here of women's participation in the anti-Somoza struggle is based largely on interviews conducted by Margaret Randall in Nicaragua with Lea Guido (former head of AMPRONAC and currently head of the Ministry of Health) and Gloria Carrión (currently head of the Nicaraguan Women's Association). These interviews will appear in a forthcoming book on women in Nicaragua by Margaret Randall, whom we thank for generously sharing her materials with NACLA. [Since the writing of this article, this book has been published as *Sandino's Daughters: Testimonies of Nicaraguan Women in Struggle* (Vancouver: New Star Press, 1981). –Ed.]

Sandinista women played a central role in forming a broad-based women's association.[8]

Known as AMPRONAC (Association of Women Confronting the National Problem), the group initially focused much of its work on the repression which had already taken on a new magnitude. They carried out petition drives, hunger strikes and clandestine activities, and led open demonstrations at a time when virtually no other organization dared even to hold a mass meeting. Even in these moments, AMPRONAC denounced the particular ways women suffered under the dictatorship, and put forth demands for an end to all discriminatory laws against women, equal pay for equal work, and an end to the commercialization of women.

By 1978, AMPRONAC's growing base of support had shifted from "concerned" middle- and upper-class women to the poorer women who were experiencing the repression more directly and were more ready to confront it in a militant fashion. This allowed AMPRONAC to define its work more directly as part of the struggle for "the people's interests." When this political orientation crystallized—the organization announced its open support for the Sandinistas in March 1978—many of its early members left.[9]

In the countryside and in the working-class *barrios* of the city, women who had not gone off to fight began to take their part in the struggle. AMPRONAC provided infrastructural support for this participation by organizing medical clinics in the hard-hit *barrios*, managing food distribution networks, and organizing Sandinista block committees. As the fighting escalated, the women guarded trenches, made bombs, delivered messages and hid Sandinista fighters in their homes.

According to Lea Guido, FSLN member who headed AMPRONAC during this period (and now Minister of Health), a key factor in the unprecedented participation of women of the popular sectors is their role as the economic pillar of the family in Nicaragua. As many as 50% of the households are headed by single women abandoned by the men who fathered their children.[10] Even when the men remain with their families, the high rate of both seasonal and permanent unemployment has hinged family survival on the ingenuity and industriousness of women. Streets in middle-class neighborhoods still are crowded with women carrying laundry back to the *patrona* and on every corner they vie with one another to sell packages of mango slices or sweet cakes. This history of primary responsibility in the daily struggle, says Guido, has forged strong and determined

---

[8] *Ibid.* See also interview with Sylvia Pérez of the Nicaraguan Women's Association, quoted in Lynn Silver, "Nicaraguan Women Organize to Defend the Revolution," *Intercontinental Press*, October 15, 1979.

[9] *Ibid.*

[10] Paula Diebold de Cruz and Mayra Pasas de Rappauoli, *Informe sobre el papel de la mujer en el desarrollo económico de Nicaragua* (Managua: U.S. Agency for International Development, November 1975), p. 8. See also, Vivian Gillespie, *Summary of Existing Information on the Roles and Status of Women in Nicaragua* (Washington, D.C.: Federation of Organizations for Professional Women, 1977), p. 4, which states that 48% of households in the poor neighborhoods of Managua are headed by women.

personalities among Nicaraguan women.[11]

Machismo is not dead in Nicaragua, however, and women are not immune to its pressures. AMPRONAC offered the women who joined its ranks a crucial source of support in facing the conflict with their husbands often created by their break with traditional roles. For some women, their activism meant separation from husbands or a difficult home situation; for others it entailed a double clandestinity (hidden from both their husbands and the Somoza forces); for others it meant that their husbands ultimately acquiesced to their new independence and even came to treat them with a new respect.

Participation also brought a sense of *self*-respect to many women. One domestic worker who had raised nine children alone said, after the victory, "Women weren't aware of anything; they only washed, ironed, cooked, had children and that was it. But now, I tell you, we're awakened." [12]

The Long View

Even in progressive movements, there is no guarantee that such participation will mean the permanent conquest of a role for women in the political sphere, or that it implies any other advance for women's equality. History is rife with proof that women's participation has all too frequently followed the ebb and flow of social crisis. Women march and bear arms alongside the men of their class, only to be encouraged to return to their homes when the crisis subsides.

Women in Nicaragua are far from equal to men, and the battle to end their oppression is a difficult and long one that has barely begun. Women still bear the responsibilities of child-rearing and housework almost alone. Even this first essential step in freeing women from their traditional role patterns is burdened with major obstacles and thus is likely to continue for some time. For one thing, Nicaragua does not have the material resources to fully socialize these tasks, though a few concrete measures are being taken as indicated below. Moreover, in addition to the already high number of female heads of household due to abandonment, the casualties produced by the war (40,000 dead) have left even more women without help. And finally, changing men's attitudes—asking them to transform relationships that have worked to their advantage—is a difficult challenge in any society, and more so in a culture permeated with machismo like Nicaragua.

But since the Sandinista victory in July 1979, Nicaragua has been undergoing a complete revolutionary transition. And as Dora María Tellez (one of the FSLN's impressive leaders who won fame as *Comandante Dos*) said, "Revolutions transform everything, make everything tremble. All the structures are disordered so that later they can be put back in order ...

---

[11] Margaret Randall, *Sandino's Daughters: Testimonies from Nicaraguan Women in Struggle* (Vancouver: New Star Press, 1981).

[12] Interview by Liz Maier quoted in "Mujeres e insurrección popular: la mitad de la revolución nicaragüense" (unpublished manuscript, 1980).

but a different, revolutionary order."[13] This upheaval opens the possibility of a social and ideological reordering that could profoundly affect the role of women in Nicaraguan society. There are positive signs that the basis for this is being laid.

First of all, the Sandinista leadership has reaffirmed its commitment to the liberation of women and has begun to talk about "the restructuring of the family and relations within it."[14] As an article in the Sandinista magazine, *Poder Sandinista,* expressed it: "Women's full integration into society constitutes the only guarantee of a true revolution in the workings of everyday life."[15]

Second, and perhaps more important, the women's mass organization is committed to insuring not only women's full participation in all aspects of the revolutionary process, but also that their interests are incorporated as well.[16] Gloria Carrión, head of AMNLAE, makes it clear that access to state power has provided vast new possibilities which must be taken advantage of from the beginning:

There are two aspects to our work to destroy the historic isolation of women—to change their socioeconomic conditions and, through political power, to change the ideology. Through participating in the reconstruction and restructuring of Nicaraguan society, women are guaranteeing their own future, in that what is created now becomes a guide for the future.[17]

Reorganized after the victory, the national mass women's group now calling itself AMNLAE counts its current membership at about 25,000. It is attempting to incorporate areas of the country where the association was never active, and to fight against the tendency for once-active women to return to their old roles, leaving revolutionary construction to the men. In the words of Sylvia Pérez of AMNLAE:

We consider that our male compañeros have very good intentions and spirit, but we have our own particular demands to fight for. Here in a revolutionary process such as the one we are now living, it is we, the organized people, the organized women in this case, who will attain our own achievements.[18]

Political participation, according to Gloria Carrión, is one of the greatest rallying cries of AMNLAE. "Our participation allows us to make films, textbooks, etc., which can transform the conception, the ideology, society has about the role that should be assigned to women."[19]

---

[13] Interview by Victoria Schultz quoted in her article, "Organizar: Women in Nicaragua," *NACLA Report on the Americas,* Vol. XIV, No. 2 (March-April), 1980.

[14] *Poder Sandinista* (Managua), March 11, 1980.

[15] *Ibid.*

[16] Pamphlet published by AMNLAE, 1980.

[17] Interview with Gloria Carrión, July 1980.

[18] Interview by Victoria Schultz with Sylvia Pérez, 1979. We thank Victoria for generously making her interview material available to NACLA.

[19] Interview with Gloria Carrión, July 1980.

Another of AMNLAE's important tasks is to see that in the formulation of Nicaragua's new government policies and programs the particular interests of women are represented. To this end, AMNLAE sits on the Council of State, the legislative body which serves as a forum for discussion of national priorities; it participates in a committee designed to coordinate policies that affect women throughout the government; and it also sits on the committees set up to advise the various government ministries on the impact of policies on particular sectors.

AMNLAE, like every other organization in Nicaragua, has mobilized its base to help advance the general priorities of the revolution, and to push for the needs of its constituency within these priorities (such as the literacy crusade, which has a particular significance for women, whose illiteracy rate is significantly higher than that of men). In addition, it has moved forward on a series of concrete programs that address women's particular needs.[20]

Child Care. In conjunction with the Ministry of Social Welfare, a program to establish daycare centers (called Centers for Infant Development) has been set up, with over a dozen opened in the first eight months. An effort is being made to employ men as well as women. AMNLAE has also proposed public laundries and dining rooms, with the long-term goal of socializing housework.

Health. In cooperation with the Ministry of Health, AMNLAE is setting up mobile health brigades to provide health care, from maternity to basic hygiene, to women throughout the country. (Prior to the revolution only 20% of women received consistent health care.)[21]

Workers. The Association has organized trade unions in the free trade zone of Managua where employees in the labor-intensive industries are almost exclusively women. AMNLAE is also organizing domestic workers with the immediate goal of alleviating the most exploitative aspects of the work, and a longer term goal of completely eliminating domestic work.

Unemployment. An urgent problem throughout Nicaragua, lack of employment is particularly severe for women. To provide immediate sources of income, AMNLAE and the Social Welfare Ministry are setting up collectively run projects such as sewing co-ops for women. In rural areas, over 30 such projects are active. AMNLAE is also starting training programs to teach women technical skills. (Prostitutes are one targeted sector for these programs.)

Political Education. Forums for political discussion are being organized in the work collectives and in the base level meetings of the association. Cadre training is being planned, and they have begun to publish a newspaper.

Juridical. A law was passed forbidding sexual exploitation of women in the media, resulting from a demand put forward by AMNLAE. Revision

---

[20] This compilation is based on various articles in *Barricada* (Managua), 1980 and NACLA interviews in Managua, March 1980.

[21] Gillespie, *Summary of Existing Information.*

of the entire legal code is being undertaken through the women's office in the Social Welfare Ministry to remove legal discrimination against women. With the support of the Sandinista Front, AMNLAE is demanding passage of a law on "responsible paternity" to force men to assume legal and financial responsibility for their children.

But, as one of the women in charge of the legal code revision warns, "It won't have any positive effect if women gain legal equality and we ourselves are not concerned that equality exists.... It is necessary not only to change the content of the law itself, but to achieve a real ideological transformation of all members of Nicaraguan society, *compañeros* and *compañeras* alike."

The most difficult changes are yet to come, and the most difficult battles yet to be fought—those that deal with the ideological underpinnings of women's oppression. The appreciation of some of the Sandinista leadership and of AMNLAE of the centrality of ideological struggle, and the creative ways in which they have thus far approached the need to make profound changes in people's way of thinking, is one of the positive signposts about the future.

Recognizing that "new ideas have been born in us, but the old ones haven't died yet," Gloria Carrión puts in profound perspective the magnitude of the struggle yet to come:

[AMNLAE] is called upon to undertake a long and profound task as much in the area of male/female relations as in the area of social and economic relations in general. It's not enough to change the structures: we must continue with a process of education, of ideological struggle.[22]

While it is true that social injustice and political repression are more intense and blatant in Latin America than in the United States, the Nicaraguan example shows that the struggle against women's oppression should not be postponed. Even if one argues for the centrality of the struggle against Latin America's system of social exploitation and political repression, the need to also fight against the particular oppression of women cannot be ignored by anyone who advocates social justice.

Through their participation in that fight women can begin to gain confidence in their ability to shape their own futures. Their incorporation into broader struggles as well provides an arena where both women and men can begin to confront sexist behavior patterns and ideas. Moreover, without women's presence in the social and political movements that hope to shape the future of Latin America, the interests of half the population in whose name the struggles are being waged will not be represented.

In sum, the continuing exclusion of women from the political sphere not only makes them bystanders in their own destinies, but also robs progressive and revolutionary movements of women's significant force.

In the past decade, Latin American women have shown that force in a variety of mobilizations. In Mexico they have been highly visible in land takeovers and squatter struggles in both urban and rural areas. In Brazil's

---

[22] NACLA interview with Sylvia Pérez, Managua, March 1980.

industrial centers like São Paulo, they have been central in organizing efforts in slum areas and in the mass protest movement against the rising cost of living. In Chile, Argentina, Brazil and other countries, women have also been a leading force in organizing on behalf of human rights in the face of severe repression. And in El Salvador today, as in Nicaragua before, unprecedented numbers of women in arms are facing the military forces in a war to end the dictatorial regime and institute a truly just society.[23] These women are not just earning their right to a voice in that new society. They are risking their lives so that all disenfranchised people can exercise that right.

Women in Revolutionary Movements: The Case of Nicaragua[*]

By Norma Stoltz Chinchilla

Norma S. Chinchilla examines in detail the reasons for women's participation in the Nicaraguan revolution. While she takes into account the structural conditions of Nicaraguan society, she also demonstrates the importance of the historical and international context of the revolution, as well as the FSLN's policy and practice of integrating women into revolutionary struggle on an egalitarian basis.

The revolutionary movements in Nicaragua, El Salvador and Guatemala represent a qualitatively new stage in Latin American revolutionary history. They also seem to represent a qualitatively new stage in the history of women's participation in revolutionary movements, not only in this hemisphere but perhaps in the world.

Women participated massively in the Nicaraguan revolution in roles that many observers have argued were more varied and significant than in any other twentieth-century revolution.[1] They were mobilized at practically every level of Nicaraguan society where opposition to the Somoza dictatorship emerged—in the neighborhoods, on the farms, in factories, offices, and schools. They were fully incorporated into the actual fighting forces of the Sandinista Liberation Front, not only in transportation, communication and logistics but in combat and positions of command, something unprecedented in Latin American history. A tiny group of "exceptional" women had been part of the foquista guerrilla organizations of the 1960s—

---

[23] For an overview of women's participation in popular struggles in Latin America in recent years, see various articles in "América Latina: la mujer en lucha, I & II," *Fem* (January-February and March-April 1980). On Brazil, see Singer, "O feminino."

[*] Abridged version of an unpublished paper written in 1981.

[1] People's Translation Service, "Interview with Nicaragua's Commander Dora," *Newsfront International*, 230 (November) 1979, pp. 11-13.

in Uruguay, Bolivia, Brazil, and before then, in Cuba[2] —and some women fought as guerrillas "just like men" in the Mexican Revolution, but never had there been so many women in combat (perhaps 30 percent) in such positions of high responsibility with men as well as women within their command. Reports out of El Salvador and Guatemala indicate that the pattern is being repeated there on an equally impressive scale.[3]

The experience of Nicaragua, and now three other Central American countries, represents an important break with past conceptions of women's proper role in socialist and revolutionary struggles and with strategies for changing the attitudes of men and women about that role. In the Popular Unity period of Chile (1970-73), for example, women were not really thought of as a major force to mobilize directly since they were not a large percentage of the unionized industrial labor force. Women were encouraged to support the struggles of their unionized and Socialist brothers, husbands, and fathers, but were not expected to contribute directly and uniquely to the overall process of socialist transformation.

The consequence of this fatal "oversight" are now well known: arch-conservative and reactionary forces moved into the vacuum and claimed the territory of "defense of the family" and the interests of women (assumed to be identical) as their own.[4] Middle- and working-class women, vulnerable because of their tenuous connection to the organization and mobilization of the strategies of socialist transformation, ended up allying with women of the bourgeoisie in helping to overthrow a socialist president in a bloody military coup that has brought in its wake untold hardship for these same middle- and working-class families.[5]

Learning from the sobering lesson of Chile and building on the experiences of Cuba, Nicaragua not only broke down the division of labor in combat but channeled significant energies into the establishment of a mass women's organization in an early stage of the struggle. Why are these developments occurring for the first time in Central America? How do we explain the high degree of participation of women in revolutionary movements in a region that is predominantly capitalist but still economically one of the most backward regions in the hemisphere? Why have women been able to organize when there seems to be little precedent for doing so— no early twentieth-century suffrage movement to speak of, for example— and where the conditions of capitalism long ago destroyed the precapitalist matrilineal, matrilocal, relatively equalitarian culture? Finding the answers to these questions will help us not only better understand how masses of

---

[2] Jane E. Jacquette, "Women in Revolutionary Movements in Latin America," *Journal of Marriage and the Family*, Vol. 35, No. 3 (May), 1973, pp. 344-353.

[3] Luz Méndez "Testimonies of Guatemalan Women," *Latin American Perspectives*, No. 25/26 (Spring/Summer 1980), pp. 160-168.

[4] María de los Angeles Crummett, "El Poder Femenino: The Mobilization of Women against Socialism in Chile," *Latin American Perspectives*, Vol. IV, No. 4 (Fall), 1977, pp. 103-113.

[5] Michele Mattelart, "Chile, The Feminine Version of the Coup d'Etat," June Nash and Helen Icken Safa (eds.), *Sex and Class in Latin America*, (New York: Praeger, 1976), pp. 279-301.

people are mobilized to participate in revolutionary movements but also how the concerns of socialists and feminists interact and intersect, in theory as well as in practice.

As a beginning, I suggest there are four developments to be taken into account in explaining the participation of women in the Nicaraguan revolution (as well as other revolutionary movements in Central America):

- the international context in which the revolutions are taking place (the impact of the international women's movement and the experience of women in revolutionary movements in other Third World countries)

- contradictions in the internal social structure of Central American societies that affect women directly (migration, male unemployment, female-headed families, influx of women into higher education, etc.)

- internal conditions for women within the revolutionary movement and in revolutionary organizations (leadership, relations between men and women, revolutionary ethics, etc.)

- the general line and strategy of the revolutionary movement, particularly, the line of "prolonged people's war."

The International Context

Both the international women's movement and the national liberation and socialist movements (particularly Cuba, Vietnam, and Angola) have shaped the international context in which revolutionary movements such as those in Central America take place.

No single international women's organization has ever emerged to put together all the separate movements and grass-roots efforts, but during the 1970s it is possible to say that the women's movement took on a loose but definite character through the exchange of travelers, distribution of literature and manifestos, and coming together in actual conferences. These contacts reinforced the process of critiquing old ideas and thinking about alternatives. Some of the most consistent male defenders of women's liberation in Nicaragua, today, for example, had contact with the women's movements of the United States and Europe as well as with the Cubans as they debated and discussed the Family Code. While Latin Americans in exile often had strong and enduring disagreements with the "narrow feminist" focus of some of the organizations they encountered, they nevertheless absorbed many of the ideas to which they were exposed and applied them to the Latin American context.

The process of thinking about alternative models of changing relationships between men and women was aided greatly by increased contacts during the 1970s between Latin American activists and other national liberation movements. In Vietnam, Angola, and Mozambique women participated in armed resistance, developed women's organizations during the anti-colonial phase of struggle and attempted to change relations between men and women in the family, in political organizations and in society at large.[6]

Most important of all, perhaps, were the theoretical contributions of the Cuban experience. The Cubans began the process of revolutionary transformation with the handicap of having seized power without mobilization of the people; as a result, organizations such as the Women's Federation got off to a slow start. When the Cuban leadership did initiate discussions about obstacles to women's full incorporation into production and political life, they did it in a bold and innovative way around a draft of a new Family Code. Women could only participate equally in social production and politics, the Cubans argued, if there were a breakdown of the division of labor in household work, a sharing of the "second shift" that had traditionally been the responsibility of working women. Poor countries like Cuba needed the contributions of women in production but could not afford to make significant investments in reducing the labor intensivity of household work. Men would simply have to share in household tasks and political men, in particular, would have to set the example. While who does the housework is not necessarily the issue during periods of crisis such as a revolutionary war where normal family life is often suspended, the question of what women can do and what men have to be willing to do to enable them to do it was given importance by the example of the debates in Cuba.

The majority of FSLN cadre could not, of course, discuss the question of women's roles in national liberation and socialism directly with representatives of other movements, and circulation of books and pamphlets was extremely limited due to censorship and repression. Nevertheless, the ideas were diffused in important, if limited ways, through cadre training and limited access to a book such as Margaret Randall's *Cuban Women Now* (*La mujer cubana de hoy*) which Comandante Dora María Tellez, FSLN, mentions as one of the ten books to which she and other cadre had access when they operated underground.[7]

Ideological influences in conflict with traditional dominant social values also came in the form of imported commercial mass media during the 1960s and 1970s. Magazines from the U.S. and Latin America discussed changing relationships between men and women and women's expectations for themselves and their mates, and this most certainly accelerated already existing contradictions between old ideologies and new realities, especially for the young and middle class. The images of North American television, though distorted and hardly liberating in the alternatives they posed, most certainly contributed to the deterioration of feudal-like norms for social behavior.

By 1979, the women's movement, the socialist movement (and the student and indigenous movements) and mass media had placed new issues and priorities on the international agenda. The Nicaraguan revolution of

---

[6] Eileen Eisen-Bergman, *Women in Vietnam* (San Francisco: People's Press, 1974). See also Stephanie Urdang, *Fighting Two Colonialisms: Women in Guinea Bissau* (New York: Monthly Review Press, 1979).

[7] Margaret Randall, *Todas estamos despiertas: testimonios de la mujer*, 1980, p. 87.

1979 took place, therefore, in a totally different international context than its predecessors in Mexico in 1910 and Cuba in 1959 and even than that of the national liberation movements of China, Vietnam, and Angola. It benefited from the richest insights in each of them. It is in this light that Dora María Tellez' comment to an interviewer from *Granma* should be understood. She says:

> ... the Nicaraguan revolution has had the largest participation of women because it is the most recent. In the next revolution, no matter where it happens, there are going to be more women.
>
> The Latin American woman has awoken and begun to take stock of herself, and as this happens, she will be able to undertake more and more tasks within her true capabilities and limitations.[8]

The Structural Contradictions in Women's Lives in Nicaragua: The 1960s and 1970s

Little is known about the social condition or political participation of women in Central America in either the immediate or more distant past. It seems certain, however, that prior to the Spanish Conquest, women in indigenous society had much greater freedom (including sexual) and access to material resources than they did afterwards. Pre-colonial societies at their height seem to have been characteristically matrilineal and matrilocal with a high degree of equality between the sexes, although these patterns were already in various degrees of decline by the time of the Conquest.[9]

While there are still elements of matrilineality and matrilocality in some indigenous groups in Guatemala[10] these formal reminders of a distant past have all but disappeared from Nicaraguan and Salvadorean mestizo society. In their place is a pattern of strict patriarchal controls on women's behavior in society and in the family.[11] At the same time, there are forces at work that tend to break down these controls such that in the last two decades, more and more young women, particularly urban women, are attending school and working at jobs outside the family unit. More and more men are unable to support their families due to unemployment and underemployment (and the alcoholism that this often brings). As a result, the rate of abandonment of families by fathers and husbands is extremely high in Central America. When fathers or husbands are present, but unable

---

[8] People's Translation Service, *op. cit.*

[9] Randall, *op. cit*; June Nash, "The Aztecs and the Ideology of Male Dominance," *Signs*, Vol. 4, No. 2 (1978), pp. 349-361; Ferdinand Anton, *Woman in Pre-Columbian America* (New York: Allanheld & Schram, 1973).

[10] John Gillian, *The Culture of Security in San Carlos: A Study of a Guatemalan Community of Indians and Ladinos* (New Orleans: Middle American Research Institute, 1951), Tulane University Publication No. 16.; and Eileen Maynard, *The Women of Palín: A Comparative Study of Indian and Ladino Women in a Guatemalan Village*, Ph.D. Dissertation, Cornell University (1963).

[11] LACWC (Latin American and Caribbean Women's Collective), *Slaves of Slaves: The Challenge of Latin American Women* (London: Zed Press, 1977).

to adequately provide, the locus of the family unit often passes to women who somehow find a way to provide for material and emotional needs.

While changes in the rate of abandonment are difficult to measure due to the lack of information on female-headed families, it seems clear that the incidence has increased dramatically and is linked to the seasonal demand for male labor, decreased access to land, and low male wages.[12] The Common Market import-substitution industrialization program of the 1960s, the encroachment of agro-export enterprises on small and medium peasant lands, and the increased seasonal demand for agricultural labor contributed to high female migration to urban areas and high concentration of women workers in service sector employment. Urban working-class women often found it easier than men to engage in subsistence activities— selling food on the streets, selling fruits, vegetables or clothing in the market, selling lottery tickets, selling services such as cooking, cleaning, waitressing, etc. Young educated urban women were an ideal reserve of labor for multinational corporations and the corresponding clerical, office and commercial needs they generated. As a result, the proportion of women officially classified as part of the economically active population increased from 14% in 1950 to 22% in 1970 and 29% in 1977.[13] The proportion of students of higher education who were women increased from 10% in 1962 to 33% in 1978. An estimated one-third of all families in Nicaragua in 1978 were headed by women. When the FSLN moved to organize women into mass organizations in 1978, the dominant ideology still defined the role of women as materially and emotionally dependent on men, restricted after marriage to the social world of the home. The reality for many Nicaraguan women, however, was clearly another.

The political situation brought into clear relief the contradiction between women's actual roles and the dominant ideology: women were expected to protect their children but their children were increasingly the targets of repression for real or imagined opposition to the dictatorship. Women increasingly had to be "in the street," outside the controlling confines of the household; but by venturing "into the street" they were increasingly subjected to sexual harassment and political repression. Sexual assaults on women known or imagined to be FSLN collaborators became commonplace in jails and on the streets. The routine transfer of National Guard soldiers from town to town every three months did little to help an already established pattern of "casual paternity."

In urban areas, young people proved to be the easiest recruits for the early FSLN due to their concentration in schools, relatively greater "leisure" time (if unemployed), and ability to pass through the streets without attracting attention. As a result, it was often sons and daughters who first exposed their parents, usually their mothers, to the ideas of the anti-Somoza movement. When sons and daughters were captured, it

---

[12] Jaime Wheelock Román, *Imperialismo y dictadura: crisis de una formación social* (México: Siglo XXI, 1975).

[13] Antonio Ybarra Rojas, "Occupational Structure of the Female Labor Force in Nicaragua," report from the Banco Central de Nicaragua, 1978.

was mostly mothers who went to jails, penitentiaries and public offices to demand their release, partly because mothers tended to be more sympathetic to the activities of their children and partly because adult men were vulnerable to being arrested themselves. Mothers who got involved in the struggle against the dictatorship because of their children were involved by the most traditional of reasons—protection or defense of an immediate family member. But once they became involved, the traditional aspect of their motivation often transformed into its opposite.

And, in this process of growing consciousness and commitment, the cycle of mothers raising daughters to be resigned and self-sacrificing mothers and wives, and sons to be successful men for whom the work of women is invisible, begins to break down. Sometimes it happens only after the death of a child. Like many other mothers, Doña Santos Buitrago, the single parent of FSLN militant Julio Buitrago, was afraid of his being killed and frequently urged him not to get so deeply involved. Julio was her only son and she was a poor woman who had worked extremely hard to put him all the way through school to the university. Friends of Julio's commented that he could not stand to see women mistreated because he always thought of his mother. Doris Tijerino recalls:

> Julio always told me that one of the things that worried him most was that his mother Doña Santos probably wouldn't be able to bear the sorrow of his death, that the day that happened, she'd die too.

But,

> When Julio died, Doña Santos survived. And not only did she survive and bear her sorrow at the death of her son but she changed radically. Doña Santos was a mother worthy of a Sandinista martyr. She went to meetings, took part in the struggle to free the prisoners, went to many assemblies with the mothers of other imprisoned comrades and helped plan popular campaigns.[14]

Sometimes it was the other way around: mothers convinced children. In other cases mothers and daughters became involved simultaneously without each other's knowledge.

Not all children, however, were able to win over their parents and had no choice but to abandon their families, or their families abandoned them. Marisol, a woman from such a family, comments:

> Look, there comes a time in the life of people in which your political ideas make you really separate from certain things. This is how it has to be. Really, it wasn't difficult for me. Little by little, I was achieving a goal which was the triumph of the Revolution and my family passed then to second place. The Revolution is before the family, before everything.[15]

Many women activists, likewise, had to choose either militancy or marriage when their husbands objected to their involvement or that of their

[14] Doris Tijerino, *Inside the Nicaraguan Revolution* (Vancouver: New Star Books, 1978), p. 117.
[15] Randall, *op. cit.*, pp. 286-7.

children. Capitalist development itself in Nicaragua made impossible the realization of bourgeois ideals of the nuclear family and economically dependent women. The expansion of capitalist relations of production during the 1960s and 1970s only made the potential conflict between dominant ideas and the reality of most Nicaraguan women more acute. But open conflict between women's views of themselves as self-sacrificing mothers with primary loyalties only to the small circle of the family broke down in the context of a revolutionary movement. Under the conditions created by this movement, what had been a traditional barrier to the participation of women—their commitments to their families—actually turned into its opposite.

Life for Women inside the FSLN

The first female militants of the Sandinista Liberation Front describe themselves as determined to demonstrate their worth as fighters in the struggle against all odds. But what made it possible not only for them, an exceptional few, but for many women to achieve important positions in cadre and mass organizations was the organizational line of the Front itself. Women were frequently recruited as collaborators and militants and were able to move up in the organization to positions of responsibility. Sandino's army in the 1930s had had some women who worked within, but never had there been a precedent for so many women being incorporated into so many important roles.

Both in Sandino's time and in the contemporary period, the roles offered to women in the movement were ahead of those available to them in society at large, but acceptance of their position was much more difficult in the earlier period. Nazaria, a 61-year-old woman who travelled with Sandino's army commented:

> There was criticism, yes, from the majority of people. They didn't understand that women could participate, be equal to men. That just like men, women can be combatants as well. Sometimes we ourselves marginalized ourselves. They said that what we were doing was incorrect, that it was crazy to go around with an army. How could a woman be able to fight, the people said, and even now you see some who think like that. But not the youth. The young ones congratulate me for participating as they do.[16]

When the Front was established in 1962 to carry on the banner of Sandino, its founding members were men. But soon afterward, perhaps because women were already participating in other guerrilla organizations on the continent, the first women were recruited into the FSLN. But the organization into which the first women were recruited was still in a "foquista" stage, isolated from the masses and frequently subject to heavy losses. This isolation and clandestine life must have been doubly hard for the women.

---

[16] Randall, *op. cit.*, p. 21.

As a consequence of the emphasis on recruitment of students in the early 1970s, a young working-class woman like Luisa Amanda Espinosa, the first female martyr of the organization, was not really at the center of the organization's work during this period and lacked the support of other women from backgrounds like her own. Later, however, as peasant and urban women began to be incorporated through their participation in mass organizations, women of all sectors and social classes eventually became part of the organization. Dora María Tellez, one of the women who eventually rose to become a *comandante*, comments:

> In our revolution, peasant women struggled in tremendously heroic ways, in spite of the repression. But in the city participation was also difficult. It was looked upon badly that a woman should be part of the political struggle (they said we were prostitutes).... More or less in 1972 or 1973 is when we began to incorporate women from the city in large numbers; this is when we created organizations such as the Association of Women Confronting the National Problem (AMPRONAC) which curiously took root at both the popular level and in the high bourgeoisie; it took root in all sectors because it was an anti-somocista response directed by the revolutionary movement against the dictatorship.[17]

The important part of the FSLN organizational line was its emphasis on "correct" relationships among cadre and between cadre and leaders. It took great care in cultivating its recruits, in basing advancement on objective skill and merit, and in motivating through political understanding. In the case of women, this support and emphasis on respect paid off. Over and over again when questioned about problems of sexism, women in the organization bring up examples of relations with men on the outside and contrast them with relations with men in the organization.

Problems arose, for example, when women with leadership responsibilities were staying in "safe houses": the collaborators in the house found it difficult to accept that female guests did not automatically offer to cook, clean and mop.

The kind of support and respect women were able to gain inside the organization contrasted greatly with the contradictory virgin/whore roles they were offered on the outside. There, once women transcended the boundaries of traditional roles they were thought to deserve whatever abuse ensued. Sexism and machismo were integral parts of the Somoza dictatorship's control of society through the National Guard. Mónica Baltodano could command a whole region of male and female troops for the FSLN, but when it came time for one of Somoza's officials to surrender he refused to negotiate with her, at first, because she was a woman.

The opportunities for respect in the movement on the basis of merit were an important reason why young women, even from high bourgeois families, rejected their class privileges (in apparently greater numbers than their male counterparts) and joined the revolutionary organization.

---

[17] Randall, *op. cit.*, p. 24.

Being treated differently within the ranks of the organization was extremely important to the morale of the women of the FSLN. Relatively more equal treatment by *compañeros* does not, in itself, guarantee long-term changes, say, in men's participation in housework or in women's equal access to employment, but it does provide an important standard and ideal which had an impact far beyond its own ranks. As Dora María Tellez comments,

> *With the revolutionary political process ideas and concepts change too. The same is true in the case of women. Women here participated in the revolution not at the level of the kitchen but at the level of combatant and at the level of political leadership. This gives another framework to women. In fact, women played another role in war and acquired a tremendous moral authority for any man to be able to respect them. It would be difficult for any woman combatant to allow some man to raise his hand to hit her, to mistreat her. Because there is an authority to her, a moral authority to the general female population that is now reflected even in intimate relations. The conception of the relationship has changed.*[18]

The General Line of the FSLN: Prolonged People's War

In the early 1970s, the FSLN, like several other Central American revolutionary organizations such as the Popular Liberation Forces (FPL) in El Salvador and the Guerrilla Army of the Poor (EGP) and Revolutionary Organization of the People in Arms (ORPA) in Guatemala, broke with the "foquista" conception of guerrilla warfare in favor of the Vietnamese-inspired conception of Prolonged People's War. In contrast to the over-reliance on military actions at the expense of political organization and a small band of full-time revolutionaries (the guerrilla *foco*) at the expense of grass-root organizations, "people's war" emphasized the long, slow (i.e., prolonged) process of accumulating forces and the organization of the masses (i.e., "people") in all sectors and at all levels under a multiplicity of tactics and organizational forms that could speak to a multiplicity of contradictions.[19] In contrast to the bureaucratism, conciliationism and dogmatism of the traditional Communist Party, "people's war" emphasized the armed struggle, the predominantly capitalist character of Nicaraguan society, and the necessity of working-class and peasant hegemony in any alliance with a sector of the bourgeoisie.

People's war adherents in Nicaragua and Guatemala followed the Vietnamese emphasis on beginning the process of accumulation of forces in the more protective environment of rural areas but the concept itself is

---

[18] Randall, *op. cit.*, p. 92.

[19] For further discussion of "foquismo" see Gerard Chaliand, *Revolution in the Third World*, (Middlesex, England: Penguin Books, 1977); and Norma Chinchilla, "Class Struggle in Central America: Background and Overview," *Latin American Perspectives*, No. 25/26 (Spring/Summer), 1980. [Also printed in abridged form in Chapter 1 of this volume. – Ed].

not inextricably linked to a choice of rural over urban, or of peasant over proletariat, as its application by revolutionary groups in more urbanized, proletarianized El Salvador demonstrates. In fact, what is important about the conception of prolonged people's war is that it generally avoids the forced dichotomous choices that characterized debates over revolutionary strategy for the previous decade. During the 1960s, it was either rural or urban guerrilla, vanguard party or mass organization, the primacy of the political or military aspect, legal or clandestine forms of work, etc. By the late 1970s the advocates of people's war had begun to demonstrate, in practice, not only the possibility but the necessity of multiple tactics for multiple fronts simultaneously coordinated in a single strategy.

This view breaks with a particular brand of Marxist thought that is mechanical, deterministic, and undialectical and replaces it with an ability to analyze and respond to the complexity of concrete social formations. The totality of the social structure can only be understood by understanding all its contradictions and their relationships to each other.

The only way to capture the multiplicity of contradictions is to study the concrete reality of a concrete social formation, and the only way to really understand that reality is to sink deep roots into it like the FSLN did early in its formation by interviewing those who had fought with Sandino and popularizing his views.

The art of revolution, then, becomes the art of coordinating or "articulating" multiple struggles against multiple contradictions in such a way that none is liquidated and the totality is strengthened. The overall class perspective for the coordination of contradictions is proletarian, but housewives, students, Christians, peasants, professionals, petty vendors, and indigenous peoples can no longer be seen as simply auxiliary to a revolution fought by the proletariat; each group can be organized directly around its concrete immediate demands in such a way that the overall revolutionary process is advanced.

The importance of responding, organizationally and politically, to all contradictions and interrelationships among contradictions is perhaps one of the most important contributions of the Central American experience.

The ability of the FSLN to organize one of the first mass women's organizations in the history of Latin America is directly related to this break with economistic, dogmatic and mechanical conceptions of Marxism and revolutionary strategy. When FSLN cadre founded AMPRONAC (the Association of Women Concerned about the National Problem), they broke with the sectarianism that demands that women's organizations be composed of only party members or only working class women or that they be totally subordinate to the party organization. It was able to break with a "liquidationist" approach to the problems of working class women which sees them only in their class aspect and not in the combination of class and gender exploitation. AMPRONAC succeeded where other organizations had failed because it was truly an organization where the masses of women could participate, obtain political education and learn leadership skills. The existence of such a mass organization and the close relationship of the vanguard organization to it reinforced and supported the work of women who were part of the cadre core, reminding them constantly that they should not see themselves as "exceptional women" but as representatives of the masses of women.

The successor of AMPRONAC, AMNLAE, is one of the three most important mass organizations in Nicaragua today. It was created by the FSLN organization and its leadership have been mostly FSLN cadre, but it is organically autonomous and its leadership gains its legitimacy from being able to lead and win the confidence of others, not through top-down directives or automatic attachment to a trademark. There are debates in AMNLAE, just as there are, from time to time, undoubtedly debates between AMNLAE and the FSLN leadership, although none have emerged into the public arena as of yet.

AMNLAE is not explicitly feminist, but there is no question that it speaks to the most immediate needs of the majority of women and is a force for the creation of conditions whereby women's demands will themselves expand. Despite a certain expected relaxing of intense commitment after the victory by some groups of women and the tendency on the part of some men to expect women to quietly retreat back into the household sphere, leaders of AMNLAE continue to raise the question of full incorporation of women into all spheres of Nicaraguan life (including combat against an expected invasion) in discussions of the future of women in Nicaragua.[20]

Conclusion

It is important not to underestimate the importance of the mass mobilization of women in a multiplicity of significant roles in the Nicaraguan Revolution. There is little precedent for it in the history of Latin America and little equal to it in the rest of the world. Men's conception of women and women's conceptions of themselves were dramatically transformed in actions that challenged and exposed the often invisible and seemingly eternal conceptions of class society.

At the same time, it is important not to substitute the mass mobilization of women in time of war for the long-term transformation of society in which women, as well as the majority of people, are liberated. As the concept implies, the war is prolonged, not only in preparing to take power but in building something new to replace the old. Women may be given the opportunity to do what men do in the new Nicaragua, but their ability to take those opportunities often depends on men doing what women do. For young women and cadre the hard choices are often mitigated by being single in the case of young women and by the availability of parents, grandparents, or neighbors for those who have children. But the majority of women, including those who are taking care of of the children of others, still face the material and attitudinal obstacles to equality in their daily lives.

---

[20] See Margaret Randall, "Women's Combat Army Mobilizes in Nicaragua," *Guardian,* 1981 for a discussion of the debate about whether women should continue to train for active combat.

Marriage is not really freely entered into until women have equal access to the means of subsistence. The alleviation of the burden of housework, especially in poor countries, cannot await the socialization of goods and services associated with reproduction; there is no other solution but to divide up the work at home so that women may work and participate politically outside the home. The position of women in the party will not be secure until their access to experience, leadership skills and top positions is fully institutionalized and until criticisms of practice in "personal" as well as "public" life are fully legitimized.

The solutions to all of these problems are linked, not only to an understanding of the sources of women's oppression and the measures by which they might be overcome, but to a basic understanding of Marxism as a method and strategy of revolutionary transformation. The Central American revolutions represent some of the most hopeful advances yet in forging this method and strategy.

From Woman-as-Object to
Woman-as-Revolutionary-Force*

At a given moment in the history of the social division of labor, women were separated from production and assigned to domestic labor. With this assignment the world of women was reduced to the atrophying dimensions of the home, to a narrow framework that was limited and individualist. In addition, they were subjected to exhausting and routinizing work. This gradually generated in women a political, technical, and social backwardness which converted them into objects propelled by history, not subjects forging their own history.

Society institutionalized this role of woman-as-object, giving it an ideological and even a legal framework, thus denying to women a voice, a consciousness, a history. This inequality, in fact and in law, converted women into easy victims and into reproductive agents of exploitative systems. Under capitalism, and for the above-mentioned reasons, women's inequality became a pillar of the system. In the first place women, by means of their domestic labor, reproduce gratis the labor power that would otherwise signify expenditures for the capitalist. Furthermore, the capitalists save money by paying lower wages to women simply because they are women. Thus women suffer the ruthlessness of the system through their double exploitation as workers and as housewives who reproduce the labor power of their spouses.

There are yet other ways in which women's inequality serves as a source of profit to the capitalist: they are taken advantage of as consumers and are utilized by the capitalist system as a transmission belt for individualist, parochial values. Therefore, it is the objective of any revolution to free this social force from commercial exploitation and from the degrading condition of object, and to return to women the right and the possibility to be complete human beings, active and strengthening components of the Revolution.

In the case of our country, our Revolution has recognized that the participation of (Nicaraguan) women has specific importance to other revolutions, not only because of the high quality of this participation (during the war all staff headquarters had women members) but also because it took an organized form: AMPRONAC (*Asociación de Mujeres Nicaragüenses ante la Problemática Nacional;* Association of Nicaraguan Women Confronting the National Problem).[1]

To maintain and deepen the level of women's participation is not only our historic duty but also a necessity of the Revolution. Massive efforts by our people are required for the consolidation of the Revolution—and half the people are women.

---

*By the Association of Nicaraguan Women, "Luisa Amanda Espinoza" (AMNLAE). Title and translation by Women's International Resource Exchange.
[1]From *Barricada*, Managua, Nicaragua, March 23, 1980.

8

Nicaragua:
The Revolutionary Option

In contrast to the bulk of the material in this book, which focuses on the tragic history of exploitation, repression and intervention suffered by the peoples and nations of Central America, a discussion of contemporary Nicaragua offers welcome relief. In fact, many Central Americans view Nicaragua as a beacon of hope, an example of what might be possible some day in the rest of Central America.

On July 19, 1979, the Nicaraguan people led by the Sandinista National Liberation Front overthrew the personal dictatorship of Anastasio Somoza. The Sandinistas had been organizing and fighting against Somoza since 1962. On the day the FSLN marched into Managua, they enjoyed the overwhelming support of the Nicaraguan people. Their support cut across class lines and involved virtually all sectors of Nicaraguan society, rich and poor. This support was especially powerful among the youth.

During the four decades of its rule, the Somoza family's corrupt and repressive regime had alienated all sectors of the Nicaraguan population, including the agro-industrial and business elite. However, it was not so much the unanimity of the Nicaraguan people's rejection of Somoza that caught the world (and above all the U.S. Department of State) off guard, as it was the bravery with which Nicaraguan youth confronted the dictatorship's formidable military machine. In a series of bloody urban insurrections which erupted in virtually every major city, entire neighborhoods took to the streets, ripping up the cobblestones to erect barricades. Teenagers pitched crude home-made contact bombs against the tanks and machine-guns that had been provided to Somoza primarily by the U.S. Parents and grandparents crept behind the barricades at night to distribute food, water and munitions to the "muchachos," as the fighters were affectionately called.

Since their triumph, the Sandinistas have begun implementing a series of economic and political programs aimed at benefiting the impoverished majority of the population, while still maintaining a mixed economy. Economically, the number one priority was declared to be the satisfaction of basic human needs. This does not mean, however, that reform was limited to concrete economic exigencies. On the contrary, the FSLN showed concern also for the subtler forms of oppression and exploitation in the cultural realm. For example, one of the first laws passed by the new government, in July, 1979, was the prohibition of any advertising which insulted the image of women. Less than a year later, another law was passed guaranteeing bilingual education to the indigenous minorities living in Nicaragua's Atlantic Coast region.

Not surprisingly, post-revolutionary reconstruction and consolidation of the Sandinista government has been neither painless nor free from contradictions. As the articles in this chapter by Richard Fagen and George Black and Judy Butler point out, the very nature of the broad-based, pluriclass support for the FSLN created problems for the fledgling government, especially when it became evident that the Sandinistas intended to implement their promise to improve the living conditions of the poor peasants and workers. This socialist orientation on the part of the FSLN alienated the wealthy business and agro-industrial elite of the country as well as the U.S. State Department. Almost immediately after the end of the fighting, therefore, the upper classes formed militant and bitterly vocal opposition parties. Some of the opposition emigrated to Miami, Honduras and Guatemala to organize armed resistance to the new government.

Criticism of the FSLN has not been limited to the privileged elite. Both in the heat of the revolutionary struggle and in the flush of victory, hopes among the Nicaraguan people were raised to unrealistic levels. This problem of overblown expectations was aggravated by the country's economic crisis, causing resentment to grow among certain sectors of the middle class and the poor, especially in the cities, when living conditions did not dramatically improve immediately following the overthrow of Somoza.

One does not have to look hard to find the causes of this problem. When the Sandinistas took over, they faced an economic catastrophe: an empty treasury and a $1.5 billion foreign debt. During the last year of the fighting Nicaragua's Gross Domestic Product dropped 25 percent; the war caused over half a billion dollars worth of direct physical damage to the infrastructure of the nation, i.e., factories, bridges, roads and hospitals. It is even claimed that in the last few weeks of the war, once Somoza knew he was going to lose, he ordered his airforce to systematically bomb the factories, hospitals and schools of the country.

The dislocation and destruction of the bloody civil war has been further exacerbated by a generalized economic recession facing all the dependent economies of Central America in the early 1980s, regardless of the character of their political regimes (see Chapter 3).

Daily life for the majority of Nicaraguans, consequently, has not yet improved in a substantial way. Once the euphoria of victory ebbed, the people were forced to return to their low wages and long hours, and moreover had to suffer the inadequate services of a wartorn country. Jobs continue to be scarce, and although education and health care are now guaranteed free of charge, life is difficult for the marginal urban dweller and the landless migrant farm worker.

Despite these substantial economic obstacles, the Sandinistas were able to begin implementing their political and economic programs immediately after coming to power. Perhaps most notable was the emergence of the "mass organizations" as bulwarks of popular democracy. Each mass organization represents a particular sector or social class and lobbies for its specific interests in the new governmental structures. In this manner, concerns among the population at the base level find an institutionalized forum for public political expression. In this vein, the article below by Fernando Cardenal and Valerie Miller offers an inside view of the Literacy Campaign and illustrates well the level of popular mobilization characteristic of post-insurrectionary Nicaragua. The mass organizations played a crucial role in implementing and even planning the Literacy Campaign; in fact, without their participation such an ambitious project would have been impossible to carry out.

In response to the growing level of mobilization on the part of the poor and formerly disenfranchised classes, the opposition parties sponsored by the wealthy elite became increasingly militant and hostile to the new government. Following a series of bombings and well-coordinated armed attacks by anti-Sandinista guerrillas, the government on March 15, 1982, declared a state of emergency. This action resulted in curbs being placed on the opposition media. Selective restrictions on the media and the detention in late 1981 of several business leaders (who were subsequently released) for violating the Law of Maintenance of Public Order and Security have elicited heavy international criticism from governments which supported the struggle against Somoza, most notably Venezuela and Costa Rica. International human rights organizations, however, unanimously recognize that the human rights record of revolutionary Nicaragua, while not perfect, is satisfactory (and by Latin American standards is excellent—see Chapter Five). In fact, one of the first laws passed by the new government was the abolition of capital punishment.

The biggest danger to the new Nicaraguan experiment, as Black and Butler point out in their article, is neither economic nor internal. It is the threat of outside intervention and covert destabilization by the U.S. or a close ally of the U.S. Evidence leaked to the press in early 1982 suggests that the Central Intelligence Agency has been financing and directing a major sabotage operation against the Sandinista government. Immediately upon coming to power, the Reagan administration took a hard line against the Sandinistas, going so far as to cut even humanitarian food aid in March, 1981. Similarly, the U.S. began increasingly to pressure multilateral lending institutions (Interamerican Development Bank, International Monetary Fund, etc.) to cut or reduce loans to Nicaragua. The signals, therefore, all indicate that the United States has decided to pursue a strategy of economic and political ostracism at the public level, and military sabotage at the covert level.

Will the Sandinistas succeed with their revolutionary project? Such success depends on a number of factors. First and foremost, it depends on the FSLN's ability to reactivate the economy and to satisfy and juggle the sometimes conflicting demands of Nicaragua's workers, peasants and urban middle classes. To some extent, it also depends on the outcomes of the popular struggles raging in El Salvador, Guatemala and other Central American Countries. Unfortunately, one of the biggest factors affecting the fate of the Nicaraguan Revolution is the behavior of the U.S. government. Will the U.S. learn to live with an independent revolutionary democracy in its "backyard" or will the historical patterns of intervention be repeated once again in Nicaragua? The answer to this last crucial question lies in the strength of the solidarity and non-intervention movements in the United States.

—Philippe Bourgois
and Hans Ulrich Hornig

Revolution and Transition in Nicaragua*
By Richard R. Fagen

Richard R. Fagen is Gildred Professor of Latin American Studies at Stanford University. He has written numerous books and articles on Latin America, comparative politics (particularly political change, development, and political economy), and United States foreign policy and relations. He has lived for periods in Mexico, Chile, Cuba and Nicaragua during the past decade.

Power and Hegemony

Who rules Nicaragua? A legalist would say that executive power resides in the Junta de Gobierno, operating through a standard array of ministries; legislative power resides in the Consejo de Estado, or Council of State, inaugurated on May 4, 1980, after a long-drawn-out controversy over its composition; and judicial power is lodged in the Supreme Court and lesser magistrates—except for special tribunals established to try ex-members of the National Guard.

This formalistic overview of the structure of government in Nicaragua would not include a separate box for or perhaps even mention the Sandinist National Liberation Front. Yet the answer to the question, "who rules Nicaragua," is: the FSLN. The FSLN named the Junta de Gobierno; FSLN commanders hold several of the most important ministerial positions; all other ministers and high officials were selected by the FSLN. The Frente decided on the composition of the Council of State (in which it has a clear majority), the armed forces (Ejército Popular Sandinista), the police, and state security are all down-the-line Sandinist organizations, and no major decision—either domestic or international—would be taken without prior approval by the National Directorate of the FSLN.

The hegemonic role exercised by the FSLN does not mean, however, that what the Frente wants the Frente gets. To the contrary, a great deal of

---

*Excerpted and abridged from *Socialist Review* 11:5 (September-October), 1981.

political bargaining takes place in Nicaragua. Policy options are constrained both by domestic and international factors. Hegemony is not the same as control; if economic realities and social forces were not so complex, for example, it certainly would not have taken the Frente months of pulling and hauling to constitute the Council of State. Nor does hegemony imply that the FSLN is actually able to govern in a direct, day-to-day manner. Not only is the new state necessarily staffed by many persons who by no means fully agree with official policies, but even with the best of will the multitude of projects under way outruns the technical and fiscal capacity of the state to respond. There is thus a sharp, double constraint on making Frente-designed policies come to life.

Additionally, the policies themselves contain substantial tensions and even contradictions. In a coffee-growing area north of Managua I witnessed sharp confrontations between peasants and landowners in the streets of the provincial capital. Peasants (not paid during much of the insurrection) were demanding back wages and better working and living conditions. They were counseled by organizers from the ATC, the Sandinist-led association of peasants and rural workers. The confrontations were being adjudicated by employees of the Ministry of Labor.

I asked a young Sandinist cadre how the Frente felt such disputes should be settled. He answered that the most important overall goal was to maintain agricultural production, that the situation on each *finca* or farm was different, that the Frente did not have nearly enough cadres to investigate individual cases, that the ATC would do a good job of representing the workers' interests, and that the final word would have to rest with the Ministry of Labor—many of whose provincial employees had served under Somoza as well. Such are some of the problems of turning hegemony into coherently implemented policies at the grass roots.

Throughout the period prior to the August 1978 assault on the National Palace, the FSLN was still not a mass organization. Although it had acquired sympathizers among high school and university youth and more radicalized sectors of the middle class, it did not command the loyalty of most of the huge number of Nicaraguans who opposed Somoza.

With the mass uprisings of September 1978, this situation changed. The uprisings, sparked by the FSLN, were truly insurrectional in the sense that thousands of citizens grabbed whatever weapon was at hand, built barricades, and launched themselves against the Guard. In many instances the major role of the thinly stretched regular FSLN combatants was simply to try to instill some order and coherence in what was a spontaneous overflowing of hostility toward Somoza and the Guard.

Somewhat chastened by this experience, the FSLN worked diligently during the fall and winter of 1978-1979 to prepare the citizenry for the next round of insurrectional activity. The response to the Frente's call was so massive, so *popular*, that the thousands of *milicianos* with their red and black kerchiefs and assorted pistols, shotguns, rifles, Molotov cocktails and contact bombs were never fully organized by Frente cadres or always led by known Sandinists. In fact, in the hour of victory, anyone who had built a barricade, thrown a bomb, fired a gun, carried a message, or cared for the wounded had earned the right—at least temporarily—to call himself or herself a Sandinist.

In July 1979, the leadership of the Frente was faced with several problems deriving from this multifold expansion of the rank and file. Most urgent was the task of putting order into the armed forces. Common criminals released by Somoza just before he fled had grabbed weapons and uniforms and were posing as combatants. Honest but untutored *muchachos* who had actually earned the right to bear arms began to give the FSLN a bad name, seizing houses and automobiles, getting drunk, firing weapons indiscriminately.

Of more lasting importance was the task of deciding how to organize the FSLN for the purpose of governing Nicaragua rather than overthrowing the dynasty. The organizational issue embodies a prior question: what should be the role of the FSLN in post-Somoza Nicaragua? The Frente has a one-line answer: *El FSLN es la organización de vanguardia del pueblo nicaragüense.* The definition of the Frente as a vanguard in turn implies a double imperative. First, it implies a continuing dominant place for the FSLN in Nicaraguan politics. It is a claim that FSLN hegemony, in the sense previously mentioned, ought to be a structural, not just a temporary, feature of the political economy of the nation. Second, it implies that membership in the FSLN must be strictly controlled. Not everyone can belong, no matter how heroic they might have been during the final insurrection.

Although not at present formally constituted as a political party, the FSLN is moving in that direction. A membership structure with three levels is envisaged: militant, pre-militant, and affiliated member. Local committees (*Comités de Base Sandinistas*) will link the party with the masses, and existing mass organizations like the CDS (Sandinist Defense Committees) and the Central Sandinista de Trabajadores (labor confederations) will then be oriented more directly by the party as well.

Ideology and Legitimacy

The objective reality of Nicaragua substantiates and reinforces the claims of the FSLN to vanguard status and thus a special place in the political life of the nation. On the other hand, the dominant ideological umbrella under which much of the struggle against Somoza was waged located the operational definition of legitimacy in an electoral process in which all come equally to contend in the "free" political marketplace. Both visions can agree on the importance of basic human rights and certain developmental goals. Both could also agree that in a transitional period after Somoza an extraordinary role would have to be taken by the group that spearheaded the dictator's downfall—the FSLN. But their longer-term understandings of the proper nature and organization of the state are in fundamental conflict.

This conflict reflects economic interests, long-standing political divisions, and international actors and forces. At least during 1979 and until late 1980, however, it was being played out largely at the ideological level. This in no way diminishes its seriousness. To the contrary, since what is at stake is nothing less than the future format of the Nicaraguan political economy, the battle is deadly serious. The ideological conflict is a sometimes murky cover through which the social forces bubbling just below the surface can be viewed. The pot has boiled over in the past, and it will undoubtedly do so again.

Interestingly, among the major open clashes of 1979 and early 1980 was a series of confrontations with the "left" opposition to the FSLN, groups which felt that the Frente was not fulfulling its class *compromiso* with the popular sectors—in wages, worker control, etc. Because the challenge to Frente hegemony was serious, the possible economic costs important, and *mano dura* easier to use against the ultra-left than against the private sector, the crackdown was swift and evidently effective. Dozens of persons were jailed and a sharp ideological campaign against the "ultras" was launched.

That voices such as the MDN (Nicaraguan Democratic Movement, headed by industrialist Alfonso Robelo) and the PSC (Social Christian Party) could speak unhindered in Nicaragua in 1980 indicates the high degree of political freedom that exists. Equally impressive and perhaps more revealing of the "tone" of politics in Nicaragua in the first year and a half of the revolution is the manner in which ordinary citizens are voicing complaints and participating in the pull and haul of reconstruction. In union halls, workplaces, neighborhoods, and on street corners, Nicaraguans are for the first time in their history speaking out in large numbers.

Economics in Command

The politics of austerity that characterizes the Sandinist economic recovery program takes different forms. For example, in a situation characterized by severe shortages of basic goods, high unemployment, and sixty per cent inflation, the official goal in 1980 was to limit salary increases to rises in the cost of living, thus keeping real wages constant. In some cases, the actual increases granted did not even meet this goal. Yet there seems to be widespread understanding and acceptance of the Sandinist slogan "la revolución no es piñata" ("the revolution isn't a bag of goodies").

In mid-1979 there were stories to the effect that Somoza's confiscated properties would amount to as much as fifty per cent of all the productive facilities of the nation. Although the holdings of the dynasty were impressive—and thus the newly formed Area of People's Property very significant—when an interim inventory became available, it was disclosed that the majority of productive facilities were still in private hands, particularly in certain key sectors of the economy. In the critical agrarian sector (the main earner of foreign exchange), 80 per cent of production remains in private hands. In manufacturing, the corresponding figure is 75 per cent. Only in mining and construction does the balance tip in favor of the state, with 95 per cent of the productive facilities of the former and 55 per cent of the latter in public hands. Overall, the Plan estimates that 59 per cent of the nation's total gross domestic product will be produced by the private sector, and 41 per cent by the state in 1980. That the state achieves even this level of participation in production is due to the large and predominantly state-run service sector.

The implications of this superficial sketch of the pattern of ownership of productive facilities in post-Somoza Nicaragua are obvious: without the cooperation of the private sector, even the modest targets of the Plan of economic reactivation cannot be met.

A special kind of mixed economy has thus developed in Nicaragua in the aftermath of Somoza's overthrow. The state controls the financial system, has important participation in other key sectors, and uses its significant instruments of pricing and credit to structure the operation of various markets. But the rules of the game are still capitalist rules—as the FSLN acknowledges; and when hard choices have to be made between production and other goals, those choices are almost always made in favor of production.

The Class Question

Within weeks after the victory, it was clear that the particular constellation of groups and organizations that came together in the anti-Somoza coalition and were thus to "share legislative functions with the Junta" did not reflect the realities of revolutionary Nicaragua. Most glaring was the omission of any mention of or representation for mass organizations—of women, youth, workers, peasants, indigenous peoples, and neighborhood committees (Committees of Sandinist Defense or CDSs). But to include mass organizations, essentially created and organized by the FSLN, was to pose a double threat to those who opposed the hegemonic role of the Frente: first, it tipped the balance of the council in favor of the FSLN and gave additional institutional legitimation to the notion of the FSLN as vanguard; second, it added a host of new voices speaking for the *clases populares* in a forum that might otherwise have overrepresented the bourgeois opposition to Somoza.

The composition of the Council became an issue which embraced the key question: in whose interest should Nicaragua be ruled? The FSLN provided for ample representation of the mass organizations on the forty-seven-seat Council. The FSLN's class position was made clear. Robelo's Nicaraguan Democratic Movement, the Social Christian Party, and the Conservative Democratic Party all initially responded by refusing to take the seats allotted to them. COSEP, the Higher Council of Private Enterprise, allotted five seats, debated for a week and then finally decided to participate.

For six months the uneasy truce remained in force. Then, early in November 1980, after the government had banned a political meeting of Robelo's MDN and some Sandinist youths had stoned the MDN's headquarters in Managua, eleven members of the Council walked out. Among them were all the representatives of COSEP as well as the representatives of the MDN, other opposition political parties, and non-Sandinist trade unions.

The position taken by COSEP vis-à-vis the Council does not mean, however, that there is an implacable and unrelenting tension between private enterprise in general on the one hand and the Sandinist state representing the *clases populares* on the other. This is well understood by both those who oppose and those who support the programs of the FSLN and the Junta. Thus, under the banner of the "sacred" defense of private property some seek to band together persons as disparate as the owners of huge agrarian estates and neighborhood shoe-repair stalls. Meanwhile, Sandinist state policies take cognizance of the importance of both the economic necessities and the values of small and not-so-small capitalists and the diffuse "middle class" to which some belong and with which many others identify.

The other key aspect of the class question is located in the relationship of the *clases populares* to the Sandinist state. The FSLN says that the new Nicaragua will be ruled in favor of the *clases populares*. But the contradictions that arise from the dual needs of austerity and benefits for the masses also complicate the relationship between long-run goals and short-run exigencies. The pressure to redistribute is very strong; worker grievances are real and poignant. "We haven't had a vacation in three hundred years," said one leader of the Association of Rural Workers. The temptation to take that vacation is great.

Furthermore, the *clases populares*, like the capitalists, are not a homogeneous and unified group. While organized workers are doing relatively well, the unemployed are not. The government's public works programs have not been able to employ more than a minority of those without jobs. The more marginal urban youth who fought so heroically during the insurrection have also caused special problems. Those who have found a place in the new Sandinist Popular Army or the police are among the most fortunate. Others have found pick-and-shovel work, usually temporary, in the physical reconstruction of the country. But many more remain on the streets. Their incorporation into a new Nicaragua will have to await future structural transformations of the society and the economy.

Conclusion: Toward Socialism

Nicaragua is not socialist. The 1980 plan was designed to revitalize capitalism and to set up an important sector of state ownership and state production. But many Nicaraguans understand that they have been given a historic opportunity to construct a socialist system that is not a Central American imitation of what has been attempted in Cuba, Eastern Europe, or elsewhere. What happens in Nicaragua will, of course, depend not only on decisions taken there, but on events and decisions in a host of other countries and institutions as well. But at a minimum there are four broad tensions that will have to be dealt with in the course of socialist construction in Nicaragua.

Centralization and decentralization. A planned economy requires a significant degree of centralization. To combine this centralization with institutions that allow for local initiative, decisional autonomy, and participation has been the most difficult task facing those who believe in socialism with a human rather than with a bureaucratic face. In war-damaged Nicaragua, there exists a powerful pull toward the centralization of decision-making. The arguments are familiar—and compelling: "a firm hand at the helm as we sail through stormy seas"; a necessary period of tutelage while the masses learn the skills and discipline needed to participate more fully in the management of their lives and labors. But even were Nicaragua not war-damaged, the pull toward centralized decisionmaking would be very strong. With its 2.5 million population, relatively homogeneous culture (with the exception of the extensive but thinly populated Atlantic coast), and uncomplicated economy, Nicaragua does not seem to offer insurmountable problems to those who advocate strong centralized control.

There are, however, tendencies that pull in the opposite direction. The massive, only partially coordinated participatory experience of the insurrection strengthens the pressures towards decentralization. Additionally, the shortage of trained cadres and bureaucrats—and the presence of holdovers from Somoza's time in the public sector—suggest that not all decisions should be taken nor all activities administered at the center.

However, basic tensions still exist: Mass organizations are charged both with implementing state policies and with representing the interests of their constituents to the state. Thinly staffed national ministries attempt to administer programs that are beyond their human and material resources; yet devolving some of these responsibilities to the citizenry is certainly not a solution that springs automatically to the bureaucratic mind. Leaders schooled for years in military discipline turn easily to command models to solve obdurate developmental problems, while at the same time appreciating the importance of mass action without necessarily knowing how or to what degree it should be encouraged in the new Nicaragua.

Consensus and dissent. No complex system ever has or ever can work on the basis of full consensus. In modern societies conflicts of interest and differences of opinion are inevitable; and even in a well-functioning socialist system, conflicts would have to be adjudicated, some voices given priority over others, and hard decisions on the allocation of scarce resources made. There will be dissent, openly expressed if the costs to the dissenters are not too high, or expressed in other ways if mechanisms of social control operate "effectively." The key question is not how much dissent will be "allowed," but what forms and channels of dissent are most compatible with the construction of a working consensus supportive of a new political-economic order.

It is precisely in this tangled area of consensus and dissent that liberal and religious fears and critiques gain their most sympathetic audiences inside and outside of Nicaragua. Socialist practice to date has emphasized national unity as a prerequisite for development. This has meant the silencing of those voices that fall outside a centrally determined view of how society should be run. What many fear is that when even tougher times come, when bedrock contradictions in the construction of socialism are reached, and when and if external and internal pressures of a clearly counter-revolutionary nature increase, among the first casualties will be the space for criticism that now exists.

Public and private property. While the incorporation of private enterprise into the process of reactivation of the economy does not mean that the private sector "commands," it does imply serious contradictions for the future. The more deeply entrenched and even legitimate a "patriotic" private enterprise becomes, the more difficult it will eventually be to gain control of its productive facilities without serious conflict. This is particularly the case for the large enterprises whose owners have very substantial political and economic resources (both domestic and international) with which to oppose the socialization of the economy. Yet it is precisely these large enterprises which eventually must pass into collective ownership if the socialist promise is to be fulfilled.

None of this is news to Nicaragua. To the contrary, as one official noted, the game being played in Nicaragua is chess, not poker. Everybody can see everyone else's hand. This means that the fragility of the alliance between the state and the private sector is evident. What can be predicted with some certainty is that the particular mix of public and private property that characterized Nicaragua at the beginning of the 1980s will not hold through much of the rest of the decade.

The present and the future. As emphasized at the outset, each of the tensions that we have mentioned must be understood historically. The past conditions the present, and the present in turn shapes—but does not determine—the future. In addition, however, there is a basic present-future tension which is not captured by this historical perspective alone. Socialism, particularly developmental socialism, elevates the dialectic of present-future to the center of its political economy. If all works well, the 1980 plan will create the initial conditions for a surplus in 1981. This surplus, in turn, will increasingly be captured by the state and will be used in ways quite different than if it were to remain in private hands. Each successive cycle—it is hoped—will thus transfer more real control over production and distribution away from the private sector and into the public domain.

This long-run political-economic dynamic involves not only the relationship of the state to private capital (particularly large capital), but also the relationship of the state to the *clases populares*. Productivity increases in both industry and agriculture are essential if significant surpluses are to be generated. And this in turn means that hard work, discipline, and sacrifice are necessarily part and parcel of the development model. Economics-in-command and a policy of austerity are required, however, not just in conventional terms (the pie is not now big enough for everyone to have a larger piece), but also in terms of collective investment in the future. The construction of socialism requires that the postponement of current gratifications—and in some cases the postponement of necessities of life—be undertaken *consciously and collectively.* This shared understanding is at the core of the cultural transformation without which the promises of structural transformations dissolve into bureaucratic and inegalitarian forms. It also implies a promise to the *clases populares* that the surplus generated by the sweat of their brows will, in fact, be used in their interests.

But to emphasize this domain of socialist construction is not to define what constitutes "proper" decisions regarding the allocation of scarce resources between what in shorthand we can call consumption and investment. All of the other tensions intercut with this. The dialectic of present and future will be resolved differently if strong, decentralized participatory institutions have been constructed. Patterns and channels of consensus and dissent are also obviously relevant, as is the particular mix and stratification of public and private property. What makes the prospect of socialist construction in Nicaragua so exciting at the moment is that none of these issues has been definitively decided. One hopes, in fact, that within certain broad boundaries they will be the subject of just as much discussion years from now as they are today, for only a dogmatist would believe that in a well-functioning socialist society these issues can or should be settled once and for all.

Nicaragua 1980:
The Battle of the ABCs*
By Fernando Cardenal, S.J.
and Valerie Miller

Father Fernando Cardenal and Valerie Miller present a vivid, first-hand account of the "battle" for literacy in Nicaragua. The authors describe the political rationale and the extensive organizational tasks of the National Literacy Crusade. Father Cardenal was nominated for a Nobel Peace Prize in 1981 for his direction of the Nicaraguan Literacy Crusade.

It is September 1980. Nicaragua recently celebrated an educational victory that over a year ago would have seemed impossible. On August 23, 1980, the nation applauded the success of students and teachers of the National Literacy Crusade. We saluted their achievements, and we also saluted thousands of people who could not stand with us, those who had given their lives in battle to free this land. The National Literacy Crusade was a living tribute to their sacrifice, commitment and hope. Their dedication and faith in the future made the campaign possible. Their memories live on in each one of us. This article is dedicated to them.

*Excerpted and abridged from *Harvard Educational Review*, Vol. 51, No. 1 (February 1981).

Development and Literacy: Yesterday

Under Somoza, Nicaragua was run as a family plantation. Development had been narrowly focused on modernizing the economy's agricultural export sector for the benefit of a small privileged minority. The promotion of universal literacy or adult education was irrelevant and potentially threatening. Under this economic system, national development programs were essentially used to enrich Somoza's personal fortune and to buttress the regime's power structure by providing his partners with lucrative business opportunities involving massive graft and corruption.

Illiteracy was both a condition and a product of this system. In 1979 a special census revealed that more than 50 percent of the population was illiterate, a figure which soared above 85 percent in some rural areas.[1] This problem was never seriously addressed during the dictatorship because the promotion of universal literacy was neither politically advisable for the maintenance of the system nor economically necessary for its functioning. The development model of export agriculture depended upon a large pool of unskilled workers, and therefore it neither required nor encouraged an educated labor force. Politically, it was unwise for Somoza to undertake a genuine nationwide literacy program. Basic education would have provided the poor and disenfranchised with the potential tools to analyze and question the unequal power relationships and economic conditions under which they had lived. An illustration from the crusade underlines this point. A peasant is speaking during the dialogue section of the lesson:

> Somoza never taught us to read—it really was ungrateful of him, wasn't it? He knew that if he taught the peasants to read we would claim our rights. Ay! But back then, people couldn't even breathe. You see, I believe that government is like the parent of a family. The parent demands the best of his children and the children demand the best of the parent, but a governor, like a parent, who does not give culture and upbringing to the child, well that means he doesn't love his child, or his people. Don't you agree?[2]

Under Somoza, literacy teaching was used as a cover for counterinsurgency operations in the north. The "Plan Waslala," according to the Ministry of Education's own report in 1978, appointed more than 100 literacy teachers to act as spies and identify peasants sympathetic to the FSLN. Many people singled out by this operation later disappeared. Waslala itself was the site of an infamous concentration camp where hundreds of peasants had been savagely tortured and killed.

Development and Literacy: Today

With the recent triumph of the Sandinista Revolution, the meaning of

---

[1] Ministry of Education, *La educación en el primer año de la revolución popular sandinista* (Managua: Author, 1980), p. 162.

[2] Auxiliadora Rivas and Asunción Suazo, conversation in literacy class, Masaya, Nicaragua, May 4, 1980.

development and education changed radically. Development in Nicaragua today requires that all aspects of society be examined and recreated to respond to the needs and aspirations of the majority. It involves a profound transformation of the social system and the creation of structures which promote permanent opportunities for learning and enhance equitable forms of economic and political participation.

We believe that in order to create a new nation we must begin with an education that liberates people. Only through knowing their past and their present, only through understanding and analyzing their reality can people choose their future. Education, therefore, must encourage people to take charge of their lives, to learn to become informed and effective decision makers, and to understand their roles as responsible citizens possessing rights and obligations. A liberating education nurtures empathy, a commitment to community, and a sense of self-worth and dignity. It involves people acquiring the knowledge, skills, and attitudes necessary for their new community responsibilities. Education for liberation means people working together to gain an understanding of and control over society's economic, political, and social forces in order to guarantee their full participation in the creation of the new nation. Literacy and permanent programs of adult learning are fundamental to these goals.

Soon after the triumph, the Government of National Reconstruction (GNR) and the FSLN proposed their first development plan. Education and literacy were among its top priorities. The program emphasized economic reactivation and national reconstruction and was founded on four major points. First, it established a socioeconomic policy based on a commitment to full employment, improved social services, universal literacy, land reform, self-sufficiency in basic foodstuffs, increased production for the common good, and a mixed economy. Second, it encouraged popular participation through a network of citizens' and workers' associations, a representative legislative body, the Council of State, and a variety of public forums for open debate and dialogue between government and citizens. Third, the program called for the birth and affirmation of the "New Nicaraguan," revolutionary men and women, characterized by sacrifice, humility, discipline, creativity, love, generosity, hard work, and a critical consciousness. Finally, to accumulate the necessary capital for domestic investment and to pay the nation's staggering debt, it emphasized austerity. Salary differentials were drastically reduced, wages controlled, and luxury imports curtailed.

Conducting a nationwide literacy campaign was one of the first priorities of the young government. In August 1979, just fifteen days after victory, Nicaragua's Literacy Crusade was born. The first goal of the campaign was to eliminate illiteracy. Specifically, this meant reducing the illiteracy rate to between 10 to 15 percent, establishing a nationwide system of adult education, and expanding primary school coverage through the country. Other important goals were to encourage an integration and understanding among Nicaraguans of different classes and backgrounds; to increase political awareness and a critical analysis of underdevelopment; to nurture attitudes and skills related to creativity, production, cooperation, discipline, and analytical thinking; to forge a sense of national consensus and of social responsibility; to strengthen channels of economic and political participation; to acquaint people with national development programs; to record oral histories and recover popular forms of culture; and to conduct research in health and agriculture for future development programming.

In its design and implementation, the campaign was eminently political and profoundly spiritual. First, it was aimed at giving the nation's poor and disenfranchised the skills and knowledge they needed to become active participants in the political process. In doing so, it consolidated a powerful new political force and challenged the power of large economic interests. Second, it was spiritual. The act of learning to read and write served to restore and nurture spiritual values which had for so long been suppressed. Dignity and self-worth took on new meaning as people began to gain confidence in themselves and their future.

The metaphors and terminology of the campaign were purposefully military—"The National Literacy Crusade: Heroes and Martyrs for the Liberation of Nicaragua," "the war on ignorance," "the cultural insurrection," and "the second war of liberation." The literacy warriors, or *brigadistas*, of the Popular Literacy Army were divided into brigades, columns and squadrons and were located along six battlefronts identical to those of the war.[3] They joined forces with the Peasant and Workers' Militias and the Urban Literacy Guerrillas. Each battle unit chose the name of a fallen combatant as a means of honoring his or her memory.

In no way was the use of military terminology designed to glorify war or violence. Anyone who lived through the horror perpetuated by Somoza's guard was acutely aware that the pain and trauma of violence and repression were not worthy of glorification. On the contrary, the choice of military metaphors was designed to help young volunteers integrate the memories of the past, transforming terms related to the war into positive associations with teaching and sharing. Military terminology also helped the brigadistas see the Crusade as a vital part of the nation's continuing liberation struggle and to understand that, as such, it demanded the seriousness, dedication and discipline of a military offensive.

The use of military terms and the naming of fallen heroes had a deeply spiritual significance. The Crusade owed its very existence to the Revolution and to the sacrifice of thousands of men and women who fought and died for liberation. By calling forth their names and memories, the young volunteers kept alive the courage and example of their fallen compatriots. A spiritual bond joined the living with the dead. It inspired greater levels of commitment and compassion and it spurred people on in moments of difficulty.

---

[3] Brigades were made up of all those brigadistas in one municipality; columns were made up of four squadrons where possible and each squadron contained thirty brigadistas and one to three education advisors.

The Challenge and the Problems

The challenge confronting the crusade staff would have discouraged most educational planners. Somoza had left the country destitute. Since the war had affected much of the nation's transportation system, and years of government corruption had impeded the development of a rural infrastructure, new methods had to be devised to maintain communication with the isolated regions of the country, to transport the tens of thousands of brigadistas to the countryside, and to distribute massive amounts of equipment and teaching materials.

The long months of battle had destroyed industry, so that supplying even the basic material necessities of the Crusade required herculean efforts. Machinery had to be imported, factories reorganized, cottage industries developed, and materials ordered from foreign markets to provide the necessary uniforms, lanterns, mosquito nets, boots, raincoats, malaria pills, water purification tablets, and study materials. Agricultural production had been interrupted, and scarcity in rural communities was commonplace. Basic foodstuffs first needed to be imported and then distributed to supply the brigadistas.

Because decades of repression had prevented the development of community groups and labor associations, the campaign had to depend on organizations that were still in their infancy for the crucial tasks of mobilizing and supporting the Crusade's volunteer personnel. To mount a campaign of such magnitude, a network of offices needed to be established. Since the number of trained and experienced administrators was limited, the Crusade would have to become a learning laboratory for educational managers.

Once launched, the Crusade confronted another series of problems. The rainy season began in May and continued throughout the duration of the campaign. As a result, many volunteers were isolated, and transportation and communication throughout the country were seriously impaired. Somoza sympathizers and former guardsmen created grave problems and tried to spread fear among the brigadistas and their families in an attempt to paralyze the Crusade. In certain regions literacy teachers and personnel were threatened and harassed; nine were assassinated.

To complete our national team we hired selected experts in education from Argentina, Colombia, Costa Rica, Mexico, Honduras, Puerto Rico and the United States. During the campaign they were joined by four Cuban specialists who had participated in the 1961 Cuban literacy campaign.

We also requested further technical assistance from a variety of organizations and institutions—UNESCO, the Organization of American States, the World Council of Churches, CELADEC (a Latin American Ecumenical group working in popular peasant education), CREFAL (Regional Center on Adult Education and Functional Literacy for Latin America), and Cuba's Ministry of Education. Cuban teachers who worked in Nicaragua's primary schools participated in the Crusade after classes. Spain, Costa Rica, and the Dominican Republic sent delegations of teachers to participate in the campaign. During the course of the program, additional international experts joined, including people from Canada, Chile, El Salvador, Peru, Spain and Uruguay. More advisors also came from Colombia, Mexico, and the United States.[4]

At the end of September the core team of seven visited Cuba for a week. We interviewed the former director of the 1961 Cuban Literacy Campaign and spent four days delving into the archives of their Literacy Museum. During October 1979 we organized an intensive one-week planning seminar with a team of experts from Mexico, Colombia, and the United States. After a careful clarification analysis of the Crusade's proposed plan, we developed some general operational guidelines and began to define program structures and tasks.

Financing the Crusade

The crusade had to be financed from sources outside the government. We called in two specialists from the Ministry of Planning. After providing them with program details such as the Crusade's proposed scope, duration, and personnel and material needs, they developed a tentative budget calling for approximately $20 million (200 million córdobas).

We immediately set up a finance office. Requests for assistance were mailed to governments, institutions, and solidarity groups around the world. Official delegations were sent to the United States and to Europe. In Nicaragua, the Crusade established a program of Patriotic Literacy Bonds and encouraged community fund-raising efforts. Employees from all sectors, public and private, tithed one day's salary each month to the campaign. Marketwomen from Managua and peasants from distant mountain villages came to the national office in order to make their contributions personally. For example, three representatives of the Revolutionary Sports Committee of Chontales, two peasants and one young student, contributed 1,000 córdobas collected from community raffles. Enthusiastic high school students filled the city streets carrying tin cans. Following some of the same tactics used in the insurrection, they set up road blocks—to collect "pennies for pencils"—and called on radio stations to read official declarations of war against ignorance and to make appeals for financial help. Dances, song fests, concerts, and poetry readings all added to the fund-raising effort.

Health Problems

For decades, life in the countryside had meant poor health and early death. Malnutrition, malaria, measles, gastroenteritis, and mountain leprosy—a widespread skin infection that causes large scabs and scars—were common and sometimes deadly. To protect the brigadistas, inoculations were given, as well as basic health training which included malaria diagnosis

---

[4] In all, the Crusade's National Office employed the services of the following international experts: 2 Argentinians, 1 Canadian, 1 Chilean, 5 Colombians, 1 Costa Rican, 4 Cubans, 2 Salvadoreans, 1 Honduran, 2 Mexicans, 1 Peruvian, 1 Puerto Rican, 4 Spaniards.

and control. Each teaching squadron was provided with a first-aid kit with supplies sufficient for the duration of the Crusade.

Health problems, however, were more extensive and complicated than anticipated. Many older people attending literacy classes suffered from poor eyesight and therefore had difficulty reading. While eyeglasses had been ordered, their delivery was delayed, causing some people to withdraw, at least temporarily, from the campaign. Other program participants suffered from debilitating illnesses, making attendance sporadic. Volunteers suffered similar ailments. In some cases, disease prevented people from enrolling in the Crusade.

The first-aid supplies which had been carefully calculated to last five months usually ran out within two weeks. When confronted with the extent of illness and disease in the countryside, the brigadistas placed their first-aid kits at the service of the community. As a result, new supplies had to be ordered and special medical brigades formed. After a brief intensive training program, some 700 university medical students were placed throughout the country to serve as mobile health teams. Besides providing basic medical attention to volunteers, they also prepared them to give community classes in elementary health education. In addition, the brigades gathered vital information on national disease patterns and health conditions to be used in future health programming.

Food was also a problem. Without the timely organization of an emergency distribution system, food shortages would also have affected the brigadistas' health. Through the Institute of Basic Grain Distribution (ENABAS) volunteers were provided with double rations of basic foodstuffs both to feed themselves and to assist their host families. Weekend visits by parents and care packages from home helped improve the community diet.

Transportation and Communication

Nicaragua's poor transportation system hampered many aspects of the Crusade. Mobilization operations, supply distribution, and communication were all affected. For the March mobilization, brigadistas were dispersed gradually, their departures staggered over a four-day period. To accomplish the massive operation, the Crusade worked in coordination with the Ministry of Transportation and the Farmworkers' Association. They located, employed, and coordinated every available means of transportation—buses, boats, ferries, trains, dump trucks, jeeps, ox carts, horses, mules, donkeys, canoes, rafts, and finally, feet. Some volunteers had to walk for two or three days to reach their assigned communities.

Communication, while always a problem, was greatly improved through a network of forty-eight shortwave radios. Department offices and selected remote municipalities were given radio equipment and their personnel provided with training. A rotating team of volunteers staffed the central office twenty-four hours a day from March 10 to August 22. Besides maintaining communication in technical and administrative matters, the network served as a lifeline in case of medical emergencies.

Establishment of Records

Since government statistics were outdated and notoriously inaccurate, one of the first campaign tasks was conducting a census to establish actual levels of literacy and to ascertain the availability of volunteer teachers. With expert assistance, the census was planned and executed. Teams of volunteer census takers were trained and sent out into the field, and the results tabulated by citizens and labor organizations. In all, the volunteers surveyed 1,434,738 people. Since the census tabulation would have absorbed all the nation's computer capacity for two weeks, a group of 2,500 volunteers received special training, and the tabulations were completed in ten days. The results indicated that 722,431 Nicaraguans were illiterate.

In addition, the census gave us a more complete picture of the country's illiteracy levels and their geographic distribution. As the Crusade progressed, however, it became clear that people's notions of illiteracy varied. Some who classified themselves as totally illiterate could recognize the alphabet and read simple words, but could not write. Exact skills were not known until brigadistas gave program applicants a qualifying test. This brief exam was the first in a series of three given during the campaign. The initial test was designed to determine the actual skill level of each participant, beginning with a simple exercise—drawing a straight line. This step was included so that those unable to continue beyond the first question would have some sense of accomplishment and understand that they too possessed the potential to master the alphabet. The next level of skill tested was the ability to write one's name, followed by reading and writing exercises—single words first, then short sentences. The test concluded with a comprehension exercise. People who completed all sections successfully were considered literate, and those who could read and write a few words were classified as semiliterates. Illiterates included people who could not read or write more than their own name.

An intermediate test was given to assess learner progress and diagnose individual study needs. The ability to read and write different syllabic families was determined so that specialized review could be oriented toward practicing those that had not yet been fully mastered. The final exam was administered by the literacy volunteer under the guidance of a technical advisor. It consisted of five parts which tested reading, writing, and comprehension skills. To be considered literate, participants had to write their name, read aloud a short text, answer three questions based on the reading, write a sentence dictated to them, and write a short composition. They were expected to be able to read with comprehension, pronouncing words as a whole and not as a series of isolated syllables. They were to write legibly, leaving appropriate space between words, and to spell phonetically. With such skills, participants were prepared within their vocabulary range to read newspapers, application forms, technical information pamphlets, and books.

Records kept on each student included such general information as name, age, sex, date of enrollment, residence, occupation, and past school attendance. A monthly progress chart indicated the lessons and exercises completed in both the primer and math workbook, as well as the total number of sessions attended. Test results for each of the three exams were recorded, as were observations about individual learning difficulties, health problems, and areas of personal interest for future study.

These reports reveal the history and progress of the Crusade. They also indicate the poor conditions under which the majority of Nicaraguans have lived and the tragic human costs of underdevelopment. According to the 1979 census, Nicaragua had an overall illiteracy rate of 50 percent, 30 percent in urban areas and 75 percent in the countryside. Children between ten and fourteen years of age accounted for 21 percent of the illiterate population. In the course of the campaign we discovered other dimensions of the illiteracy problem. As much as we did not want to accept the fact, some people simply did not have the capacity to master reading and writing skills in the campaign. Reports from volunteers and technical advisers indicated widespread learning difficulties and cases of disability. Poor health was the principal cause. Extensive malnutrition handicaps many Nicaraguans, impairing sight and hearing, limiting memory, and often causing early senility. About 9 percent of the population had severe learning disabilities that prevented them from studying.

Despite debilitating health problems and extreme hardships, 406,056 Nicaraguans learned basic reading and writing skills—an achievement that testifies to the creative power and determination of students and teachers alike. But initial statistics revealed that Nicaragua still had an illiteracy rate of 13 percent to overcome (6 urban and 21 percent rural). We believe, however, that by 1981 the rate will decrease as a result of the Crusade's follow-up program and the campaigns in English, Miskito, and Sumo.

Structural Organization: From Mountaintops to Managua

The success of the Crusade's administrative and support structure depended primarily on the participation of the citizen and labor associations. Though we did not know the kind of structure that would facilitate their involvement or exactly how to organize it, we learned much from the process. Since the campaign was an intensive, short-run nationwide project, it required setting up a massive organizational network that could effectively reach from isolated mountaintops down to the neighborhoods of Managua. With that it mind, we tried to develop a system that would be flexible and responsive at the local level and yet maintain a clear central direction and control. A single national coordinating structure took on the general management functions. Operational responsibilities were decentralized through a regional institutional network. In the field, the teachers' organization, ANDEN, and the Sandinista Young People's Association carried out organizational and implementation functions. Citizen groups, labor federations, and public institutions participated and supported the work at all levels. Two national congresses were held which brought together participants and staff to discuss program needs, problems, and solutions. Conferences began at the community level, proceeded to the municipal, on to the departmental, and finally to the national. In all, over 100,000 people participated.

Pedagogy in Practice: Revolution and Education

In designing the materials and methodologies for the Crusade, the liberation struggle served as inspiration and teacher. Its lessons were many, some pedagogical and some philosophical. Educational experiences carried out over the long years of fighting and community organizing had demonstrated the validity of a variety of teaching approaches and learning principles. Small study groups had met throughout the struggle to analyze, plan, and carry out war-related tasks; clandestine literacy efforts had been conducted as well. Learning in this context had been based on action and reflection. Lessons had a direct, urgent, and immediate application to reality. These experiences had combined such methods and techniques as experiential learning, dialogue, group discussions, and collective problem solving. They also revealed the tremendous creativity and capacity for learning that existed within people regardless of their educational background.

These experiences were enriched by the ideas and practice of Paulo Freire and others. At the beginning of the campaign, Freire had challenged us to create the best learning program we could. He stressed the importance of providing opportunities for learners to practice their creativity and added that within a liberating revolutionary process people would learn to read and write even with mediocre materials. With his challenge in mind, we faced two technical questions: how to design literacy materials for use by volunteer teachers and how to translate young people's enthusiasm and commitment into a minimum set of pedagogical skills.

The Crusade's education team attempted to address these questions first by studying Nicaragua's experiences in clandestine literacy teaching and then by analyzing other countries' programs in light of local need. Cuba's literacy campaign was examined closely, as was that of Guinea-Bissau, both of which had been greatly inspired by Freire.

To help volunteers promote the process of dialogue we provided them with concrete, step-by-step guidelines. The five-step process contained a series of suggested questions designed to help participants develop both analytical skills and a profound sense of social responsibility. The questions proceeded from simple to difficult and encouraged the students to describe the contents of a photograph; analyze the situation portrayed; relate the particular situation to the life of the learner, to the community, and to the problems facing them; solve problems around issues identified by the group; and engage participants in transforming reality, committing themselves to solving the problem, and becoming active in the national programs of social change. During the course of the Crusade, however, we came to realize the obvious—that dialogue occurred both during the literacy teaching process itself as well as in the daily living experience, and that the latter was perhaps the richer and more profound exchange.

After twenty minutes or so of dialogue, the direct study of reading and writing skills began—first with a sentence, then a word, and finally a syllabic family. We expanded Freire's single-word approach by using a short phrase or sentence based on the photograph's theme as the starting point for literacy practice. The team felt that a sentence provided a smoother transition from complex discussion to the concrete study of syllables. Because sentences encompassed a whole thought, they were considered more appropriate for adult learning as well as more flexible in generating the study of syllabic families. After reading the sentence, a key word from each phrase was chosen and divided into syllables, from which one family of syllables was selected and studied. For example, in the second lesson the name Fonseca was divided, Fon-se-ca, initiating a study of the syllabic family, sa, se, si, so, and su. Writing exercises were introduced and recognition exercises were used to help the participants identify the syllables as phonetic units. As learners mastered the individual syllables, they went on to use them to build new words, thus practicing their creativity and skills in manipulating the written language.

A Pedagogy of Shared Responsibility

To prepare the immense teacher corps to use the program's materials and methods, a national training program of short, intensive workshops was conducted. The first training materials explained to the brigadistas their revolutionary educational role as literacy promoters:

> You will be a catalyst of the teaching-learning process. Your literacy students will be people who think, create, and express their ideas. Together, you will form a team of mutual learning and human development....The literacy process is an act of creation in which people offer each other their thoughts, words, and deeds. It is a cultural action of transformation and growth.[5]

Training, therefore, required that all participants take on new educational roles in what we called a pedagogy of shared responsibility. The traditional model of the active, all-wise professor and passive, ignorant pupil was specifically rejected and replaced by one in which the traditional teacher became a type of learning coordinator. The role of the workshop director was one of facilitator, a role that involved motivating, inspiring, challenging, and working with the participants who were encouraged to become active problem solvers. Participants were the foundation and wellspring of the process. Their responsibilities were to explore, research, and create. Small-group study, team-teaching, and problem-solving affirmed this new relationship.

---

[5] Cruzada Nacional de Alfabetización, *Cuaderno de orientaciones* (Managua: Ministry of Education, 1979), p. 1.

To implement the training program, a decentralized four-stage model was designed. The program's success depended on its multiplier effect: beginning with seven national trainers, it was expected that in less than four months almost 100,000 people would be prepared. From December to March, workshops were held across the country. The driving force behind the training was the "group of eighty." Forty university students and forty teachers were specially selected for an intensive two-week preparation program and a one-month field experience. From their ranks, forty were chosen to train approximately 600 students and teachers in the next phase. During late February these 600 people prepared more than 12,000 people, most of whom were teachers. They, in turn, conducted the eight-day intensive workshops for thousands of literacy volunteers. Once the Crusade began, permanent training workshops were given for those people who still wished to enter the program. A radio show broadcast twice daily, together with special Saturday seminars conducted by squadron technical advisors, provided a continuing in-service training for the volunteers.

The Continuing Challenge

We are presently involved in designing and establishing a permanent system of adult education. In October 1980 three new Crusades began—in English, Miskito, and Sumo—for Nicaraguans who do not speak Spanish as their native language; and in 1981 we are hoping to launch a Health Crusade along the same lines as the literacy campaign. So much needs to be done. The hundreds of thousands of Nicaraguans who mastered basic reading and writing skills have just begun their studies. Their skills are still fragile.

The challenge for the future is awesome. Expectations are great, problems complex, and resources scarce. In the face of new tasks, the example and lessons of the campaign provide the inspiration and hope for tomorrow. As one young literacy volunteer expressed in August, "The Crusade is like the source of a river of popular knowledge which will flow onward forever."

What Difference Could a Revolution Make?
Farming in the New Nicaragua*

By Joseph Collins

Joseph Collins is co-author with Frances Moore Lappé of Food First: Beyond the Myth of Scarcity, World Hunger: Ten Myths *and* Aid as Obstacle *(all available through the Institute for Food and Development Policy, 1885 Mission Street, San Francisco, Ca. 94103). Over the last two years the Institute for Food and Development Policy has been studying food and agriculture policies in the new Nicaragua and advising the*

---

*Excerpted from a forthcoming book *What Difference Could a Revolution Make? Food and Farming in the New Nicaragua* to be published by the Institute for Food and Development Policy, 1885 Mission Street, San Francisco, Ca. 94103 (415) 648-6090.

government there on agrarian planning. The Institute recently published a Food First Action Alert on Nicaragua and is also preparing a major book, What Difference Could a Revolution Make? Food and Farming in the New Nicaragua. This article is excerpted from the forthcoming book.

Imagine yourself born into a family in rural Nicaragua in 1960. Your family would most likely either have no land at all to farm or have too little land, hilly and with poor soil, to be able to grow even enough food for the family. This was the bitter reality for well over two thirds of rural families in Nicaragua. Moreover, even if your family does farm a little plot of marginal land, your father in all likelihood would have to pay a steep cash rent or hand over half or even more of what he grows to the owner.

Not surprisingly, your family is always in debt. To buy a few simple tools, some cooking oil, sugar, salt and kerosene your father has to borrow from the local moneylender at rates always over 50 percent and often much more. Without land to grow enough food for the year and always in debt, your family is forced to work on the coffee, sugar or cotton estates. Even then, such work is available only during harvest time—three to four months a year. The pay is miserable—only about a dollar for working from sunup to sundown—and therefore your mother also has to work in the harvests (over 40 percent of the coffee harvest workers are women and girls), as well as your grandmother, your older sister and your brother. You too have to start picking coffee or cotton when you are six. The owner wants as many workers as possible since he pays not by the hour but by weight of the coffee beans at 16 cents for a 20-pound can. Seven days a week, work starts at 5:30 a.m., after a breakfast of black coffee and two fried bananas. With your mother, you go from bush to bush, picking only the mature coffee beans. At 3 p.m., you take the coffee beans to the weighing station. After a small lunch it is back to picking until nightfall.

After dark and the final weighing, you and your family are crowded into a long, windowless barrack built out of roughhewn unpainted planks. There with the other exhausted workers—men, women, old people and children, sick and well—you sleep on plywood slabs. You call them "drawers" because four or five are stacked on top of each other with only 20 inches of space between them. There is no privacy for there are no partitions. There is no flooring, no windows, not a single electric bulb. There are a few nails in the wall where clothes can be hung. The only toilet is the bushes. Filth all the day long. For three to four months a year this is home for you and for over 400,000 other Nicaraguans.

Work on the coffee estates is at least in the hillier, cooler regions. Some years, however, rather than harvest coffee, your family goes down to the Pacific coastal plains to pick cotton. The fields are open, with the blinding tropical sun in a cloudless sky bringing temperatures to well over 100 degrees. You have nothing to protect you from the pointed cotton branches, the pesticide-saturated fields and the maddening swirl of gnats and jiggers.

Your mother places your infant sister on the edge of the hot, dusty field and picks cotton as fast as she can, filling her sack and rushing to the weighing station so she can hurry back to nurse. What you will not know is that tests would probably show that your mother's breast milk has over 500 times the DDT considered safe for consumption by the World Health Organization, a frightening contamination due to 20 to 40 aerial sprayings a year of the cotton fields with DDT.

The meals you get on the plantations leave you hungry. Served on banana leaves are small portions of beans and fried bananas, and rarely some rice or corn tortillas or a bit of smoked cheese in place of the bananas. And for this you have to pay the equivalent of three or more hours' work a day—you're sure the owner makes profits even selling you the food. You get meat only once during the harvest: on the final day the owner and his family drive to the estate and awkwardly put on a "feast" to celebrate the close of the harvest.

As you have grown up you have learned—quite possibly through the Catholic priest—that even though your family owns no land, it is not because Nicaragua is land-poor. There are more than six agricultural acres per person with a potential of possibly twice that. But 2 percent of those owning land own over 50 percent of the land in farms and ranches. While 70 percent of those owning land own only two percent of the land, and that doesn't include your father who only rents his miserable plot.

Your father tells you that when he was a little boy your grandparents had a small farm near Chinandega on the Pacific Coastal plains. It was small, to be sure, but the land was good: that area of the country had been known as the breadbasket of the country. Your grandparents grew beans, corn and some vegetables, had a few fruit trees and raised some pigs and chickens.

Then in the late 1940's "white gold fever" struck Nicaragua. White gold, of course, was what the rich called cotton. But it was anything but golden for your grandparents who like tens of thousands of other small farmers fell victim to one of the biggest and most rapid waves of land grabbing in Latin America. Cotton acreage grew from just 3,000 acres to over 500,000 acres in only twenty years. You heard that Nicaraguan agriculture was considered the most successful in Latin America. First a lawyer came and said your grandparents' title to their farm wasn't in order and that they would have to go. Your grandfather refused. Then came Somoza's National Guard and forced your grandparents off the land, burned their home and pulled up the fences. Your father hates the National Guard.

You watch your little sister become repeatedly ill with diarrhea. She is so much smaller than she should be; there is never enough food to nourish her little body. Your parents see her losing her strength but there is no one to help. In all of rural Nicaragua there are only five clinics with beds, and one doesn't even have a permanent doctor. Once again your little sister barely pulls through. But weakened, she is then hit by measles and over four short days you watch your little sister die. You know that your mother and father have watched five children die. You see so many little coffins in the countryside.

You hardly know anyone who can read and write—except the priest, of course, but he's not a Nicaraguan. You'd like to learn but there is no school. Anyway, you must work.

Finally, throughout your entire childhood you cannot remember a day when your mother was not worried about having enough food for your family—and, of course, you never really did or your little sister wouldn't have died from measles. You heard once on a neighbor's little transistor that Nicaragua was importing more and more corn, beans and sorghum and you had heard about the huge stores called *supermercados* in Managua— but without money you can't buy food no matter how much there is. Going hungry seems to be part of everyday life.

That was before July 19, 1979, the date of the Sandinista-led overthrow of the U.S.-installed Somoza dynasty.

By the late 1960s more and more poor farmers and landless plantation workers were declaring they had had enough—*basta!* This groundswell of campesino opposition had its roots in the Church, as did the Sandinista National Liberation Movement.

In the wake of Vatican II (1962) and the Medellín Conference of Latin American Bishops, the church in Nicaragua sought ways to make the Gospel a living reality for rural people.

In 1968, the Jesuit Fathers, with the support of the bishops, created CEPA, the Educational Center for Agrarian Advancement. Initially CEPA trained campesino leaders in appropriate agricultural techniques and they did this in the context of Biblical reflection. CEPA published in cartoon form *Cristo, Campesino* which interpreted the social and political implications of the Christian gospel for those who worked the land. "You have a right to land," was a recurring message of *Cristo, Campesino.*

With so few priests, the Catholic Church in Nicaragua has never been able to place many priests in the rural areas. But with the Vatican Council's emphasis on the priesthood of every Christian, the Nicaraguan Church formally sought to train and authorize lay persons to perform many sacramental and other religious functions in the countryside where there were no priests. These "Delegates of the Word" would form "Christian Base Communities" to discuss the realities in the countryside in light of Bible reading. The Delegates were also trained to teach literacy and health awareness. Some Delegates also took part in CEPA training sessions. In one province alone, by 1975 there were over 900 active Delegates working closely with Capuchin Fathers from the United States.

No political impact was intended. Nonetheless, more and more CEPA activists and Delegates came to understand that no matter how hard they worked at it, campesinos could not substantially better their conditions since the society was fundamentally structured against their interests. Gradually the CEPA activists and the Delegates of the Word began to understand that campesinos would have to unite and organize political action. Similarly, the Delegates among the coffee plantation workers soon concluded that "to hunger and thirst for justice" meant that workers had to organize to demand basic health services, drinking water, livable wages and year-round employment.

In this way a number of Christians working in CEPA became militantly anti-Somoza and supporters of the Sandinista National Liberation Front. Several key CEPA activists became directors of the Association of Rural Workers (ATC) which, as we will see, the Sandinistas established in 1977. Others associated with CEPA opted to become guerrilla freedom fighters. As this logic of commitment progressed, the Catholic hierarchy attempted to restrict the activities of CEPA and to discourage it from moving toward collaboration with the Sandinistas. When the bishops left no other option, CEPA cut its ties with the hierarchy and became an independent Christian organization, closely allied to the Sandinistas.

Early on the Somoza regime sensed the dangers of a socially interpreted Gospel. The National Guard labeled Delegates of the Word subversives and began to harass them. Campesinos disappeared in areas with a strong Delegate presence. Eventually the National Guard repression claimed the lives of Delegates, too, provoking the official church into opposing Somoza. As the repression intensified, many Delegates and Christian Base Communities were forced to go underground. After 1975, in some northern areas, the National Guard regularly banned all religious meetings. Yet such conditions actually fostered these Christians' collaboration with the Sandinistas.

From its founding in the early 1960's, the Sandinista Front worked with campesinos. The Sandinista guerrillas depended on the campesinos for their very existence. No one who wants to understand the Sandinistas in victory can afford to overlook this dependence in war. What would have happened to the guerrillas pursued by the National Guard without the help of campesinos who knew the lay of the land? Campesinos forewarned Sandinistas of the Guard's attacks. Campesinos were key in provisioning the guerrillas. Both campesino minifundistas and landless agricultural workers joined the guerrillas. One of the earliest Sandinista strikes was carried out by a guerrilla column almost totally made up of minifundistas and landless workers under the direction of Colonel Santos Lopez, a campesino who had fought the U.S. Marines with Sandino in the 1920s.

Building on the awareness in part engendered by CEPA and the Delegates, the Sandinistas started in 1976 to organize Committees of Agricultural Workers. They started first among the coffee workers in the Carazo and Masaya regions. The Committees sought to collectively demand better working and living conditions. Committees were formed on some 20 coffee estates during the harvest period when growers needed both minifundistas and landless workers. Although these first confrontations were over economic conditions, they soon became political, especially because the landowners frequently called in the National Guard, who beat, tortured, imprisoned and murdered Committee members. It became apparent that Somoza was standing behind the landowners.

The repression backfired. The Committees of Agricultural Workers spread south into the department of Rivas and north to Chinandega, from the coffee estates to cotton and sugar plantations. By late 1977, the northern Pacific zone, completely dominated by export estates, was the most militant area in the country.

In response to the National Guard's "cleanup," rural recruits swelled the guerrilla ranks; they sought just vindication for years of forced misery and for the Guard's murder of relatives and comrades. Of the 50,000 killed in the fight against Somoza's National Guard, untold thousands were small farmers, landless rural laborers and their families. Several top Sandinista leaders were born campesinos.

What difference, then, is the Nicaraguan revolution making for the vast majority of rural people?

The record of these first three years shows the Sandinista government carrying out its pre-liberation promise of agrarian reform—both out of its commitment to social justice and its recognition that without the great sacrifices of many Nicaraguan rural people victory over the dictatorship would not have been possible. At the same time the Sandinistas have sought to take measures that would balance rather than interrupt production out of a recognition of the debt-burdened, war-devastated economic situation of the country. Moreover, because of the U.S. government's hostility to the new government, the Sandinistas have given priority to building national unity against external threats. Thus in practice the new government, far from pushing a radical program down the throats of its people, repeatedly finds itself working to dissuade many rural people from making changes too fast.

Many tenant farmers and other landless rural people, for example, having all their lives seen good land lie fallow while they went hungry, were disappointed that the government did not immediately expropriate and redistribute the land. The farms belonging to the Somozas and their close collaborators, such as officers, were nationalized immediately following victory. They were made into state farms primarily to avoid the drop likely if these generally mechanized estates were parcelled out to small producers. Achievements to date vary from farm to farm. One major problem lies outside the control of Nicaraguans: the sharp decline in world prices for the exports produced by these farms.

But no ceiling was placed on the amount of land anyone can own. A full 64 percent of the agricultural land remained in the hands of large and medium-sized farms. The government did bring under public control the international marketing of Nicaragua's principal agricultural exports so that more benefits would be more likely to wind up benefiting the development of Nicaragua rather than fattening a Miami bank account. In order to encourage production by these commercial producers, virtually 100 percent government financing of production costs was made available and guaranteed minimum prices for export crops established through negotiations with the big growers' associations. If the international price unexpectedly falls, the government absorbs the loss. If the price rises, part of that increase goes to producers. As a further incentive, as of 1982 part of the export price is paid to producers in dollars. Private commercial producers are, however, required to respect minimum wage laws and the freedom of workers to form labor unions.

Despite these favorable conditions for profits, all too many of the larger growers during the first two years, especially with the launching of the Reagan administration's de-stabilization campaign, cut back on their production, converting producer credits into dollars to steal out of the country. Some switched from cotton and tobacco to crops requiring fewer hired laborers, sold off machinery, slaughtered livestock and illegally sent the proceeds out of the country.

For the nation's small farmers, the government immediately extended unprecedented amounts of credit on liberal terms. In many areas the flood of cheap institutional credit has freed farmers from the clutches of exploitative moneylenders. For tenants, rent limits were established that worked out to be about one-sixth the previous levels that inhibited production as well as impoverished most family farmers. Evictions without due cause were outlawed as well as the refusal to rent to those who would farm idle land (in practice this measure came to include idle land on state farms). In the first two years, over 12,000 landless families gained access to land to grow food crops.

To benefit small farmers and to stimulate food production, the government guarantees prices, although sale to private wholesalers and retailers is permitted. In the case of important items that have been scarce, such as beans, the guaranteed price has been doubled—although that price is still much less costly than using scarce dollars to import beans from the United States. Government resale to wholesalers and retailers is done at prices that make reasonable profits possible even though retail prices for 39 basic items are set at a level that most Nicaraguans can afford. This government subsidy worked to the benefit of both small farmers and consumers.

Farmers have responded well to the mix of liberal credit and reasonable guaranteed prices: despite significantly increased national food consumption, Nicaragua is likely this year to achieve self-sufficiency in all its basic foods—beans, corn, rice and sorghum.

Nicaragua is also intent on developing its export potential, especially in beans and white corn, for which foreign markets are much more promising than for cotton, coffee and sugar. Such a strategy could greatly enhance the earnings of Nicaragua's family farmers and give them new dignity as dollar-earners for the nation, in a country where food production has up until the revolution been considered a second-class activity.

The experiences of the first two years and countless formal and informal meetings with large commercial producers, small farmers and agricultural laborers led Nicaragua's legislative body, the Council of State, to pass the Agrarian Reform Law in August 1981.

The law guarantees the right to private property. Unlike land reforms in many other countries, the pragmatic Nicaraguan reform sets no ceilings on the size of landholdings. The new law, however, makes it very clear that abandoned land and land left idle or under-used can be redistributed. Moreover, the government can redistribute lands rented to tenants on large farms above a specified size. Large farms that are entirely rented out by absentee owners (mainly cotton plantations) can be nationalized and then rented out to the same producers but with the rent going to the public good rather than to the absentee landlord.

It is estimated that once the law is fully implemented (which should take several years), as many as 4 million acres will be redistributed, with 160,000 families receiving land.

Who will get the land? The new reform law legalizes the possession by the poor peasants, tenants and cooperatives of idle lands they had already seized and have been productively working. Future seizures, however, are prohibited.

As other lands are available for distribution, first priority will go to the over 100,000 small farmers who do not have enough land to meet their basic needs. Many have been tenants and sharecroppers. Those who organize themselves into cooperatives will get preference, although land titles are being given to individuals.

Second priority are landless farmworkers, especially extended families. The farmworkers union, the Association of Rural Workers, estimates that 60,000 families will benefit from the new law.

Third priority is the creation or enlargement of government-operated farms.

The fact that the landless get second priority indicates the government's fear that any seasonal farmworkers given land to farm for themselves will not work in the harvests; that work is critical to the country's foreign exchange earnings. Therefore seasonal workers who get land will be asked to agree to work, for pay, in the harvests, which fortunately come at different times of year than the work on food crops.

The priority for cooperatives reflects the view that, at least in the long term, cooperatives rather than individuals can take better advantage of economies of scale as well as new facilities for health, education and crop-processing. Finally, putting government-run farms last reflects the government's judgment that it has enough on its hands with the farms it is already responsible for.

The vision of the Sandinista leadership is that of a farm economy in which eventually 50 percent of the farmland will be in independent cooperatives; 30 percent in private, individually owned farms of various sizes; and 20 percent in government-owned farms.

Creating a just and productive Nicaraguan countryside is a difficult, long-range undertaking. But the pragmatic, one-step-at-a-time approach of the new Nicaraguan government offers dramatic hope to the people so long forced to live in misery.

Miskitus in Nicaragua:
Who Is Violating Human Rights?

By Roxanne Dunbar Ortiz

*The Sandinista's relationship to their largest indigenous minority, the Mis-
kitu Indians, has become a subject of polemics. The following article
was published in the inaugural edition of the American Indian journal Indigenous World (Number 1, Spring 1982). The article places the "Miskitu
question" in the context of U.S. government hostility towards the Sandinistas. Roxanne Dunbar Ortiz is a professor in Native American Studies at
California State University, Hayward.*

During January and February, 1982, media coverage of the Miskitu situation in Nicaragua began with a January 3 press release claiming that the
Honduran government had announced that 200 Miskitus had been massacred by Sandinista soldiers inside Honduras. The following day, the
Honduras government denied making the statement as well as denying its
accuracy. The correction was not well publicized, and the notion of a
"massacre" was widely believed in the United States. For instance, the
San Francisco Nicaraguan community held a well-attended mass to com-
memorate the "200 slain Miskitus." The source of the false statement is
still not known.

On February 19, Secretary of State Haig claimed that "atrocious and
genocidal actions are being taken by Nicaragua against the Indians on their
east coast"; on February 25, Assistant Secretary of State for Human Rights
and Humanitarian Affairs, Elliot Abrams, told the Senate Subcommittee
on Western Hemisphere Affairs that the "Miskitus are now subject to massive assaults by the Sandinistas"; on February 4, U.S. Ambassador to the
United Nations, Jeane Kirkpatrick, stated on the MacNeil-Lehrer television show that "... the Mestizo [sic] Indians—are being so badly repressed
that concentration camps have been built on the coast of Nicaragua in the
effort to try to imprison them, to eliminate their opposition." On March 1,
the Ambassador reiterated her charge in the United Nations, saying that
the Nicaraguan government's "assault" on the Miskitus "is more massive
than other human rights violations that I'm aware of in Central America."
In Geneva, the United Nations Human Rights Commission, in its annual
meeting, heard U.S. representative, Richard Schifter (former U.S. attorney
in Indian land cases), condemning the Sandinistas for "atrocities" against
the Miskitus. And, in an extraordinary manner, even President Reagan
himself referred to the alleged "human rights violations" by Sandinistas
against the Miskitus in an address to the Organization of American States
(OAS).

In addition to allegations by the Reagan administration, widely publicized in the media, Steadman Fagoth Mueller was in Washington the week
of February 22, sponsored by the American Security Council and heavily

promoted by U.S. State Department, which arranged many of his interviews with members of Congress and the media. Fagoth had been the representative to the Nicaraguan Council of State of MISURASATA, the Nicaraguan Indian mass organization, before his arrest in February, 1981, on suspicion of conspiring to overthrow the Revolutionary government. He fled Nicaragua in May, 1982, when he was released with restrictions, and joined the pro-Somoza paramilitary forces in Honduras and Miami.

U.S.-Financed Terrorism

The pronouncements and media coverage followed a series of events which culminated in the evacuation of some 12,000 Miskitus from their Coco River villages on the Honduran border to 50 miles south of the area. However, the media also reported the U.S. plan for destabilizing Nicaragua (*Washington Post,* February and March.).

"Navidad Roja" or "Red Christmas" was the name given by the counter-revolutionary paramilitary groups in Honduras to their project to disrupt, destabilize and discredit the Sandinista Revolution, investigative journalists reported. Terrorism hit Nicaragua full force in early December when a Nicaraguan passenger plane in the Mexican airport exploded on the ground, the bomb having been set to go off in midair, but the plane was late in boarding. Another plane was bombed in the Managua airport a month later, killing three. Attempts were made to blow up a plant and a refinery near Managua. Armed commandos began terrorizing Miskitus in their villages along the Coco River in early December, and by Christmas, 45 Sandinista soldiers and 15 civilians had been slain by the terrorists. There were also kidnappings and raping of Miskitus.

The new realities created by the terrorism, and the state of military emergency which was required in the Coco River region, brought general confusion to supporters of the Sandinistas, which was further complicated by the evacuation of Miskitus from their villages along the river. Miskitu leaders in the villages explain that it was impossible for the Sandinista armed forces to protect the Miskitu people in the villages without firing into Honduras, which they could not do without risking direct U.S. military intervention. Also, they explain, the Somocista radio "September 15" in Honduras was terrifying many Miskitus into leaving the villages to join Miskitu dissidents in the camps in Honduras; perhaps as many as 10,000 crossed over to Honduras.

Tasba Pri—Free Land

The Nicaraguan government evacuated the 16 Miskitu villages from the river border area during a six-week period in January and February, creating five new settlements some 50 miles from the border, still well within the region of the Miskitu traditional land area. In early March, a 26-member delegation from Nicaragua visited Washington and New York to talk with groups (including representatives of nearly a dozen American Indian groups) and explain the situation. The delegation included a broad representation from the churches, including the Moravian bishop of the Atlantic coast. They strongly condemned U.S. intervention as well as the Miskitu and Moravian elements involved, and expressed support for the Sandinista actions in the crisis, giving assurances that no massacres, killings, nor even human rights violations by Sandinistas had occurred before, during or after the evacuation. The delegation stated that a feasibility study, completed in November, 1980, exploring the possibility of emergency or permanent relocation of several Miskitu villages near Cabo Gracias a Dios, villages that are flooded annually, facilitated the efficiency of the emergency evacuation. The region for potential relocation had been identified through soil and other studies, and this area was quickly prepared for the crisis resettlement.

During March, 1982, a number of international observers visited the new Miskitu settlements, and made positive reports on the efforts being made by the Sandinista government in the crisis. Attorney Juan Mendez, an international human rights expert, representing Americas Watch, following his visit to the resettlement area in late March, stated that human rights standards were being observed, and that health care is particularly impressive. Education is by Miskitu teachers in the Miskitu language. The people go out daily to hunt, fish, and to farm, Mendez stated, observing that little security and no force is imposed upon them.

Background to the Crisis

What led to this crisis and present situation? What role did the errors of the new revolutionary government play in leading to the crisis and what role was played by the destabilization project? A brief review of what took place in the Atlantic Coast region from the time of the victory in July, 1979, to the end of 1981, puts the present crisis in perspective.

In November, 1979, MISURASATA was formed in a general meeting of the indigenous population of the Atlantic Coast. The Sandinista leadership was represented by Comandante Daniel Ortega, Coordinator of the Government, and Ernesto Cardenal, Minister of Culture. An indigenous organization, ALPROMISU already existed, having been active internationally from 1975 and 1979 through its affiliation with the World Council of Indigenous Peoples, based in Canada. Leading activists in ALPROMISU became the directorate of MISURASATA since the Sandinista government recognized the right of the indigenous to select their own representatives.

MISURASATA presented its first statement of principles and demands in the Summer of 1980, arguing strenuously and effectively for literacy in the indigenous languages, and they won that demand of the government. MISURASATA was reserved a seat in the newly-formed legislative national body, the Council of State, and Steadman Fagoth Mueller, Director of MISURASATA, was selected by the organization to take that seat. MISURASATA was also seated in the Government House (Casa de Gobierno) with MISURASATA directorate member, Armstrong Wiggins, selected by the organization to hold that position. During the same period, the Ministry for the Atlantic Coast (INNICA) was established to oversee the activities of all parts of the government in relation to the Atlantic Coast. The government accepted in principle the confirmation of indigenous ownership of their traditional villages and lands, and awaited a study and proposal from MISURASATA to formulate the confirmation. MISURASATA surged as a mass movement, particularly among the Miskitus, and it had a positive influence nationally in making the majority population in the Pacific zone, themselves poor and living in war-torn, deprived conditions, aware of the special cultural, political and economic needs and rights of the indigenous of the Atlantic Coast.

Yet, in August, 1980, in New York at United Nations headquarters, in a meeting called by the International YMCA and the World Council of Indigenous Peoples in conjunction with the UN Special Session on Development, a press release was circulated calling for condemnation of the Sandinistas in Nicaragua for alleged "massacres" and general repression against the Miskitus.

During October, 1980, there were mass demonstrations by Creoles in Bluefields against the Sandinista government, resulting in a military emergency. Captured organizers of the demonstration admitted links to foreign and domestic covert actions planned to destabilize the Sandinista revolution. However, the protests also indicated some real problems and dissatisfaction, and extended discussions between the Creole community and government leaders took place. Many of the problems being exploited by enemies of the revolution were worked out, and others openly discussed, a pattern that has prevailed since that time between the indigenous groups and the government.

At the conclusion of the Miskitu literacy campaign, serious problems rose between MISURASATA and the government when "Plan 81" of MISURASATA was interpreted by the government to be a separatist movement with links with the Somocista/CIA covert action plans. Fagoth and some 30 other MISURASATA activists were arrested. In the Miskitu town of Prinzapolka, eight men were killed in a fracas over the arrest of one of the MISURASATA literacy workers. When Fagoth was arrested, some 3000 young Miskitu men crossed over into Honduras and joined the Somocistas.

Sandinista responses to tension with MISURASATA sharpened during the first year of the Reagan administration with the intense, steadily accelerating attacks on the Sandinista government as being "totalitarian," "Soviet, Cuban-controlled," "repressive," and allegedly building up its army to attack its neighbors—all this in addition to allegedly supplying arms to the Salvadorean opposition. In May, 1981, with an agreement between the MISURASATA directorate (all released from prison) and the government, Fagoth was released from prison, but he fled illegally to Honduras, then Miami, publicly linking himself with Somocista and U.S. State Department elements. Another MISURASATA leader, Armstrong Wiggins, went into voluntary exile to Washington, D.C., where he was given an office in the Indian Law Resource Center, a consultative non-governmental organization in the UN, based in the New York Iroquois movement that publishes *Akwesasne Notes.*

The remaining members of the MISURASATA Directorate, under the leadership of Brookly Rivera, presented a document to the government in July, 1981, demanding political autonomy for all the Department of Zelaya (nearly half of Nicaragua) to be administered by MISURASATA. The Sandinista government refused to negotiate with this demand and decertified MISURASATA as a legal organization. Rivera and hundreds of his followers joined Fagoth in Honduras, claiming to establish MISURASATA in exile. From Honduras, Rivera distributed a long statement world-wide, strongly denouncing the Sandinistas for human rights violation and reasserting the demand for Zelaya as a separate territory.

With these events, the Sandinista government developed a different approach to the Atlantic Coast, relating to and negotiating with each village separately, with the Ministry for the Atlantic Coast (INNICA) coordinating relations. Miskitu and other indigenous activists work within the Ministry. With this approach, the government announced the "Declaration of Principles Regarding the Indigenous Communities of the Atlantic Coast," in which they reaffirm commitment to respect the cultural distinctions in the region and to promote their growth; a commitment to bilingual education and affirmative action for the region and the people; and a commitment to guarantee village lands in community ownership.

Let Us Breathe*
By George Black and Judy Butler

George Black lives and works in Managua, Nicaragua. Judy Butler is a staff member of NACLA.

"Were it not for imperialism," said an FSLN leader in November, as Haig was noisily refusing to rule out options against Nicaragua, "we could talk to the business sector, establish rates of profit based on their productive experience and say to them, this is the new situation of Nicaragua. And with the popular power that the revolution has, these businessmen could accept it as a real consequence of the political phenomenon that Nicaragua has lived through.

"But those that are trying to sabotage the revolution, that are boycotting it, that are capitalizing the economy, do so because they are energized, supported and pushed from outside by a power that makes them feel confident. That is the imperialist policy."[1]

Indeed it is. In October 1980, the Heritage Foundation, a right-wing think tank, published policy recommendations for Nicaragua that have become a virtual blueprint for U.S. policy. Author Cleto Di Giovanni, a former CIA officer in Latin America, identified real or possible allies that

---

*This article consists of brief excerpts from *NACLA Report on the Americas*, Vol. XVI, No. 1 (January-February), 1982 (52 pages, illustrated).

[1] Vice Minister of Atlantic Coast Humberto Campbell in Washington press conference, March 5, 1982.

should be supported in a "well orchestrated program targeted against the Marxist Sandinista government. The Catholic Church is influential. There are many political parties ... united in their opposition to the Sandinistas. There is one free newspaper in Nicaragua, *La Prensa*. ... Free labor unions are competing successfully for the loyalty of workers. The private sector is united under an umbrella organization, COSEP, which speaks authoritatively for it. ... Finally, among the free democratic forces in Nicaragua is the Permanent Commission on Human Rights, headed by José Esteban González."[2]

Conversely, these same sectors saw in the election of Ronald Reagan the opportunity to finally press their case with vehemence. They had been biding their time under Carter, but now the honeymoon with the Sandinistas was over.

Two weeks after the U.S. elections, COSEP issued a 30-page document charging the regime with monopolizing political power, reneging on a promise to hold early elections and preparing to "implement in Nicaragua a Communist political-economic project with totalitarian state capitalism (sic) and consequent restrictions on all civil liberties."[3] . It was followed a few weeks later by the arrest and conviction of eight people, most of them business leaders, who admitted conspiring to overthrow the Nicaraguan junta. In a press conference called by Interior Minister Tomás Borge, the president of the Chamber of Commerce and Industry—one of those arrested—admitted that the plotters had made contact with ex-Guardsmen and representatives of other Central American government and military officials. Another testified that Jorge Salazar, a vice president of COSEP, had given $50,000 to buy arms for the movement. The plot had been aborted a few days earlier with the killing of Salazar in a gun battle between his driver and Sandinista security police when they tried to stop his car, reportedly full of weapons.[4]

Only a month later, Managua's Archbishop Obando y Bravo risked splitting the Church by publicly demanding that four priests serving in ministerial posts in the government choose between politics and the Church. Obando y Bravo, no stranger to temporal politics, is an adversary the Sandinistas would prefer not to have. Widely identified with years of opposition to Somoza, he is still an important voice of authority in Nicaragua, even though a majority of priests and other religious workers have left his side to work within the revolutionary process. Initially subdued in his criticism of the Sandinistas, he suddenly became more outspoken. "In the long run, we could fall into Marxism," he said in an interview in early January 1981, "and by long run I don't mean 20 years, I mean three years."[5] In a conference sponsored by the Northeast Pastoral Center for Hispanics in New York City in January of this year, after blithely equating Marxism with

---

[2] Cleto Di Giovanni, "U.S. Policy and the Marxist Threat to Central America," *The Heritage Foundation Backgrounder,* October 15, 1980, pp. 4-5.

[3] *New York Times,* November 28, 1980.

[4] *Miami Herald,* November 23, 1980.

[5] *Miami Herald,* January 2, 1981.

totalitarianism, he even refused to admit that the conditions of human rights were better than they had been under Somoza! On that same trip, the archbishop received an award bestowed on him and the Nicaraguan Council of Catholic Bishops in July of last year by the Washington-based Institute on Religion and Democracy (IRD), a new organization of the neoconservative stripe. The first recipient of IRD's Religious Freedom Award, Obando was praised for his "fight for human rights against both the Right and the Left," according to the Institute. IRD, which recently published and widely distributed a pamphlet called "Nicaragua—A Revolution Against the Church?", has as one of its main objectives to isolate progressive sectors within the U.S. religious community.

Then there was the action of Heritage Foundation darling José Esteban González. González' Permanent Human Rights Commission in Managua had received substantial international funding toward the end of the Somoza regime. But after the victory the money dried up and many of the early members of the executive committee took high posts in the new government.[6] González was clearly sidelined. In February 1981, after an audience with Pope John Paul II, González captured international headlines with the news that he had delivered a document to Vatican officials charging that there were 8,000 political prisoners in Nicaragua, that the "Sandinista regime applies methods of torture and repression very similar to those applied in the past by the Somoza dictatorship," and that he had compiled figures showing that 800 people in Nicaragua had mysteriously "disappeared" since Somoza was overthrown.[7]

In fact, the Sandinistas had abolished the death penalty and had just concluded laboriously trying over 6,000 followers of Somoza, mainly National Guardsmen, as war criminals, convicting some 4,000 to sentences ranging from one to thirty years. The government, as well as much of the population which had wanted to avenge the brutal murders of friends and relatives at the hands of the Guards in a less generous way, was enraged. González was arrested on his return for spreading false and dangerous propaganda. At his trial, González backed off, saying that his remarks in Rome had been "misinterpreted." But of course, as is the case with such headlines, the damage was done both internationally and internally among those already primed to be suspicious of the Sandinistas.

The Heritage Foundation neglected to mention the three indigenous groups on the Atlantic Coast. They have been isolated from the western side of Nicaragua for centuries by geography, language, religion, and different colonial experience and the supreme neglect of the Somoza regime. Though they certainly shared the poverty, these people neither suffered the repression nor experienced the resistance that characterized the unfolding of the revolution in the Pacific region. The Sandinistas, unfamiliar with their customs and social organization, had for a year and a half been grappling with the question of how to appropriately incorporate them into the new

---

[6] *Miami Herald*, January 3, 1981.

[7] *Los Angeles Times*, February 13, 1981; *New York Times*, March 5, 1981.

revolutionary process, making many errors of cultural insensitivity along the way.

Turning the Economic Screws

The private sector derives its greatest muscle from majority control of the economy—75 percent of industrial and 80 percent of agricultural production.[8] With the exception of a few properties confiscated on grounds of decapitalization, the FSLN has restricted state control to former Somoza properties, natural resources and the financial system.

These entrepreneurs have been happy to take their risks with state-supplied investment capital. In fact, since 1979, the great majority of government credits have flowed into private business.

But the terms of economic coexistence provided for guaranteed profit margins in exchange for uninterrupted production, and the agreement has faltered. Private investment has plummeted to an all-time low, from 80 percent of total investment in 1978 to only 10 percent in 1981. It is business' way to serve notice of its discontent with the FSLN's conscious strategy of not letting economic influence be translated into corresponding political power. The *Guardian Weekly* reported that "What Robelo cannot pardon is that wealth no longer brings with it power."[9]

What does this mean in practice? One young executive, who boasts that he has salted away $80,000 abroad since the revolution, made it clear: "Why shouldn't I? The government gives us economic incentives, but what we want is a climate of political confidence."

Masters of Economic War

But the battle is not going on at the ideological and political levels alone, and it is not being fought out primarily among Nicaraguans with merely aid and comfort from the Reagan Administration. Underpinning all these attempts to break the fragile national unity in Nicaragua is the first and most basic level of the U.S. assault: economic warfare. The hoped-for sequence of events is that the disruption of economic activities will lead to social unrest, which in turn will include political turmoil.

The Heritage Foundation had put it in a nutshell: Nicaraguan workers continue to have an emotional attachment to the revolutionary movement. This attachment can be expected to weaken as the economy deteriorates.... There are some indications of growing broadly based support to take to arms to overthrow the Sandinista government, and this support could increase as further economic problems develop.[10]

Sixty percent of the $75 million fiscal 1981 U.S. foreign aid had been designated for the private sector. Of the balance, $30 million, only half

---

[8] *Plan Económico 1981*, Ministry of Planning (Managua).

[9] *Guardian Weekly* (England), August 2, 1981.

[10] Di Giovanni, "U.S. Policy and the Marxist Threat," p. 3.

actually made it to the Nicaraguan government before being suspended just as the reins were handed over to Reagan.

Following the suggestion of the Heritage Foundation—"economic short-comings might provoke at least limited civil unrest by the end of the current harvest season (May-June 1981)"—Reagan turned the suspension into outright cancellation in April. In addition, Reagan also halted PL-480 credits for the purchase of $9.6 million worth of U.S. wheat. But the maneuver backfired. There was civil unrest alright but it was aimed at Reagan, not the Sandinistas. Furthermore, Western and socialist countries alike rushed to fill the wheat deficit.[11]

Before leaving office, Carter prepared the aid request for fiscal 1982. It included $53.3 million in development assistance (usually administered by a local AID office for specific infrastructural or basic human needs projects) and Economic Support Funds (normally provided to governments for such items as offsetting military expenditures or balance of payments deficits). By the time Reagan submitted the request to Congress, it had been cut to $33.3 million. And by the time it passed Congress, the $20 million in Economic Support Funds had been designated specifically to the private sector for raw materials or capital goods imports. The remaining $13.3 million of development assistance has been designated for the private sector as well. But none has been disbursed.

The explanation is simple, according to AID. These funds were to provide the private sector with foreign exchange in order to facilitate its import needs. But once they would be funneled through the government, which imports far more than this amount for private sector use anyway, there is no way to document that this money is additional.[12]

Outright grants administered by the AID office in Managua and turned over directly to the private sector have been continued. In 1980 the figure was $5 million, in 1981 it was $7 million and so far in 1982, $2.4 million. The lion's share of this goes to the Nicaraguan Development Foundation (FUNDE), one of the groups under the umbrella organization, COSEP. Funding includes one three-year $5 million project for agricultural and small manufacturing cooperatives managed paternalistically by FUNDE. FUNDE is also listed as the Nicaraguan cooperating agency for several U.S. privately funded projects whose goal is similar.[13]

Another $2 million AID-funded project has been allocated to other branches of COSEP including the chambers of commerce and industry, the cattlemen's organization and similar agricultural associations. Tradition-ally comprising large capitalists, COSEP has realized it must extend its legitimacy and broaden its base among the smaller growers in competition with the FSLN-inspired agricultural and cattle ranchers' association.

---

[11] "Central America, No Road Back," *NACLA Report on the Americas,* Vol. XV, No. 3 (May-June), 1981.

[12] Phone conversation with AID official at Nicaragua desk.

[13] For information on programs of 47 private, non-profit organizations in Nicaragua see *Development Assistance Programs of U.S. Non-Profit Organizations, Nicaragua, May 1981* (New York: Technical Assistance Information Clearing House, 1981).

The Invisible Blockade Strikes Again

Like all of Central America, Nicaragua's economy is based on export crops which have confronted plummeting world market prices, while the cost of machinery imports has increased. As Daniel Ortega explained in his speech to the United Nations, 47 percent more cotton was required to buy one tractor in 1981 than in 1977; or 54 percent more sugar; or 145 percent more coffee. This, coupled with the breakdown of regional markets and the resulting capital flight in all the countries, has left all near bankruptcy. In the case of Nicaragua, decapitalization has resulted in a capital flight of some $140 million.

Productivity has remained low (labor problems were estimated to have cost $100 million in 1981); unemployment and inflation, which had bottomed out at 18 percent and 25 percent respectively by 1980, both began to rise again; state bureaucracy had mushroomed from 33,000 to 61,000 employees (Much, but not all, of the bureaucratic growth results from the expansion or creation of ministries which provide the vast new social services.) Reserves had hit rock-bottom and it was impossible to generate any internal surplus without resorting to ever-increasing foreign aid.

These problems, most of which are shared regionally, and are even worse in Costa Rica and El Salvador than in Nicaragua, come on top of and are exacerbated by the situation the Sandinistas inherited from Somoza: a $1.6 billion foreign debt, the highest debt *per capita* in the Americas; wholesale destruction of the country's productive infrastructure (factories and croplands); the dislocation of export crop cycles, and Somoza's looting of reserves (both by mortgaging Somocista properties to get liquid capital in the later period of the war and by the blatant robbery of all but $3.5 million from the Central Bank just before he fled).

In U.S. policy, "doves" and "hawks" alike have exploited this weakness and dependency. Nicaragua's "integration into the international economic system is one of the greatest deterrents to the consolidation of a Marxist system," wrote former Assistant Secretary of State for Inter-American Affairs Viron Vaky (1978-80), adding in a footnote that the Sandinista government's agreement on the rescheduling of $600 million in debts contracted by Somoza with some 120 American, European and Japanese creditor banks "locked Nicaragua into the private money market."[14] To be thus locked means to be subjected to international interest rates, exchange rates, loans procedures, creditor ratings, etc. Tied, in short, to a set of objective conditions determined by Western finance capital, and above all by the United States.

But not to be tied is even rougher. Forgetting the medium and long-term investment loans which carry high interest rates, there are also the crucial short-term credits which allow a country to carry on daily international trade. A U.S. blockade of external financing (imposed against Cuba,

---

[14] Viron P. Vaky, "Hemispheric Relations: 'Everything Is Part of Everything Else,'" *Foreign Affairs*, Vol. 59, No. 3 (1980), p. 621.

Allende's Chile, Grenada and now Nicaragua), which in turn implies a blockade of foreign investment, is thus one of the deadliest weapons in the economic arsenal.

Despite the fact that the Sandinistas agreed to accept Somoza's debts, and actually received favorable rescheduling terms, both private credits and investments were effectively halted when the Administration cut off aid. It is automatic in such situations that Ex-Im Bank trade guarantees and Overseas Private Investment Corporation (OPIC) investment guarantees are halted as well. Without them, banks and investors are loath to take risks.

Because the major U.S. banks have inordinate influence on the international banking community, the Sandinistas have received virtually no private credits, even short-term ones, since the triumph. And in what can only be viewed as overkill, the State Department is now rumored to be directly pressuring the banks not to change their minds.[15]

In effect, this means that the Nicaraguan government must put up cash for all import purchases, from food to tractors to horseshoe nails. Since Nicaragua has few manufacturing plants for spare parts and most of the machinery is from the United States, it only takes a few breakdowns before an entire fishing fleet is docked, buses and taxis are out of commission and factory production is operating at less than full capacity. Not only does this decrease production, but it puts workers out of jobs. INPESCA, the state fishing industry, had to close one of its processing plants because so many boats were not operating.

The Reagan Administration has now begun to move on the multilateral lending institutions. First, in early November, the newly-appointed U.S. representative, Cuban exile José Manuel Casanova, forced Nicaragua to withdraw a loan application to the Inter-American Development Bank for $40 million to renovate and invest in Nicaragua's fishing industry, centered mainly along the Atlantic Coast. While the stated reasons for opposing the loan were "technical," U.S. sources revealed that the United States and some other countries had an "overall political problem with the direction" of the Nicaraguan government.[16]

In the World Bank, where the United States holds fewer votes, its "no" did not prevent other members from approving a $16 million loan for the improvement of Managua slum districts in January 1982.[17] State Department spokesperson Sue Pittman confirmed in that month that the Reagan Administration would oppose any Nicaraguan credit or aid request to any international lending institution.[18] It did not appear to matter that

---

[15] This pressure is admitted by U.S. banks asked to participate in a $130 million loan to Nicaragua being syndicated by a London-based consortium named Intermex. One banker admitted the loan might be politically impossible, adding, "We are listening to what happens in Mexico and Washington." The loan would be guaranteed by the Banco Nacional de México (*Journal of Commerce*, March 9, 1982).

[16] Center for International Policy (CIP) *Aid Memo*, November 12, 1981.

[17] *World Bank News Release*, No. 82-41, January 14, 1982.

[18] *Unomásuno* (Mexico), January 17, 1982.

the social impact on the Nicaraguan poor is immediate. The IDB still has seven loan and technical assistance projects worth $87.6 million under consideration for Nicaragua, and the World Bank more than $70 million.[19]

Underdeveloped countries are also linked into world capitalist commodity markets, opening a further structural vulnerability easily exploited through trade embargoes. In Nicaragua's case, the embargoes will be selective. Nicaragua's two leading export crops (coffee and cotton) have relatively diversified markets, but its next highest earners are wide open to U.S. pressures: 75 percent of Nicaragua's meat goes to the United States, with virtually all the rest going to Puerto Rico, while the U.S. market also accounts for 82.7 percent of sugar exports.[20] Early threats were waved at beef exports, but lifted when Nicaragua cancelled the planned purchase of high-grade, low-cost breeding bulls from Cuba. The Cuban connection also lay behind threats to suspend U.S. export of resins used in Nicaragua's PVC manufacturing industry—because Nicaragua might sell Cuba its surplus stocks of plastics.

A final, and more dramatic facet of economic warfare is direct sabotage. Here, the forms of attack are multiple. At one extreme, sabotage is the withdrawal of industrial capital through any number of difficult-to-detect means. The Philadelphia-based chemicals corporation, Pennsalt, and the Sears Roebuck department store are two U.S. multinationals accused by their Nicaraguan workers of decapitalization.[21] At the other extreme lies the bombing of a Nicaraguan state-owned passenger jet in Mexico City in December 1981.

Economic Emergency, Political Confrontation

By mid-1981, the economic situation was headed from bad to worse. By the end of the year, some analysts suggested that Nicaragua would need $500 million over and above currently predicted export earnings and foreign aid receipts simply to maintain current levels of economic activity in 1982.[22] Exports for 1981 were predicted at $540 million and imports at $900 million, a full 20 percent higher than first expected.[23]

The crisis presented the FSLN with an acute political dilemma. Even without calling in the International Monetary Fund (IMF) and their infamous restrictions, the Nicaraguan people were seeing liberation followed by austerity. The redistributive reforms put into effect by the government had yet to hit the middle class really hard. On September 9 the government decreed a State of Economic and Social Emergency. The decree set out to cut government expenditure, raise tax revenues, halt capital flight and increase productivity—the latter by means of a controversial no-strike clause.

[19] *CIP Memo*, undated.

[20] InterPress Service (Managua), November 27, 1981.

[21] *Multinational Monitor* (Vol. 2, No. 5), May 1981.

[22] *Washington Post*, November 23, 1981.

[23] Interview with Xavier Gorostiaga, reprinted in Instituto Histórico Centroamericano bulletin (Managua), 1981.

The strike freeze, as well as seven other restrictions, made it illegal to carry out any act that would effect the precarious economic situation whether by sabotage, land invasions, speculation, or spreading of false information. Violation carried penalties of one to three years in prison.[24]

The World Bank, in an unpublished report dated October 9, 1981, endorsed the Nicaraguan economic reforms which it said are "expected to define a framework wherein private sector business can satisfactorily operate." Within Nicaragua, the only initial complaint came from some who felt the step might have been taken earlier. COSEP welcomed the decree as "the first step toward solving the national crisis."[25]

Yet hard on the heels of the decree came a four-week sequence of events which convinced the FSLN that a major coordinated U.S. plan of destabilization was finally falling into place, and that the opposition had gained enough confidence from external attacks to force the economic crisis onto a political battleground.

On September 29 and October 1, La Prensa was twice closed for its most serious provocation yet: the publication of false allegations by a convicted "decapitalizer." Days later COSEP heard its complaints of Junta mismanagement cited in the U.S. Senate as the FY82 Foreign Aid Amendment approving the $33.3 million to the Nicaraguan private sector was passed.[26]

Over the first three weeks of the month, an unprecedented 16 cross-border raids by Somocista terrorists from Honduras were registered and on October 7-9, the United States and Honduras staged two days of joint military maneuvers off Puerto Cortez on Honduras' Atlantic Coast. As of October 5, the details of the maneuvers involving patrol boats and aircraft "had not been concretized," and would therefore not become public information, but the exercise involved training in ocean search and interception. The objective, according to a Navy memo, was to train 130 U.S. military personnel and their Honduran counterparts in sea and air tactics, communications and joint command. Samuel Dickens, past staff member of the Inter-American Defense Board, said at the time that the maneuvers were a signal of U.S. support in case Honduras goes to war with Nicaragua.[27]

Three weeks later the U.S. military carried out an unusually large exercise with 38 ships and 200 aircraft, with maneuvers running from Norfolk, Virginia, headquarters of the Second fleet, to the Caribbean Sea. The operations, involving the aircraft carriers Kennedy and Eisenhower, were designed to "improve fleet readiness in coordinated dual carrier battleground operations with Navy and Marine Corps personnel on weapons systems under realistic conditions."[28]

Meanwhile, on October 8, the U.S. Deputy Ambassador to the United

24 Barricada Internacional (Managua), September 15, 1981.

25 Miami Herald, September 15, 1981.

26 Washington Post, November 9, 1981.

27 Diario de Las Americas, October 6, 1981.

28 U.S. Navy Press Release and Miami Herald, November 26, 1981.

Nations leveled a vicious attack against Nicaragua in the General Assembly; on October 12, the IAPA arrived in Managua and received *La Prensa's* accusations of sharply falling FSLN support and on October 19, a column in the *Washington Post* by Evans and Novak insinuated Cuba had sent troops via Nicaragua to blow up an important Salvadorean bridge: The climax of mounting domestic dissent had come on October 19. Six COSEP leaders signed an open letter to Junta coordinator Daniel Ortega denouncing government policies.

Far from simply "accusing the Sandinista Junta of Marxist-Leninist tendencies" as the U.S. press would have us believe, the signatories accused the FSLN of creating the economic crisis, "preparing a new genocide" and leading the country to the verge of disaster. The letter was not only widely disseminated within Nicaragua, but was forwarded to a number of international organizations, including the UN, the OAS and the International Labor Organization, a direct challenge to stipulations of the Emergency Decree. The change of political climate the private sector demanded was nothing less than gaining state power.

Even Nicaraguan Ambassador to the United States Arturo Cruz, who resigned in part because of disagreement with the actions taken by the government against his COSEP friends, was the first to admit that the letter had had a destabilizing effect. "If they wanted to criticize the government, they could have sent the letter directly to the Junta," he said to a group of journalists at the Center for Inter-American Relations.[29]

Facing the most serious political challenge to date, the FSLN moved swiftly to assert its authority, knowing in advance that to do so would have clear international consequences. Junta member Sergio Ramírez had already pointed out that, "We can't decide everything in terms of international opinion while we are being destabilized. There are times when it is better to show that the authority of the revolution does exist and that it can hit back at its foes. Our reactions are going to get harder as the harrassment gets more aggressive."[30] The three COSEP signatories who did not go into hiding were tried and sentenced to seven months in jail (though this was commuted after four months).

The reassertion of authority was validated by impressive mass mobilization. Nationwide anti-intervention rallies in October brought 250,000 Nicaraguans into the streets, the target of their wrath as much domestic enemies of the revolution as the Halcon Vista naval maneuvers which they saw as a dry run for intervention.

Signs are that this newest crisis has left the opposition, as before, in some disarray. Retreating from the brink, *La Prensa* changed tack in mid-November, denouncing Haig's "interfering and threatening attitude" in an editorial.[31] Even Robelo positioned himself as far from the U.S.

---

[29] Presentation by former Nicaraguan Ambassador to the United States Arturo Cruz to the Center for Inter-American Relations, December 1, 1981.

[30] *Le Monde Diplomatique*, July 19, 1981.

[31] *La Prensa* (Managua), November 15, 1981.

Administration as he could. With a new law governing the activities of political parties on the table for debate, some opposition groups found their way back to the Council of State, while others remained adrift. The new COSEP board took a conciliatory tone. And the FSLN, in no doubt about the most pressing task at hand, dubbed 1982 the "Year of National Unity Against Aggression."

Managing the Message

Why has the propaganda offensive become such a key tool of Reagan's destabilization efforts against Nicaragua? Once again, reference to the Heritage Foundation provides the clue. "In the near future," advises Di Giovanni, "the U.S. must revert to a more traditional view of Central America if the spread of Marxism is to be contained.... As long as it exists in any great strength in anyone of [countries], the others will be in danger. Thus, although the Marxist government in Nicaragua might fall eventually of its own failures, the security of El Salvador requires the acceleration of the removal of the government in Managua." [32]

Furthermore, it had become clear that the Administration was opting for a military solution to the situation in El Salvador, and with the gains of the insurgents that would mean far greater U.S. involvement. The hitch was that close to half of the U.S. population feared a war under Reagan.

The campaign portraying Nicaragua as a totalitarian bastion carrying out the bidding of the Soviet Union in El Salvador would thus serve several ends. It could hope to explain away the successes of the Salvadorean insurgents, help mobilize public opinion in support of increased U.S. involvement and begin to construct a rationale for the eventual regionalization of the conflict. Most importantly it could drive a wedge between support for the struggle in El Salvador and the triumphant Sandinistas. Haig pushed at this in a speech in Palm Beach, Florida in mid-November: "The Reagan Administration is very worried about the totalitarian course the Nicaraguan regime is adopting. El Salvador is going to follow that same road if the United States doesn't increase economic and military assistance to the Duarte junta." [33]

Within Congress this effort has taken its toll. Liberal members of Congress who had fought on behalf of the $75 million aid package to Nicaragua during Carter's last year began to speak of being betrayed by the Sandinistas. In debate over Senator Zorinsky's proposed amendment to the fiscal 1982 foreign aid request that all $33 million for Nicaragua go to the private sector, Senator Kennedy endorsed it with the following remark: "Nicaragua has experienced the lion's share of social and political injustice under two regimes—including first a corrupt tyrant of the right and now an authoritarian regime of the left." [34]

---

[32] Di Giovanni, "U.S. Policy and the Marxist Threat," p. 2.

[33] *Diario de Las Americas*, November 15, 1981.

[34] *Congressional Record—Senate*, October 20, 1981, p. S11665.

Suggested Readings

General Readings

Bell, John. *Crisis in Costa Rica*. Austin: Woodward, 1971.

Biesanz, Richard. *The Costa Ricans*. New Jersey: Prentice Hall, 1982.

Catholic Relief Services. *Eyewitness Report: Turmoil in Central America*. Catholic Relief Services, 1981.

Galeano, Eduardo. *Guatemala: Occupied Country*. New York: Monthly Review, 1969.

Gettleman, Marvin E. et al. *El Salvador: Central America in the New Cold War*. New York: Grove Press, 1981.

Grant, Cedric H. *The Making of Modern Belize: Politics, Society and British Colonialism in Central America*. New York: Cambridge University Press, 1976.

Holland, O. Nigel. *The Formation of a Colonial Society: Belize, from Conquest to Crown Colony*. Baltimore: Johns Hopkins University Press, 1977.

Jonas, Susanne and David Tobis, eds. *Guatemala*. New York: NACLA, 1974.

Krehm, William. *Democracia y tiranías en el Caribe*. Ed. Vicente Saénz, Mexico: Unión Democrática Centroamericana, 1949.

Menjívar, Rafael. *El Salvador: el eslabón más pequeño*. San José, Costa Rica: Editorial Universitaria Centroamericana, 1980.

Meza, Víctor. *Política y sociedad en Honduras*. Tegucigalpa, Honduras: Editorial Guaymuras, 1981.

Setzekorn, William David. *Formerly British Honduras: A Profile of the New Nation of Belize*. Athens, Ohio: Ohio University Press, 1981.

Torres Rivas, Edelberto. *Crisis del poder en Centroamérica*. San José, Costa Rica: EDUCA, 1981.

Webre, Stephen. *José Napoleón Duarte and the Christian Democratic Party in Salvadorean Politics*. Baton Rouge, Louisiana: Louisiana State University Press, 1979.

Wheaton, Philip. *The Iron Triangle: The Honduran Connection*. Washington, D.C.: EPICA, 1981.

Wheelock Román, Jaime. *Imperialismo y dictadura: crisis de una formación social*. 3rd ed. Mexico: Siglo XXI, 1979.

White, Alastair. *El Salvador*. New York: Praeger, 1973.

Woodward, Jr., Ralph Lee. *Central America: A Nation Divided*. New York: Oxford University Press, 1976.

Wortman, Miles L. *Government and Society in Central America, 1680-1840.* New York: Columbia University Press, 1982.

Zammit, J. Ann. *The Belize Issue.* London: Latin America Bureau, 1978.

Chapter 1. The Rise of Revolution

Adams, Richard N. *Crucifixion by Power.* Austin: Univ. of Texas Press, 1970.

Aguilera Peralta, Gabriel. "Terror and Violence as Weapons of Counterinsurgency in Guatemala." *Latin American Perspectives,* VII, Nos. 2 & 3, Issues 25 & 26 (Spring/Summer 1980), 91-113.

Albízurez, Miguel Angel. "Struggles and Experiences of the Guatemalan Trade-Union Movement, 1976-June 1978." *Latin American Perspectives,* VII, Nos. 2 & 3, Issues 25 & 26 (Spring/Summer 1980), 145-159.

Alegría, Claribel. "The Insurrection and Holocaust of 1932." *Third World,* No. 7.

Anderson, Thomas P. *Matanza: El Salvador's Communist Revolt of 1932.* Lincoln, Nebraska: University of Nebraska Press, 1971.

Armstrong, Robert, and Janet Shenk. *El Salvador: The Face of Revolution.* Boston: South End Press, 1982.

CAMINO. *El Salvador—Background to the Crisis.* Boston: Central America Information Office, 1982.

Cardoza y Aragón, Luis. *La revolución guatemalteca.* Montevideo: Pueblos Unidos, 1956.

Center for Information, Documentation and Analysis of the Latin American Workers' Movement (CIDAMO). "The Workers' Movement in Guatemala." *NACLA Report on the Americas,* XIV, No. 1 (Jan.-Feb. 1980), 28-33.

Contemporary Marxism, No. 3. *Revolution and Intervention in Central America.* San Francisco: Synthesis Publications, 1981.

Crawley, Eduardo. *Dictators Never Die: A Portrait of Nicaragua and the Somozas.* New York: St. Martin's Press, 1979.

EPICA. *Nicaragua: A People's Revolution.* Washington, D.C.: EPICA, 1980.

Estudios Centroamericanos. Guatemala: drama y conflicto social, special issue nos. 356-357. San Salvador: Universidad Centroamericana José Simeón Cañas, 1978.

Fonseca Amador, Carlos. "Zero Hour in Nicaragua." *Tricontinental* (Cuba), No. 14 (Sept.-Oct. 1969).

Jonas, Susanne. "An Overview: 50 Years of Revolution and Intervention in Central America." *Contemporary Marxism,* No. 3 (Summer 1981), pp. iii-xxiv.

Jung, Harald, "Class Struggles in El Salvador." *New Left Review,* No. 122, July-August 1980, pp. 3-25.

Karmali, Jan et al. *Nicaragua: Dictatorship and Revolution.* London: Latin America Bureau, 1979.

Latin America Bureau. *Violence and Fraud in El Salvador: A Report on Current Political Events in El Salvador.* London: Latin America Bureau, 1977.

MacEoin, Gary. "North of Salvador, Another Cauldron." *Christianity and Crisis,* Vol. 41, No. 3 (March 2, 1981).

Medina, Susana. "Guatemala: contrainsurgencia y revolución." *Revista Ter-*

ritorios, No. 5, Universidad Autónoma Metropolitana—Xochimilco, Mexico City (Nov.-Dec. 1980).

Melville, Thomas and Marjorie Melville. *Guatemala—Another Vietnam?* London: Penguin, 1971.

Millett, Richard. *Guardians of the Dynasty: A History of the U.S.-Created Guardia Nacional de Nicaragua and the Somoza Family.* Maryknoll, New York: Orbis Books, 1977.

Montgomery, T.S. *Revolution in El Salvador: Origins and Evolution.* Boulder, Colorado: Westview Press, 1982.

NACLA Latin America and Empire Report, "Nicaragua," Vol. X, No. 2 (February 1976), 2-40.

Ortega Saavedra, Humberto. *50 años de lucha sandinista.* Mexico City: Editorial Diógenes, 1979.

Ovidio Medina, León, ed. *El Salvador: revolución y muerte.* Medellín, Colombia: Ediciones Hombre Nuevo, 1981.

Paz Salinas, María Emelia. *Belize: el despertar de una nación.* Mexico City: Siglo XXI, 1979.

Plant, Roger. *Guatemala: Unnatural Disaster.* London: Latin America Bureau, 1978.

Scroggs, William O. *Filibusters and Financiers: The Story of William Walker and His Associates.* New York: MacMillan, 1916.

Selser, Gregorio. *Sandino.* Translated by Cedric Belfrage. New York: Monthly Review Press, 1981.

Socialist Review. "El Salvador and the Central American War" (Interview with John Womack, Jr.). *Socialist Review,* Vol. 12, No. 2 (March-April 1982), 9-28.

Torres Rivas, Edelberto. "Problemas de la contrarrevolución y la democracia en Guatemala." *Nueva Sociedad,* No. 53 (March-April 1981).

Chapter 2. U.S. Policy: The Politics of Intervention

Arnson, Cynthia. *El Salvador: A Revolution Confronts the United States.* Washington, D.C.: Institute for Policy Studies, 1982.

Blasier, Cole. *The Hovering Giant: U.S. Responses to Revolutionary Change in Latin America.* Pittsburgh: University of Pittsburgh Press, 1976.

Fagen, Richard et al. "Caribbean Strategies: Critiques of Left and Right, Christian and Social Democrats." *Caribbean Review,* Vol. XI, No. 2 (Spring 1982).

Feinberg, Richard E., ed. *Central America: International Dimensions of the Crisis.* New York: Holmes and Meier, 1982.

Fontaine, Roger, et al. "Castro's Specter." *Washington Quarterly,* 3:4 (Autumn 1980).

Gettleman, Marvin E. et al., eds. *El Salvador: Central America in the New Cold War.* New York: Grove Press, 1981.

Hadar, Arnon. *The United States and El Salvador: Political and Military Involvement.* Berkeley: U.S.-El Salvador Research and Information Center, 1981.

Immerman, Richard H. *The CIA in Guatemala: The Foreign Policy of Interven-*

tion. Austin: University of Texas Press, 1982.

Joseph, Paul. *Cracks in the Empire: State Politics in the Vietnam War.* Boston: South End Press, 1981.

Kamman, William. *A Search for Stability: United States Diplomacy toward Nicaragua, 1925-1933.* Notre Dame, Indiana: University of Notre Dame Press, 1968.

Klare, Michael T. and Cynthia Arnson. *Supplying Repression: U.S. Support for Authoritarian Regimes Abroad.* Washington, D.C.: Institute for Policy Studies, 1981.

LaFeber, Walter. *The Panama Canal: The Crisis in Historical Perspective.* New York: Oxford University Press, 1978.

Lawton Casals, Jorge. "Crisis de la hegemonía: la política de Carter hacia Nicaragua 1977-1979." *Cuadernos Semestrales—Estados Unidos: Perspectiva Latinoamericana,* No. 6 (2 semestre, 1979).

Lowenthal, Abraham F. et al. "The Caribbean Basin Initiative." *Foreign Policy,* No. 47 (Summer 1982), pp. 114-38.

Maira, Luis. "Fracaso y reacomodo de la política de Estados Unidos hacia Centroamérica." *Foro Internacional,* 20:4 (April-June 1980).

Munro, Dana. *Intervention and Dollar Diplomacy, 1900-1921.* Princeton: Princeton University Press, 1964.

————. *The United States and the Caribbean Republics, 1921-1933.* Princeton: Princeton University Press, 1974.

Pastor, Robert A. "Our Real National Interests in Central America." *Atlantic,* July 1982, pp. 27-39.

Pearce, Jenny. *Under the Eagle: U.S. Intervention in Central America and the Caribbean.* London: Latin America Bureau, 1981.

Poelchau, Warner, ed. *White Paper Whitewash: Interviews with Philip Agee on the CIA and El Salvador.* New York: Deep Cover Books, 1981.

Schlesinger, Stephen and Stephen Kinzer. *Bitter Fruit: The Untold Story of the American Coup in Guatemala.* Garden City, New York: Doubleday, 1982.

Sklar, Holly, ed. *Trilateralism: The Trilateral Commission and Elite Planning for World Management.* Boston: South End Press, 1980.

Wolfe, Alan and Jerry Sanders. "Resurgent Cold War Ideology: The Case of the Committee on the Present Danger." In Richard R. Fagen, ed., *Capitalism and the State in U.S.-Latin American Relations.* Stanford: Stanford University Press, 1979.

Chapter 3. Dependent Development and Economic Imperialism

Ashcraft, Norman. *Colonialism and Underdevelopment: Processes of Political-Economic Change in British Honduras.* New York: Teachers College Press, 1973.

Bauer Paiz, Alfonso. *Cómo opera el capital yanqui en Centroamérica: el caso de Guatemala.* Mexico: 1956.

Burbach, Roger and Patricia Flynn. *Agribusiness in the Americas.* New York: NACLA and Monthly Review Press, 1980.

Fallas, Helio. *Crisis económica en Costa Rica.* San José, Costa Rica: Editorial Nueva Década, 1981.

Kepner, Charles and Jay Soothill. *The Banana Empire.* New York: Russell, 1935.

Monteforte Toledo, Mario. *Centroamérica: subdesarrollo y dependencia.* 2 vols. Mexico: Universidad Nacional Autónoma de Mexico, 1972.

Ortiz-Buonafina, Marta. *The Impact of Import Substitution Policies on Marketing Activities: A Case Study of the Guatemalan Commercial Sector.* Washington, D.C.: University Press of America, 1982.

Raynolds, David R. *Rapid Development in Small Economies: The Example of El Salvador.* New York: Praeger, 1967.

Slutzky, Daniel and Esther Alonso. *Les transformations récentes de l'enclave bananière au Honduras.* Paris: CETRAL, 1979.

Torres Rivas, Edelberto. *Interpretación del desarrollo social centroamericano.* 5th ed. San José, Costa Rica: EDUCA, 1977.

Wheelock Román, Jaime and Luis Carrión. *Apuntes sobre el desarrollo económico y social de Nicaragua.* Managua: 1980.

Wynia, Gary. *Politics and Planners: Economic Development in Central America.* Madison, Wisconsin: University of Wisconsin Press, 1972.

Chapter 4. Heritage of Hunger: Population, Land and Survival

Anderson, Thomas P. *War of the Dispossessed: Honduras and El Salvador, 1969.* Lincoln, Nebraska: University of Nebraska Press, 1981.

Arbingast, Stanley A. et al. *Atlas of Central America.* Austin, Texas: University of Texas, Bureau of Business Research, 1979.

Behm, H. and D. Primante. "Mortalidad en los primeros años de vida en la América Latina." *Notas de Población,* Año 6, No. 16 (1978).

Browning, David. *El Salvador: Landscape and Society.* Oxford: Clarendon Press, 1971.

Burke, Melvin. "El sistema de plantación y la proletarización del trabajo agrícola en El Salvador."

Capa, Cornell and J. Mayone Stycos. *Margin of Life: Population and Poverty in the Americas.* New York: Grossman, 1974.

CSUCA/Programa Centroamericano de Ciencias Sociales. *Estructura agraria, dinámica de población y desarrollo capitalista en Centroamérica.* San José, Costa Rica: EDUCA, 1978.

Deere, Carmen Diana. "A Comparative Analysis of Agrarian Reform in El Salvador and Nicaragua, 1979-81." *Development and Change,* Vol. 13 (1982), 1-41.

Durham, William H. *Scarcity and Survival in Central America: Ecological Origins of the Soccer War.* Stanford: Stanford University Press, 1979.

Figueroa Ibarra, Carlos. *El proletariado rural en el agro guatemalteco.* Guatemala: Instituto de Investigaciones Económicas y Sociales de la Universidad de San Carlos, 1976.

Inter-American Development Bank. *Economic and Social Progress in Latin America, 1978-79.* Washington, D.C.: IDB, 1980.

Janvry, Alain de. *The Agrarian Question and Reformism in Latin America.* Baltimore: Johns Hopkins University Press, 1982.

Karush, Gerald E. "Plantations, Population, and Poverty: The Roots of the

Demographic Crisis in El Salvador." *Studies in Comparative International Development*, Vol. XIII, No. 3, 1978.

Lappé, Frances Moore and Joseph Collins, with Cary Fowler. *Food First: Beyond the Myth of Scarcity*. San Francisco: Institute for Food and Development Policy, 1977.

Peckenham, Nancy. "Land Settlement in the Petén." *Latin American Perspectives*, Issues 25 and 26 (Spring/Summer 1980), Vol. VII, Nos. 2 & 3, 169-77.

Puffer, R. R. and Carlos V. Serrano. *Patterns of Mortality in Childhood*. Washington, D.C.: Pan American Health Organization, 1973.

Ramírez, Marco Antonio. *Los alimentos en Centroamérica*. San Salvador: Organización de los Estados Centroamericanos (ODECA), 1968.

Roberts, Bryan. *Organizing Strangers: Poor Families in Guatemala City*. Austin, Texas: University of Texas Press, 1973.

Riba, Jorge Ricardo. *La vivienda en Centroamérica*. San Salvador: Organización de Estados Centroamericanos (ODECA), 1969.

Richter, Ernesto. "Social Classes, Accumulation, and the Crisis of 'Overpopulation' in El Salvador." *Latin American Perspectives*, Vol. VII, Nos. 2 and 3 (Spring/Summer 1980).

Simon, L. and J. Stephens. *El Salvador Land Reform 1980-1981: Impact Audit*. Boston: OXFAM-America, 1981.

Teller, Charles et al. "Population and Nutrition: Implications of Sociodemographic Trends and Differentials for Food and Nutrition Policy in Central America and Panama." *Ecology of Food and Nutrition*, Vol. 8 (1979), 95-109.

United Nations/Economic Commission for Latin America. *Nicaragua: Economic Repercussions of Recent Political Events*. CEPAL (ECLA), 1979.

————. *Statistical Yearbook for Latin America–1979*. New York: CEPAL (ECLA), 1981.

Valverde, Victor, et al. "Life Styles and Nutritional Status of Children from Different Ecological Areas of El Salvador." *Ecology of Food and Nutrition*, Vol. 9 (1980), 167-77.

Winson, Anthony. "Class Structure and Agrarian Transition in Central America." *Latin American Perspectives*, Vol. V (Fall 1978), 27-48.

Chapter 5. Violations of Human Rights: The Price of Stability

Aguilera Peralta, Gabriel. *Dialéctica del terror en Guatemala*. San José, Costa Rica: EDUCA, 1981.

Americas Watch Committee and the American Civil Liberties Union. *Report on Human Rights in El Salvador*. New York: Vintage Books, 1982.

Chomsky, Noam and Edward S. Herman. *The Washington Connection and Third-World Fascism*. Boston: South End Press, 1979.

CISPES (U.S. Committee in Solidarity with the People of El Salvador). *El Salvador: No Refuge*. Washington, D.C.: CISPES, 1981.

House of Commons. *Human Rights in El Salvador*. London: Parliamentary Human Rights Group, 1979.

Klare, Michael T. and Cynthia Arnson. *Supplying Repression: U.S. Support for Authoritarian Regimes Abroad*. Washington, D.C.: Institute for Policy Studies, 1981.

Langguth, A. J. *Hidden Terrors*. New York: Pantheon Books, 1978.

National Lawyers Guild and La Raza Legal Alliance. *Guatemala: Repression and Resistance*. New York: National Lawyers Guild, 1980.

O'Malley, William. *The Voice of Blood*. Maryknoll, New York: Orbis Books, 1980.

Organization of American States. *Report on the Situation of Human Rights in Nicaragua*. Washington, D.C.: Organization of American States, 1978.

The Political-Diplomatic Commission of the FMLN/FDR of El Salvador. *A Massacre in El Salvador's Morazán Province*. San Francisco: Solidarity Publications, 1982.

Schoultz, Lars. *Human Rights and United States Policy toward Latin America*. Princeton, New Jersey: Princeton University Press, 1981.

U.S. Congress, House, Subcommittee on International Organizations. *Religious Persecution in El Salvador: Hearings on July 21 and 29, 1977*.

Vogelgesang, Sandy. *American Dream, Global Nightmare: The Dilemma of U.S. Human Rights Policy*. New York: W.W. Norton, 1980.

Chapter 6. The Church and Liberation

Arias, Esther and Mortimer Arias. *The Cry of My People: Out of Captivity in Latin America*. New York: Friendship Press, 1980.

Assman, Hugo, ed. *El juego de los reformismos frente a la revolución en Centroamérica*. San José, Costa Rica: Departamento Ecuménico de Investigaciones, 1981.

Cardenal, Ernesto. *The Gospel in Solentiname*. Translated by Donald D. Walsh. Maryknoll, New York: Orbis Books, 1977.

Dahlin, Therrin C. et al. *The Catholic Left in Latin America: A Comprehensive Bibliography*. Boston: G.K. Hall, 1981.

Departamento Ecuménico de Investigaciones. *Apuntes para una teología nicaragüense*. San José, Costa Rica: Departamento Ecuménico de Investigaciones, 1981.

Dodson, Michael and T.S. Montgomery. "The Churches in the Nicaraguan Revolution." In Thomas W. Walker, ed., *Nicaragua in Revolution*. New York: Praeger, 1982.

Eagleson, John, ed. *Christians and Socialism*. Maryknoll, New York: Orbis Books, 1975.

Ecumenical Program for Interamerican Communication and Action (EPICA). *Reflections and Problems of a Church Being Born among the People*. Washington, D.C.: EPICA.

Erdozaín, Plácido. *Archbishop Romero: Martyr of Salvador*. Maryknoll, New York: Orbis Books, 1981.

Gheerbrant, Alain. *The Rebel Church in Latin America*. London: Penguin Books, 1974.

Gutiérrez, Gustavo. *A Theology of Liberation*. Maryknoll, New York: Orbis Books, 1973.

Instituto Histórico Centroamericano. *Fé cristiana y revolución sandinista en Nicaragua*. Managua: Instituto Histórico Centroamericano, 1979.

Lernoux, Penny. *Cry of the People.* New York: Doubleday, 1982.

Levine, Daniel H., ed. *Churches and Politics in Latin America.* Beverly Hills, California: Sage Publications, 1979.

Machovec, Milan. *A Marxist Looks at Jesus.* Translated by Peter Hebblethwaite. London: Darton, Longman and Todd, 1976.

Míguez Bonino, José. *Doing Theology in a Revolutionary Situation.* Philadelphia: Fortress Press, 1975.

New Catholic World. "The Church in Central America." *New Catholic World,* Vol. 224, No. 1343 (Sept.-Oct. 1981).

Romero, Archbishop Oscar Arnulfo. *A Martyr's Message of Hope: Six Homilies by Archbishop Oscar Romero.* Translated by National Catholic Reporter Publishing Company. Kansas City, Missouri: Celebration Books, 1981.

Torres, Sergio and John Eagleson, eds. *The Challenge of Basic Christian Communities.* Maryknoll, New York: Orbis Books, 1981.

Torres, Sergio and John Eagleson, eds. *Theology in the Americas.* Maryknoll, New York: Orbis Books, 1976.

Chapter 7. Women in Revolution

AMES (Association of Salvadorean Women). "Participation of Latin American Women in Social and Political Organizations: Reflections of Salvadorean Women." *Monthly Review,* Vol. 34, No. 2 (June 1982), 11-25.

Latin American and Caribbean Women's Collective. *Slaves of Slaves: The Challenge of Latin American Women.* London: Zed Press, 1980.

Nicaragua Solidarity Campaign. *Women in Nicaragua.* London: Nicaragua Solidarity Campaign, 1980.

Nieves, Isabel. "Household Arrangements and Multiple Jobs in San Salvador." *Signs,* Vol. 5, No. 1 (May 1979).

Randall, Margaret. *Sandino's Daughters: Testimonies of Nicaraguan Women in Struggle.* Vancouver: New Star Books, 1981.

Ramírez-Horton, Susan E. "The Role of Women in the Nicaraguan Revolution." In Thomas W. Walker, ed., *Nicaragua in Revolution.* New York: Praeger, 1982, pp. 147-159.

Rivera, María Amalia Irías de and Irma Violeta Alfaro de Carpio. "Guatemalan Working Women in the Labor Movement." *Latin American Perspectives,* Vol. IV, Nos. 1 and 2 (Winter and Spring 1977), Issues 12 and 13, 194-202.

Women's International Resource Exchange Service. *Nicaraguan Women and Revolution* (packet). New York: Women's International Resource Exchange Service.

————. *Women and War: El Salvador* (packet). New York: Women's International Resource Exchange.

Youssef, Nadia Haggag. *Women and Work in Developing Societies.* Population Monograph Series No. 15. Berkeley: University of California, 1974.

Chapter 8. The Revolutionary Option: Nicaragua

Black, George. *Triumph of the People: The Sandinista Revolution in Nicaragua.* London: Zed Press, 1981.

Castañeda, Jorge G. *Nicaragua, contradicciones en la revolución.* Mexico: 1980.

Collins, Joseph. *What Difference Could a Revolution Make? Farming and Food in the New Nicaragua.* San Francisco: Institute for Food and Development Policy, 1982.

EPICA Task Force. *Nicaragua: A People's Revolution.* Washington, D.C.: EPICA, 1980.

Fagen, Richard R. *The Nicaraguan Revolution: A Personal Report.* Washington, D.C.: Institute for Policy Studies, 1981.

Gelly, Adolfo. *La nueva Nicaragua: antiimperialismo y lucha de clases.* Mexico: Editorial Nueva Imagen, 1980.

Ramírez, Sergio, ed. *El pensamiento vivo de Sandino.* 5th ed. San José, Costa Rica: EDUCA, 1980.

Sunol, Julio. *Insurrección en Nicaragua: la historia no contada.* San José, Costa Rica: Editorial Costa Rica, 1981.

Walker, Thomas W., ed. *Nicaragua in Revolution.* New York: Praeger, 1982.

Weber, Henri. *Nicaragua: The Sandinist Revolution.* London: Verso Editions, 1981.

Selected Journals and Periodicals

Between the Lines
Guatemala Information Center
P.O. Box 15052
Long Beach, CA 90815

Boletín de ciencias económicas y sociales
(San Salvador: UCA)
Apartado 668
San Salvador, El Salvador

Central America Monitor
CISPES
1151 Massachusetts Avenue
Cambridge, MA 02138

Central America Update
P.O. Box 2207, Station P
Toronto, Ontario
Canada M5S2T2

Christianity and Crisis
537 W. 121st Street
New York, NY 10027

Contemporary Marxism
(Journal of the Institute for the Study of Labor and Economic Crisis)
Synthesis Publications
P.O. Box 40099
San Francisco, CA 94140

Diálogo Social
Ediciones CCS
Apartado 9A-192
Panamá, R.P.

El Salvador Alert!
CISPES
P.O. Box 12056
Washington, DC 20005

Estudios Centroamericanos
(San Salvador: UCA)
Apartado 668
San Salvador, El Salvador

Estudios Sociales Centroamericanos
Apartado 37
Ciudad Universitaria
Costa Rica

Guatemala!
Guatemala News and Information Bureau
P.O. Box 4126
Berkeley, CA 94704

In These Times
1509 Milwaukee Avenue
Chicago, IL 60622

Inforpress Centroamericana
9a Calle "A," 3-56, z.1
Guatemala

Institute for Policy Studies Resource
    Materials on U.S. Military Assis-
    tance in Central America
Institute for Policy Studies
1901 Q Street, N.W.
Washington, D.C. 20009

LADOC
Latinamerica Press
Apartado 5594
Lima 100, Perú

Latin America Update
Washington Office on Latin America
110 Maryland Avenue, N.W.
Washington, D.C. 20002

Latin American Perspectives
P.O. Box 792
Riverside, CA 92502

Latin America Weekly Report and
    Latin America Regional Reports:
    Mexico and Central America
Latin American Newsletters Ltd.
91-93 Charterhouse Street
London ECIM 6HR, England

Monthly Review
62 W. 14th Street
New York, N.Y. 10011

NACLA Report on the Americas
North American Congress on Latin
    America
151 W. 19th Street, 9th Floor
New York, N.Y. 10011

The Nation
P.O. Box 1953
Marion, Ohio 43305

The National Catholic Reporter
P.O. Box 281
Kansas City, MO 64141

News from Guatemala
P.O. Box 335, Station R
Toronto, Ontario, Canada M4G 4C3

New Left Review
7 Carlisle Street
London W1V6NL
England

Newsletter of the Religious Task Force
    for El Salvador
1747 Connecticut Ave., N.W.
Washington, D.C. 20009

Nicaraguan Perspectives
Nicaragua Information Center
P.O. Box 1004
Berkeley, CA 94704

Socialist Review
4228 Telegraph Avenue
Oakland, CA 94609

Washington Report on the
    Hemisphere
(Council of Hemispheric Affairs)
1900 L Street, N.W., Suite 201
Washington, D.C. 20006

Chronology of Events*

1821—Central America follows the example of Agustín Iturbide in Mexico and declares independence from Spain.

1822—Central America joins Iturbide's Mexican Empire.

1823—Iturbide is overthrown and Central America declares itself independent as the United Provinces of Central America.

1823—President James Monroe, fearing an attempt by Spain to restore its authority over its rebellious New World colonies, declares that the United States will tolerate no further European intervention in the affairs of the nations of Central and South America.

1833—The first major peasant rebellion in El Salvador occurs. It is led by the Indian Anastasio Aquino.

1838—The United Provinces of Central America collapses, and conservative *caudillos* come to power.

1846—California is seized by the United States, starting talk of an interoceanic passageway through Nicaragua as a way to shorten the journey from New York to the West Coast.

1848—Cornelius Vanderbilt establishes the Atlantic and Pacific Steam Co., which transports passengers across Nicaragua.

1854—The U.S. military destroys the Nicaraguan city of San Juan del Norte in retaliation for an insult to the American Minister to Nicaragua.

1855—North American adventurer William Walker invades Nicaragua, with the aim of establishing a slave state there, and declares himself President.

1857—The U.S. military, with help from Vanderbilt, invades Nicaragua in an attempt to overthrow Walker. Walker is ultimately defeated by a force of Costa Ricans at Rivas.

1880-1910—The feudal hacienda system of El Salvador usurps large tracts of communal peasant land for coffee-growing. Peasants evicted from these lands are forced to become sharecroppers and bondservants.

---

*Sources from which this chronology was taken include the following: *El Salvador: Background to the Crisis* (Central American Information Office, 1982); Arnon Hadar, *The United States and El Salvador: Political and Military Involvement* (U.S.-El Salvador Research and Information Center, 1981); *San Francisco Examiner*, "The Tortured Land: Key Dates in the History of Central America," July 25, 1982; and the articles appearing in this volume.

1894-1899—A series of four U.S. military interventions in Nicaragua to protect U.S. interests.

1899—Minor Keith, a North American, founds the United Fruit Company in Honduras.

1903—U.S. military intervention in Honduras to protect U.S. interests.

1903—The United States sponsors a revolt in Panama resulting in Panama's independence from Colombia, which clears the way for the construction of the Panama Canal.

1903-04—A series of U.S. military interventions in Panama during and following the revolt against Colombia.

1904—President Theodore Roosevelt adds the Roosevelt Corollary to the Monroe Doctrine. Under the Corollary, the U.S. takes on the role of an "international police force" in Central America.

1907—U.S. military intervention in Honduras during a war between Honduras and Nicaragua.

1909—Conservative revolt supported by U.S. marines in Nicaragua overthrows Liberal government of José Santos Zelaya.

1914—Panama Canal opens.

1912-25—Presence of U.S. Marines maintains Conservatives in power in face of continued Liberal rebellion in Nicaragua.

1920—U.S. military intervention in Guatemala during a period of fighting between trade unionists and the government.

1921—Unrest in San Salvador. Women strikers are killed and a shoemakers' strike is brutally crushed.

1924—Regional Federation of Workers of El Salvador is established with 80,000 members; it affiliates with the Central American Workers Federation.

1925—Strikes and rent riots in Panama lead to the landing of about 600 U.S. troops.

1928-34—Augusto Sandino leads a guerrilla war against U.S. forces in Nicaragua. The U.S. forces leave in 1934, but Sandino is killed by the U.S.-trained National Guard of Anastasio Somoza García after having been tricked into disbanding his guerrilla army. Somoza initiates a dynasty which rules Nicaragua for the next 45 years.

1931—The Communist Party of El Salvador wins a number of municipal elections. General Martínez, the military dictator, refuses to accept the electoral results.

1931-44—Martínez rules El Salvador for 13 years, his policies preventing industrialization.

1932—Brutal suppression of a peasant uprising in El Salvador results in the massacre of up to 30,000 men, women and children. The vast majority of the victims are killed after the uprising has been stamped out. Indians are the target of especially brutal repression, and the massacre has the effect of wiping out indigenous culture. The massacre has become known as *la matanza,* the slaughter. Agustín Farabundo Martí, a leader of the peasants, was arrested by the government a few days before the massacre.

1944—Nervous about popular unrest in El Salvador, the United States advises General Martínez to resign. Military rule continues.

1948—The Partido Revolucionario de Unificación Democrática (Revolutionary Party of Democratic Unification—PRUD) is founded in El Salvador. Its leader, Oscar Osorio, is president from 1950 to 1956. This is the beginning of a period of industrialization.

1954—The democratically elected, progressive government of President Arbenz in Guatemala is overthrown in a U.S.-sponsored coup carried out by the CIA, initiating a string of military governments that has continued up to the present.

1961—Frente Sandinista de Liberación Nacional (Sandinista National Liberation Front) is founded in Nicaragua.

1961—The right-wing anti-communist group ORDEN is founded in El Salvador by General José Alberto Medrano.

1961—The Central American Common Market is formed.

1969—The Soccer War breaks out between El Salvador and Honduras. The Central American Common Market collapses.

1970-present—Period of increasing violence and civil war throughout the region. Civil wars in Guatemala, Nicaragua and El Salvador. Intensified repression by government forces and right-wing death squads. Growth of popular movements and guerrilla organizations.

1977—Carter Administration cuts off military aid to Guatemala because of continuing human rights violations there.

Jan. 10, 1978—Managua newspaper editor Pedro Joaquín Chamorro, leading critic of the Somoza regime, is assassinated, presumably at the orders of dictator Anastasio Somoza Debayle. The death of the widely respected editor sparks rioting and serves as a catalyst in bringing together anti-Somoza forces.

Aug. 22, 1978—A group of 25 Sandinistas led by Commander Zero—Edén Pastora—takes the National Palace in Managua, holding 1,500 hostages, including 49 deputies of the national assembly. The two-day occupation focuses world attention on Nicaragua and the Sandinistas.

May 19, 1979—Sandinista forces begin their final offensive from Costa Rica.

June 20, 1979—ABC correspondent Bill Stewart is murdered by a National Guardsman in Managua in full view of U.S. television cameras.

July 17, 1979—Somoza resigns and goes into exile in Miami. His National Guard surrenders to the Sandinistas two days later.

Oct. 15, 1979—Reform-minded officers in El Salvador overthrow the dictatorship of General Carlos Humberto Romero.

Jan. 3, 1980—Mass resignations from the Salvadorean government, including the three civilians in the junta.

Jan. 10, 1980—A second junta is formed in El Salvador; two prominent Christian Democrats fill vacancies in the junta.

March 6, 1980—The Salvadorean junta announces plans for agrarian reform. This is followed by an upsurge in government repression.

March 9, 1980—A third Salvadorean junta is formed. José Napoleón Duarte of the PDC joins the junta. Mass PDC defections by members unwilling to be associated with the government follow.

March 24, 1980—Salvadorean Archbishop Oscar Arnulfo Romero, an outspoken opponent of government repression and spokesman for the needs of the poor of El Salvador, is assassinated by a sniper while celebrating mass.

March 27, 1980—USAID grants 13 million dollars in aid to El Salvador.

April 1, 1980—U.S. House of Representatives Appropriations Committee approves $5.7 million in military aid to El Salvador.

April 18, 1980—The Frente Democrático Revolucionario (Democratic Revolutionary Front—FDR) is formed in El Salvador.

May 14, 1980—Massacre of Salvadorean peasants trying to flee into Honduras at the Río Sumpul. Six hundred killed by Salvadorean troops acting in unison with Honduran forces.

Oct. 4, 1980—The Salvadorean Army begins a military offensive in Morazán, resulting in 3000 peasants killed and over 20,000 refugees.

Nov. 27, 1980—Six leaders of the FDR are kidnapped in San Salvador with the assistance of the military; later their tortured bodies are found.

Dec. 2, 1980—Four religious workers from the U.S. are killed after returning to El Salvador from a short trip. Their bodies are found in shallow graves near the airport. Members of El Salvador's National Guard are blamed for their deaths. Three days later President Carter suspends all aid to El Salvador. The women's murderers have yet to be brought to justice.

Dec. 13, 1980—José Napoleón Duarte, a member of the junta since March, is named president.

Dec. 15, 1980—U.S. economic aid to El Salvador is resumed. Total for 1980 is $150 million.

Jan. 5, 1981—North Americans Michael Hammer and Mark Pearlman, working as advisers to El Salvador's agrarian reform program, together with José Viera, head of the Salvadorean agrarian reform agency, are gunned down in San Salvador.

Jan. 10, 1981—Guerrillas' unsuccessful "final offensive" launched in El Salvador.

Feb. 10, 1981—The new Reagan administration gives an aid package of $64 million to El Salvador and suspends aid disbursement of $15 million to Nicaragua.

Feb. 23, 1981—State Department releases a white paper showing what it calls "definitive evidence" that leftist rebels of El Salvador are receiving arms and training from communist countries, especially Cuba, with the help of Nicaragua.

March 3, 1981—Reagan administration announces that 20 more U.S. military advisers will be sent to El Salvador, bringing the total number to more than 50. It also announces $25 million in additional military aid to El Salvador.

June 1981—Credibility of State Department's white paper destroyed by several articles in the U.S. press which refute it on every point.

Aug. 28, 1981—Mexico and France issue a joint communique recognizing the FDR-FMLN, the umbrella organization of the Salvadorean opposition, as a "representative political force."

Nov. 29, 1981—Roberto Suazo Cordova elected president of Honduras.

March 15, 1982—Amid growing tension with the United States, the Sandinista government declares a state of emergency in Nicaragua.

March 23, 1982—A military coup in Guatemala overthrows the lame-duck government of Romeo Lucas García after García's candidate, Gen. Aníbal Guevara, had been declared the winner in allegedly fraudulent elections. A three-man junta takes over, led by retired General Efraín Ríos Montt, a born-again Christian with ties to U.S. evangelical organizations.

March 28, 1982—In the midst of civil war and government repression, and under a state of siege, elections are held in El Salvador. They result in a victory by right-wing parties which threaten to squeeze the Christian Democrats remaining in the government out of power. Roberto D'Aubuisson, former death-squad leader, becomes head of the new Constituent Assembly.

May 19, 1982—The Salvadorean Constituent Assembly, now dominated by parties to the right of the Christian Democrats, calls a halt to the agrarian reform.

June 9, 1982—Ríos Montt drops the other members of the junta and takes over as sole leader of Guatemala.

June 30, 1982—Montt announces a state of siege in Guatemala and declares war on leftist guerrillas, whom he says will be executed upon conviction.

July 27, 1982—Reagan certifies that the human rights situation is improving in El Salvador and that reforms are proceeding there, contrary to evidence from international human rights monitoring agencies and other groups. In the period immediately following the certification, government killings of civilians soar.

Index